THE DEMAND FOR ALCOHOL, TOBACCO AND MARIJUANA

With sincere gratitude to our PhD supervisor and mentor throughout our academic career over the past 20 years:

Professor Kenneth William Clements
Director, Economic Research Centre,
The University of Western Australia
Western Australia
Australia

The Demand for Alcohol, Tobacco and Marijuana:
International Evidence

SAROJA SELVANATHAN and ELIYATHAMBY A. SELVANATHAN
Griffith University, Australia

ASHGATE

© Saroja Selvanathan and Eliyathamby A. Selvanathan 2005
© Kenneth W. Clements and Mert Daryal 2005

Published by
Ashgate Publishing Company Ltd
Gower House
Croft Road
Aldershot
Hants GU11 3HR
England

Ashgate Publishing Company
Suite 420
101 Cherry Street
Burlington, VT 05401-4405
USA

Ashgate website: http://www.ashgate.com

British Library Cataloguing in Publication Data
Selvanathan, Saroja
   The demand for alcohol, tobacco and marijuana :
   international evidence
   1.Drinking of alcoholic beverages - Econometric models
   2.Tobacco habit - Econometric models 3.Marijuana abuse -
   Econometric models 4.Alcoholic beverage industry -
   Econometric models 5.Tobacco industry - Econometric models
   6.Marijuana industry - Econometric models 7.Consumption
   (Economics) - Econometric models 8.Demand (Economic theory)
   - Econometric models
   I.Title II.Selvanathan, E. Antony, 1954-
   339.4'864121

Library of Congress Cataloging-in-Publication Data
Selvanathan, Saroja.
   The demand for alcohol, tobacco and marijuana : international evidence / by Saroja
Selvanathan and Eliyathamby A. Selvanathan.
        p. cm.
   Includes bibliographical references and index.
   ISBN 0-7546-4438-3
   1.   Alcoholic beverage industry--Econometric models. 2. Tobacco industry--
Econometric models. 3. Marijuana industry--Econometric models. 4. Drinking of
alcoholic beverages--Econometric models. 5. Tobacco habit--Econometric models. 6.
Consumption (Economics)--Econometric models. 7. Demand (Economic theory)--Econometric
models. I. Selvanathan, E. Antony, 1954- II. Title.

   HD9350.5.S455 2005
   339.4'86337--dc22

2004028580
ISBN 0 7546 4438 3

Printed and bound in Great Britain by Antony Rowe Ltd, Chippenham, Wiltshire

Contents

About the Authors

Eliyathamby A. Selvanathan is a Professor in Econometrics in the Department of International Business and Asian Studies at Griffith University, Queensland, Australia. He has also taught previously at the University of Jaffna (Sri Lanka), Murdoch University (Australia), The University of Western Australia and the University of Queensland (Australia). He was educated at the University of Jaffna, University of Bucharest (Romania) and Murdoch University (Australia). He has published four research monographs and has published widely in international refereed journals and book chapters.

Saroja Selvanathan is Head of Economics and Business Statistics Discipline; Deputy Head of the Department of Accounting, Finance and Economics and the Director of the Statistics and Research Design (STARDS) Unit at Griffith University, Queensland, Australia. She has also taught previously at the University of Jaffna (Sri Lanka), Murdoch University (Australia) and The University of Western Australia. She was educated at the University of Jaffna, Murdoch University and The University of Western Australia. She has published three research monographs and has published widely in international refereed journals and book chapters.

Acknowledgements

We wish to express our sincere gratitude to Professor Ken Clements of The University of Western Australia for many stimulating and helpful comments on various chapters of the book. We would also like to thank Professor Ken Clements and Mert Daryal for contributing Chapter 10 of this book.

We also acknowledge the comments and suggestions of the anonymous reviewers and the editor of the book at *Ashgate Publishing Limited*, which have helped improve the quality and presentation of the book. We would like to thank Renuka Mahadevan and Tanya Tietze for excellent research assistance during various stages of the project. The data collection and preliminary analysis for Chapters 8 and 9 were funded by an Australian Research Council (Small) grant, Griffith University.

The authors of Chapter 10, Clements and Daryal would like to thank Juraj Hiric, Yew Liang Lee, Chee Ming Mak, Paul Miller, Anthony Phillips, and especially Barbara Moyser for their help with the survey reported in this chapter. Clements and Daryl would also like to acknowledge the help of Mark Hazell, Yihui Lan, Ye Qiang, Jan Smith, Greg Swensen, Clare Yu, Paul Williams and Robin Wong. The research for Chapter 10 was supported in part by the Australian Research Council.

Our special thanks to our loving children, *Arthavan* (12 years) and *Prabha* (10 years), for their patience, support and clerical assistance throughout the duration of this project.

Technical Notes

This book contains thirteen chapters and a bibliography. To aid the reader, each chapter has been written so that it is more or less self-contained.

Each chapter contains a number of sections, subsections and a list of references. The sections in each chapter are numbered at two levels. The first level refers to the chapter and the second to the order of occurrence of the section within the chapter. For example, Section 3.4 is the fourth section in Chapter 3. Subsections are unnumbered.

Equations are indicated by two numbers, the first refers to the section and the second to the order of occurrence within that section. For example, 'equation (2.3)' of Chapter 7 denotes the third equation in the second section of that chapter (Section 7.2). This equation is referred to in Chapter 7 as 'equation (2.3)'. If this equation is referred to in another chapter, then we use the terminology 'equation (2.3) of Chapter 7'.

Tables and figures are indicated by two numbers, the first refers to the chapter and the second to the order of occurrence. For example, 'Table 5.5' refers to the fifth table of Chapter 5 and 'Figure 4.2' refers to the second figure of Chapter 4.

Matrices are indicated by a boldface uppercase symbol (e.g., $\mathbf{X}$). Vectors are indicated by a boldface lowercase symbol (e.g., $\boldsymbol{x}$). The notation $[x_{ij}]$ refers to a matrix whose $(i,j)^{\text{th}}$ element is x_{ij}, while $\boldsymbol{x} = [x_i]$ refers to a column vector whose i^{th} element is x_i.

Chapter 1

Introduction

For many governments around the world, consumption of various types of drugs (licit drug such as tobacco and alcohol and illicit drugs such as marijuana, heroin, ecstasy etc.) by their citizens is a matter of concern for a number of reasons. Even though, in most countries, taxes on tobacco and alcohol sales are being used as instruments to generate government revenue, many governments are now realizing that the cost associated with the use of tobacco and excessive use of alcohol is a far greater burden on the society as a whole than the revenue they generate. This has resulted in the introduction of a number of control policies and the formation of specific bodies to control the use and abuse of tobacco and alcohol consumption in most countries. Similarly in the case of illicit drugs, new policies have been developed to control and rehabilitate the users of illicit drugs in an attempt to minimise the impact of drug use on families and society as a whole. The cost of developing and administering these policies is added to by the fact that the government does not collect revenue from illicit drugs. Even though the use of illicit drugs is considered as harmful as licit drugs not only to individuals but also to the society as a whole, the shift in perception and attitude of the society is changing. It is now acknowledged that illicit drugs are readily available in the community and in some cases with drug addicts it is becoming a necessity to make such drugs available to those people.

Food is one of the necessities of any human-being. While the amount a person spends on purchasing food may vary depending on whether the person comes from a rich or poor country, it would be interesting to know how these different types of consumers react to changes in income and prices in purchasing food items. While the type of food items consumed by people may also vary from country to country, for an economist what is important is finding the answers to questions such as 'What proportion of his/her income does a consumer allocates on his/her food purchase?', 'How do changes in one's income affect their food purchase?', 'How do these allocations change with varying income over time?', 'To what extent does the price of food affect a consumer's decision in terms of the quantity of food purchased?' etc.

The main focus of this book is to study the economic factors that affect the demand for food, soft drinks, tobacco, alcohol (as a whole as well as beer, wine and spirits, individually) and marijuana, using a diverse database consisting of a number of countries and utilizing the modern system-wide approach. The book also considers the control measures in place in these countries with respect to drugs. As many of the issues related to the consumption of food, soft drinks, tobacco, alcohol and marijuana are common to most countries, the cross-country analysis involving a number of countries with similar lifestyles provides convincing evidence regarding the consumption of these commodities and will sheds some light towards finding solutions to a number of social problems related to tobacco, alcohol and marijuana. This book uses two groups of countries consisting of *developed countries* (high-income/industrialized) and *developing countries* (low income/less-developed) as they share a number of common features within each group. This book does not attempt to find answers to general questions such as, 'Is alcohol a significant contributor to declining health?' or 'Does tobacco consumption cause death?' etc. The focus of the book is to provide answers to economic questions such as, 'To what extent does a consumer's level of income determine the level of consumption of food, soft drinks, tobacco, alcohol and marijuana?' and 'Do prices of these goods determine the level of their consumption?', 'What are the control policies introduced by various governments to curb excessive drinking and smoking?' etc. As the findings of this book will come from a number of countries, rather than a single country, one can be more confident in the reliability of the results and their general applicability.

Understanding consumer behaviour with regard to the consumption of food, soft drinks, tobacco, alcohol and marijuana is significantly important to policy makers in various government bodies such as health departments, social security departments, treasury and the tobacco, alcohol and soft drinks industries. This book is the first study to present an analysis of the demand for these five commodities in a system-wide framework. To our knowledge, very little research has been published on this topic at a cross-country level. Consequently, this book makes a significant contribution to the knowledge in this area.

1.1 A System-wide Approach

The primary objective of consumption theory is to determine the factors that influence the demand for consumer goods and services, measure the level of influence and test various hypotheses about the change in consumption due to changes in those factors. The two major economic factors considered in this book are income of the consumer and prices he/she pays for the goods and services he/she purchases. The theory and measurement of consumer demand both have a long history. A number of researchers have made significant contributions to the theory and measurement, including, in the early stages, the works of Cournot (1838), Gossen (1854), Engel (1857), Menger (1871), Edgeworth (1881), Marshall (1898), Fisher (1892), Warlas (1896), Pareto (1909), Slutsky (1915), Jevons (1931), Frisch (1932), Dupuit (1934), Hicks and Allen (1934), Working (1943), Houthakker (1952), Stone (1954), Wold (1953) and Samuelson (1965). The classical consumption theory is concerned with a single consumer and assumes that his/her preferences can be described by means of a utility function and the consumer attempts to maximize his/her utility subject to his/her budget constraint. This maximization problem yields a unique demand function, one for each good. The change in the demand for a commodity due to a change in the price of another commodity can be divided into two components, namely, the income effect (the reduction in real income due to the price increase) and the substitution effect. These substitution effects are symmetric, known as Slutsky symmetry, and means that the effect of a small increase in the price of good i on the demand for good j is the same as that of an equal increase in the price of j on the demand for i, assuming that the income effects due to the two price changes are equally compensated. Under the traditional single equation approach cross-equation restrictions such as symmetry were ignored. The modern system-wide approach (Theil, 1975/76, 1980) to consumption economics emphasizes equation system rather than single equations under which cross-equation restrictions can be imposed and tested.

The system-wide approach has in recent years been used for international consumption comparisons in book-length publications by several authors including Barnett (1981), Bewley (1986), Deaton and Muelbauer (1980a), Phlips (1974), Powell (1974), Lluch, Powell and Williams (1977), Theil and Suhm (1981), Theil and Clements (1987), Theil at. al (1989), Pollak and Wales (1992), S. Selvanathan (1993), Chen (2001) and Selvanathan and Selvanathan (2003).

1.2   A Preview of the Book

The book focuses on the international consumption comparisons of food, soft drinks, alcohol, tobacco and marijuana across a number of developed and developing countries. Chapters 2-5 of the book, present detailed statistics and background information on the consumption of food, soft drinks, tobacco, alcohol and marijuana in a number of countries. Chapters 6 and 7 present the theory and parameterisation of demand equations and estimation methods for a complete analysis of the data. Chapter 8 presents the demand model estimates and the implied income and price elasticities for food, tobacco, alcohol and soft dinks using the demand equations and estimation methods presented in Chapters 6 and 7. Chapter 9 disaggregates the alcoholic beverages group into individual beverages, beer, wine and spirits, and analyses the demand for these beverages. Chapter 10 presents an analysis of marijuana consumption. Chapters 11 and 12 discuss the alcohol and tobacco control policies in place in a number of countries and the final chapter presents an overall summary of the conclusions of the analysis presented in the book.

Firstly in Chapter 2, we present an overview of the consumption patterns of the five commodities, food, soft drinks, tobacco, alcohol and marijuana. Initially we look at individual commodities across a number of countries and later we compare the consumption across commodities. We also analyse the consumption patterns of alcohol, tobacco and marijuana across various age groups, various ethnic groups and consumers acceptability and perceptions in a number of selected countries.

In Chapter 3, we consider tobacco consumption in detail using time-series and cross-country data. We first present a global picture of tobacco consumption in the form of cigarettes, cigars and all other tobacco products over the years 1950 to 1997 and a number of survey results on the smoking population. We then closely analyse tobacco consumption statistics based on various age groups, ethnic groups, income groups and educational groups, in a number of selected countries.

A comparison of the recent alcohol consumption data across countries is presented in detail in Chapter 4. We start this chapter by presenting a global picture of alcohol consumption. We then look at the consumption of alcohol into beer, wine and spirits in a number of selected countries. We cover a number of international survey results across various age groups and socio economic groups, We also analyse the drinkers' perceptions about alcohol consumption from surveys from a number of selected countries.

Chapter 5 considers marijuana consumption in detail. Initially, we present a cross-country analysis based on international surveys. We then present an analysis at individual country level for a number of selected countries. In this chapter, we also present cross-country survey results on marijuana consumption behaviour in relation to consumers' education level, employment status, cultural background, marital status etc.

In Chapter 6, we present the differential approach to demand analysis which is the key to deriving demand equations for estimation. This chapter starts with introducing various Divisia indices and derives the Barten's fundamental matrix equation. We then derive the demand systems in relative and absolute prices. We also consider special cases of the utility function such as block independence and preference independence to analyse the demand for individual beverages within the alcoholic beverages group. We then derive the demand equation for a group of goods and for a good within a group.

We consider the parameterization, estimation and testing hypotheses of the demand systems in Chapter 7. The issue of parameterisation of the demand equations are very important as the demand equations derived in Chapter 6 are in infinitesimal changes whereas the data to be used in Chapters 8 to 10 are available only in finite time interval (annual). In light of this requirement, we convert all the demand equations required for estimation in Chapters 8 to 10 in finite-changes. In this chapter, we also discuss the estimation methods of these equations. Finally, we explain how to test demand theory hypotheses such as homogeneity, symmetry and preference independence using the traditional statistical tests and simulation experiments.

In Chapter 8, we present a detailed demand analysis of the four commodities food, tobacco, alcohol and soft drinks by estimating a system of demand equations using data from 44 countries. We present a basic data analysis of the consumption data and then estimate various forms of system of demand equations and test the demand theory hypotheses. This chapter also presents the income and price elasticities of the four commodity groups. These demand elasticities are key inputs for economic policy analysis used by various governments and industry bodies.

We disaggregate the alcoholic beverages group we considered in Chapter 8 into three individual beverages, namely, beer, wine and spirits, in Chapter 9. We initially present consumption data for beer, wine and spirits for 126 countries. We then present a detailed analysis on the demand for beer, wine and spirits for a number of selected countries using a new data set. We start with a preliminary data analysis and then estimate a system of demand equations and test the demand theory hypotheses. This chapter also presents the income and price elasticities of the three individual beverages beer, wine and spirits. These demand elasticities are key inputs in determining tax rates on individual beverages. This chapter further presents a comparison of the results of this chapter with the results reported in a number of other previous studies for the same countries.

Chapter 10 presents a detail analysis of marijuana combined with beer, wine and spirits under a system-wide framework. By estimating a system of demand equations, we analyse the demand for these four commodities and obtain the income and price elasticities of the four commodities. In this chapter, we also review a number of marijuana studies and compare their results with ours. We then present an analysis on the marijuana consumption based on a unique survey data set.

We consider the alcohol misuse issues and alcohol control policies at a cross-country level in Chapter 11. We compare alcohol misuse indicators such as liver cirrhosis deaths and road accidents statistics across a number of countries. We also compare various alcohol control policies in place in various countries in relation to alcohol sale, licensing requirements, alcohol (beer, wine and spirits) advertising, drinking and driving and taxation of alcohol.

In Chapter 12, we consider tobacco control policies in various countries. We first discuss the smoking related issues and then present various statistics of prevalence of tobacco use. We discuss various tobacco control measures put in place by various governments to reduce tobacco demand including tobacco taxation, restrictions on direct and indirect tobacco advertising, support made available to quit smoking, health warning labels on tobacco products, restrictions on smoking in public places and restrictions on tobacco sales.

Finally, in Chapter 13 we present a summary of the results and conclusions of all the previous chapters to give an overall picture of the problems associated with the consumption of alcohol, tobacco and marijuana as well the measures which have been imposed by many governments to reduce the associated social cost.

Chapter 2

Food, Soft Drinks, Tobacco, Alcohol and Marijuana Consumption: An Overview

Many of the issues related to the consumption of food, soft drinks, tobacco, alcohol and marijuana are common to most countries. In this chapter, we present an overview of the consumption patterns of food, soft drinks, tobacco, alcohol and marijuana using data over time and over various consumer characteristics across countries. The reason for the selection of the five commodities is that, in terms of a consumer's purchase decision, the first four goods, food, soft drinks, tobacco and alcohol, are closely related while the consumption of the fifth commodity, marijuana, as we will show later in the book, is clearly linked to the consumption of tobacco and alcohol.

Sections 2.1-2.5 present a cross-country comparison of the consumption patterns of food, soft drinks, tobacco, alcohol and marijuana, respectively. In Section 2.6, we present a comparison of the consumption patterns of tobacco, alcohol and marijuana. The analysis presented in Section 2.7 looks at the consumption patterns of tobacco, alcohol and marijuana among various age groups and groups with various ethnic backgrounds in Australia. Section 2.8 considers the acceptability and perceptions of the consumption of these drugs among consumers and, finally, in Section 2.9 we present our concluding comments.

2.1   Food Consumption

According to a recent international consumption study (Selvanathan and Selvanathan, 2003), food is the most important commodity in any average world consumer's budget. According to the results reported in the study, world consumers allocate almost one-third of their income to food (food, soft drinks, tobacco and alcohol combined). The next closest commodity item competing with food is housing which consumes about one-seventh of a world consumer's income followed by transport, which consumes about one-eighth of their income. The study also found that there are significant differences in the budget allocation of food between rich and poor countries to the extent that, on the one hand, consumers from rich countries such as the US allocate only one-sixth of their income on food, while on the other, consumers from some poor countries like Sri Lanka allocate about 60 percent of their income on food. Therefore, a scientific analysis of the demand for food at cross-country level becomes very important.

Table 2.1 presents the proportion of income allocated by consumers from a number of selected countries on their food (excluding Soft drinks, tobacco and alcohol) purchases and the average growth rates of food consumption and food prices. In column 1, we list the countries in alphabetical order but in two groups. The first 22 countries are developed countries (from the Organization for Economic Co-operation and Development, OECD) and the last 21 countries are developing (developing) countries (LDC). In columns 2 and 5 of the table we present the beginning (year 1) and end (year T) of the sample period of the data set and the two middle columns present the proportions of income (in percentages) allocated to food during those two years. Column 6 presents the average income allocation on food, averaged over the whole sample period. As can be seen, in all countries (except South Africa and Venezuela), the proportion of income allocation on food has fallen over the years. Furthermore, a general trend appears that the income allocation on food is usually higher in most of the developing countries compared to the developed countries. It can also be seen from column 6 that, on average, the Americans allocate the least proportion of income on food (12 percent) followed by the New Zealanders (12.3 percent) and the British (12.6 percent). The highest proportion of income allocated for food is by the Philippinos (53.1 percent) followed by the Indians (50.8 percent) and the Sri Lankans (48.7 percent) which are more than four times the proportion spent by the Americans, New Zealanders and the British. Based on the last row of the table, we can see that an average world consumer would allocate about one-fourth of his/her income on food.

The last two columns of Table 2.1 present the growth rates in food prices and food consumption. As can be seen, in general, food prices grew at a faster rate (about twice) in the developing countries compared to the developed countries. The growth in food consumption is positive in most of the developed countries while it is negative in a number of developing countries. Around the world, on average, food prices grew at a rate of 8 percent per annum while food consumption grew at a rate of only 0.8 percent per annum.

2.2   Soft Drinks

Soft drinks (carbonated) are becoming the favourite refreshment, more popular than tea, coffee and fruit juice, especially with the younger age group. Soft drinks started appearing on the shop shelves when the soft drinks industry began experimenting with 'soda water' in the 1700s. The soft drinks industry plays an important role in the economic growth of many economies by generating thousands of jobs worldwide. While soft drinks refresh people, it is also now being debated among the medical profession that frequent consumption contributes to obesity in children. Furthermore, some research studies also report that frequent consumption of soft drinks also leads to weak bones in teenage girls. Whatever the downside is,

Table 2.1 Proportion of income allocation on food expenditure and average price and quantity growth rates in 43 countries (in percentages)

Country	First sample period		Final sample period		At	Average growth rates	
	Year 1	$\overline{w}_1$	$\overline{w}_T$	Year T	sample mean	Price	Quantity
(1)	(2)	(3)	(4)	(5)	(6)	(7)	(8)
Developed countries (OECD)							
1. Australia	1974	17.84	14.77	1998	15.64	6.66	1.28
2. Austria	1964	26.37	12.68	1996	18.86	3.30	1.10
3. Belgium	1986	17.57	12.97	1997	14.90	0.91	0.52
4. Canada	1961	18.82	10.37	1995	14.10	4.84	0.47
5. Denmark	1966	21.85	14.33	1995	17.42	5.78	0.77
6. Finland	1970	24.88	13.31	1996	19.60	6.00	0.72
7. France	1970	21.97	13.68	1997	17.33	5.58	0.84
8. Germany	1961	32.61	18.02	1994	24.58	2.51	1.64
9. Greece	1980	35.37	28.84	1995	31.96	14.67	0.87
10. Iceland	1977	20.23	16.32	1996	18.14	22.50	0.15
11. Ireland	1970	28.54	16.56	1995	23.23	7.79	1.48
12. Italy	1970	31.81	15.08	1997	23.45	8.98	0.68
13. Luxembourg	1970	23.81	10.94	1991	17.12	5.16	-0.41
14. Netherlands	1977	16.73	10.70	1996	13.31	0.78	0.94
15. New Zealand	1983	13.38	10.93	1995	12.31	5.18	0.93
16. Norway	1989	17.27	15.52	1997	16.61	1.82	1.81
17. Portugal	1986	27.70	21.45	1995	24.11	6.73	2.96
18. Spain	1980	24.97	16.55	1994	20.69	6.68	0.16
19. Sweden	1963	23.53	13.36	1996	18.69	5.63	0.60
20. Switzerland	1961	25.14	18.84	1993	21.82	3.57	1.15
21. UK	1980	16.42	10.45	1996	12.63	4.01	0.49
22. US	1961	17.47	7.55	1996	11.99	3.95	0.39
OECD Mean		22.92	14.69		18.57	6.05	0.89
Less-developed countries (LDC)							
23. Colombia	1972	33.75	28.55	1992	31.86	21.36	1.47
24. Cyprus	1985	24.82	20.40	1996	21.92	4.00	2.40
25. Ecuador	1973	35.34	31.11	1993	31.96	27.53	-0.04
26. Fiji	1977	28.75	26.84	1991	27.69	7.24	-0.44
27. Honduras	1973	41.25	41.21	1982	41.23	8.95	-0.16
28. Hong Kong	1970	31.99	13.20	1995	21.35	7.07	2.25
29. India	1981	54.05	48.18	1996	50.82	8.15	1.32
30. Israel	1986	24.26	18.23	1997	20.72	11.12	1.69
31. Jamaica	1974	34.02	30.72	1988	31.98	14.91	-1.03
32. Korea	1988	24.83	13.93	2001	18.39	5.76	0.95
33. Malta	1973	26.87	20.98	1996	23.93	3.54	3.96
34. Mexico	1988	27.02	21.10	2000	23.27	15.82	1.96
35. Philippines	1983	53.92	51.08	1997	53.14	10.45	1.02
36. Puerto Rico	1963	25.96	16.21	1996	22.35	5.75	-0.22
37. Singapore	1980	20.05	10.33	1997	15.19	1.29	0.11
38. South Africa	1980	24.63	25.70	1997	25.19	13.28	-0.74
39. Sri Lanka	1984	49.13	46.65	1996	48.74	8.77	2.61
40. Taiwan	1988	26.35	22.27	1997	23.71	4.07	4.44
41. Thailand	1980	37.18	20.01	1996	26.09	4.09	1.56
42. Venezuela	1984	27.08	34.50	1995	32.03	32.52	0.40
43. Zimbabwe	1975	25.02	13.41	1987	18.87	12.59	-10.38
LDC Mean		32.20	26.41		29.07	10.87	0.63
Overall Mean		27.45	20.41		23.70	8.40	0.76

these days daily consumption of soft drinks is part and parcel of many people's lives, in particular, among the younger generation in developed countries. In recent years, the multinational companies to a significant extent have managed to infiltrate the beverages market in the developing countries, which was previously dominated by non-soft drinks such as milk, tea, coffee and fruit juice.

Table 2.2 presents the proportion of income allocated to soft drinks by consumers in a number of selected developed and developing countries. These data are collected from Selvanathan and Selvanathan (2003) which originated from the *Year Book of National Accounts* (United Nations, various issues). As can be seen, as with the consumption of food, consumers from the developing countries allocate

Table 2.2 Proportion of income allocation on soft drinks expenditure and average price and quantity growth rates (in percentages) in 42 countries

Country	Percentage of income allocation					Average growth rates	
	First sample period		Final sample period		At	Price	Quantity
	Year 1	$\overline{w}_1$	$\overline{w}_T$	Year T	sample mean		
(1)	(2)	(3)	(4)	(5)	(6)	(7)	(8)
Developed countries (OECD)							
1. Austria	1964	0.71	0.61	1996	0.65	2.01	4.23
2. Belgium	1983	0.43	0.52	1997	0.49	1.75	4.10
3. Denmark	1966	0.67	0.82	1995	0.64	6.45	2.26
4. Finland	1970	0.62	0.50	1996	0.52	7.58	0.72
5. France	1970	0.55	0.60	1997	0.52	5.07	3.43
6. Greece	1980	1.00	1.21	1995	1.05	14.40	3.79
7. Iceland	1977	1.78	2.73	1996	2.40	22.11	3.93
8. Ireland	1970	0.95	1.25	1995	1.30	8.49	4.08
9. Italy	1970	0.40	0.41	1997	0.35	9.01	3.56
10. Luxembourg	1970	0.64	0.64	1991	0.54	4.19	4.32
11. Netherlands	1977	0.51	0.55	1996	0.55	0.59	3.88
12. Spain	1980	0.42	0.49	1994	0.45	7.06	3.71
13. Sweden	1963	0.72	0.59	1996	0.60	4.54	2.79
14. UK	1980	0.86	0.83	1996	0.85	2.30	4.76
15. US	1961	0.24	0.93	1996	0.75	8.87	1.77
OECD Mean		0.70	0.85		0.78	6.96	3.42
Less-developed countries (LDC)							
16. Colombia	1972	0.81	1.15	1992	1.04	23.28	2.14
17. Ecuador	1973	1.17	1.60	1993	1.46	27.71	1.98
18. India	1981	0.07	0.19	1996	0.11	7.94	8.75
19. Israel	1986	1.89	1.96	1997	2.13	9.15	6.59
20. Jamaica	1974	1.32	1.34	1988	1.22	18.87	-4.13
21. Korea	1988	0.58	0.73	2001	0.72	2.86	10.12
22. Malta	1973	3.10	2.30	1996	2.54	6.24	1.03
23. Mexico	1988	1.78	2.81	2000	2.33	20.18	3.47
24. Singapore	1980	1.27	1.06	1997	1.16	1.32	2.93
25. South Africa	1980	1.30	1.66	1997	1.46	13.97	-0.24
26. Sri Lanka	1984	0.63	1.49	1996	0.69	6.74	12.30
27. Thailand	1980	2.79	2.77	1996	3.06	2.75	6.73
LDC Mean		1.39	1.59		1.49	11.75	4.31
Overall Mean		1.01	1.18		1.10	9.09	3.81

a larger proportion of their income on soft drinks (on average, about one and a half times) compared to the consumers in developed countries. In most countries, in contrast to income allocation on food, the income allocation on soft drinks is on the increase. On average, consumers around the world allocate about 1.1 percent of their income on soft drinks. The prices of soft drinks in a country have increased at an average rate of 9.1 percent per annum. It should be noted that, prices of soft drinks in developing countries have grown at a rate of more than one and a half times that of the developed countries. The soft drinks consumption has increased at an average rate of 3.8 percent per annum, which is almost five times that of the food consumption (see last row of Table 2.1).

Figure 2.1 presents the global beverages market change in volume by beverage type for the period 1997-2001. Figure 2.2 depicts the same information for the Asian market. As can be seen from Figures 2.1 and 2.2, there is a significant growth in the volume of soft drinks in the Asian as well as the global markets. The change in volume of soft drinks in the last few years is high in the Asian markets compared to the overall global market.

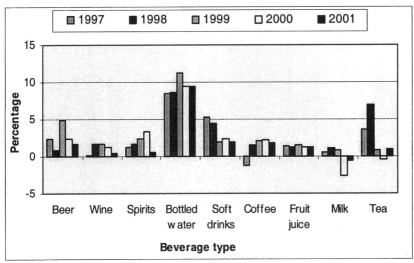

Figure 2.1 Change in volume by beverage type, global beverages market, 1997-2001

2.3   Tobacco Consumption

In the last four decades, there has been a lot of debate about issues associated with the dangers of smoking. There is increasing general public awareness about the effects of smoking on individuals as well as the effect of passive smoking on the well being of non-smokers at home, at the workplace and at public places such as

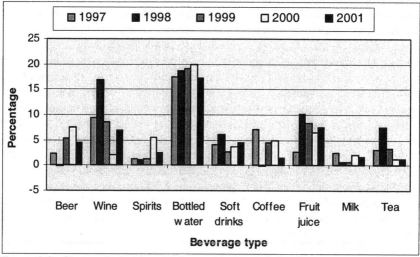

Figure 2.2   Change in volume by beverage type, Asian beverages market, 1997-2001

hospitals, restaurants, cinemas and hotels etc. Medical practitioners claim that, in many countries, (tobacco) smoking is a major contributor to the number of deaths due to lung cancer and other diseases. They also claim that cigarette smoking is addictive and increases the risk of several types of cancer, heart disease and chronic lung disease. Furthermore, according to the health professionals, frequent passive smoking harms non-smokers' health and, even the health of an unborn baby will be harmed if the mother smokes during pregnancy. In many countries, the tobacco companies are required to print health warning messages on the outside cover of the cigarette packets such as 'SMOKING CAUSES LUNG CANCER', 'SMOKING CAUSES HEART DISEASE', 'SMOKING DAMAGES YOUR LUNGS' etc. and printed material as well as advertisements in the media are used to educate people about the harmful effects of smoking. But still a significant proportion of the population smoke and a significant number of young people start smoking every day.

An extensive cross-country survey, the European Schools Survey Project on Alcohol and Drugs (ESPAD, 2000) was carried out by the *Swedish Council for Information on Alcohol and Other Drugs* in 1999. This survey was conducted among 95,000 students in the 10th grade in the 30 participating countries in Europe and the US.

Figure 2.3 presents the summary results from the ESPAD (2000) survey. This figure shows a comparison of the proportion of the 10th grade students who reported smoking cigarettes in the past 30 days of the survey in the US, Europe and the various regions of Europe. As can be seen, the proportion of students who reported smoking in the past 30 days is 11 percent higher in Europe (37 percent)

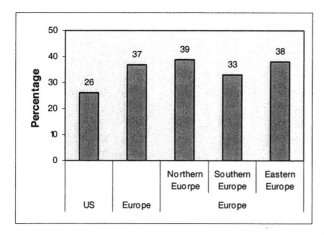

Figure 2.3   Proportion of 10th grade students who reported smoking cigarettes in the past 30 days, US vs Europe, 1999

than in the US (26 percent). Within Europe, the proportion of the 10th graders who smoked in the last 30 days in Northern (39 percent) and Eastern (38 percent) Europe are higher than that in Southern Europe (33 percent).

Figure 2.4 presents the percentage among 10th grade students who smoked daily, based on the ESPAD (2000) survey. As can be seen, one in every 5 students in the UK is a daily smoker. The highest percentage of daily smokers is in the UK (20 percent) followed by Ireland, which is about 18 percent. The lowest percentage of daily smokers among students is in FYROM[1], Greece and Romania. Figure 2.5 presents the proportion of students who have 'smoked in the last 30 days', for a number of countries considered in the ESPAD survey. As can be seen, the percentage of students who have 'smoked in the last 30 days' across countries varies between 16 percent (Cyprus) and 67 percent (Greenland) with most countries in the range of 25 to 45 percent.

Table 2.3 presents the per capita cigarettes smoked by an individual in years 1970, 1980, 1990 and a recent year (the last year in the database) and the price of a packet of (20) cigarettes for a selected number of countries grouped by regions, namely, Africa, America, East Mediterranean, Europe, South East (SE) Asia and Western Pacific (Source: American Cancer Society; www5.who.int/tobacco). The last row for each region gives the average for the countries in that region. As can be seen, based on average, in all regions except SE Asia, there is a significant decline in the per capita cigarette consumption from 1980 onwards. Based on the 1990 values, the average per capita consumption (number of cigarettes per capita) is the highest in the European (2166 cigarettes) and Western Pacific (2059 cigarettes)

---

[1] The country FYROM refers to Former Yugoslav Republic of Macedonia.

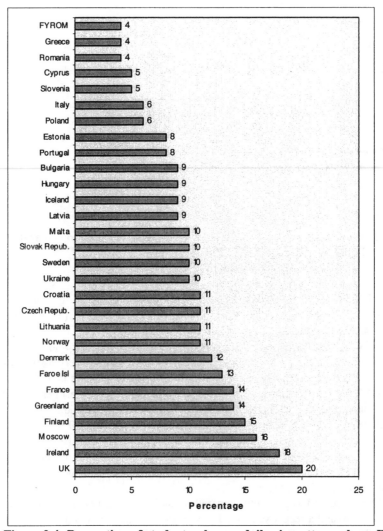

Figure 2.4 Proportion of students who are daily cigarette smokers, European countries, 1999

regions. In 1990, the average per capita consumption in the African (640 cigarettes) and the SE Asian (595 cigarettes) regions are the lowest, which are about half of that of the American (1216 cigarettes) and the East Mediterranean (1118 cigarettes) regions and one-fourth that of the European region (2116 cigarettes). The average domestic price of a pack of cigarettes is lower in the SE Asian (U$0.81), African

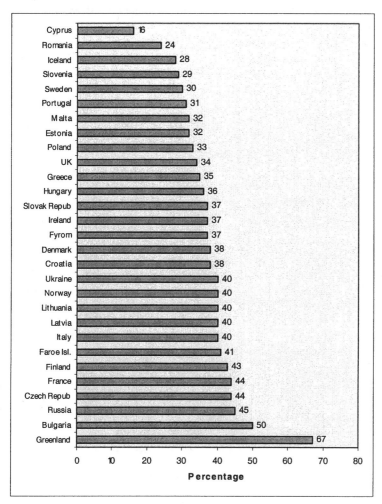

Figure 2.5 Proportion of students reported to have smoked in the last 30 days, European countries, 1999

(U$0.92), East Mediterranean (U$1.01) and American (U$1.11) regions and higher in the European (U$2.47) and Western Pacific (U$2.26) regions.

Figures 2.6 and 2.7 present the average annual per capita consumption and the average price information presented in the last row of Table 2.3 for each group in the form of a bar chart.

Table 2.3 Annual per capita cigarette consumption (cigarette sticks) and price per packet*

Region (1)	Country (2)	Per capita consumption				Latest year in database (7)	Price per packet ($)	
		1970 (3)	1980 (4)	1990 (5)	Latest (6)		Domestic (8)	Foreign (9)
Africa								
	Algeria	866	1499	1298	1021	1994	1.86	2.38
	Angola	731	694	571			1.08	2.70
	Cameroon	258	281	760	652	1998	0.96	1.60
	Congo	337	188	183	135	1995	1.09	1.48
	Cote Divoire	812	842	681	580	1998	0.78	0.94
	Gabon	757	1002	623	519	1995	1.37	1.48
	Kenya	410	546	532	200	1995	0.80	1.59
	Malawi	190	164	215	123	1997	0.51	0.51
	Mauritius	1292	1558	1305	1556	1995	1.60	6.85
	Nigeria	314	315	223	189	1993	0.83	0.83
	Senegal	509	1094	813			0.32	0.80
	Sierra Leone	377	1237	465			0.41	0.41
	South Africa	1384	1746	1932	1516	1997	1.37	1.37
	Togo	831	530	692	492	1998	0.98	0.98
	Uganda	292	93	152	180	1997	0.69	0.69
	Tanzania	358	376	269	177	1997	0.75	1.50
	Zambia	508	442	408			0.75	2.03
	Zimbabwe	719	476	404	399	1998	0.33	0.98
	Mean	608	727	640	553		0.92	1.62
America								
	Argentina	1788	1976	1462	1527	1998	1.35	1.60
	Barbados	1047	891	774	542	1995	3.12	4.44
	Belize	1453	2249	1173	1092	1994	0.62	1.39
	Brazil	1277	2009	1802			0.63	0.92
	Canada	3366	3537	2025	1976	1995	2.67	3.50
	Chile	1142	1554	1111	1202	1997	1.14	1.90
	Colombia	1699	1387	625	521	1997	0.53	0.81
	Costa Rica	1616	1620	1047	690	1995	0.64	0.69
	Cuba	3368	2223	1914			0.25	0.25
	Dominican Repub	918	1027	1017	754	1997	0.38	0.86
	Ecuador	417	842	663	232	1995	0.53	0.62
	El Salvador	1022	2576	1657	1832	1995	0.75	0.75
	Guatemala	718	723	413	464	1995	0.86	1.03
	Guyana	1318	1339	625	590	1994	0.61	0.61
	Honduras	1250	1327	1081	595	1997	0.50	0.50
	Jamaica	1299	951	879	735	1998	2.02	2.02
	Mexico	1501	1470	1068	754	1997	0.86	1.07
	Nigaragua	1212	1454	1167	793	1998	0.80	1.22
	Paraguay	1301	1421	1136			0.79	1.06
	Peru	393	380	194	195	1997	0.88	1.18
	Suriname	1168	2281	1888	2627	1995	0.62	0.62
	Trinidad	1482	1312	850	645	1995	1.12	1.28
	USA	3681	3544	2762	2255	1998	3.26	3.38
	Uruguay	1552	1881	1648	1396	1995	1.54	3.25
	Venezuela	1797	2367	1418	1079	1995	1.28	1.44
	Mean	1511	1694	1216	1023		1.11	1.46

Table 2.3 Annual per capita cigarette consumption (cigarette sticks) and price per packet* (continued)

Region	Country	Per capita consumption				Latest year in database	Price per packet ($)	
		1970	1980	1990	Latest		Domestic	Foreign
(1)	(2)	(3)	(4)	(5)	(6)	(7)	(8)	(9)
East Mediterranean								
	Bahrain	2510	2647				1.46	1.46
	Egypt	581	1387	1177	1275	1997	1.16	1.16
	Iran	774	924	792	765	1995	0.77	2.50
	Jordan	1037	1544	1237	1174	1995	0.77	1.76
	Kuwait	4740	3357	1228	2286	1998	1.11	1.11
	Morocco	1317	1132		800	1998	1.45	2.84
	Pakistan	636	720	463	564	1998	0.50	1.04
	Saudi Arabia	1973	3091	1920	810	1995	1.32	1.32
	Syria	833	1557	1008	1283	1997	0.58	1.74
	Mean	1600	1818	1118	1120		1.01	1.66
Europe								
	Austria	2347	2651	2171	2073	1995	3.26	3.49
	Belgium	2455	2434	2350	2428	1995	2.89	3.14
	Bulgaria	1550	2416	1892	2574	1997	0.43	1.14
	Croatia			2634	2578	1998	1.38	2.20
	Czech Republic			2879	2306	1997	1.15	1.29
	Denmark	1937	1972	1860	1919	1998	4.30	4.37
	Estonia			1425	1983	1995	0.43	1.21
	Finland	1776	1613	1923	1351	1995	3.68	3.96
	France	1850	2236	2170	2058	1995	2.76	3.26
	Germany	2470	2471	2171	1702	1998	2.79	2.87
	Greece	2575	3439	3355	4313	1995	1.86	2.18
	Hungary	2742	3399	3022	2431	1997	0.89	1.01
	Iceland	2854	2436	2531	1915	1998	4.97	4.97
	Ireland	2377	2893	2378	2236	1995	4.24	4.24
	Israel	2010	2180	2335	2162	1995	1.75	3.07
	Italy	1850	2350	1997	1901	1997	2.16	3.03
	Netherlands	2003	2885	1154	2323	1998	2.61	2.93
	Norway	824	846	853	725	1998	7.28	7.28
	Poland	3039	3525	3405	3291	1995	0.99	1.21
	Portugal	1362	1805	2211	2079	1995	1.98	2.04
	Romania			1752	1676	1997	0.80	1.53
	Russia			1108	1702	1997	0.49	0.81
	Spain	2243	2688	2427	2364	1997	1.26	2.30
	Sweden	1723	1946	1650	1202	1995	4.20	4.32
	Switzerland	3460	3696	3064	2720	1997	2.88	2.94
	Turkey	1804	2237	2009	2394	1998	0.99	1.32
	UK	3057	2727	2109	1748	1998	6.27	6.27
	Yugoslavia			1822	1548	1995	0.40	1.25
	Mean	2196	2493	2166	2132		2.47	2.84

Table 2.3 Annual per capita cigarette consumption (cigarette sticks) and price per packet* (continued)

Region	Country	Per capita consumption				Latest year in database	Price per packet ($)	
		1970	1980	1990	Latest		Domestic	Foreign
(1)	(2)	(3)	(4)	(5)	(6)	(7)	(8)	(9)
South East Asia								
	Bangladesh	253	294	203	245	1995	0.85	1.37
	India	190	178	101	129	1997	0.91	1.24
	Indonesia	469	906	1137	1405	1998	0.61	0.73
	Nepal	172	224	645	619	1997	0.24	0.87
	Sri Lanka	417	545	464	374	1997	1.53	1.81
	Thailand	796	1107	1021	1067	1995	0.73	1.09
	Mean	383	542	595	640		0.81	1.19
Western Pacific								
	Australia	3024	3291	2719	1907	1998	3.37	3.84
	China	782	1187	1972	1791	1998	1.80	1.85
	Hong Kong	3195	2483	1562	1016	1998	3.86	3.86
	Fiji	1146	1434	1182	976	1995	1.54	3.01
	Japan	2812	3441	3126	2403	1998	2.30	2.58
	Malaysia	1377	1963	1563	910	1997	0.76	1.11
	New Zealand	2788	2710	1724	1213	1997	3.62	3.81
	Philippines	1938	2105	1841	1849	1995	0.61	0.80
	Korea	2139	2778	3019	2918	1995	1.68	2.69
	Singapore	2741	2309	1883	1230	1998	3.08	3.31
	Mean	2194	2370	2059	1621		2.26	2.69

* A packet contains 20 cigarettes.

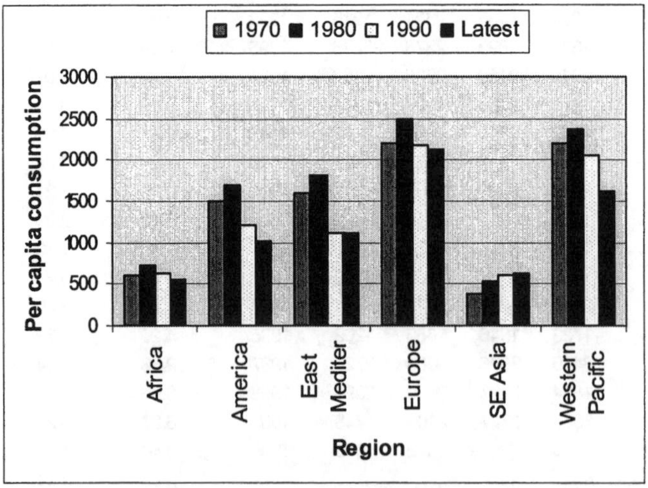

Figure 2.6 Per capita cigarette consumption in various regions of the world, 1970, 1980, 1990 and the latest year

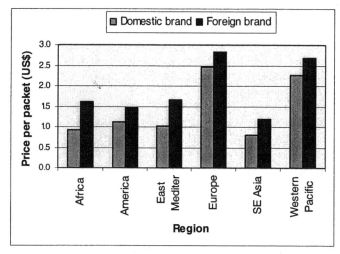

Figure 2.7 Average price of a packet of cigarettes

2.4   Alcohol Consumption

As with tobacco, alcohol consumption has also been part of the human culture for centuries and is deeply integrated into most people's daily lives in most countries of the world (for example, wine in France, Poland, Portugal, Luxembourg and Italy; beer in Germany, Denmark, Ireland, Belgium and Australia and spirits in Russia, Hungary, Romania, Poland and the Slovak Republic). While most drinkers mainly consume alcohol in moderate quantities, some drink heavily, inappropriately, and with adverse and sometimes tragic results. Alcohol-related problems constitute a major cause for concern at local, national and international level. Due to pressure from the public and welfare groups, governments have introduced various control measures (for example, bans on alcohol advertising, increased tax on alcoholic beverages, raising the minimum legal drinking age, random breath testing - RBT, etc.) to reduce the level of alcohol misuse. However, the problems associated with alcohol misuse continue to increase. On the other hand, the alcohol industry argues that control policies such as higher taxes and prices do not affect alcohol abusers or the level of alcohol abuse but only penalises the moderate drinking majority.

The bright side of alcohol consumption is that, in most countries, alcoholic beverage consumption provides relaxation and facilitates social interaction for millions of people; and the alcohol industry provides employment to thousands of people and sizeable revenue to government treasuries resulting in benefits to the society as a whole. Many recent medical studies have also concluded that moderate consumption of red wine significantly reduces the risk of cardiovascular disease and early death. Most governments raise revenue through various levels of taxation on alcohol. For example, Italy raises 0.6 percent and Ireland raises 6.3 percent of their total revenue from alcohol taxes.

The dark side of alcohol consumption is that it continues to be one of the significant contributors to road accidents/fatality; alcoholic cirrhosis; work absenteeism, low productivity, family break-ups, domestic violence, crime, etc. resulting in devastating effects to families and society as a whole. Excessive alcohol consumption has resulted in alcohol addiction in tens of thousands of people around the world. Sadly, the trend of alcohol abuse in many countries is still on the increase. In many countries, the proportion of women drinking alcohol is also increasing. The drinking population 'at risk' varies between 2 percent (in Australia) and 30 percent (in Poland). The social costs associated with alcoholism and alcohol abuse are very high. According to a recent ILO (1998) report, the economic cost of alcohol abuse in different countries was estimated at US$70 billion in the US; US$2.6 billion in the UK; US$5.7 billion in Japan; US$3.4 billion in Australia; US$3.3 billion in Germany; and US$5.5 billion in Canada. Inevitably, society has to carry this burden, even if the majority of society does not cause the problems related to excessive alcohol drinking or alcohol abuse.

According to the AIHW (2000) survey, in Australia, approximately 18 percent of the male and 7 percent of the female population consumed alcohol at dangerous levels. Between 1995 and 1998, the proportion of Australians who consumed alcohol, rose from 78 percent to 81 percent. The hazardous and harmful use of alcohol led to the deaths of more than 3,600 Australians in 1997, which is almost 3 percent of all deaths in Australia. Between 1995 and 1998, the proportion of the population aged 14 years and older who drove a motor vehicle while under the influence of alcohol, increased from 10 percent to 18 percent. More than 400 road deaths and 7,700 serious road injuries each year are linked to high-risk alcohol consumption at a cost to the community of A$1.34 ($\approx$U$0.9) billion. These statistics clearly show the enormity of the alcohol-related problems faced by the Australian government and the society as a whole. The same problem is faced by most high-income countries. Most governments attempt to reduce the social cost due to alcohol abuse by introducing various control measures that would reduce the demand for alcohol. Some of these control policies are extremely controversial indeed.

Alcohol taxes in some countries are used as a tool to increase prices, which in turn reduces alcohol consumption, while in some other countries, they are used as an instrument to raise revenue, and in some others, they are used for both purposes. The level of alcohol taxes imposed varies from country to country. For example, wine tax per gallon of pure alcohol in Italy is just US$7 while it is US$48 in Australia and US$165 in Ireland (Scales et. al., 1995). In Australia, wine is taxed at a lower rate than beer and spirits. Wine producers argue that as moderate consumption of wine is beneficial to health and wine is mostly consumed in the home environment, wine consumption does not add much to the social cost and hence should not be taxed. Furthermore, wine producers also argue that as the wine industry provides livelihood for many grape growers/small wine producers, an increase in wine tax would destroy this aspect of regional development. On the other hand, brewers and the distilled spirits industry argue that, as the three beverages are considered to be pair-wise substitutes, the difference in tax rates encourages consumers to buy wine which is favoured by the differential tax system. It is also argued that as wine is favoured by the tax system, more of the community resources will be put into the production of wine.

In a number of countries (for example, in Australia, Canada, Denmark, Ireland, New Zealand and UK), due to the recognition of growing concern of the general public over alcohol advertising, new guidelines or codes have been introduced by the alcohol industry, news media and governments. From the social and health points of view there is a strong criticism of alcohol advertising. On the other hand, the alcohol industry argues that advertising affects brand and beverage choice only and not the total consumption. Furthermore, the alcohol industry argues that any advertising ban denies consumers the right product information and wider choice information. Research studies published for the UK by Johnson (1985), Duffy (1987, 2001) and Selvanathan (1989) support the alcohol industry's claim. These studies conclude that the role of advertising is just to reshuffle a fixed amount of total alcohol consumption among the three beverages - it does not increase the total alcohol consumption.

Figure 2.8 presents the proportion of 10th grade students who reported to have consumed any alcohol consumption in the past 30 days in the US, Europe and in Europe by regions. The data are compiled from the ESPAD (2000) survey. As can be seen, the proportion of 10th grade students who consumed alcohol in the last 30 days is lower in the US than in Europe, almost 50 percent higher in Europe than in the US. Within Europe, there is some noticeable difference between Eastern Europe (58 percent) and Northern (62 percent) and Southern (63 percent) Europe. A lesser proportion of students in Eastern Europe consumed alcohol in the last 30 days compared to those in Northern and Southern Europe.

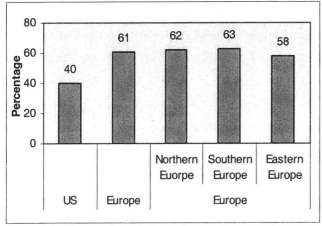

Figure 2.8 Proportion of the students who report any alcohol consumption in the past 30 days

Table 2.4 presents the per capita total pure alcohol consumption during the period 1996-2000 for a number of countries. As can be seen, Luxembourg leads all other countries in 1996 and 1998 with the per capita total pure alcohol consumption of 11.8 and 13.3 litres, respectively. However, per capita alcohol consumption in Luxembourg has fallen slightly in 2000 to 12.1 litres to make it the number 2 ranked in that year. In Ireland, the total pure alcohol consumption has increased steadily from 9.1 litres per capita in 1996 to 10.8 litres per capita in 1998 and then to 12.3 litres per capita in 2000 to be ranked first in that year, which is the highest among all countries in 2000. As can be seen from the average alcohol consumption presented in the last row of Table 2.4, the per capita total pure alcohol consumption around the world has, on average, increased from 6.2 litres in 1996 to 7.2 litres in 2000.

From Table 2.4, we can also see a noticeable difference in per capita pure alcohol consumption between the developed and the developing countries. Most of the developed countries appear with higher ranks while most of the developing countries appear with lower ranks.

Figure 2.9 presents the percentage of students from a selected number of European countries who have reported using any alcoholic beverage 10 times or more in the last 30 days of the ESPAD (2000) survey. As can be seen, the highest percentage reported (about 20 percent) was from Malta followed by Denmark (18 percent) and the UK (16 percent). The least proportion of students are from Finland (1 percent) and Iceland (1 percent). In general, a significant proportion of 10th grade students in a number of European countries have consumed alcohol at least once in the last 30 days.

In Figure 2.10, we present the proportion of 10th grade students in the European countries who reported to have been drunk at least 3 times in the last 30 days of the ESPAD (2000) Survey. As can be seen, one in every 3 students in Denmark and one in every 4 students in the UK and Ireland have reported being drunk at least 3 times in the last 30 days. The proportion is relatively low in countries like Romania (2 percent), Cyprus (3 percent), Greece (3 percent) and Italy (3 percent).

2.5   Marijuana Consumption

The use of marijuana also has a long history like alcohol and tobacco and was, until the turn of this century, largely used for medical purposes in countries such as India, China, the Middle East, South East Asia, South Africa and South America. By the early 1900s, its use for medical purposes had begun to decline and it became a prohibited substance. Marijuana is one of the illicit drugs most commonly used by a significant proportion of the world population. It is the most used illegal drug in a number of countries, including Australia, the UK and the US. According to UNODCCP (1999, p.91), 141 million people around the world (i.e., about 2.5 percent of the world population) use marijuana. A number of medical findings reveal that, like tobacco, regular use of marijuana also plays a role in cancer and problems in the respiratory, and immune systems. When nursing mothers use

Table 2.4 Per capita pure alcohol consumption and the country ranking in 1996, 1998 and 2000

	Country	1996		1998		2000	
		Litres	Rank	Litres	Rank	Litres	Rank
	(1)	(2)	(3)	(4)	(5)	(6)	(7)
1.	Argentina	6.8	23	6.8	25	6.3	29
2.	Australia	7.5	20	7.6	19	7.8	19
3.	Austria	9.8	7	9.2	11	9.4	10
4.	Belgium	9.0	13	8.9	14	8.4	15
5.	Brazil	3.5	39	4.0	41	4.5	37
6.	Bulgaria	7.8	18	6.8	26	5.2	33
7.	Canada	6.0	30	6.2	30	6.6	27
8.	Chile	5.0	32	5.1	32	5.3	31
9.	China	3.7	38	3.8	42	4.0	42
10.	Colombia	4.5	35	4.4	37	4.5	38
11.	Cuba	2.7	41	2.3	47	n.a.	n.a.
12.	Cyprus	7.5	21	6.8	24	7.7	20
13.	Czech Republic	10.1	4	10.2	6	10.6	5
14.	Denmark	10.0	5	9.5	9	9.5	9
15.	Estonia	2.3	43	2.4	46	n.a.	n.a.
16.	Finland	6.7	24	7.1	23	7.1	24
17.	France	11.1	3	10.8	4	10.5	7
18.	Germany	9.8	6	10.6	5	10.5	6
19.	Greece	8.7	14	9.1	13	8.0	18
20.	Guyana	n.a.	n.a.	2.7	45	2.9	45
21.	Hungary	9.5	8	9.4	10	9.2	12
22.	Iceland	3.7	37	4.3	38	4.4	39
23.	Ireland	9.1	12	10.8	3	12.3	1
24.	Israel	0.9	48	n.a.	n.a.	n.a.	n.a.
25.	Italy	8.2	16	7.7	18	7.5	21
26.	Japan	6.6	26	6.5	28	6.5	28
27.	Latvia	n.a.	n.a.	7.1	22	7.4	22
28.	Luxembourg	11.8	1	13.3	1	12.1	2
29.	Malta	n.a.	n.a.	5.1	33	5.2	32
30.	Mexico	3.4	40	3.2	43	3.1	44
31.	Netherlands	8.0	17	8.1	16	8.2	16
32.	New Zealand	6.8	22	7.6	20	7.4	23
33.	Norway	4.0	36	4.3	40	4.3	41
34.	Paraguay	2.1	44	2.3	48	n.a.	n.a.
35.	Peru	1.2	46	1.4	50	n.a.	n.a.
36.	Poland	6.2	29	6.2	29	6.9	25
37.	Portugal	11.2	2	11.2	2	10.8	4
38.	Romania	8.7	15	9.5	8	11.7	3
39.	Russia	6.2	27	7.9	17	8.1	17
40.	Singapore	1.6	45	1.7	49	n.a.	n.a.
41.	Slovak Republic	9.2	11	8.3	15	8.5	13
42.	South Africa	4.9	34	4.8	36	4.7	35
43.	Spain	9.3	10	10.1	7	10.0	8
44.	Sweden	4.9	33	4.9	34	4.9	34
45.	Switzerland	9.3	9	9.2	12	9.2	11
46.	Taiwan	2.7	42	3.0	44	3.1	43
47.	Thailand	0.7	50	4.3	39	4.4	40
48.	Turkey	0.9	49	n.a.	n.a.	n.a.	n.a.
49.	Ukraine	1.0	47	n.a.	n.a.	n.a.	n.a.
50.	UK	7.6	19	7.5	21	8.4	14
51.	Uruguay	6.2	28	4.8	35	5.9	30
52.	US	6.6	25	6.5	27	6.7	26
53.	Venezuela	5.5	31	5.2	31	4.7	36
54.	Mean	6.2		6.6		7.2	

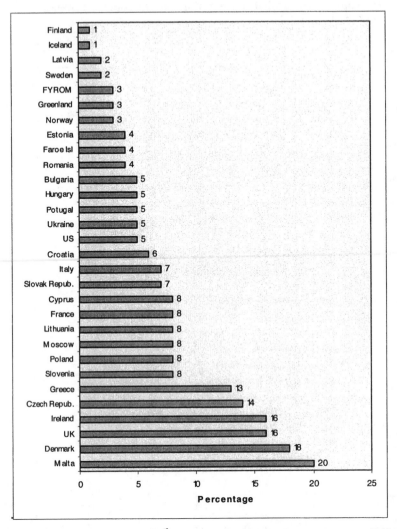

Figure 2.9 Proportion of 10th grade students who have used any alcoholic beverage 10 times or more during the last 30 days, 1999

marijuana, it is believed that some of the marijuana contents are passed to the baby in her breast milk.

Using data compiled from the ESPAD (2000) Survey, in Figure 2.11, we present the proportion of the 10th grade students who have 'ever used' marijuana in the US, Europe as a whole and the different (Northern, Southern and Eastern) regions in Europe. Comparing the 10th graders in the US and Europe as a whole, we can see that the proportion of 10th graders who have 'ever used' marijuana in the

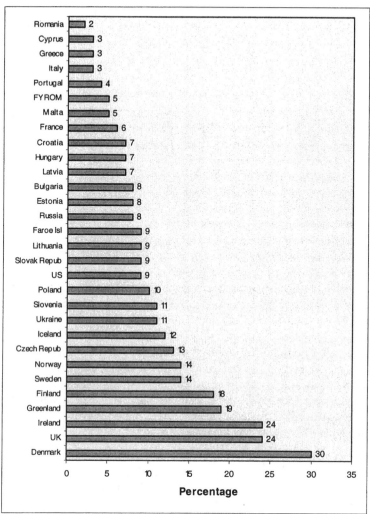

Figure 2.10   Proportion of students who have been drunk 3 times or more during the last 30 days, 1999

US is much (about two and a half times) higher than that in Europe. Within Europe, the proportion is highest (19 percent) in Northern Europe and lowest (14 percent) in Southern Europe.

Marijuana is usually smoked as a cigarette or in a pipe or a bong. According to surveys, it is believed that one in four high school students in developed countries is a current marijuana user. Long-term marijuana use is believed to lead to addiction in some people. Prices for commercial-grade marijuana have remained relatively stable over the past decade.

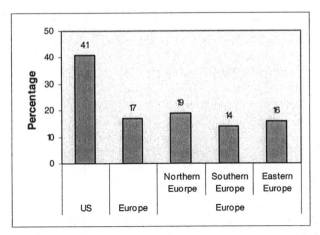

**Figure 2.11   Proportion of students who ever used marijuana,
US vs Europe, 1999**

Figure 2.12 presents a comparison between the frequency of use of marijuana among 14-25 year olds by gender (male/female) in Australia and the UK. These figures are based on the CDHFS (1997). As can be seen, while the percentage of once a week use of marijuana is similar for males and females across the two countries, a higher proportion of males and females in Australia use marijuana twice a month than the British. The proportion of less frequent use category (once every two months) is smaller in Australia than in the UK. In both countries, male teenagers use marijuana more frequently (twice a month and once a week) than their female counterparts. The frequency of marijuana use once every two months is higher among female teenagers than the male teenagers.

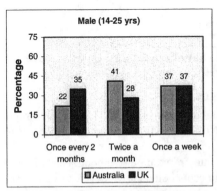
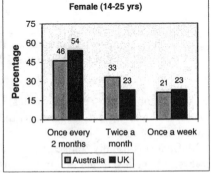

**Figure 2.12   Frequency of marijuana use among the 14-25 age group by
gender, Australia vs the UK, 1997**

Based on the ESPAD (2000) Survey, Figure 2.13 presents a summary of the survey in relation to the proportion of students reported to have used marijuana in the last 30 days. As can be seen, the proportion of students who have used marijuana in the last 30 days is higher in France, the US and the UK compared to most other countries in the study. About one in five students in France and the US have used the drug in the last 30 days. The lowest usages of the drug in the last 30 days were reported in Cyprus (1 percent), Faroe Island (1 percent), Romania (1 percent), Finland (2 percent) and Sweden (2 percent).

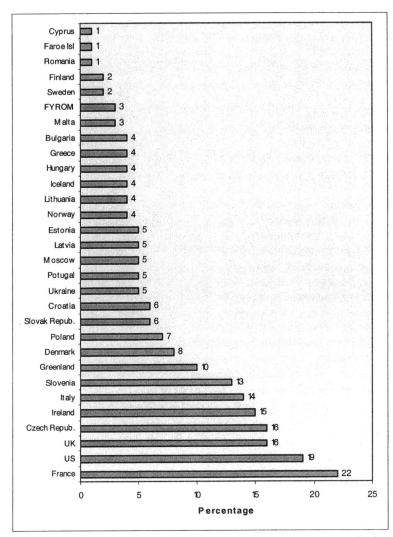

Figure 2.13   Proportion of students who have used marijuana during the last 30 days, European countries and the US, 1999

Figure 2.14 presents the percentage of students who have used marijuana at least once in their lifetime in a number of European countries (ESPAD, 2000). As can be seen, about one in three students in Ireland, the UK, France and the Czech Republic have used marijuana at least once in their lifetime. The least percentage of people who have used marijuana in Europe are from Romania (1 percent) and Cyprus (2 percent).

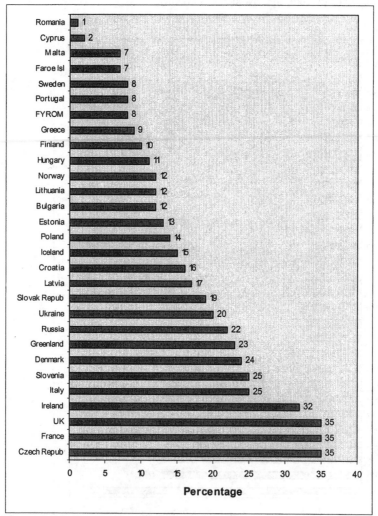

Figure 2.14   Proportion of students who have used marijuana at least once in their lifetime, European countries, 1999

Table 2.5 presents the percentage of the adult population (15 years and over) who have used various types of illicit drugs in the past 12 months for a number of selected countries during 2000-2001. As can be seen, marijuana is the most popular illicit drug in these countries followed by amphetamines, ecstasy and opiates. Furthermore, the use of illicit drugs appears to be higher in Australia and New Zealand than in Canada, the UK and the US. While marijuana appears to be the most popular drug in all five countries, it also appears that amphetamines and ecstasy are also very popular in Australia and New Zealand.

Table 2.5   Summary of drug use in the past 12 months: percentage of the population aged 15 years and over, selected countries, 2000–2001[1]

Substance (1)	Australia (2)	Canada (3)	NZ (4)	UK[2] (5)	US (6)
Marijuana/cannabis	15.0	8.9	20.0	9.4	9.3
Amphetamines	4.0	n.a.	5.0	1.9	1.1
Ecstasy	3.4	1.5	3.4	1.6	1.4
Opiates[3]	0.6	0.3	1.0	0.6	0.5

[1] Australia, New Zealand and United States 2001; Canada and United Kingdom 2000. [2] United Kingdom figures for marijuana/cannabis, amphetamines and ecstasy relate to persons aged 16–59 years. [3] Includes heroin, opium, morphine and synthetic opiates.
Source: AIHW (2002a) and UNODCCP (2002).

2.6   A Comparison of Tobacco, Alcohol and Marijuana Consumption

In Figure 2.15, we present a comparison of the tobacco, alcohol and marijuana consumption in Australia during 1998 and 2001. The data are compiled from the AIHW (2002a) survey. As can be seen, in Australia, the proportion of the population (14 years and over) who have recently used alcohol has increased slightly between 1998 and 2001 while the proportion has fallen for tobacco and marijuana. Figure 2.16 shows a similar picture to Figure 2.15 for the US during 1997 and 1999. In contrast to Australia, in the US, the proportion of the population who have recently used alcohol has fallen which is also the case with tobacco and marijuana.

Figures 2.17-2.18 plot the information on the comparison of tobacco, alcohol and marijuana with respect to the percentage of Australians who used tobacco/alcohol/marijuana (1) had the opportunity to use them and (2) age of their initiation. As can be seen, the opportunity to use alcohol among all groups (all persons, male and female) is higher compared to tobacco and marijuana. The opportunity to have access to all three drugs is higher for the male population compared to their female counterparts. In contrast, the age of initiation of tobacco use is the lowest at 16 years with the higher age of initiation of marijuana use of 19 years. Most Australians initiate alcohol consumption when they are about 17 years old.

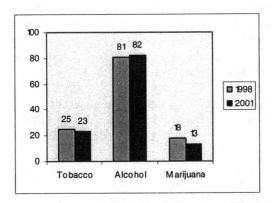

Figure 2.15   Percentage of persons 14 years and over who have used drugs in the last 12 months by drug type, Australia, 1998 and 2001

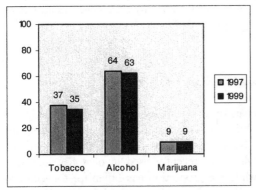

Figure 2.16   Percentage of persons aged 12 years and over who have used drugs in the last 12 months, US, 1997 and 1999

2.7   Drug Use Among Different Ethnic Groups

Based on various published statistics it is also becoming evident that the drug use differs among various type of populations such as English/non-English speaking background, European/non-European background, different age groups, different gender groups, aboriginal/non-aboriginal groups etc. For implementing drug control policies it is also important to devise different polices to target such diverse groups of drug users. Below we look at the drug use statistics based on these differing characteristics of various segments of the population.

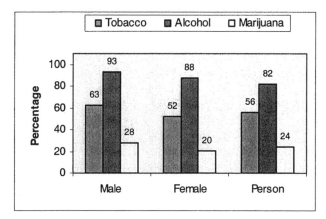

Figure 2.17 **Percentage of adult population who had the opportunity to use drugs by drug type and gender, Australia, 2001**

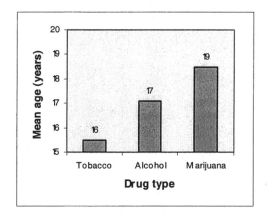

Figure 2.18 **Average age at initiation of drug use by the Australian population by drug type, 2001**

In Table 2.6, we present the survey results based on Australian data, where we make a comparison of the use of alcohol, tobacco and marijuana across a number of population characteristics, such as English/non-English speaking background, major city/non-major city location and aboriginal/non-aboriginal. A number of observations can be made with regard to the type of drug used and the population characteristics from Table 2.6 for Australia. As can be seen, adults from an English-speaking background are heavy users of all types of drugs compared to those from a non-English speaking background. A comparison of alcohol, tobacco and marijuana consumption shows that, irrespective of the population

**Table 2.6 Summary of drug use in the last 12 months: proportion of people
from different sections of the Australian population, 2001
(in percentages)**

	Language		Location		Indigenous	
Substance (1)	English speaking (2)	Non-English speaking (3)	Major city (4)	Non-major city (5)	Aboriginal (6)	Non- Aboriginal (7)
Tobacco	24	18	22	25	50	23
Alcohol	84	58	82	83	79	83
Marijuana	13	5	13	13	27	13

Source: National Drug Strategy Household Survey 2001; Table 8.4, 8.8 and 8.9.

characteristic, a higher proportion of Australians use alcohol followed by tobacco and then by marijuana. This order of use is as expected as alcohol is more easily accessible than tobacco while the accessibility of marijuana is further restricted as it is a prohibited drug. From columns 2 and 3, it is evident that the use of alcohol, tobacco and marijuana is higher among the English speaking Australians than the non-English speaking Australians. There is a significant difference in the marijuana use between English speaking and non-English speaking Australians in the sense that the percentage of users from the former group is three times higher than that of the latter group.

A comparison of column 4 with 5 reveals that while the percentage of alcohol and tobacco users in the non-major cities is higher than the percentage in the major cities, there is not much difference in the percentage of marijuana users. The values in columns 6 and 7 indicate that with regard to the percentage of alcohol users, there is not much difference between Aboriginal and non-aboriginal population. However, there are some significant differences with regard to the use of tobacco and marijuana; there is a higher percentage of tobacco and marijuana users among the aboriginal population than the non-aboriginal population.

Table 2.7 presents a summary of drugs used by various age groups. A comparison between columns 2 to 7 reveals that, while the percentage of alcohol users is higher in the 40-49 age group, the percentage of marijuana users is higher in the 14-39 age group than any other age groups.

In Table 2.8, we present a cross-usage matrix of all drugs divided into male/female/persons categories. The first two rows present the percentage of tobacco users who use alcohol (row 1) and marijuana (row 2). As can be seen, a higher percentage of smokers reported that they use alcohol more compared to the use of marijuana. Furthermore, among both males and females, a larger number of smokers than non-smokers tend to use alcohol as well as marijuana. A remarkable difference appears between smokers and non-smokers in the use of marijuana which may be due to the fact that many smokers may tend to mix marijuana with their tobacco smoking habit. The middle two rows show the percentage of alcohol users who use tobacco (row 3) and marijuana (row 4). The values in these two rows indicate that a higher percentage of alcohol users also use tobacco compared to marijuana. As before, the percentage is higher among the alcohol users than the non-alcohol users who also use tobacco and marijuana. The last two rows present the percentage of marijuana users who use alcohol and tobacco. As can be seen, compared to marijuana users, a lower percentage of non-marijuana users tend to use alcohol and tobacco. In all categories, the percentages are less for females than males.

Table 2.7 Summary of drug use in the last 12 months: younger and older persons aged 14 years and over, Australia, 2001

Substance	Age group					
(1)	14-39yrs (2)	40-49yrs (3)	50-59yrs (4)	60-69yrs (5)	70-79yrs (6)	80+ yrs (7)
Tobacco	29	25	20	13	7	4
Alcohol	85	86	83	77	68	65
Marijuana	23	9	3	1	–	–

Source: AIHW (2002a); Table 8.10.

Table 2.8 Recent cross-drug use: proportion of the population aged 14 years and over, by sex, Australia, 2001

Substances used	Males	Females	Persons	Males	Females	Persons
Tobacco		**Smokers**			**Non-smokers**	
Alcohol	92.5	88.2	90.5	83.6	76.8	80.0
Marijuana	35.2	31.7	27.6	9.2	5.4	7.2
Alcohol		**Drinkers**			**Non-drinkers**	
Tobacco	27.6	23.2	13.6	25.5	11.8	12.5
Marijuana	17.9	12.2	15.1	3.3	1.9	2.4
Marijuana		**Users**			**Non-users**	
Alcohol	97.1	96.1	96.7	83.9	77.4	80.5
Tobacco	56.9	57.2	57.0	19.8	16.7	18.2

Source: AIHW (2002a); Tables 11.1 and 11.3.

2.8   Perceptions and Acceptability of Drug Use

Various surveys have shown that, worldwide, people's perceptions, attitude towards and acceptability about the use of drugs as well as towards the drug users is changing over time. Table 2.9 presents the results of a survey which explores the

Table 2.9 Proportion of persons aged 14 years and over, by age and gender Australia, 2001 (in percentages)

Drug	Age group												All ages	
	14–19		20–29		30–39		40–49		50–59		60+			
	M	F	M	F	M	F	M	F	M	F	M	F	M	F

	Drugs most likely to be associated with a 'drug problem'													
Tobacco	4.5	3.5	2.1	1.3	1.9	1.7	2.4	2.8	2.5	2.7	4.0	3.7	2.8	2.6
Alcohol	9.3	6.8	7.0	5.9	7.0	6.3	7.3	7.3	8.1	9.4	9.3	10.4	7.9	7.7
Marijuana	40.0	39.7	24.2	23.6	19.4	19.6	21.2	22.0	22.7	21.8	21.5	21.3	23.8	23.5
	Form of drug use thought to be of most serious concern for the general community													
Tobacco	22.5	24.0	18.2	16.2	19.1	15.1	20.8	16.8	20.9	17.9	21.4	18.4	20.3	17.6
Alcohol	15.1	16.7	19.1	20.6	20.8	24.8	22.2	27.5	21.3	27.3	19.5	27.0	20.0	24.6
Marijuana	11.9	14.0	5.5	6.0	3.7	4.8	3.7	4.9	4.2	4.3	4.3	3.4	5.1	5.6
	Drugs thought to either directly or indirectly cause the most deaths													
Tobacco	36.9	33.4	43.2	37.4	46.2	37.6	48.8	42.7	47.7	41.6	41.1	34.3	44.5	37.9
Alcohol	24.0	23.7	24.5	21.5	23.6	22.5	22.1	22.6	21.8	22.9	19.2	20.8	22.4	22.2
Marijuana	3.1	4.4	1.2	0.9	0.8	0.8	1.1	0.8	1.2	1.2	2.3	2.2	1.5	1.5
	Personal approval of the regular use by an adult of selected drugs													
Tobacco	44.8	47.8	53.6	50.3	50.6	45.2	42.9	35.1	37.5	27.4	25.0	19.3	42.5	36.8
Alcohol	79.7	76.3	85.6	78.3	84.2	72.9	82.7	67.8	83.0	64.4	72.3	52.6	81.4	68.0
Marijuana	31.6	27.3	44.8	35.6	37.1	26.6	28.0	20.7	16.9	9.4	4.5	3.5	27.4	20.1

Source: AIHW (2002a); Tables 11.1 and 11.3.

opinions and perceptions over a variety of drug related issues such as personal approval of drug use, the impact of drugs on the general community and on morality; and their perceptions of health risks from alcohol, tobacco and marijuana consumption. The results presented in this table are also grouped across different age groups.

The first section of the table presents the percentage of Australians who associate tobacco, alcohol and marijuana use with a 'drug problem'. As can be seen, most of the Australians consider marijuana to be associated with a 'drug problem' but only a small percentage consider alcohol and tobacco to be associated with a 'drug problem'. The percentages are higher among the 14-19 age group while they are lower for the females in general but increasing with the aging female population.

The next section of the table presents the percentage of Australians who thought tobacco/alcohol/marijuana to be a most serious concern for the general community. The figures show that most younger age groups consider tobacco to be the most serious problem to the general community while older age groups consider alcohol to be the most serious concern. In most age groups the percentage is lower for the female age groups than the male age groups.

The third section of the table presents the percentage of the Australian population who think tobacco/alcohol/marijuana causes the most deaths. Overwhelmingly, Australians from all age groups consider tobacco as the leading drug that causes most deaths followed by alcohol. Only a small proportion of Australians think that marijuana leads to some deaths. There is not much difference in the opinion between males and females irrespective of age groups.

The last section of the table gives the percentage of Australians approval for an adult to regularly use tobacco/alcohol/marijuana. Most Australians (about 70 to 85 percent) support the regular use of alcohol by adults. About half of the younger age group (14-39) support regular use of tobacco by adults however it declines to 25 percent with the 60+ age group. About one-third of younger Australians also support the regular use of marijuana by adults but the percentage evaporates to about 5 percent when we reach the 60+ age group. In general, the support for regular use of any one of tobacco/alcohol/marijuana is higher among the males than females.

2.9   Concluding Comments

In this chapter, we have presented an overview on the consumption patterns of food, soft drinks, tobacco, alcohol and marijuana and highlighted the problems most governments are facing due to excessive alcohol use, tobacco consumption as well as marijuana consumption, especially by young adults and children. All these goods play a significant role in the economic growth in many countries and the daily lives of many people directly or indirectly. While alcohol and tobacco are the most easily accessible drugs in most countries, marijuana is also available if desired. While governments around the world have set-up several policies to control the use and misuse of tobacco, alcohol and illicit drugs such as marijuana, they are still available at various levels to the society. In the following chapters, we look at the consumption of tobacco, alcohol and marijuana in detail.

Chapter 3

Tobacco Consumption

Statistics show that with the strong health awareness and educational campaign of the anti-smoking lobby in the high-income countries, the rate of smoking is on the decline, especially among the male population. However, the rate of smoking is on the increase among the male population in the middle-income and the low-income countries and among the female population worldwide. Many people commence smoking at an early age with a significant proportion developing an addiction which makes breaking the habit of smoking very difficult. Tobacco manufacturers argue that people must have the freedom of choice and claim that their advertisements are aimed at shifting people's preference from one brand to another, rather than encouraging tobacco consumption. The anti-smoking lobby argues that governments should intervene and ban smoking altogether. Their stance is based on the claim that smoking is additive and poses a cost burden to a society as a whole. Smokers counteract this argument by stating that they pay high tax as tobacco is one of the most highly taxed commodities around the world, and hence they pay their share of the medical expenses associated with smoking. However, this ignores the health care costs arising from declining non-smokers' health as a result of passive smoking. From the governments' point of view, while many governments acknowledge the high cost of smoking to the society, they are also happy to see the revenue continue to fill the purse of the treasuries. Another factor for consideration is the large number of jobs provided by the tobacco industry. The policy of increasing the tax on tobacco may reduce the demand for tobacco among the poor but may have little impact on the rich consumers. Tax policies, which increase the price of tobacco products, will be more effective in developing countries as consumers in these countries are more responsive to changes in the price of goods they purchase. To date, not much action has been taken to control the supply of tobacco. The only policy initiative in this direction is to control the sale of tobacco to minors.

This chapter presents an overview of tobacco consumption around the world. In Section 3.1, we present summary statistics on tobacco consumption in a number of countries around the world. In the remaining sections of this chapter, we present a detailed analysis of tobacco consumption patterns in a number of countries. In the final section, we give an overall picture of smoking patterns.

3.1   A Global Picture

In this section, we consider tobacco (cigarettes as well as all other forms of tobacco) consumption at a global level.

Table 3.1 presents the per adult (aged 15 or more) consumption of cigarettes for the years 1986, 1991 and 1996 for a number of countries, listed in alphabetical order (compiled from AIHW, 2001). It also provides a ranking for each country within the group of countries analysed based on the number of cigarettes consumed. As the consumption reflects the number of cigarettes per adult per year, it is comparable across time as well as across countries. As can be seen from the table, among the countries considered, the Greeks consumed the highest number of cigarettes followed by consumers in Poland and Japan. A comparison of columns 2, 4 and 6, reveals that a majority of countries have experienced a decline in per adult consumption of cigarettes over the 10-year period since 1986. It can also be seen that, between 1986 and 1996, there is significant improvement (measured by the reduction in per adult cigarette consumption) in the ranking of Australia (from 9th to 17th), Canada (from 8th to 16th), Czech Republic (from 17th to 31st), Iceland (from 11th to 29th), Italy (from 19th to 27th), Syria (25th to 36th) and the US (from 6th to 14th). On the other hand, a decline in performance can be noticed in the ranking for China (from 35th to 20th), Germany (from 27th to 15th), Netherlands (from 38th to 30th), Portugal (from 32nd to 18th), Tunisia (from 31st to 21st) and Turkey (from 24th to 9th). In general, the per adult consumption of cigarettes has fallen in most countries during the period 1986 to 1996.

Table 3.2 presents the historical time-series data for per capita daily consumption of cigarettes (number/adult/day) and the consumption of all tobacco products (cigarettes, cigars, pipe smoking etc) combined (grams/adult/day) in a number of countries (compiled from Forey et al, 2002, and AIHW, 2003). For each country, the first column gives the number of cigarettes consumed and the second column gives the total weight of all tobacco products consumed per adult per day. The entries in Table 3.2 are also comparable over time and across countries. As can be seen, in most countries, consumption has increased for a number of years until the late 1970s and after that it has decreased.

Figure 3.1 plots the daily per adult cigarette consumption for these countries (from the first column entries of each country in Table 3.2). As can be seen, for most countries, cigarette consumption peaked during the mid to late 1970s and started to decline from then onwards. Figure 3.2 presents the percentage sales of tobacco in different forms (by weight of cigarettes, cigars and other tobacco) for selected years between 1925 and 1995 in a number of countries (also compiled from Forey et al, 2002). As can be seen, in most countries, cigarettes became the most commonly consumed form of tobacco product from the 1960s. In recent years, in some countries like Austria, Italy, Japan, Poland, Portugal and Romania, almost all tobacco consumption is consumed in the form of cigarettes. It can also be seen that, in most countries, consuming tobacco in the form of cigar has become non-existence.

Table 3.1 Per adult consumption of number of cigarettes among the population aged 15 and over in selected countries and the country ranking, 1986, 1991 and 1996

	Country	1986		1991		1996	
		Number	Rank	Number	Rank	Number	Rank
	(1)	(2)	(3)	(4)	(5)	(6)	(7)
1.	Albania	1157	39	1243	37	1314	39
2.	Argentina	1876	29	1537	34	1616	32
3.	Australia	2710	9	2585	8	2017	17
4.	Austria	2506	13	2322	13	1973	19
5.	Belgium	2115	21	2091	21	1848	24
6.	Bulgaria	2429	14	2312	14	2509	8
7.	Canada	2783	8	1878	27	2053	16
8.	China	1710	35	1958	25	1904	20
9.	Cyprus	3197	5	2346	12	2531	7
10.	Czech Republic	2355	17	2070	22	1646	31
11.	Denmark	1865	30	1637	31	1840	25
12.	Egypt	1587	36	1221	38	1212	40
13.	France	2152	20	2136	18	1848	23
14.	Germany	1977	27	2186	17	2087	15
15.	Greece	3757	1	3560	2	3474	1
16.	Hungary	3253	3	3153	4	2645	6
17.	Iceland	2667	11	2388	11	1789	29
18.	Indonesia	1093	40	1186	39	1464	34
19.	Ireland	2367	16	2403	10	2333	10
20.	Israel	2406	15	2267	15	2261	13
21.	Italy	2247	19	1880	26	1810	27
22.	Japan	3213	4	3226	3	3193	2
23.	Jordan	1769	34	1439	35	1419	35
24.	Malaysia	1797	33	1609	33	1349	37
25.	Netherlands	1351	38	1619	32	1658	30
26.	Poland	3553	2	3690	1	3180	3
27.	Portugal	1816	32	1996	24	1996	18
28.	Romania	2073	23	1381	36	1874	22
29.	Saudi Arabia	1882	28	2122	19	1812	26
30.	Singapore	1988	26	1678	30	1468	33
31.	South Africa	1411	37	1706	29	1335	38
32.	South Korea	2671	10	3021	5	2993	4
33.	Spain	2595	12	2710	7	2324	11
34.	Switzerland	2918	7	2902	6	2658	5
35.	Syria	2037	25	935	40	1380	36
36.	Taiwan	2314	18	2252	16	2284	12
37.	Tunisia	1837	31	1791	28	1878	21
38.	Turkey	2069	24	2119	20	2362	9
39.	UK	2080	22	2056	23	1797	28
40.	US	3092	6	2571	9	2258	14
Mean		2267		2130		2035	

Table 3.2 Daily consumption of manufactured cigarettes (number/adult/day) and all tobacco products (grams/adult/day)

Year	Australia Cig (1)	Tob (2)	Austria Cig (3)	Tob (4)	Belgium Cig (5)	Tob (6)	Bulgaria Cig (7)	Tob (8)	Canada Cig (9)	Tob (10)	Czech Republic Cig (11)	Tob (12)	Denmark Cig (13)	Tob (14)	Finland Cig (15)	Tob (16)	France Cig (17)	Tob (18)	Germany Cig (19)	Tob (20)
1950	3.5	7.8	3.0	4.0	3.4	7.7			4.9	9.4			3.5	9.9	4.4	4.4	2.6	5.1	1.8	5.4
1951	4.1	8.6	3.4	4.4	3.3	7.6			4.4	8.9			3.0	8.8	4.5	4.5	2.8	5.2	2.2	5.9
1952	4.1	8.5	3.6	4.5	3.2	8.0			4.9	9.8			3.3	9.2	5.0	4.8	2.8	5.1	2.3	6.0
1953	3.9	8.4	3.7	4.6	3.3	7.9			5.7	10.0			3.4	9.3	4.9	4.6	3.1	5.4	2.6	6.2
1954	4.5	8.9	3.2	4.1	3.3	8.0			5.8	9.9			3.2	9.3	5.2	4.9	3.1	5.4	2.8	6.2
1955	4.8	8.9	3.6	4.5	3.4	7.9			6.4	10.4			3.2	9.1	5.3	4.8	3.2	5.5	3.2	6.5
1956	5.2	8.8	4.0	4.8	3.6	8.2			6.8	10.4			3.2	9.1	5.4	4.9	3.4	5.7	3.5	6.8
1957	5.6	9.1	4.2	4.9	3.9	8.4			7.4	11.0			3.3	9.1	5.1	5.1	3.6	5.9	3.9	7.0
1958	5.8	9.2	4.5	5.1	4.1	8.5			7.8	11.5			3.6	9.5	4.8	4.5	3.7	6.1	4.0	7.0
1959	6.1	9.2	4.6	5.3	4.0	8.5			8.0	11.7			3.8	9.8	5.3	4.8	3.5	5.8	4.3	7.1
1960	6.5	9.6	4.7	5.4	4.3	8.7	4.0	4.0	7.9	11.7	5.1		4.0	9.9	5.6	4.9	3.7	6.1	4.7	7.3
1961	6.8	9.7	4.6	5.5	4.4	8.8	4.3	4.3	8.3	12.1	5.3		4.0	9.8	5.8	5.3	3.8	6.2	5.1	7.7
1962	6.9	9.5	4.8	5.6	4.6	9.0	4.5	4.5	8.6	12.4	4.9		4.1	10.1	5.8	5.3	3.8	6.2	5.1	7.4
1963	7.0	9.4	5.0	5.7	4.8	8.8	4.9	4.9	8.7	12.4	5.0		4.3	9.8	6.1	6.1	3.9	6.3	5.2	7.3
1964	7.2	9.4	5.1	5.8	4.9	9.1	4.5	4.5	8.7	12.2	4.6		4.0	10.1	4.6	5.1	3.9	6.2	5.5	7.5
1965	7.3	9.2	5.3	5.9	5.4	9.4	3.9	3.9	9.0	12.6	5.0		4.1	10.1	5.4	5.7	4.1	6.4	5.8	7.7
1966	7.6	9.2	5.7	6.3	5.7	9.5	5.1	5.1	9.4	12.6	5.1		4.2	10.0	5.2	5.7	4.3	6.6	6.0	8.0
1967	7.3	8.7	5.8	6.4	5.8	9.9	3.4	3.4	9.3	12.3	5.1		4.2	10.0	5.4	6.0	4.5	6.8	5.9	7.7
1968	7.6	9.0	5.9	6.5	5.9	9.7	4.7	4.7	8.9	12.0	5.4		4.3	9.9	5.1	5.9	4.6	7.0	6.3	8.1
1969	7.8	9.1	6.1	6.6	6.2	9.7	6.3	6.3	8.8	11.7	4.6		4.6	10.1	5.2	6.1	4.7	7.0	6.6	8.2
1970	8.0	9.1	6.4	6.9	6.6	9.7	4.1	4.1	9.2	12.2	5.1		4.6	10.0	5.1	6.0	4.9	7.1	6.9	8.4
1971	7.9	9.1	6.6	7.1	6.8	10.0	5.1	5.1	9.2	12.2	5.2		4.7	9.8	5.5	6.3	5.1	7.2	7.3	8.7
1972	8.1	9.2	6.5	6.9	7.0	10.2	5.3	5.3	9.4	12.3	5.1		5.0	10.0	5.8	6.7	5.0	7.1	7.3	8.7
1973	8.4	9.3	7.0	7.4	7.4	10.4	5.5	5.5	9.5	12.4	5.2		5.1	10.0	5.6	6.4	5.2	7.3	7.1	8.5
1974	9.1	9.3	6.9	7.2	7.3	10.2	6.7	6.7	9.6	10.3	5.3		4.9	8.8	6.0	4.9	5.5	7.6	7.2	8.4
1975	8.8	9.1	6.6	7.0	6.8	9.7	5.3	5.3	9.5	10.1	5.5		5.1	8.7	6.1	4.8	5.7	7.9	7.0	8.2
1976	8.2	8.8	6.8	7.1	6.6	9.5	5.6	5.6	9.8	10.4	5.6		5.4	8.7	4.8	4.2	5.6	7.8	7.3	8.4
1977	8.9	8.7	6.9	7.2	6.3	9.2	6.7	6.7	9.7	10.2	5.7		5.3	8.6	4.9	4.3	5.8	8.0	6.5	7.9
1978	8.8	8.4	7.0	7.3	5.5	8.3	5.6	5.6	9.5	8.9	5.6		5.1	8.2	4.9	4.2	5.6	7.7	6.8	8.2
1979	8.7	7.9	7.2	7.5	5.9	8.5	5.6	5.6	9.7	8.9	5.7		5.1	8.0	5.1	4.3	5.8	7.9	6.9	8.2
1980	9.0	7.9	7.1	7.4	5.9	8.4	5.2	5.2	9.6	8.7	5.7		4.8	7.9	5.1	4.1	5.7	7.8	7.0	8.2
1981	8.7	7.6	7.2	7.4	5.8	8.3	5.1	5.1	9.7	8.8	6.7		4.9	7.9	4.7	3.9	5.6	7.6	7.0	8.2
1982	8.4	7.7	7.1	7.3	6.2	9.1	5.1	5.1	9.6	8.7	6.7		5.3	8.3	4.9	3.9	5.6	7.5	6.0	7.7
1983	7.9	7.2	7.1	7.4	5.9	9.0	5.7	5.7	8.9	8.2	6.7		4.9	7.6	5.0	4.0	5.7	7.6	6.3	7.8
1984	7.7	6.9	6.9	7.2	5.9	9.2	6.3	6.3	8.6	7.9	6.9		5.1	7.7	5.2	4.1	5.7	7.6	6.3	7.7
1985	7.7	6.7	6.9	7.2	5.4	8.6	6.6	6.6	8.1	7.6	6.5		5.1	7.7	4.7	3.8	6.0	7.9	6.4	7.7
1986	7.7	6.5	6.9	7.1	5.3	8.1	7.1	7.1	7.6	7.3	6.5		4.9	7.5	5.0	3.9	5.9	7.7	6.2	7.5
1987	7.3	6.1	6.7	6.9	4.9	7.6	6.2	6.2	7.1	6.9	6.4		4.7	7.3	5.3	4.1	5.8	7.5	6.2	7.5
1988	7.4	6.0	6.3	6.5	5.0	7.6	5.3	5.3	6.8	6.7	6.4		4.5	7.1	5.1	4.0	5.7	7.3	6.2	7.3
1989	7.3	5.7	6.1	6.3	4.8		5.4	5.4	6.3	6.2	6.1		4.4	7.0	5.3	4.1	5.7	7.4	6.3	7.3
1990	7.4	5.7	6.2	6.4	4.6		4.7	4.7	6.1	5.9	6.6		4.2	6.9	4.9	3.8	5.7	7.4	6.2	7.3
1991	7.0	5.3	6.3	6.4	4.7		6.0	6.0	5.5	5.4	6.0		4.2	6.7	4.7	3.7	5.8	7.4	5.4	6.8
1992	7.1	5.3	6.0	6.2	4.5		7.1	7.1	5.5	5.1	6.5		4.3	6.7	4.6	3.8	5.7	7.3	5.2	6.3
1993	6.5	4.7	5.7	5.9	4.2		7.5	7.5	5.3	4.8			4.1	6.4	3.9	3.4	5.5	7.1	5.5	6.4
1994	6.4	4.6	5.8	6.0	4.0		6.0	6.0	5.9	5.3			4.1	6.3	3.7	3.2	5.3	6.8	5.4	6.3
1995	6.2		5.5	5.6	4.1	7.0	6.4	6.4	5.3	4.8			4.1	6.2	3.4	3.0	5.1	6.7		
1996							7.6	7.6												
1997							8.1	8.1												
:																				
2001		3.7								3.9				4.4		2.6		5.2		6.2

Table 3.2 continues on next page

Table 3.2 Daily consumption of manufactured cigarettes (number/adult/day) and all tobacco products (grams/adult/day) (continued)

Year	Greece		Hungary		Iceland		Ireland		Israel		Italy		Japan		Netherlands		New Zealand		Norway	
	Cig	Tob	Cig	Tob	Cig	Tob	Cig	Tob	Cig	Tob	Cig	Tob	Cig	Tob	Cig	Tob	Cig	Tob	Cig	Tob
	(21)	(22)	(23)	(24)	(25)	(26)	(27)	(28)	(29)	(30)	(31)	(32)	(33)	(34)	(35)	(36)	(37)	(38)	(39)	(40)
1950	4.4	5.0			4.1	6.1	6.8	8.5			1.8	2.5	3.3	3.8	9.4	3.1	4.0	9.2	1.4	5.4
1951	4.4	5.0			3.8	5.4	7.7	9.4			2.7	3.3	3.7	4.1	8.8	3.2	4.3	9.6	1.4	5.3
1952	4.3	4.9			3.8	5.4	7.3	8.6			2.7	3.3	3.9	4.3	9.3	3.6	4.1	9.3	1.5	5.6
1953	4.2	4.8			4.3	6.1	7.1	8.6			2.7	3.3	4.3	4.6	9.6	3.8	4.0	9.4	1.4	5.5
1954	4.3	4.8			3.8	5.5	6.9	8.2			2.7	3.3	4.5	4.8	10.0	4.2	4.4	9.6	1.5	5.4
1955	4.2	4.8			3.9	5.7	7.3	8.7			2.7	3.3	4.5	4.8	9.6	4.3	4.8	9.8	1.5	5.4
1956	4.3	4.9			4.4	6.1	6.8	8.0			3.0	3.6	4.4	4.6	10.1	4.7	4.8	9.2	1.4	5.2
1957	4.3	4.8			5.0	7.1	6.6	7.8			3.2	3.7	4.5	4.7	10.2	4.8	5.0	9.7	1.5	5.4
1958	4.4	5.0			4.9	6.7	6.6	7.8			3.3	3.8	4.6	4.8	10.1	4.6	4.6	9.0	1.5	5.4
1959	4.6	5.2			4.8	6.9	6.9	8.0			3.4	3.9	4.8	5.0	10.5	4.6	4.4	8.7	1.5	5.5
1960	4.7	5.3	5.8		4.7	6.5	7.2	8.3			3.5	4.0	5.1	5.3	10.7	4.7	5.3	9.7	1.5	5.6
1961	4.7	5.4	6.1		5.1	7.0	7.5	8.6			3.7	4.2	5.6	5.7	11.0	4.9	5.3	9.7	1.5	5.8
1962	4.8	5.4	6.0		5.3	7.6	7.4	8.4			4.0	4.4	5.7	5.8	10.7	5.0	5.5	9.6	1.5	5.9
1963	4.9	5.5	5.7		5.5	7.9	7.8	8.7			4.0	4.5	5.9	6.0	11.2	5.2	5.9	9.9	1.4	5.7
1964	5.1	5.8	5.8		4.5	7.5	7.5	8.5			4.1	4.5	6.2	6.2	10.4	4.4	6.0	9.5	1.3	5.6
1965	5.1	5.9	6.5		5.1	8.1	7.4	8.3			4.2	4.6	6.4	6.5	11.7	5.6	6.3	9.5	1.4	5.9
1966	5.3	6.1	7.2		5.5	8.7	7.6	8.3	5.4		4.5	4.8	6.7	6.7	10.1	4.3	6.9	10.0	1.5	6.0
1967	5.6	6.3	7.2		5.6	8.8	7.7	8.2	5.5		4.6	4.9	7.0	7.1	10.9	5.0	6.8	9.6	1.6	6.1
1968	5.7	6.5	7.5		5.1	8.4	7.8	8.1	5.9		4.7	5.0	7.0	7.1	11.5	5.5	6.8	9.5	1.7	6.3
1969	5.9	6.6	7.0		4.5	8.3	8.1	8.1	6.0	6.2	4.7	5.0	7.5	7.5	10.3	4.8	7.0	9.5	1.8	6.4
1970	6.0	6.8	7.5		5.1	8.8	8.2	7.9	6.2		4.7	5.0	7.8	7.8	11.1	5.4	7.1	9.5	1.7	6.1
1971	6.3	7.1	8.0		5.0	8.6	8.2	8.0	6.4		4.7	5.0	8.2	8.2	11.0	5.6	7.2	9.5	1.6	5.9
1972	6.4	7.2	8.6		5.6	9.4	8.6	8.2	7.1		4.9	5.2	8.6	8.6	11.6	6.1	7.3	9.5	1.7	6.3
1973	6.6	7.5	7.7		5.6	9.4	9.1	8.5	7.2		5.3	5.5	8.9	9.0	12.2	6.5	7.4	9.5	1.7	6.2
1974	7.0	7.9	7.7		6.3	8.6	9.7	8.8	6.6	6.7	5.7	5.9	9.5	9.5	12.2	6.4	7.5	9.5	1.7	6.2
1975	7.3	8.3	8.4		6.0	8.4	9.6	8.4	6.4		5.7	5.9	9.5	9.6	12.0	6.4	7.9	9.9	1.7	6.2
1976	7.5	8.5	8.6		6.2	8.4	9.2	8.0	6.2		5.7	5.9	9.4	9.4	11.6	6.0	7.7	9.6	1.6	6.0
1977	7.9	8.9	8.4		5.8	7.7	8.8	7.6	6.5		5.7	5.9	9.7	9.7	12.7	7.0	7.9	9.8	1.8	6.2
1978	8.1	9.2	8.3		6.0	7.7	9.2	8.1	6.2		5.6	5.7	9.6	9.6	11.4	6.0	7.7	9.4	1.7	5.8
1979	8.4	9.5	8.5		6.3	7.9	8.9	7.8	5.6	5.7	6.0	6.2	9.6	9.6	12.0	6.8	7.4	9.1	1.9	6.1
1980	8.3	9.4	9.4		6.3	7.8	8.7	7.7	6.2		6.1	6.2	9.4	9.4	10.6	5.7	7.2	8.8	2.0	6.3
1981	8.1	9.2	9.2		6.6	8.2	8.3	7.4	6.2	6.2	6.1	6.3	9.5	9.5	10.2	5.2	7.3	8.9	1.8	6.0
1982	7.1	8.1	8.7		6.7	8.1	7.7	6.9	6.4	6.5	6.2	6.3	9.4	9.5	10.2	5.4	7.1	8.7	1.8	5.7
1983	8.6	8.6	8.2		6.9	8.3	7.3	6.6	6.6	6.6	6.2	6.3	9.3	9.3	10.9	5.6	7.0	8.5	1.9	6.0
1984	9.0	9.0	9.0		7.0	8.3	7.0	6.3	6.4	6.5	6.3	6.4	9.2	9.2	9.1	3.8	7.0	8.5	2.1	6.1
1985	9.5	9.5	8.9		6.7	7.9	6.8	6.2	6.3	6.4	6.3	6.4	9.0		9.0	3.8	7.6		2.3	6.2
1986	9.7	9.7	8.9		6.6	7.6	6.4	5.9	6.4	6.4	6.2	6.3	8.8		8.9	3.8	5.8	7.1	2.6	6.3
1987	9.9	9.9	8.9		6.6	7.6	6.1	5.6	5.3	5.4	6.0	6.1	8.7		8.5	3.7	5.8	7.1	2.7	6.1
1988	9.6	9.6	8.7	8.8	6.3	7.2	6.0	5.5	4.7	4.7	5.6	5.7	8.6		8.3	3.7	5.8	7.1	2.8	6.1
1989	9.1	9.1	8.9		6.0	6.9	6.1	5.5	4.7		5.6	5.7	8.6		8.2	3.7	4.6	5.7	2.8	6.1
1990	8.7	8.7	9.6		5.9	6.8	6.2	5.6	4.5		5.2	5.3	8.8		8.2	3.9	4.7	6.0	2.8	6.1
1991	8.3	8.3	8.7		5.9	6.7	6.6	5.9	4.4		5.1	5.2	8.9		8.6	4.1	4.2	5.5	2.9	6.1
1992	8.0	8.0	8.5		5.6	6.4	6.3	5.6	4.1		5.0	5.1	8.8		7.9	3.9	3.6	4.9	2.7	5.6
1993	7.1	7.1	9.1		5.3	6.1	5.9	5.3	4.1		5.0	5.1	8.8		7.2	3.5	3.5	4.8	2.8	5.8
1994	6.7	6.7	9.4		5.2	6.0	6.1	5.4	3.5		5.1	5.1	8.8		7.4	3.6	3.5	4.6	2.6	5.4
1995	9.3	9.3	9.1		5.0	5.7	6.4	5.7			5.1	5.1	8.8		7.4	3.7	3.2	4.4	2.7	5.4
1996	8.8	8.8																		
:																				
2001		9.9	5.6		4.8		5.0								6.8			3.7		4.1

Table 3.2 continues on next page

Table 3.2 Daily consumption of manufactured cigarettes (number/adult/day) and all tobacco products (grams/adult/day) (continued)

Year	Poland Cig (41)	Tob (42)	Portugal Cig (43)	Tob (44)	Romania Cig (45)	Tob (46)	Spain Cig (47)	Tob (48)	Sweden Cig (49)	Tob (50)	Switzerland Cig (51)	Tob (52)	UK Cig (53)	Tob (54)	US Cig (55)	Tob (56)	USSR Cig (57)	Tob (58)	Yugoslavia Cig (59)
1950			1.7	2.4			1.2	3.9	2.2	5.1	4.1	7.5	6.0	7.0	9.0	12.7			
1951			1.7	2.4			1.3	3.5	2.2	4.8	4.3	7.6	6.3	7.3	9.4	13.0			
1952			1.9	2.6			1.5	4.3	2.6	5.3	4.7	8.0	6.4	7.4	9.7	13.3			
1953			1.9	2.5			1.7	3.4	2.6	5.2	4.6	7.8	6.5	7.5	9.4	12.9			
1954			1.9	2.4			1.8	3.8	2.6	5.2	4.6	7.6	6.7	7.6	8.9	12.2			
1955			2.0	2.5			2.0	4.0	2.7	5.2	4.8	7.9	6.9	7.8	9.1	12.4			
1956			2.2	2.6			1.9	3.7	2.8	5.2	5.1	8.0	6.9	7.9	9.2	12.3			
1957			2.2	2.6			2.3	4.0	2.9	5.1	5.3	7.7	7.1	8.1	9.5	12.5			
1958			2.4	2.7			2.8	4.5	2.9	5.2	5.8	8.3	7.2	8.2	9.9	13.0			
1959			2.5	2.8			2.9	4.3	3.0	5.3	5.9	8.3	7.3	8.3	10.2	13.1			
1960	6.2	6.2	2.7	3.1	4.3	4.3	3.1	4.4	3.2	5.6	6.6	8.8	7.6	8.5	10.4	13.0			4.3
1961	6.9	6.9	2.4	2.7	4.5	4.5	3.4	4.6	3.4	5.7	7.2	9.4	7.7	8.5	10.7	13.4	3.9	2.7	4.8
1962	7.2	7.2	2.5	2.8	4.5	4.5	3.7	4.7	3.5	5.7	7.6	9.9	7.3	8.1	10.6	13.1	4	2.7	4.7
1963	7.1	7.1	2.9	3.2	4.3	4.3	4.1	5.0	3.6	5.7	7.6	10.5	7.6	8.2	10.8	13.8	3.7	2.5	4.8
1964	6.1	6.1	3.0	3.3	4.4	4.4	4.4	5.2	3.5	5.8	7.2	10.2	7.5	8.0	10.3	13.5	4.2	2.8	4.8
1965	6.7	6.7	3.2	3.4	4.5	4.5	4.8	5.6	3.7	5.8	8.5	11.4	7.3	7.6	10.5	13.3	4.7	3.2	5.2
1966	7.4	7.4	3.4	3.6	4.9	4.9	5.0	5.8	3.9	6.0	6.7	9.5	7.7	7.6	10.5	12.9	5.3	3.6	5.7
1967	7.1	7.1	3.5	3.7	4.7	4.7	5.3	6.0	3.9	5.8	7.7	10.4	7.8	7.6	10.5	12.5	5.2	3.5	5.6
1968	7.6	7.6	3.7	3.9	4.7	4.7	5.4	6.1	4.2	5.8	8.1	10.8	7.9	7.5	10.2	12.3	4.9	3.3	5.9
1969	8.0	8.0	3.7	3.9	4.8	4.8	5.4	6.0	4.4	5.8	9.0	11.7	8.1	7.3	9.8	11.7	4.8	3.5	6.2
1970	8.0	8.0	4.0	4.1	4.7	4.7	5.6	6.3	4.4	5.6	9.5	12.1	8.3	7.3	10.0	11.5	5.2	3.7	6.2
1971	7.7	7.7	4.0	4.2	4.7	4.7	5.7	6.3	4.3	5.3	10.3	12.8	7.9	7.0	9.7	11.0	5.5	4	6.4
1972	9.1	9.1	4.2	4.3	4.8	4.8	5.9	6.6	4.8	5.7	10.7	13.3	8.4	7.3	10.0	11.3	5.9	4.5	6.4
1973	8.3	8.3	4.5		4.9	4.9	6.2	6.9	3.9	5.0	9.3	11.8	8.8	7.7	10.5	11.4	5.9	4.5	6.4
1974	8.7	8.7	4.7		5.0	5.0	6.6	7.4	4.7	5.0	9.2		8.8	7.5	10.5	11.2	6.0	4.6	7.1
1975	8.8	8.8	4.8		5.2	5.2	6.3	7.2	4.9	5.2	8.6		8.5	7.1	10.3	10.8	6.0	4.9	7.0
1976	9.4	9.4	4.6		5.3	5.3	6.6	7.4	5.0	5.3	8.5		8.3	6.9	10.2	10.3	6.0	4.9	7.1
1977	9.4	9.4	4.9		5.4	5.4	6.9	7.7	4.7	5.1	8.8		8.0	6.6	10.1	10.0	6.1	5.0	7.9
1978	9.4	9.4	4.9		5.6	5.6	6.4	7.1	4.9	5.2	8.5		7.9	7.1	9.9	9.6	6.2	5.0	8.8
1979	9.5	9.5	4.6	4.7	5.6	5.6	7.1	7.7	4.9	5.2	8.2		7.8	7.0	9.8	9.8	6.0	5.1	9.7
1980	9.6	9.6	4.5	4.5	5.7	5.7	6.9	7.6	4.9	5.2	8.3		7.5	6.8	9.8	9.5	5.8	4.9	8.9
1981	9.1	9.1	4.7	4.8	5.9	5.9	6.3	6.9	4.7	5.1	8.4		6.8	6.3	9.8	9.2	5.8	4.9	8.1
1982	9.2	9.2	4.8	4.8	6.0	6.0	6.6	7.2	4.9	5.3	8.4		6.2	5.8	9.6	9.1	5.9	5.2	7.9
1983	8.6	8.6	5.0	5.0	5.9	5.9	6.7	7.3	4.7	5.2	8.5		6.2	5.7	9.0	8.8	5.8	5.0	8.9
1984	8.8	8.8	4.9	4.9	5.8	5.8	6.9	7.5	4.6	5.4	8.4		6.0	5.6	8.9	8.4	5.9	5.1	8.4
1985	9.2	9.2	4.9	4.9	5.8	5.8	7.3	7.9	4.5	5.4	8.1		5.9	5.5	8.7	8.4	6.0	5.2	8.6
1986	9.7	9.7	4.9		5.7	5.7	7.1	7.7	4.5	5.3	8.1		5.7	5.1	8.5	8.0	5.9	5.2	8.8
1987	10.1	10.1	5.3		4.6	4.6	7.2	7.7	4.4	5.3	8.0		5.8	5.3	8.2	7.7	5.9	5.2	8.5
1988	9.2	9.2	5.1		4.9	4.9	6.9	7.4	4.4	5.2	7.9		5.8	5.2	8.0	7.5	5.6	4.9	8.9
1989	9.3	9.3	5.1	5.1	5.0	5.0	7.0		4.3	5.1	7.9		5.7	5.1	7.6	7.0	5.4	4.7	8.5
1990	9.9	9.9	5.4	5.4	5.0	5.0	7.2		4.1	5.0	7.8		5.8	5.2	7.4	6.9	5.1	4.5	8.5
1991	10.7	10.7	5.5	5.6	3.6	3.6	7.3		4.1	5.1	7.8		5.6	5.0	7.1	6.8	4.8	4.2	8.0
1992	9.1	9.1	5.7	5.8	4.3	4.3	6.9		4.2	5.2	8.2		5.3	4.7	6.9	6.6	4.9	4.2	6.8
1993	9.7	9.7	5.8		5.5	5.5	6.3	6.7	3.4	4.6	7.6		5.3	4.7	6.6	6.6	4.5	4.0	7.6
1994	8.9	8.9	6.0		5.7	5.7	6.8		3.3	4.7	7.4		5.1	4.4	6.6	6.0	4.1	3.6	
1995	9.3	9.3	5.5		6.3	6.3	6.3		3.1	4.6	7.4		4.6	4.0	6.5	6.1	4.4	3.9	
2001									3.4	4.5									

Source: Forey et al (2002).

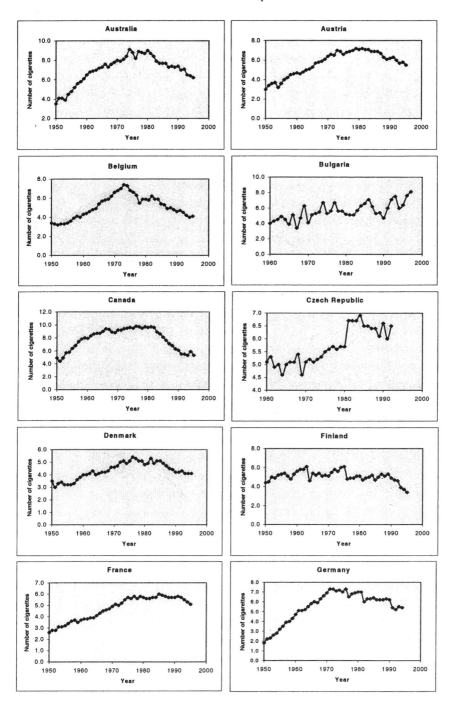

Figure 3.1 Daily consumption of manufactured cigarettes (number/adult/day)

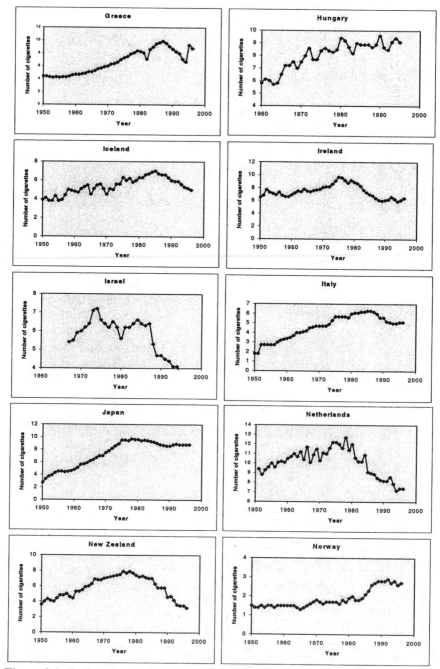

Figure 3.1   Daily consumption of manufactured cigarettes (number/adult/day) (continued)

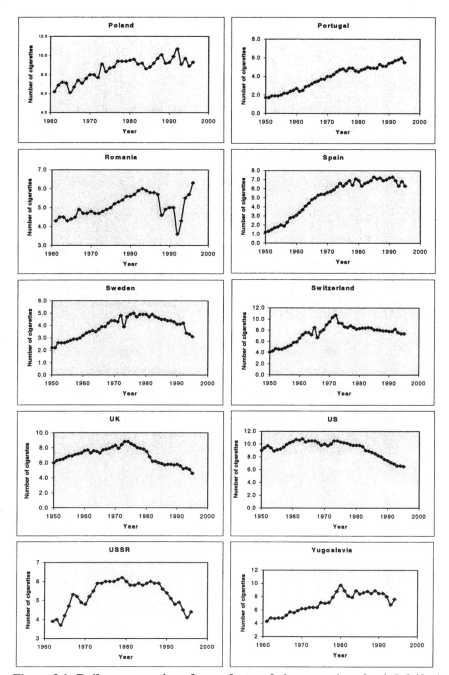

Figure 3.1 Daily consumption of manufactured cigarettes (number/adult/day) (continued)

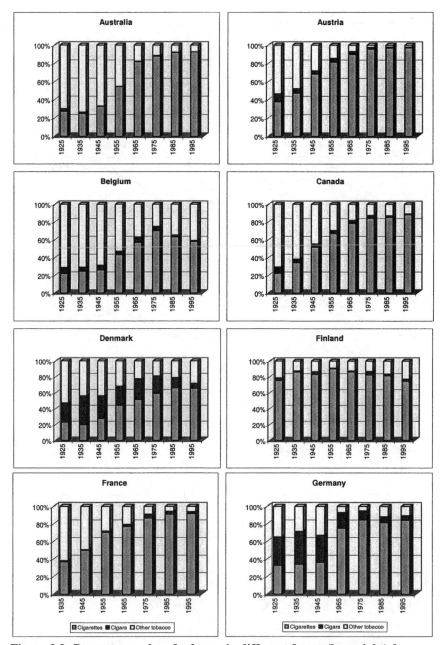

**Figure 3.2 Percentage sales of tobacco in different forms (by weight) for
selected years between 1925-1995 in selected countries**

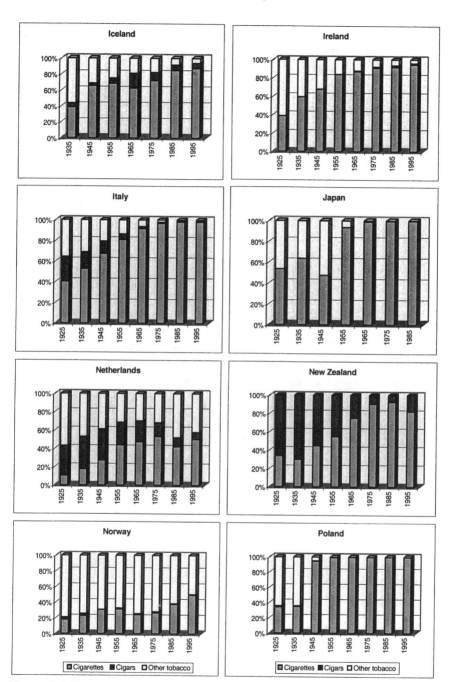

Figure 3.2 Percentage sales of tobacco in different forms (by weight) for selected years between 1925-1995 in selected countries (continued)

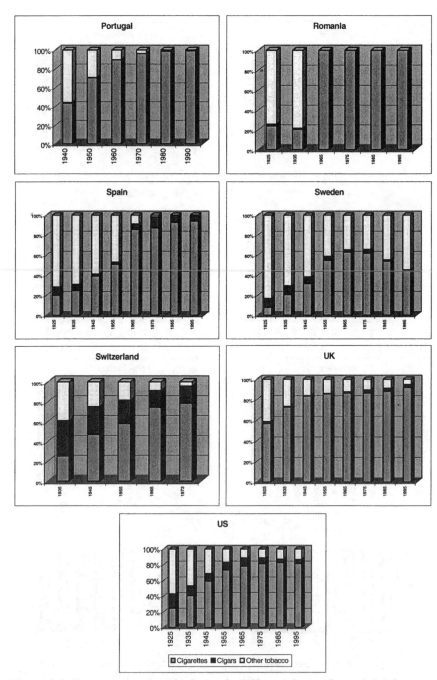

Figure 3.2 Percentage sales of tobacco in different forms (by weight) for selected years between 1925-1995 in selected countries (continued)

In Table 3.3, we present a cross-country comparison of prevalence of daily smoking of the adult population in a number of OECD countries over the years 1971 to 2001. As can be seen, in all countries, in general, the prevalence of daily smoking has declined from 1971 to 2001. The ratio of people smoking daily also varies across countries ranging from about one in three of the adult population in Japan, Korea, Luxembourg, Netherlands and Norway, to less than one in five in Australia, Canada, Sweden and the US in 2001.

Table 3.3 Proportion of daily smokers among the population aged 15 and over, selected OECD countries, 1971 to 2001 (in percentages)

Country (1)	1971 (2)	1981 (3)	1991 (4)	2001 (5)
Australia	37.0	36.0	26.7	19.8
Austria	27.7	28.1	27.5	n.a.
Belgium	n.a.	40.5	28.5	28.0
Canada	39.5	32.8	25.9	19.8
Czech Republic	n.a.	n.a.	26.1	23.5
Denmark	56.0	49.0	44.0	30.5
Finland	n.a.	27.2	27.0	23.4
France	n.a.	31.4	28.5	27.0
Germany	n.a.	45.4	23.7	24.7
Hungary	n.a.	n.a.	35.5	30.1
Iceland	n.a.	n.a.	30.5	23.6
Ireland	45.6	n.a.	28.5	27.0
Italy	n.a.	n.a.	25.7	24.4
Japan	46.1	43.1	37.7	34.3
Korea	n.a.	n.a.	34.7	33.5
Luxembourg	n.a.	n.a.	33.0	32.0
Netherlands	55.0	42.0	38.0	33.0
New Zealand	n.a.	32.0	26.0	22.0
Norway	41.0	35.0	34.0	32.0
Sweden	n.a.	30.4	25.1	18.9
UK	46.5	39.0	30.0	27.0
US	37.3	33.5	22.0	19.0

Source: AIHW (2003).

Figure 3.3 presents[1] a cross-country comparison of the proportion of daily smokers among 10th grade boys and girls during 1999 in a number of European countries. As can be seen, the highest percentage of daily smokers among girls is 24 percent in the UK, which also exceeds the highest percentage of 18 percent for boys in Moscow. The lowest percentage for girls is 2 percent (Romania) and for boys is 5 percent (Italy, Slovenia and Greece).

In Sections 3.2-3.5, we consider the tobacco consumption patterns in detail in Australia, the US, the UK and New Zealand.

---

[1] Data are compiled from the ESPAD (2000) Survey. The country FYROM refers to Former Yugoslav Republic of Macedonia.

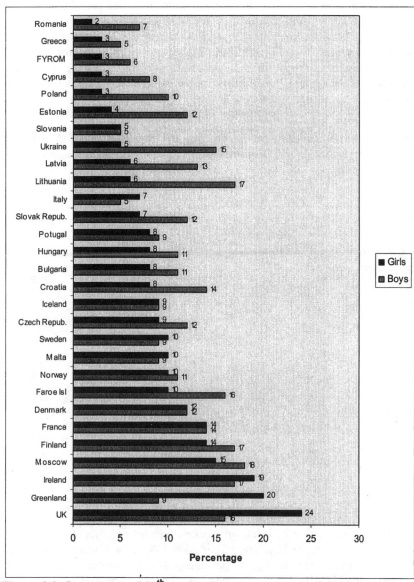

Figure 3.3   Percentage of 10th grade students who smoked daily, European countries, 1999

3.2   Tobacco Consumption in Australia

As in many other countries, various government and non-government organizations in Australia are progressively introducing a range of control measures to reduce the harmful effects of smoking to the public. According to recently released health department statistics, about 40 percent of the adult Australian population are regular smokers while about one-tenth of them are addicted to tobacco smoking. Tobacco is the second most accessible drug in Australia after alcohol, which is the most readily available drug. In 2001, one in every two Australians aged 14 and over were offered or had the opportunity to use tobacco. About half of the Australians aged 14 and above had smoked more than 100 cigarettes at some time in their lifetime. Most of the data used in this section are compiled from the *Australian Institute of Health and Welfare (AIHW) Publication*, 2000a, 2000b, 2001, 2002a, 2002b and 2003.

Figure 3.4 presents the proportion of the Australian adult population who smoke daily by gender. As can be seen, for the male adult population, the percentage has increased from 27 percent in 1991 to 29 percent in 1993 and has steadily decreased since then to 21 percent in 2001. For the female population, the proportion of daily smokers has declined from 22 percent in 1991 to 18 percent in 2001. While the percentage of male daily smokers has decreased by 8 percent between 1993 and 2001, the percentage of female daily smokers has decreased by only 3 percent during the same period.

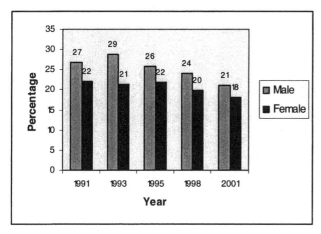

Figure 3.4 Proportion of daily smokers among the population aged 14 or over, Australia, 1991-2001

Figure 3.5 presents the proportion of the Australian adult population who nominated smoking as a drug problem. As can be seen, the proportion of Australians who associate smoking as a drug problem has decreased from 4.2 percent in 1998 to 2.7 percent in 2001. This could be due to the fact that more and more smokers are willing to give up smoking in recent years and many people still consider tobacco as a soft drug compared to the use of illicit drugs such as marijuana. The fall in this proportion is very similar among men and women.

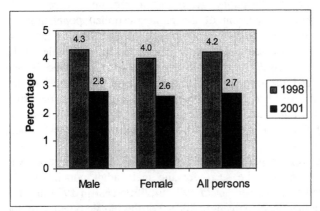

Figure 3.5 Proportion of Australians who associate smoking as a drug problem, by gender, Australia, 1998 and 2001

Figure 3.6 presents the proportion of adult Australians who find regular use of tobacco acceptable, by gender, in 1998 and 2001. As can be seen, overall, this proportion was stable during 1998 to 2001. This proportion increased slightly for male Australians while it decreased slightly for female Australians. That is, men appear to be more tolerant towards smoking than women. The difference in proportion between males and females is on the increase and was about 6 percent in 2001.

Table 3.4 presents the smoking status of males, females and all persons in Australia for the years 1998 and 2001, disaggregated by age groups. As can be seen from the last column for 'all persons', one in every five Australians aged 14 or

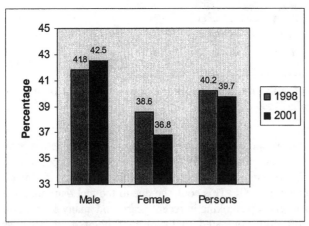

Figure 3.6 Proportion of Australians who find regular smoking acceptable by gender, Australia, 1998 and 2001

Table 3.4 Proportion of smokers aged 14 and over by age group and gender (in percentages) and mean number of cigarettes smoked per week, Australia, 1998 and 2001

Smoking status (1)	1998 All ages (2)	Age groups, 2001						
		14–19 (3)	20–29 (4)	30–39 (5)	40–49 (6)	50–59 (7)	60+ (8)	All (9)
Male								
Daily	24.2	14.1	28.5	27.3	23.6	20.3	10.2	21.1
Occasional[1]								
Weekly	*2.0*	*2.7*	*3.3*	*2.8*	*1.3*	*1.2*	*0.7*	*2.0*
Less than weekly	*1.6*	*3.4*	*5.1*	*2.8*	*2.3*	*1.7*	*0.6*	*2.6*
All smokers	27.8	20.2	36.9	32.9	27.2	23.2	11.5	25.7
Ex-smoker[2]	28.3	4.0	12.4	21.8	33.9	44.2	53.0	29.6
Never smoked[3]	43.9	75.9	50.7	45.4	38.9	32.5	35.5	44.7
Average number of cigarettes/week		71.2	86.7	118.4	129.9	142.4	115.4	111.8
Female								
Daily	19.6	16.2	23.7	24.3	20.8	16.1	7.8	18.0
Occasional								
Weekly	*1.6*	*2.0*	*2.3*	*1.7*	*1.1*	*0.7*	*0.2*	*1.3*
Less than weekly	*1.1*	*2.4*	*3.2*	*1.8*	*1.2*	*0.8*	*0.3*	*1.5*
All smokers	22.3	20.6	29.2	27.8	23.1	17.6	8.3	20.8
Ex-smoker	28.4	4.7	17.1	25.6	29.0	26.0	26.6	22.9
Never smoked	54.3	74.7	53.7	46.7	47.8	56.4	65.2	56.4
Average number of cigarettes/week		72.2	83.0	105.4	128.4	137.4	120.0	106.5
All persons								
Daily	21.8	15.1	26.1	25.7	22.2	18.2	8.9	19.5
Occasional								
Weekly	*1.8*	*2.3*	*2.8*	*2.2*	*1.2*	*1.0*	*0.4*	*1.6*
Less than weekly	*1.3*	*2.9*	*4.1*	*2.3*	*1.8*	*1.2*	*0.4*	*2.0*
All smokers	24.9	20.3	33.0	30.2	25.2	20.4	9.7	23.1
Ex-smoker	25.9	4.4	14.7	23.7	31.5	35.3	38.7	26.2
Never smoked	49.2	75.3	52.2	46.1	43.3	44.3	51.6	50.6
Average number of cigarettes/week		71.7	85.1	112.3	129.2	140.3	117.5	109.4

[1] Occasional smoker is a person who smokes less than daily, that is, weekly or less than weekly. [2] Ex-smoker is a person who has smoked at least 100 cigarettes or the equivalent amount of tobacco in their life, and is no longer smoking. [3] Never smoked is a person who has never smoked 100 cigarettes or the equivalent amount of tobacco in their life. Source: *Statistics on Drug Use in Australia*, 2002; AIHW (2002b) and AIHW (2003).

older smoked daily in 2001. Overall, the proportion of weekly or less than weekly smokers is about 4 percent. A comparison across the different age groups among males and females shows that the highest percentage of daily smokers among the male population was in the 20-29 age group (28.5 percent) while the highest percentage of daily smokers among the female population was in the 30-39 age group (24.3 percent). Females in the 14-19 age group were more likely to smoke daily than males in the same age group. With respect to all ages, more males (21.1 percent) smoked daily than females (18.0 percent). The proportion of daily smokers among the male as well as the female population increases at the early age groups and decreases afterwards. A comparison of entries in column 2 with column 9 reveals that the proportion of smokers among the Australian adult population has decreased between 1998 and 2001. The reduction in the proportion of smokers for the Australian male population between 1998 and 2001 is one and a half times that for the Australian female population.

The last row under each category, male, female and all persons, of Table 3.4 shows the average number of cigarettes smoked per week by each age group. A comparison of the entries for males and females shows that, an average male smokes more cigarettes than an average female. As can be seen, the average number of cigarettes smoked per week by various age groups of the Australian population indicates a common trend among male, female and all (persons) smokers. The average number of cigarettes smoked per week increased with age until the 50-59 age group (142 cigarettes/week for male, 137 for female and 140 for all persons) and then decreased. The male and female teenage smokers, on average, smoked about 72 cigarettes per week. Except for the 14-19 and 60+ age groups, on average, males smoke a higher number of cigarettes than females.

In Table 3.5 we present the tobacco smoking status of Australians grouped into indigenous and non-indigenous Australians. A comparison of the two respective columns of the table reveals that an indigenous Australian is more than twice likely to smoke daily than a non-indigenous Australian. While one in every two indigenous Australians (49 percent) is a smoker, only one in every four non-indigenous Australians (23 percent) is a smoker.

Table 3.6 presents the smoking status of Australians in 2001 by various socio-economic characteristics such as education, labour force status, income level,

Table 3.5 Proportion of smokers among indigenous and non-indigenous persons aged 14 and over by smoking status and gender, Australia, 2001

Smoking status	Indigenous Australians			Non-indigenous Australians		
	Male	Female	Persons	Male	Female	Persons
(1)	(2)	(3)	(4)	(5)	(6)	(7)
All smokers						
Daily	43	47	45	21	18	19
Occasional	6	3	4	5	3	4
Ex-smoker	12	13	12	30	23	26
Never smoked	39	37	38	45	57	51

See footnote to Table 3.4. Indigenous Australians refers to the Aboriginal and Torres Strait islander people in Australia. Source: AIHW (2003).

Table 3.6 Proportion of smokers aged 14 and over by smoking status, and mean number of cigarettes smoked by gender for various socio-economic characteristics, Australia, 2001

Characteristics	Percentage by smoking status			Average number of cigarettes smoked per week		
	Never smoked	Ex-smoker	Smoker	Male	Female	Persons
(1)	(2)	(3)	(4)	(5)	(6)	(7)
Education						
Without post-school qualification	53.3	22.4	24.2	116.6	111.6	114.0
With post-school qualification	48.4	29.6	22.0	106.7	97.6	103.2
Labour force status						
Currently employed	47.0	27.1	25.9	111.1	98.3	106.3
Student	74.6	7.3	18.1	54.9	64.6	59.5
Unemployed	37.6	18.2	44.3	121.1	116.5	119.5
Retired/pension/home duties	49.4	32.7	17.9	137.6	127.0	130.4
Main language spoken at home						
English	49.3	27.1	23.6	112.9	107.2	110.3
Other	68.0	14.2	17.8	91.0	75.7	86.8
Socioeconomic status						
1st quintile	48.0	26.2	25.8	128.8	115.2	122.4
2nd quintile	49.2	25.7	25.1	122.0	113.6	118.1
3rd quintile	50.0	26.3	23.7	107.2	106.5	106.9
4th quintile	50.1	26.3	23.6	110.4	99.3	105.3
5th quintile	54.9	26.7	18.4	85.6	87.9	86.6
Geography						
Urban	52.1	25.4	22.5	108.5	103.0	106.0
Rural/remote	46.7	28.3	25.0	118.1	113.7	116.2
Marital status						
Never married	61.5	10.4	28.0	93.3	86.5	90.5
Divorced/separated/widowed	45.0	28.2	26.7	133.4	130.1	131.6
Married/de facto	47.0	32.5	20.5	118.8	109.8	114.8
Indigenous status						
Indigenous	37.7	12.4	49.9	132.6	119.2	125.4
Non-Indigenous	50.8	26.4	22.8	110.8	105.3	108.3

Source: AIHW (2002b).

marital status etc and the number of cigarettes smoked per week by gender. Columns 2-4 of the table present the percentages of smokers by smoking status and various characteristics of adult Australians. As can be seen, in 2001, the percentage of smokers without post-school qualification was slightly higher than the percentage of smokers with post-school qualification. The possibility of an unemployed person being a smoker is twice as likely to that of a currently employed person. An Australian whose main spoken language at home is not English (non-English speaking background) is less likely to smoke than a person who spoke mainly English (English speaking background) at home. In terms of the socio-economic status, a higher proportion of the lower-income group smoke than the high-income group. With increasing socio-economic status, the percentage of smokers has fallen in 2001.

In terms of the geographic location, it is more likely for a person to be a smoker in the rural area than a person in the urban area. Considering the marital status of the population, three in five Australians (62 percent) who have never married have never smoked while one in two divorced/separated/widowed and married/de facto (47 percent) have never smoked. On the other hand, it is also more likely to find a never married person to be a smoker than a married/de facto person to be a smoker. Columns 5-7 of Table 3.6 provide information on the average number of cigarettes smoked per week by gender, socio-economic and other characteristics. The average number of cigarettes smoked by an Australian without post-school qualification is 114 cigarettes per week while that for an Australian with post-school qualification is 103 cigarettes per week. On average, an Australian student smokes 60 cigarettes per week, half that of an unemployed (120 cigarettes) or a retired (130 cigarettes per week) person. There is significant difference between the English and non-English speaking groups in terms of the average number of cigarettes they smoke. On average, a person with English speaking background smokes about 25 cigarettes per week more than a person from a non-English speaking background.

It can also be seen from Table 3.6 that Australians living in the rural areas are more likely to smoke more cigarettes than those living in urban areas. On average, a divorced/separated/widowed person smokes (132 cigarettes/week) more cigarettes than a never married (91 cigarettes/week) or married/de facto (115 cigarettes/week) person. It can also be noted that, on average, an Aboriginal person smokes a higher number of cigarettes (125 cigarettes/week) than a non-Aboriginal person (108 cigarettes/week). From columns 5 and 6 of Table 3.6, another general observation can be made with respect to smoking status and gender. That is, male smokers smoke more cigarettes than female smokers with the exception of students, where, on average, female students smoke (65 cigarettes/week) more cigarettes than male students (55 cigarettes/week).

In Table 3.7, we present the tax revenue raised by the Australian government from tobacco excise, customs clearance and state business franchise fees. As can be seen, the revenue comes mostly from excise and state franchise fees.

3.3　　Tobacco Consumption in the UK

The increasing smoking habit among school children is a major concern to many governments in the developed countries, especially in the UK, where the problem is severe. Recent *UK National Statistics* (NS, 2003) reveals that an alarming proportion of school children, especially girls aged between 11 and 15 smoke regularly. The UK government is determined to bring down this percentage to

Table 3.7 Government revenue from excise, customs clearances, and state business franchise fees related to the sale of tobacco, Australia, 1996-2002*

Duty	1996	1997	1998	1999	2000	2001	2002
Excise	1,617	1,629	4,052	4,696	4,693	4,616	4,685
Customs	108	111	242	255	286	376	399
State franchise taxes	2,621	2,855	n.a.	n.a.	n.a.	48	n.a.
Total	4,346	4,595	4,294	4,951	4,979	5,040	5,085

*The year 1996, for example, refers to the financial year in Australia, 1 July 1995 to 30 June 1996.
Source: AIHW (2003).

below 9 percent in 2010. In this section, we analyse the tobacco consumption patterns of the UK population based on various characteristics such as gender, socio-economic status, age group etc. The data used in this section are compiled mainly from the *UK National Statistics* (NS, 2002).

Table 3.8 presents the cigarette smoking status by gender over the years 1996-2001 in the United Kingdom (UK). As can be seen, the percentage of current smokers in the UK has fallen from 28 percent in 1996 to 24 percent in 2001. The fall in the percentage of current female smokers (from 28 to 23 percent) is much higher than the fall in the percentage of current male smokers (from 28 to 26 percent). The percentage of persons who have never smoked cigarettes has increased from 46 percent in 1996 to 50 percent in 2001.

Table 3.8 Proportion of smokers by cigarette smoking status and gender, UK, 1996-2001

Cigarette smoking status	Year				
(1)	1996 (2)	1997 (3)	1999 (4)	2000 (5)	2001 (6)
Male					
Current smoker	28	26	27	26	26
Ex-regular smoker	32	32	34	34	32
Never smoked	39	41	39	40	43
Female					
Current smoker	28	27	26	26	23
Ex-regular smoker	19	23	22	22	21
Never smoked	52	50	52	51	56
All persons					
Current smoker	28	26	27	26	24
Ex-regular smoker	26	27	28	28	25
Never smoked	46	46	46	46	50

Figure 3.7 shows the smoking status by gender and socio-economic group. As can be seen, across all socio-economic groups, the percentage of non-smokers among females is higher than the percentage of smokers and ex-smokers. Furthermore, the percentage of non-smokers among females is higher than that among males across each socio-economic group. The percentage of smokers among the professionals and managers is slightly higher among females than males; and it is the opposite among skilled and unskilled workers.

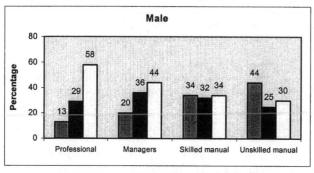

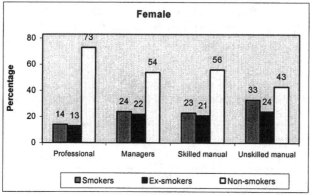

Figure 3.7   Proportion of smokers by smoking status and socio-economic status, males and females, UK, 1999

Table 3.9 shows the prevalence of cigarette smoking by gender and different age groups for the years 1996-2001. Considering the various age groups, in recent years, the prevalence of smoking was higher among the 25-34 age group. The percentage of prevalence of smoking was stable over the years across most age groups. Figure 3.8 shows the prevalence of smoking for males and females over a long period of time from 1974-1998. As can be seen, the percentage of prevalence of smoking has generally fallen but is higher among males than females, with the gap between males and females narrowing in recent years.

Table 3.9 Proportion of smokers among various age groups by gender, UK, 1996-2001 (percentages)

Age group	1996		1997		1999		2000		2001	
	M	F	M	F	M	F	M	F	M	F
(1)	(2)	(3)	(4)	(5)	(6)	(7)	(8)	(9)	(10)	(11)
16–24 yrs	39	36	31	26	39	35	38	33	30	26
25–34 yrs	39	34	35	35	33	34	35	36	40	35
35–44 yrs	29	32	27	29	31	28	28	28	28	31
45–54 yrs	26	27	26	23	30	26	24	27	31	28
55–64 yrs	23	27	26	16	22	26	24	21	20	23
65–74 yrs	15	22	18	12	17	19	16	17	14	23
75+ yrs	10	10	8	10	9	6	13	10	7	8
All ages	28	28	26	23	27	26	26	26	26	27

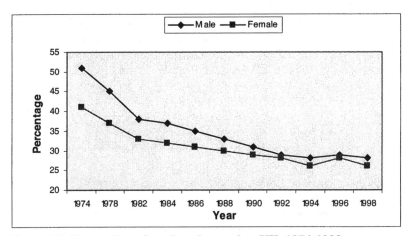

Figure 3.8 Proportion of smokers by gender, UK, 1974-1998

Table 3.10 presents the prevalence of cigarette smoking by gender and socio-economic status for the year 2001. The percentage of prevalence was lower for the managerial occupations (males) and for the 'never worked' category (females) when compared to the other two socio-economic groups. Among males and females, the percentage of prevalence of cigarette smoking was higher for males than females except for the managerial category.

Table 3.11 presents the daily cigarette consumption by gender over the years 1996-2001. Among both, male and female, a higher percentage smoke more than 10 cigarettes per day. In 2001, 77 percent of males and 66 percent of females smoked at least 10 cigarettes per day in the UK. About one-fourth of males and about one-third of females smoked less than 10 cigarettes per day.

In Figure 3.9, we show the percentage of smokers who would like to give up smoking altogether by gender and number of cigarettes smoked per day over the

Table 3.10 Proportion of smokers by socio-economic classification and gender, 2001 (in percentages)

Social-economic classification	Male	Female	All persons
(1)	(2)	(3)	(4)
Managerial & Professional	17	20	18
Intermediate	26	22	24
Routine and manual	33	27	30
Never worked [1]	26	14	19
Total	26	23	24

[1] Never worked and long-term unemployed.

Table 3.11 Proportion of daily smokers by number of cigarettes smoked per day and gender, UK, 1996-2001

Number of cigarettes/day	1996		1997		1999		2000		2001	
	M	F	M	F	M	F	M	F	M	F
(1)	(2)	(3)	(4)	(5)	(6)	(7)	(8)	(9)	(10)	(11)
1. 20+/day	38	28	32	29	36	24	34	32	37	25
2. 10–19/day	37	41	43	42	38	47	39	37	40	41
3. <10/day	25	31	25	29	25	29	27	31	23	34

period 1992-2001. As can be seen, people who smoke between 10-19 cigarettes per day are more likely to give up smoking than the other two age groups. However, the proportion of people who would give up smoking increased up to 2000 and then decreased in 2001 for both the male and female population, regardless of the number of cigarettes smoked per day.

The time series plot in Figure 3.10 shows the tax revenue from tobacco and that revenue as a percentage of all government tax revenues for the UK during the years, 1978 to 1998. As can be seen, while the tax revenue increased about four-fold during the 20-year period, the tax revenue from tobacco as a proportion of all tax revenue fell by about one-third.

3.4   Tobacco Consumption in the US

The United States (US) is one of the countries in the industrialized world allocating a large proportion of its resources to combat tobacco consumption. In 2001, about 67 million Americans were reported to be current users of tobacco. In many medical research publications, cigarette smoking has been identified as the most important contributor to premature mortality in the US. It is also reported that

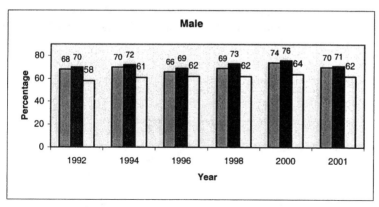

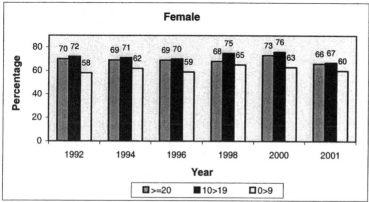

Figure 3.9 Proportion of smokers who would like to give up smoking altogether by number of cigarettes smoked per day and gender, UK, 1992-2001

smoking directly contributes to the death of 470,000 Americans every year due to diseases related to smoking. Smoking is reported as responsible for the death of one in five Americans and costs the US economy 100 billion dollars per year in health care costs and lost productivity. In terms of packets of cigarettes sold in the US, this cost is estimated to be equivalent to US$7.18 per pack. It is also estimated that smoking during pregnancy has resulted in estimated 1007 infant deaths annually in the US. In this section, we look at tobacco consumption patterns by Americans with respect to age, race, gender and various social characteristics.

Like many other western governments, the US government spends a significant amount of resources to educate its people about the effects of cigarette smoking on their health. Despite all the efforts, a very high proportion of Americans still continue to smoke. According to the *National Household Survey* (NHSDA, 2003a), 30 percent of those aged 12 and over or about 67 million Americans are reported to have used tobacco products in the past 12 months. Figure 3.11 presents the details about the number of tobacco consumers with respect to the type of tobacco product in the US. As can be seen, the majority of Americans smoke cigarettes followed by cigars, smokeless tobacco and pipes.

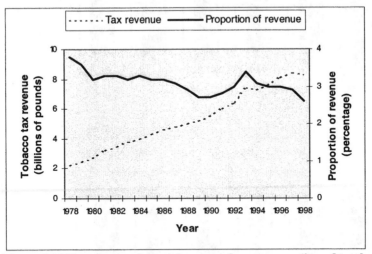

Figure 3.10 Tax revenue from tobacco and as a proportion of total revenue, UK, 1978-1998

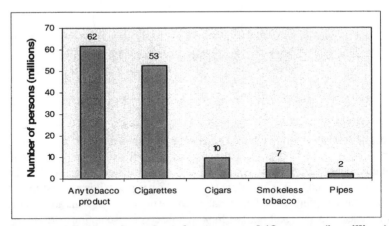

Figure 3.11 Estimated number of persons aged 18 or over (in millions) who have smoked in the past month, US, 2000

Figure 3.12 shows the plot of age category against the percentage of lifetime, past year and past month use of cigarettes for the year 2001. As can be seen, the percentages of lifetime smokers, past year smokers and past month smokers have all increased up to age 21. While the percentage of lifetime users remains steady for those aged 30 and over, there is a sharp fall in the percentage of past year and past month smokers among those aged 30 and over.

Figure 3.13 shows the percentage of persons aged 12 or older who used tobacco in the past month by product type over the period 1999 to 2001. As can be seen, for each product type, the percentage of people who have used it in the past month is stable over the three years. Altogether, about 30 percent of adult Americans have used tobacco products in the past month.

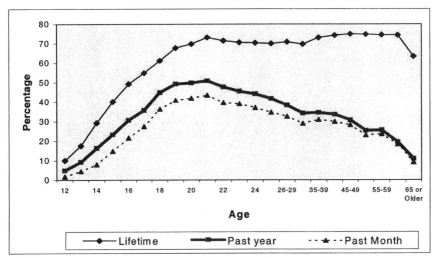

Figure 3.12 **Percentage of persons reporting lifetime, past year and past month use of cigarettes by age groups, US, 2001**

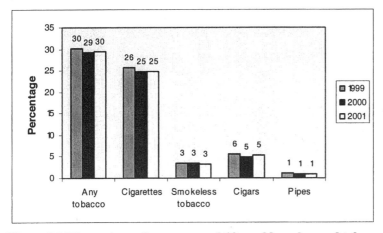

Figure 3.13 **Percentage of persons aged 12 or older who used tobacco in the past month by product type, US, 1999-2001**

Figure 3.14 presents the percentage of tobacco users by product type in the past month for the 12-17 age group for the three years 1999 to 2001. As can be seen, over the years 1999-2001, among the 12-17 age group, the percentage of cigarette smokers has fallen from 15 percent to 13 percent and the percentage who have used any form of tobacco has fallen from 17 percent to 15 percent.

Figure 3.15 presents the percentage of tobacco users among the 12-17 age group by gender. The figure reveals that the percentage of cigarette use in the past month among male as well as female fell in recent years.

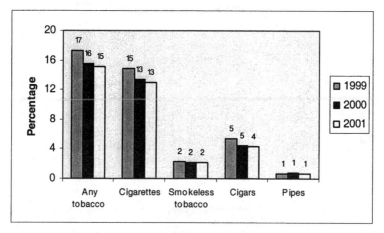

Figure 3.14 Percentage of youths aged 12-17 who have used tobacco in the past month by product type, US, 1999-2001

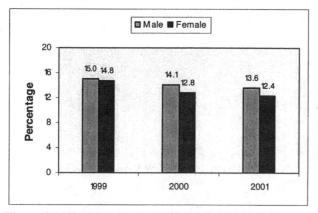

Figure 3.15 Percentage of youths aged 12-17 who have used tobacco in the past month by gender, US, 1999-2001

In Figure 3.16, we show the percentage of adults (aged 12 and over) who smoked tobacco in the past month by product type and age groups. As can be seen, with all product types the percentage is high for the 18-25 age group. About 15 percent of the 12-17 age group, 44 percent of the 18-25 age group and 29 percent of the 26+ age group consumed some kind of tobacco product in the US during 2001. Across all age groups, cigarette consumption is higher than the consumption of any other product type.

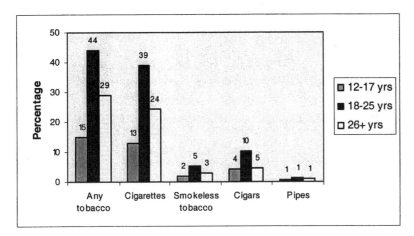

Figure 3.16 Percentage of persons aged 12 or older who have used tobacco in the past month by product type and age groups, US, 2001

Figure 3.17 shows the percentage of American current smokers over the period 1970 to 1997, disaggregated by age groups. Over time a clear downward trend appears across all age groups, except the 18-24 age group during 1990-1997. The percentage of current smokers in the 18-24 age group fell from 38 percent in 1970 to 25 percent in 1990 and increased to 29 percent in 1997. There was a significant fall in the percentage of current smokers in the 25-44 age group (fell from 45 percent 1970 to 29 percent in 1997) and 45-64 age group (from 39 percent in 1970 to 24 percent in 1997) while only a fall of 4 percent (from 16 percent in 1970 to 12 percent in 1997) in the 64+ age group.

Figure 3.18 depicts the percentage of persons among smokers and non-smokers who used other drugs in the past month. As can be seen, it is more likely for smokers to use any other illicit drugs, binge alcohol or heavy alcohol than non-smokers. While about 40 percent of smokers tend to be binge alcohol drinkers, only about 14 percent of non-smokers tend to do the same.

Figure 3.19 presents the percentage of adult Americans who used cigarettes in the past month in 2001 by ethnic group. The percentage of smokers among the native Indian Americans is 40 percent, which is higher than the proportion of smokers among any other ethnic group. Twenty seven percent of the Puerto Rican

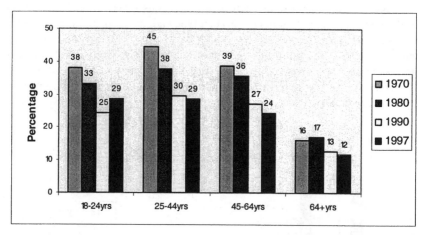

Figure 3.17 Percentage of current smokers by age groups, US, 1970-1997

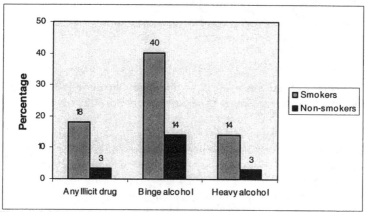

**Figure 3.18 Percentage of smokers and non-smokers aged 12 or older who
have used illicit drugs, binge alcohol and heavy alcohol, US, 2001**

Americans and 26 percent of the white Americans are the next two highest groups. Only 10 percent of the Chinese Americans used cigarettes in the past month during 2001. Figure 3.20 presents the movements in the percentage of white and black American smokers during the years 1970-1997. As can be seen, while the percentage of black smokers was higher than the percentage of white smokers during 1970 to 1980, the percentages were about the same in the last 20-year period.

Figures 3.21-3.23 present the percentage of smokers by their socio-economic status. Figure 3.21 shows the distribution of consumers of the four product types

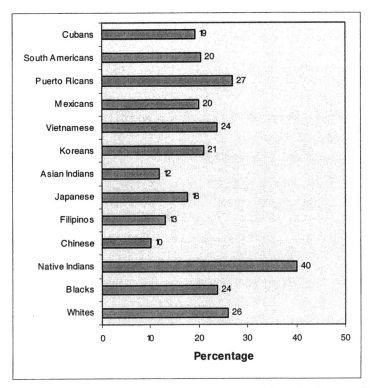

Figure 3.19 Percentage of persons aged 12 or older who have used cigarettes in the past month by race/ethnicity, US, 2000/2001

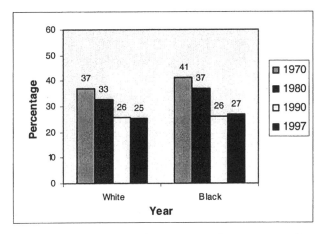

Figure 3.20 Percentage of current smokers among white and black adults, US, 1970-1997

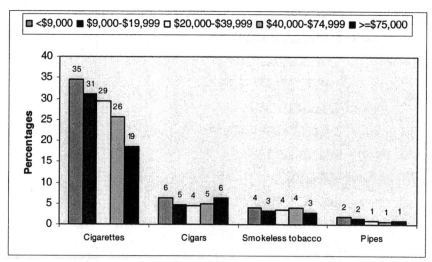

Figure 3.21 Percentage of persons aged 18 or over who have used tobacco in the past month by level of family income, US, 2000

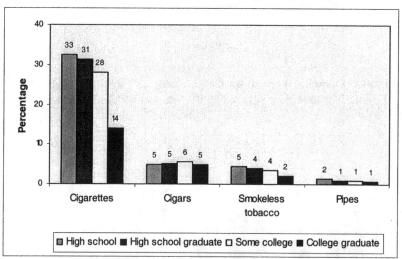

Figure 3.22 Percentage of persons aged 18 or over who have used tobacco in the past month by level of education, US, 2000

according to their income level. As can be seen, with increasing income the consumption of tobacco products generally decreases with the exception of the use of cigars with the over $75,000 income group. As in Figure 3.21, Figure 3.22 shows the distribution of smokers for each product type with respect to educational

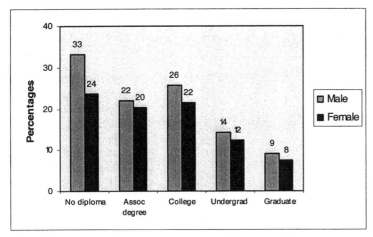

Figure 3.23 Percentage of persons aged 18 or over who were current smokers by level of education, US, 2000

level. With increasing educational level, the percentage of smokers falls under each tobacco product type, with the exception that a slightly higher percentage of college qualified persons who smoke cigars among the cigar smokers group. Figure 3.23 shows the percentage of male and female smokers with respect to the educational level. As can be seen, generally, at all educational levels, the percentage of males is higher than the females and with increasing level of education the percentage of smokers falls. For example, about one third of males and one fourth of females who do not have a diploma smoke. In comparison, only about 9 percent of graduate males and 8 percent of graduate females smoke.

3.5 Tobacco Consumption in New Zealand

Teenage smoking in New Zealand, especially among females, has been on the increase and is a concern to New Zealand Government. Currently, while only one in every four New Zealanders is a smoker, the proportion of women smokers in the 15-24 age group is higher than the proportion for males in the same age. According to the Ministry of Health statistics, there are about 388 deaths attributable to second-hand smoke ('passive smoking') in year 2000, which is about 75 percent of the number of people killed each year on the roads of New Zealand in recent years. In this section we look at various statistics regarding tobacco consumption patterns in New Zealand.

Table 3.12 gives the loose tobacco and manufactured cigarettes expressed as number of cigarettes equivalent per adult (15+) available for consumption. As can be seen, the tobacco released in the form of loose tobacco has been more than halved from 534 cigarettes equivalent per adult in 1970 to 251 cigarettes equivalent

Table 3.12 Tobacco consumption, NZ, 1970-1999

Year	Loose Tobacco	Manufactured Cigarettes	Total
(1)	(2)	(3)	(4)
1970	534	2581	3115
1971	493	2615	3108
1972	468	2705	3173
1973	416	2697	3113
1974	371	2740	3111
1975	347	2885	3232
1976	319	2835	3154
1977	300	2857	3157
1978	272	2794	3066
1979	255	2715	2970
1980	239	2617	2856
1981	239	2666	2905
1982	230	2603	2833
1983	228	2541	2769
1984	219	2560	2779
1985	200	2293	2493
1986	202	2102	2304
1987	203	2125	2328
1988	217	2101	2318
1989	216	1662	1878
1990	233	1738	1971
1991	243	1495	1738
1992	283	1277	1560
1993	295	1232	1527
1994	249	1221	1470
1995	287	1187	1474
1996	230	1280	1510
1997	253	1191	1444
1998	259	1118	1377
1999	251	1062	1313

Source: NZHIS (2001).

per adult in 1999. The number of manufactured cigarettes released has also fallen by about 60 percent from 2581 cigarettes per adult in 1970 to 1062 cigarettes per adult in 1999. In total, the tobacco released for consumption has fallen by 58 percent from 3115 cigarettes equivalent per adult in 1970 to 1313 cigarettes per adult in 1999.

Figure 3.24 plots the number of cigarettes released per adult for consumption against the price index. As can be seen, there appears an opposite movement in terms of the number of cigarettes released and the tobacco price index. Figure 3.25 shows the percentage of adult population smokers by ethnicity. As can be seen, the proportion of indigenous Maori population smokers is almost twice that of the proportion of the non-Maori (European) population. While there has been a significant fall in the proportion of smokers in the non-Maori population, the proportion of smokers in the Maori population still remains high and has increased from 1996 onwards.

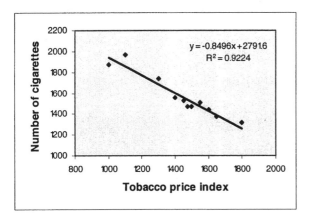

Figure 3.24 Available cigarettes per adult against tobacco price index, NZ, 1989-1998

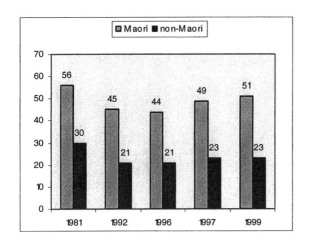

Figure 3.25 Percentage of smoking adult population by ethnicity, NZ, 1981-1999

Table 3.13 presents the percentage of cigarette smokers by age, gender and ethnicity based on the New Zealand 1996 census. Clearly the Maori group has the highest percentage of smokers and the Asians has the lowest percentage of smokers. In all ethnic groups, the 25-44 age group has the highest percentage of smokers while the 65+ age group has the lowest. With the exception of the 15-24 age group, males have a higher percentage of smokers than females.

Figure 3.26 shows the percentage of cigarette smokers by personal income groups. The middle-income group ($20,000-$30,000) has the highest percentage of smokers and lowest percentage of those who have never smoked.

Table 3.13 Percentage of cigarette smokers by age, gender and ethnicity, NZ, 1996 census

Age group (1)	European		Maori		Pacific		Asian		Other		All	
	M (2)	F (3)	M (4)	F (5)	M (6)	F (7)	M (8)	F (9)	M (10)	F (11)	M (12)	F (13)
15–24yrs	24	25	37	47	27	24	13	5	18	14	26	28
25–44yrs	27	25	45	53	40	29	23	5	30	16	30	28
45–64yrs	21	18	36	40	37	19	18	4	23	16	23	20
65+yrs	12	9	21	19	24	11	16	5	16	11	12	9
All ages	22	20	40	47	35	25	19	5	26	15	25	23
All persons	21		44		30		11		21		24	

Source: *Statistics New Zealand*, Census of Population and Dwellings, 1996; and NZHIS (2001).

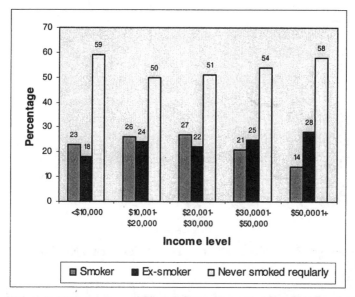

Figure 3.26 Percentage of cigarette smokers by personal income group, NZ, 1996

Table 3.14 shows the percentage prevalence of cigarette smoking over the years 1976-1998, by gender and differing age groups. As can seen, prevalence percentage is high among both males and females in the 25-34 age group. The percentage prevalence is lower among the 55+ age male and female groups.

Table 3.14 Percentage prevalence of cigarette smoking, NZ, 1976–1998

Year	15–24	25–34	35–54	55+	Total males	15–24	25–34	35–54	55+	Total females	Total population
	Age groups: Males					Age groups: Females					
(1)	(2)	(3)	(4)	(5)	(6)	(7)	(8)	(9)	(10)	(11)	(12)
1976	35	43	44	35	40	34	38	35	21	32	36
1981	33	38	38	30	35	35	34	32	19	29	32
1983	34	38	37	29	35	40	35	31	21	31	33
1984	35	39	35	27	34	40	34	29	22	31	32
1985	31	35	31	24	30	40	34	29	19	30	30
1986	31	32	29	24	29	37	34	32	21	31	30
1987	32	34	34	22	31	36	35	26	19	28	30
1988	27	38	31	20	29	39	35	28	16	29	29
1989	28	30	28	20	27	37	33	25	16	27	27
1990	30	32	30	18	28	34	32	28	16	27	28
1991	28	35	27	18	27	33	30	24	16	26	26
1992	25	34	29	18	27	33	36	27	14	27	27
1993	28	35	30	19	28	30	34	26	16	26	27
1994	28	36	30	17	28	34	33	25	16	26	27
1995	25	35	29	19	27	33	36	25	14	26	27
1996	27	33	26	19	26	36	35	26	13	26	26
1997	27	30	28	16	26	35	36	26	14	27	26
1998	27	34	28	16	26	30	31	26	12	24	25

Source: NZHIS (2001).

3.6   Concluding Comments

In this chapter we presented a cross-country analysis of tobacco consumption. We have used time-series cross-country and survey data from various government departments and statistical office sources for this purpose. We also looked at the tobacco consumption within individual countries, Australia, UK, the USA and New Zealand. The time-series and cross-country data reveal that, in most countries, total per adult tobacco consumption has peaked and is decreasing in the last 25 years. The market share of different types of tobacco products is also changing to the extent that, in some countries, cigarette consumption has taken over all other tobacco product types such as cigars, pipes etc. We also found that in a number of European countries, the percentage of lifetime use of cigarettes and daily smoking is higher among girls than boys. Furthermore, we found the prevalence of daily smoking is falling in most countries.

At the individual country level, in Australia the proportion of daily smokers is decreasing every year and currently the proportion is 21 percent for males and 18 percent for females. The proportion of smokers with respect to various age groups increases with increasing age up to 29 for males and 39 for females and then starts to decline. On average, males smoke more cigarettes than females with the exception of females in the 14-19 and 60+ age groups, where females smoke more than males. An Australian, on average, adult smokes about 110 cigarettes per week. In terms of social characteristics, people at a lower education level, unemployed and retired people, low-income groups, people living in the rural area, divorced/separated/widowed people, indigenous people all tend to smoke more cigarettes than the corresponding other groups.

As in Australia, the prevalence of daily smoking in the UK shows that more males (26 percent) than females (23 percent) smoke daily. The proportion of smokers with respect to various age groups increases with increasing age up to 34 for males and females and then starts to decline. In terms of social characteristics unskilled workers tend to smoke more than skilled workers. About 40 percent of males and females smoke 70-133 cigarettes per week, while 37 percent of males and 25 percent of females smoke more than 140 cigarettes per week.

As in Australia and the UK, the trend in the US is that the percentage of smokers is on the decline. The proportion of current smokers in the 25-44 age group is higher than the proportion of current smokers in any other age group, which is similar to Australia and the UK. While the current smokers in all age groups are on the decline, the percentage is recently on the increase for the 18-24 age group. In terms of social characteristics, a higher proportion of low income groups smoke than the higher income groups; a higher proportion of native Indian and Black population also tend to smoke more than the white population; people with lower education level also smoke more than the people with higher education level.

As observed with Australia, the UK and the US, the proportion of smokers in New Zealand is highest in the 25-44 age group and among the local Maori population. We also found that the proportion of smokers decreases with increasing income as observed in the other countries, Australia, the UK and the US.

Chapter 4

Alcohol Consumption

Alcohol is the most commonly consumed licensed drug in the world. Second only to caffeine, alcohol is used by more people and in larger quantities than any other substance. According to archaeological evidence, alcohol has a long history in human civilization dating back to 6400BC. There were times when alcohol was unsuccessfully outlawed as well as times when alcohol was conditionally accepted in the society. A number of governments were greatly concerned about alcohol consumption during World War 1, as they feared that drunkenness may hamper the war efforts. For example, Russia outlawed the sale of vodka and the British government restricted the availability of alcohol by imposing restrictions on the Public Houses opening times (before the war started, it was 5am to mid-night and then, during the war, it was changed to 12:00-2.30pm and 6.30-9.30pm) and increased tax on alcohol (the rate of tax was increased to five times what it was before the war). Due to these restrictions in the UK from 1914 to 1918, total alcohol consumption fell from 89 million gallons to 37 million gallons and the number of convictions of being drunk in London fell from 67,103 in 1914 to 16,567 persons in 1918 (Learning Curve, *The UK National Archives*, London). However, a similar attempt by the Russian government to control alcohol sales ended up in failure as people started producing their own alcohol which resulted in only the reduction (about 30 percent) of the government's tax revenue.

Alcohol related research shows that drinking amongst young people and women are on the increase. This raises growing concerns to health authorities and social service departments of individual governments and international bodies such as the World Health Organization (WHO), United Nations Children Fund (UNICEF), etc. According to WHO (2003), while alcohol consumption is declining overall in most of the developed countries, it is on the increase in most of the developing countries and countries in the central and eastern Europe. The male population in these countries do most of the drinking to the extent that alcohol use is contributing to a major decline in the male life expectancy. Among those who drink alcohol, 10 percent are heavy drinkers who consume more than 50 percent of all alcohol consumed.

Worldwide manufacturing and supply of beer and spirits is being handled by a small number of multinational companies, especially in the developing countries. They cleverly market their products to simulate demand under the name of free market reforms in these countries in order to achieve their aim of increasing alcohol sales worldwide at a high cost to the local social structure of these countries. If alcohol consumption is not properly managed, excessive alcohol consumption can lead to various social, health and economic problems. Long term health problems associated with excessive alcohol consumption include irreparable damage to the brain and liver. Like tobacco, alcohol is also linked to the development of some types of cancer, high blood pressure and cardiac conditions. Alcohol is considered as a major factor responsible for death and injury on the roads, drowning, assaults, domestic violence and family disputes, divorce etc. The extent of alcohol's influence on issues such as those above is highlighted by a recent interview to the BBC by a spokesperson for the British Association of Accident and Emergency Medicine mentioning that 'I cannot underestimate the importance of alcohol in the workload of emergency departments - we would be out of business if it was not for alcohol' (BBC News, 2000).

Another important aspect of alcohol is its misuse by young children as alcohol is easily available at home like any food items. In some countries, children as young as 8-10 have been reported as having consumed alcohol. According to the BBC report (2000) on 'Alcohol Concern', the average weekly alcohol consumption among 11-15 year old drinkers is on the increase. Unlike tobacco consumption, which has no support from the medical profession, there is some support for alcohol consumption from certain sections of the medical profession who believe that a limited amount of consumption is good for people's health. While some medical scientists claim that 'beer/wine is good for human health' and others claim that 'moderate drinking protects bones', a majority of the medical profession support only a properly managed alcohol consumption habit.

In this chapter, we first present a global picture of alcohol consumption and then look more closely at the consumption patterns of alcohol in a selected number of countries.

4.1   A Global Picture

In this section, we present a cross-country comparison of alcohol consumption patterns at a global level.

Table 4.1 presents the per adult (15+) pure alcohol consumption (in litres) for the years 1961, 1971, 1981, 1991 and 2001, in a selected number of OECD countries. For some countries the data are incomplete due to unavailability of information. A comparison of entries in columns 2-6 for each country reveals that, in a majority of countries, alcohol consumption is on the decline during the last 30 years, while the level in 2001 is higher than the 1961 level for some countries. Also in some countries the change over the 40 years is huge. For example, between 1961 and 2001, alcohol consumption in Denmark and Iceland had doubled and in Finland and Netherlands it is tripled while in France and Italy alcohol consumption had been halved during the same period. Table 4.2 presents the same information but according to ranking in each time period. A general observation of this table is

Table 4.1 Per adult (15+) pure alcohol consumption (in litres) for years 1961, 1971, 1981, 1991 and 2001 in OECD countries

	Country	1961	1971	1981	1991	2001
	(1)	(2)	(3)	(4)	(5)	(6)
1.	Australia	9.3	11.6	13.0	10.0	9.8
2.	Austria	10.9	15.5	13.7	12.8	11.3
3.	Belgium	9.0	12.5	13.5	11.5	10.2
4.	Canada	7.2	9.0	10.8	8.8	7.6
5.	Czech Republic	n.a.	n.a.	12.3	11.5	11.8
6.	Denmark	5.8	9.3	12.0	11.6	11.6
7.	Finland	2.9	6.4	8.0	9.2	8.9
8.	France	25.1	22.5	19.7	16.2	12.9
9.	Germany	7.5	13.4	12.5	12.4	10.5
10.	Greece	7.2	7.0	12.7	10.6	9.4
11.	Hungary	8.1	11.9	14.8	13.3	11.1
12.	Iceland	2.5	4.1	4.4	5.1	6.3
13.	Ireland	7.8	11.2	13.0	10.6	12.3
14.	Italy	16.6	18.2	13.0	10.7	8.7
15.	Japan	n.a.	6.9	8.1	8.9	8.3
16.	Luxembourg	10.4	12.7	12.4	15.2	14.9
17.	Netherlands	3.7	8.5	11.3	10.0	10.0
18.	New Zealand	5.3	10.4	11.7	10.3	8.9
19.	Norway	3.5	4.9	5.3	4.9	5.6
20.	Poland	6.3	8.0	8.7	8.8	8.5
21.	Portugal	17.2	20.0	15.6	15.8	13.0
22.	Slovak Republic	7.1	13.6	14.5	13.7	9.2
23.	Spain	9.6	16.0	17.6	13.2	11.7
24.	Sweden	5.1	7.0	6.3	6.3	6.2
25.	Switzerland	12.7	14.2	13.7	12.9	11.2
26.	Turkey	0.9	1.2	1.6	1.4	1.4
27.	UK	n.a.	7.4	9.1	9.4	10.2
28.	US	7.8	9.8	10.5	9.7	8.3
Mean		8.4	10.9	11.4	10.5	9.6

Source: AIHW (2003).

the huge difference in the amount of alcohol consumed between the countries in the top and bottom of the tables. For example, in 1961, per adult consumption of alcohol in France (Rank 1: 25.1 litres) was three times that of the US (Rank 12: 7.8 litres). In 2001, per adult alcohol consumption in Luxembourg (Rank 1: 14.9 litres) was twice that of the US (Rank 23: 8.3 litres). As can be seen, during 1961-1991, the French consumed a higher amount of alcohol (on a per adult basis) than any other OECD country but its rank 1 status was replaced by Luxembourg in 2001. Portugal is ranked second, except in 1981 when it was replaced by Spain. Italy was

Table 4.2 Per adult (15+) pure alcohol consumption (in litres) by country ranking for the years 1961, 1971, 1981, 1991 and 2001 in OECD countries

	1961		1971		1981		1991		2001	
Rank	Country	Litres	Country	Litres	Country	Litres	Country	Litres	Country	Litres
	(1)	(2)	(3)	(4)	(5)	(6)	(7)	(8)	(9)	(10)
1	France	25.1	France	22.5	France	19.7	France	16.2	Luxembourg	14.9
2	Portugal	17.2	Portugal	20.0	Spain	17.6	Portugal	15.8	Portugal	13.0
3	Italy	16.6	Italy	18.2	Portugal	15.6	Luxembourg	15.2	France	12.9
4	Switzerland	12.7	Ireland	17.2	Hungary	14.8	Slovak Republic	13.7	Ireland	12.3
5	Austria	10.9	Spain	16.0	Slovak Republic	14.5	Hungary	13.3	Czech Republic	11.8
6	Luxembourg	10.4	Austria	15.5	Austria	13.7	Spain	13.2	Spain	11.7
7	Spain	9.6	Switzerland	14.2	Switzerland	13.7	Switzerland	12.9	Denmark	11.6
8	Australia	9.3	Slovak Republic	13.6	Belgium	13.5	Austria	12.8	Austria	11.3
9	Belgium	9.0	Germany	13.4	Australia	13.0	Germany	12.4	Switzerland	11.2
10	Hungary	8.1	Luxembourg	12.7	Ireland	13.0	Denmark	11.6	Hungary	11.1
11	Ireland	7.8	Belgium	12.5	Italy	13.0	Belgium	11.5	Belgium	10.5
12	US	7.8	Hungary	11.9	Greece	12.7	Czech Republic	11.5	Germany	10.5
13	Germany	7.5	Germany	11.6	Germany	12.5	Italy	10.7	UK	10.2
14	Canada	7.2	New Zealand	10.4	Luxembourg	12.4	Greece	10.6	Netherlands	10.0
15	Greece	7.2	US	9.8	Czech Republic	12.3	Ireland	10.6	Australia	9.8
16	Slovak Republic	7.1	Denmark	9.3	Denmark	12.0	New Zealand	10.3	Greece	9.4
17	Poland	6.3	Canada	9.0	New Zealand	11.7	Australia	10.0	Slovak Republic	9.2
18	Denmark	5.8	Netherlands	8.5	Netherlands	11.3	Netherlands	10.0	Finland	8.9
19	New Zealand	5.3	Poland	8.0	Canada	10.8	US	9.7	New Zealand	8.9
20	Sweden	5.1	UK	7.4	US	10.5	UK	9.4	Italy	8.7
21	Netherlands	3.7	Greece	7.0	UK	9.1	Finland	9.2	Poland	8.5
22	Norway	3.5	Sweden	7.0	Poland	8.7	Japan	8.9	Japan	8.3
23	Finland	2.9	Japan	6.9	Japan	8.1	Canada	8.8	US	8.3
24	Iceland	2.5	Finland	6.4	Finland	8.0	Poland	8.8	Canada	7.6
25	Turkey	0.9	Norway	4.9	Sweden	6.3	Sweden	6.3	Iceland	6.3
26			Iceland	4.1	Norway	5.3	Iceland	5.1	Sweden	6.2
27			Turkey	1.2	Iceland	4.4	Norway	4.9	Norway	5.6
28					Turkey	1.6	Turkey	1.4	Turkey	1.4

occupying the third place until 1981, when Italy was replaced by Portugal, by Luxembourg (in 1991) and France (in 2001).

Table 4.3 presents the estimated per adult beer, wine and spirits consumption in terms of pure alcohol in 1996 for 151 countries. Columns 2-4 give the consumption figures for beer, wine and spirits, individually, and column 5 presents the total of the three columns. Countries listed in column 1 are arranged according to the values of the total alcohol consumption in column 5 in descending order. In terms of per capita total pure alcohol consumption, Luxembourg (17.05 litres of pure alcohol) is ranked first, followed by Slovenia (15.15 litres of pure alcohol) and then South Korea (14.4 litres of pure alcohol). At sample means (across countries), average world per adult consumption in 1996 was 2 litres pure alcohol of beer, 1.5 litres pure alcohol of wine and 2.0 litres of pure alcohol of spirits, giving a total of about 5 litres of total pure alcohol. A closer look at the ranking of the countries reveals that most of the developed countries are on the top of the list and the developing countries as well as the countries influenced by the prohibition of alcohol based on religious beliefs are at the bottom of the list as expected.

Table 4.3 Per adult beer, wine, spirits and total alcohol consumption in terms of pure alcohol (in litres), ranked by total alcohol consumption in 151 countries, 1996

Rank	Country	Beer	Wine	Spirits	Total²
(1)	(2)	(3)	(4)	(5)	(6)
1	Luxembourg	6.63	8.47	1.95	17.05
2	Slovenia	5.76	8.50	0.89	15.15
3	South Korea	2.41	0.02	11.97	14.40
4	Czech Rep	9.83	2.49	2.03	14.35
5	Guyana	0.98		13.05	14.03
6	France	2.45	8.91	3.01	13.74
7	Portugal	3.75	8.81	0.97	13.57
8	Yugoslavia	3.48	5.12	4.57	13.17
9	Slovak Rep	5.79	2.07	5.14	13.00
10	Hungary	4.83	4.38	3.65	12.85
11	Denmark	7.15	4.13	1.35	12.15
12	Bahamas	1.08	1.18	9.82	12.09
13	Austria	7.04	4.59	1.82	11.90
14	Ireland	9.32	2.35	2.22	11.90
15	Croatia	4.38	5.62	1.75	11.75
16	Germany	8.01	3.26	2.50	11.67
17	Switzerland	3.65	6.30	1.81	11.27
18	New Caledonia	5.57	4.91	0.78	11.26
19	Spain	3.86	4.34	2.86	11.09
20	Belgium	6.20	3.65	1.34	10.94
21	Romania	2.37	3.49	5.01	10.88
22	Greece	2.33	4.88	3.23	10.41
23	Cyprus	3.40	2.05	4.55	10.00
24	Netherlands	5.13	2.51	2.16	9.80
25	Paraguay	3.19	0.37	6.15	9.71
26	Italy	1.41	7.74	1.06	9.62
27	Argentina	2.05	7.11	0.42	9.58
28	Australia	6.07	2.78	1.72	9.55
29	Bulgaria	3.25	3.18	3.09	9.52
30	UK	6.34	1.94	1.72	9.41
31	Venezuela	5.84	0.06	3.51	9.41
32	US	5.36	1.12	2.43	8.90
33	New Zealand	6.11	2.59	1.51	8.85
34	Netherlands Antilles	4.61	0.80	3.37	8.78
35	Latvia	2.01	0.98	5.72	8.70
36	Thailand	0.88	0.02	7.73	8.64
37	Rep. of Moldova	0.34	7.84	0.43	8.62
38	Barbados	2.82	0.45	5.10	8.37
39	Finland	5.06	1.12	2.40	8.26
40	Bosnia-Herzegovina	2.57	0.84	4.84	8.25
41	Uruguay	1.78	5.07	1.32	8.17
42	Belarus	1.08	0.57	6.49	8.14
43	Russian Federation	0.96	0.45	6.67	8.08
44	Estonia¹	2.08	0.14	5.85	8.07
45	Poland	2.62	1.06	4.24	7.93
46	Japan	3.21	0.14	2.62	7.85
47	South Africa	4.42	1.72	1.59	7.72
48	Kazakhstan	0.47	0.16	7.09	7.71
49	Canada	4.23	1.19	2.16	7.52
50	Chile	2.40	2.68	1.98	7.06
51	Malta	3.34	1.50	2.06	6.91
52	Philippines	1.51	0.01	5.25	6.77
53	Gabon	3.94	1.84	0.99	6.76
54	Haiti	0.01	0.01	6.53	6.55
55	Colombia	4.27	0.02	2.11	6.41
56	Lithuania	1.94	0.75	3.54	6.23
57	Sweden	3.64	1.97	1.44	6.04
58	Dominican Rep	2.12	0.08	3.70	5.90
59	Belize	2.62	0.09	3.14	5.85
60	Panama	3.45	0.09	2.19	5.74
61	Costa Rica	0.92	0.12	4.67	5.72
62	Liberia	0.18		5.49	5.68
63	Brazil	2.96	0.33	2.28	5.57
64	Lebanon	0.52	1.81	3.10	5.43
65	China	0.95	0.06	4.38	5.39
66	Mexico	4.11	0.04	0.89	5.04
67	Norway	3.27	1.13	1.02	4.97
68	Iceland	2.14	0.81	1.98	4.88
69	Yugoslavia (old)	1.92	2.32	0.62	4.86
70	Suriname	3.07	0.06	1.55	4.68
71	Georgia	0.19	3.38	0.93	4.50
72	Mauritius	2.01	0.19	2.14	4.33
73	Azerbaijan	0.12	0.65	3.39	4.16
74	Laos	0.33		3.79	4.12
75	Peru	1.63	0.17	2.21	4.00
76	Jamaica	1.78	0.06	2.06	3.90
77	Cape Verde	1.39	2.02	0.45	3.86
78	Trinidad & Tobago	1.48	0.07	2.14	3.69
79	Cuba	1.00	0.22	2.31	3.53
80	Bolivia	1.73	0.06	1.55	3.35
81	UAE	1.20	0.16	1.70	3.06
82	Zimbabwe	0.19	0.05	2.53	2.78
83	Botswana	1.97	0.21	0.50	2.68
84	Albania	1.02	0.80	0.77	2.59
85	North Korea	0.19		2.37	2.56
86	El Salvador	1.30	0.03	1.20	2.54
87	Honduras	1.24	0.02	1.15	2.41
88	Nicaragua	0.54	0.01	1.79	2.34
89	Ukraine	0.30	0.38	1.63	2.31
90	Kyrgyzstan	0.27	0.36	1.57	2.20
91	Singapore	1.33	0.12	0.65	2.10
92	Maldives	0.60	0.26	1.22	2.08
93	Guatemala	0.78	0.02	1.19	1.99
94	Mongolia	0.13		1.82	1.95
95	Fiji	1.62	0.18	0.02	1.82
96	Tajikistan	0.04	0.59	1.15	1.78
97	Israel	0.81	0.52	0.42	1.75
98	Ecuador	0.63	0.13	0.89	1.66
99	Kenya	0.87	0.01	0.77	1.66
100	Guinea-Bissau	0.39	0.47	0.73	1.59
101	Angola	0.62	0.55	0.41	1.58
102	Cameroon	1.53	0.05		1.58
103	Congo	1.22	0.30	0.05	1.56
104	Uzbekistan		1.48	0.07	1.55
105	Côte dIvoire	1.06	0.33	0.04	1.43
106	Benin	0.75	0.06	0.58	1.39
107	Turkey	0.82	0.10	0.43	1.35
108	Madagascar	0.16	0.13	0.95	1.25
109	Vietnam	0.38		0.83	1.21
110	Swaziland			1.18	1.18
111	Burundi	1.16	0.01	0.01	1.17
112	Turkmenistan	0.09	0.13	0.95	1.17
113	Lesotho	0.75	0.04	0.33	1.12
114	Ethiopia	0.88		0.14	1.02
115	PNG	0.90	0.03	0.10	1.02
116	Togo	0.66	0.15	0.20	1.01
117	India	0.04		0.95	0.99
118	Vanuatu	0.29	0.57	0.09	0.96
119	Eritrea	0.95			0.95
120	Tunisia	0.34	0.46	0.09	0.89
121	Malaysia	0.76	0.01	0.10	0.87
122	Armenia		0.56	0.27	0.84
123	Brunei	0.20	0.03	0.52	0.75
124	Rwanda	0.70		0.01	0.71
125	C African Rep	0.62	0.04	0.04	0.70
126	Nigeria	0.65		0.01	0.66
127	Zambia	0.62		0.01	0.63
128	Iraq	0.30		0.32	0.61
129	Tanzania	0.51		0.09	0.60
130	Morocco	0.25	0.28	0.05	0.58
131	Solomon Islands	0.41	0.04	0.10	0.56
132	Egypt	0.05	0.01	0.47	0.53
133	Djibouti	0.26	0.11	0.10	0.47
134	Uganda	0.22		0.24	0.46
135	Mozambique	0.23	0.04	0.19	0.45
136	Burkina Faso	0.34		0.11	0.45
137	Malawi	0.12		0.30	0.42
138	Ghana	0.33	0.06	0.02	0.41
139	Senegal	0.30	0.09	0.03	0.41
140	Cambodia	0.14		0.20	0.34
141	Algeria	0.15	0.10	0.02	0.27
142	Sudan			0.26	0.26
143	Chad	0.22	0.01		0.23
144	Syria	0.07	0.01	0.14	0.21
145	Sri Lanka	0.06		0.15	0.21
146	Myanmar	0.05		0.16	0.21
147	Congo (DR)	0.20			0.21
148	Guinea	0.16	0.01		0.17
149	Gambia	0.05	0.06	0.05	0.16
150	Yemen	0.11		0.04	0.15
151	Indonesia	0.06		0.07	0.13
	Mean	1.98	1.46	2.01	5.02

¹ The estimates for Estonia are for the year 1995, and *Statistical Yearbook of Estonia 1996* (Tallinn, Statistical Office of Estonia, 1996). ² Rows may not total exactly due to variations in estimates.
Source: Data are published by WHO but compiled from *FAO Statistical Databases1998*; Produktschap voor Distilleerde Dranken, 1997.

Table 4.4 presents the ranking of the countries in Table 4.3 by amount of consumption of pure alcohol for beer, wine and spirits. As can be seen, based on per adult pure alcohol consumption of beer, the Czech Republic (9.83 litres) is ranked as number one followed by Ireland (9.32 litres) and then Germany (8.01 litres). With respect to wine, France (8.91 litres) is ranked as number one followed by Portugal (8.81 litres) and Slovenia (8.5 litres). With respect to spirits, Guyana

Table 4.4 Per adult consumption of beer, wine, spirits in terms of pure alcohol (in litres), ranked by consumption levels in 147 countries, 1996

	Beer			Wine			Spirits	
Rank	Country	Litres	Rank	Country	Litres	Rank	Country	Litres
(1)	(2)	(3)	(4)	(5)	(6)	(7)	(8)	(9)
1	Czech Rep	9.83	1	France	8.91	1	Guyana	13.05
2	Ireland	9.32	2	Portugal	8.81	2	South Korea	11.97
3	Germany	8.01	3	Slovenia	8.50	3	Bahamas	9.82
4	Denmark	7.15	4	Luxembourg	8.47	4	Thailand	7.73
5	Austria	7.04	5	Rep of Moldova	7.84	5	Kazakhstan	7.09
6	Luxembourg	6.63	6	Italy	7.74	6	Russian Federation	6.67
7	United Kingdom	6.34	7	Argentina	7.11	7	Haiti	6.53
8	Belgium	6.20	8	Switzerland	6.30	8	Belarus	6.49
9	New Zealand	6.11	9	Croatia	5.62	9	Paraguay	6.15
10	Australia	6.07	10	Yugoslavia	5.12	10	Estonia2	5.85
11	Venezuela	5.84	11	Uruguay	5.07	11	Latvia	5.72
12	Slovakia	5.79	12	New Caledonia	4.91	12	Liberia	5.49
13	Slovenia	5.76	13	Greece	4.88	13	Philippines	5.25
14	New Caledonia	5.57	14	Austria	4.59	14	Slovakia	5.14
15	US	5.36	15	Hungary	4.38	15	Barbados	5.10
16	Netherlands	5.13	16	Spain	4.34	16	Romania	5.01
17	Finland	5.06	17	Denmark	4.13	17	Bosnia-Herzegovina	4.84
18	Hungary	4.83	18	Belgium	3.65	18	Costa Rica	4.67
19	Netherlands Antilles	4.61	19	Romania	3.49	19	Yugoslavia	4.57
20	South Africa	4.42	20	Georgia	3.38	20	Cyprus	4.55
21	Croatia	4.38	21	Germany	3.26	21	China	4.38
22	Colombia	4.27	22	Bulgaria	3.18	22	Poland	4.24
23	Canada	4.23	23	Australia	2.78	23	Lao	3.79
24	Mexico	4.11	24	Chile	2.68	24	Dominican Rep	3.70
25	Gabon	3.94	25	New Zealand	2.59	25	Hungary	3.65
26	Spain	3.86	26	Netherlands	2.51	26	Lithuania	3.54
27	Portugal	3.75	27	Czech Rep	2.49	27	Venezuela	3.51
28	Switzerland	3.65	28	Ireland	2.35	28	Azerbaijan	3.39
29	Sweden	3.64	29	Yugoslavia	2.32	29	Netherlands Antilles	3.37
30	Yugoslavia	3.48	30	Slovakia	2.07	30	Greece	3.23
31	Panama	3.45	31	Cyprus	2.05	31	Belize	3.14
32	Cyprus	3.40	32	Cape Verde	2.02	32	Lebanon	3.10
33	Malta	3.34	33	Sweden	1.97	33	Bulgaria	3.09
34	Norway	3.27	34	UK	1.94	34	France	3.01
35	Bulgaria	3.25	35	Gabon	1.84	35	Spain	2.86
36	Japan	3.21	36	Lebanon	1.81	36	Japan	2.62
37	Paraguay	3.19	37	South Africa	1.72	37	Zimbabwe	2.53
38	Suriname	3.07	38	Malta	1.50	38	Germany	2.50
39	Brazil	2.96	39	Uzbekistan	1.48	39	US	2.43
40	Barbados	2.82	40	Canada	1.19	40	Finland	2.40
41	Belize	2.62	41	Bahamas	1.18	41	North Korea	2.37
42	Poland	2.62	42	Norway	1.13	42	Cuba	2.31
43	Bosnia-Herzegovina	2.57	43	Finland	1.12	43	Brazil	2.28
44	France	2.45	44	US	1.12	44	Ireland	2.22
45	South Korea	2.41	45	Poland	1.06	45	Peru	2.21
46	Chile	2.40	46	Latvia	0.98	46	Panama	2.19
47	Romania	2.37	47	Bosnia-Herzegovina	0.84	47	Canada	2.16
48	Greece	2.33	48	Iceland	0.81	48	Netherlands	2.16
49	Iceland	2.14	49	Albania	0.80	49	Mauritius	2.14

Table 4.4 continued on next page

Table 4.4 Per adult consumption of beer, wine, spirits in terms of pure alcohol (in litres), ranked by consumption levels in 147 countries, 1996 (cont)

Beer			Wine			Spirits		
Rank	Country	Litres	Rank	Country	Litres	Rank	Country	Litres
(1)	(2)	(3)	(4)	(5)	(6)	(7)	(8)	(9)
50	Dominican Rep	2.12	50	Netherlands Antilles	0.80	50	Trinidad&Tobago	2.14
51	Estonia	2.08	51	Lithuania	0.75	51	Colombia	2.11
52	Argentina	2.05	52	Azerbaijan	0.65	52	Jamaica	2.06
53	Latvia	2.01	53	Tajikistan	0.59	53	Malta	2.06
54	Mauritius	2.01	54	Belarus	0.57	54	Czech Rep	2.03
55	Botswana	1.97	55	Vanuatu	0.57	55	Chile	1.98
56	Lithuania	1.94	56	Armenia	0.56	56	Iceland	1.98
57	Yugoslavia	1.92	57	Angola	0.55	57	Luxembourg	1.95
58	Jamaica	1.78	58	Israel	0.52	58	Austria	1.82
59	Uruguay	1.78	59	Guinea-Bissau	0.47	59	Mongolia	1.82
60	Bolivia	1.73	60	Tunisia	0.46	60	Switzerland	1.81
61	Peru	1.63	61	Barbados	0.45	61	Nicaragua	1.79
62	Fiji	1.62	62	Russian Federation	0.45	62	Croatia	1.75
63	Cameroon	1.53	63	Ukraine	0.38	63	Australia	1.72
64	Philippines	1.51	64	Paraguay	0.37	64	UK	1.72
65	Trinidad&Tobago	1.48	65	Kyrgyzstan	0.36	65	UAE	1.70
66	Italy	1.41	66	Brazil	0.33	66	Ukraine	1.63
67	Cape Verde	1.39	67	Côte dIvoire	0.33	67	South Africa	1.59
68	Singapore	1.33	68	Congo	0.30	68	Kyrgyzstan	1.57
69	El Salvador	1.30	69	Morocco	0.28	69	Bolivia	1.55
70	Honduras	1.24	70	Maldives	0.26	70	Suriname	1.55
71	Congo	1.22	71	Cuba	0.22	71	New Zealand	1.51
72	UAE	1.20	72	Botswana	0.21	72	Sweden	1.44
73	Burundi	1.16	73	Mauritius	0.19	73	Denmark	1.35
74	Bahamas	1.08	74	Fiji	0.18	74	Belgium	1.34
75	Belarus	1.08	75	Peru	0.17	75	Uruguay	1.32
76	Côte dIvoire	1.06	76	Kazakhstan	0.16	76	Maldives	1.22
77	Albania	1.02	77	UAE	0.16	77	El Salvador	1.20
78	Cuba	1.00	78	Togo	0.15	78	Guatemala	1.19
79	Guyana	0.98	79	Estonia	0.14	79	Swaziland	1.18
80	Russian Federation	0.96	80	Japan	0.14	80	Honduras	1.15
81	China	0.95	81	Ecuador	0.13	81	Tajikistan	1.15
82	Eritrea	0.95	82	Madagascar	0.13	82	Italy	1.06
83	Costa Rica	0.92	83	Turkmenistan	0.13	83	Norway	1.02
84	PNG	0.90	84	Costa Rica	0.12	84	Gabon	0.99
85	Ethiopia	0.88	85	Singapore	0.12	85	Portugal	0.97
86	Thailand	0.88	86	Djibouti	0.11	86	India	0.95
87	Kenya	0.87	87	Algeria	0.10	87	Madagascar	0.95
88	Turkey	0.82	88	Turkey	0.10	88	Turkmenistan	0.95
89	Israel	0.81	89	Belize	0.09	89	Georgia	0.93
90	Guatemala	0.78	90	Panama	0.09	90	Ecuador	0.89
91	Malaysia	0.76	91	Senegal	0.09	91	Mexico	0.89
92	Benin	0.75	92	Dominican Rep	0.08	92	Slovenia	0.89
93	Lesotho	0.75	93	Trinidad&Tobago	0.07	93	Viet Nam	0.83
94	Rwanda	0.70	94	Benin	0.06	94	New Caledonia	0.78
95	Togo	0.66	95	Bolivia	0.06	95	Albania	0.77
96	Nigeria	0.65	96	China	0.06	96	Kenya	0.77
97	Ecuador	0.63	97	Gambia	0.06	97	Guinea-Bissau	0.73
98	Angola	0.62	98	Ghana	0.06	98	Singapore	0.65

Table 4.4 continued on next page

Table 4.4 Per adult consumption of beer, wine, spirits in terms of pure alcohol (in litres), ranked by consumption levels in 147 countries, 1996 (continued)

	Beer			Wine			Spirits	
Rank	Country	Litres	Rank	Country	Litres	Rank	Country	Litres
(1)	(2)	(3)	(4)	(5)	(6)	(7)	(8)	(9)
99	C African Rep	0.62	99	Jamaica	0.06	99	Yugoslavia	0.62
100	Zambia	0.62	100	Suriname	0.06	100	Benin	0.58
101	Maldives	0.60	101	Venezuela	0.06	101	Brunei	0.52
102	Nicaragua	0.54	102	Cameroon	0.05	102	Botswana	0.50
103	Lebanon	0.52	103	Zimbabwe	0.05	103	Egypt	0.47
104	Tanzania	0.51	104	C African Rep	0.04	104	Cape Verde	0.45
105	Kazakhstan	0.47	105	Lesotho	0.04	105	Rep of Moldova	0.43
106	Solomon Islands	0.41	106	Mexico	0.04	106	Turkey	0.43
107	Guinea-Bissau	0.39	107	Mozambique	0.04	107	Argentina	0.42
108	Viet Nam	0.38	108	Solomon Islands	0.04	108	Israel	0.42
109	Burkina Faso	0.34	109	Brunei	0.03	109	Angola	0.41
110	Rep of Moldova	0.34	110	El Salvador	0.03	110	Lesotho	0.33
111	Tunisia	0.34	111	PNG	0.03	111	Iraq	0.32
112	Ghana	0.33	112	Colombia	0.02	112	Malawi	0.30
113	Lao	0.33	113	Guatemala	0.02	113	Armenia	0.27
114	Iraq	0.30	114	Honduras	0.02	114	Sudan	0.26
115	Senegal	0.30	115	South Korea	0.02	115	Uganda	0.24
116	Ukraine	0.30	116	Thailand	0.02	116	Cambodia	0.20
117	Vanuatu	0.29	117	Burundi	0.01	117	Togo	0.20
118	Kyrgyzstan	0.27	118	Chad	0.01	118	Mozambique	0.19
119	Djibouti	0.26	119	Egypt	0.01	119	Myanmar	0.16
120	Morocco	0.25	120	Guinea	0.01	120	Sri Lanka	0.15
121	Mozambique	0.23	121	Haiti	0.01	121	Ethiopia	0.14
122	Chad	0.22	122	Kenya	0.01	122	Syria	0.14
123	Uganda	0.22	123	Malaysia	0.01	123	Burkina Faso	0.11
124	Brunei	0.20	124	Nicaragua	0.01	124	Djibouti	0.10
125	Congo	0.20	125	Philippines	0.01	125	Malaysia	0.10
126	North Korea	0.19	126	Syria	0.01	126	PNG	0.10
127	Georgia	0.19				127	Solomon Islands	0.10
128	Zimbabwe	0.19				128	Tanzania	0.09
129	Liberia	0.18				129	Tunisia	0.09
130	Guinea	0.16				130	Vanuatu	0.09
131	Madagascar	0.16				131	Indonesia	0.07
132	Algeria	0.15				132	Uzbekistan	0.07
133	Cambodia	0.14				133	Congo	0.05
134	Mongolia	0.13				134	Gambia	0.05
135	Azerbaijan	0.12				135	Morocco	0.05
136	Malawi	0.12				136	C African Rep	0.04
137	Yemen	0.11				137	Côte dIvoire	0.04
138	Turkmenistan	0.09				138	Yemen	0.04
139	Syria	0.07				139	Senegal	0.03
140	Indonesia	0.06				140	Algeria	0.02
141	Sri lanka	0.06				141	Fiji	0.02
142	Egypt	0.05				142	Ghana	0.02
143	Gambia	0.05				143	Burundi	0.01
144	Myanmar	0.05				144	Nigeria	0.01
145	India	0.04				145	Rwanda	0.01
146	Tajikistan	0.04				146	Zambia	0.01
147	Haiti	0.01						

(13.05 litres) ranked as number 1, South Korea (11.97 litres) as number 2 and Bahamas (9.82 litres) as number 3. A cross-country comparison based on the table reveals that, in general, people from developed countries consume more beer and wine than people from developing countries, while people from developing countries consume more spirits than people from developed countries.

Figure 4.1 presents a comparison of total alcohol consumption by world regions during 1990-1995, for which the data are compiled from *World Drink Trends 1997* (WDT, 1997). As can be seen, alcohol consumption is falling in most countries in Europe, North America and Australasia while it is on the increase in the Latin American countries and the rest of the world. During 1990-1995, growth in alcohol consumption in Western Europe was –5 percent; Eastern Europe –2 percent; North America –8 percent; Australasia –6 percent and Latin America 3 percent. Even though people in the rest of the world consume only a small amount of pure alcohol compared to the other regions, the amount has increased from 2 litres per capita to 4 litres per capita during 1990-1995 giving a growth of 64 percent. For the world as a whole, on average, per capita consumption has increased from 4 litres in 1990 to 5 litres in 1995.

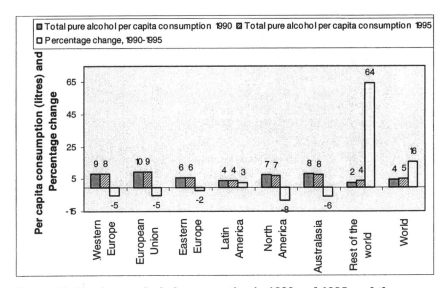

Figure 4.1 Total pure alcohol consumption in 1990 and 1995, and the percentage change in consumption

Figure 4.2 presents the proportion of 10th grade students in the European countries who have used any alcoholic beverages 10 times or more during the last 30 days taken from the survey based on ESPAD (2000) by gender. In all countries, the proportion of male students who consume alcohol is higher than the proportion of female students. The proportion of male students who have used any alcohol 10

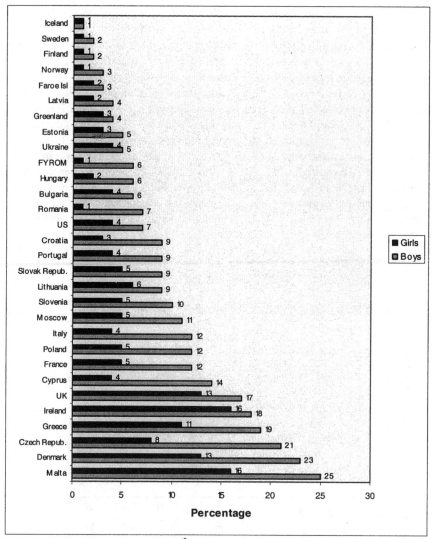

Figure 4.2 Percentage among 10th grade students who have used any alcoholic beverage 10 times or more during the last 30 days by gender, European countries, 1999

times or more is highest in Malta (25 percent) and lowest in Iceland (1 percent). The proportion of female students who have used any alcohol 10 times or more is highest in Malta and Ireland (equally at 16 percent) and lowest in Romania, FYROM (Former Yugoslav Republic of Macedonia), Norway, Sweden, Finland and Iceland (all are 1 percent).

In Figure 4.3 we present the proportion of 10th grade students in the European countries who have been drunk at the age of 13 or younger, by gender, also from the same survey, ESPAD (2000). In all countries, the proportion of male students who have been drunk at the age of 13 or younger is higher than the proportion of female students. The proportion of male students is highest in Denmark

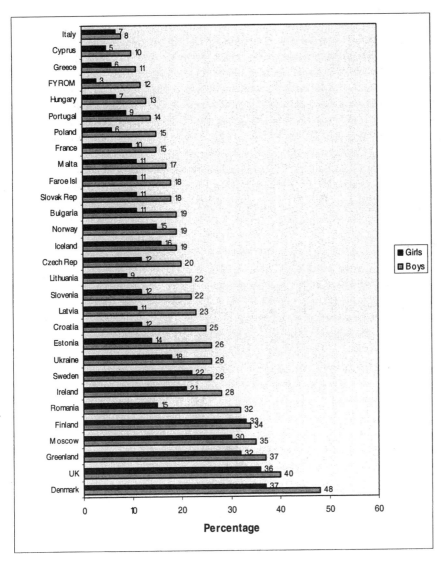

Figure 4.3 Proportion of 10th grade students who have been drunk at the age of 13 or younger, by gender, 1999, European countries

48 percent) and lowest in Italy (8 percent). The proportion of female students is also highest in Denmark (37 percent) and lowest in FYROM (3 percent).

In the remaining sections of this chapter, we consider the consumption of alcohol in detail for Australia, the UK, the US and New Zealand.

4.2   Alcohol Consumption in Australia

Alcohol is one of the most commonly used drugs in Australia. More than half of the adult (15+) Australian population drinks at least weekly. In 2001, on a per adult basis Australians consumed about 10 litres of pure alcohol per person. About 80 percent of Australian teenagers try alcohol at least once. In 1999, one out of four drivers involved with road accidents were over the legal limit for blood alcohol concentration. Australians are one of the major beer and wine consumers in the world. In this section we look at the alcohol consumption patterns of Australians over time and across various consumer characteristics.

Figure 4.4 presents the per adult pure alcohol consumption of Australia in 2001, compared to a number of other OECD countries and the percentage change in alcohol consumption over the 1980-2000 period. As can be seen, the Australian per adult consumption of pure alcohol is about half a litre below the UK consumption and one and a half litres above the US consumption. Like most other countries Australian alcohol consumption has also fallen and by about 19 percent during 1980-2000.

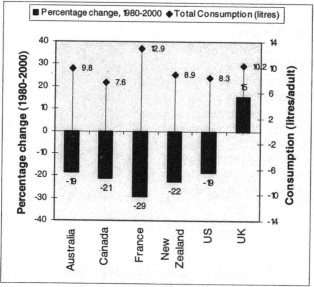

Figure 4.4 Total consumption of pure alcohol (litres/per adult), 2001, and percentage change in consumption in 6 countries, 1980-2000

In Figure 4.5 we plot the per adult pure alcohol consumption of beer, wine, spirits and total alcohol over the years 1961-1999 for Australia obtained from WHO (2003). As can be seen, in recent years, total alcohol consumption has fallen while consumption of wine and spirits are on the increase at the expense of beer in Australia. In 1999, Australians consumed 10.3 litres of pure alcohol per adult made up of 5.2 litres of pure alcohol of beer, 3.4 litres of pure alcohol of wine and 1.7 litres of pure alcohol of spirits.

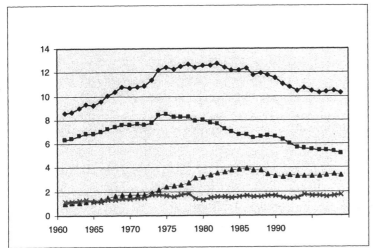

Figure 4.5 Per adult (pure alcohol) consumption of beer, wine, spirits and total alcohol, Australia, 1961-1999

Figure 4.6 presents the alcohol drinking status in Australia during 1991-2001. The proportion of adult Australians who drink daily has fallen from 10.2 percent in 1991 to 8.3 percent in 2001. The proportion of adult population who have reported drinking alcohol weekly has also fallen during the period from 41 percent to 39.5 percent. However, the proportion of 'less than weekly' drinkers have increased during the early 1990s from 30.4 percent in 1991 to 34.6 percent in 2001.

Table 4.5 presents the alcohol drinking status by gender and age groups in Australia. The last column of the table gives the summary measure corresponding to all ages. As can be seen, the proportion of Australian males drinking alcohol daily is about twice that of the proportion of Australian women. The proportion of Australian males who drink weekly is also higher than the corresponding Australian female proportion. A comparison of the numbers in the first row of the male section and female section of the table shows that the proportion of daily alcohol drinking increases with age. Among the weekly drinkers, the higher proportions of drinkers are from the middle age groups 20-29, 30-39 and 40-49. Overall, one in twelve Australians drink alcohol daily while about one in three Australians drink alcohol 'weekly' or 'less than weekly'. Furthermore, one in every ten Australians appear to be a non-alcohol drinker.

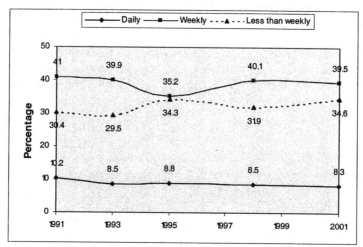

Figure 4.6 Proportion of adults (15+) by alcohol drinking status, Australia, 1991-2001

Table 4.5 Alcohol drinking status: proportion of the population aged 14 or over, by age and gender, Australia, 2001

Alcohol drinking status	Age group						All ages
(1)	14–19 (2)	20–29 (3)	30–39 (4)	40–49 (5)	50–59 (6)	60+ (7)	(8)
Male							
Daily	0.3	4.2	6.6	11.5	17.6	22.7	11.1
Occasional[1]							
Weekly	31.2	54.8	54.0	48.2	47.0	36.3	46.0
Less than weekly	41.2	32.5	30.5	28.8	22.9	20.8	28.8
Ex-drinker[2]	5.6	3.2	4.6	7.2	7.7	11.9	6.8
Never a full serve of alcohol	21.7	5.2	5.3	4.3	4.8	8.2	7.4
Female							
Daily	0.5	1.8	2.9	6.3	9.1	10.6	5.6
Occasional[1]							
Weekly	25.4	39.4	35.2	39.0	33.6	25.2	33.2
Less than weekly	48.7	47.5	45.9	38.2	35.3	30.7	40.3
Ex-drinker[2]	3.9	5.8	9.5	8.0	11.5	13.5	9.2
Never a full serve of alcohol	21.5	5.6	6.5	8.4	10.5	20.0	11.7
All persons							
Daily	0.4	3.0	4.7	8.9	13.4	16.1	8.3
Occasional[1]							
Weekly	28.3	47.2	43.9	43.7	40.4	30.3	39.5
Less than weekly	44.9	39.9	38.4	33.4	29.0	26.2	34.6
Ex-drinker[2]	4.8	4.5	7.1	7.6	9.6	12.8	8.0
Never a full serve of alcohol	21.6	5.4	5.9	6.3	7.6	14.6	9.6

[1] Occasional drinkers are those who drink alcohol less than daily, that is, weekly or less than weekly. [2] Ex-drinkers are those who have consumed at least a full serve of alcohol, but not in the last 12 months. Source: AIHW (2003).

In Table 4.6 we present usual place of consumption of alcohol by adult drinkers, by age and gender. As can be seen, a majority of male and female adult Australians drink alcohol at their own home, at their friend's home or at private parties. Australians in the higher age group tend to consume alcohol at home and the younger age group tend to consume alcohol at private parties. A significant proportion of younger Australians consume alcohol in a car than older Australians. Male Australians are twice as likely to have consumed alcohol at their workplace than their female counterparts. The 20-29 age group, both males and females, are highly likely to consume alcohol at licensed premises.

Table 4.6 Usual place of consumption of alcohol, drinkers aged 14 or over, by age and gender, Australia, 2001

	Age group							
Location	14–19		20–29		30–39		40+	
(1)	M (2)	F (3)	M (4)	F (5)	M (6)	F (7)	M (8)	F (9)
In my home	61.5	61.1	74.3	76.6	85.5	84.4	88.7	84.4
At friend's house	62.9	63.9	67.7	66.2	64.2	65.4	48.4	52.4
At private parties	67.8	70.2	62.7	60.7	54.0	55.4	39.6	43.3
At raves/dance parties	22.9	24.5	18.0	12.2	4.2	3.1	2.2	1.3
At restaurants/cafes	22.4	25.5	55.4	61.6	57.3	63.1	48.7	56.9
At licensed premises	37.1	38.8	75.5	73.7	59.9	51.1	46.9	37.6
At school/TAFE/uni	6.2	3.4	6.3	2.7	0.7	0.3	0.3	0.4
At workplace	5.8	2.7	14.3	8.6	14.0	4.7	5.5	2.7
In public places	14.1	10.6	8.5	2.9	4.2	2.9	2.2	1.4
In a car	12.2	7.0	8.8	2.5	4.3	1.3	1.3	0.3
Somewhere else	8.3	7.2	5.1	1.6	3.3	1.1	1.6	0.9

Note: Respondents could select more than one response. Source: AIHW (2002b).

Table 4.7 shows the type of alcohol consumed by Australian adult drinkers by age and gender. A comparison of the numbers in the last column reveals that males consume a higher proportion of regular beer, followed by bottled wine and bottled spirits. Bottled wine is the most popular drink among female Australians followed by bottled spirits and cask wine. Among all Australians, bottled wine is the most popular alcoholic drink followed by bottled spirits and regular beer. Among the male (female) Australians, cask wine is most popular among the over 50 age groups (over 60 age group), bottled wine is popular among the 50-59 age group (over 30 age groups), regular beer is popular among the 20-29 age group (14-29 age groups), bottled spirits is popular among the 14-29 age groups (14-29 age groups) and the fruit flavoured 'coolers' among the younger 14-19 age group. Overall, bottled wine, regular beer and bottled spirits are the three most favourite drinks of Australians.

Table 4.7 Type of alcohol consumed: proportion of recent drinkers aged 14 or over by age and gender, Australia, 1998

Type of Alcohol	Age group						All ages
	14–19	20–29	30–39	40–49	50–59	60+	
(1)	(2)	(3)	(4)	(5)	(6)	(7)	(8)
Male							
Cask wine	11.3	12.5	16.8	17.0	27.9	26.6	18.7
Bottled wine	13.9	37.9	45.4	45.0	50.7	38.2	40.6
Regular beer	66.9	73.7	60.1	52.2	45.9	25.2	54.3
Mid-strength beer	13.4	15.8	24.1	26.7	20.7	15.2	20.0
Low-alcohol beer	11.2	10.7	22.8	35.9	27.8	39.4	25.1
Premixed spirits	30.6	19.5	8.9	7.1	6.1	1.6	11.0
Bottled spirits	62.3	59.2	37.8	30.2	30.7	22.3	39.4
Alcoholic soda	22.0	16.2	3.7	1.2	0.2	0.2	6.3
Cider	5.5	6.1	4.6	4.3	3.4	1.8	4.3
Fruit-flavoured 'coolers'	11.2	6.5	2.6	0.2	3.7	1.4	3.7
Other	10.4	4.5	4.4	3.8	1.6	2.8	4.2
Female							
Cask wine	13.7	15.8	24.7	26.9	25.2	34.6	23.8
Bottled wine	24.6	53.3	63.5	63.9	63.0	61.9	57.4
Regular beer	28.1	28.8	17.9	12.7	8.9	11.1	17.9
Mid-strength beer	8.3	5.8	6.9	4.7	4.5	5.0	5.8
Low-alcohol beer	6.8	5.2	13.9	17.2	12.9	22.0	13.2
Premixed spirits	44.3	24.4	9.6	3.6	3.7	3.8	13.2
Bottled spirits	62.9	57.8	45.4	25.7	15.9	21.3	38.2
Alcoholic soda	46.3	25.6	6.2	2.3	0.9	2.1	12.0
Cider	13.3	8.8	6.9	3.8	2.1	2.9	6.1
Fruit-flavoured 'coolers'	24.8	20.7	11.3	7.5	9.2	4.0	12.4
Other	15.7	8.6	4.9	6.3	7.8	5.2	7.4
All persons							
Cask wine	12.5	14.1	20.6	21.9	26.6	30.3	21.1
Bottled wine	19.3	45.3	54.1	54.4	56.3	49.2	48.7
Regular beer	47.4	52.2	39.7	32.7	29.1	18.6	36.8
Mid-strength beer	10.8	11.0	15.8	15.8	13.4	10.5	13.2
Low-alcohol beer	9.0	8.1	18.5	26.6	21.1	31.3	19.4
Premixed spirits	37.5	21.8	9.3	5.3	5.0	2.6	12.1
Bottled spirits	62.6	58.5	41.5	28.0	24.0	21.8	38.9
Alcoholic soda	34.2	20.7	4.9	1.7	0.6	1.1	9.1
Cider	9.4	7.4	5.7	4.0	2.8	2.3	5.1
Fruit-flavoured 'coolers'	18.0	13.3	6.8	3.8	6.2	2.6	7.8
Other	13.1	6.5	4.7	5.0	4.4	3.9	5.7

Note: Base equals all recent drinkers. Alcohol contents of regular beer is more than 4% Alc/Vol; mid-strength beer is 3.0%–3.9% Alc/Vol, and low-alcohol beer is 1%–2.9% Alc/Vol. Source: AIHW (2000).

In Table 4.8 we present the amount of alcohol usually consumed by age and gender. As can be seen one in four Australians drink 3-4 standard drinks and one in two Australians drink 1-2 standard drinks. The proportion of males consuming 1-2 standard drinks and 3-4 standard drinks are about the same. The majority of the women consume 1-2 standard drinks. Among males (females) people in the 40-49 age group (14-39 age groups) are more likely to consume 3-4 standard drinks than

Table 4.8 Amount of alcohol usually consumed: proportion of recent drinkers aged 14 or over, by age and gender, Australia, 1998

Amount	Age group						All ages
(1)	14–19 (2)	20–29 (3)	30–39 (4)	40–49 (5)	50–59 (6)	60+ (7)	(8)
Male							
13+ standard drinks	14.2	10.8	2.4	2.4	0.4	1.0	4.6
9 to 12 standard drinks	18.8	9.1	6.5	2.5	5.4	1.6	6.4
7 to 8 standard drinks	14.2	11.3	7.0	6.3	4.4	1.6	7.1
5 to 6 standard drinks	15.0	16.7	15.0	20.0	14.4	8.0	15.1
3 to 4 standard drinks	17.3	25.0	33.2	40.6	31.1	28.9	30.5
1 to 2 standard drinks	20.5	27.0	35.8	28.2	44.2	59.0	36.3
Female							
13+ standard drinks	6.0	3.8	0.6	1.2	—	—	1.7
9 to 12 standard drinks	8.2	4.1	1.2	1.1	—	0.1	2.1
7 to 8 standard drinks	12.7	6.2	2.1	0.8	0.1	0.1	3.1
5 to 6 standard drinks	19.1	14.5	8.0	4.3	6.7	0.6	8.4
3 to 4 standard drinks	25.2	26.8	26.6	19.6	15.1	17.4	22.3
1 to 2 standard drinks	28.8	44.7	61.5	73.0	78.2	81.8	62.4
All persons							
13+ standard drinks	10.1	7.4	1.5	1.8	0.2	0.5	3.3
9 to 12 standard drinks	13.5	6.7	3.9	1.8	3.0	0.9	4.4
7 to 8 standard drinks	13.4	8.9	4.6	3.6	2.5	0.9	5.2
5 to 6 standard drinks	17.1	15.7	11.6	12.3	10.9	4.6	11.9
3 to 4 standard drinks	21.3	25.9	30.0	30.4	24.0	23.6	26.6
1 to 2 standard drinks	24.7	35.5	48.2	50.0	59.4	69.6	48.7

Note: Base equals all recent drinkers. Source: AIHW (2000).

any other group. The older age groups are more likely to have 1-2 standard drinks than the younger age groups.

Table 4.9 correlates the use of alcohol with various characteristics of the Australian adult population. A comparison of the numbers in the education section shows that the lower the education level of a person it is more likely for the person to be a 'never' drinker, ex-drinker or occasional drinker but is less likely for the person to be a regular drinker. An Australian student is more likely to be an occasional drinker and a currently employed Australian is more likely to be a regular drinker. While one in two Australian-born is mostly a regular drinker, only one in three non-English-speaking born is a regular drinker. About one in two Australians are regular drinkers irrespective of their socio-economic status. It is also about equally likely that an Australian living in urban or rural areas will be a regular alcohol drinker. About one in two never married, divorced or presently married Australians is likely to be a regular drinker.

We give the proportion of adult Australians' alcohol related risk of harm in the long term by age and gender in Table 4.10. For males, 'low risk' is defined as the consumption of up to 28 standard drinks per week on average in 12 months before the survey period. For females, this is the consumption of up to 14 standard drinks per week on average over the same period. As can be seen from the table, about

Table 4.9 Correlates of alcohol use: proportion of the population aged 14 or over, Australia, 1998

Characteristics	Drinking status			
(1)	Never (2)	Ex-drinker (3)	Occasional (4)	Regular (5)
Education				
No qualification	10.3	13.6	35.8	40.3
HSC or equivalent	8.1	8.3	30.1	53.5
Trade/diploma	4.6	8.2	27.9	59.3
Tertiary	5.6	7.0	27.6	59.8
Employment status				
Currently employed	4.9	7.0	30.0	58.2
Student	21.9	6.6	40.5	31.1
Unemployed	12.5	10.9	34.4	42.2
Retired/pension	12.4	16.5	32.3	38.8
Occupational status				
Upper (white)	4.8	7.7	27.0	60.4
Middle	7.0	9.0	32.4	51.6
Lower (blue)	9.4	12.8	36.6	41.2
Country of birth				
Australian born	8.0	10.0	32.8	49.2
Other English-speaking born	3.6	10.8	26.8	58.8
Non-English-speaking born	24.5	10.3	32.7	32.5
Socioeconomic area				
1st quintile	8.7	13.4	31.2	46.7
2nd quintile	11.3	10.9	33.6	44.2
3rd quintile	8.9	9.9	34.2	47.0
4th quintile	8.8	9.7	33.7	47.8
5th quintile	8.6	7.1	28.3	56.1
Geography				
Urban	10.7	9.4	30.5	49.4
Rural/remote	6.0	11.7	35.6	46.7
Marital status				
Never married	11.6	7.8	35.6	45.0
Widowed	23.0	10.7	34.3	32.0
Divorced/separated	4.6	10.7	34.7	49.9
Presently married	8.0	11.0	29.5	51.5
Social influences				
At least 50% friends use	3.9	6.0	31.1	59.1
Less than 50% friends use	24.7	22.5	35.3	15.2

Source: AIHW (2000).

76 percent of male and 70 percent of female adult Australians consumed alcohol at levels in which there is low risk of alcohol related harm. Overall, 6.7 + 3.5 = 10.2 percent of Australian adult males consume alcohol at 'risky' or 'high risk' level.

The corresponding proportion for females is 7.2 + 2.2 = 9.4 percent. Among different age groups, 10.2 + 4.5 = 14.7 percent of 20-29 age group consumed alcohol at 'risky' or 'high risk' level, which is the highest percentage among all groups.

Table 4.11 presents the tax revenue from alcohol consumption in Australia during the years 1995/96 to 2002/2003. As can be seen, most of the tax revenue for the Australian government is generated from beer and spirits. Tax revenue from alcohol taxes has increased from 2.4 billion dollars in 1995/96 to 3.1 billion dollars in 2001/2002 and fell slightly in 2002/2003.

Table 4.10 Risk of harm in the long term: proportion of the population aged 14 or over, by age and gender, Australia, 2001

Age group	Abstainers			Low risk			Risky			High risk		
	M	F	All	M	F	All	M	F	All	M	F	All
(1)	(2)	(3)	(4)	(5)	(6)	(7)	(8)	(9)	(10)	(11)	(12)	(13)
14–19yrs	27.2	25.3	26.2	64	60.1	62.1	6.1	9.9	8	2.7	4.7	3.7
20–29yrs	8.4	11.3	9.9	77.1	73.7	75.4	9.5	10.9	10.2	5	4	4.5
30–39yrs	9.8	16	13	81.4	75.4	78.3	5.8	6.8	6.3	3.1	1.9	2.5
40–49yrs	11.4	16.4	13.9	79	73.9	76.5	6.4	7.8	7.1	3.2	1.9	2.6
50–59yrs	12.5	21.9	17.1	75.8	70.7	73.3	7.3	5.9	6.6	4.3	1.5	2.9
60+yrs	20.1	33	27.1	71.9	62.6	66.8	5.4	3.7	4.4	2.6	0.7	1.6
All ages	14.1	20.8	17.5	75.6	69.8	72.7	6.7	7.2	7	3.5	2.2	2.9

Note: Abstainers are those who did not consume alcohol in the last 12 months. For males, the consumption of up to 28 standard drinks per week is considered 'Low risk', 29 to 42 per week 'Risky', and 43 or more per week 'High risk'. For females, the consumption of up to 14 standard drinks per week is considered 'Low risk', 15 to 28 per week 'Risky' and 29 or more per week 'High risk'.
Source: AIHW (2002a).

Table 4.11 Government revenue from excise, customs and state franchise taxes, Australia, 1996-2002

Type of tax	1996	1997	1998	1999	2000	2001	2002
(1)	(2)	(3)	(4)	(5)	(6)	(7)	(8)
Excise							
Beer	864	870	882	873	878	1705	1654
Spirits	201	163	142	144	150	201	101
Customs							
Beer	7	9	12	14	14	36	45
Wine	4	3	4	4	4	3	4
Spirits	565	645	717	720	751	1074	1062
State Franchise taxes	735	774	532	921	973	97	n.a.
Total	2377	2464	2288	2675	2772	3116	2867

Source: AIHW (2003).

4.3   Alcohol Consumption in the UK

In the last section (see Figure 4.4), we observed that the British consume about the same amount of pure alcohol as Australians but higher than the Americans. The impact of alcohol on the British society is very similar to those in the other developed countries. In this section we look closely at the alcohol consumption pattern in the UK over time and in relation to various consumer characteristics.

Figure 4.7 shows per adult consumption (in litres of pure alcohol) of beer, wine and spirits in the United Kingdom (UK) over the years 1961 to 1999 obtained from WHO (2003). As can be seen, the total alcohol consumption has increased from 6.5 litres per adult in 1961 to 10.5 litres per adult in 1979 and fell to a low level of 9.3 litres in 1982 and since then fluctuates between 9.5 and 10 litres. Beer consumption peaked in 1979 and has been falling ever since. Currently it is about 5 litres per capita (about the same level as in the early 1960s). Wine consumption has sharply increased from 0.3 litres per adult in 1961 to 2.3 litres per adult in 1999. Spirits consumption also increased until 1979 but has stabilized to around 2 litres per adult since then.

In Figure 4.8 we plot the average household expenditure per week on alcohol (at constant 1999 prices) and the income allocation to alcohol (the budget share of alcohol). As can be seen, the average weekly expenditure on alcohol has increased from about 13 pounds per week in 1978 to about 15 pounds a week in 1999. The budget share on alcohol has fallen from 4.9 percent to about 4.3 percent during the same period.

Table 4.12 presents various price indices and the alcohol affordability index for the years 1978-2000 (1978=100). Column 2 of the table gives the alcohol price index. As can be seen, alcohol prices in the UK have increased more than four-fold

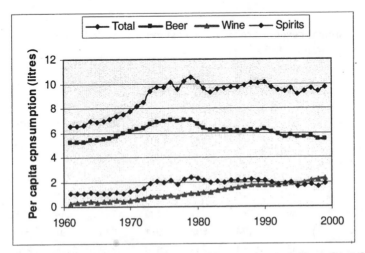

Figure 4.7 Per adult consumption of beer, wine, spirits and total alcohol, UK, 1961-1999

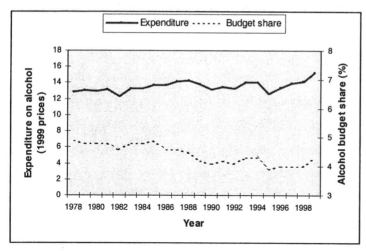

Figure 4.8 Per capita expenditure on alcohol (in 1999 prices) and alcohol budget share, UK, 1978-1999

in the last two decades. Columns 3 and 4 give the retail price index of all consumer goods and the relative price index of alcohol. The price of alcohol relative to the price of all other consumer goods fell slightly initially for two years and has since increased by 24 percent during 1978-2000. The last two columns of the table present the household real disposable income and the affordability of alcohol index (obtained by column 5 divided by column 4). As can be seen, the affordability of alcohol fell below the 1978 level during 1982 and 1983 but increased by about 50 percent during the period 1978 to 2000.

In Table 4.13, we give information on the tax revenue collected by the British government over the years 1978 to 1999. Columns 2-4 of the table give the revenue from beer, wine and spirits and column 5 gives their total. As can be seen, throughout the years, beer is the major contributor to the total tax revenue. Until the mid-1990s, the contribution of spirits to the revenue was higher than that of wine but was taken over by wine from then onwards. Column 6 presents the total government tax revenue and column 7 expresses the alcohol tax revenue as a proportion of the total revenue. As can be seen from the values in the last column, the contribution of alcohol revenue to the total revenue in the UK has fallen from 4.9 percent in 1978 to a low 3.4 percent in 1999.

Table 4.14 presents the survey results on the proportion of number of drinking days in last week by age and gender in 2001 obtained from NS (2003) survey. The age group 65 and over, both males and females, are more likely to drink throughout the whole week than any other age group. The 16-24 age group is most likely to drink one day in a week. A significant proportion of the male and the female population have abstained from drinking in a whole week (i.e. 0 days in a week). It can also be seen that among all age groups, a higher proportion of males drink on more days per week than females.

Table 4.12 Indices of alcohol price, retail price, relative alcohol price, real household's disposable income and affordability of alcohol, UK, 1978-2000

Year	Alcohol price index	Retail price index	Relative alcohol price index	Disposable income index	Affordability of alcohol index
(1)	(2)	(3)	(4)	(5)	(6)
1978	100.0	100.0	100.0	100.0	100.0
1979	110.8	113.4	97.7	105.6	108.1
1980	133.6	133.8	99.9	107.4	107.5
1981	156.2	149.7	104.3	106.9	102.5
1982	174.0	162.6	107.0	106.6	99.6
1983	186.9	170.0	109.9	109.2	99.4
1984	197.8	178.5	110.8	113.2	102.1
1985	210.3	189.3	111.1	117.0	105.3
1986	219.7	195.8	112.2	122.1	108.8
1987	228.7	204.0	112.1	126.6	112.9
1988	240.4	214.0	112.3	133.2	118.6
1989	253.9	230.6	110.1	138.9	126.2
1990	278.4	252.4	110.3	144.1	130.7
1991	313.0	267.2	117.1	146.3	124.9
1992	333.0	277.2	120.1	151.8	126.4
1993	347.9	281.6	123.5	156.4	126.6
1994	356.4	288.4	123.6	158.4	128.2
1995	369.9	298.4	124.0	162.5	131.1
1996	380.5	305.6	124.5	166.0	133.3
1997	391.0	315.2	124.0	172.3	138.9
1998	404.3	326.0	124.0	172.5	139.1
1999	414.8	331.1	125.3	178.6	142.6
2000	421.4	340.9	123.7	184.0	148.9

Source: *Statistics on Alcohol: England*, Statistical Bulletin 2001/13, Department of Health, United Kingdom, July 2001.

Figure 4.9 presents the average weekly alcohol consumption of the British by gender and economic activity status in 2001 obtained from the NS (2003) survey. It can be easily seen from the graph that, irrespective of economic activity status, males consume alcohol almost twice that of the amount of alcohol consumed by females. There is not much difference between the amount of alcohol consumed by British working and unemployed persons. But those who are economically inactive consume about 30 percent less than those who are working or unemployed. Based on the NS (2003) survey data, in Figure 4.10, we plot the average weekly alcohol consumption by gender and gross weekly household income level. For both males and females, alcohol consumption generally increases with increasing income.

Table 4.13 Tax revenue from alcoholic drinks, current prices, UK, 1978-1999 (millions of pounds)

Year	Tax revenue				Total govt tax revenue	Proportion of alcohol tax revenue
	Beer	Wine	Spirits	Total alcohol		
(1)	(2)	(3)	(4)	(5)	(6)	(7)
1978	1200	430	1145	2775	56284	4.9%
1979	1383	537	1372	3292	67746	4.9%
1980	1700	640	1478	3817	83051	4.6%
1981	2072	796	1579	4448	96736	4.6%
1982	2332	913	1667	4912	106993	4.6%
1983	2579	1025	1736	5340	115953	4.6%
1984	2803	1083	1849	5734	124223	4.6%
1985	3033	1170	1986	6188	135425	4.6%
1986	3129	1217	2020	6366	144581	4.4%
1987	3203	1240	2049	6492	155442	4.2%
1988	3415	1352	2185	6952	173197	4.0%
1989	3523	1384	2166	7074	189240	3.7%
1990	3778	1503	2358	7640	203571	3.8%
1991	4155	1680	2452	8286	212136	3.9%
1992	4301	1844	2458	8603	213535	4.0%
1993	4200	1987	2550	8737	217837	4.0%
1994	4576	2106	2570	9252	234110	4.0%
1995	4773	2283	2492	9548	254162	3.8%
1996	4841	2455	2410	9706	267592	3.6%
1997	5053	2587	2414	10053	288783	3.5%
1998	5109	2847	2440	10396	317609	3.3%
1999	5275	3191	2772	11237	334049	3.4%

Source: *Statistics on Alcohol: England*, Statistical Bulletin 2001/13, Department of Health, United Kingdom, July 2001.

Table 4.14 Proportion of adults (15+) who drank last week by number of drinking days, gender and age, UK, 2001

Number of drinking days last week	Age group: Male				Age group: Female			
	16-24	25-44	45-64	65+	16-24	25-44	45-64	65+
(1)	(2)	(3)	(4)	(5)	(6)	(7)	(8)	(9)
0	30	22	24	32	41	34	39	55
1	21	18	18	17	23	21	19	16
2	17	18	15	12	13	17	12	7
3	11	13	10	8	9	10	9	4
4	8	9	7	5	5	6	5	2
5	5	6	6	3	3	4	4	2
6	4	4	5	3	2	2	2	1
7	5	9	15	21	3	5	11	12
Percentage who drank last week	70	78	76	68	59	66	61	45

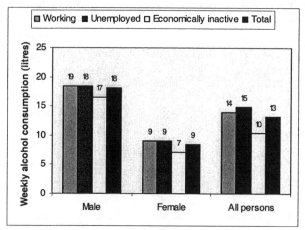

Figure 4.9   Average weekly alcohol consumption by gender and economic activity status, UK, 2001

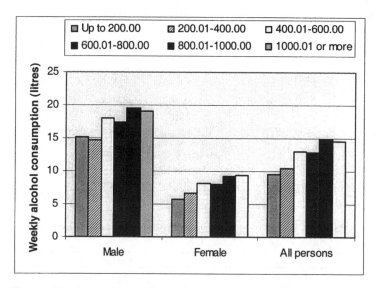

Figure 4.10 Average weekly alcohol consumption by usual gross weekly household income and gender, UK, 2001

In Table 4.15 we present the average weekly alcohol consumption over the period 1992-1998 by gender and age group, compiled from NS (2003). During 1992-1998, the average weekly alcohol intake has increased for both males and females and across all age groups, except the male 25-44 age group. In 1998, males consumed about two and a half times that of females weekly alcohol consumption, irrespective of age group.

Table 4.15 Mean number of units of alcohol consumption per week by adults (aged 16 or older), UK, 1992-1998

Age group	Mean number of units per week			
	1992	1994	1996	1998
(1)	(2)	(3)	(4)	(5)
Male				
16-24yrs	19.1	17.4	20.3	23.6
25-44yrs	18.2	17.5	17.6	16.5
45-64yrs	15.6	15.5	15.6	17.3
65+yrs	9.7	10.0	11.0	10.7
Total	15.9	15.4	16.0	16.4
Female				
16-24yrs	7.3	7.7	9.5	10.6
25-44yrs	6.3	6.2	7.2	7.1
45-64yrs	5.3	5.3	5.9	6.4
65+yrs	2.7	3.2	3.5	3.3
Total	5.4	5.4	6.3	6.4
All persons				
16-24yrs	12.9	12.3	14.7	16.6
25-44yrs	11.8	11.4	11.9	11.4
45-64yrs	10.2	10.2	10.5	11.6
65+yrs	5.6	6.0	6.8	6.5
Total	10.2	10.0	10.7	11.0

Figure 4.11 presents the percentage of adult drinking above the recommended alcohol guidelines by gender and ethnic groups. As can be seen, except for the Chinese ethnic group, the proportion of males is higher than the females in terms of

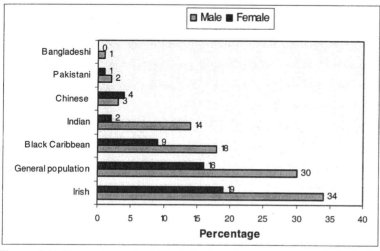

Figure 4.11 Percentage of adults drinking above recommended alcohol guidelines: by ethnic group and gender, UK, 1999

drinking alcohol above the recommended limit. While among all other ethnic groups, for every two men, one woman consumes alcohol above the recommended amount, among Indians only one woman for every seven men drinks above the recommended amount. In general, the Irish tend to exceed the limit more than any other ethnic group.

Table 4.16 presents the percentage of British drinking last week by gender and marital status. The first part of the table gives the percentage of British who drank the week before the survey. As can be seen, the proportion who drank last week is higher among the married population than the single, divorced or widowed population. The proportion is also higher among the 16-44yrs age group than the 45 and over age group. The second part of the table gives the percentage of British who drank 5 or more days during the survey week. As before, a higher proportion of married men and women tend to drink 5 or more days in a week than the singles and divorced but a higher proportion of the 45+ age group consume alcohol 5 or more days in a week than the 16-44 age group. The last two sections of the table

Table 4.16 Alcohol consumption patterns of persons (16+) by marital status, gender and age, UK, 2001

Marital status	Male			Female			All persons		
	16-44yrs	45+yrs	All ages	16-44yrs	45+yrs	All ages	16-44yrs	45+yrs	All ages
(1)	(2)	(3)	(4)	(5)	(6)	(7)	(8)	(9)	(10)
Percentage who drank last week									
Single	73	62	71	61	43	58	68	54	66
Married/cohabiting	79	75	76	67	60	63	72	68	70
Divorced/separated	73	73	73	58	50	54	64	60	61
Widowed	*	66	66	*	43	43	69	48	48
Total	76	73	75	64	54	59	70	63	67
Percentage who drank on five or more days last week									
Single	14	28	16	9	14	9	12	22	13
Married/cohabiting	21	26	24	12	18	15	16	22	19
Divorced/separated	13	26	21	9	12	11	11	18	15
Widowed	*	22	21	*	14	14	7	16	16
Total	18	26	22	11	16	13	14	21	17
Percentage who drank more than 3-4 units on at least one day last week									
Single	50	30	47	39	10	35	45	21	41
Married/cohabiting	45	29	36	30	16	23	37	23	29
Divorced/separated	49	39	43	29	12	19	36	23	28
Widowed	*	20	21	*	6	7	40	9	10
Total	47	30	39	32	13	22	40	21	30
Percentage who drank more than 6-8 units on at least one day last week									
Single	35	14	32	24	4	21	30	10	27
Married/cohabiting	27	12	18	13	4	9	20	8	13
Divorced/separated	29	20	23	15	4	8	20	11	14
Widowed	*	6	6	*	1	1	16	2	2
Total	30	12	21	17	3	10	23	7	15

present the percentage who drank more than 3-4 units and 6-8 units at least one day during the past week, respectively. The numbers show that a higher proportion of single and divorced male populations and single and married female populations consumed 3-4 or 6-8 units of alcohol on at least one day of a week.

Table 4.17 presents the proportion of young students who drank alcohol in the week before the survey by gender and age. As can be seen, there is not much difference in the proportion between male and female students when they get older. Among the 11 year olds, in most years, the proportion of boys is twice that of girls. Among both boys and girls, the percentage increased over time mostly among the 13-15 age group.

Table 4.17 Proportion of students who drank alcohol in the last week by gender and age, UK, 1988-2002

Age	1988	1990	1992	1994	1996	1998	1999	2000	2001	2002
(1)	(2)	(3)	(4)	(5)	(6)	(7)	(8)	(9)	(10)	(11)
Boys										
11yrs	7	8	8	8	7	4	7	5	8	7
12yrs	12	9	13	10	12	14	10	11	14	12
13yrs	20	17	15	22	27	16	16	18	22	20
14yrs	25	32	32	34	37	28	28	34	35	34
15yrs	45	42	49	52	50	48	48	52	54	49
11-15yrs	24	22	24	26	27	23	22	25	28	25
Girls										
11yrs	4	4	5	4	6	2	4	5	4	4
12yrs	7	6	7	9	9	6	8	9	11	9
13yrs	11	19	11	16	22	14	17	19	22	21
14yrs	19	32	25	26	35	29	28	31	35	34
15yrs	36	39	40	48	55	40	41	46	50	45
11-15yrs	17	20	17	22	26	18	20	23	25	23
Boys & girls										
11yrs	5	6	6	6	7	3	6	5	6	5
12yrs	9	8	10	9	11	10	9	10	12	11
13yrs	16	18	13	19	24	15	16	19	22	20
14yrs	22	32	29	30	36	29	28	32	35	34
15yrs	40	40	45	50	53	44	45	49	52	47
11-15yrs	20	21	21	24	27	21	21	24	26	24

4.4   Alcohol Consumption in the US

According to *US Health Statistics*, in 2000, about 7 million (or one in five) Americans in the 12-20 age group was a binge drinker (drink 5 or more drinks on the same occasion at least once in 30 days). American students spend annually about 6 billion dollars on alcohol, which is more than what they spend on soft drinks, tea, milk, juice, coffee or books combined. Each year, the US alcohol industry spends about 2 billion dollars on alcohol advertising and the Americans spend over 90 billion dollars on alcohol each year. These statistics show that, like many other countries, alcohol plays an important role in the US, it continues to make a significant contribution to the national economy. In this section, we look at the alcohol consumption patterns in the US.

Figure 4.12 plots the per adult American consumption of pure alcohol beer, wine, spirits and total alcohol (in litres), for the period 1961-2000, where the data are compiled from WHO (2003). As can be seen, the total alcohol consumption has reached the maximum level of 10.5 litres per adult in 1980 and has steadily declined until 2000. The consumption of beer, wine and spirits, all followed the same pattern as the total alcohol. Total alcohol consumption was 6.8 litres per adult in 1961 and was 9.1 litres per adult in 2000. Per adult consumption of beer, wine and spirits were 3.9, 0.7 and 2.2 litres in 1961 and 5.1, 1.7 and 2.3 litres in 2000, respectively.

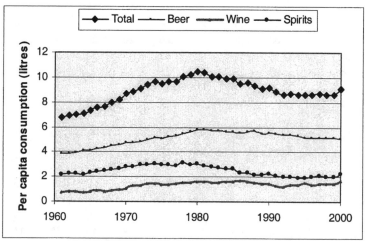

Figure 4.12   Per adult consumption of beer, wine, spirits and total alcohol, US, 1961-2000

In Figure 4.13, we present the proportion of alcohol users among persons (18+) by type of alcohol use and gender in 2000 and 2001. As can be seen, for all types of alcohol use, the proportion of use is higher for males than females. Also the proportion of 'any alcohol use' for both males and females has increased slightly from 2000 to 2001. The proportion of binge use among the males has slightly fallen while the female proportion remains the same between 2000 and 2001.

Figure 4.14 plots the percentage reporting the past month alcohol use from 2000 and 2001 surveys by educational level, lower high school, high school graduate, some college qualification and college graduation. As can be seen, the

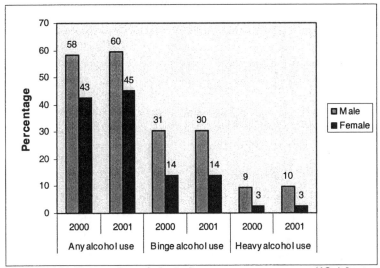

Figure 4.13 **Proportion of alcohol users among persons (18+) by type of alcohol use and gender, US, 2000-2001**

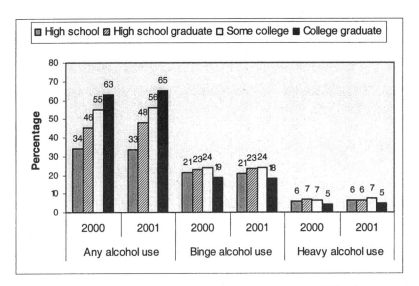

Figure 4.14 **Proportion of alcohol users among persons (18+) by type of alcohol use and educational level, US, 2000-2001**

proportion of any alcohol use increases with educational level and generally the proportion is higher in 2001 than in 2000. The proportion of binge alcohol use and heavy alcohol use increases up to a certain educational level and then falls with increasing educational level. The proportions do not change much between 2000 and 2001.

Figure 4.15 presents the percentage reporting past month alcohol use in the 2001 survey of NHSDA (2003a) by current employment level, full-time, part-time, unemployed and retired, students etc. As can be seen, the proportion of 'any alcohol use' is the highest among the full-time job holders followed by part-timers,

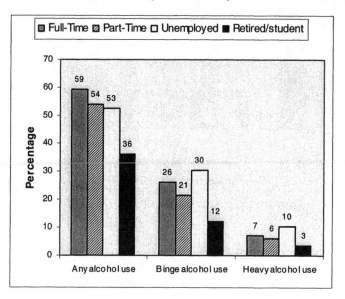

Figure 4.15   Proportion of alcohol users among persons (18+) by type of alcohol use and employment status, US, 2001

unemployed persons and retired persons and students. The proportion of binge alcohol use is the highest among the unemployed persons followed by full-time job holders, part-timers, and retired persons and students. The order of proportion of heavy alcohol use is the same as the proportion of binge alcohol use. Figure 4.16 shows the proportion of past month alcohol use among youths aged 12 to 20, by race/ethnicity. As can be seen the proportion is highest among the white Americans followed by Cubans, American Indians and Mexicans. The least percentage corresponds to the Vietnamese ethnic group.

4.5   Alcohol Consumption in New Zealand

According to an official survey in 2000, 85 percent of New Zealanders reported that they were drinkers. The same survey also revealed that 88 percent of male New Zealanders and 83 percent of female New Zealanders of the 14-65 age group

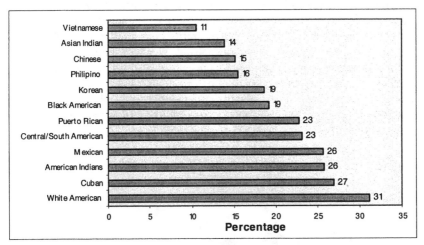

Figure 4.16 **Proportion among youths aged 12-20 who have used alcohol in the past month by race/ethnicity, US, 2000-2001 averages**

of the population were drinkers in 2000. In 2000, an average drinker consumed about 11.4 litres of pure alcohol. Male drinkers consumed about 66 percent and females consumed 34 percent of the total volume of the absolute alcohol consumed by all New Zealand drinkers. In this section we consider the alcohol consumption pattern of New Zealanders.

Figure 4.17 plots the beer, wine, spirits and total alcohol consumption (pure alcohol litres/adult) in New Zealand over the period 1961 to 2000, data compiled

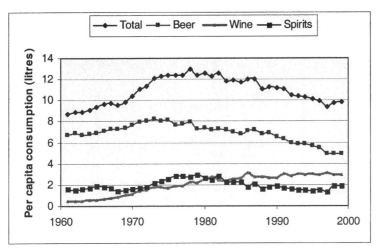

Figure 4.17 **Per adult consumption of beer, wine, spirits and total alcohol, NZ, 1961-1999**

from WHO (2003). As can be seen, the total alcohol consumption increased until the early 1980s and fell from then onwards. Beer consumption reached its peak around the mid 1970s and then declined. Spirits consumption also fell in New Zealand from the late 1970s. On the other hand, wine consumption continues to grow throughout the years. Figure 4.18 presents the annual volume of alcohol consumption by men and women in 2000 by age group. As can be seen, the 18-19 and the 20-24 age groups consume the highest amount of alcohol among both males and females in New Zealand. In general, across all age groups men consume more alcohol than women.

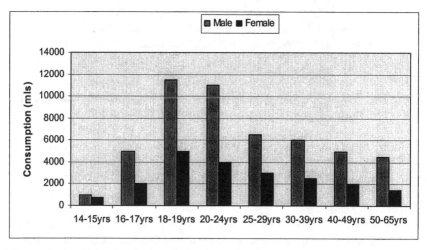

Figure 4.18   Annual volume of absolute alcohol consumed by men and women, NZ, 2000

Figure 4.19 presents the proportion of the total volume of alcohol consumed by men and women New Zealanders at each drinking location in 2000. As can be seen, a major portion of total alcohol is consumed at people's own home followed by other's home and then pub/tavern. About 75 percent of total consumption of alcohol is takes place in the above three places combined.

4.6 Concluding Comments

In this chapter, we presented the consumption patterns of alcoholic beverages, beer, wine, spirits and total alcohol in a number of countries. We found that, in most developed (OECD) countries, per adult alcohol consumption is steadily falling over the last 40 years. However, we found that per adult alcohol consumption is on the increase in most developing countries. Comparing the level of alcohol consumption in all countries, we found that per adult alcohol consumption is still much higher in the developed countries than the developing countries.

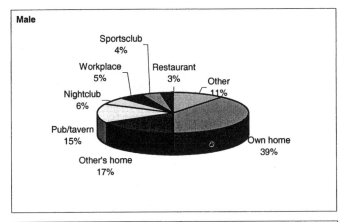

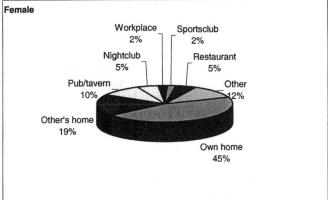

Figure 4.19 Proportion of the total volume of alcohol consumed by males and females at each drinking location, NZ, 2000

Looking at the consumption patterns of the individual alcoholic beverages, beer, wine and spirits in Australia over the last two decades, we found that per adult consumption of wine and spirits have increased while beer consumption has fallen. Comparing the various types of beer, wine and spirits, we found that bottled wine, regular beer and bottled spirits are the three most favourite drinks of Australians. We also found that male Australians are more likely to be a drinker compared to female Australians, and regardless of their socio-economic status, one in two Australian adults are regular drinkers.

In the UK, we found that per adult consumption of beer has been declining and that of wine is sharply increasing while spirits consumption has been stable in the past 2 decades. During the same period, alcohol prices in the UK has increased more than four fold. We also found that among all age groups, a higher proportion of males drink more alcohol and on more days than females in the UK. Also, regardless of their gender, alcohol consumption increases with increasing income.

Among 11-15 year old boys and girls, we found that as they get older, the proportion of boys who drinks alcohol tend to increase sharply compared to the proportion of girls who drinks alcohol which increases very slowly.

In the US, we found that per adult consumption of beer has slightly decreased, while that of wine has steadily increased and that of spirits is stable in the past 20 years. Male Americans are heavy drinkers compared to female Americans. Comparing the alcohol drinking habits of various ethnic groups in the US, we found that a higher proportion of white Americans drink alcohol, followed by the Cubans, Americans Indians and Mexicans, while a very low proportion of Asian Americans drink alcohol.

In the past 2 decades, total alcohol consumption in New Zealand has steadily decreased. Beer and spirits consumption has decreased while wine consumption has increased slightly during the same period. In terms of volume of alcohol, 18-24 year old males consumed the highest amount of alcohol (more than 11,000 litres) compared to all other age groups. In all age groups, with the exception of the 14-15 year olds, female New Zealanders consumed less than half of the amount of alcohol consumed by male New Zealanders. We also found that a very high proportion of New Zealanders tend to drink alcohol at their home than in other places.

In Chapter 8, we further analyse the alcohol consumption patterns by estimating the demand models for alcohol as a commodity and, in Chapter 9, we analyse the consumption patterns of the three beverages, beer, wine and spirits, test demand model hypothesis and present income and price elasticities for the alcoholic beverages group as a whole and for the individual beverages in a number of countries. In Chapter 11, we present a review of a number of alcohol control policies and other measures put in place to reduce alcohol consumption in a number of countries.

Chapter 5

Marijuana Consumption

Marijuana, though illegal, is one of the illicit drugs most commonly used by a significant proportion of the world population. It is the most used illegal drug in a number of countries, including Australia, the UK and the US. About 2.5 percent of the world population use marijuana (UNODCCP, 1999, p.91). It is usually a green, brown, or grey mixture of dried, shredded leaves, stems, seeds, and flowers of hemp plant, *cannabis sativa*. All forms of marijuana are mind altering. The main active chemical in marijuana is THC (Delta-9-Tetrahydrocannabinol). Today's marijuana is considered to be 10 to 15 times stronger in terms of the THC concentration than that which was available 30-40 years ago. The use of marijuana has a long history and was until the turn of the century, largely used for medical purposes mostly in Asia, Africa and the Middle East. Towards the end of 19th century only Western societies took a serious interest in marijuana. During the period 1880-1900, several research studies were published on the therapeutic use of marijuana. Its medical uses varied from its use in the treatment of malaria to the relief of pain during childbirth. However, the unreliable supply and the discovery of alternative medicines for pain relief led to a reduced level of use of marijuana in the medical field.

While marijuana does not generate revenue to governments directly, it is considered as a cash crop in many countries. Across the world it has been found that marijuana is the second most common drug after alcohol, present in the blood stream of non-fatal and fatally injured persons. According to recent surveys, it is believed that one in four high school students in developed countries is a current marijuana user. The short term effects of marijuana include problems with memory and learning, distorted perceptions, trouble with thinking and problem solving, loss of motor co-ordination and increased heart beat and breathing problems. These effects are considered even greater when marijuana is mixed with other drugs. In the long term, regular use of marijuana, like smoking, could develop cancer and problems in lungs and airways and increase the risk of developing infections in the immune system. The long-term use of marijuana could lead to addiction in some people.

In this chapter, we first present a global picture of marijuana consumption and then look more closely at the consumption patterns of alcohol in a selected number of countries.

5.1   A Global Picture

Using data compiled from the ESPAD (2000) survey, in Figure 5.1, we present the proportion of the 10th grade students who have 'ever used' marijuana in the US, the Europe as a whole and the different (Northern, Southern and Eastern) regions in Europe. Comparing the 10th graders in the US and the Europe as a whole, we can see that the proportion of 10th graders who have 'ever used' marijuana in the US is much higher (about two and a half times) than that in Europe. Within Europe, the proportion is highest (19 percent) in the Northern Europe and lowest (14 percent) in the Southern region.

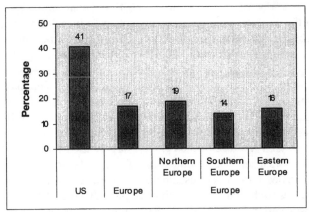

Figure 5.1   Proportion of students who ever used marijuana, US vs Europe, 1999

Figure 5.2 presents the proportion of boys and girls who have used marijuana at least once in their lifetime in the European countries and the US, based on the 1999 survey (ESPAD, 2000). As can be seen, boys and girls in the US have the highest lifetime experience of marijuana compared with any other country. It appears that, in all countries, the percentage of boys who have used marijuana at least once in their lifetime is significantly higher than that of girls. The proportions, for both boys and girls, are quite high in countries like Ireland, France, the UK, Czech Republic and the US, and are quite low in Romania and Cyprus.

Figure 5.3 shows the proportion of boys and girls who have used marijuana during the last 30 days of the survey. In all countries, as before, the proportion of boys who have used marijuana in the past 30 days is significantly higher than that of the girls. It can also be seen that the proportion of boys and girls in France who had used marijuana in the last 30 days is higher than that in any other country including the US.

Figure 5.4 presents a comparison of the frequency of using marijuana over time across the two countries, Australia and the US using data compiled from CDHFS (1997). As can be seen, the proportion of people who use marijuana occasionally in

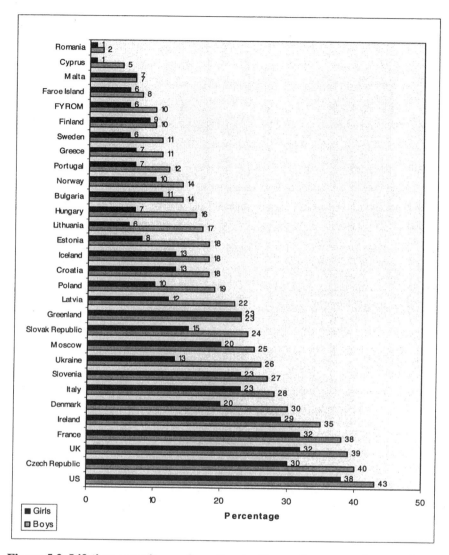

Figure 5.2 Lifetime experience of marijuana: Proportion among boys and girls, 1999

the US is higher than that in Australia in any particular year. This proportion is on the decline in the US but fluctuating around 4 percent in Australia. The proportion of monthly users is also higher in the US than in Australia. While this proportion over the time period is declining in the US, it is increasing in Australia. The proportion of weekly users is higher in Australia than in the US. This proportion is falling over time in the US but fluctuating around 4 to 5 percent in Australia. In Figure 5.5, we present the proportion of people who have used marijuana in the

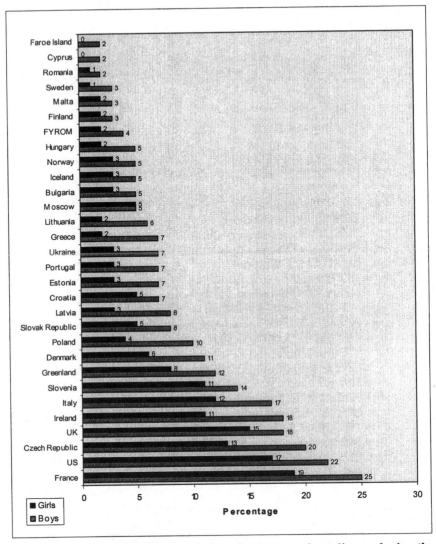

Figure 5.3 Proportion of boys and girls who have used marijuana during the last 30 days, 1999

past 12 months to 2000/2001 in Australia, Canada, New Zealand, the UK and the US, using data compiled from AIHW (2003). As can be seen, the percentage of people who have used marijuana in the past 12 months is highest in New Zealand (20 percent) followed by Australia (15 percent), and in the remaining three countries the proportion is only about 9 percent.

In the following sections we look at marijuana consumption patterns in Australia, the US, the UK and New Zealand in more detail.

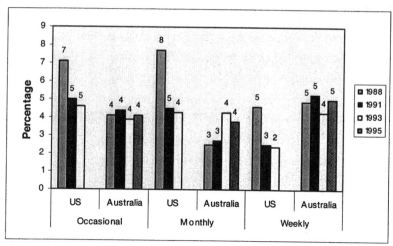

Figure 5.4 Frequency of using marijuana, Australia and the US

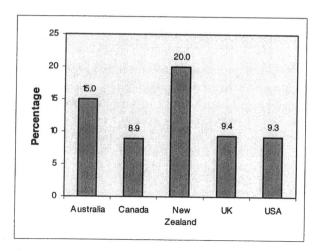

Figure 5.5 Proportion of adults who have used marijuana in the past 12 months, 5 countries, 2001

5.2   Marijuana Consumption in Australia

Marijuana is one of the widely available and accepted illicit drugs in the Australian community. While about 30 percent of Australians have tried marijuana, about 12 percent of Australians have reported that they have used it in the past 12 months (AIHW, 2003). Men and young people are more likely to try marijuana than the women and older people in Australia. As marijuana use is also spreading among school children, it is becoming a major concern to parents and education providers. In this section, we look at the consumption patterns of marijuana in Australia over time and with respect to various consumer characteristics.

Figures 5.6 and 5.7 show the recent use and lifetime use, respectively, of various types of illicit drugs by Australian adults (14+). As can be seen, marijuana is the dominant illicit drug used by many Australians, which is three to four times higher than the next closest drug, amphetamines. About 13 percent of adult Australians are current users of marijuana (see Figure 5.6) and about 33 percent of Australians have used marijuana at least once in their lifetime (see Figure 5.7).

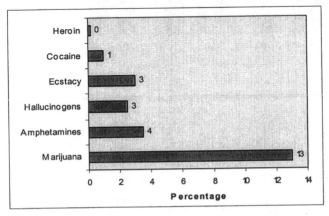

Figure 5.6 Proportion of adults (aged 14 or over) who have used illicit drugs recently by drug type, Australia, 2001

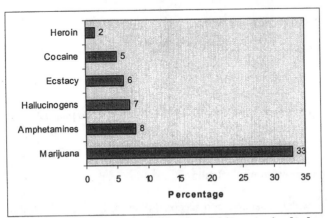

Figure 5.7 Proportion of adults (aged 14 or over) who have used illicit drugs at least once in their lifetime by drug type, Australia, 2001

Table 5.1 presents the proportion of adults (14+) who have used marijuana in the past 12 months over the years 1995-2001, by age and gender. The proportion in the last 3 years, during 1998-2001, is generally falling for both males and females.

Furthermore, in general, the percentage is higher for the male population than the female population. For all ages, the proportion for male marijuana users increased from 18.0 percent in 1995 to 21.3 percent in 1998 and then fell to 15.8 percent in 2001, and for females, the proportion has increased from 8.6 percent in 1995 to 14.7 percent in 1998 and has then fallen to 10.0 percent in 2001.

In Figure 5.8, we present the frequency of marijuana use in 2001 by age groups. The proportion of 'every day' users or 'once a week or more' users of marijuana

Table 5.1 Proportion of the adult population (aged 14+) who have used marijuana in the past 12 months, by age and gender, Australia, 1995-2001

Age group	Males			Females		
	1995	1998	2001	1995	1998	2001
(1)	(2)	(3)	(4)	(5)	(6)	(7)
14-19	35.9	35.0	26.6	20.1	34.2	22.6
20-29	43.7	43.7	35.1	23.4	29.3	23.2
30-39	19.0	24.1	20.8	8.2	16.3	11.7
40-49	8.0	16.6	10.7	2.2	6.3	6.6
50-59	1.9	5.6	4.5	1.2	7.6	2.0
60+	1.1	0.7	0.5	1.2	0.3	0.0
All ages	18.0	21.3	15.8	8.6	14.7	10.0

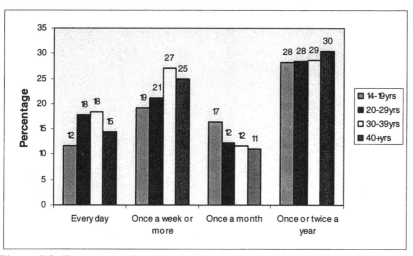

Figure 5.8 Frequency of marijuana use by age group, Australia, 2001

increases with the age up to 40 years of age and then starts to fall beyond 40+. The proportion of 'once a month' marijuana users declines from 17 percent for the 14-19 years age group to 11 percent for the 40+ years age group. The proportion of 'once or twice a year' marijuana users increases slightly with increasing age.

Figure 5.9 presents the frequency of marijuana use by gender. As can be seen, a male Australian is more likely to use marijuana more frequently (every day or once a week or more) than a female. The proportion of infrequent (once or twice a year) marijuana use is higher among females than males.

Figure 5.10 shows the proportion of Australians who have used marijuana in the past 12 months by ethnic groups such as Australian born, European born migrants and other migrants. As can be seen, the proportion of marijuana users among the

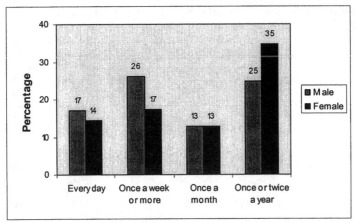

Figure 5.9   Frequency of Marijuana use by gender, Australia, 2001

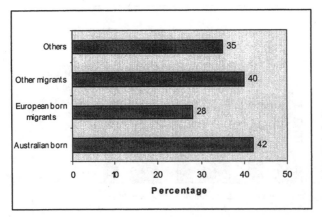

Figure 5.10   Proportion of marijuana users by ethnicity, Australia, 2001

Australian born people and other migrants are much higher at about 40 percent while only 28 percent of the European born migrants have used marijuana in the past 12 months.

Figure 5.11 also presents the marijuana use in the past 12 months but by marital status. As can be seen, the proportion of Australians who have used marijuana in the past 12 months among the 'never married' marital status is much higher than the proportion for any other marital status. This proportion for the 'widowed' population is only a third of the proportion for the 'never married' population.

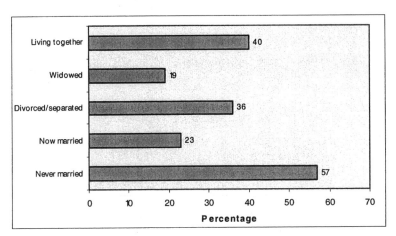

Figure 5.11   Proportion of marijuana users by marital status, Australia, 2001

Figures 5.12-5.14 present some other interesting observations about the use of marijuana among Australians, namely, the usual place of use of marijuana, usual source of obtaining marijuana and other types of drug use in conjunction with marijuana. As can be seen from Figure 5.12, the majority of adult Australians (both male and female) use marijuana at their home and private parties. Another significant proportion is the adult Australians who have used marijuana in other places such as in a vehicle, at parks, workplace, at public establishments and dance parties. Female Australians are more likely to consume marijuana at home than male Australians.

Figure 5.13 shows that the major source of marijuana supply to most Australians (both males and females) is their friends. The other sources of obtaining marijuana are through relatives, dealers and by growing marijuana themselves.

As Figure 5.14 shows, about 95 percent of male and female Australians consume marijuana along with alcohol. The other types of drugs mostly consumed simultaneously with marijuana are amphetamines, ecstasy, cocaine and heroin, but the last two are to a lesser extent.

Table 5.2 presents the proportion of Australians who have reported to have used marijuana never/lifetime/recent against various characteristics such as educational

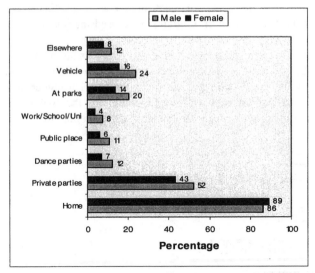

Figure 5.12   Proportion of marijuana users among adults (aged 14 or over) by place of use and gender, Australia, 2001

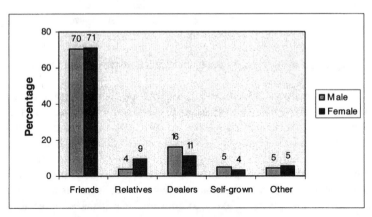

Figure 5.13   Proportion of recent marijuana users among adults (aged 14 or over) by access type, Australia, 2001

level, employment status, socio-economic status etc. The results from the table can be summarized as follows:

♦ It is more likely that an Australian with HSC equivalent qualification has recently used marijuana than an Australian with any other qualification or no qualification.
♦ An unemployed Australian is more likely to have used marijuana recently than an employed person.

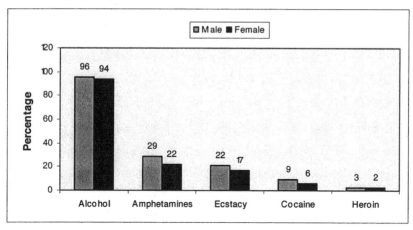

Figure 5.14 **Proportion of adult (aged 14 or over) marijuana users who also use other drugs, Australia, 2001**

♦ Blue-collar workers are more likely to have used marijuana recently than white-collar workers.
♦ People from a non-English speaking born are less likely to have used marijuana in their lifetime or recently than those from an English speaking or Australian born.
♦ High income Australians are more likely to use marijuana during their lifetime or recently than any other income group.
♦ A never married person is more likely to have used marijuana either recently or during their lifetime than others.

5.3 Marijuana Consumption in the UK

Compared to the US and Australia, not much statistical data on illicit drug use is available for the United Kingdom (UK). The main source of information on the use of illicit drug use comes from the *British Crime Survey* (BCS) and the *Annual Health Survey of England* (HSE) conducted by the *National Centre for Social Research* (Natcen). Furthermore, these surveys targeted only the population in England and Wales instead of the whole of Great Britain and mostly collected information on the impact of government policies on illicit drug use.

In a recent report by Natcen (2003) based on the BCS, it was reported that marijuana was by far the most likely illicit drug to be taken by the British. About 25 percent of the population has reported using marijuana at least once in their lifetime, 9 percent reported use in the preceding year and 5 percent used it in the previous month.

Table 5.2 Correlates of marijuana use: Proportion of marijuana users among the population aged 14 and over, Australia, 1998

Characteristics (1)	Never used (2)	Lifetime use (3)	Recent use (4)
Education			
No qualification	68.1	31.9	13.9
HSC or equivalent	51.1	48.9	23.4
Trade/diploma	57.1	42.9	19.8
Tertiary	54.2	45.8	15.9
Employment status			
Currently employed	51.6	48.4	20.6
Student	57.0	43.0	29.2
Unemployed	52.9	47.1	32.1
Retired/pension	80.0	20.0	6.2
Occupational status			
Upper (white)	57.9	42.1	16.4
Middle	60.4	39.6	16.9
Lower (blue)	60.0	40.0	20.7
Cultural background			
Australian born	58.9	41.1	19.3
Other English-speaking born	55.0	45.0	, 18.6
Non-English-speaking born	79.3	20.7	8.0
Socioeconomic area			
1st quintile	64.5	35.5	16.7
2nd quintile	64.3	35.7	15.3
3rd quintile	57.7	42.3	19.0
4th quintile	59.8	40.2	18.5
5th quintile	57.3	42.7	20.4
Geography			
Urban	61.0	39.0	18.3
Rural/remote	60.6	39.4	16.9
Marital status			
Never married	46.7	53.3	36.1
Widowed	90.2	9.8	1.8
Divorced/separated	53.2	46.8	17.9
Presently married	66.7	33.3	10.1

The proportion of boys taking drugs was higher than the proportion of girls who were taking drugs in 2001. Thirteen percent of young people in the 11-15 age group had taken marijuana in 2001. Marijuana was the illicit drug most likely to have been offered (about 28 percent of youngsters were offered marijuana in 2001) to younger people in England during 2001.

Figure 5.15 presents the number of marijuana seizures as a proportion of total number of drug seizures in the UK over the 1991-2001 period. As can be seen,

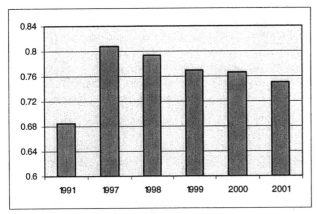

Figure 5.15   Number of marijuana seizures as a proportion of total number of drug seizures, UK, 1991-2001

marijuana is the most seized illicit drug item in the UK. In 1997, about 80 percent of the drugs seized cases were related to marijuana. While the percentage of seizures is fell from 1997 onwards, currently the percentage is about 75 percent. That is, three in four drug seizures are related to marijuana. In Figure 5.16, we present the estimated number of drug users among the 16-24 age group by drug type. As can be seen, a larger number of 16-24 year olds use marijuana (1,525,000 persons) compared to the next popular illicit drug, Ecstasy (used by about 384,000 persons).

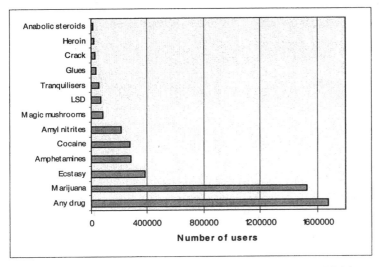

Figure 5.16   Estimates of last year drug users among the 16-24 age group, UK, 2002

Table 5.3 presents a comparison of last year use of marijuana and any drug as well as the last month use of marijuana and any other drug by age groups. As can be seen, in the UK, persons in the 16-24 age group are the more active users of marijuana or any other drug, both in terms of last year use and last month use, than the persons in the other two age groups, 25-34 years and 35-59 years. The proportion of people in the 25-34 age group who have used marijuana or any other drug in the last year or last month is about half the corresponding proportions for the 16-24 age group.

Table 5.3 Prevalence estimates for last year and last month use of marijuana for different age groups, UK, 2002

Age group	Last year		Last month	
	Marijuana	Any drug	Marijuana	Any drug
(1)	(2)	(3)	(4)	(5)
16-24	26.9	29.6	17.1	18.8
25-34	13.5	15.4	8.6	9.7
35-59	4.1	4.9	2.4	2.9

Figure 5.17 presents the proportion of illicit drug use among the 16-59 years age group in England and Wales by drug type. As can be seen, the most popular drug used at least once in their lifetime or in the preceding year is marijuana followed by amphetamines, LSD etc. About 25 percent of the 16-59 years age group are lifetime marijuana users and 9 percent of this age group have used marijuana in the preceding year.

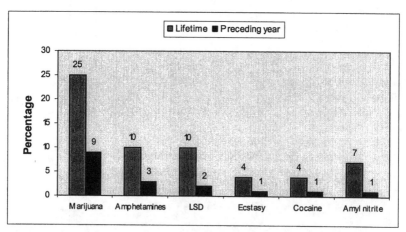

Figure 5.17   Proportion of illicit drug users among the 16-59 age group, England and Wales, 1998

Figure 5.18 plots the mean age at initiation of illicit drug use of the 16-24 age group in the UK. The lowest mean age is for marijuana (15.5 years) and the highest is for Cocaine (18.2 years). In Figure 5.19, we present the proportion of people who are reported to have 'easy' access to various types of illicit drugs. About 68 percent of the people reported that they had 'easy' access to marijuana, followed by ecstasy (43 percent) and amphetamines (42 percent). The least accessibility reported is for methadone (12 percent).

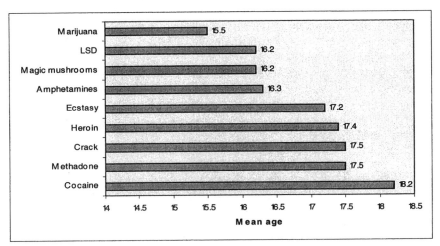

Figure 5.18   Mean age at initiation of drug use, 16-24 age group, UK, 2001/2002

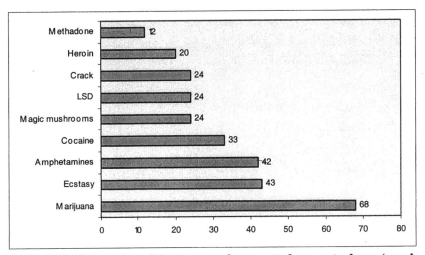

Figure 5.19   Proportion of drug users who reported access to drugs 'easy', UK, 2002

Table 5.4 presents information on the percentage of people aged 16-59 who used a drug in the last year by drug type and over the years 1994 to 2000. As can be seen, while the percentage is on the increase for the three drugs, marijuana (from 8.4 percent in 1994 to 9.4 percent in the year 2000), ecstasy (from 1 percent in 1994 to 1.6 percent in 2000) and cocaine (from 0.5 percent in 1994 to 1.7 percent in 2000), it is decreasing for amphetamines (from 2.4 percent in 1994 to 1.9 percent in 2000) and LSD (from 1.3 percent in 1994 to 0.6 percent in 2000). The proportion of marijuana users in 2000 is about 6 times that of ecstasy, 5 times that of amphetamines and cocaine, 16 times that of LSD and 30 times that of heroin.

Figure 5.20 presents the percentage of persons in the 16-59 years age group using various types of drugs in their lifetime by ethnic groups in the UK. As can be seen, the whites dominate the proportion of users of any type of drug compared to any other ethnic group. In the UK, 28 percent of whites, 24 percent of blacks, 10 percent of Indians and 6 percent of migrants from Pakistan/Bangladesh have used

Table 5.4 Percentage of people aged 16-59 using various drugs in the last year, 1994-2000, UK

Drug type	1994	1996	1998	2000
(1)	(2)	(3)	(4)	(5)
Marijuana	8.4	8.7	9.0	9.4
Ecstasy	1.0	1.4	1.2	1.6
Amphetamines	2.4	2.9	2.6	1.9
Cocaine	0.5	0.6	1.1	1.7
LSD	1.3	0.9	0.6	0.6
Heroin	0.2	0.2	0.1	0.3

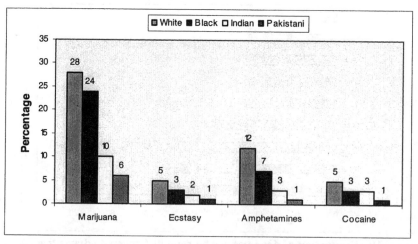

Figure 5.20   Proportion of respondents aged 16-59 using various drugs in their lifetime by ethnic group, UK, 2000

marijuana in their lifetime. Figure 5.21 presents the same information for the 16-29 age group. A comparison of Figures 5.20 and 5.21 shows that the proportion of the different types of drug users in the two age groups appear to be the same. A noticeable difference among the ethnic groups is that the Indians in the 16-59 age group use less ecstasy and cocaine than the blacks in the same age group. In the 16-29 age group, the proportion of Indians who use ecstasy and cocaine is greater than that of the blacks.

Table 5.5 presents the percentage of people who had taken marijuana last month and last year, by age and gender. As can be seen, the percentage is higher for the younger age groups, 16-19, 20-24 and 25-29, compared to the older groups. Furthermore, the proportion is higher for males than females.

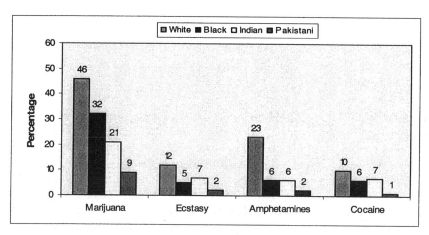

Figure 5.21   Proportion of respondents aged 16-29 using various drugs in their lifetime by ethnic group, UK, 2000

5.4   Marijuana Consumption in the US

In the US, marijuana has been prohibited since 1937. Nearly 69 million Americans over the age of 12 have tried marijuana at least once. According to the *US National Household Survey on Drug Abuse (NHSDA) 2001*, marijuana was used by 76 percent of current illicit drug users. An estimated 37 percent of Americans aged 12 or older have used marijuana at least once in their lifetime. Over 1 million youths aged 12 to 17 and half-a-million young adults aged 18 to 25 used marijuana for the first time in 1999. Based on the survey (NHSDA, 2003b), adult dependence on marijuana was more likely among individuals who first used marijuana at age 14 or younger than among those who first used marijuana after the age 14. According to the *MTF (2002)* study, 6 percent of 12th, 4 percent of 10th, 1 percent of 8th graders had used marijuana daily in the past 30 days of the survey. In 2000, it was estimated that Americans used 1009 metric tons of marijuana worth an estimated

Table 5.5 Percentage of men and women who had taken marijuana in the last year, by age group, 2000

Age group	Last month		Last Year	
	Male	Female	Male	Female
(1)	(2)	(3)	(4)	(5)
16-19	20	11	28	21
20-24	21	15	30	24
25-29	17	6	23	12
30-34	9	3	15	6
35-39	5	1	9	4
40-44	4	1	6	3
45-59	2	0	3	1
16-59	8	4	12	7
16-29	19	10	27	18

value of U$10.4 billion. In 1999, over 220,000 people who entered the drug treatment programme have reported marijuana as their primary drug of abuse.

Figures 5.22 and 5.23 plot the estimated number of marijuana initiatives and the mean age at first marijuana use during 1965-1999 in the US. As can be seen, the number of estimated marijuana initiatives peaked first during the late 1970s and fell to a low level in the early 1990s and then reached another peak during the late 1990s but somewhat lower than the late 1970s peak level and is now again on the decline. The mean age at first use for the American marijuana users has fallen from about mean age of 20 years in 1965 to 17 years in 1999 (see Figure 5.23).

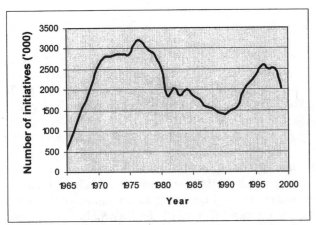

Figure 5.22   Estimated number of marijuana initiatives, US, 1965-1999

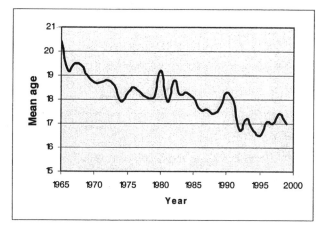

Figure 5.23   Mean age at first marijuana use, US, 1965-1999

Table 5.6 presents information on the frequency of drug use among US high school seniors. Among the high school seniors, it appears that marijuana is the most popular drug followed by stimulants, LSD and cocaine. About 24 percent of the seniors have reported that they have used marijuana in the past month and about 5 percent reported to have used stimulants, 3 percent LSD and 2 percent cocaine.

Table 5.6 Proportion of drug users among US high school seniors by frequency of use, 1998

Drug (1)	Ever used (2)	Past year (3)	Past month (4)
Marijuana	49.6	38.5	23.7
Cocaine	8.7	5.5	2.3
Crack	3.9	2.4	0.9
Stimulants	16.5	10.2	4.8
LSD	13.6	8.4	3.1
PCP	3.9	2.3	0.7
Heroin	2.1	1.2	0.5

Source: *Fact Sheet: Drug Data Summary*, White House Office of National Drug Policy, February 1998.

Figure 5.24 plots the proportion of Americans who used marijuana in the past month, by age groups during the period 1978-2000, compiled from ONDCP (2003). As can be seen, for all age groups the proportion is initially falling until 1990 and while it is stable from then onwards for the older age groups, 26-34 and 35+ years, the proportion is on the increase for the younger age groups 12-17 and 18-25 years.

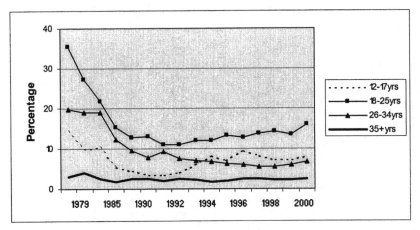

Figure 5.24   Percentage reporting past month use of marijuana, by age of respondents, US, 1979-2001

In Figure 5.25, we present the distribution of frequency of use of marijuana by students at 8th, 10th and 12th grades. As expected, at all frequency types (daily, 30-day and annual) the higher the grade, the higher the proportion of students consuming marijuana. We plot the proportion of the 8th, 10th and high school seniors in the US who have reported the use of marijuana in the past month during 1975-2001, compiled from ONDCP (2003), in Figure 5.26. As can be seen, the proportion of seniors who have reported using marijuana and any drug peaked during 1978-1979 and then fell sharply until 1992. The proportion then increased until in recent years the proportion seems to have stabilised. The same trend can be noticed for the 8th and 10th graders between 1990 and 2001.

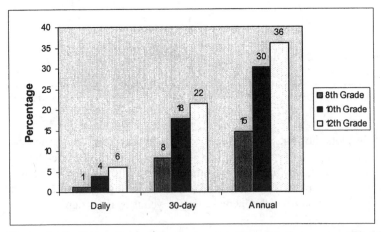

Figure 5.25   Percentage of students reporting marijuana use, US, 2002

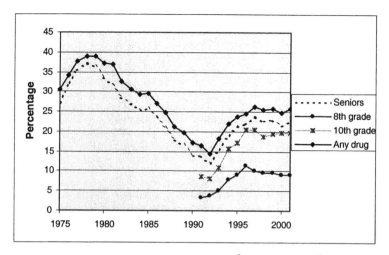

Figure 5.26 Past month marijuana use, 8th grade and 10th grade students, US

Figure 5.27 presents the percentage of Americans aged 12 to 25 reporting past month marijuana use by age in year 2000, compiled from NHSDA (2003b). As can be seen, the proportion increases from about 1 percent (12 years) up to 18 percent (18 and 19 years) and then starts to decline to its lowest level of 8 percent at 25 years. Table 5.7 presents the average price per ounce of marijuana in the US over the period 1981-1997. As can be seen, the price of marijuana in the US increased sharply in the 1980s, was stable during the 1990s and then started to fall in 1997.

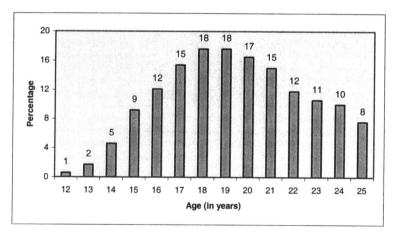

Figure 5.27 Percentage of persons aged 12-25 reporting past month marijuana use, by age, US, 2000

Table 5.7 Price of Marijuana in the US

Year	Price per ounce (US$)
1981	2.56
1988	7.58
1995	7.69
1996	8.39
1997	5.24

Source: *Fact Sheet: Drug Data Summary*, White House Office of National Drug Policy, February 1998.

5.5   Marijuana Consumption in New Zealand

As in many countries, marijuana is an illegal drug in New Zealand. Marijuana is the third most popular drug in New Zealand followed by alcohol and tobacco (see Figure 5.28). According to the *New Zealand Ministry of Health Survey* of 1998, 43 percent of males and 27 percent of females in the 18-24 years age group had used marijuana in the past 12 months. Most people started using marijuana when they were between 14 and 18 years old.

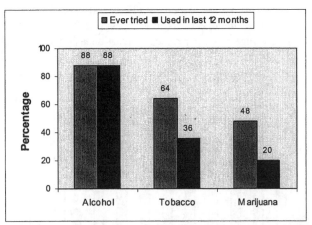

Figure 5.28   Proportion of drug use by frequency, New Zealand, 1998

Figure 5.29 presents the proportion of marijuana users in 1990 and 1998 by age group and by gender. As can be seen, at all age levels, a higher proportion of New Zealand males consume marijuana than females. The proportion of users in 1998 is higher than that in 1990 regardless of their gender and age group, with the difference being significant for the 18-24 age groups. The proportion of marijuana users among New Zealanders decreases with increasing age from 19 years onwards.

In Figure 5.30 we present the source of obtaining marijuana by New Zealand marijuana users. As can be seen, 42 percent of the people obtained marijuana from

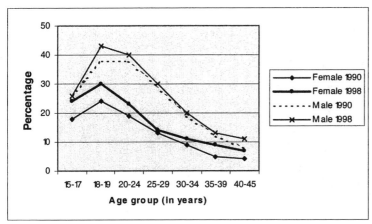

Figure 5.29   Proportion of marijuana users by age group and gender, NZ, 1990 and 1998

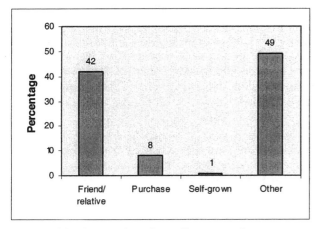

Figure 5.30   Proportion of marijuana use by access type, NZ, 1998

friends and relatives, another 8 percent of New Zealanders purchased marijuana directly in the black market and one percent grew marijuana themselves.

According to the NZHIS (2001) report, an average New Zealand marijuana user smoked about 80 percent of a joint on a typical occasion. Figure 5.31 presents the average consumption of marijuana by age in 1998. Generally, the average amount smoked is less among the 25+ age groups compared to the other younger groups. Among the older groups, the 35-39 age group smoked more than the other 25-29, 30-34 and 40-45 age groups. At age 15-17 years, average consumption was 97 percent of a joint.

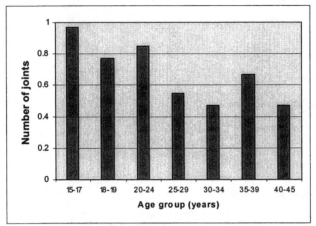

Figure 5.31   Average number of joints smoked on a typical occasion, by age group, NZ, 1998

Table 5.8 presents the proportion of the location of marijuana use by New Zealanders in the past 12 months of 1998 obtained from NZHIS (2001). As can be seen, marijuana is most commonly smoked at home, about two thirds (=32+30) of those who had used marijuana in the past 12 months smoked 'all' or 'most' of their marijuana at home. About 24 percent had smoked 'some' of their marijuana in a public place and 11 percent reported to have used 'some' of their marijuana while driving. About 3 (=1+2) percent had smoked 'all' or 'most' of their marijuana while driving. In other words, a significant proportion of New Zealanders are driving under the influence of marijuana on New Zealand roads.

Table 5.8 Distribution of individuals by level of marijuana use at four locations in previous 12 months, NZ, 1998

	Amount smoked	Homes	Public places	Driving	Work
1.	All	32	6	1	0
2.	Most	30	12	2	0
3.	Some	13	24	11	2
4.	Hardly any	11	16	19	2
5.	None	14	42	67	95

Figure 5.32 presents the proportion of persons reporting marijuana use in 10 or more occasions in the last 30 days of the survey by gender and age groups. As can be seen, the proportion of males who have used marijuana in 10 or more occasions in the last 30 days is higher than that for the females. Among the male population, the proportion is higher (11 percent) for the 18-19 age group than any other age group, while among the female population, the proportion is higher (8 percent) for the 20-24 age group than any other age group.

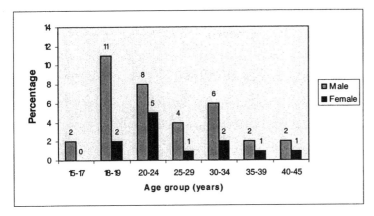

Figure 5.32 Proportion of people reporting marijuana use on 10 or more occasions in the last 30 days by gender and age group, NZ, 1998

5.6 Concluding Comments

In this chapter, we looked at marijuana consumption at a cross-country level as well as in a selected number of individual countries. The cross-country comparison of marijuana consumption among school students reveals that, in most countries, the proportion of children who have used marijuana is higher among boys than girls. The proportions of both boys and girls who have used marijuana are highest in the US, followed by the Czech Republic, the UK and France in that order. About one in every two boys and one in every three girls in the US reported to have consumed marijuana.

Among Australians, Canadians, New Zealanders, the British and the Americans, the proportion of adults who have reported to have used marijuana in the last thirty days is highest in New Zealand (one in every five adult) followed by Australia, the UK, the US and Canada, in that order.

The data used in this chapter also reveals that marijuana use is correlated with consumer characteristics such as level of education, employment status, socio-economic status, cultural background and marital status. In terms of marital status, the proportion of marijuana users is high among the 'never married' category. Most of the regular adult user have used marijuana at home and private parties and is mostly supplied by friends. It is also evident that marijuana goes hand in hand with alcohol in most situations than marijuana with any other drug. Among all drugs, marijuana has the lowest mean age of initiation of drug use. The mean age of initiation of marijuana use has been fallen in many countries, from 20 years to 17 years, in the last four decades.

In Chapter 10, Clements and Daryal explore the economic aspects of marijuana consumption by estimating the demand elasticities for marijuana in a system-wide framework with beer, wine and spirits.

Chapter 6

A Differential Approach to Demand Analysis

The consumer demand function for a single good explains how changes in consumers' income and prices of all goods affect the quantity purchased of that good. Two of the main objectives of consumer demand theory are to (1) derive testable hypotheses about the demand functions, and (2) obtain income and price elasticities to measure consumer response to income and price changes. These hypotheses take the form of theoretical restrictions on the demand functions, for example, demand homogeneity, Slutsky symmetry, etc. These restrictions come from the utility-maximizing theory of consumer behaviour. Consequently, the objective of this chapter is to set out the theory of the utility-maximizing consumer and the derivation of the demand equations. There are a number of ways one could derive demand equations. This chapter focusses on the application of the differential approach to derive demand equation.

Major book-length works on the theory and measurement of consumer demand include Barnett (1979, 1981), Bewley (1986), Chen (2001), Deaton (1974, 1975), Deaton and Muellbauer (1980a, 1980b), Goldberger (1987), Lluch, Powell and Williams (1977), Phlips (1974), Pollak and Wales (1992), Powell (1974), Selvanathan, S. (1993), Selvanathan, E.A., and Clements (1995), Selvanathan and Selvanathan (1994, 2003), Theil (1975/76), Theil, Chung and Seale (1989), Theil and Clements (1987) and Theil and Suhm (1981). Survey articles in this area are provided by Barten (1977), Blundell (1988), Brown and Deaton (1972), Clements and S. Selvanathan (1994), Clements, Selvanathan and Selvanathan (1996), Deaton (1986) and Thomas (1987).

This chapter is structured as follows. Section 6.1 introduces the well-known Divisia (1925) moments to be used to measure the movements of prices and consumption. Section 6.2 presents a popular example of directly specified demand equations, the *double-log demand system*. In Sections 6.3 and 6.4, we consider the utility approach to derive the general form of demand equations and Barten's fundamental matrix equation. Section 6.5 deals with the derivation of the demand equation in relative prices using the differential approach. This approach requires no initial algebraic specification of any function. As a result, the demand equations of this approach are completely general, having coefficients which are not necessarily constant. Of course, the estimation of these equations requires some parameterization, but this only comes as the last step. In Section 6.6, we derive the demand equation in absolute prices. Section 6.7 considers one of the most restrictive forms of the utility structure, additive consumer preferences, and derives the demand equations. We then consider a relaxed form of the utility function known as block independence and present the applications of the differential approach to the demand for groups of goods and to goods within a group in Sections 6.8 and 6.9. The flexibility of the differential approach is illustrated in Chapter 7, where we consider the parameterization of the differential demand equations.

This chapter draws mainly on Clements (1987a, 1987b) and Selvanathan (1987).

6.1   Divisia Indexes

In this section, we introduce the Divisia (1925) indexes which will be later used in deriving demand equations in the remaining sections of this chapter and other parts of this book.

Let q_i be the quantity consumed of good i (i=1,..., n) and p_i be the price of good i. Then the total consumption expenditure on the n goods, M, which we shall refer to as *income* for short, will be given by

$$M = \sum_{i=1}^{n} p_i q_i . \tag{1.1}$$

Therefore, the proportion of income devoted to good i, to be referred to as the *budget share* of i, is given by

$$w_i = \frac{p_i q_i}{M} . \tag{1.2}$$

The budget shares are positive and, in view of (1.1), have a unit sum.

The Divisia price and Divisia volume index are defined, respectively,

$$d(\log P) = \sum_{i=1}^{n} w_i d(\log p_i) \tag{1.3}$$

and

$$d(\log Q) = \sum_{i=1}^{n} w_i d(\log q_i) . \tag{1.4}$$

The price index defined in (1.3) is a weighted average of the n logarithmic price changes $d(\log p_1)$, ..., $d(\log p_n)$, the weights being the budget shares. We have also used the identity $dx/x = d(\log x)$ to denote the logarithmic change in a variable X. Similarly, the volume index (1.4) is a weighted average of the quantity log-changes.

To see the link between the Divisia volume and price index, we consider the differential of (1.1)

$$\sum_{i=1}^{n} p_i dq_i + \sum_{i=1}^{n} q_i dp_i = dM.$$

Dividing both sides of this by M, using the identity $dx/x = d(\log x)$ and using (1.2), we obtain

$$d(\log Q) + d(\log P) = d(\log M). \tag{1.5}$$

Equation (1.5) decomposes the change in income into a volume and price index.

The Divisia price index $d(\log P)$ is defined in (1.3) as a budget-share-weighted-average of the n logarithmic price changes $d(\log p_1)$, ..., $d(\log p_n)$. This can be viewed as a weighted first-order moment of the price changes. The corresponding second-order moment is the Divisia price variance

$$\Pi = \sum_{i=1}^{n} w_i [d(\log p_i) - d(\log P)]^2. \tag{1.6}$$

This Π vanishes when all prices change proportionately and it increases when the prices change more disproportionately. In other words, Π is a measure of the changes in relative prices. Similarly, the Divisia volume index $d(\log Q)$, defined in (1.4), is the Divisia (i.e. budget-share-weighted) mean of the quantity changes. There is also the Divisia quantity variance

$$K = \sum_{i=1}^{n} w_i [d(\log q_i) - d(\log Q)]^2. \tag{1.7}$$

To measure the co-movement of quantities and prices, we define the Divisia price-quantity covariance

$$\Gamma = \sum_{i=1}^{n} w_i [d(\log p_i) - d(\log P)][d(\log q_i) - d(\log Q)] \tag{1.8}$$

and the corresponding price-quantity correlation is

$$\rho = \frac{\Gamma}{\sqrt{K \Pi}}. \tag{1.9}$$

This correlation measures the co-movement of prices and quantities. As those commodities having above-average price increases would tend to experience below-average increases in consumption and vice versa, ρ will usually be negative. However, as ρ includes a real-income component, in certain cases it may be positive. See Theil (1975/76, Chapter 11).

6.2   Demand Systems without Utility Reference

As we mentioned earlier, this book focuses its analysis on the basis of a utility function. Under the utility based demand analysis we derive demand equations by postulating that the consumer behaves as if he chooses the consumption basket to maximize a utility function subject to a budget constraint. This approach gives rise to elegant and intuitive interpretations of the coefficients of the demand equations in terms of the utility function.

On the other hand, there is an older tradition, which goes back to Cassel (1932) and Workings (1943), which specifies the demand equations directly, without any reference to the utility function. Under this pragmatic approach, the demand for a good is specified as a simple function of income and prices. In this section we consider two such well-known demand specifications, namely, *double-log demand system* and the *Working's Model*.

Double-Log Demand System

The double-log demand system takes the form

$$\log q_i = \alpha_i + \eta_i \log M + \sum_{j=1}^{n} \eta_{ij} \log p_j, \qquad i=1,\ldots,n, \qquad (2.1)$$

where q_i is the quantity consumed of good i (i=1,...,n): p_j is the price of good j; and M is income; and α_i, η_i and η_{ij} are constant coefficients. In (2.1), the coefficient of income is

$$\eta_i = \frac{\partial(\log q_i)}{\partial(\log M)} = \frac{\partial q_i / q_i}{\partial M / M}, \qquad i=1,\ldots,n. \qquad (2.2)$$

This is known as the *income elasticity* of demand for good i and answers the question: If income rises by 1 percent with prices constant, what is the percentage change in consumption of i?

We classify the commodities as necessities, luxuries or inferior goods according to the value of the income elasticity. When $\eta_i < 1$, from (2.2), we have

$$p_i \frac{\partial q_i}{\partial M} < \frac{p_i q_i}{M},$$

which means that the marginal propensity to spend on good i is less than the corresponding average propensity (or w_i). Therefore, commodities with income elasticity less than unity are called *necessities*, while those with income elasticity greater than unity are known as *luxuries*. If the income elasticity is negative, then the good is said to be *inferior* as its consumption falls with increasing income.

Similarly, the coefficient η_{ij} measures the percentage change in q_i resulting from a 1 percent change in p_j while income and the other prices remain constant;

$$\eta_{ij} = \frac{\partial(\log q_i)}{\partial(\log p_j)} = \frac{\partial q_i / q_i}{\partial p_j / p_j}, \qquad i,j = 1,\ldots,n.$$

The coefficient η_{ij} is known as the *cross-price elasticity* - the elasticity of demand for i with respect to the price of j. As (2.1) holds constant money income M, the η_{ij}'s include both the income and substitution effects of the price changes. This is expressed by saying that the η_{ij}'s are the *uncompensated price elasticities*. If $i = j$, according to the law of demand, we would expect η_{ii} to be negative (ruling out Giffin goods). If an increase in the price of commodity j increases (decreases) the demand for i, that is $\eta_{ij} > 0$ (<0), then i and j are called *gross substitutes* (*gross complements*).

Several kinds of price elasticities will be encountered in this book and η_{ij} in (2.1) is one such elasticity. As this equation has money income M on the right-hand side, the income effect of the change in the jth price is included in η_{ij}. This η_{ij} is called the *Cournot price elasticity*.

Multiplication of the budget share by the corresponding income elasticity yields

$$w_i\eta_i = \frac{p_iq_i}{M} \frac{\partial q_i / q_i}{\partial M / M} = p_i\frac{\partial q_i}{\partial M} = \frac{\partial(p_iq_i)}{\partial M}, \qquad (2.3)$$

where we have used (1.2) and (2.2) in the second step and the last step follows from the fact the p_i is held constant. The term on the far right of (2.3) answers the question: If income rises by one dollar how much of this is spent on commodity i? We write this as

$$\theta_i = \frac{\partial(p_iq_i)}{\partial M}, \qquad i=1,\ldots,n, \qquad (2.4)$$

which shall be referred to as the ith *marginal share*. Similar to the budget shares, the marginal shares also have a unit sum; this can be verified by differentiating both sides of (1.1) with respect to income. In contrast to the budget shares, the marginal shares are not always positive; θ_i is negative if i is an inferior good.

Combining (2.3) and (2.4) shows that the income elasticity can also be expressed as the ratio of the marginal share to the corresponding budget share,

$$\frac{\theta_i}{w_i} = \eta_i. \tag{2.5}$$

As the marginal shares have a unit sum, it follows from (2.3) that a budget-share-weighted average of the income elasticities is equal to unity:

$$\sum_{i=1}^{n} w_i \eta_i = 1. \tag{2.6}$$

Equation (2.6) is called the *Engle aggregation.*
   The differential of equation (1.2) gives

$$d(\log w_i) = d(\log q_i) + d(\log p_i) - d(\log M).$$

With constant prices, using (2.2), the above equation can be simplified to

$$d(\log w_i) = (\eta_i - 1)d(\log M). \tag{2.7}$$

Equation (2.7) states that the income elasticity of the budget share of commodity i is $(\eta_i - 1)$. For necessities $(\eta_i < 1)$, this means that an increase in income will reduce the budget share of i; and conversely for luxuries $(\eta_i > 1)$, an increase in income will increase the budget share of i. For example, when the consumer becomes more affluent, then the amount he spends on food, a necessity, will rise less rapidly than income, causing the food budget share to fall. This inverse relationship between the food budget share and income is known as the *Engel's Law*, after Engel (1857).

Working's Model

Above we considered the double-log demand system, an example of a system of directly specified demand equations. Another example of directly specified demand equations is the Working's (1943) model, which expresses the budget shares as linear functions of the logarithm of income:

$$w_i = \alpha_i + \beta_i \log M, \qquad\qquad i=1,...,n. \tag{2.8}$$

As the budget shares sum to unity, it follows from (2.8) that the constant coefficients α_i and β_i satisfy $\sum_{i=1}^{n} \alpha_i = 1$ and $\sum_{i=1}^{n} \beta_i = 0$. When $M = 1$, the above equation reduces to $w_i = \alpha_i$. Therefore, α_i can be interpreted as the budget share of the ith household whose income equals 1. Taking the differentials of both sides of equation (2.8), we can write $dw_i = \beta_i d(\log M)$; thus we can interpret β_i as 100 times the change in w_i resulting from a 1 percent increase in income M. It is to be noted that (2.8) does not contain prices. Consequently, it can be applied to household surveys, where prices are approximately constant. However, the model needs to be extended by adding a substitution term in situations where prices are not constant, as in a time-series application. We shall come back to this issue in Chapter 7.

We multiply both sides of (2.8) by M to give

$$p_i q_i = \alpha_i M + \beta_i \log M,$$

and then differentiate with respect to M to obtain

$$\theta_i = \frac{\partial (p_i q_i)}{\partial M} = \alpha_i + \beta_i (1 + \log M).$$

Substituting from (2.8) we get

$$\theta_i = w_i + \beta_i. \tag{2.9}$$

Thus under Working's model the marginal share and the budget share for commodity i differ by the constant coefficient β_i. Furthermore, as the budget share w_i is not a constant over time, neither is the marginal share θ_i defined in (2.9). Dividing both sides of (2.9) by w_i, we obtain the income elasticity of commodity i

$$\eta_i = 1 + \frac{\beta_i}{w_i}. \tag{2.10}$$

This shows that a commodity is a necessity (luxury) if β_i is negative (positive).

As the budget share of a luxury increases with income, prices remaining constant, it follows from (2.10) that increasing income causes the income elasticity η_i of such a good to fall towards 1. The income elasticity of a necessity also declines with increasing income under (2.10). Thus as the consumer becomes more affluent, all goods become less luxurious under Working's model, which is plausible.

6.3 Utility Maximization and Demand Constraints

In this section, we first derive demand equations by considering the consumer's utility maximizing problem. The utility function takes the form

$$u = u(q_1, \dots q_n), \tag{3.1}$$

where, as before, q_i is the quantity consumed of good i. We assume that this function is differentiable and that there is nonsatiation, so that each marginal utility is positive,

$$\frac{\partial u}{\partial q_i} > 0, \qquad\qquad\qquad i=1,\ldots,n. \qquad (3.2)$$

We further assume that there is generalized diminishing marginal utility, so that the Hessian matrix of the utility function is negative definite. As Hessians are symmetric, we have

$$U = \left[\frac{\partial^2 u}{\partial q_i \partial q_j}\right] \qquad\qquad (3.3)$$

is a symmetric negative definite $n \times n$ matrix. The total expenditure on the n goods $p_1 q_1 + \ldots + p_n q_n$ must equal a fixed total M:

$$M = \sum_{i=1}^{n} p_i q_i . \qquad\qquad\qquad (3.4)$$

To maximize (3.1) subject to the budget constraint (3.4) we form the Lagrangian expression

$$u^*(q_1, \ldots, q_n, \lambda) = u(q_1, \ldots, q_n) - \lambda\left[\sum_{i=1}^{n} p_i q_i - M\right], \qquad (3.5)$$

where λ is a Lagrangian multiplier. The first-order conditions for a maximum of (3.5) are (3.4) and

$$\frac{\partial u}{\partial q_i} = \lambda p_i, \qquad\qquad\qquad i=1,\ldots,n, \qquad (3.6)$$

which states that each marginal utility is proportional to the corresponding price. As the prices are positive, it follows from (3.2) and (3.6) that $\lambda > 0$. By dividing both sides of (3.6) by p_i, we obtain

$$\lambda = \frac{\partial u}{\partial (p_i q_i)}, \qquad\qquad\qquad i=1,\ldots,n.$$

This shows that a one-dollar increase in income causes utility to rise by λ when this increase is spent on any of the n goods. Accordingly, λ is known as the *marginal utility of income*. The second-order conditions for a maximum are satisfied by (3.3).

The first-order conditions (3.4) and (3.6) constitute $(n + 1)$ equations which can in principle be solved for the $(n + 1)$ unknowns $q_1,\ldots, q_n$ and λ; we assume that the resulting quantities are unique and positive for relevant values of prices and income. The optimal quantities depend on income and the prices, so that we can write

$$q_i = q_i (M, p_1, \dots p_n), \qquad\qquad i=1,\dots,n. \qquad (3.7)$$

This is a system of n demand equations.

There are a number of constraints that demand equations (3.7) must satisfy. These constraints come directly from the above utility maximization problem. They are formulated in terms of the income and price derivatives of (3.7).

The first constraint is that the demand equations must satisfy the budget constraint for all values of income and prices. Thus, differentiating (3.4) with respect to M and $p_1, \dots, p_n$, we obtain

$$\sum_{i=1}^{n} p_i \frac{\partial q_i}{\partial M} = 1 \qquad\qquad (3.8)$$

and

$$\sum_{i=1}^{n} p_i \frac{\partial q_i}{\partial p_j} = - q_j, \qquad\qquad j=1,\dots,n. \qquad (3.9)$$

The second constraint is known as *demand homogeneity* which comes from the fact that demand functions are homogeneous of degree zero. The economic interpretation of this is that an equiproportionate change in income and prices leaves consumption of each good unchanged; in other words, the consumer does not suffer from money illusion. Thus, if we apply Euler's theorem to (3.7), we obtain

$$M \frac{\partial q_i}{\partial M} + \sum_{j=1}^{n} p_j \frac{\partial q_i}{\partial p_j} = 0, \qquad\qquad i=1,\dots,n. \qquad (3.10)$$

Dividing both sides of (3.10) by q_i yields

$$\frac{\partial q_i / q_i}{\partial M / M} + \sum_{j=1}^{n} \frac{\partial q_i / q_i}{\partial p_j / p_j} = 0, \qquad\qquad i=1,\dots,n.$$

Thus, demand homogeneity can be expressed in elasticity form as

$$\eta_i + \sum_{j=1}^{n} \eta_{ij} = 0, \qquad\qquad i=1,\dots,n. \qquad (3.11)$$

The Slutsky equation decomposes the total substitution effect of a price change in commodity j on the demand for i as

$$\frac{\partial q_i}{\partial p_j} = \frac{\partial q_i^*}{\partial p_j} - q_j \frac{\partial q_i}{\partial M}, \qquad\qquad i,j=1,\ldots,n, \qquad\qquad (3.12)$$

where the superscript * denotes that utility remains constant, that is,

$$\frac{\partial q_i^*}{\partial p_j} = \frac{\partial q_i}{\partial p_j}\bigg|_{du=0}.$$

As holding utility constant is equivalent to keeping real income unchanged, $\partial q_i^*/\partial p_j$ in (3.12) is known as the *substitution effect of a change in the price of commodity j on the demand for i*. The remaining term on the right of (3.12), $-q_j(\partial q_i/\partial M)$, is the effect on the demand for i on account of the fall in real income; real income falls as a result of the increase in price of j as nominal income M is held constant. This term is known as the *income effect of a change in the price of j on the demand for i*.

Equation (3.12) can be expressed in elasticity form as

$$\eta_{ij} = \eta_{ij}^* - w_j \eta_i, \qquad\qquad i,j=1,\ldots,n, \qquad\qquad (3.13)$$

where

$$\eta_{ij}^* = \frac{\partial(\log q_i^*)}{\partial(\log p_j)}$$

is called the *compensated price elasticity of i with respect to the price of j*. If $\eta_{ij}^* > 0$ (< 0), then the pair of goods i and j are called *net substitutes (net complements)*. If we sum both sides of (3.13) over j=1,...,n, and then use (3.11) and the sum of budget shares is equal to 1, we obtain

$$\sum_{j=1}^{n} \eta_{ij}^* = 0, \qquad\qquad i=1,\ldots,n. \qquad\qquad (3.14)$$

The third constraint is the *Slutsky symmetry*. This states that, when real income is held constant, the effect of an increase in the price of commodity j on the demand for i is equal to the effect of a price increase of i on the demand for j. In other words, as the commodity subscripts can be interchanged, the substitution effects are symmetric in i and j:

$$\frac{\partial q_i^*}{\partial p_j} = \frac{\partial q_j^*}{\partial p_i}, \qquad\qquad i,j=1,\dots,n. \qquad (3.15)$$

In elasticity form, this constraint becomes

$$w_i \eta_{ij}^* = w_j \eta_{ji}^*, \qquad\qquad i,j=1,\dots,n. \qquad (3.16)$$

The last constraint is that the $n \times n$ matrix of compensated price derivatives is negative semidefinite.

Combining (3.14) and (3.16) yields

$$(1/w_i) \sum_{j=1}^{n} w_j \eta_{ji}^* = 0.$$

Multiplying through by w_i and switching subscripts, this becomes

$$\sum_{i=1}^{n} w_i \eta_{ij}^* = 0, \qquad\qquad j=1,\dots,n. \qquad (3.17)$$

From (3.13) we have, $\eta_{ij}^* = \eta_{ij} + w_j \eta_i$, which we substitute in (3.17) to give

$$\sum_{i=1}^{n} w_i \eta_{ij} + w_j = 0, \qquad\qquad j=1,\dots,n, \qquad (3.18)$$

where we have also used (2.6). Equations (3.17) and (3.18) are known as *Cournot aggregation.*

6.4   Barten's Fundamental Matrix Equation

Now, we apply the method of comparative static to obtain information about the demand equations (3.7) in the form of partial derivatives. This involves the use of the first-order conditions (3.4) and (3.6) to ask, how do the values of the endogenous variables $q_1,\dots, q_n$ and λ, respond to changes in the exogenous variables $M, p_1, \dots, p_n$? We proceed in three steps.

We first differentiate the budget constraint (3.4) with respect to p_j and M to yield

$$\sum_{i=1}^{n} p_i \frac{\partial q_i}{\partial p_j} = -q_j, \quad j=1,\dots,n, \quad \text{and} \quad \sum_{i=1}^{n} p_i \frac{\partial q_i}{\partial M} = 1.$$

These can be expressed in matrix form as

$$p' \frac{\partial q}{\partial p'} = -q' \quad \text{and} \quad p' \frac{\partial q}{\partial M} = 1, \tag{4.1}$$

where $\partial q/\partial p' = [\partial q_j/\partial p_i]$ is the $n \times n$ matrix of price derivatives of the demand functions; and $\partial q/\partial M = [\partial q_j/\partial M]$ is the vector of n income slopes of the demand functions.

Second, we differentiate the proportionality conditions (3.6) with respect to p_j and M to give

$$\sum_{k=1}^{n} \frac{\partial^2 u}{\partial q_i \partial q_k} \frac{\partial q_k}{\partial p_j} = \lambda \delta_{ij} + p_i \frac{\partial \lambda}{\partial p_j}, \qquad i,j=1,\dots,n,$$

and

$$\sum_{k=1}^{n} \frac{\partial^2 u}{\partial q_i \partial q_k} \frac{\partial q_k}{\partial M} = p_i \frac{\partial \lambda}{\partial M}, \qquad i=1,\dots,n,$$

where δ_{ij} is the Kronecker delta (= 1 if i=j, 0 otherwise). We write these in matrix form as

$$U \frac{\partial q}{\partial p'} = \lambda I + p \frac{\partial \lambda}{\partial p'} \qquad \text{and} \qquad U \frac{\partial q}{\partial M} = \frac{\partial \lambda}{\partial M} p, \tag{4.2}$$

where U is the Hessian matrix (3.3); I is the $n \times n$ identity matrix; and $\partial \lambda/\partial p' = [\partial \lambda/\partial p_j]$.

Third, we combine (4.1) and (4.2) to give

$$\begin{bmatrix} U & p \\ p' & 0 \end{bmatrix} \begin{bmatrix} \dfrac{\partial q}{\partial M} & \dfrac{\partial q}{\partial p'} \\ -\dfrac{\partial \lambda}{\partial M} & -\dfrac{\partial \lambda}{\partial p'} \end{bmatrix} = \begin{bmatrix} 0 & \lambda I \\ 1 & -q' \end{bmatrix} \tag{4.3}$$

Equation (4.3) is known as *Barten's fundamental matrix equation* in consumption theory, after Barten (1964). The matrix immediately to the left of the equal sign contains the derivatives of all the endogenous variables with respect to all exogenous variables. Our next objective is to solve (4.3) for this matrix.

The inverse of the matrix on the far left of (4.3) is

$$\begin{bmatrix} U & p \\ p' & 0 \end{bmatrix}^{-1} = \frac{1}{p'U^{-1}p}\begin{bmatrix} (p'U^{-1}p)U^{-1} - U^{-1}p(U^{-1}p)' & U^{-1}p \\ (U^{-1}p)' & -1 \end{bmatrix}.$$

Using this inverse the solution of (4.3) is

$$\begin{bmatrix} \dfrac{\partial q}{\partial M} & \dfrac{\partial q}{\partial p'} \\ -\dfrac{\partial \lambda}{\partial M} & -\dfrac{\partial \lambda}{\partial p'} \end{bmatrix} = \frac{1}{p'U^{-1}p}\begin{bmatrix} (p'U^{-1}p)U^{-1} - U^{-1}p(U^{-1}p)' & U^{-1}p \\ (U^{-1}p)' & -1 \end{bmatrix}\begin{bmatrix} 0 & \lambda I \\ 1 & -q' \end{bmatrix}.$$

Carrying out the matrix multiplication block by block, we obtain

$$\frac{\partial q}{\partial M} = \frac{1}{p'U^{-1}p}U^{-1}p, \tag{4.4}$$

$$\frac{\partial q}{\partial p'} = \lambda U^{-1} - \frac{\lambda}{p'U^{-1}p}U^{-1}p(U^{-1}p)' - \frac{1}{p'U^{-1}p}U^{-1}pq', \tag{4.5}$$

$$\frac{\partial \lambda}{\partial M} = \frac{1}{p'U^{-1}p}, \tag{4.6}$$

and

$$\frac{\partial \lambda}{\partial p} = -\frac{\lambda}{p'U^{-1}p}U^{-1}p - \frac{1}{p'U^{-1}p}q. \tag{4.7}$$

To simplify these expressions, we use (4.6) to substitute $\partial\lambda/\partial M$ for the reciprocal of $p'U^{-1}p$ in (4.4), (4.5) and (4.7). Equation (4.4) then becomes

$$\frac{\partial q}{\partial M} = \frac{\partial \lambda}{\partial M}U^{-1}p. \tag{4.8}$$

Next, we replace $U^{-1}p$ in (4.5) and (4.7) with $\partial q/\partial M$ divided by $\partial\lambda/\partial M$, which follows from (4.8). This yields

$$\frac{\partial q}{\partial p'} = \lambda U^{-1} - \frac{\lambda}{\partial \lambda / \partial M} \frac{\partial q}{\partial M} \frac{\partial q'}{\partial M} - \frac{\partial q}{\partial M} q' \tag{4.9}$$

and

$$\frac{\partial \lambda}{\partial p} = -\lambda \frac{\partial q}{\partial M} - \frac{\partial \lambda}{\partial M} q . \tag{4.10}$$

Equations (4.8) and (4.9) give the income and price derivatives of the demand functions. We write equation (4.9) in scalar form as

$$\frac{\partial q_i}{\partial p_j} = \lambda u^{ij} - \frac{\lambda}{\partial \lambda / \partial M} \frac{\partial q_i}{\partial M} \frac{\partial q_j}{\partial M} - \frac{\partial q_i}{\partial M} q_j, \quad i,j=1,\dots,n, \tag{4.11}$$

where u^{ij} is the $(i,j)^{th}$ element of U^{-1}. This shows that the effect of a change in p_j on q_i, with income and the other prices constant, is made up of three terms. The third term on the right of (4.11), $-q_j(\partial q_i/\partial M)$, is the *income effect* of the price change. The remaining two terms thus represent the *total substitution effect*, the response of q_i to a change in p_j with real income (and the other prices) held constant. This total substitution effect comprises the *specific substitution effect*, λu^{ij}, and the general substitution effect,

$$-\frac{\lambda}{\partial \lambda / \partial M} \frac{\partial q_i}{\partial M} \frac{\partial q_j}{\partial M},$$

with the terminology from Houthakker (1960). The latter effect is concerned with the competition of all goods for an extra dollar of the consumer's income, while the former deals with the interaction of goods i and j in the utility function.

For future reference, we write (4.8) in scalar terms as

$$\frac{\partial q_i}{\partial M} = \frac{\partial \lambda}{\partial M} \sum_{j=1}^{n} u^{ij} p_j, \qquad i=1,\dots,n. \tag{4.12}$$

6.5   A Differential Demand System

In this section we use the solution to the fundamental matrix equation presented in the previous section to derive a general system of differential demand equations.

The total differential of (3.7) is

$$dq_i = \frac{\partial q_i}{\partial M} dM + \sum_{j=1}^{n} \frac{\partial q_i}{\partial p_j} dp_j, \qquad i=1,\dots,n.$$

We transform this to logarithmic-differential form by multiplying both sides by p_i/M and using $w_i = p_i q_i/M$,

$$w_i \, d(\log q_i) = \theta_i \, d(\log M) + \sum_{j=1}^{n} \frac{p_i p_j}{M} \frac{\partial q_i}{\partial p_j} d(\log p_j), \quad i=1,\dots,n. \tag{5.1}$$

We use (1.2), (2.4) and (3.18) to express the second term on the right of (5.1) as

$$\sum_{j=1}^{n} \frac{p_i p_j}{M} \frac{\partial q_i}{\partial p_j} d(\log p_j) = \sum_{j=1}^{n} \frac{p_i p_j}{M} \left[\lambda u^{ij} - \frac{\lambda}{\partial \lambda/\partial M} \frac{\partial q_i}{\partial M} \frac{\partial q_j}{\partial M} \frac{\partial q_i}{\partial M} q_j \right] d(\log p_j)$$

$$= \sum_{j=1}^{n} \left[\frac{\lambda p_i p_j u^{ij}}{M} - \frac{\lambda/M}{\partial \lambda/\partial M} \theta_i \theta_j - w_j \theta_i \right] d(\log p_j).$$

Substituting this in (5.1) and rearranging gives

$$w_i \, d(\log q_i) = \theta_i \left[d(\log M) - \sum_{j=1}^{n} w_j d(\log p_j) \right]$$

$$+ \sum_{j=1}^{n} \left[\frac{\lambda p_i p_j u^{ij}}{M} - \frac{\lambda/M}{\partial \lambda/\partial M} \theta_i \theta_j \right] d(\log p_j). \tag{5.2}$$

In view of (1.3) and (1.5) the term in the first square brackets on the right hand side of equation (5.2) is the Divisia volume index $d(\log Q)$, which enables us to write

$$\theta_i \left[d(\log M) - \sum_{j=1}^{n} w_j d(\log p_j) \right] = \theta_i d(\log Q). \tag{5.3}$$

To simplify the price substitution term of (5.2), we define

$$\phi = \frac{\lambda/M}{\partial \lambda/\partial M} = \left[\frac{\partial(\log \lambda)}{\partial(\log M)} \right]^{-1} < 0 \tag{5.4}$$

as the reciprocal of the *income elasticity of the marginal utility of income*. For brevity, we shall refer to ϕ as the income flexibility. We also define

$$v_{ij} = \frac{\lambda}{M} p_i p_j u^{ij}, \quad i,j=1,\dots,n. \tag{5.5}$$

We will show below that these coefficients satisfy

$$\sum_{j=1}^{n} v_{ij} = \phi\theta_i, \qquad\qquad i=1,\ldots,n. \qquad\qquad (5.6)$$

To show that ϕ is negative, as stated in equation (5.4), we use (5.5) and (5.6) to write

$$\sum_{j=1}^{n} \frac{\lambda}{M} p_i p_j u^{ij} = \phi\theta_i, \qquad i=1,\ldots,n.$$

In view of $\sum_{i=1}^{n} \theta_i = 1$, summing both sides of the above over $i=1,\ldots,n$ yields

$$\phi = \frac{\lambda}{M} \sum_{i=1}^{n}\sum_{j=1}^{n} p_i p_j u^{ij}. \qquad\qquad (5.7)$$

The right-hand side is proportional to a quadratic form with matrix U^{-1} and vector p. In view of (3.3), this matrix is negative definite, so that the quadratic form is negative. As the factor of proportionality λ/M on the right of (5.7) is positive, we conclude that $\phi < 0$.

To verify constraint (5.6), we multiply both sides of (4.12) by p_i, which yields

$$\theta_i = \frac{\partial\lambda}{\partial M} \sum_{j=1}^{n} p_i p_j u^{ij}, \qquad i=1,\ldots,n.$$

We then use (5.5) and re-arrange the equation to obtain (5.6).

Using (5.5) and (5.6), the substitution term of (5.2) can then be expressed as

$$\sum_{j=1}^{n}\left[\frac{\lambda p_i p_j u^{ij}}{M} - \frac{\lambda/M}{\partial\lambda/\partial M}\theta_i\theta_j\right]d(\log p_j) = \sum_{j=1}^{n} v_{ij}d(\log p_j) - \phi\theta_i d(\log P')$$

$$= \sum_{j=1}^{n} v_{ij}[d(\log p_j) - d(\log P')], \qquad (5.8)$$

where

$$d(\log P') = \sum_{i=1}^{n} \theta_i d(\log p_i) \qquad\qquad (5.9)$$

is the *Frisch (1932) price index*. This index is different from the Divisia price index (1.3), which uses budget shares as weights rather than marginal shares.

Using (5.3) and (5.9) in (5.2) the demand equation for good i becomes

$$w_i \, d(\log q_i) = \theta_i \, d(\log Q) + \sum_{j=1}^{n} v_{ij} d\left[\log \frac{p_j}{P'} \right], \qquad i=1,\ldots,n, \qquad (5.10)$$

where $d[\log(p_j/P')]$ is interpreted as $d(\log p_j) - d(\log P')$.

The first term on the right of (5.10) gives the effect of real income on the demand for good i. This term is a multiple θ_i of the Divisia volume index $d(\log Q)$. As this volume index equals $d(\log M) - d(\log P)$, where $d(\log P)$ is the Divisia price index, it follows that the Divisia price index transforms the change in money income into the change in real income. Furthermore, as the Divisia price index is budget-share-weighted, it follows that this index measures the income effect of the n price changes on the demand for the ith good.

The second term on the right of (5.10), $\sum_{j=1}^{n} v_{ij} \, d[\log(p_j/P')]$, deals with the effects of relative prices. The Frisch price index acts as a deflator of each price change, so that we refer to $d[\log(p_j/P')]$ as the change in the *Frisch-deflated price of j*. From equation (5.8), it can also be seen that the substitution term can be written as the difference between $\sum_{j=1}^{n} v_{ij} \, d(\log p_j)$, which is the specific substitution effect of the n prices on the demand for good i, and $\phi d(\log P')$, which is the general substitution effect. Accordingly, the general substitution effect acts as the deflator of the specific effect by transforming absolute prices into Frisch-deflated prices.

In the substitution term of (5.10), v_{ij} is the coefficient of the jth relative price, which shall be called the $(i,j)^{th}$ price coefficient. These price coefficients satisfy $\sum_{i=1}^{n} \sum_{j=1}^{n} v_{ij} = \phi$, which follows from (5.6) and the fact that $\sum_{i=1}^{n} \theta_i = 1$. If $v_{ij} > 0$, then an increase in the Frisch-deflated price of j causes consumption of i to increase. Consequently, we follow Houthakker (1960) and define goods i and j as specific substitutes (complements) if $v_{ij} > 0 \, (< 0)$.

To further interpret the v_{ij}'s, we use (5.5) to define the $n \times n$ matrix

$$[v_{ij}] = \frac{\lambda}{M} P'U^{-1}P, \qquad (5.11)$$

where P is the diagonal matrix with $p_1,\ldots, p_n$ on the diagonal and U^{-1} is the inverse of the Hessian of the utility function. On the right of (5.11), $\lambda, M > 0$; P is a symmetric positive definite matrix and U^{-1} is symmetric negative definite. Therefore,

$$[v_{ij}] \text{ is a symmetric negative definite } n \times n \text{ matrix.} \qquad (5.12)$$

Inverting both sides of (5.11), we obtain

$$v^{ij} = \frac{M}{\lambda} \frac{\partial^2 u}{\partial(p_i q_i) \partial(p_j q_j)}, \qquad i,j=1,\ldots,n, \qquad (5.13)$$

where v^{ij} is the $(i,j)^{th}$ element of $[v_{ij}]^{-1}$. Since $\partial u/\partial(p_i q_i)$ is the marginal utility of a dollar spent on good i, $\partial^2 u/\partial(p_i q_i)\partial(p_j q_j)$ on the right of (5.13) is interpreted as the change in this marginal utility when spending on good j increases by one dollar. Accordingly, (5.13) shows that $[v_{ij}]$ is inversely proportional to the Hessian matrix of the utility function in expenditure terms.

   In contrast to the other approaches to generating demand equations, the differential approach requires no algebraic specification of the utility function. Consequently, the coefficients of the demand equations (5.10) need not be constant; they may be functions of income and prices. The decision how to parameterize differential demand equations comes as the final step, which will be illustrated in the next chapter.

6.6   Demand Equations in Absolute Prices

The substitution term of equation (5.10) is formulated in terms of deflated prices. We use (5.9) to express the substitution term in absolute (or undeflated) prices as

$$\sum_{j=1}^{n} v_{ij} d\left[\log \frac{p_j}{P'}\right] = \sum_{j=1}^{n} \pi_{ij} d(\log p_j), \tag{6.1}$$

where

$$\pi_{ij} = v_{ij} - \phi \theta_i \theta_j, \qquad\qquad i,j=1,\dots,n, \tag{6.2}$$

is the $(i,j)^{th}$ *Slutsky (1915) coefficient.* This coefficient gives the total substitution effect on the demand for good i of a change in the jth price. It can be easily verified that

$[\pi_{ij}]$ is a symmetric negative semi-definite $n \times n$ matrix with rank n-1.   (6.3)

Using (6.1) in (5.10) yields the demand equation for good i in terms of absolute prices,

$$w_i\, d(\log q_i) = \theta_i\, d(\log Q) + \sum_{j=1}^{n} \pi_{ij} d(\log p_j), \qquad i=1,\dots,n. \tag{6.4}$$

In view of (6.3), the Slutsky coefficients are symmetric in i and j,

$$\pi_{ij} = \pi_{ji}, \qquad\qquad i,j=1,\dots,n, \tag{6.5}$$

which is known as Slutsky symmetry. These coefficients also satisfy

$$\sum_{j=1}^{n} \pi_{ij} = 0, \qquad\qquad i=1,...,n, \qquad\qquad (6.6)$$

which follows from (5.6) and (6.2). Constraint (6.6) reflects the homogeneity property of the demand functions that a proportionate change in all prices has no effect on the demand for any good under the condition that real income is constant. Accordingly, (6.6) is known as *demand homogeneity*. As stated in (6.3), the Slutsky matrix $[\pi_{ij}]$ is *symmetric negative semidefinite with rank n-1*; the cause of the singularity is (6.6).

Dividing both sides of (6.4) by w_i, we find that the income and compensated price elasticities are

$$\eta_i = \frac{\theta_i}{w_i}, \qquad\qquad \eta_{ij} = \frac{\pi_{ij}}{w_i}, \qquad\qquad i,j=1,...,n. \qquad\qquad (6.7)$$

These elasticities satisfy demand homogeneity and Slutsky symmetry.

6.7 Preference Independence

When the consumer's tastes can be described by means of a utility function which is the sum of n sub-utility functions, one for each good, the utility function (3.1) takes the form

$$u(q_1,..., q_n) = \sum_{i=1}^{n} u_i(q_i), \qquad\qquad (7.1)$$

and the marginal utility of good i is independent of the consumption of j, $i \neq j$. Accordingly, (7.1) is known as *preference independence*. If the commodities are fairly broad groups, such as food, housing, clothing and so on, then (7.1) could be a reasonable working hypothesis as it conveys the idea that total utility is obtained from the utility derived from food and utility from housing and utility from clothing and so on. These broad commodity groups can be interpreted as representing the *basic wants* of the consumer, which could be expected to exhibit little interaction in the utility function. The number of unknown coefficients in a general system of demand equations such as (5.10) and (6.4) is of the order of n^2, where n is the number of commodities. This number of coefficients can only be estimated precisely with data when n is very small; even for moderate-sized systems (n in the vicinity of 6), it is impossible to estimate such a large number of coefficients. The hypothesis of preference independence comes to the rescue as it serves to simplify the form of the demand equations by greatly reducing the number of unknown coefficients to be estimated. Accordingly, there are two distinct justifications of preference independence: (i) the economic justification, in terms of preference independence being plausible when applied to broad aggregates; and (ii) the statistical justification when n is not small.

We now analyse the implications of preference independence of the utility function for the demand equation (5.10). Under (7.1) the Hessian matrix U and its inverse are both diagonal. As $u^{ij} = 0$ for $i \neq j$, it follows from (5.5) that $v_{ij} = 0$ for $i \neq j$. Equation (5.6) then implies $v_{ii} = \phi\theta_i$, so that the demand equation (5.10) takes the simpler form

$$w_i \, d(\log q_i) = \theta_i \, d(\log Q) + \phi\theta_i d\left[\log \frac{p_i}{P'} \right], \qquad i=1,\ldots,n. \qquad (7.2)$$

Therefore, preference independence implies that only the own deflated price appears in each demand equation, rather than all n such prices. In other words, preference independence implies that no pair of goods (i,j) can be either a specific substitute or a specific complement. In addition, for $[v_{ij}]$ to be a negative definite matrix with diagonal elements $\phi\theta_1, \ldots, \phi\theta_n$ and off-diagonal elements zero, each marginal share θ_i must be positive. Consequently, the hypothesis of preference independence rules out inferior goods.

6.8   Block Independence and Group Demand Equations

In the previous section, we analysed the case when preferences can be represented by a utility function that is additive in the n goods. This form of the utility function is known as preference independence as the marginal utility of good i is independent of the consumption of good j for $i \neq j$. Under preference independence, the Hessian matrix of the utility function and its inverse are both diagonal and it then follows that $v_{ij} = 0$ for $i \neq j$ and $v_{ii} = \phi\theta_i$. It follows from (7.2) that, under preference independence, only the own Frisch-deflated price appears in each demand equation, so that no pair of goods is either a specific substitute or complement. Furthermore, preference independence implies that each θ_i is positive, which rules out inferior goods. As can be seen, the implications of the preference independence assumption are rather drastic. A weaker version of preference independence is *block independence*, whereby the additive specification (7.1) is applied to groups of goods rather than to individual goods. Let the n goods be divided into $G < n$ groups, written $S_1,\ldots,S_G$ such that each good belongs to only one group. Further, let the consumer's preferences be such that the utility function is the sum of G group utility functions, each involving the quantities of only one group,

$$u(q_1,\ldots, q_n) \;=\; \sum_{g=1}^{G} u_g(q_g), \qquad (8.1)$$

where q_g is the vector of the q_i's that fall under S_g. Under (8.1), the marginal utility of a good depends only on the consumption of goods belonging to the same group. When the goods are numbered appropriately, the Hessian of the utility function and its inverse become block-diagonal. Accordingly, specification (8.1) is known as *block-independent preferences*.

In view of (5.5), block independence implies that $[v_{ij}]$ is block-diagonal. Therefore, if i belongs to S_g, equations (5.10) and (5.6) can now be written as

$$w_i \, d(\log q_i) = \theta_i \, d(\log Q) + \sum_{j \in S_g} v_{ij} d\left[\log \frac{p_j}{P'} \right], \qquad i \in S_g, \qquad (8.2)$$

and

$$\sum_{j \in S_g} v_{ij} = \phi \theta_i, \qquad i \in S_g. \qquad (8.3)$$

Thus block independence implies that the only deflated prices that appear in the ith demand equation are those of goods belonging to the same group as the commodity in question. As $v_{ij} = 0$ for i and j in different groups, under block independence no good is a specific substitute or complement of any good that belongs to a different group.

We write the group budget share and the group marginal share as

$$W_g = \sum_{i \in S_g} w_i \quad \text{and} \quad \Theta_g = \sum_{i \in S_g} \theta_i.$$

Hence, the conditional budget share and conditional marginal share can be written as

$$w_i' = \frac{w_i}{W_g} \quad \text{and} \quad \theta_i' = \frac{\theta_i}{\Theta_g}, \qquad i \in S_g, \qquad (8.4)$$

for the budget and marginal shares of group S_g. The marginal share Θ_g tells us the increase in expenditure on S_g as a result of a one-dollar increase in income. Summing both sides of (8.3) over $i \in S_g$ shows that

$$\sum_{i \in S_g} \sum_{j \in S_g} v_{ij} = \phi \Theta_g < 0, \qquad (8.5)$$

where the inequality sign is based on the negative definiteness of the matrix $[v_{ij}]$. Accordingly, block independence means that no group as a whole can be inferior; members of the group can be inferior, however.

We define the group Divisia volume, Divisia price and Frisch price indexes as

$$d(\log Q_g) = \sum_{i \in S_g} w_i' \, d(\log q_i), \quad d(\log P_g) = \sum_{i \in S_g} w_i' \, d(\log p_i) \qquad (8.6)$$

and

$$d(\log P_g') = \sum_{i \in S_g} \theta_i' \, d(\log p_i). \qquad (8.7)$$

These two indexes aggregate consistently since a budget-share-weighted average of $d(\log Q_1),\ldots,d(\log Q_G)$ equals the Divisia volume index of all the n goods $d(\log Q)$; and a marginal-share-weighted average of $d(\log P_1'),\ldots,d(\log P_G')$ equals the overall Frisch price index $d(\log P')$. That is,

$$d(\log Q) = \sum_{g=1}^{G} W_g \, d(\log Q_g)$$

and

$$d(\log P') = \sum_{g=1}^{G} \Theta_g \, d(\log P_g').$$

We obtain the demand equation for the group S_g as a whole under block independence by simply adding over $i \in S_g$ both sides of the demand equation for good i under block independence, equation (8.2). In view of (8.4) and (8.6) this yields

$$W_g \, d(\log Q_g) = \Theta_g \, d(\log Q) + \sum_{i \in S_g} \sum_{j \in S_g} \nu_{ij} d\left[\log \frac{p_j}{P'}\right], \qquad g=1,\ldots,G. \qquad (8.8)$$

Our objective is to simplify the price substitution term of this equation. As ν_{ij} is symmetric in i and j [see equation (5.12)], (8.3) can be expressed as

$$\sum_{i \in S_g} \nu_{ij} = \phi \theta_j, \qquad\qquad j \in S_g,$$

so that

$$\sum_{i \in S_g} \sum_{j \in S_g} \nu_{ij} d\left[\log \frac{p_j}{P'}\right] = \phi \sum_{j \in S_g} \theta_j d\left[\log \frac{p_j}{P'}\right] = \phi \Theta_g d\left[\log \frac{P_g'}{P'}\right],$$

where the second step is based on (8.4) and (8.7). Accordingly, (8.8) can be expressed as

$$W_g \, d(\log Q_g) = \Theta_g \, d(\log Q) + \phi \Theta_g d\left[\log \frac{P_g'}{P'} \right], \qquad g=1,\dots,G. \qquad (8.9)$$

This is the *composite demand equation* for S_g as a group.

Equation (8.9) shows that under block independence, the demand for a group of goods as a whole depends on real income and the relative price of the group $d[\log(P_g'/P')]$. This relative price is the *Frisch-deflated Frisch price index* of the group. It is to be noted that the relative prices of goods outside the group in question play no role in equation (8.9). By dividing both sides of this equation by W_g, we find that

$$\eta_g = \frac{\Theta_g}{W_g} \quad \text{and} \quad \eta_{gg} = \frac{\phi \Theta_g}{W_g}, \qquad g=1,\dots,G, \qquad (8.10)$$

are the income elasticity of demand and the own-price elasticity, respectively, for the group. This latter elasticity is the elasticity of the Divisia volume index of the group with respect to the Frisch-deflated Frisch price index of the group.

It is instructive to compare equation (8.9) with (7.2), the demand equation for an individual good under preference independence. This comparison reveals that both equations have the same general form: $w_i d(\log q_i)$ on the left side of (7.2) becomes $W_g d(\log Q_g)$ in (8.9), and $\theta_i d(\log Q)$ and $\phi \theta_i d[\log (p_i/P')]$ on the right in (7.2) are replaced with $\Theta_g d(\log Q)$ and $\phi \Theta_g d[\log (P_g'/P')]$ in (8.9). Therefore in going from (7.2) to (8.9), each variable is replaced by the corresponding group concept, making the latter equation an uppercase version of the former. The reason for this is that the demand equation for the group (8.9) is based on block independence, while (7.2) holds under preference independence, and the utility function under block independence (8.1) exhibits preference independence with respect to groups of goods, rather than the individual commodities. Another way of expressing this is to note that if S_g consists of only one good, let it be the ith, then (8.9) for this group coincides with (7.2).

6.9   Conditional Demand Equations

As there are G groups of goods, there are G composite demand equations, each of the form (8.9). These equations give the allocation of income to each of the G groups. This allocation depends only on income and the G relative prices of the groups. Given the demand for a group, the next question is how expenditure on the group is allocated to the commodities within the group. This question is answered by the *conditional demand equations*. In this section we analyse the form of the conditional demand equations under the assumption of block independence. To obtain the conditional demand equations, we first rearrange (8.9):

$$d(\log Q) = \frac{W_g}{\Theta_g} d(\log Q_g) - \phi d\left[\log \frac{P_g'}{P'}\right].$$ (9.1)

It follows from (5.12) that the price coefficients are symmetric in i and j for commodities belonging to the same group.

$$\nu_{ij} = \nu_{ji}, \qquad\qquad i,j \in S_g.$$ (9.2)

The ν_{ij}'s within S_g are also constrained by (8.3) which we repeat here:

$$\sum_{j \in S_g} \nu_{ij} = \phi \theta_i, \qquad\qquad i \in S_g.$$ (9.3)

To derive the conditional demand equation, we first substitute the right side of (9.1) for $d(\log Q)$ in the unconditional equation (8.2). This yields

$$w_i d(\log q_i) = \theta_i\left[\frac{W_g}{\Theta_g} d(\log Q_g) - \phi d\left[\log \frac{P_g'}{P'}\right]\right] + \sum_{j \in S_g} \nu_{ij} d\left[\log \frac{p_j}{P'}\right]$$

$$= \theta_i' W_g \, d(\log Q_g) - \phi\theta_i[d(\log P_g') - d(\log P')]$$
$$+ \sum_{j \in S_g} \nu_{ij}[d(\log p_j) - d(\log P')], \qquad i=1,\dots,n.$$ (9.4)

In view of (9.3), the second term on the right in (9.4) can be expressed as

$$-\phi\theta_i[d(\log P_g') - d(\log P')] = \sum_{j \in S_g} \nu_{ij}[d(\log P_g') - d(\log P')].$$ (9.5)

Therefore, using (9.5), equation (9.4) can be simplified as

$$w_i \, d(\log q_i) = \theta_i' W_g \, d(\log Q_g) + \sum_{j \in S_g} \nu_{ij} d\left[\log \frac{p_j}{P_g'}\right], \qquad i \in S_g,$$ (9.6)

where

$$\theta_i' = \frac{\theta_i}{\Theta_g}, \qquad\qquad i \in S_g,$$ (9.7)

is the *conditional marginal share* of good i within the group S_g, with $\sum_{i \in S_g} \theta_i' = 1$. This conditional share answers the question: If income increases by one dollar, resulting in a certain additional amount spent on the group S_g, what is the proportion of this additional amount that is allocated to commodity i?

Equation (9.6) is the demand equation for $i \in S_g$, given the demand for the group as a whole $W_g d(\log Q_g)$. It is known as the *conditional demand equation* for $i \in S_g$. This equation shows that the allocation of expenditure to goods within the gth group depends on the total consumption of the group, as measured by $W_g d(\log Q_g)$, and the relative prices of goods within the group. The deflator for these relative prices is the Frisch price index of the group $d(\log P_g')$, defined in (8.7). Consumption of other groups and the prices of goods outside S_g do not appear in (9.6). Consequently, the within-group allocation of expenditure depends only on variables pertaining to the group in question.

The conditional demand equation (9.6) is to be contrasted with (8.2) which can be described as the corresponding *unconditional demand equation*. The variables on the left of these two equations are the same, but the real income term in (8.2), $\theta_i d(\log Q)$ is replaced by $\theta_i' W_g d(\log Q_g)$ in (9.6). Also, the price substitution terms are identical, except that the Frisch price index of all goods acts as the deflator in (8.2), while the corresponding group concept $d(\log P_g')$ plays this role in (9.6).

Block-independent preferences imply that the consumer's problem can be solved in two steps. The first decision involves the allocation of income to the G groups, as described by the G group demand equations (8.9). Each of these demand equations contains real income and the relative price of the group in question but not the prices of the individual goods. Then in the second decision, for each of the groups, expenditure is allocated to the goods within the group. The conditional demand equations (9.6) describe this allocation and they contain total consumption of the group, as determined by the previous decision, and relative prices within the group. Accordingly, there is a decision hierarchy under block independence.

The conditional demand equations (9.6) were obtained under block independence. These results also hold, however, under the weaker condition of blockwise dependence; see, e.g., Theil (1975/76).

Equation (9.6) is in relative prices. To obtain the conditional demand equations in absolute prices, we define the (i,j)th *conditional Slutsky coefficients* as

$$\pi_{ij}^g = \nu_{ij} - \phi\Theta_g\, \theta_i'\theta_j', \qquad i,j \in S_g. \qquad (9.8)$$

This coefficient measures the effect of a change in the price of good j on the consumption of i ($i,j \in S_g$) under the condition that other prices and total consumption of the group remain constant. The conditional Slutsky coefficients satisfy demand homogeneity,

$$\sum_{j \in S_g} \pi_{ij}^g = 0, \qquad\qquad i \in S_g, \qquad\qquad (9.9)$$

which follows from (9.3) and (9.8) and Slutsky symmetry,

$$\pi_{ij}^g = \pi_{ji}^g, \qquad\qquad i,j \in S_g, \qquad\qquad (9.10)$$

which follows from (9.2) and (9.8).

The absolute price version of the conditional demand equation can be written as

$$w_i \, d(\log q_i) = \theta_i' W_g \, d(\log Q_g) + \sum_{j \in S_g} \pi_{ij}^g d(\log p_j), \qquad i \in S_g. \qquad (9.11)$$

6.10 Concluding Comments

In this chapter we used the differential approach to derive demand systems starting from the maximization of the consumer's utility function subject to his/her budget constraint. We derived the demand equations in relative prices as well as absolute prices. We also derived demand theory hypotheses, demand homogeneity and Slutsky symmetry.

We also derived the demand equations under most restrictive form of the utility structure, preference independence. We then considered a less restrictive utility structure, block preference independence, and derived the demand equations for a group of goods (called the group demand equation) as well as for a good within the group (called the conditional demand equations).

In Chapter 7, we will discuss the parameterization, estimation and testing of the demand theory hypotheses.

Chapter 7

Parameterization, Estimation and Testing Hypotheses

In Chapter 6, we presented a number of Divisia indexes and several forms of demand equations, which were formulated in infinitesimal changes. However, in practice, data are available only in finite time intervals (monthly, quarterly, yearly etc.). In the first part of this chapter, we discuss various approaches of converting the variables in infinitesimal form to finite-change form and estimating the demand systems. In the second half of the chapter, we consider the testing of the demand theory hypotheses demand homogeneity, Slutsky symmetry and the preference independent utility structure.

7.1   Finite-change Version of the Divisia Indexes

Divisia indexes formulated in Chapter 6 are in terms of infinitesimal changes. To apply these indexes to finite-change data, we write $Dx_t = log\ x_t - log\ x_{t-1}$ for the finite log-change from period t-l to t for any positive variable x. As can be seen from equations (1.3) and (1.4) of Section 6.1, the budget share w_i in these indexes does not involve a change. Therefore, we could use $w_{i,t-l}$, w_{it} or a combination thereof which treats t and t-l symmetrically. The natural choice is to use the arithmetic average of $w_{i,t-l}$ and w_{it}, $\overline{w}_{it} = \frac{1}{2}(w_{i,t} + w_{i,t-1})$, which is mid-way between the two extremities. With these changes, the finite-change versions of the Divisia price and volume indexes defined in (1.3) and (1.4), respectively, of Section 6.1 take the form

$$DP_t = \sum_{i=1}^{n} \overline{w}_{it} Dp_{it} \tag{1.1}$$

and

$$DQ_t = \sum_{i=1}^{n} \overline{w}_{it} Dq_{it}, \tag{1.2}$$

where $Dp_{it} = ln\ p_{it} - ln\ p_{it-1}$ and $Dq_{it} = ln\ q_{it} - ln\ q_{it-1}$ are the price and quantity log-changes and $\overline{w}_{it} = \frac{1}{2}(w_{it} + w_{it-1})$ is the arithmetic average of the budget share during periods t and t-1.

The finite-change version of the Divisia price variance, quantity variance; price-quantity covariance and price-quantity correlation, defined in (1.6), (1.7), (1.8) and (1.9), respectively, of Section 6.1 can be written as

$$\Pi_t = \sum_{i=1}^{n} \overline{w}_{it}[Dp_{it} - DP_t]^2, \qquad (1.3)$$

$$K_t = \sum_{i=1}^{n} \overline{w}_{it}[Dq_{it} - DQ_t]^2, \qquad (1.4)$$

$$\Gamma_t = \sum_{i=1}^{n} \overline{w}_{it}[Dp_{it} - DP_t][Dq_{it} - DQ_t], \qquad (1.5)$$

and

$$\rho_t = \frac{\Gamma_t}{\sqrt{K_t \Pi_t}}, \qquad t=1,\dots,T. \qquad (1.6)$$

The conditional version of the Divisia price and quantity indexes for a group of commodities S_g defined in (8.6) of Section 6.8 in finite-change form are

$$DP_{gt} = \sum_{i \in S_g} \overline{w}'_{it} Dp_{it} \qquad (1.7)$$

and

$$DQ_{gt} = \sum_{i \in S_g} \overline{w}'_{it} Dq_{it}, \qquad (1.8)$$

where $\overline{w}'_{it} = \frac{1}{2}(w'_{it} + w'_{it-1})$ is the arithmetic average of the conditional budget share during periods t and t-1 with $w'_{it} = w_{it}/W_{gt}$ being the conditional budget share of i; and Dp_{it} and Dq_{it} are the price and quantity log-changes, as before. The finite-change version of the conditional Divisia price variance, quantity variance, price-quantity covariance and price-quantity correlation, respectively, are

$$\Pi_{gt} = \sum_{i \in S_g} \overline{w}'_{it}[Dp_{it} - DP_{gt}]^2, \qquad (1.9)$$

$$K_{gt} = \sum_{i \in S_g} \overline{w}'_{it}[Dq_{it} - DQ_{gt}]^2, \qquad (1.10)$$

$$\Gamma_{gt} = \sum_{i \in S_g} \overline{w}'_{it}[Dp_{it} - DP_{gt}][Dq_{it} - DQ_{gt}], \qquad (1.11)$$

and

$$\rho_{gt} \quad = \quad \frac{\Gamma_{gt}}{\sqrt{K_{gt}\Pi_{gt}}}, \qquad t=1,\dots,T. \qquad (1.12)$$

7.2   Rotterdam Parameterization of the Demand Systems

The demand equations derived in Sections 6.5 to 6.9 in Chapter 6 are formulated in terms of infinitesimal changes; the *Rotterdam model*, due to Barten (1964) and Theil (1965), is a finite-change version of these demand equations.

Unconditional Rotterdam Demand Equations

We initially base our discussions on the relative price version of the unconditional demand equation (5.10) of Section 6.5, which we reproduce below.

$$w_i \, d(log \; q_i) = \theta_i \, d(log \; Q) + \sum_{j=1}^{n} v_{ij} d\left[log \; \frac{p_j}{P'} \right], \qquad i=1,\dots,n. \qquad (2.1)$$

To obtain the finite-change version of equation (2.1), we replace the variables w_i and $d(log \; q_i)$ on the left of (2.1) with $\overline{w}_{it}$ and Dq_{it}, respectively; $d(log \; Q)$ is replaced by DQ_t defined in (1.2) and $d[log \; (p_j/P')]$ with $Dp_{jt} - DP'_t$, where $DP'_t = \sum_{i=1}^{n} \theta_i Dp_{it}$ is a finite-change version of the Frisch price index. The finite-change version of (2.1) is then

$$\overline{w}_{it} \, Dq_{it} \quad = \quad \theta_i \, DQ_t + \sum_{j=1}^{n} v_{ij}(Dp_{jt} - DP'_t), \qquad i=1,\dots,n. \qquad (2.2)$$

When the coefficients of (2.2), θ_i and v_{ij}, are treated as constants, it is known as the ith *unconditional demand equation of the relative price version of the Rotterdam model;* see Theil (1975/76).

As stated in Section 6.5, the $n \times n$ matrix of price coefficients $[v_{ij}]$ satisfy

$$[v_{ij}] \text{ is a symmetric negative definite } n \times n \text{ matrix.} \qquad (2.3)$$

These coefficients also satisfy

$$\sum_{j=1}^{n} v_{ij} \quad = \quad \phi\theta_i, \qquad i=1,\dots,n. \qquad (2.4)$$

Constraint (2.4) and the constancy of the coefficients v_{ij} and θ_i imply that ϕ is also a constant in the model.

The absolute price version of the Rotterdam model (2.2) is the finite-change version of the differential demand equation in absolute prices (6.4) of Section 6.6:

$$\overline{w}_{it}\, Dq_{it} \;=\; \theta_i\, DQ_t \;+\; \sum_{j=1}^{n} \pi_{ij} Dp_{jt}, \qquad\qquad i=1,...,n, \qquad (2.5)$$

where π_{ij} is the Slutsky coefficient defined as

$$\pi_{ij} \;=\; v_{ij} \,-\, \phi\theta_i\theta_j, \qquad\qquad i,j=1,...,n. \qquad (2.6)$$

These coefficients also satisfy demand homogeneity,

$$\sum_{j=1}^{n}\pi_{ij} \;=\; 0, \qquad\qquad i=1,...,n, \qquad (2.7)$$

and are symmetric in i and j,

$$\pi_{ij} \;=\; \pi_{ji}, \qquad\qquad i,j=1,...,n, \qquad (2.8)$$

which is known as *Slutsky symmetry*. The Slutsky matrix

$[\pi_{ij}]$ is *symmetric negative semidefinite with rank n-1*.

When the coefficients θ_i and π_{ij} in (2.5) are specified as constants, equation (2.5) is known as the ith *unconditional demand equation of the absolute price version of the Rotterdam model*.

The two versions of the unconditional Rotterdam model each have their own attractions. The absolute price version and constraints (2.7) and (2.8) are linear in the parameters, which makes estimation and testing straightforward. However, when n becomes larger, the number of π_{ij}'s grows rapidly, making the absolute price version of the model suitable for small systems only. For larger models, it is necessary to use the relative price version of the model (which is nonlinear in the parameters) with suitable constraints on the v_{ij}'s. These constraints take the form of postulating that certain goods do not interact in the consumer's utility function; a special case of this is preference independence when no good interacts with another.

Analysis of Income Elasticities

From equation (2.7) of Section 6.2, we have

$$d(log\ w_i) \;=\; (\eta_i - 1)\ d(log\ M). \qquad (2.9)$$

The income elasticity of commodity i implied by the unconditional demand model (2.2) or (2.5) is

$$\eta_i = \frac{\theta_i}{w_i}. \tag{2.10}$$

Under the Rotterdam parameterization the marginal share θ_i is a constant. Taking the differential of both sides of (2.10), we get

$$d(log\ \eta_i) = -d(log\ w_i), \tag{2.11}$$

as θ_i under the Rotterdam parameterization is a constant. Equation (2.11) shows that the income elasticity is inversely proportional to the corresponding budget share, under the Rotterdam parameterization.

Substituting (2.9) in (2.11) gives

$$d(log\ \eta_i) = -(\eta_i - 1)\ d(log\ M), \tag{2.12}$$

which shows that the income elasticity of η_i is $-(\eta_i - 1)$. Equation (2.12) holds under the conditions of constant marginal shares and constant prices. This equation shows that for luxuries (i.e., for $\eta_i > 1$), the income elasticity falls with income growth; and conversely for necessities. Accordingly, if we specify the marginal shares as constants as in the case of Rotterdam parameterization, then the income elasticity of demand for food, a necessity, would increase with increasing income. In other words, greater affluence causes food to become less of a necessity, that is, more of a luxury. This is implausible.

In many applications the budget share changes only gradually over time, so that the implied changes in the income elasticities will not be very large. Consequently, in such applications, the assumption of constant marginal shares does not create serious problems. In other situations, however, there will be major problems. See Theil (1987) for further details.

Preference Independent Version of the Rotterdam Demand Equations

Under preference independence, the utility function takes the form (7.1) of Section 6.7, so that all second-order cross-derivatives vanish. Therefore, in view of the fact that $v_{ij} = \lambda p_i p_j u^{ij}/M$ and the constraint (2.4), $v_{ij} = 0$ for $i \neq j$ and $v_{ii} = \phi\theta_i$. Then, the relative price version of the Rotterdam model (2.2) takes the form

$$\overline{w}_{it}\ Dq_{it} = \theta_i\ DQ_t + \phi\theta_i(Dp_{it} - DP'_t), \qquad i=1,\dots,n. \tag{2.13}$$

When the coefficients ϕ and θ_i are specified as constants, equation (2.13) is known as the ith *preference independence version of the Rotterdam model.*

The number of unconstrained coefficients in (2.13) for i=1,...,n is n, which is made up of n-1 unconstrained θ_i's (1 is constrained by $\sum_{i=1}^{n} \theta_i = 1$) and ϕ. Note that (2.13) is simply a finite-change version of (7.2) of Section 6.7.

Group Rotterdam Demand Equations

The finite change version of the group demand equation (8.9) of Section 6.8 is

$$\overline{W}_{gt} DQ_{gt} = \Theta_g DQ_t + \phi\Theta_g [DP'_{gt} - DP'_t], \qquad g=1,...,G, \qquad (2.14)$$

where $\overline{W}_{gt} = \frac{1}{2}(W_{gt} + W_{gt-1})$ is the arithmetic average of the group budget share during the periods t and t-1; DQ_t and DQ_{gt} are defined in equations (1.2) and (1.8); and

$$DP'_{gt} = \sum_{i \in S_g} \theta'_i Dp_{it} \qquad (2.15)$$

is the *Frisch price index of the group in terms of finite changes*; $DP'_t = \sum_{i=1}^{n} \theta_i Dp_{it}$ is the finite-change version of the Frisch price index; and all other notations are as before. When the coefficients, group marginal share Θ_g and ϕ in (2.14) are treated as constants, it is known as the *Group Rotterdam demand model* for group S_g.

Conditional Rotterdam Demand Equations

The finite-change version of the conditional demand equation (9.6) of Section 6.9 in relative prices is

$$\overline{w}_{it} Dq_{it} = \theta'_i \overline{W}_{gt} DQ_{gt} + \sum_{j \in S_g} v_{ij} (Dp_{jt} - DP'_{gt}), \qquad i \in S_g, \qquad (2.16)$$

where DQ_{gt} and DP'_{gt} are defined in equations (1.8) and (2.15); and the other notations are as before. When the conditional marginal share θ'_i and price coefficients v_{ij}'s in (2.16) are treated as constants, it is known as the *i^{th} relative price equation of the conditional version of the Rotterdam model*; it is the conditional demand equation for commodity i belonging to the group S_g

Equation (2.16) is analogous to the unconditional Rotterdam model given in (2.2). The price coefficients v_{ij} in these two equations are identical, and the constraint on the v_{ij}'s within S_g, similar to (2.4) is

$$\sum_{j \in S_g} v_{ij} = \phi\theta_i = \phi\Theta_g\theta'_i, \qquad i \in S_g. \qquad (2.17)$$

Furthermore, as $[v_{ij}]$ is symmetric, the price coefficients within the group are also symmetric.

The finite-change version of the absolute price version of the conditional demand equation defined in (9.11) of Section 6.9 takes the form

$$\overline{w}_{it} Dq_{it} = \theta_i' \overline{W}_{gt} DQ_{gt} + \sum_{j \in S_g} \pi_{ij}^g Dp_{jt}, \qquad i \in S_g, \qquad (2.18)$$

where

$$\pi_{ij}^g = v_{ij} - \phi \Theta_g \theta_i' \theta_j', \qquad i,j \in S_g, \qquad (2.19)$$

is the $(i,j)^{th}$ conditional Slutsky coefficient and satisfies Slutsky symmetry,

$$\pi_{ij}^g = \pi_{ji}^g, \qquad i,j \in S_g, \qquad (2.20)$$

and demand homogeneity,

$$\sum_{j \in S_g} \pi_{ij}^g = 0, \qquad i \in S_g. \qquad (2.21)$$

Equation (2.18) is a conditional version of (2.5). When the coefficients π_{ij}^g and θ_i' are specified as constants, equation (2.18) is known as the ith *conditional demand equation of the absolute price version of the Rotterdam model*. It should be noted that, in contrast to the price coefficients, the v_{ij}'s, which are the same in the unconditional demand equation (2.2) as well as the conditional demand equation (2.16), the Slutsky coefficients in (2.18) differ from those in the unconditional demand equation (2.5).

7.3   An Alternative Parameterization of the Conditional Demand Equations

Comparing the unconditional demand equations (2.2) and (2.5) with the corresponding conditional demand equations (2.16) and (2.18), respectively, we see that the left-hand variable for both is $\overline{w}_{it} Dq_{it}$. It is, however, more natural to have as the left-hand variable of the conditional demand equations, $\overline{w}_{it}' Dq_{it}$. In this section, we shall modify the conditional demand equation (2.16) and (2.18), so that $\overline{w}_{it}' Dq_{it}$ is the left-hand variable.

The Relative Price Version

To get a conditional demand equation with left-hand variable $\overline{w}_{it}' Dq_{it}$, we divide both sides of (2.16) by $\overline{W}_{gt}$ to give

$$\overline{w}_{it}' Dq_{it} = \theta_i' DQ_{gt} + \sum_{j \in S_g} v_{ij}' (Dp_{jt} - DP_{gt}'), \qquad i \in S_g, \qquad (3.1)$$

where

$$v_{ij}' = \frac{v_{ij}}{\overline{W}_{gt}}. \qquad (3.2)$$

We shall refer to equation (3.1) as the *modified relative price version of the conditional Rotterdam demand equations*. The coefficients defined by (3.2) are referred to as *modified price coefficients*. We shall now discuss the properties of the modified price coefficients. If we sum both sides of (3.2) over $j \in S_g$, we get

$$\sum_{j \in S_g} v'_{ij} = \frac{1}{\overline{W}_{gt}} \sum_{j \in S_g} v_{ij} = \eta_{gg} \theta'_i, \qquad (3.3)$$

where we have used (2.17) and

$$\eta_{gg} = \frac{\phi \Theta_g}{\overline{W}_{gt}} = \phi \eta_g \qquad (3.4)$$

is the own-price elasticity of the group S_g, where $\eta_g = \Theta_g / \overline{W}_{gt}$ is the income elasticity of the group S_g. This interpretation of η_{gg} can be verified by going back to equations (8.9) (the group demand equation under block independence) and (8.10) of Section 6.8.

From (3.2), we also have that the modified price coefficient matrix

$$[v'_{ij}] = \frac{1}{\overline{W}_{gt}} [v_{ij}], \qquad (3.5)$$

is symmetric negative definite. This follows from the facts that $1/\overline{W}_{gt} > 0$ and that $[v_{ij}]$ is symmetric negative definite. Furthermore, if we sum both sides of (3.3) over $i \in S_g$ and use $\sum_{i \in S_g} \theta'_i = 1$, we get

$$\sum_{i \in S_g} \sum_{j \in S_g} v'_{ij} = \eta_{gg}. \qquad (3.6)$$

Equation (3.6) means that under block independence, the sum of all modified price coefficients of a group is equal to the own-price elasticity of demand for the group as a whole.

The difference between (2.2) and (3.1) is twofold. First, as we discussed at the beginning of this section, the dependent variables differ: $\overline{w}_{it} Dq_{it}$ in (2.2) and $\overline{w}'_{it} Dq_{it}$ in (3.1). Second, they differ in parameterization. In (2.2), the price coefficients (v_{ij}) are specified as constants, while the modified price coefficients (v'_{ij}) are constants in (3.1). As $v'_{ij} = v_{ij} / \overline{W}_{gt} =$ constant, it follows that, according to the parameterization adopted in (3.1), the original price coefficients (v_{ij}'s) are variable over time and proportional to $\overline{W}_{gt}$.

The Absolute Price Version

To obtain the absolute price version of (3.1), we divide both sides of (2.18) by $\overline{W}_{gt}$ to give

$$\overline{w}'_{it} Dq_{it} = \theta'_i DQ_{gt} + \sum_{j \in S_g} \pi'_{ij} Dp_{jt}, \qquad i \in S_g, \qquad (3.7)$$

where

$$\pi'_{ij} = \frac{\pi^g_{ij}}{\overline{W}_{gt}} = v'_{ij} - \eta_{gg}\,\theta'_i\theta'_j, \qquad\qquad i,j \in S_g, \qquad (3.8)$$

and we have used (2.19), (3.2) and (3.4).

We shall refer to equation (3.7) as the *modified absolute price version of the conditional Rotterdam demand equation* for $i \in S_g$. The coefficients defined by (3.8) are referred to as *modified conditional Slutsky coefficients*. We shall now discuss the properties of these coefficients.

If we sum both sides of equation (3.8) over $i \in S_g$ we obtain

$$\sum_{j \in S_g} \pi'_{ij} = \frac{1}{\overline{W}_{gt}} \sum_{j \in S_g} \pi^g_{ij} = 0, \qquad\qquad i \in S_g, \qquad (3.9)$$

where we have used (2.21). Thus the modified Slutsky coefficients also satisfy the demand homogeneity property. Using equation (3.8), we can write the modified conditional Slutsky matrix as

$$[\pi'_{ij}] = \frac{1}{\overline{W}_{gt}}[\pi^g_{ij}], \qquad\qquad (3.10)$$

is symmetric negative semidefinite with rank $n_g - 1$. This follows from the facts that $1/\overline{W}_{gt} > 0$ and that $[\pi^g_{ij}]$ is symmetric negative semidefinite with rank $n_g - 1$.

7.4   The Generalized Rotterdam Model

In this section we introduce another parameterization of the differential demand system by adding a price substitution term to the Working's model to yield the generalized Rotterdam model. This is a generalization of the Rotterdam model as the marginal shares are no longer constant.

The Working's (1943) model discussed in Section 6.2 specifies that the budget share of each good is a linear function of the logarithm of income:

$$w_i = \alpha_i + \beta_i \log M, \qquad\qquad i=1,\dots,n, \qquad (4.1)$$

where α_i and β_i are constants satisfying $\sum_{i=1}^{n} \alpha_i = 1$ and $\sum_{i=1}^{n} \beta_i = 0$. The marginal shares implied by (4.1) take the form

$$\theta_i = w_i + \beta_i, \qquad\qquad i=1,\dots,n. \qquad (4.2)$$

In finite-change form with a time subscript added, the above equation becomes

$$\theta_{it} = \overline{w}_{it} + \beta_i, \qquad\qquad i=1,\dots,n. \qquad (4.3)$$

Under Working's model the implied income elasticity for good i takes the form

$$\eta_i = 1 + \frac{\beta_i}{w_i}, \qquad\qquad i=1,\dots,n, \qquad\qquad (4.4)$$

which shows that a good with a positive (negative) β_i has an income elasticity larger (smaller) than one. Moreover (4.4) shows that under Working's model, a good cannot change from being a luxury to a necessity or vice versa; if η_i starts out above (below) 1, it always stays there. This is not necessarily true under the Rotterdam model.

Adding a Substitution Term

Working's model (4.1) represents an incomplete specification of the demand function because it contains no price term, although it can be applied to the analysis of household budget data where all participating families pay the same price for each commodity. Now we endow this model with a price substitution term.

Unconditional Version

If we substitute θ_{it} from (4.3) in (2.5) we get

$$\overline{w}_{it}(Dq_{it} - DQ_t) = \beta_i DQ_t + \sum_{j=1}^{n} \pi_{ij} Dp_{jt}, \qquad i=1,\dots,n. \qquad (4.5)$$

This is the ith equation of Working's model with a substitution term added. We shall refer to equation (4.5) as the *absolute price version of the unconditional generalized Rotterdam model*. Note that the only difference between (4.5) and the Rotterdam model (2.5) is the variable on the left. Although we previously referred to (4.1) as Working's model, there will be no confusion if, from now on, we refer to (4.5) for i=1,...,n as Working's model. For further details of (4.5), see Clements (1987a) and Keller and van Driel (1985).

Preference Independent Version

If we substitute θ_{it} from (4.3) in (2.13), we get

$$\overline{w}_{it}(Dq_{it} - DQ_t) = \beta_i DQ_t + \phi(\beta_i + \overline{w}_{it})(Dp_{it} - DP'_t), \qquad i=1,\dots,n. \qquad (4.6)$$

This is the ith equation of Working's model under preference independence with a substitution term added. We shall refer to equation (4.6) as the *preference independent version of the generalized Rotterdam model*.

Conditional Version

Let the n goods be divided into G groups $S_1,\dots,S_G$ and let $w_i' = w_i/W_g$ be the conditional budget share of $i \in S_g$. The conditional version of (4.1) is

$$w_i' = \alpha_i' + \beta_i' \, log \, M_g, \qquad\qquad i \in S_g, \qquad\qquad (4.7)$$

where α_i' and β_i' are constants satisfying $\sum_{i=1}^{n_g} \alpha_i' = 1$ and $\sum_{i=1}^{n_g} \beta_i' = 0$; $M_g = \sum_{i \in S_g} p_{it} q_{it}$ is total expenditure on the group S_g; and n_g is the number of goods in S_g. The marginal shares implied by (4.7) take the form

$$\theta_i' = w_i' + \beta_i', \qquad\qquad i \in S_g, \qquad\qquad (4.8)$$

which is of the same form as the unconditional version of the marginal shares given in (4.2). Under conditional Working's model (4.7) the implied income elasticity for good $i \in S_g$ takes the form

$$\eta_i' = 1 + \frac{\beta_i'}{w_i'}, \qquad\qquad\qquad (4.9)$$

which is in the same form as its unconditional counterpart given in (4.4). From equations (4.8) and (4.9), we see that good $i \in S_g$ is a conditional luxury or necessity according to $\beta_i' > 0$ or < 0.

Clements et al (1985) shows that equation (4.7) can be derived as an approximation from (4.1) under the assumption that the income elasticity of demand for the group is approximately unity. Consequently, the result is that Working's model implies a conditional model of the same form under unitary income elasticity of the group.

In finite-change form with a time subscript added, the above equation can be written as

$$\theta_{it}' = \overline{w}_{it}' + \beta_i'. \qquad\qquad\qquad (4.10)$$

If we substitute θ_{it}' from (4.10) in the conditional demand equation (2.18), we get

$$\overline{w}_{it}(Dq_{it} - DQ_{gt}) = \beta_i' \overline{W}_{gt} DQ_{gt} + \sum_{j \in S_g} \pi_{ij}^g Dp_{jt}, \qquad i \in S_g, \qquad (4.11)$$

where β_i' and π_{ij}^g are constants; and the other notation is as before. We shall refer to equation (4.11) as the *first conditional version of the generalized Rotterdam model in absolute prices.*

In Section 7.3 we discussed a modified version of the Rotterdam model, which has $\overline{w}_{it}' Dq_{it}$ as dependent variable rather than $\overline{w}_{it} Dq_{it}$. Under Working's model, the modified conditional version takes the form

$$\overline{w}_{it}'(Dq_{it} - DQ_{gt}) = \beta_i' DQ_{gt} + \sum_{j \in S_g} \pi_{ij} Dp_{jt}, \qquad i \in S_g. \qquad (4.12)$$

We shall refer to equation (4.12) as the *second conditional version of the generalized Rotterdam model in absolute prices*.

7.5   Estimation

Estimating a system of demand equations in an unrestricted fashion requires the estimation of an impossibly large number of coefficients, especially with large demand systems. As discussed earlier, one way of reducing the number of coefficients to be estimated is to impose *a priori* restrictions such as demand homogeneity, symmetry or preference independence. In this section we shall discuss the procedure for estimating the absolute price version of the unconditional demand equation (2.5), without any restrictions imposed and with homogeneity or Slutsky symmetry or preference independence imposed. However, the estimation of the other parameterizations can be estimated in a similar manner.

One Equation is Redundant

For estimation, we write equation (2.5) with an error term ε_{it} added.

$$\overline{w}_{it}\, Dq_{it} \;=\; \theta_i\, DQ_t + \sum_{j=1}^{n} \pi_{ij} Dp_{jt} + \varepsilon_{it}, \qquad\qquad i=1,\dots, n;\ t=1,..,T. \qquad (5.1)$$

In the context of (5.1) the adding up restrictions imply that

$$\sum_{i=1}^{n} \theta_i \;=\; 1 \qquad\text{and}\qquad \sum_{i=1}^{n} \pi_{ij} \;=\; 0, \qquad j=1,\dots, n. \qquad (5.2)$$

The second adding-up restriction in (5.2) can be obtained by summing both sides of (5.1) and using the first adding-up restriction in (5.2).

If we sum both sides of (5.1) over $i=1,\dots, n$, we get

$$\sum_{i=1}^{n} \overline{w}_{it}\, Dq_{it} \;=\; \sum_{i=1}^{n} \theta_i\, DQ_t + \sum_{i=1}^{n}\sum_{j=1}^{n} \pi_{ij} Dp_{jt} + \sum_{i=1}^{n} \varepsilon_{it}.$$

Using equation (5.2) and the fact that $DQ_t = \sum_{i=1}^{n} \overline{w}_{it} Dq_{it}$, we obtain

$$\sum_{i=1}^{n} \varepsilon_{it} \;=\; 0 \qquad\qquad\qquad t=1,\dots,T,$$

where T is the number of observations. This shows that the disturbances ε_{it}'s, $i=1,\dots,n$ are linearly dependent, which means that one of the equations is redundant and can be deleted. Barten (1969) shows that it doesn't matter which equation is deleted. So we delete the last equation from system (5.1). Hence the reduced version of (5.1) takes the form

$$\overline{w}_{it} \, Dq_{it} \;=\; \theta_i \, DQ_t + \sum_{j=1}^{n} \pi_{ij} Dp_{jt} + \varepsilon_{it}, \qquad i=1,...,n-1; \, t=1,...,T. \quad (5.3)$$

Assumption on the Error Term

We make the following assumption about the disturbances in (5.3). We assume that the ε_{it}'s are independently distributed with

$$E[\varepsilon_{it}] = 0, \qquad\qquad E[\varepsilon_{is}\,\varepsilon_{jt}\,] = \sigma_{ij}\delta_{st}, \qquad\qquad (5.4)$$

where σ_{ij} is a constant and δ_{st} is the Kronecker delta. Under these assumptions, we have

$$V[\,\epsilon_t^*\,] = \Sigma, \qquad\qquad (5.5)$$

where $\epsilon_t^* = [\varepsilon_{1t} \; ..... \; \varepsilon_{n-1,t}]'$ and $\Sigma = [\sigma_{ij}]$ is a non-singular $(n-1)\times(n-1)$ contemporaneous covariance matrix. From (5.4) and (5.5) we also have

$$E[\varepsilon] = 0, \qquad E[\varepsilon\varepsilon'] = \Sigma^*, \qquad\qquad (5.6)$$

where $\varepsilon = [\,\epsilon_t^*\,]$; I_T is the identity matrix of order T; and $\Sigma^* = \Sigma \otimes I_T$.

In general, Σ is unknown. For estimation and hypothesis testing, it is common practice to approximate this matrix by its unbiased estimator S, the matrix of mean squares and cross products of the LS residuals.

Unrestricted Estimation

Denoting $y_{it} = \overline{w}_{it} \, Dq_{it}$, $\gamma_i = [\theta_i \; \pi_{i1} \; ... \; \pi_{in}]'$ and $x_t = [DQ_t \, Dp_{1t} \, ... \, Dp_{nt}]'$, equation (5.3) can be written for $t=1,...,T$ as

$$y_i \;=\; X\gamma_i + \varepsilon_i, \qquad\qquad i=1,...,n-1, \qquad (5.7)$$

where $y_i = [y_{it}]$ is a T-vector; X is a $T \times (n+1)$ matrix whose t^{th} row is x_t'; and $\varepsilon_i = [\varepsilon_{it}]$ is a T-vector. We write (5.7) for $i=1,...,n-1$ as

$$y \;=\; (I_{n-1} \otimes X)\gamma + \varepsilon$$
$$=\; X^*\gamma + \varepsilon, \qquad\qquad (5.8)$$

where I_{n-1} is the identity matrix of order $(n-1)$; $y = [y_i]$; $\gamma = [\gamma_i]$; $\varepsilon = [\varepsilon_i]$ are vectors consisting of $(n-1)$ subvectors; $\otimes$ is the Kronecker product; and $X^* = (I_{n-1} \otimes X)$.

We now proceed to estimate γ of (5.8) by generalized least squares (GLS) estimation method. Thus the unrestricted estimator of γ is given by

$$
\begin{aligned}
\hat{\gamma} &= (X^{*\prime} \Sigma^{*-1} X^*)^{-1} (X^{*\prime} \Sigma^{*-1} y) \\
&= [(I_{n-1} \otimes X')(\Sigma^{-1} \otimes I_T)(I_{n-1} \otimes X)]^{-1} [(I_{n-1} \otimes X')(\Sigma^{-1} \otimes I_T)y] \\
&= [\Sigma^{-1} \otimes (X'X)]^{-1} [(\Sigma^{-1} \otimes X')y] \\
&= [I \otimes (X'X)^{-1} X']y
\end{aligned}
\tag{5.9}
$$

and

$$
\mathrm{Var}\,[\hat{\gamma}] = (X^{*\prime} \Sigma^{*-1} X^*)^{-1} = [\Sigma \otimes (X'X)^{-1}].
$$

The Homogeneity Restriction

Here we reproduce the homogeneity restriction (2.7):

$$
\sum_{j=1}^{n} \pi_{ij} = 0, \qquad\qquad i=1,\ldots,n. \tag{5.10}
$$

Let $a = [0\ 1\ \ldots\ 1]'$ be a $(n+1)$-vector. Then, demand homogeneity, (5.10), can be written in vector form as

$$
a'\gamma_i = 0, \qquad\qquad i=1,\ldots,n.
$$

For $i=1,\ldots,n-1$, this can be expressed as

$$
R\gamma = 0, \tag{5.11}
$$

where $R = I_{n-1} \otimes a'$.

Now we consider estimating the model (5.8) subject to the $n-1$ linear restrictions given by (5.11). Let $\gamma^* = (X^{*\prime} X^*)^{-1} X^{*\prime} y$ be the unrestricted least squares estimator of γ. The homogeneity constrained (GLS) estimator of γ (see Theil, 1971, p.285) is

$$
\hat{\gamma}^H = \gamma^* - (X^{*\prime} \Sigma^{*-1} X^*)^{-1} R'[R(X^{*\prime} \Sigma^{*-1} X^*)^{-1} R']^{-1} R\gamma^*,
$$

or equivalently,

$$
\hat{\gamma}^H = \gamma^* - [\Sigma \otimes (X'X)^{-1}]R' \left\{ R[\Sigma \otimes (X'X)^{-1}]R' \right\}^{-1} R\gamma^*. \tag{5.12}
$$

The Slutsky Symmetry Restriction

We now take homogeneity as given and consider symmetry. The homogeneity-constrained version of model (5.3) is obtained by imposing the homogeneity restriction (5.10) on (5.3):

$$y_{it} = \theta_i DQ_t + \sum_{j=1}^{n-1} \pi_{ij}(Dp_{jt} - Dp_{nt}) + \varepsilon_{it}, \qquad i=1,\dots,n-1; \; t=1,\dots,T. \quad (5.13)$$

Let $\boldsymbol{\gamma}_i^H = [\theta_i \; \pi_{i1} \; \dots \; \pi_{in-1}]'$ and $\mathbf{x}_t^H = [DQ_t \; (Dp_{1t} - Dp_{nt}) \; \dots \; (Dp_{n-1,t} - Dp_{nt})]'$. Then, (5.13) can be written as

$$y_i = \mathbf{X}^H \boldsymbol{\gamma}_i^H + \varepsilon_i, \qquad\qquad i=1,\dots,n-1, \quad (5.14)$$

where $\mathbf{X}^H$ is a $T \times n$ matrix whose t^{th} row is $\mathbf{x}_t^H$ '; and y_i and ε_i are as before. As for the unconstrained case, it can be shown that the best linear unbiased estimator of $\boldsymbol{\gamma}_i^H$ in (5.14) is the single-equation LS estimator (Theil, 1971).

As before, we write (5.14) in matrix form as

$$y = (\mathbf{I} \otimes \mathbf{X}^H)\boldsymbol{\gamma}^H + \varepsilon, \quad (5.15)$$

where $\mathbf{I}$ is the identity matrix of order $(n-1)$; $\boldsymbol{\gamma}^H = [\boldsymbol{\gamma}_i^H]$ is a vector consisting of $(n-1)$ subvectors; and y and ε are as before. Let $\hat{\boldsymbol{\gamma}}_i^H$ be the LS estimator of $\boldsymbol{\gamma}_i^H$ for $i=1,\dots,n$; and $\hat{\boldsymbol{\gamma}}^H = [\hat{\boldsymbol{\gamma}}_i^H]$ be the vector consisting of $(n-1)$ subvectors.

Here, we reproduce the Slutsky symmetry restriction, given by (2.8)

$$\pi_{ij} = \pi_{ji}, \qquad\qquad i,j=1,\dots,n. \quad (5.16)$$

In vector form, for $i,j=1,\dots,n-1$, the symmetry restrictions (5.16) can be written as

$$\mathbf{R}\boldsymbol{\gamma}^H = \mathbf{0}, \quad (5.17)$$

where $\mathbf{R}$ is a $q \times n(n-1)$ matrix with $q = \frac{1}{2}(n-1)(n-2)$ and each row of $\mathbf{R}$ consists of zeros except for a 1 and a -1 corresponding to π_{ij} and π_{ji} for some $i \neq j$.

We can now write the homogeneity- and symmetry-constrained GLS estimator of γ for model (5.15) as in (5.12) with the new definition of $\mathbf{R}$ and $\mathbf{X}^*$ replaced by $(\mathbf{I}_{n-1} \otimes \mathbf{X}^H)$.

The Preference Independence Restriction

Under preference independence, the Slutsky coefficients take the form

$$\pi_{ij} = \phi\theta_i (\delta_{ij} - \theta_j), \qquad\qquad i,j=1,\dots,n, \quad (5.18)$$

where we have used equations (2.6) and the fact that $v_{ij} = 0$ for $i \neq j$; and $v_{ij} = \phi\theta_i$ for i=j. Substituting (5.18) for π_{ij} in (5.3) and adding a constant term α_i, the preference independent version of (5.3) can be written as

$$\overline{w}_{it} \, Dq_{it} = \alpha_i + \theta_i \, DQ_t + \phi\theta_i [Dp_{it} - \sum_{j=1}^{n}\theta_j Dp_{jt}] + \varepsilon_{it}, \quad i=1,\ldots,n\text{-}1; \, t=1,\ldots,T. \quad (5.19)$$

As can be seen, equation (5.19) is non-linear in its parameters. Therefore, we apply the maximum likelihood estimation procedure.

We write equation (5.19) in the following form

$$y_{it} = \alpha_i + \theta_i \, DQ_t + \phi z_{it} + \varepsilon_{it}, \qquad i=1,\ldots,n\text{-}1; \, t=1,\ldots,T, \qquad (5.20)$$

where $y_{it} = \overline{w}_{it} \, Dq_{it}$;

$$z_{it} = \theta_i \, [Dp_{it}^* - \sum_{j=1}^{n-1}\theta_j Dp_{jt}^*];$$

and $Dp_{it}^* = Dp_{it} - Dp_{nt}$, and we have also used $\sum_{i=1}^{n}\theta_i = 1$.

In vector form, (5.20) can be written as

$$y_t = X_t \gamma + \varepsilon_t,$$

where $y_t = [y_{it}]$; $X_t = [DQ_t I_{n-1} \; z_t \; I_{n-1}]$ with I_{n-1} being the identity matrix of order n-1; $z_t = [z_{it}]$; $\gamma = [\theta' \; \phi \; \alpha']' = [\theta_1 \ldots \theta_{n-1} \mid \phi \mid \alpha_1 \ldots \alpha_{n-1}]'$; and $\varepsilon_t = [\varepsilon_{it}]$.

Assuming that the ε_t's are independent normal errors with zero mean and non-singular covariance matrix Σ, the log-likelihood function of the y_t's is given by

$$\ell(\gamma, \Sigma; y) = C + \frac{T}{2}\ell n |\Sigma^{-1}| - \frac{1}{2}\sum_{t=1}^{T}(y_t - X_t\gamma)'\Sigma^{-1}(y_t - X_t\gamma), \qquad (5.21)$$

where C is a constant and T is the sample size. The first-order conditions for a maximum of (5.21) are

$$\frac{\partial \ell}{\partial \Sigma^{-1}} = \frac{T}{2}\Sigma - \frac{1}{2}\sum_{t=1}^{T}(y_t - X_t\gamma)(y_t - X_t\gamma)' = 0 \qquad (5.22)$$

and

$$\frac{\partial \ell}{\partial \gamma'} = \sum_{t=1}^{T}(y_t - X_t\gamma)'\Sigma^{-1}\frac{\partial(X_t\gamma)}{\partial \gamma'} = 0, \qquad (5.23)$$

where

$$\frac{\partial(X_t\gamma)}{\partial \gamma} = \left[DQ_t I + \phi\frac{\partial z_t}{\partial \theta'} \quad z_t \quad I \right]; \qquad (5.24)$$

$$\frac{\partial \mathbf{z_t}}{\partial \boldsymbol{\theta}'} = \left[\frac{\partial z_{it}}{\partial \theta_j}\right];$$

and

$$\frac{\partial z_{it}}{\partial \theta_j} = -\theta_i Dp^*_{jt} + \delta_{ij}\left[Dp^*_{it} - \sum_{k=1}^{n-1}\theta_k Dp^*_{kt}\right].$$

From the first order condition (5.22), we have

$$\hat{\boldsymbol{\Sigma}} = \frac{1}{T}\sum_{t=1}^{T}(\mathbf{y_t} - \mathbf{X_t}\hat{\boldsymbol{\gamma}})(\mathbf{y_t} - \mathbf{X_t}\hat{\boldsymbol{\gamma}})'.$$

This is the usual ML estimator of Σ.

It follows from (5.23) that

$$\frac{\partial^2 \ell}{\partial \Sigma^{-1}\partial \gamma'} = \sum_{t=1}^{T}(\mathbf{y_t} - \mathbf{X_t}\gamma)\left[\frac{\partial(\mathbf{X_t}\gamma)}{\partial \gamma'}\right]'. \tag{5.25}$$

Since $E[(\mathbf{y_t} - \mathbf{X_t}\gamma)] = E[\varepsilon_t] = 0$, the expected value of the right-hand side of (5.25) vanishes, so that the information matrix of the ML procedure is block-diagonal with respect to γ and Σ^{-1}. From (5.23), we also have

$$\frac{\partial^2 \ell}{\partial \gamma \partial \gamma'} = -\sum_{t=1}^{T}\frac{\partial(\mathbf{X_t}\gamma)'}{\partial \gamma}\Sigma^{-1}\frac{\partial(\mathbf{X_t}\gamma)}{\partial \gamma'} + \sum_{t=1}^{T}(\mathbf{y_t} - \mathbf{X_t}\gamma)'\Sigma^{-1}\left[\frac{\partial^2(\mathbf{X_t}\gamma)}{\partial \gamma \partial \gamma'}\right].$$

The second term on the right-hand side has zero expectation. Therefore, the asymptotic covariance matrix of the ML estimator of γ is

$$\mathbf{V} = -\left[E\left[\frac{\partial^2 \ell}{\partial \gamma \partial \gamma'}\right]\right]^{-1} = \left[\sum_{t=1}^{T}\frac{\partial(\mathbf{X_t}\gamma)'}{\partial \gamma}\Sigma^{-1}\frac{\partial(\mathbf{X_t}\gamma)}{\partial \gamma'}\right]^{-1}.$$

The ML estimator of γ is obtained by means of Newton's iterative scheme based on successive estimates of $\mathbf{V}$ and Σ. The asymptotic standard errors are the square roots of the diagonal elements of $\mathbf{V}$ with ML-estimates substituted for the unknown parameters in $\mathbf{V}$.

7.6   Testing Homogeneity, Symmetry and Preference Independence

One problem associated with the tests of demand homogeneity, Slutsky symmetry and preference independent utility structure is the test procedure, which is usually based on the asymptotic distribution of the test statistic without correction for small-sample bias and, therefore, the results are biased towards rejection. In a review article on systems of consumer demand functions, Barten (1977) summarizes the results from various empirical applications, which test the validity of the hypotheses of homogeneity and symmetry. These results show that homogeneity is generally not acceptable, while symmetry is a bit more acceptable. Barten concludes that one reason for these negative results is that since the test procedures are usually based on the asymptotic distribution of the test statistic without correction for small-sample bias, the results are biased towards rejection. Simulations by Bera et al. (1981), Bewley (1983), Laitinen (1978) and Meisner (1979) have confirmed this conclusion. In view of these difficulties, Laitinen (1978) developed a finite-sample test for testing homogeneity and Theil (1987) developed alternative distribution-free testing procedures for testing homogeneity and symmetry. S. Selvanathan (1987) developed an alternative distribution-free testing procedure for preference independence based on Barnard's (1963) Monte Carlo simulation procedure. In this section, we present a detailed account of the conventional tests and the simulation based tests used for testing demand theory hypotheses: homogeneity, symmetry and preference independence.

Testing Demand Homogeneity

The demand homogeneity (5.10), can be written in vector form as (5.11).

The Asymptotic Test

The test statistic for testing the homogeneity restriction (5.10) is

$$\frac{(\mathbf{R}\hat{\gamma})'\Sigma^{-1}(\mathbf{R}\hat{\gamma})/\mathbf{a}'(\mathbf{X}'\mathbf{X})^{-1}\mathbf{a}}{\operatorname{tr}\Sigma^{-1}\mathbf{S}}, \tag{6.1}$$

where $\hat{\gamma}$ is the LS estimator of γ, Σ is the error covariance matrix; and $\mathbf{S}$ is the LS residual moment matrix, an unbiased estimator of Σ (Theil, 1971). When Σ is known, under the null hypothesis, (6.1) is distributed as F with $(n-1)$ and $(n-1)(T-n-2)$ degrees of freedom. Usually, the error covariance matrix Σ is unknown and is replaced by its estimator $\mathbf{S}$. The test statistic for homogeneity then becomes

$$\Psi_H = \frac{(\mathbf{R}\hat{\gamma})'\mathbf{S}^{-1}(\mathbf{R}\hat{\gamma})}{\mathbf{a}'(\mathbf{X}'\mathbf{X})^{-1}\mathbf{a}}. \tag{6.2}$$

Under the null hypothesis, it can be easily shown that, Ψ_H has an asymptotic χ^2 distribution with $(n-1)$ degrees of freedom. It is worth noting that as (6.2) involves $\mathbf{S}^{-1}$, $\mathbf{S}$ must be non-singular. The necessary condition for $\mathbf{S}$ to be non-singular is that $T-2n \geq 1$ (Laitinen, 1978).

Laitinen's Exact Test

Laitinen (1978) derived the exact finite-sample distribution of Ψ_H in (6.2) under the null hypothesis of demand homogeneity restriction. Laitinen showed that Ψ_H is distributed as a Hotelling's T^2, which itself is distributed as a constant multiple $(n\text{-}1)(T\text{-}n\text{-}2)/(T\text{-}2n)$ of $F(n\text{-}1,T\text{-}2n)$. This exact test is very useful in applications where the sample size is relatively small.

Testing Symmetry

The symmetry hypothesis is given by equation (5.17). The test statistic for symmetry is

$$\frac{(R\hat{\gamma}^H)'\{R[\Sigma \otimes (X^H{}'X^H)^{-1}]R'\}^{-1}(R\hat{\gamma}^H)}{[q/(n\text{-}1)]\text{tr}\,\Sigma^{-1}S}, \tag{6.3}$$

where Σ is the error covariance matrix of model (5.13) for i=1,...,n-1 (Theil, 1971). Under the null, (6.3) is distributed as F with q and $(n\text{-}1)(T\text{-}n)$ degrees of freedom. As before, we replace Σ by its estimator S (when S is non-singular) and the test statistic becomes

$$\Psi_S = (R\hat{\gamma}^H)'\{R[S \otimes (X^H{}'X^H)^{-1}]R'\}^{-l}(R\hat{\gamma}^H), \tag{6.4}$$

which has an asymptotic χ^2 distribution with q degrees of freedom. Using simulation experiments, Meisner (1979) showed that the asymptotic test is biased against symmetry, particularly in large demand systems. Since (6.4) involves cross-equation restrictions, the exact distribution of Ψ_S is complicated and has not yet been derived.

Testing Preference Independence

The Asymptotic Test

To test preference independence, a standard likelihood ratio test could be used. The likelihood values of the unrestricted model (5.3) and restricted model under preference independence, equation (5.20) can be used to calculate the test statistic which follows an asymptotic χ^2 distribution with $k = \frac{1}{2}\,n(n\text{-}1)\text{-}1$ degrees of freedom.

Monte Carlo Test

It is now well accepted in the econometrics literature that the negative results of various hypothesis testing in demand systems are at least in part due to the failure of asymptotic tests which use the moment matrix S that could be singular (or near-singular) with insufficient data (for a review, see Barten, 1977).

To overcome the problems associated with the asymptotic tests, distribution-free tests based on Barnard's (1963) Monte Carlo simulation procedure have recently been developed for demand theory hypotheses homogeneity, Slutsky symmetry (Theil, 1987) and preference independence (Selvanathan, 1987, 1993).

The basic idea behind the Monte Carlo tests is to simulate a large number of values of the test statistic under the null hypothesis to construct its empirical distribution. The observed value of the test statistic is then compared to this distribution, rather than its asymptotic counterpart. Below, we set out this Monte Carlo procedure and then in the next chapter we present its application to preference independence.

Using the standard notation, consider the system of equations $y = X\beta + \varepsilon$. Suppose we are interested in testing the null hypothesis $R\beta = b$ using a test statistic τ. Obviously τ is a function of the estimate of the parameter vector β. In general, the Monte Carlo procedure can be summarized as follows:

Step 1: Estimate the unrestricted model and obtain the data-based value τ_1 of τ.

Step 2: Estimate the model under the null hypothesis $R\beta = b$ and obtain the estimate S of the covariance matrix Σ of the disturbances.

Step 3: Generate quasi-normal error terms with zero means and covariance matrix S and use these errors together with the observed value of X and the restricted estimates to generate a new data set for y under the null. Use the generated data to estimate the unrestricted model.

Step 4: Repeat Step 3 a certain number of times, N say, and in each case calculate the simulated value of the test statistic τ.

Step 5: Let $\tau_2, \tau_3 \ldots \tau_M$ be the values of the test statistic τ obtained from the simulated data, where $M=N+1$. For a one-tailed test, we reject the null hypothesis for the observed sample at the α percent significance level if τ_1 is among the M' largest values of the τ_i's such that $(M'/M) \times 100 = \alpha$.

The number of replications (N) is usually chosen to be sufficiently large to reduce the 'blurring effect', which leads to loss of power (see Marriot, 1979). However, after a certain number of replications, the return for increased computing time diminishes. According to Besag and Diggle (1977), the suggested number of replications to reduce the 'blurring effect' for a 5 percent significance test is 999. If we use $\alpha = 5$ percent significance level and $N = 999$ simulations, for a one-tailed test, we reject the null hypothesis if the rank of τ_1 is 951,....,999 or 1000. For $\alpha = 1$ percent and $N = 999$ simulations, for a one-tailed test, we reject the null if the rank of τ_1 is 991, ..., 999 or 1000.

7.7   Concluding Comments

In this chapter, we discussed the parameterisation of the unconditional and conditional demand equations. We also discussed the estimation of these demand systems. Finally, we presented various recently developed procedures for testing demand homogeneity, symmetry and preference independence hypotheses.

Chapter 8

Demand for Food, Tobacco, Alcohol and Soft Drinks

In this chapter, we analyse the consumption patterns of consumers in 44 countries in relation to the four commodity groups, namely, food, tobacco, alcohol and soft drinks. In Section 8.1, we present the details of the data source and its characteristics and a summary of the data in the form of Divisia indices in Section 8.2. In Section 8.3, we present the estimation results based on a double-log demand system. In Section 8.4, we estimate the demand systems introduced in Chapters 6 and 7, and test demand theory hypotheses such as demand homogeneity and Slutsky symmetry. We also test the assumption of preference independence. In Sections 8.5 and 8.6, we present the final estimates and the implied income and price elasticities of the four commodity groups and the concluding comments. The results presented in this chapter are obtained using the *Demand Analysis Package 2000* (DAP2000, Yang *et al*, 2003) and *DEMMOD* (Barten *et al*, 1989).

8.1 Data Source

The basic data, consisting of annual consumption expenditures (in current and constant prices) and the population for the 44 countries, listed in column 1 of Table 8.1, considered in this book are compiled from the *Yearbook of National Account Statistics* (United Nations: New York, various issues); *National Accounts of OECD Countries* (OECD: Paris, various issues) and *International Financial Statistics Yearbook* (various issues). Almost half of the countries considered in this study are from the Organisation of Economic Co-operation and Development (OECD), which are considered to be high-income, industrialized and developed (rich) countries. The remaining half of the countries considered in this study are low-income, developing (poor) countries.

One of the most important empirical regularities in consumption economics is the *Engel's Law*. This law sates that the budget share for food (w_{Ft}) falls with increasing income (M_t). Working (1943) and then Leser (1963) modelled the *Engel's Law* into a linear regression framework, which is known as the *Working's model*,

$$w_{Ft} \quad = \quad \alpha_F + \beta_F \log M_t. \qquad\qquad (1.1)$$

Choosing $M_t = 1$ for some year t in equation (1.1), α_F can be interpreted as the budget share of food during that year t. The coefficient β_F gives 100 times the change in the budget share of food resulting from a 1 percent increase in income. Model (1.1) is also applicable across countries, where we replace the subscript t by the country subscript c.

Column 1 of Table 8.1 lists the 44 countries in the order of decreasing per capita real GDP (Gross Domestic Product) in US dollars presented in column 2. Column 3 presents the GDP for the 44 countries relative to the US with the GDP for the US=100. In the next column we present the logarithm of the GDP. Columns 5-9 gives the budget shares for the 4 commodities, food, tobacco, alcohol and soft drinks and for the 'food group' (the 4 commodities combined) for the year 1992. Figure 8.1 presents the plot of budget shares against the logarithm of the per capita GDP for the 'food group' in the 44 countries. As can be seen, a clear inverse relationship exists between budget share for each item and the per capita real GDP. This clearly provides support to the *Engel's Law*. However, the support is stronger in the case of food than the other three commodities, tobacco, alcohol or soft drinks.

8.2   Divisia Summary Measures

Let there be n commodities. Let p_{it} be the price and q_{it} be the per capita quantity consumed of commodity i $(=1,...,n)$ and M_t be the total expenditure on the n commodities during period t $(=1,...,T)$. Therefore, the total expenditure $M_t = \sum_{i=1}^{n} p_{it} q_{it}$. The proportion of total expenditure devoted to commodity i, the budget share of i, is

$$w_{it} = \frac{p_{it} q_{it}}{M_t}, \qquad\qquad t=1, ..., T.$$

The number of commodities considered in this chapter is $n=5$, namely, food, tobacco, alcohol, soft drinks and all other goods. As disaggregated data for food are not available for Japan, from now onwards in this chapter, only 43 countries are considered.

Table 8.2 presents the budget share of food, tobacco, alcohol and soft drinks for each country at the beginning and end of the sample periods for 43 countries. As can be seen, falling budget share appears to be a universal phenomena for food (except for South Africa and Venezuela). In the case of tobacco also the budget share is falling with the exception of a number of countries such as Cyprus, Ecuador, Greece, India, Luxembourg, Norway, Portugal, South Africa, Spain, Sri Lanka and Zimbabwe. Consumer allocation of their income on alcohol is also falling in most countries except Colombia, Cyprus, Greece, Israel, South Africa,

Table 8.1 The logarithm of real GDP per capita and the budget shares for the 4 commodities, 44 countries, 1992

Country	Real GDP per capita 1992			Budget share in 1992				Overall food group
	($US)	US=100	Ln(GDP)	Food	Tobacco	Alcohol	Soft drinks	
(1)	(2)	(3)	(4)	(5)	(6)	(7)	(8)	(9)
Developed countries								
1. US	23220	100	10.05	8.32	1.21	1.23	0.97	11.73
2. Switzerland	21631	93	9.98	19.23	7.29			26.52
3. Luxembourg	21144	91	9.96	10.94	5.74	1.25	0.64	18.57
4. Hong Kong	21034	91	9.95	13.62	0.61	0.64		14.87
5. Canada	20970	90	9.95	10.68	2.56	2.59		15.83
6. Germany	20197	87	9.91	19.03	1.73			20.76
7. Japan	19920	86	9.90					18.60
8. Denmark	18730	81	9.84	14.98	2.74	2.97	0.62	20.69
9. Australia	18500	80	9.83	14.42	1.84	4.26		20.52
10. Sweden	18387	79	9.82	14.33	1.86	3.00	0.58	19.77
11. France	18232	79	9.81	14.70	1.17	1.91	0.55	18.33
12. Belgium	18091	78	9.80					17.53
13. Netherlands	17373	75	9.76	11.47	1.48	1.52	0.58	15.05
14. Norway	17094	74	9.75					22.11
15. Austria	16989	73	9.74	14.54	1.83	1.71	0.67	18.08
16. Singapore	16736	72	9.73	12.60	1.55	1.56	1.05	16.76
17. Italy	16724	72	9.72	17.17	1.40	1.03	0.41	20.01
18. Iceland	16324	70	9.70	18.02	1.80	2.72	2.94	25.48
19. UK	16302	70	9.70	11.26	2.72	6.34	0.95	21.27
20. Finland	15619	67	9.66	16.34	2.41	4.64	0.53	23.92
21. New Zealand	15502	67	9.65	12.32	2.40		4.08	18.80
22. Spain	12986	56	9.47	17.04	1.48	1.29	0.49	20.30
23. Israel	12783	55	9.46	20.11	1.42	0.68	2.12	24.33
24. Ireland	12259	53	9.41	18.09	3.93	11.09	1.38	34.49
25. Cyprus	11742	51	9.37	18.57	2.49	2.58	1.85	25.49
Mean (developed)	17540		9.76	14.90	2.35	2.79	1.20	20.39
Developing countries								
26. Taiwan	9850	42	9.20	23.34	1.39	3.26		27.99
27. Korea	9358	40	9.14	20.17	2.10	0.78	0.75	23.80
28. Portugal	9005	39	9.11	22.53	2.20	3.28		28.01
29. Greece	8658	37	9.07	28.44	3.83	2.94	1.14	36.35
30. Venezuela	8449	36	9.04	34.26	1.57	4.47		40.30
31. Mexico	7867	34	8.97	23.06	0.66	2.50	2.25	28.47
32. Malta	7625	33	8.94	21.76	2.59	3.60	2.55	30.50
33. Puerto Rico	7120	31	8.87	17.89	1.43	2.86		22.18
34. Fiji	5288	23	8.57	24.46	1.86	3.94	2.38	32.64
35. Thailand	5018	22	8.52	21.61	1.93	3.88	3.15	30.57
36. Colombia	4254	18	8.36	28.55	0.81	3.72	1.15	34.23
37. South Africa	3885	17	8.26	25.83	2.47	6.58	1.55	36.43
38. Ecuador	3420	15	8.14	32.26	1.80	2.97	1.59	38.62
39. Jamaica	2978	13	8.00	30.72	4.34	3.61	1.34	40.01
40. Sri Lanka	2783	12	7.93	50.07	5.85	2.73	0.56	59.21
41. Philippines	2172	9	7.68	52.57	2.77	2.37		57.71
42. Honduras	1792	8	7.49	41.21	0.66	3.15		45.02
43. India	1633	7	7.40	50.31	2.32	0.70	0.12	53.45
44. Zimbabwe	1479	6	7.30	13.41	9.67	7.01		30.09
Mean (less-developed)	5402		8.42	31.20	2.72	3.61	1.66	38.63
Mean (all countries)	12298		9.18	21.51	2.50	3.15	1.37	27.23

Source: GDP are from Penworld Tables by Heston and Summers. For Honduras, the entries are from 'The World Fact Book', www.odci.goc/cia/publications/factbook; and GDP and budget share entries for Puerto Rico are for 1985 and for Taiwan are for 1990. The countries are grouped into developed and developing countries using a cut-off of 1992 real per capita GDP at US$10,000.

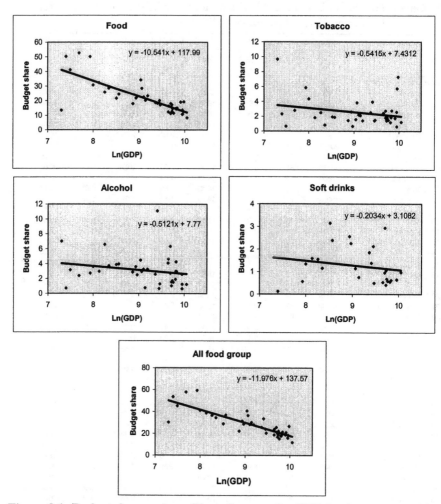

Figure 8.1 Budget share vs logarithm of per capita GDP for four commodities in 44 countries

Thailand, Venezuela and Zimbabwe. On the other hand the budget share for soft drinks is on the increase in a majority of countries.

Columns 2-5 of Table 8.3 presents the budget shares at sample means for each of the four commodities calculated as

$$\overline{w}_i = \frac{1}{T}\sum_{t=1}^{T} w_{it}, \qquad i=1(\text{food}), 2(\text{tobacco}), 3(\text{alcohol}), 4(\text{softdrinks})$$

Table 8.2 Budget shares at start and end of the sample periods for 43 countries (in percentages)

Country	Year	Food	Tobacco	Alcohol	Soft drinks	Country	Year	Food	Tobacco	Alcohol	Soft drinks
1. Australia	1974	17.84	2.46	6.07		23. Luxembourg	1970	23.81	1.75	1.91	0.64
	1998	14.77	1.84	4.11			1991	10.94	5.73	1.25	0.64
2. Austria	1964	26.37	2.83	5.95	0.71	24. Malta	1973	26.87	4.04	4.98	3.10
	1996	12.68	1.62	1.88	0.61		1996	20.98	2.62	2.95	2.30
3. Belgium	1986	17.57	1.69	1.86		25. Mexico	1988	27.02	0.70	2.60	1.78
	1997	12.97	1.55	1.78			2000	21.10	0.50	1.86	2.81
4. Canada	1961	18.82	3.09	3.76		26. Netherlands	1977	16.73	2.00	2.24	0.51
	1995	10.37	1.75	2.41			1996	10.70	1.45	1.44	0.55
5. Colombia	1972	33.75	1.76	3.38	0.81	27. New Zealand	1983	13.38	2.30		3.57
	1992	28.55	0.81	3.72	1.15		1995	10.93	1.99		3.58
6. Cyprus	1985	24.82	1.80	2.06		28. Norway	1989	17.27	2.24	2.83	
	1996	20.40	2.26	2.71			1997	15.52	2.51	2.58	
7. Denmark	1966	21.85	5.84	4.12	0.67	29. Philippines	1983	53.92	2.94	2.27	
	1995	14.33	2.31	2.53	0.82		1997	51.08	2.25	2.05	
8. Ecuador	1973	35.34	1.11	4.39	1.17	30. Portugal	1986	27.70	2.29	3.55	
	1993	31.11	1.75	3.20	1.60		1995	21.45	2.45	3.13	
9. Fiji	1977	28.75	2.54	4.33		31. Puerto Rico	1963	25.96	2.87	5.59	
	1991	26.84	1.86	3.94			1996	16.21	1.57	2.31	
10. Finland	1970	24.88	2.84	4.37	0.62	32. Singapore	1980	20.05	2.25	2.22	1.27
	1996	13.31	1.76	3.88	0.50		1997	10.33	1.36	1.46	1.06
11. France	1970	21.97	1.50	3.07	0.55	33. South Africa	1980	24.63	2.43	4.67	1.30
	1997	13.68	1.53	1.89	0.60		1997	25.70	2.51	6.59	1.66
12. Germany	1961	32.61	3.37			34. Spain	1980	24.97	1.17	1.25	0.42
	1994	18.02	1.76				1994	16.55	1.70	1.27	0.49
13. Greece	1980	35.37	2.38	2.31	1.00	35. Sri Lanka	1984	49.13	6.61	2.96	0.63
	1995	28.84	3.84	2.69	1.21		1996	46.65	6.80	2.98	1.49
14. Honduras	1973	41.25	0.65	3.12		36. Sweden	1963	23.53	2.89	3.89	0.72
	1982	41.21	0.66	3.15			1996	13.36	1.89	2.59	0.59
15. Hong Kong	1972	31.99	1.98	2.93		37. Switzerland	1961	25.14	10.08		
	1997	13.20	0.52	0.64			1993	18.84	7.10		
16. Iceland	1977	20.23	2.21	3.17	1.78	38. Taiwan	1988	26.35	2.03	3.81	
	1996	16.32	1.67	2.63	2.73		1997	22.27	1.03	2.94	
17. India	1981	54.05	2.46	1.34	0.07	39. Thailand	1980	37.18	2.70	4.12	2.79
	1996	48.18	2.94	0.60	0.19		1996	20.01	1.67	4.36	2.77
18. Ireland	1970	28.54	7.37	12.10	0.95	40. UK	1980	16.42	3.52	7.27	0.86
	1995	16.56	4.04	11.32	1.25		1996	10.45	2.56	6.07	0.83
19. Israel	1986	24.26	1.41	0.60	1.89	41. US	1961	17.47	2.16	1.97	0.24
	1997	18.23	1.35	0.96	1.96		1996	7.55	0.98	1.13	0.93
20. Italy	1970	31.81	2.82	3.22	0.40	42. Venezuela	1984	27.08	1.91	3.80	
	1997	15.08	1.70	0.92	0.41		1995	34.50	1.56	4.52	
21. Jamaica	1974	34.02	4.90	3.58	1.32	43. Zimbabwe	1975	25.02	8.89	1.98	
	1988	30.72	4.34	3.61	1.34		1987	13.41	9.67	7.01	
22. Korea	1988	24.83	3.11	0.92	0.58						
	2001	13.93	1.75	0.52	0.73						

for the 43 countries. As can be seen from Table 8.3, on average, consumers in the US (row 41) spend only about 12 percent of their income on food while those in India (row 17) and the Philippines (row 29) spend more than half of their income on food. Looking at the allocation of income to tobacco consumption from column 3 of the table, among the developed countries, the Swiss (about 9 percent) and, among the developing countries, the Zimbabwians (10 percent) and the Sri Lankans (6 percent) lead in allocating a significantly higher proportion of their income to tobacco consumption. Looking at the allocation of income to alcohol consumption presented in column 4, the Irish (about 12 percent) lead all other countries followed by the British (7 percent) and the South Africans (6 percent). For example, the Irish allocate about seven times the share allocated by the Americans on alcohol

Table 8.3 Budget shares and price and quantity growth rates for food, tobacco, alcohol and soft drinks

Country	Budget shares				Price log-change				Quantity log-change			
	Food	Tobacco	Alcohol	Softdrinks	Food	Tobacco	Alcohol	Softdrinks	Food	Tobacco	Alcohol	Softdrinks
(1)	(2)	(3)	(4)	(5)	(6)	(7)	(8)	(9)	(10)	(11)	(12)	(13)
1. Australia	15.64	1.99	4.94		6.66	10.96	7.51		1.28	-3.44	-0.41	
2. Austria	18.86	2.34	3.18	0.65	3.30	3.78	2.11	2.01	1.10	1.18	0.97	4.23
3. Belgium	14.90	1.51	1.80		0.91	5.62	1.61		0.52	-2.22	2.19	
4. Canada	14.10	2.37	3.32		4.84	6.60	4.94		0.47	-1.21	0.82	
5. Colombia	31.86	1.23	3.62	1.04	21.36	22.90	22.25	23.28	1.47	-3.11	1.89	2.14
6. Cyprus	21.92	2.21	2.46		4.00	5.37	4.71		2.40	4.88	5.96	
7. Denmark	17.42	3.64	3.72	0.64	5.78	5.10	4.03	6.45	0.77	-0.29	2.29	2.26
8. Ecuador	31.96	1.58	3.34	1.46	27.53	30.78	26.29	27.71	-0.04	-0.36	0.24	1.98
9. Fiji	27.69	2.28	3.77		7.24	9.09	7.71		-0.44	-4.05	-1.09	
10. Finland	19.60	2.24	4.28	0.52	6.00	9.03	7.09	7.58	0.72	-1.75	1.57	0.72
11. France	17.33	1.20	2.23	0.52	5.58	7.25	6.33	5.07	0.84	1.00	0.04	3.43
12. Germany	24.58	2.42			2.51	3.20			1.64	0.77		
13. Greece	31.96	3.25	2.64	1.05	14.67	18.35	15.52	14.40	0.87	1.76	2.39	3.79
14. Honduras	41.23	0.65	3.14		8.95	9.41	8.52		-0.16	-0.51	0.39	
15. Hong Kong	21.35	1.12	1.38		7.07	11.66	7.54		2.25	-4.16	-0.76	
16. Iceland	18.14	2.01	2.65	2.40	22.50	23.72	21.07	22.11	0.15	-1.41	1.74	3.93
17. India	50.82	2.20	0.98	0.11	8.15	10.51	7.53	7.94	1.32	0.92	-2.67	8.75
18. Ireland	23.23	4.61	11.45	1.30	7.79	9.87	9.27	8.49	1.48	-0.83	1.91	4.08
19. Israel	20.72	1.31	0.72	2.13	11.12	12.32	13.30	9.15	1.69	2.89	6.32	6.59
20. Italy	23.45	1.93	1.74	0.35	8.98	8.97	8.73	9.01	0.68	1.59	-0.92	3.56
21. Jamaica	31.98	4.59	3.72	1.22	14.91	17.57	17.05	18.87	-1.03	-3.83	-2.36	-4.13
22. Korea	18.39	2.08	0.70	0.72	5.76	6.77	5.07	2.86	0.95	-0.02	1.74	10.12
23. Luxembourg	17.12	4.55	1.64	0.54	5.16	8.80	4.88	4.19	-0.41	5.29	1.57	4.32
24. Malta	23.93	3.41	4.24	2.54	3.54	4.26	5.29	6.24	3.96	2.43	1.01	1.03
25. Mexico	23.27	0.63	2.33	2.33	15.82	16.66	14.38	20.18	1.96	0.39	2.65	3.47
26. Netherlands	13.31	1.69	1.77	0.55	0.78	4.98	1.87	0.59	0.94	-2.58	-0.11	3.88
27. New Zealand	12.31	2.27		3.85	5.18	12.21		5.46	0.93	-5.61		2.35
28. Norway	16.61	2.37	2.65		1.82	8.15	3.45		1.81	-1.76	0.33	
29. Philippines	53.14	2.90	2.27		10.45	10.33	10.04		1.02	-0.39	1.06	
30. Portugal	24.11	2.29	3.50		6.73	10.86	12.65		2.96	2.44	-1.52	
31. Puerto Rico	22.35	1.90	4.22		5.75	5.67	4.92		-0.22	-0.54	-0.63	
32. Singapore	15.19	1.89	1.83	1.16	1.29	6.65	2.85	1.32	0.11	-4.29	0.02	2.93
33. South Africa	25.19	2.31	5.86	1.46	13.28	14.29	12.88	13.97	-0.74	-1.80	1.44	-0.24
34. Spain	20.69	1.43	1.29	0.45	6.68	8.82	8.21	7.06	0.16	3.64	1.70	3.71
35. Sri Lanka	48.74	6.03	2.75	0.69	8.77	14.97	13.20	6.74	2.61	-2.92	-1.34	12.30
36. Sweden	18.69	2.34	3.90	0.60	5.63	7.27	6.31	4.54	0.60	-0.62	0.40	2.79
37. Switzerland	21.82	8.76			3.57	3.81			1.15	0.72		
38. Taiwan	23.71	1.41	3.26		4.07	0.86	1.22		4.44	1.96	6.27	
39. Thailand	26.09	2.25	3.86	3.06	4.09	3.75	4.45	2.75	1.56	2.74	5.43	6.73
40. UK	12.63	2.98	6.68	0.85	4.01	8.60	6.45	2.30	0.49	-3.27	-0.25	4.76
41. US	11.99	1.43	1.62	0.75	3.95	5.77	4.24	8.87	0.39	-1.29	0.90	1.77
42. Venezuela	32.03	1.82	3.99		32.52	29.87	31.90		0.40	-0.98	0.39	
43. Zimbabwe	18.87	9.96	5.17		12.59	16.93	26.79		-10.38	-8.83	-8.83	
Mean	23.70	2.64	3.22	1.22	8.40	10.52	9.60	9.23	0.76	-0.64	0.82	3.75

consumption. The budget share of soft drinks is lower compared to tobacco or alcohol in most countries, varying in the range of 0.1 percent (India) to 3.1 percent (Thailand) whereas the alcohol share varies in the range 0.7 percent (Korea and Israel) to 11.5 percent (Ireland), and the tobacco share varies in the range 0.6 percent (Mexico) to 10.0 percent (Zimbabwe). As can be seen from the last row, on average, people around the world allocate about 23.7 percent of their income on food, 2.6 percent on tobacco, 3.2 percent on alcohol and 1.2 percent on soft drinks.

We define price and quantity log-changes as

$$Dp_{it} = \ln p_{it} - \ln p_{it-1} \quad \text{and} \quad Dq_{it} = \ln q_{it} - \ln q_{it-1},$$

respectively, so that when multiplied by 100, these log-changes can be interpreted as percentage growth rates from year t-1 to t. Here and elsewhere *ln* refers to the natural logarithm.

Columns 6-9 of Table 8.3 present the annual mean log-changes in prices of each commodity

$$D\overline{p}_i = \frac{1}{T}\sum_{t=1}^{T} Dp_{it}, \qquad \text{i=1(food), 2(tobacco), 3(alcohol), 4(soft drinks)}$$

for the 43 countries. As can be seen, the average growth in food prices varies from 0.8 percent (Netherlands) per annum to 32.5 percent per annum (Venezuela). The price of tobacco has grown faster than the price of the other three commodities. On average, tobacco price has increased at various rates from 0.9 percent in Taiwan to 30.8 percent in Ecuador. Alcohol prices have also increased in most countries but to a somewhat lesser extent than tobacco. Prices of soft drinks have increased at a faster rate in the developing countries compared to the price increases in the developed countries. As can be seen from the last row, on average in all countries, the price of food has increased at a rate of 8.4 percent per annum, the price of tobacco at 10.5 percent per annum, the price alcohol at 9.6 percent per annum and soft drinks at a rate of 9.2 percent per annum.

Columns 10-13 of Table 8.3 present the mean log-changes in per capita consumption of each commodity

$$D\overline{q}_i = \frac{1}{T}\sum_{t=1}^{T} Dq_{it}, \qquad \text{i=1(food), 2(tobacco), 3(alcohol), 4(soft drinks)}$$

for the 43 countries. As can be seen, the growth rate in per capita consumption of food has fallen in a number of, mainly developing, countries (Ecuador, Fiji, Honduras, Jamaica, Luxembourg, Puerto Rico, South Africa and Zimbabwe). The average growth in consumption of food varies between –10.4 percent (Zimbabwe) per annum and 4.4 percent per annum (Taiwan). Tobacco consumption, on average, has fallen in 27 out of the 43 countries. The overall average tobacco consumption growth is negative (-.64 percent). This could be due to the increasing awareness about the harmful effects of smoking on one's health and the increasing number of tobacco control policies implemented by many governments during the last two decades. In most countries, alcohol consumption is on the increase with a cross-country average of 0.86 percent. As alcohol is not considered as harmful as long as it is consumed in moderation, this positive consumption growth is expected in contrast to tobacco, as any level of smoking is considered to be harmful to one's health. On average, soft drink consumption has grown at a moderate rate in most countries, with the exception of India, Israel, Korea, Sri Lanka and Thailand. It is interesting to see that soft drink consumption has grown at a faster rate in these developing countries than the developed countries, which could be due to globalization and multinational soft drinks companies investing in these developing countries in the last couple of decades. As can be seen from row 43, on average in all countries, the consumption of food, alcohol and soft drinks have increased at the rates of 0.8 percent, 0.8 percent and 3.8 percent, respectively, per annum while consumption of tobacco has fallen at a rate of 0.6 percent per annum.

Columns 2 and 3 of Table 8.4 present the mean Divisia price index,

$$\overline{DP} = \frac{1}{T} \sum_{t=1}^{T} DP_t ,$$

where

$$DP_t = \sum_{i=1}^{n} \overline{w}_{it} Dp_{it} , \qquad t=1,\dots,T;$$

and the mean Divisia volume index,

$$\overline{DQ} = \frac{1}{T} \sum_{t=1}^{T} DQ_t ,$$

where

$$DQ_t = \sum_{i=1}^{n} \overline{w}_{it} Dq_{it} , \quad t=1,\dots,T,$$

with $\overline{w}_{it} = \frac{1}{2}(w_{it} + w_{it-1})$ being the arithmetic average of the budget shares of commodity i in periods t and t-1. As can be seen, the overall prices grew positively and vary widely between developed and developing countries, between 2 percent (Singapore) and 31 percent (Venezuela), while overall consumption grew at a somewhat smaller rate, less than 7 percent, in most countries with an average overall consumption growth of 2.1 percent. This is reflected in the values of the Divisia price and quantity variances presented in columns 4 and 5 of the table. These two variances measure the degree to which the quantities and prices of the individual commodities change disproportionately. When all quantities and prices change proportionately, these two variances will vanish.

To measure the co-movement of prices and quantities, we present the Divisia price-quantity correlation

$$\rho_t = \frac{\Gamma_t}{\sqrt{K_t \Pi_t}} , \qquad t=1, \dots, T,$$

where $\Gamma_t = \sum_{i=1}^{n} \overline{w}_{it} [Dp_{it} - DP_t][Dq_{it} - DQ_t]$ is the Divisia price-quantity covariance between price and quantities. The last column of Table 8.4 presents the mean correlation for each country averaged over the whole sample period. As can be seen, with the exception of three countries, the correlations presented in the

Table 8.4 Divisia moments in 43 countries

	Country	Divisia price index $D\overline{P}$	Divisia quantity index $D\overline{Q}$	Divisia price variance $\overline{\Pi}$	Divisia quantity variance $\overline{K}$	Divisia price-quantity correlation $\overline{\rho}$
	(1)	(2)	(3)	(4)	(5)	(6)
1.	Australia	6.85	1.88	2.46	2.07	-0.59
2.	Austria	4.23	2.46	5.07	3.86	-0.02
3.	Belgium	2.60	1.59	2.06	1.31	-0.16
4.	Canada	4.82	2.24	2.84	2.58	-0.61
5.	Colombia	22.06	1.61	5.77	2.64	-0.32
6.	Cyprus	3.69	4.48	1.95	7.93	-0.52
7.	Denmark	6.33	1.68	3.12	3.78	-0.36
8.	Ecuador	26.66	1.46	15.99	4.98	-0.15
9.	Fiji	7.16	0.13	12.28	21.57	-0.68
10.	Finland	7.18	1.94	4.17	3.92	-0.31
11.	France	5.78	2.40	1.22	1.38	-0.32
12.	Germany	3.34	2.61	0.97	1.02	0.05
13.	Greece	15.50	1.40	4.58	3.58	-0.22
14.	Honduras	8.93	-0.12	0.76	0.69	-0.87
15.	Hong Kong	8.10	4.77	5.66	12.49	-0.24
16.	Iceland	22.78	1.00	5.56	9.90	-0.28
17.	India	7.96	2.28	2.37	6.54	-0.20
18.	Ireland	9.31	2.14	11.32	10.66	-0.23
19.	Israel	12.35	3.06	5.34	4.70	-0.40
20.	Italy	10.38	2.05	4.62	1.80	0.16
21.	Jamaica	13.95	0.67	37.61	50.06	-0.52
22.	Korea	6.46	4.70	3.21	6.20	0.08
23.	Luxembourg	5.61	2.84	7.02	8.90	-0.03
24.	Malta	4.08	4.50	8.62	31.98	-0.36
25.	Mexico	17.77	2.08	6.81	1.88	-0.32
26.	Netherlands	2.91	1.16	3.91	1.05	-0.22
27.	New Zealand	6.17	1.62	4.18	5.35	-0.48
28.	Norway	2.53	2.44	1.38	1.84	-0.50
29.	Philippines	10.90	0.94	4.02	0.46	-0.24
30.	Portugal	8.80	3.73	6.17	6.13	-0.18
31.	Puerto Rico	4.09	2.86	4.86	11.73	-0.60
32.	Singapore	2.32	2.99	1.89	7.93	-0.11
33.	South Africa	12.28	0.01	6.10	7.25	-0.37
34.	Spain	8.00	1.78	9.32	4.69	-0.12
35.	Sri Lanka	9.95	1.86	60.36	61.30	-0.37
36.	Sweden	6.81	1.14	2.89	1.91	-0.35
37.	Switzerland	4.12	1.51	1.07	0.68	-0.05
38.	Taiwan	3.52	6.85	1.93	4.17	-0.05
39.	Thailand	4.51	5.01	7.52	11.16	-0.16
40.	UK	5.05	2.27	1.92	3.34	-0.42
41.	US	4.50	2.24	5.12	1.79	-0.24
42.	Venezuela	30.84	-0.12	18.92	7.24	-0.24
43.	Zimbabwe	11.19	-3.78	275.20	241.75	-0.42
Mean		8.89	2.10	13.45	13.63	-0.29

All entries in columns 2 and 3 are to be divided by 100 and columns 4 and 5 by 10000.

table are negative with a cross-country average of -0.3. This reflects the tendency of the consumer to move away from those commodities having above average price increases.

The first 4 columns of Table 8.5 present the mean relative price log-changes $(D\overline{p}_i - D\overline{P})$ and the mean relative quantity log-changes $(D\overline{q}_i - D\overline{Q})$ for the 4 commodity groups for each of the 43 countries. The last row of the table presents the average of the averages over the 43 countries. As can be seen, on average, the relative prices of food and soft drinks has fallen by 0.5 percent and 0.4 percent per annum while relative prices of tobacco and alcohol have increased at a rate

Table 8.5 Relative prices and relative quantities for food, tobacco, alcohol and soft drinks in 43 countries

Country	Relative price				Relative quantity			
	Food	Tobacco	Alcohol	Soft drinks	Food	Tobacco	Alcohol	Soft drinks
(1)	(2)	(3)	(4)	(5)	(6)	(7)	(8)	(10)
1. Australia	-0.19	4.11	0.66		-0.59	-5.32	-2.29	
2. Austria	-0.93	-0.45	-2.12	-2.22	-1.36	-1.28	-1.49	1.77
3. Belgium	-1.69	3.01	-0.99		-1.08	-3.81	0.60	
4. Canada	0.02	1.78	0.12		-1.77	-3.46	-1.42	
5. Colombia	-0.69	0.84	0.20	1.22	-0.14	-4.73	0.28	0.53
6. Cyprus	0.31	1.68	1.02		-2.09	0.40	1.48	
7. Denmark	-0.54	-1.23	-2.29	0.12	-0.91	-1.98	0.61	0.58
8. Ecuador	0.86	4.11	-0.37	1.05	-1.50	-1.82	-1.22	0.52
9. Fiji	0.08	1.94	0.56		-0.58	-4.18	-1.22	
10. Finland	-1.19	1.84	-0.09	0.39	-1.22	-3.68	-0.37	-1.22
11. France	-0.20	1.47	0.55	-0.70	-1.56	-1.39	-2.36	1.03
12. Germany	-0.83	-0.14			-0.97	-1.83		
13. Greece	-0.83	2.84	0.02	-1.10	-0.53	0.36	0.99	2.39
14. Honduras	0.03	0.49	-0.41		-0.04	-0.39	0.50	
15. Hong Kong	-1.02	3.57	-0.56		-2.64	-22.87	1.98	
16. Iceland	-0.28	0.94	-1.71	-0.68	-0.85	-2.41	0.74	2.92
17. India	0.19	2.55	-0.43	-0.02	-0.96	-1.36	-4.95	6.47
18. Ireland	-1.52	0.56	-0.04	-0.82	-0.66	-2.96	-0.23	1.95
19. Israel	-1.24	-0.04	0.95	-3.20	-1.36	-0.37	3.26	3.53
20. Italy	-1.39	-1.41	-1.65	-1.36	-1.37	-0.46	-2.97	1.51
21. Jamaica	0.97	3.63	3.10	4.92	-1.70	-4.50	-3.04	-4.80
22. Korea	-0.70	0.32	-1.39	-3.60	-3.75	-4.73	-2.97	5.41
23. Luxembourg	-0.45	3.19	-0.73	-1.42	-3.26	2.45	-1.27	1.47
24. Malta	-0.53	0.19	1.21	2.16	-0.54	-2.07	-3.49	-3.47
25. Mexico	-1.94	-1.11	-3.38	2.42	-0.11	-1.69	0.57	1.40
26. Netherlands	-2.13	2.07	-1.04	-2.32	-0.22	-3.74	-1.28	2.72
27. New Zealand	-1.00	6.03		-0.71	-0.69	-7.23		0.73
28. Norway	-0.71	5.62	0.92		-0.63	-4.19	-2.10	
29. Philippines	-0.46	-0.57	-0.87		0.07	-1.34	0.12	
30. Portugal	-2.07	2.06	3.85		-0.77	-1.29	-5.25	
31. Puerto Rico	1.65	1.58	0.82		-3.08	-3.41	-3.50	
32. Singapore	-1.02	4.33	0.53	-0.99	-2.88	-7.28	-2.97	-0.06
33. South Africa	1.00	2.00	0.60	1.69	-0.75	-1.81	1.43	-0.25
34. Spain	-1.32	0.82	0.22	-0.94	-1.62	1.86	-0.08	1.92
35. Sri Lanka	-1.18	5.02	3.25	-3.21	0.75	-4.79	-3.20	10.44
36. Sweden	-1.18	0.46	-0.50	-2.27	-0.53	-1.76	-0.74	1.65
37. Switzerland	-0.55	-0.31			-0.35	-0.79		
38. Taiwan	0.55	-2.66	-2.30		-2.42	-4.90	-0.59	
39. Thailand	-0.42	-0.76	-0.06	-1.75	-3.45	-2.26	0.43	1.72
40. UK	-1.04	3.54	1.39	-2.76	-1.78	-5.54	-2.52	2.49
41. US	-0.55	1.27	-0.26	4.37	-1.85	-3.53	-1.33	-0.47
42. Venezuela	1.69	-0.97	1.07		0.51	-0.87	0.51	
43. Zimbabwe	1.40	5.75	15.60		-6.60	-5.05	-5.05	
Mean	-0.49	1.63	0.39	-0.43	-1.34	-3.07	-1.11	1.59

of 1.6 percent and 0.4 percent per annum, respectively. The relative consumption has fallen at a rate of 1.3 percent for food, 3.1 percent for tobacco and 1.1 percent for alcohol per annum while consumption of soft drinks has increased at a rate of 1.6 percent per annum.

In Section 7.4, we derived the finite-change version of the Working's model (4.6) under preference independence, which we reproduce here,

$$\overline{w}_{it}(Dq_{it} - DQ_t) = \beta_i DQ_t + \phi(\beta_i + \overline{w}_{it})(Dp_{it} - DP'_t), \quad i=1,\ldots,n, \quad (2.1)$$

where $DP'_t = \sum_{j=1}^{n}(\beta_j + \overline{w}_{jt})Dp_{jt}$. Under the assumption of unitary income elasticity of commodity i, we have

$$\eta_{it} = 1 + \frac{\beta_i}{\overline{w}_{it}} = 1,$$

which implies that $\beta_i = 0$. Therefore, under the assumption of unitary income elasticity, equation (2.1) for a particular country c ($=1,\ldots,43$) becomes

$$(Dq_{it}^c - DQ_t^c) = \phi^c(Dp_{it}^c - DP_t^c), \quad i=1,\ldots,n; \ t=1,\ldots,T, \quad (2.2)$$

where $DP_t^c = \sum_{j=1}^{n} \overline{w}_{jt}^c Dp_{jt}^c$ is the Divisia price index for country c. For a given i, if we regress the growth in relative consumption of i, $(Dq_{it}^c - DQ_t^c)$, against the growth in relative price of i, $(Dp_{it}^c - DP_t^c)$, for $t=1,\ldots,T$, the slope of the regression line can be interpreted as ϕ^c, the income flexibility.

In the above regression model (2.2), if we assume that $\phi^c (= \phi)$ is a constant for all countries, we can also perform a restricted pooled regression. For each country, if we sum both sides of (2.2) over $t=1,\ldots,T$ and divide by T, we obtain

$$(D\overline{q}_i^c - D\overline{Q}^c) = \phi(D\overline{p}_i^c - D\overline{P}^c), \quad i=1,\ldots,n; \ c=1,\ldots,43, \quad (2.3)$$

where $D\overline{q}_i^c = (1/T)\sum_t Dq_{it}^c$; $D\overline{Q}^c = (1/T)\sum_t DQ_t^c$; $D\overline{p}_i^c = (1/T)\sum_t Dp_{it}^c$ and $D\overline{P}^c = (1/T)\sum_t DP_t^c$. Figure 8.2 presents the plots of $(D\overline{q}_i^c - D\overline{Q}^c)$ against $(D\overline{p}_i^c - D\overline{P}^c)$ for $c=1,\ldots,43$ for each commodity i. As can be seen, there is a strong negative relationship between relative prices and relative consumption. The slope of each plot can be interpreted as the respective income flexibility for the 4 commodities. That is, the estimated income flexibility of food, tobacco, alcohol and soft drinks are -0.44, -0.66, -0.32 and -0.92, respectively, with an average income flexibility of -0.6, which is well in agreement with many previous findings, Theil and Suhm (1981), Theil and Clements (1987), Selvanathan (1993) and Selvanathan and Selvanathan (2003).

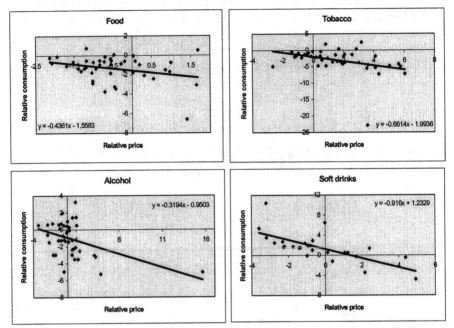

Figure 8.2 Relative quantity against relative price for food, tobacco, alcohol and soft drinks, 43 countries

Table 8.6 presents a summary frequency distribution (in percentages) of joint signs of relative consumption and relative prices for the raw data of the 43 countries. For example, in Canada, relative prices and consumption move in the same direction for 13 + 11 = 24 percent of the time, while they move in the opposite directions 38 + 39 = 77 percent of the time. Column 6 of the table presents the percentage of relative prices and relative consumption moving in the opposite direction. As can be seen, in 39 of the 43 countries, a majority of relative prices and their corresponding relative consumption move in the opposite direction. On average, 60 percent of the relative prices and relative consumption move in the opposite direction. These results clearly support the *law of demand*, which states that, all other things being equal, an increase in the relative price of a commodity causes its consumption to fall.

8.3   Elasticities from Double-Log Demand Equations

In Chapter 6, we introduced the double-log demand equations as an example of the demand equations without specifying the form of the utility function. In this section, we use them to obtain preliminary estimates for the income and price elasticities. In Section 8.5, we use the differential demand systems introduced in

Table 8.6 Frequencies of joint signs of relative consumption and relative price changes, 43 countries

	Country (1)	Positive consumption		Negative consumption		Opposite signs (3)+(4) (6)
		Positive (2)	Negative (3)	Positive (4)	Negative (5)	
1.	Australia	17	28	44	11	72
2.	Austria	19	30	24	27	54
3.	Belgium	16	27	36	20	63
4.	Canada	13	38	39	11	77
5.	Colombia	22	27	35	16	62
6.	Cyprus	14	41	32	14	73
7.	Denmark	15	41	25	19	66
8.	Ecuador	24	27	25	24	52
9.	Fiji	20	29	43	9	72
10.	Finland	22	30	32	17	62
11.	France	14	24	38	24	62
12.	Germany	24	25	22	28	47
13.	Greece	19	25	33	23	58
14.	Honduras	6	39	44	11	83
15.	Hong Kong	22	25	31	22	56
16.	Iceland	18	26	35	21	61
17.	India	24	36	21	19	57
18.	Ireland	21	31	28	20	59
19.	Israel	18	31	27	24	58
20.	Italy	17	28	23	32	51
21.	Jamaica	16	34	37	13	71
22.	Korea	14	32	22	32	54
23.	Luxembourg	19	20	26	35	46
24.	Malta	17	28	33	22	61
25.	Mexico	22	27	28	23	55
26.	Netherlands	25	29	24	21	53
27.	New Zealand	17	33	31	19	64
28.	Norway	16	25	41	19	66
29.	Philippines	14	29	25	32	54
30.	Portugal	31	11	22	36	33
31.	Puerto Rico	17	30	38	15	68
32.	Singapore	21	20	28	31	48
33.	South Africa	25	28	32	15	60
34.	Spain	20	23	29	29	52
35.	Sri Lanka	22	33	32	13	65
36.	Sweden	15	33	33	18	66
37.	Switzerland	18	34	31	17	65
38.	Taiwan	11	25	28	36	53
39.	Thailand	19	34	23	25	57
40.	UK	19	25	34	23	59
41.	US	16	30	28	26	58
42.	Venezuela	20	36	27	16	63
43.	Zimbabwe	8	33	42	17	75
	Mean	18	29	31	22	60

Chapters 6 and 7 to obtain final estimates for the demand elasticities and then compare the two sets of estimates.

The double-log demand equation (2.1) given in Section 6.2 (with cross-price elasticities set to zero) for commodity i in finite-change form can be written as

$$Dq_{it} = \alpha_i + \eta_i DQ_t + \gamma_i [Dp_{it} - DP_t], \qquad i=1,\dots,n, \qquad (3.1)$$

where $DQ_t = DM_t - DP_t$; α_i is an autonomous trend term; η_i is the income elasticity of commodity i; γ_i is the Slutsky own-price elasticity. It is worth noting that this double-log demand equation includes only the own-relative price and not other prices. Equation (3.1) can also be considered as the preference independent version of the Rotterdam demand system given by equation (2.13) of Section 7.2, where both sides of (2.13) has been divided by $\overline{w}_{it}$ so that the coefficients of the model become the elasticities, income elasticity $\eta_i = \theta_i / \overline{w}_{it}$ and own-price elasticity $\gamma_i = \phi\theta_i / \overline{w}_{it}$; and DP_t' is replaced with DP_t. We estimate (3.1) by least squares (LS) for each country separately.

Tables 8.7-8.8 present the estimates for the income elasticity (η_i) and own-price elasticity (γ_i), respectively, for each commodity. The last row of the table presents the elasticities for each commodity averaged over the 43 countries. As can be seen from Table 8.7, all the income elasticites for food, except for Fiji, Honduras and Philippines, are less than one with a cross-country average of 0.6, indicating that food is a necessity for consumers around the world. The income elasticity of tobacco is also positive and less than one in all but 10 countries with a cross-country average of 0.64, indicating that tobacco is also considered to be a necessity by world consumers. The income elasticity of alcohol is near or greater than unity in about half of the countries. The average income elasticity of alcohol is about unity, indicating that alcohol is neither a luxury nor a necessity in many countries. The income elasticity of soft drinks is above unity in most countries with a cross-country average of 1.14, indicating that soft drinks are a luxury.

In Table 8.8, most of the own-price elasticities (196 out of 207) are negative as they should be. On average, most of the price elasticities are negative and less than one in absolute value, indicating that demand for food, tobacco, alcohol and soft drinks are all price inelastic. The average own-price elasticities across countries are -0.34 (for food), -0.58 (for tobacco), -0.50 (for alcohol) and -0.55 (for soft drinks).

8.4 Testing Demand Theory Hypotheses

Consider the absolute price version of the Rotterdam model from equation (2.5) of Section 7.2, which we reproduce here:

$$\overline{w}_{it} Dq_{it} = \theta_i DQ_t + \sum_{j=1}^{n} \pi_{ij} Dp_{jt}, \qquad i=1,\dots,n,$$

Table 8.7 Income elasticities for 4 commodities based on double-log demand equations, 43 countries (standard errors are in parentheses)

	Country (1)	Food (2)		Tobacco (3)		Alcohol (4)		Soft drinks (5)		Other (6)	
1.	Australia	0.704	(0.220)	0.346	(0.346)	1.113	(0.310)			1.085	(0.060)
2.	Austria	0.424	(0.162)	0.718	(0.223)	0.241	(0.321)	0.687	(0.401)	1.205	(0.047)
3.	Belgium	0.712	(0.242)	-0.813	(0.835)	0.472	(1.639)			1.095	(0.066)
4.	Canada	0.674	(0.087)	0.485	(0.187)	0.950	(0.172)			1.082	(0.019)
5.	Colombia	0.844	(0.135)	0.003	(0.868)	0.551	(0.409)	1.467	(0.803)	1.115	(0.075)
6.	Cyprus	0.456	(0.143)	1.628	(0.700)	1.744	(0.450)			1.123	(0.043)
7.	Denmark	0.352	(0.142)	0.626	(0.246)	0.645	(0.228)	1.158	(0.376)	1.193	(0.036)
8.	Ecuador	0.674	(0.157)	2.448	(0.436)	1.525	(0.277)	1.059	(0.562)	1.127	(0.097)
9.	Fiji	1.164	(0.142)	0.362	(0.918)	1.483	(0.411)			0.940	(0.063)
10.	Finland	0.420	(0.114)	0.659	(0.381)	0.937	(0.207)	0.984	(0.309)	1.170	(0.039)
11.	France	0.348	(0.034)	0.455	(0.127)	0.085	(0.123)	1.239	(0.282)	1.196	(0.009)
12.	Germany	0.730	(0.078)	0.662	(0.258)					1.123	(0.026)
13.	Greece	0.192	(0.270)	1.372	(0.787)	1.908	(0.590)	2.181	(1.055)	1.362	(0.140)
14.	Honduras	1.004	(0.010)	1.207	(0.265)	0.982	(0.030)			0.995	(0.006)
15.	Hong Kong	0.319	(0.148)	-0.146	(0.517)	1.380	(0.490)			1.252	(0.049)
16.	Iceland	0.338	(0.168)	0.608	(0.191)	0.603	(0.371)	1.428	(0.385)	1.171	(0.056)
17.	India	0.787	(0.139)	1.787	(0.789)	0.375	(0.881)	3.084	(0.642)	1.225	(0.172)
18.	Ireland	0.324	(0.144)	0.238	(0.271)	0.609	(0.180)	0.953	(0.423)	1.430	(0.074)
19.	Israel	0.554	(0.077)	0.295	(0.349)	1.962	(0.789)	1.196	(0.455)	1.120	(0.037)
20.	Italy	0.541	(0.098)	0.037	(0.374)	0.759	(0.237)	1.397	(0.483)	1.169	(0.033)
21.	Jamaica	0.684	(0.190)	0.745	(0.256)	0.830	(0.475)	2.090	(0.437)	1.173	(0.094)
22.	Korea	0.688	(0.094)	0.216	(0.221)	0.932	(0.198)	0.684	(0.589)	1.090	(0.023)
23.	Luxembourg	0.302	(0.254)	1.537	(1.675)	0.292	(0.948)	-0.524	(1.064)	1.186	(0.107)
24.	Malta	0.416	(0.178)	0.855	(0.270)	1.744	(0.501)	-0.823	(0.408)	1.224	(0.057)
25.	Mexico	0.679	(0.107)	0.229	(0.345)	1.513	(0.268)	0.982	(0.259)	1.085	(0.034)
26.	Netherlands	0.384	(0.120)	0.956	(0.228)	1.199	(0.545)	1.181	(0.587)	1.092	(0.029)
27.	New Zealand	0.501	(0.225)	0.677	(0.595)			0.522	(0.658)	1.121	(0.052)
28.	Norway	0.348	(0.346)	0.430	(0.753)	2.359	(0.577)			1.090	(0.047)
29.	Philippines	1.027	(0.066)	0.585	(0.309)	0.839	(0.195)			1.003	(0.069)
30.	Portugal	0.319	(0.332)	0.384	(0.806)	0.214	(1.128)			1.298	(0.169)
31.	Puerto Rico	0.967	(0.175)	0.988	(0.354)	1.370	(0.287)			0.974	(0.063)
32.	Singapore	0.848	(0.137)	0.086	(0.317)	0.576	(0.237)	0.423	(0.359)	1.079	(0.030)
33.	South Africa	0.659	(0.139)	0.621	(0.451)	1.432	(0.476)	0.775	(0.537)	1.110	(0.077)
34.	Spain	0.156	(0.144)	0.669	(0.964)	0.945	(0.570)	1.956	(0.734)	1.197	(0.027)
35.	Sri Lanka	0.602	(0.245)	0.527	(1.151)	0.445	(1.180)	1.014	(2.861)	1.395	(0.260)
36.	Sweden	0.401	(0.090)	0.518	(0.228)	1.114	(0.268)	0.935	(0.415)	1.155	(0.031)
37.	Switzerland	0.969	(0.101)	1.126	(0.149)					1.007	(0.036)
38.	Taiwan	0.634	(0.071)	0.329	(0.243)	0.882	(0.137)			1.153	(0.026)
39.	Thailand	0.389	(0.193)	0.545	(0.488)	2.109	(0.630)	0.978	(0.391)	1.058	(0.082)
40.	UK	0.401	(0.109)	0.173	(0.189)	0.799	(0.265)	1.265	(0.447)	1.140	(0.032)
41.	US	0.272	(0.170)	0.466	(0.327)	0.740	(0.267)	1.806	(0.613)	1.128	(0.026)
42.	Venezuela	0.492	(0.236)	0.563	(0.479)	1.297	(0.462)			1.312	(0.120)
43.	Zimbabwe	0.521	(0.298)	1.185	(0.135)	1.616	(0.338)			1.015	(0.100)
Mean		0.563	(0.037)	0.637	(0.085)	1.039	(0.087)	1.115	(0.152)	1.146	(0.016)

Table 8.8 Own-price elasticities for 4 commodities based on double-log demand equations, 43 countries (standard errors are in parentheses)

Country (1)	Food (2)		Tobacco (3)		Alcohol (4)		Soft drinks (5)		Other (6)	
1. Australia	-0.277	(0.129)	-0.432	(0.079)	-0.715	(0.147)			-0.355	(0.146)
2. Austria	-0.298	(0.119)	-0.613	(0.133)	-0.221	(0.135)	-0.362	(0.178)	-0.324	(0.128)
3. Belgium	-0.265	(0.120)	-1.212	(0.485)	-0.463	(1.159)			-0.321	(0.181)
4. Canada	-0.569	(0.087)	-0.349	(0.062)	-0.831	(0.182)			-0.680	(0.108)
5. Colombia	-0.363	(0.077)	-0.678	(0.256)	-0.199	(0.188)	-0.162	(0.313)	-0.303	(0.082)
6. Cyprus	-0.748	(0.399)	-0.558	(0.624)	-0.321	(0.549)			-0.801	(0.408)
7. Denmark	-0.366	(0.131)	-0.513	(0.175)	-0.814	(0.221)	-0.984	(0.272)	-0.387	(0.133)
8. Ecuador	-0.151	(0.090)	-0.245	(0.099)	-0.161	(0.186)	-0.163	(0.239)	-0.178	(0.106)
9. Fiji	-0.581	(0.140)	-1.762	(0.251)	-1.045	(0.173)			-0.439	(0.148)
10. Finland	-0.243	(0.114)	-0.530	(0.189)	-0.643	(0.116)	-0.785	(0.198)	-0.191	(0.130)
11. France	-0.130	(0.063)	-0.338	(0.057)	-0.170	(0.111)	-0.542	(0.350)	-0.215	(0.069)
12. Germany	-0.248	(0.161)	-0.427	(0.119)					-0.351	(0.141)
13. Greece	-0.463	(0.205)	-0.347	(0.164)	-0.322	(0.272)	-0.118	(0.384)	-0.475	(0.248)
14. Honduras	-0.812	(0.195)	-0.895	(0.221)	-0.864	(0.039)			-1.073	(0.136)
15. Hong Kong	-0.729	(0.247)	-0.668	(0.175)	-0.294	(0.203)			-0.680	(0.212)
16. Iceland	-0.222	(0.257)	-0.311	(0.124)	-0.435	(0.270)	-0.533	(0.404)	-0.430	(0.305)
17. India	0.334	(0.446)	-0.836	(0.381)	-1.241	(0.462)	-0.856	(0.132)	0.334	(0.546)
18. Ireland	-0.191	(0.147)	-0.386	(0.174)	-0.222	(0.162)	-0.597	(0.185)	-0.133	(0.157)
19. Israel	-0.084	(0.113)	-0.630	(0.112)	-0.941	(0.530)	-0.937	(0.354)	-0.245	(0.194)
20. Italy	-0.183	(0.070)	-0.272	(0.105)	-0.128	(0.093)	0.266	(0.338)	-0.170	(0.058)
21. Jamaica	-0.679	(0.177)	-1.305	(0.140)	-0.880	(0.357)	-0.632	(0.331)	-0.805	(0.146)
22. Korea	-0.070	(0.181)	-0.362	(0.143)	-0.857	(0.282)	-1.381	(0.634)	-0.115	(0.145)
23. Luxembourg	-0.125	(0.233)	-0.328	(0.149)	-0.875	(0.415)	-0.457	(0.433)	-0.389	(0.201)
24. Malta	-1.006	(0.324)	-1.376	(0.227)	-1.212	(0.510)	-1.406	(0.217)	-0.861	(0.255)
25. Mexico	-0.080	(0.134)	-0.257	(0.091)	-0.313	(0.217)	-0.459	(0.176)	-0.079	(0.136)
26. Netherlands	-0.038	(0.054)	-0.425	(0.088)	-0.212	(0.246)	-0.332	(0.236)	-0.013	(0.062)
27. New Zealand	-0.700	(0.219)	-0.366	(0.210)			-1.141	(0.285)	-0.625	(0.199)
28. Norway	-0.069	(0.419)	-1.697	(0.308)	-0.435	(0.401)			-0.343	(0.203)
29. Philippines	-0.144	(0.079)	-0.030	(0.162)	0.017	(0.141)			-0.135	(0.070)
30. Portugal	0.410	(0.561)	-0.477	(0.530)	-0.016	(0.291)			0.545	(0.718)
31. Puerto Rico	-0.505	(0.204)	-0.812	(0.232)	-1.376	(0.263)			-0.302	(0.233)
32. Singapore	0.006	(0.429)	-0.561	(0.516)	0.154	(0.510)	-0.999	(0.588)	0.059	(0.371)
33. South Africa	-0.590	(0.121)	-0.108	(0.266)	-0.535	(0.507)	-0.230	(0.565)	-0.649	(0.170)
34. Spain	-0.217	(0.071)	-0.709	(0.137)	-0.488	(0.117)	-0.481	(0.156)	-0.020	(0.064)
35. Sri Lanka	-0.410	(0.176)	-0.317	(0.443)	0.355	(1.039)	-0.395	(0.451)	-0.625	(0.151)
36. Sweden	-0.274	(0.065)	-0.609	(0.111)	-0.529	(0.218)	-0.133	(0.144)	-0.309	(0.094)
37. Switzerland	-0.445	(0.101)	-0.346	(0.166)					-0.401	(0.102)
38. Taiwan	-0.323	(0.237)	0.149	(0.557)	-0.128	(0.256)			-0.465	(0.305)
39. Thailand	0.064	(0.156)	-0.825	(0.226)	-0.902	(0.323)	-0.374	(0.340)	0.166	(0.180)
40. UK	-0.334	(0.149)	-0.496	(0.132)	-0.112	(0.378)	-0.380	(0.221)	-0.066	(0.232)
41. US	-0.264	(0.084)	-0.473	(0.145)	-0.193	(0.128)	-0.187	(0.045)	-0.400	(0.101)
42. Venezuela	-0.037	(0.192)	-0.138	(0.146)	-0.907	(0.342)			-0.181	(0.165)
43. Zimbabwe	-2.366	(0.999)	-1.165	(0.097)	-0.667	(0.062)			-1.085	(0.163)
Mean	-0.344	(0.065)	-0.582	(0.063)	-0.504	(0.064)	-0.547	(0.077)	-0.338	(0.051)

where θ_i is the marginal share of commodity i and π_{ij} is the Slutsky coefficient. In this section we consider the demand theory hypotheses, demand homogeneity, given by

$$\sum_{j=1}^{n} \pi_{ij} = 0, \qquad\qquad i=1,...,n,$$

Slutsky symmetry, given by

$$\pi_{ij} = \pi_{ji}, \qquad\qquad i,j=1,...,n,$$

and preference independent utility structure, which can be written as

$$\pi_{ij} = \phi\theta_i (\delta_{ij} - \theta_j), \qquad\qquad i,j=1,...,n.$$

In Section 7.6, we discussed the procedures that can be used to test hypotheses such as demand homogeneity, Slutsky symmetry and preference independence. In this section, we apply these procedures to test the three hypotheses using the data for the 5 commodity groups, namely, food, tobacco, alcohol, soft drinks and all other goods in 43 countries.

Tests of Demand Homogeneity

The test statistic for testing homogeneity is given by equation (6.2) of Section 7.6, which we reproduce here,

$$\Psi_H = \frac{(R\hat{\gamma})' S^{-1} (R\hat{\gamma})}{a' (X' X)^{-1} a}, \qquad\qquad (4.1)$$

where $R = I_{n-1} \otimes a'$; $a = [0 \; 1 \; ... \; 1]'$ is a $(n+1)$-vector; $\hat{\gamma}$ is the LS estimator of the demand equation given by $\hat{\gamma} = [I \otimes (X' X)^{-1} X']y$; $y = [y_i]$, $y_i = [y_{it}]$ is a T-vector, $y_{it} = \overline{w}_{it} Dq_{it}$; X is a $T \times (n+1)$ matrix whose t^{th} row is $x'_t = [DQ_t \; Dp_{1t} \; ... \; Dp_{nt}]$; $\hat{\gamma}$ is the LS estimator of $\gamma = [\gamma_i]$, $\gamma_i = [\theta_i \; \pi_{i1} \; ... \; \pi_{in}]'$; and S is the LS residual moment matrix.

We now calculate the test statistic (4.1) to test homogeneity. The results from the homogeneity test are shown in Table 8.9. The observed values of the test statistic are presented in column 2 of the table. The critical values at the 5 percent level of significance for the asymptotic χ^2-test are presented in column 3. Comparing column 2 with column 3, we see that homogeneity is acceptable for about two-thirds of the 43 countries. These results are consistent with the results from most previous studies where the asymptotic test was used to test homogeneity (e.g., Selvanathan, 1993; Theil and Clements, 1987; and Chen, 2001), which is biased towards rejecting homogeneity.

Table 8.9 Testing homogeneity in 43 countries

Country	Asymptotic χ^2 test			Laitinen's exact test		
	Data-based Ψ_H	Critical $\chi^2(n\text{-}1,.05)$	Conclusion	Data-based T^2	Critical $F(n\text{-}1,T\text{-}2n,\alpha)$	Conclusion
(1)	(2)	(3)	(4)	(5)	(6)	(7)
1. Australia	8.94	$\chi^2(3)$=11.34*	Do not rej*	2.65	F(3,16)=3.24	Do not rej
2. Austria	2.90	$\chi^2(4)$=9.49	Do not rej	0.64	F(4,22)=2.82	Do not rej
3. Belgium	1.93	$\chi^2(3)$=7.82	Do not rej	0.39	F(3,3)=9.28	Do not rej
4. Canada	1.31	$\chi^2(3)$=7.82	Do not rej	0.40	F(3,26)=2.98	Do not rej
5. Colombia	0.29	$\chi^2(4)$=9.49	Do not rej	0.05	F(4,10)=3.48	Do not rej
6. Cyprus	7.03	$\chi^2(3)$=7.82	Do not rej	1.41	F(3, 3)=9.28	Do not rej
7. Denmark	14.68	$\chi^2(4)$=9.49	Reject	3.17	F(4,19)=4.50*	Do not rej*
8. Ecuador	14.08	$\chi^2(4)$=9.49	Reject	2.71	F(4,10)=3.48	Do not rej
9. Fiji	3.25	$\chi^2(3)$=7.82	Do not rej	0.81	F(3,6)=4.76	Do not rej
10. Finland	9.04	$\chi^2(4)$=9.49	Do not rej	1.90	F(4,16)=3.01	Do not rej
11. France	12.32	$\chi^2(4)$=13.28*	Do not rej*	2.62	F(4,17)=2.96	Do not rej
12. Germany	2.02	$\chi^2(2)$=5.99	Do not rej	0.97	F(2,27)=3.35	Do not rej
13. Greece	9.00	$\chi^2(4)$=9.49	Do not rej	1.50	F(4,5)=5.19	Do not rej
14. Honduras	17.48	$\chi^2(3)$=7.82	Reject	2.91	F(3,1)=215.7	Do not rej
15. Hong Kong	11.44	$\chi^2(3)$=7.82	Reject	3.41	F(3,17)= 5.19*	Do not rej*
16. Iceland	7.90	$\chi^2(4)$=9.49	Do not rej	1.48	F(4,9)=3.63	Do not rej
17. India	4.15	$\chi^2(4)$=9.49	Do not rej	0.69	F(4,5)= 5.19	Do not rej
18. Ireland	5.39	$\chi^2(4)$=9.49	Do not rej	1.12	F(4,15)=3.06	Do not rej
19. Israel	153.24	$\chi^2(4)$=9.49	Reject	15.32	F(4,1)=224.6	Do not rej
20. Italy	8.25	$\chi^2(4)$=9.49	Do not rej	1.75	F(4,17)=2.96	Do not rej
21. Jamaica	2.70	$\chi^2(4)$=9.49	Do not rej	0.39	F(4,4)=6.39	Do not rej
22. Korea	5.75	$\chi^2(4)$=9.49	Do not rej	0.72	F(4,3)=9.12	Do not rej
23. Luxembourg	16.16	$\chi^2(4)$=9.49	Reject	3.17	F(4,11)=3.36	Do not rej
24. Malta	8.81	$\chi^2(4)$=9.49	Do not rej	1.80	F(4,13)=3.18	Do not rej
25. Mexico	147.83	$\chi^2(4)$=9.49	Reject	14.78	F(4,2)=19.25	Do not rej
26. Netherlands	4.12	$\chi^2(4)$=9.49	Do not rej	0.77	F(4,9)=3.63	Do not rej
27. New Zealand	8.08	$\chi^2(3)$= 11.34*	Do not rej*	1.80	F(3,4)= 6.59	Do not rej
28. Norway	2689.62	$\chi^2(3)$=7.82	Reject	298.63	F(3,1)=5403*	Do not rej*
29. Philippines	2.75	$\chi^2(3)$=7.82	Do not rej	0.71	F(3,6)=4.76	Do not rej
30. Portugal	0.22	$\chi^2(3)$=7.82	Do not rej	0.03	F(3,1)=215.7	Do not rej
31. Puerto Rico	9.30	$\chi^2(3)$=11.34*	Do not rej*	2.88	F(3,25)=2.99	Do not rej
32. Singapore	13.87	$\chi^2(4)$=9.49	Reject	2.43	F(4,7)=4.12	Do not rej
33. South Africa	15.67	$\chi^2(4)$=9.49	Reject	2.74	F(4,7)=4.12	Do not rej
34. Spain	23.35	$\chi^2(4)$=9.49	Reject	3.34	F(4,4)=6.39	Do not rej
35. Sri Lanka	76.36	$\chi^2(4)$=9.49	Reject	7.64	F(4,2)=19.25	Do not rej
36. Sweden	8.70	$\chi^2(4)$=9.49	Do not rej	1.92	F(4,23)=2.80	Do not rej
37. Switzerland	0.18	$\chi^2(2)$=5.99	Do not rej	0.08	F(2,26)=3.37	Do not rej
38. Taiwan	44.06	$\chi^2(3)$=7.82	Reject	7.34	F(3,1)=215.7	Do not rej
39. Thailand	2.83	$\chi^2(4)$=9.49	Do not rej	0.47	F(4,6)=4.53	Do not rej
40. UK	24.58	$\chi^2(4)$=9.49	Reject	4.10	F(4,6)=4.53	Do not rej
41. US	2.24	$\chi^2(4)$=9.49	Do not rej	0.50	F(4,25)=2.76	Do not rej
42. Venezuela	5.93	$\chi^2(3)$=7.82	Do not rej	1.19	F(3,3)=9.28	Do not rej
43. Zimbabwe	5.52	$\chi^2(3)$=7.82	Do not rej	1.31	F(3,4)=6.59	Do not rej

The level of significance α = 0.05. A * denotes critical value and conclusion at α = 0.01.

Now we employ Laitinen's (1978) exact test discussed in Section 7.6 to test the hypothesis of demand homogeneity. As pointed out earlier, Laitinen showed that Ψ_H is distributed as a Hotelling's T^2, which itself is distributed as a constant multiple $(n\text{-}1)(T\text{-}n\text{-}2)/(T\text{-}2n)$ of $F(n\text{-}1,T\text{-}2n)$. The observed and critical values based on exact distributions are presented in columns 5 and 6 of Table 8.9. Comparing the observed values of the test statistic in column 5 with the critical values in column 6, we can see that homogeneity is now acceptable for all countries. These results support the view of Barten (1977) that the rejection of homogeneity is due to the failure of the asymptotic test.

Testing Slutsky Symmetry

The test statistic for testing symmetry is given by equation (6.4) of Section 7.6, which we reproduce here,

$$\Psi_S = (R\hat{\gamma}^H)'\{R[S \otimes (X^{H'}X^H)^{-1}]R'\}^{-1}(R\hat{\gamma}^H), \tag{4.2}$$

which has an asymptotic χ^2 distribution with q ($=\frac{1}{2}(n-1)(n-2)$) degrees of freedom. Here $\hat{\gamma}^H = [\hat{\gamma}_i^H]$, $\hat{\gamma}_i^H$ is the LS estimator of $\gamma_i^H = [\theta_i\ \pi_{i1}\ \ldots\ \pi_{in-1}]'$ for i=1,...,n; and X^H is a $T \times n$ matrix whose t^{th} row is $x_t^H = [DQ_t\ (Dp_{1t} - Dp_{nt})\ \ldots\ (Dp_{n-1,t} - Dp_{nt})]'$. Using the test statistic (4.2) with the data from the 43 countries, we test symmetry and the results are shown in Table 8.10. A comparison of the observed values in column 2 with the χ^2-critical values for the asymptotic test presented in column 3 shows that Slutsky symmetry is acceptable for all countries, except four countries, Italy, Korea, Venezuela and Zimbabwe. That is, the symmetry hypothesis is acceptable in more than 90 percent of the countries.

Testing Preference Independence

Under preference independence, the Rotterdam model takes the form (see (2.13) in Section 7.2),

$$\overline{w}_{it} Dq_{it} = \theta_i DQ_t + \phi\theta_i(Dp_{it} - DP'_t), \qquad i=1,...,n, \tag{4.3}$$

where $DP'_t = \sum_{j=1}^n \theta_j Dp_{jt}$ and the coefficients ϕ and θ_i are specified as constants.

In this section, we test the hypothesis of preference independence, initially using a likelihood ratio test, which is an asymptotic test. We then check the validity of these results using Monte Carlo simulations proposed in Selvanathan (1987).

Asymptotic test

We now test the preference independence hypothesis using the likelihood ratio test. The test statistic has an asymptotic χ^2 distribution with $k = \frac{1}{2}n(n-1)-1$ degrees of freedom. The results for this test for the 43 countries are presented in columns 2-4 of Table 8.11. As can be seen, based on the asymptotic test, preference independence is not supported by the data for a number of countries at the 5 percent level. This result is consistent with previous studies which uses the asymptotic test (for example, see Barten, 1977). Below, we shall investigate this matter further.

Table 8.10 Testing symmetry in 43 countries

Country (1)	Data-based Ψ_s (2)	Critical $\chi^2(q)$ (3)	Conclusion (4)
1. Australia	1.82	$\chi^2(3)=7.82$	Do not reject
2. Austria	6.79	$\chi^2(6)=12.59$	Do not reject
3. Belgium	2.15	$\chi^2(3)=7.82$	Do not reject
4. Canada	2.18	$\chi^2(3)=7.82$	Do not reject
5. Colombia	4.70	$\chi^2(6)=12.59$	Do not reject
6. Cyprus	5.35	$\chi^2(3)=7.82$	Do not reject
7. Denmark	3.37	$\chi^2(6)=12.59$	Do not reject
8. Ecuador	2.68	$\chi^2(6)=12.59$	Do not reject
9. Fiji	1.16	$\chi^2(3)=7.82$	Do not reject
10. Finland	5.54	$\chi^2(6)=12.59$	Do not reject
11. France	1.88	$\chi^2(6)=12.59$	Do not reject
12. Germany	0.34	$\chi^2(1)=3.84$	Do not reject
13. Greece	13.19	$\chi^2(6)=16.81^*$	Do not reject*
14. Honduras	0.54	$\chi^2(3)=7.82$	Do not reject
15. Hong Kong	11.02	$\chi^2(3)=11.34^*$	Do not reject*
16. Iceland	1.75	$\chi^2(6)=12.59$	Do not reject
17. India	6.36	$\chi^2(6)=12.59$	Do not reject
18. Ireland	5.47	$\chi^2(6)=12.59$	Do not reject
19. Israel	7.29	$\chi^2(6)=12.59$	Do not reject
20. Italy	19.09	$\chi^2(6)=12.59$	Reject
21. Jamaica	15.62	$\chi^2(6)=16.81^*$	Do not reject*
22. Korea	34.27	$\chi^2(6)=12.59$	Reject
23. Luxembourg	3.88	$\chi^2(6)=12.59$	Do not reject
24. Malta	5.36	$\chi^2(6)=12.59$	Do not reject
25. Mexico	2.95	$\chi^2(6)=12.59$	Do not reject
26. Netherlands	5.48	$\chi^2(6)=12.59$	Do not reject
27. New Zealand	0.17	$\chi^2(3)=7.82$	Do not reject
28. Norway	6.80	$\chi^2(3)=7.82$	Do not reject
29. Philippines	9.04	$\chi^2(3)=11.34^*$	Do not reject*
30. Portugal	3.96	$\chi^2(3)=7.82$	Do not reject
31. Puerto Rico	2.10	$\chi^2(3)=7.82$	Do not reject
32. Singapore	2.75	$\chi^2(6)=12.59$	Do not reject
33. South Africa	6.11	$\chi^2(6)=12.59$	Do not reject
34. Spain	7.29	$\chi^2(6)=12.59$	Do not reject
35. Sri Lanka	6.09	$\chi^2(6)=12.59$	Do not reject
36. Sweden	6.56	$\chi^2(6)=12.59$	Do not reject
37. Switzerland	0.95	$\chi^2(1)=3.84$	Do not reject
38. Taiwan	0.94	$\chi^2(3)=7.82$	Do not reject
39. Thailand	3.70	$\chi^2(6)=12.59$	Do not reject
40. UK	6.23	$\chi^2(6)=12.59$	Do not reject
41. US	4.02	$\chi^2(6)=12.59$	Do not reject
42. Venezuela	12.32	$\chi^2(3)=7.82$	Reject
43. Zimbabwe	21.34	$\chi^2(3)=7.82$	Reject

$q = \frac{1}{2}(n-1)(n-2)$. The level of significance $\alpha = 0.05$. A * denotes critical value and conclusion at $\alpha = 0.01$.

Monte Carlo test

It is now well accepted in the econometrics literature that the negative results of various hypothesis testing in demand systems are at least in part due to the failure of asymptotic tests which use the moment matrix **S** that could be singular (or near-singular) with insufficient data (for a review, see Barten, 1977).

To overcome the problems associated with the asymptotic tests, we now apply the distribution-free tests based on Barnard's (1963) Monte Carlo simulation

Country	Asymptotic χ^2 (k) test			Monte Carlo Simulations	
	Data-based	Critical	Conclusion	Rank	Conclusion
(1)	(2)	(3)	(4)	(5)	(6)
1. Australia	3.34	$\chi^2(5)$=11.07	Do not reject	225	Do not reject
2. Austria	16.99	$\chi^2(9)$=21.67*	Do not reject*	888	Do not reject
3. Belgium	15.56	$\chi^2(5)$= 11.07	Reject	817	Do not reject
4. Canada	4.39	$\chi^2(5)$= 11.07	Do not reject	398	Do not reject
5. Colombia	16.04	$\chi^2(9)$=16.92	Do not reject	718	Do not reject
6. Cyprus	11.88	$\chi^2(5)$=15.09*	Do not reject	655	Do not reject
7. Denmark	14.37	$\chi^2(9)$= 16.92	Do not reject	752	Do not reject
8. Ecuador	26.70	$\chi^2(9)$=16.92	Reject	963	Do not reject*
9. Fiji	8.47	$\chi^2(5)$= 11.07	Do not reject	645	Do not reject
10. Finland	6.55	$\chi^2(9)$= 16.92	Do not reject	165	Do not reject
11. France	18.08	$\chi^2(9)$= 21.67*	Do not reject*	876	Do not reject
12. Germany	4.06	$\chi^2(2)$= 5.99	Do not reject	851	Do not reject
13. Greece	16.99	$\chi^2(9)$= 21.67*	Do not reject*	722	Do not reject
14. Honduras	14.25	$\chi^2(5)$=15.09*	Do not reject*	649	Do not reject
15. Hong Kong	14.81	$\chi^2(5)$=15.09*	Do not reject*	950	Do not reject
16. Iceland	14.26	$\chi^2(9)$= 16.92	Do not reject	616	Do not reject
17. India	11.87	$\chi^2(9)$=16.92	Do not reject	459	Do not reject
18. Ireland	8.27	$\chi^2(9)$= 16.92	Do not reject	281	Do not reject
19. Israel	32.02	$\chi^2(9)$=16.92	Reject	944	Do not reject
20. Italy	16.68	$\chi^2(9)$=16.92	Do not reject	830	Do not reject
21. Jamaica	48.89	$\chi^2(9)$=16.92	Reject	997	Reject
22. Korea	20.26	$\chi^2(9)$=21.67*	Do not reject*	641	Do not reject
23. Luxembourg	3.39	$\chi^2(9)$= 16.92	Do not reject	19	Do not reject
24. Malta	21.42	$\chi^2(9)$=21.67*	Do not reject*	937	Do not reject
25. Mexico	12.99	$\chi^2(9)$=16.92	Do not reject	229	Do not reject
26. Netherlands	25.39	$\chi^2(9)$= 16.92	Reject	952	Do not reject*
27. New Zealand	6.59	$\chi^2(5)$= 11.07	Do not reject	410	Do not reject
28. Norway	20.18	$\chi^2(5)$= 11.07	Reject	852	Do not reject
29. Philippines	3.98	$\chi^2(5)$=11.07	Do not reject	246	Do not reject
30. Portugal	2.16	$\chi^2(5)$= 11.07	Do not reject	49	Do not reject
31. Puerto Rico	7.71	$\chi^2(5)$=11.07	Do not reject	761	Do not reject
32. Singapore	24.85	$\chi^2(9)$=16.92	Reject	912	Do not reject
33. South Africa	16.08	$\chi^2(9)$=16.92	Do not reject	680	Do not reject
34. Spain	31.87	$\chi^2(9)$= 16.92	Reject	942	Do not reject
35. Sri Lanka	20.00	$\chi^2(9)$=21.67*	Do not reject*	596	Do not reject
36. Sweden	11.64	$\chi^2(9)$= 16.92	Do not reject	601	Do not reject
37. Switzerland	0.90	$\chi^2(2)$= 5.99	Do not reject	324	Do not reject
38. Taiwan	6.71	$\chi^2(5)$=11.07	Do not reject	342	Do not reject
39. Thailand	28.34	$\chi^2(9)$=16.92	Reject	948	Do not reject
40. UK	14.68	$\chi^2(9)$= 16.92	Do not reject	523	Do not reject
41. US	39.74	$\chi^2(9)$=16.92	Reject	998	Reject
42. Venezuela	4.31	$\chi^2(5)$=11.07	Do not reject	169	Do not reject
43. Zimbabwe	18.78	$\chi^2(5)$=11.07	Reject	962	Do nor reject*

Degrees of freedom $k = \frac{1}{2}n(n-1)-1$. The level of significance $\alpha = 0.05$. A * denotes critical value and conclusion at $\alpha = 0.01$.

procedure described in Section 7.6. The basic idea behind the Monte Carlo tests is to simulate a large number of values of the test statistic under the null hypothesis to construct its empirical distribution. The observed value of the test statistic is then compared to this distribution, rather than its asymptotic counterpart.

We now apply this Monte Carlo simulation procedure to test the preference independence. The results are reported in columns 5 and 6 of Table 8.11. As can be seen from the table, preference independence is now acceptable for 41 out of the 43 countries.

Summary Results

In this section so far, we have tested the demand theory hypotheses, demand homogeneity and Slutsky symmetry and a special type of utility structure preference independence. We used the asymptotic tests as well as the finite-sample exact tests (for homogeneity) and Monte Carlo test for preference independence. Table 8.12 summarises our findings regarding the three hypothesis tests. As can be seen, all three hypotheses are generally acceptable.

8.5   Estimation Results

In the last section, we found that the homogeneity, symmetry and preference independence hypotheses are widely acceptable for most countries. In this section, we present the estimation results of the demand system under preference independence, equation (4.3) with an intercept term and error term added,

$$\overline{w}_{it}\, Dq_{it} = \alpha_i + \theta_i\, DQ_t + \phi\theta_i\,[Dp_{it} - \sum_{j=1}^{n}\theta_j\, Dp_{jt}] + \varepsilon_{it},\ \ i=1,\ldots,n\text{-}1;\, t=1,\ldots,T,\quad (5.1)$$

based on the estimation procedure described in Section 7.5.

Parameter Estimates

Table 8.13 presents the estimation results of the Rotterdam demand model under preference independence for the 43 countries. Columns 2-6 of the table present the estimates of the intercept terms for the 5 commodities. As can be seen, for most countries, the intercept terms for food, tobacco and alcohol are negative while the intercept terms for soft drinks and all other goods are positive. This indicates that, in most countries, there is an autonomous trend in consumption out of food, tobacco and alcohol into soft drinks and all other goods.

Columns 7-12 of Table 8.13 present the estimates for the marginal shares, θ_i, $i=1,\ldots,5$, and the estimates for income flexibility. As can be seen, for most countries, the marginal share estimates for food, tobacco and alcohol are positive. For example, the marginal shares for Australia are 0.071 (food), 0.010 (tobacco) and 0.043 (alcohol). This means that if an Australian's income increases by $1, out of that additional dollar, 7 cents will be allocated to food expenditure, 1 cent to tobacco and 4 cents to alcohol. The remaining 88 cents will be allocated to other goods. The average marginal shares across countries are 0.14 (food), 0.02 (tobacco), 0.03 (alcohol) and 0.10 (soft drinks). The income flexibility estimates

Table 8.12 Summary results: Testing demand theory hypotheses 43 countries

Country (1)	Demand homogeneity (2)	Slutsky symmetry (3)	Preference independence
1. Australia	Do not reject	Do not reject	Do not reject
2. Austria	Do not reject	Do not reject	Do not reject
3. Belgium	Do not reject	Do not reject	Do not reject
4. Canada	Do not reject	Do not reject	Do not reject
5. Colombia	Do not reject	Do not reject	Do not reject
6. Cyprus	Do not reject	Do not reject	Do not reject
7. Denmark	Do not reject*	Do not reject	Do not reject
8. Ecuador	Do not reject	Do not reject	Do not reject*
9. Fiji	Do not reject	Do not reject	Do not reject
10. Finland	Do not reject	Do not reject	Do not reject
11. France	Do not reject	Do not reject	Do not reject
12. Germany	Do not reject	Do not reject	Do not reject
13. Greece	Do not reject	Do not reject*	Do not reject
14. Honduras	Do not reject	Do not reject	Do not reject
15. Hong Kong	Do not reject*	Do not reject*	Do not reject
16. Iceland	Do not reject	Do not reject	Do not reject
17. India	Do not reject	Do not reject	Do not reject
18. Ireland	Do not reject	Do not reject	Do not reject
19. Israel	Do not reject	Do not reject	Do not reject
20. Italy	Do not reject	Reject	Do not reject
21. Jamaica	Do not reject	Do not reject*	Reject
22. Korea	Do not reject	Reject	Do not reject
23. Luxembourg	Do not reject	Do not reject	Do not reject
24. Malta	Do not reject	Do not reject	Do not reject
25. Mexico	Do not reject	Do not reject	Do not reject
26. Netherlands	Do not reject	Do not reject	Do not reject*
27. New Zealand	Do not reject	Do not reject	Do not reject
28. Norway	Do not reject*	Do not reject	Do not reject
29. Philippines	Do not reject	Do not reject*	Do not reject
30. Portugal	Do not reject	Do not reject	Do not reject
31. Puerto Rico	Do not reject	Do not reject	Do not reject
32. Singapore	Do not reject	Do not reject	Do not reject
33. South Africa	Do not reject	Do not reject	Do not reject
34. Spain	Do not reject	Do not reject	Do not reject
35. Sri Lanka	Do not reject	Do not reject	Do not reject
36. Sweden	Do not reject	Do not reject	Do not reject
37. Switzerland	Do not reject	Do not reject	Do not reject
38. Taiwan	Do not reject	Do not reject	Do not reject
39. Thailand	Do not reject	Do not reject	Do not reject
40. UK	Do not reject	Do not reject	Do not reject
41. US	Do not reject	Do not reject	Reject
42. Venezuela	Do not reject	Reject	Do not reject
43. Zimbabwe	Do not reject	Reject	Do not reject*

The level of significance used is $\alpha = 0.05$. A * denotes conclusion at $\alpha = 0.01$.

presented in the last column of Table 8.13 are all negative as they should be with an average value of -0.62, which is in line with the findings of several previous econometric studies and also close to the preliminary estimates of ϕ presented in Section 8.2.

Table 8.13　Estimates of the demand model under preference independence, 43 countries

Country	Constant term					Marginal shares					Income flexibility
	Food	Tobacco	Alcohol	Softdrinks	Other	Food	Tobacco	Alcohol	Softdrinks	Other	
(1)	(2)	(3)	(4)	(5)	(6)	(7)	(8)	(9)	(10)	(11)	(12)
1. Australia	0.057	-0.051	-0.079		0.073	0.071	0.010	0.043		0.876	-0.820
	(0.060)	(0.010)	(0.027)		(0.083)	(0.021)	(0.003)	(0.011)		(0.032)	(0.202)
2. Austria	-0.042	-0.017	-0.003	0.013	0.049	0.086	0.019	0.011	0.004	0.881	-0.646
	(0.100)	(0.018)	(0.029)	(0.009)	(0.111)	(0.028)	(0.005)	(0.005)	(0.002)	(0.031)	(0.129)
3. Belgium	-0.065	-0.039	0.034		0.070	0.083	0.005	0.003	0.909		-0.085
	(0.074)	(0.022)	(0.036)		(0.101)	(0.034)	(0.011)	(0.018)	(0.047)		(0.110)
4. Canada	-0.114	-0.032	-0.017	0.162		0.090	0.008	0.027	0.875		-0.864
	(0.042)	(0.012)	(0.017)	(0.058)		(0.012)	(0.002)	(0.004)	(0.016)		(0.133)
5. Colombia	-0.053	-0.058	0.042	0.005	0.064	0.285	0.015	0.015	0.013	0.672	-0.374
	(0.089)	(0.023)	(0.027)	(0.015)	(0.098)	(0.038)	(0.007)	(0.010)	(0.005)	(0.043)	(0.077)
6. Cyprus	0.112	-0.055	-0.016		-0.041	0.099	0.039	0.039		0.823	-0.375
	(0.191)	(0.064)	(0.062)		(0.208)	(0.030)	(0.009)	(0.009)		(0.032)	(0.199)
7. Denmark	-0.007	-0.065	-0.030	0.003	0.099	0.059	0.022	0.034	0.008	0.877	-0.822
	(0.068)	(0.027)	(0.035)	(0.007)	(0.071)	(0.020)	(0.006)	(0.007)	(0.002)	(0.022)	(0.131)
8. Ecuador	-0.316	-0.049	-0.061	0.005	0.422	0.236	0.032	0.055	0.014	0.663	-0.123
	(0.138)	(0.019)	(0.024)	(0.020)	(0.160)	(0.042)	(0.006)	(0.008)	(0.006)	(0.050)	(0.040)
9. Fiji	-0.158	-0.040	-0.036		0.234	0.285	0.055	0.064		0.596	-0.611
	(0.123)	(0.077)	(0.051)		(0.131)	(0.031)	(0.010)	(0.010)		(0.033)	(0.083)
10. Finland	-0.083	-0.047	-0.023	-0.006	0.159	0.083	0.016	0.044	0.005	0.851	-0.671
	(0.084)	(0.023)	(0.027)	(0.005)	(0.103)	(0.018)	(0.004)	(0.007)	(0.001)	(0.023)	(0.102)
11. France	-0.048	-0.002	-0.014	0.003	0.061	0.082	0.007	0.007	0.006	0.898	-0.442
	(0.034)	(0.005)	(0.010)	(0.006)	(0.034)	(0.012)	(0.001)	(0.003)	(0.002)	(0.012)	(0.089)
12. Germany	-0.119	-0.027			0.146	0.186	0.020			0.795	-0.392
	(0.066)	(0.016)			(0.070)	(0.018)	(0.005)			(0.020)	(0.131)
13. Greece*						0.120	0.039	0.044	0.019	0.778	-0.225
						(0.088)	(0.024)	(0.016)	(0.009)	(0.093)	(0.113)
14. Honduras	-0.008	0.001	0.007		0.001	0.413	0.008	0.032		0.547	-0.711
	(0.014)	(0.006)	(0.006)		(0.020)	(0.003)	(0.001)	(0.001)		(0.004)	(0.030)
15. Hong Kong	-0.249	-0.052	-0.052		0.354	0.124	0.006	0.009		0.861	-0.937
	(0.202)	(0.021)	(0.036)		(0.187)	(0.026)	(0.002)	(0.003)		(0.026)	(0.252)
16. Iceland	-0.027	-0.031	0.016	0.038	0.003	0.055	0.012	0.014	0.032	0.887	-0.488
	(0.140)	(0.015)	(0.043)	(0.039)	(0.180)	(0.025)	(0.003)	(0.008)	(0.007)	(0.032)	(0.134)
17. India*						0.426	0.040	0.013	0.004	0.517	-0.432
						(0.087)	(0.019)	(0.008)	(0.001)	(0.085)	(0.125)
18. Ireland	0.082	-0.075	0.062	0.012	-0.081	0.073	0.018	0.064	0.015	0.830	-0.543
	(0.145)	(0.042)	(0.081)	(0.023)	(0.166)	(0.028)	(0.007)	(0.016)	(0.004)	(0.037)	(0.170)
19. Israel*						0.046	0.009	0.005	0.026	0.912	-1.203
						(0.009)	(0.001)	(0.003)	(0.003)	(0.008)	(0.152)
20. Italy	-0.166	0.011	-0.047	0.006	0.197	0.144	0.012	0.014	0.003	0.828	-0.257
	(0.077)	(0.019)	(0.017)	(0.004)	(0.092)	(0.026)	(0.006)	(0.006)	(0.001)	(0.031)	(0.087)
21. Jamaica	-0.263	-0.070	-0.033	0.016	0.350	0.234	0.037	0.023	0.016	0.689	-0.908
	(0.344)	(0.100)	(0.090)	(0.042)	(0.286)	(0.043)	(0.007)	(0.009)	(0.004)	(0.042)	(0.099)
22. Korea	-0.309	-0.029	-0.019	0.019	0.338	0.104	0.008	0.006	0.007	0.875	-0.669
	(0.139)	(0.025)	(0.009)	(0.018)	(0.161)	(0.021)	(0.003)	(0.001)	(0.002)	(0.024)	(0.198)
23. Luxembourg	-0.134	0.202	-0.026	0.018	-0.060	0.029	0.015	0.016	0.002	0.938	-0.673
	(0.090)	(0.107)	(0.035)	(0.011)	(0.150)	(0.025)	(0.014)	(0.010)	(0.002)	(0.036)	(0.481)
24. Malta*						0.169	0.026	0.038	0.018	0.749	-1.588
						(0.025)	(0.006)	(0.016)	(0.005)	(0.031)	(0.271)
25. Mexico	0.047	-0.008	-0.038	0.037	-0.038	0.165	0.004	0.038	0.025	0.768	-0.192
	(0.105)	(0.009)	(0.027)	(0.022)	(0.099)	(0.022)	(0.001)	(0.006)	(0.005)	(0.021)	(0.065)

* No constant model　　　　　　　　　　　　　　　　　　　　　*Table continues on next page*

Implied Income and Price Elasticities

Now, we present the implied income and own-price elasticitiy estimates based on the estimates presented in Table 8.13 and the mean budget shares presented in Table 8.3.

Table 8.13 Estimates of the demand model under preference independence, 43 countries (continued)

Country	Constant term					Marginal shares					Income flexibility
	Food	Tobacco	Alcohol	Softdrinks	Other	Food	Tobacco	Alcohol	Softdrinks	Other	
(1)	(2)	(3)	(4)	(5)	(6)	(7)	(8)	(9)	(10)	(11)	(12)
26. Netherlands	0.039	-0.059	-0.044	0.008	0.057	0.045	0.020	0.027	0.007	0.900	-0.268
	(0.033)	(0.009)	(0.020)	(0.006)	(0.047)	(0.013)	(0.004)	(0.008)	(0.002)	(0.021)	(0.071)
27. New Zealand	-0.062	-0.071		0.019	0.114	0.053	0.006		0.025	0.916	-1.771
	(0.072)	(0.033)		(0.057)	(0.117)	(0.022)	(0.003)		(0.012)	(0.036)	(0.761)
28. Norway*						0.030	0.088	0.024		0.859	-0.808
						(0.017)	(0.021)	(0.010)		(0.024)	(0.267)
29. Philippines*						0.545	0.015	0.020		0.421	-0.085
						(0.035)	(0.009)	(0.004)		(0.030)	(0.064)
30. Portugal	-0.077	0.030	-0.048		0.095	0.144	0.013	0.003		0.840	-0.879
	(0.239)	(0.042)	(0.081)		(0.306)	(0.028)	(0.009)	(0.003)		(0.034)	(0.260)
31. Puerto Rico*						0.133	0.014	0.052	0.801		-1.209
						(0.032)	(0.004)	(0.009)	(0.039)		(0.229)
32. Singapore	-0.300	-0.062	-0.017	-0.001	0.380	0.099	0.007	0.007	0.010	0.877	-0.890
	(0.119)	(0.033)	(0.026)	(0.026)	(0.142)	(0.016)	(0.005)	(0.004)	(0.003)	(0.020)	(0.325)
33. South Africa	-0.030	-0.037	0.109	0.007	-0.049	0.165	0.004	0.065	0.007	0.759	-0.776
	(0.108)	(0.031)	(0.081)	(0.024)	(0.155)	(0.030)	(0.006)	(0.017)	(0.006)	(0.040)	(0.160)
34. Spain	-0.047	0.024	0.002	0.002	0.019	0.030	0.020	0.012	0.007	0.931	-0.294
	(0.072)	(0.034)	(0.018)	(0.007)	(0.048)	(0.014)	(0.007)	(0.004)	(0.002)	(0.016)	(0.115)
35. Sri Lanka	0.570	-0.173	-0.039	0.075	-0.433	0.280	0.017	0.026	0.011	0.666	-0.512
	(0.451)	(0.246)	(0.114)	(0.073)	(0.418)	(0.088)	(0.024)	(0.019)	(0.004)	(0.088)	(0.116)
36. Sweden	-0.061	-0.031	-0.052	0.013	0.131	0.099	0.023	0.055	0.001	0.822	-0.476
	(0.048)	(0.012)	(0.025)	(0.006)	(0.058)	(0.019)	(0.004)	(0.010)	(0.002)	(0.025)	(0.095)
37. Switzerland	-0.114	-0.090			0.204	0.218	0.100			0.681	-0.445
	(0.050)	(0.031)			(0.055)	(0.021)	(0.013)			(0.025)	(0.088)
38. Taiwan*						0.156	0.003	0.025		0.816	-0.670
						(0.018)	(0.002)	(0.004)		(0.015)	(0.252)
39. Thailand	-0.193	-0.141	-0.290	0.000	0.623	0.098	0.037	0.099	0.039	0.727	-0.261
	(0.270)	(0.057)	(0.120)	(0.050)	(0.237)	(0.047)	(0.009)	(0.020)	(0.008)	(0.041)	(0.091)
40. UK	-0.106	-0.103	-0.080	0.003	0.285	0.056	0.014	0.045	0.009	0.877	-0.591
	(0.043)	(0.017)	(0.038)	(0.013)	(0.067)	(0.012)	(0.005)	(0.011)	(0.003)	(0.020)	(0.172)
41. US	-0.049	-0.034	-0.008	0.005	0.085	0.043	0.010	0.011	0.002	0.934	-0.317
	(0.055)	(0.010)	(0.010)	(0.006)	(0.060)	(0.018)	(0.004)	(0.003)	(0.001)	(0.020)	(0.121)
42. Venezuela	0.234	-0.021	0.058		-0.271	0.113	0.010	0.049		0.828	-0.417
	(0.236)	(0.032)	(0.064)		(0.233)	(0.040)	(0.005)	(0.012)		(0.043)	(0.142)
43. Zimbabwe*						0.157	0.104	0.029		0.710	-0.971
						(0.064)	(0.015)	(0.008)		(0.065)	(0.146)
Mean	-0.061	-0.038	-0.023	0.019	0.110	0.144	0.023	0.030	0.097	0.792	-0.621
	(0.028)	(0.010)	(0.011)	(0.007)	(0.034)	(0.017)	(0.004)	(0.003)	(0.047)	(0.019)	(0.056)

The *income elasticity* implied by model (5.1) can be calculated as

$$\eta_{it} = \frac{\theta_i}{\overline{w}_{it}}, \qquad i=1,\ldots,n. \qquad (5.2)$$

When the budget shares are fairly stable over time, $\overline{w}_{it}$ in (5.2) can be replaced by its sample mean $\overline{\overline{w}}_i = (1/T)\sum_{t=1}^{T}\overline{w}_{it}$ and the implied income elasticity can then be written as

$$\eta_i = \frac{\theta_i}{\overline{\overline{w}}_i}, \qquad i=1,\ldots,n. \qquad (5.3)$$

When η_i is less than one, good i will be a necessity. On the other hand, when η_i is greater than one, good i will be a luxury.

The *Slutsky (or compensated) own-price elasticity* of good i implied by model (5.1) at sample means is

$$\eta_{ii} = \frac{\phi\theta_i(1-\theta_i)}{\overline{\overline{w}}_i}, \qquad\qquad i=1,\ldots,n. \qquad (5.4)$$

To calculate these elasticities, we use the ML estimates of the marginal shares (θ_i) and income flexibility (ϕ) presented in Table 8.13 and the budget shares presented in Table 8.3. We present these income and price elasticity estimates for the 43 countries in Table 8.14.

Overall, all the income elasticities presented in Table 8.14 are positive. As can be seen from column 2 of Table 8.14, the income elasticity estimates for food are all less than one for all countries except Fiji, Honduras and Philippines. The average income elasticity for food is 0.57. This means that food is considered to be a necessity by consumers around the world. The average income elasticity for tobacco is 0.83, alcohol 0.96 and soft drinks 1.12. As can be seen from columns 7-11 of Table 8.14, almost all the own-price elasticities are negative as they should be and most of them are less than one in absolute value, indicating that, in general, demand for food, tobacco, alcohol and soft drink is also price inelastic. A comparison of the preliminary income and price elasticity estimates presented in Tables 8.7 and 8.8 with the estimates presented in this section reveals that they are very similar.

In Table 8.15, we reproduce the elasticity estimates from Table 8.14 as well as the income flexibility estimates from Table 8.12 grouped by developed and developing countries. As in Table 8.1, the countries are presented in declining GDP order. Comparing the group average of the income elasticities for the four commodities presented in columns 2-5 for the developing and developed countries, we can conclude that food is a necessity in both groups, tobacco is a necessity in the developed countries and close to a luxury in developing countries, alcohol is a necessity in developed countries and a luxury in the developing countries, and soft drinks are a luxury in developing countries. Comparing the average own-price elasticities of the four commodities for the two groups presented in columns 7-10, the estimates for the four commodities are similar for developed and developing countries. The negative estimates indicating that demand for food, tobacco, alcohol and soft drink is also price inelastic in all countries, regardless of the country's income level. Finally, comparing the income flexibilities (ϕ), we see that the averages are similar for the developed and developing countries, indicating that ϕ is an international constant with a value of around -0.6.

8.6   Concluding Comments

In this chapter, we analysed the consumption patterns of the 4 commodities, food, tobacco, alcohol and soft drinks in 43 countries. The countries considered included 24 developed countries and 19 developing countries.

Table 8.14 Income and own-price elasticity estimates for 4 commodities under preference independence, 43 countries

Country	Income elasticity					Own-price elasticity				
	Food	Tobacco	Alcohol	Soft drinks	Other	Food	Tobacco	Alcohol	Soft drinks	Other
(1)	(2)	(3)	(4)	(5)	(6)	(7)	(8)	(9)	(10)	(11)
1. Australia	0.455	0.498	0.872		1.131	-0.346	-0.404	-0.685		-0.115
2. Austria	0.456	0.792	0.345	0.564	1.174	-0.269	-0.503	-0.221	-0.363	-0.090
3. Belgium	0.560	0.306	0.163		1.111	-0.044	-0.026	-0.014		-0.009
4. Canada	0.636	0.352	0.821	1.090	-0.500	-0.302	-0.690	-0.118		
5. Colombia	0.893	1.230	0.410	1.287	1.080	-0.239	-0.454	-0.151	-0.475	-0.133
6. Cyprus	0.452	1.778	1.577		1.120	-0.153	-0.641	-0.568		-0.074
7. Denmark	0.341	0.616	0.908	1.194	1.175	-0.264	-0.495	-0.721	-0.974	-0.119
8. Ecuador	0.739	2.039	1.661	0.971	1.073	-0.069	-0.242	-0.193	-0.118	-0.044
9. Fiji	1.029	2.415	1.708		0.899	-0.449	-1.394	-0.977		-0.222
10. Finland	0.425	0.731	1.017	1.023	1.161	-0.261	-0.482	-0.653	-0.682	-0.116
11. France	0.475	0.574	0.332	1.098	1.140	-0.193	-0.252	-0.146	-0.482	-0.052
12. Germany	0.756	0.811			1.088	-0.241	-0.312			-0.088
13. Greece	0.377	1.187	1.662	1.795	1.274	-0.075	-0.257	-0.357	-0.396	-0.064
14. Honduras	1.004	1.167	1.000	0.995		-0.474	-0.933	-0.780		-0.363
15. Hong Kong	0.581	0.571	0.656		1.130	-0.477	-0.531	-0.610		-0.147
16. Iceland	0.301	0.581	0.527	1.343	1.186	-0.139	-0.280	-0.254	-0.635	-0.065
17. India	0.838	1.867	1.369	3.359	1.124	-0.208	-0.774	-0.584	-1.447	-0.235
18. Ireland	0.314	0.398	0.557	1.119	1.398	-0.158	-0.212	-0.283	-0.598	-0.129
19. Israel	0.225	0.729	0.745	1.218	1.214	-0.258	-0.870	-0.893	-1.428	-0.128
20. Italy	0.613	0.606	0.797	0.752	1.142	-0.135	-0.154	-0.202	-0.193	-0.050
21. Jamaica	0.699	1.057	1.045	1.519	1.146	-0.480	-0.770	-0.587	-0.809	-0.366
22. Korea	0.570	0.388	0.842	0.980	1.118	-0.342	-0.257	-0.560	-0.651	-0.094
23. Luxembourg	0.170	0.331	1.001	0.289	1.232	-0.111	-0.219	-0.662	-0.194	-0.052
24. Malta	0.704	0.761	0.894	0.718	1.137	-0.927	-1.173	-1.362	-1.116	-0.451
25. Mexico	0.712	0.646	1.602	1.078	1.074	-0.114	-0.123	-0.296	-0.202	-0.048
26. Netherlands	0.339	1.214	1.532	1.308	1.088	-0.087	-0.318	-0.399	-0.348	-0.029
27. New Zealand	0.430	0.276		0.634	1.124	-0.721	-0.486		-1.095	-0.167
28. Norway	0.528	1.253	0.910		1.096	-0.388	-0.980	-0.717		-0.125
29. Philippines	1.025	0.497	0.864		1.011	-0.040	-0.042	-0.072		-0.050
30. Portugal	0.599	0.585	0.074		1.197	-0.451	-0.507	-0.065		-0.168
31. Puerto Rico	0.594	0.751	1.243		1.119	-0.622	-0.894	-1.422		-0.270
32. Singapore	0.650	0.353	0.398	0.850	1.098	-0.522	-0.312	-0.352	-0.749	-0.120
33. South Africa	0.656	0.162	1.101	0.483	1.165	-0.425	-0.125	-0.799	-0.372	-0.217
34. Spain	0.145	1.382	0.915	1.631	1.223	-0.041	-0.399	-0.266	-0.477	-0.025
35. Sri lanka	0.574	0.281	0.946	1.671	1.592	-0.212	-0.142	-0.472	-0.846	-0.272
36. Sweden	0.529	1.003	1.408	0.101	1.104	-0.227	-0.466	-0.633	-0.048	-0.094
37. Switzerland	0.985	1.178				0.982	-0.388	-0.414		-0.127
38. Taiwan	0.661	0.224	0.762		1.138	-0.373	-0.149	-0.497		-0.140
39. Thailand	0.378	1.629	2.585	1.264	1.120	-0.089	-0.410	-0.608	-0.317	-0.080
40. UK	0.445	0.454	0.669	1.081	1.140	-0.248	-0.265	-0.378	-0.633	-0.083
41. US	0.402	0.276	0.558	1.139	1.105	-0.273	-0.288	-0.535	-0.165	-0.055
42. Venezuela	0.351	0.570	1.230		1.334	-0.130	-0.236	-0.488		-0.096
43. Zimbabwe	0.830	1.038	0.555		1.078	-0.678	-0.901	-0.522		-0.302
Mean	0.569	0.827	0.957	1.123	1.111	-0.262	-0.459	-0.500	-0.586	-0.135

We found that a clear inverse relationship exists between budget share for each commodity and the per capita real GDP, supporting the *Engel's Law*. On average, price of the four commodities have grown but at varying levels, tobacco at faster rate (10.5 percent per annum) than food, alcohol and soft drinks. Prices of soft drinks have increased at a faster rate in the developing countries compared to the price increases in the developed countries. Consumption of food, alcohol and soft drinks has gown while that of tobacco has fallen.

Table 8.15 Income and own-price elasticity, and income flexibility estimates for 4 commodities under preference independence, developed vs developing countries

Country	Income elasticity					Own-price elasticity					Income flexibility
	Food	Tobacco	Alcohol	Soft drinks	Other	Food	Tobacco	Alcohol	Soft drinks	Other	
(1)	(2)	(3)	(4)	(5)	(6)	(7)	(8)	(9)	(10)	(11)	(12)
Developed countries											
1. US	0.402	0.276	0.558	1.139	1.105	-0.273	-0.288	-0.535	-0.165	-0.055	-0.317
2. Switzerland	0.985	1.178				0.982	-0.388	-0.414		-0.127	-0.445
3. Luxembourg	0.170	0.331	1.001	0.289	1.232	-0.111	-0.219	-0.662	-0.194	-0.052	-0.673
4. Hong Kong	0.581	0.571	0.656		1.130	-0.477	-0.531	-0.610		-0.147	-0.937
5. Canada	0.636	0.352	0.821	1.090	-0.500	-0.302	-0.690	-0.118			-0.864
6. Germany	0.756	0.811			1.088	-0.241	-0.312			-0.088	-0.392
7. Denmark	0.341	0.616	0.908	1.194	1.175	-0.264	-0.495	-0.721	-0.974	-0.119	-0.822
8. Australia	0.455	0.498	0.872		1.131	-0.346	-0.404	-0.685		-0.115	-0.820
9. Sweden	0.529	1.003	1.408	0.101	1.104	-0.227	-0.466	-0.633	-0.048	-0.094	-0.476
10. France	0.475	0.574	0.332	1.098	1.140	-0.193	-0.252	-0.146	-0.482	-0.052	-0.442
11. Belgium	0.560	0.306	0.163		1.111	-0.044	-0.026	-0.014		-0.009	-0.085
12. Netherlands	0.339	1.214	1.532	1.308	1.088	-0.087	-0.318	-0.399	-0.348	-0.029	-0.268
13. Norway	0.528	1.253	0.910		1.096	-0.388	-0.980	-0.717		-0.125	-0.808
14. Austria	0.456	0.792	0.345	0.564	1.174	-0.269	-0.503	-0.221	-0.363	-0.090	-0.646
15. Singapore	0.650	0.353	0.398	0.850	1.098	-0.522	-0.312	-0.352	-0.749	-0.120	-0.890
16. Italy	0.613	0.606	0.797	0.752	1.142	-0.135	-0.154	-0.202	-0.193	-0.050	-0.257
17. Iceland	0.301	0.581	0.527	1.343	1.186	-0.139	-0.280	-0.254	-0.635	-0.065	-0.488
18. UK	0.445	0.454	0.669	1.081	1.140	-0.248	-0.265	-0.378	-0.633	-0.083	-0.591
19. Finland	0.425	0.731	1.017	1.023	1.161	-0.261	-0.482	-0.653	-0.682	-0.116	-0.671
20. New Zealand	0.430	0.276		0.634	1.124	-0.721	-0.486		-1.095	-0.167	-1.771
21. Spain	0.145	1.382	0.915	1.631	1.223	-0.041	-0.399	-0.266	-0.477	-0.025	-0.294
22. Israel	0.225	0.729	0.745	1.218	1.214	-0.258	-0.870	-0.893	-1.428	-0.128	-1.203
23. Ireland	0.314	0.398	0.557	1.119	1.398	-0.158	-0.212	-0.283	-0.598	-0.129	-0.543
24. Cyprus	0.452	1.778	1.577		1.120	-0.153	-0.641	-0.568		-0.074	-0.375
Mean (developed)	0.467	0.711	0.796	0.967	1.082	-0.203	-0.416	-0.442	-0.567	-0.090	-0.628
Developing countries											
25. Taiwan	0.661	0.224	0.762		1.138	-0.373	-0.149	-0.497		-0.140	-0.670
26. Korea	0.570	0.388	0.842	0.980	1.118	-0.342	-0.257	-0.560	-0.651	-0.094	-0.669
27. Portugal	0.599	0.585	0.074		1.197	-0.451	-0.507	-0.065		-0.168	-0.879
28. Greece	0.377	1.187	1.662	1.795	1.274	-0.075	-0.257	-0.357	-0.396	-0.064	-0.225
29. Venezuela	0.351	0.570	1.230		1.334	-0.130	-0.236	-0.488		-0.096	-0.417
30. Mexico	0.712	0.646	1.602	1.078	1.074	-0.114	-0.123	-0.296	-0.202	-0.048	-0.192
31. Malta	0.704	0.761	0.894	0.718	1.137	-0.927	-1.173	-1.362	-1.116	-0.451	-1.588
32. Puerto Rico	0.594	0.751	1.243		1.119	-0.622	-0.894	-1.422		-0.270	-1.209
33. Fiji	1.029	2.415	1.708		0.899	-0.449	-1.394	-0.977		-0.222	-0.611
34. Thailand	0.378	1.629	2.585	1.264	1.120	-0.089	-0.410	-0.608	-0.317	-0.080	-0.261
35. Colombia	0.893	1.230	0.410	1.287	1.080	-0.239	-0.454	-0.151	-0.475	-0.133	-0.374
36. South Africa	0.656	0.162	1.101	0.483	1.165	-0.425	-0.125	-0.799	-0.372	-0.217	-0.776
37. Ecuador	0.739	2.039	1.661	0.971	1.073	-0.069	-0.242	-0.193	-0.118	-0.044	-0.123
38. Jamaica	0.699	1.057	1.045	1.519	1.146	-0.480	-0.770	-0.587	-0.809	-0.366	-0.908
39. Sri lanka	0.574	0.281	0.946	1.671	1.592	-0.212	-0.142	-0.472	-0.846	-0.272	-0.512
40. Philippines	1.025	0.497	0.864		1.011	-0.040	-0.042	-0.072		-0.050	-0.085
41. Honduras	1.004	1.167	1.000	0.995		-0.474	-0.933	-0.780		-0.363	-0.711
42. India	0.838	1.867	1.369	3.359	1.124	-0.208	-0.774	-0.584	-1.447	-0.235	-0.432
43. Zimbabwe	0.830	1.038	0.555		1.078	-0.678	-0.901	-0.522		-0.302	-0.971
Mean (developing)	0.696	0.973	1.134	1.343	1.149	-0.337	-0.515	-0.568	-0.614	-0.190	-0.611
Mean (all countries)	0.569	0.827	0.957	1.123	1.111	-0.262	-0.459	-0.500	-0.586	-0.135	-0.621

We also tested the demand theory hypotheses, homogeneity, Slutsky symmetry and preference independent utility structure and found that, in general, they are acceptable for all countries. Based on this, we used the differential demand model implied by the three hypotheses as our preferred demand model and derived the demand elasticity estimates for the 4 commodities in 43 countries.

Table 8.16 summarises some of the results of this chapter grouped by developed and developing countries. As can be seen, consumers in the developing countries spend a higher proportion of their income on food than consumers in developed countries. The proportion of expenditure allocated to the other three commodities, tobacco, alcohol and soft drinks, are similar across all countries. As can be seen, on average, people around the world allocate about 23.7 percent of their income on food, 2.6 percent on tobacco, 3.2 percent on alcohol and 1.2 percent on soft drinks. Comparing the income elasticities it can be seen that food is a necessity in all countries, while tobacco is a necessity in developed countries and a near luxury in developing countries. Alcohol is a necessity in the developed countries and a luxury in developing countries. Soft drinks are a luxury in developing countries and a near luxury in the developed countries. The own-price elasticities show that demand for all four commodities is price inelastic in all countries.

In the next chapter, we analyse the consumption patterns within the alcoholic beverages group across a number of countries.

Table 8.16 Summary results: Average GDP, budget shares and, income elasticities, own-price elasticities and income flexibility estimates, developed vs developing countries

Statistic	Countries		
	Developed	Developing	All
(1)	(2)	(3)	(4)
GDP ($US in 1992)	17 539.6	5401.8	12 298.3
Budget shares			
Food	14.90	31.20	23.70
Tobacco	2.35	2.72	2.64
Alcohol	2.79	3.61	3.22
Soft drinks	1.20	1.66	1.22
Total food	20.39	38.63	30.78
Income flexibility	-0.63	-0.61	-0.62
Income elasticities			
Food	0.47	0.70	0.57
Tobacco	0.71	0.97	0.83
Alcohol	0.80	1.13	0.96
Soft drinks	0.97	1.34	1.12
Price elasticities			
Food	-0.20	-0.34	-0.26
Tobacco	-0.42	-0.52	-0.46
Alcohol	-0.44	-0.57	-0.50
Soft drinks	-0.57	-0.61	-0.59

Chapter 9

Demand for Beer, Wine and Spirits

In Chapter 8, we considered the alcoholic beverages group as one commodity and analysed the demand for alcohol as a whole at a cross-country level. We found that consumers' income and the price of alcohol are the two major economic factors that influence alcohol consumption. In that chapter we also estimated the income and price elasticities of alcohol for each country and found that alcohol as a whole is a necessity and the demand for alcohol is price inelastic. In most economic policy applications, for example, the taxation of alcoholic beverages, the demand elasticity estimates are required at the individual beverage level such as for beer, wine and spirits. The price of an alcoholic beverage is heavily dependant on the level of tax charged on it by the government. Taxes on alcoholic beverages are imposed for different reasons. In some countries they are used for revenue collection or for economic considerations and in some others as instruments to control alcohol misuse (either to reduce the consumption of all alcoholic beverages or to shift the consumption from one type of beverage to another), while in some others alcohol taxes are used as a combination of the two. The level of taxation on alcoholic beverages differs from beverage to beverage and also from country to country. To determine the appropriate level of taxation placed on each alcoholic beverage, the demand elasticities are used as key inputs. Consequently, obtaining estimates of demand elasticities is of crucial importance for taxation purposes at the micro and macro level of the economy.

In this chapter, we analyse the demand for the three alcoholic beverages, beer, wine and spirits, across countries. In Section 9.1, we present the consumption of beer, wine, spirits and total alcohol for 123 countries in 2000. In the following section, we focus our analysis on 10 selected countries by presenting a number of summary statistics of the data. In Section 9.3 we present the Divisia moments of alcohol consumption and, in the following section, we analyse the movements of relative consumption and relative prices. In Section 9.5 we obtain preliminary estimates of the income and price elasticities for beer, wine and spirits using a double-log demand system. In Section 9.6 we estimate the differential demand systems, test various demand theory hypotheses and based on these test results, we also derive the preferred demand system and present the estimates and the implied income and price elasticities for beer, wine and spirits for the 10 countries. In Section 9.7, we present a comparison of the demand elasticities from the current study with those from a number of previous studies. In the last section we present our concluding comments.

9.1   Consumption Data

In this section we present the most recent data (for the year 2000) for per adult (15 years and over) pure alcohol consumption of beer, wine and spirits and their total in 123 countries (see WHO, 2003, which originated from the *United Nations Food and Agriculture Organisation's Statistical Database, World Drink Trends* and *Produktschap voor Gedistilleerde Dranken*, Netherlands, and government statistical departments of a number of countries). As the data are expressed in terms of litres of pure alcohol per adult, they are comparable across countries, across beverages and across time.

Column 1 of Table 9.1 lists the 123 countries which are ranked by beverage type based on the per adult pure alcohol consumption of total alcohol and the three individual beverages, beer, wine and spirits presented in columns (2), (4), (6) and (8). As can be seen from the table, in terms of beer consumption Ireland (8.80 litres of pure alcohol per adult of beer), Czech Republic (8.60 litres of pure alcohol per adult of beer) and Swaziland (6.93 litres of pure alcohol per adult of beer) lead the world. In terms of wine, Luxembourg (8.89 litres of pure alcohol per adult of wine), France (8.25 litres of pure alcohol per adult of wine) and Portugal (7.22 litres of pure alcohol per adult of wine); and in terms of spirits Bahamas (12.77 litres of pure alcohol per adult of spirits), Thailand (12.45 litres of pure alcohol per adult of spirits) and Guyana (8.83 litres of pure alcohol per adult of spirits) lead the world. Looking at the table, it can also be seen that, in terms of total per adult pure alcohol consumption in 2000, Luxembourg had the highest consumption (17.04 litres) followed by Portugal (16.59 litres) and Ireland (15.80 litres). The last row of the table presents the world average consumption. As can be seen, on average, an adult world consumer consumes 2.34 litres of pure alcohol of beer, 1.46 litres of pure alcohol of wine, 2.09 litres of pure alcohol of spirits to give a total of 6.12 litres of pure alcohol during 2000.

9.2   Alcohol Consumption in Ten Countries

In this section, we present the alcohol consumption data for the ten countries, Australia, Canada, Finland, France, Japan, New Zealand, Norway, Sweden, the UK and the US. We have selected these countries on the basis of availability of consumption, expenditure and price data over a certain number of years.

Figure 9.1 plots the consumption of the three beverages for individual countries over time. As can be seen, in most countries (except in Finland, Japan and Norway) the per capita beer consumption peaked during the mid 1970s and fell since then. Among the group of ten countries considered here, the per capita wine consumption

Table 9.1 Ranking of countries by per adult volume of pure alcohol in total alcohol, beer, wine and spirits in 123 countries, 2000

Rank	Country (1)	Total alcohol (2)	Country (3)	Beer (4)	Country (5)	Wine (6)	Country (7)	Spirits (8)
1	Luxembourg	17.04	Ireland	8.80	Luxembourg	8.89	Bahamas	12.77
2	Portugal	16.59	Czech Republic	8.60	France	8.25	Thailand	12.45
3	Ireland	15.80	Swaziland	6.93	Portugal	7.22	Guyana	8.83
4	Bahamas	15.26	Germany	6.82	Italy	7.11	Réunion	8.67
5	Czech Republic	14.94	Austria	5.96	Argentina	6.92	Russian Federation	8.05
6	Saint Lucia	14.56	Luxembourg	5.96	Switzerland	6.43	Saint Lucia	7.43
7	Thailand	13.59	Saint Lucia	5.85	Uruguay	6.23	Latvia	6.71
8	Réunion	13.39	Denmark	5.58	Croatia	5.69	Belarus	6.50
9	France	13.31	UK	5.46	South Africa	5.04	Slovakia	5.37
10	Uganda	13.10	Belgium	5.40	Greece	4.82	Lao	5.31
11	Slovenia	12.60	Australia	5.18	Georgia	4.78	Portugal	5.27
12	Germany	12.45	New Caledonia	5.18	Slovenia	4.66	Haiti	5.17
13	Croatia	12.20	US	5.11	Cyprus	4.64	Barbados	4.44
14	Slovakia	12.11	Croatia	4.96	Spain	4.61	Poland	4.38
15	Austria	12.00	New Zealand	4.95	Austria	4.47	China	4.04
16	South Africa	11.51	Slovakia	4.95	Hungary	4.37	Czech Republic	3.96
17	Hungary	11.50	Uganda	4.94	Denmark	4.36	North Korea	3.88
18	Switzerland	11.45	Venezuela	4.86	Ireland	4.35	Liberia	3.71
19	Denmark	11.30	Netherlands Antilles	4.63	Chile	4.25	Hungary	3.64
20	Spain	11.17	Netherlands	4.62	New Caledonia	3.53	Costa Rica	3.57
21	Russian Federation	10.70	French Polynesia	4.56	Australia	3.41	Paraguay	3.41
22	Australia	10.29	Guam	4.44	Romania	3.39	South Africa	3.41
23	New Caledonia	10.08	Finland	4.41	Germany	3.27	Slovenia	3.30
24	Guyana	9.95	Gabon	4.27	Réunion	3.19	Estonia	3.15
25	New Zealand	9.80	Portugal	3.87	Bulgaria	3.16	France	2.96
26	UK	9.73	Estonia	3.86	French Polynesia	3.04	Bulgaria	2.94
27	Finland	9.72	Canada	3.80	New Zealand	2.97	Zimbabwe	2.93
28	Belgium	9.64	Slovenia	3.76	Belgium	2.88	Dominican Republic	2.85
29	Argentina	9.59	Spain	3.76	Netherlands	2.72	Suriname	2.85
30	Latvia	9.54	Colombia	3.75	Finland	2.57	Japan	2.81
31	Netherlands	9.45	Botswana	3.68	Czech Republic	2.35	Spain	2.79
32	Greece	9.16	Panama	3.56	UK	2.29	Finland	2.73
33	Italy	9.16	Hungary	3.55	Sweden	2.19	Ireland	2.65
34	US	9.08	Sweden	3.29	Gabon	1.90	Belize	2.63
35	Cyprus	8.96	Paraguay	3.26	Slovakia	1.75	Philippines	2.56
36	Uruguay	8.95	Switzerland	3.25	US	1.67	Colombia	2.54
37	Estonia	8.81	Romania	3.22	Bahamas	1.63	Germany	2.38
38	Swaziland	8.46	Burkina Faso	3.18	Cape Verde	1.59	Venezuela	2.34
39	Belarus	8.31	Poland	2.99	Canada	1.55	Cuba	2.30
40	Poland	8.26	South Africa	2.99	Swaziland	1.34	US	2.29
41	French Polynesia	8.11	Malta	2.95	Norway	1.33	Greece	2.24
42	Romania	7.96	Mexico	2.92	Iceland	1.14	Canada	2.23
43	Bulgaria	7.70	Norway	2.84	Angola	1.09	Mauritius	2.23
44	Canada	7.58	Zambia	2.72	Saint Lucia	1.09	Netherlands Antilles	2.18
45	Barbados	7.50	Cyprus	2.70	Russian Federation	1.07	Netherlands	2.05
46	Netherlands Antilles	7.48	Dominican Republic	2.67	Lebanon	1.06	Brazil	2.03
47	Venezuela	7.28	Tanzania	2.64	Estonia	1.01	Panama	2.01
48	Paraguay	7.23	Iceland	2.62	Poland	0.90	South Korea	2.01
49	Gabon	7.01	Suriname	2.53	Latvia	0.70	Luxembourg	1.94
50	South Korea	6.78	Brazil	2.40	Netherlands Antilles	0.64	Mongolia	1.93
51	Sweden	6.71	Barbados	2.35	Barbados	0.62	Peru	1.91
52	Nigeria	6.67	Japan	2.30	Tunisia	0.57	UK	1.89
53	Colombia	6.37	Argentina	2.26	Paraguay	0.52	New Zealand	1.88
54	Japan	6.26	Peru	2.25	Vanuatu	0.52	El Salvador	1.80
55	Chile	6.05	France	2.10	Guinea-Bissau	0.50	UAE	1.79
56	Lao	5.78	Greece	2.10	Malta	0.49	Switzerland	1.77
57	Panama	5.72	Mauritius	2.04	Albania	0.42	Lebanon	1.76
58	Georgia	5.71	Uruguay	2.01	Japan	0.41	Australia	1.70
59	Dominican Republic	5.64	Latvia	1.94	Brazil	0.36	Austria	1.70
60	Suriname	5.46	Bulgaria	1.85	Belarus	0.35	Nicaragua	1.70
61	Lebanon	5.38	South Korea	1.78	Côte D'Ivoire	0.33	Trinidad	1.60
62	Iceland	5.21	Cape Verde	1.73	Mauritius	0.33	Croatia	1.50

Table 9.1 continues on next page

Table 9.1 Ranking of countries by per adult volume of pure alcohol in total alcohol, beer, wine and spirits in 123 countries, 2000 (continued)

Rank	Country (1)	Total alcohol (2)	Country (3)	Beer (4)	Country (5)	Wine (6)	Country (7)	Spirits (8)
63	Haiti	5.18	Russian Federation	1.67	Botswana	0.30	Cyprus	1.49
64	China	5.17	Singapore	1.60	Mexico	0.30	Bahrain	1.48
65	Norway	5.00	Fiji	1.57	Singapore	0.30	Iceland	1.45
66	Mauritius	4.93	Jamaica	1.50	Fiji	0.28	Belgium	1.36
67	Botswana	4.91	Italy	1.47	Israel	0.25	Denmark	1.36
68	Brazil	4.79	Réunion	1.46	Morocco	0.24	New Caledonia	1.33
69	Rwanda	4.65	Ghana	1.45	UAE	0.21	Romania	1.31
70	Malta	4.62	Bolivia	1.30	Algeria	0.17	Bolivia	1.26
71	Guam	4.50	Samoa	1.28	Bahrain	0.17	Oman	1.23
72	Costa Rica	4.39	Guinea-Bissau	1.21	Trinidad	0.16	Sweden	1.23
73	Peru	4.31	Belize	1.18	Peru	0.15	Guatemala	1.18
74	North Korea	4.13	Chile	1.18	Madagascar	0.14	Malta	1.09
75	Mexico	4.01	Belarus	1.17	Panama	0.12	India	0.98
76	Liberia	3.93	Malawi	1.17	Dominican Republic	0.11	Jamaica	0.91
77	Zimbabwe	3.91	Lesotho	1.14	Togo	0.11	Viet Nam	0.88
78	Belize	3.90	Thailand	1.12	China	0.09	Israel	0.87
79	Cape Verde	3.81	El Salvador	1.11	Samoa	0.09	Honduras	0.83
80	Cuba	3.42	Guyana	1.11	Belize	0.08	Norway	0.83
81	Burkina Faso	3.39	Kenya	1.11	Colombia	0.08	Gabon	0.82
82	Philippines	3.33	Honduras	1.10	Jamaica	0.08	Madagascar	0.80
83	Tanzania	3.04	Angola	1.09	Suriname	0.08	Turkey	0.80
84	El Salvador	2.96	Cuba	1.09	Bolivia	0.07	Mexico	0.79
85	Zambia	2.92	Ecuador	1.04	Venezuela	0.07	Singapore	0.70
86	UAE	2.75	Nigeria	1.04	Costa Rica	0.06	Uruguay	0.69
87	Singapore	2.73	China	1.03	Guam	0.06	Botswana	0.64
88	Bahrain	2.63	Rwanda	1.03	Turkey	0.06	Georgia	0.64
89	Bolivia	2.63	Albania	1.00	Lesotho	0.05	Chile	0.63
90	Nicaragua	2.62	Bahrain	0.98	Zimbabwe	0.05	Guinea-Bissau	0.60
91	Angola	2.56	Côte D'Ivoire	0.98	El Salvador	0.04	Italy	0.58
92	Jamaica	2.48	Israel	0.93	Ghana	0.04	Albania	0.57
93	Mongolia	2.33	Zimbabwe	0.93	Malaysia	0.04	Ecuador	0.57
94	Guinea-Bissau	2.30	Nicaragua	0.88	Mozambique	0.04	French Polynesia	0.48
95	Israel	2.06	Bahamas	0.78	PNG	0.04	Kenya	0.48
96	Fiji	2.02	PNG	0.77	Cuba	0.03	Vanuatu	0.46
97	Albania	1.99	Malaysia	0.76	Ecuador	0.03	Argentina	0.42
98	Honduras	1.96	UAE	0.75	Honduras	0.03	Cape Verde	0.42
99	Guatemala	1.91	Philippines	0.74	Nicaragua	0.03	Angola	0.37
100	Trinidad	1.75	Costa Rica	0.73	Burkina Faso	0.02	Lesotho	0.29
101	Ghana	1.64	Guatemala	0.72	Kenya	0.02	Mozambique	0.23
102	Ecuador	1.63	Turkey	0.71	Mongolia	0.02	Sudan	0.22
103	Kenya	1.61	Togo	0.63	South Korea	0.02	Malawi	0.20
104	Turkey	1.58	Lao	0.47	Zambia	0.02	Fiji	0.19
105	Lesotho	1.47	Viet Nam	0.45	Guatemala	0.01	Burkina Faso	0.18
106	Samoa	1.42	Lebanon	0.33	Haiti	0.01	Uganda	0.18
107	Malawi	1.38	Mongolia	0.32	Liberia	0.01	Zambia	0.18
108	Côte D'Ivoire	1.32	Tunisia	0.32	Malawi	0.01	Malaysia	0.15
109	Oman	1.32	Mozambique	0.29	Philippines	0.01	Sri Lanka	0.12
110	Viet Nam	1.32	Georgia	0.28	Thailand	0.01	Togo	0.09
111	Vanuatu	1.17	Mali	0.27	North Korea	0.00	Tanzania	0.07
112	Madagascar	1.10	North Korea	0.25	Guyana	0.00	Samoa	0.05
113	India	1.01	Liberia	0.21	India	0.00	Morocco	0.04
114	Tunisia	1.01	Morocco	0.20	Lao	0.00	PNG	0.03
115	Malaysia	0.95	Vanuatu	0.17	Mali	0.00	Algeria	0.01
116	PNG	0.85	Madagascar	0.15	Nigeria	0.00	Côte D'Ivoire	0.01
117	Togo	0.85	Oman	0.08	Oman	0.00	Nigeria	0.01
118	Mozambique	0.56	Sri Lanka	0.06	Rwanda	0.00	Ghana	0.00
119	Morocco	0.51	Algeria	0.04	Sri Lanka	0.00	Guam	0.00
120	Mali	0.28	India	0.03	Sudan	0.00	Mali	0.00
121	Algeria	0.22	Trinidad	0.02	Tanzania	0.00	Rwanda	0.00
122	Sudan	0.22	Haiti	0.01	Uganda	0.00	Swaziland	0.00
123	Sri Lanka	0.19	Sudan	0.00	Viet Nam	0.00	Tunisia	0.00
Mean		6.12		2.34		1.46		2.09

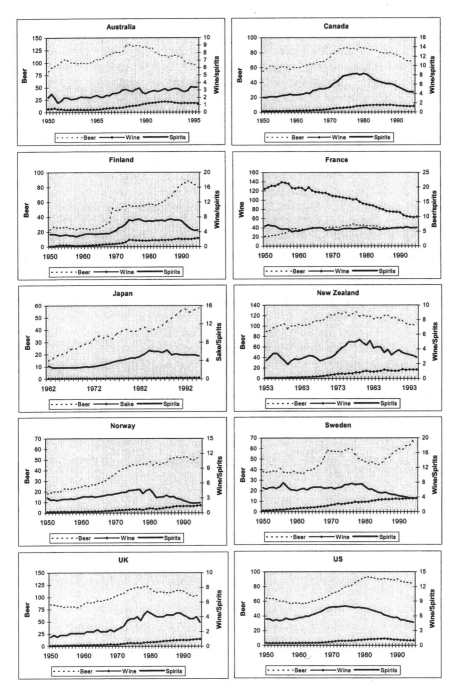

Figure 9.1 Per capita consumption of beer, wine and spirits in 10 countries, 1950-1996

is high in France compared to all other nine countries. While the per capita wine consumption in France has almost halved from 125 litres per capita in 1950 to 63.5 litres per capita in 1995, the per capita wine consumption in all other countries has increased. In most countries, like per capita beer consumption, the per capita spirits consumption also increased up to the mid 1970s and has declined ever since. An overall picture emerges that, in most countries, there is a shift in consumption into wine at the expense of beer and spirits. This could be due to the awareness campaign by the health profession against excessive alcohol drinking, the ban on alcohol advertising in the media and the introduction of new legislative laws regarding drinking and driving in most countries. These measures have had the effect of shifting consumption from high alcohol content beverages to low alcohol content beverages and the consumption of alcohol mostly at home. We will revisit this observation again when we consider the market shares of the three beverages later in the chapter.

Now we present the time series data for alcohol consumption, price and expenditure for the 10 countries. These annual consumption, expenditure and price data for beer, wine and spirits are collected from various issues of government publications. Details of the data sources are reported in the Appendix to this chapter. The sample periods used in the analysis of the ten countries are presented in column 2 of Table 9.2. For all countries, except Japan, we consider three beverages beer, wine and spirits and for Japan wine is replaced by sake. The wine market in Japan is not as significant as the other three beverages.

Figure 9.2 plots the price indices of beer, wine and spirits in each of the 10 countries. As can be seen, the prices of all three beverages have mostly increased rapidly in the last 3 decades. In columns 3-8 of Table 9.2 we present the quantities consumed (q_{it}) of beer (i=1), wine (i=2) and spirits (i=3) and the corresponding

Table 9.2 Price and quantity log-changes (at sample means), 10 countries*

	Country	Sample period	Price			Quantity		
			Beer	Wine	Spirits	Beer	Wine	Spirits
	(1)	(2)	(3)	(4)	(5)	(6)	(7)	(8)
1.	Australia	1955-1998	5.98	5.61	5.87	-0.30	3.05	1.02
2.	Canada	1953-1999	4.59	4.35	2.96	0.18	3.66	0.77
3.	Finland	1969-1985	10.24	10.40	9.23	1.96	3.66	3.06
4.	France	1971-1995	7.71	5.58	3.07	-0.29	-2.21	0.60
5.	Japan	1963-2002	2.67	2.71	2.33	2.17	-1.34	0.85
6.	New Zealand	1965-1982	10.96	10.82	8.33	0.85	9.26	3.07
7.	Norway	1963-1996	6.81	4.67	6.50	2.18	5.15	-1.13
8.	Sweden	1961-1999	7.21	5.51	6.31	1.70	4.34	-1.62
9.	UK	1955-2002	6.82	5.92	4.96	0.29	4.52	2.22
10.	US	1950-2000	0.63	1.35	-0.07	3.30	3.59	3.02
Mean			6.36	6.02	4.95	1.20	3.89	1.19

* For Japan, 'wine' should be replaced by 'sake'. The last row, mean, calculation for 'wine' excludes Japan. All entries in columns 3-8 are multiplied by 100.

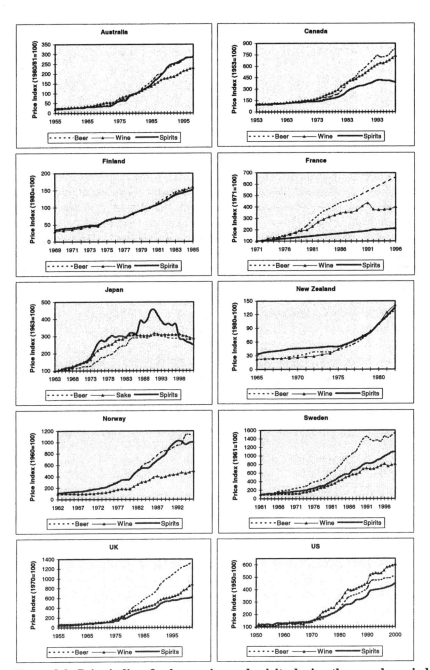

Figure 9.2 Price indices for beer, wine and spirits during the sample period, 10 countries

prices (p_{it}) in log-change form

$$Dq_{it} = \ln q_{it} - \ln q_{it-1} \quad \text{and} \quad Dp_{it} = \ln p_{it} - \ln p_{it-1},$$

at sample means (all are multiplied by 100). These mean values are the annual average growth rates of consumption and prices of the three beverages. It can be seen from columns 3-5 of Table 9.2 that the prices of the three beverages in all countries have increased (except for spirits in the US). From the last row of columns 3-5 of the table, it can be seen that, on average, prices of beer, wine and spirits have risen at a rate of 6.4 percent, 6.0 percent and 5.0 percent, respectively, per annum. Looking at columns 6 to 8 of the table, it can be seen that per capita consumption of beer, wine and spirits have increased in all countries except beer consumption in Australia and France, wine consumption in France, sake consumption in Japan and spirits consumption in Norway and Sweden, where the average consumption growth rate for those beverages is negative. For example, in Australia, on average, the prices of beer, wine and spirits have increased at a rate of 6.0 percent, 5.6 percent and 5.9 percent per annum, respectively, while beer consumption has fallen by .3 percent per annum and wine and sprits consumption have increased by 3.1 and 1.0 percent, per annum, respectively. As can be seen from the last row of the table, on average, the consumption of beer, wine and spirits in the ten countries have increased at a rate of 1.2 percent, 3.9 percent and 1.2 percent per annum, respectively. In most countries, wine consumption and beer prices have the fastest growth.

The first half of Table 9.3 presents the average unconditional budget shares for the three beverages as well as the budget share for total alcohol (alcohol as a whole) averaged over the respective sample periods. The unconditional budget share of beverage i is defined as

$$w_{it} = \frac{p_{it} q_{it}}{M_t}$$

where $p_{it} q_{it}$ is the expenditure on beverage i (=1 for beer, 2 for wine and 3 for spirits) and $M_t = \sum_{i=1}^{n} p_{it} q_{it}$ is the total consumption expenditure on all goods. The budget share of alcohol is then defined as

$$W_{At} = \sum_{i=1}^{3} w_{it}.$$

As can be seen from Table 9.3, on average, consumers in Australia allocate about 3.5 percent of their income on beer, Canada 1.4 percent, Finland 2.5 percent, France 0.3 percent, Japan 2.0 percent, New Zealand 4.0 percent, Norway 2.2 percent, Sweden 1.4 percent, UK 3.7 percent and the US 1.5 percent. Looking at the row for 'wine' we see that, on average, consumers in Australia, Finland, New Zealand and Sweden allocate about 0.9 percent of their income on wine, Canada 0.4 percent, France 1.2 percent, Norway 0.7 percent, the UK 1.3 percent and the US 0.2 percent. The third row for 'spirits' shows that, on average, consumers in

Table 9.3 Mean Unconditional and conditional budget shares for beer, wine, spirits and total alcohol in 10 countries*, selected years

Beverage type	Australia	Canada	Finland	France	Japan	New Zealand	Norway	Sweden	UK	US	Mean
Unconditional budget shares											
Beer	3.50	1.42	2.53	0.33	2.02	3.96	2.17	1.40	3.68	1.53	2.25
Wine	0.88	0.37	0.91	1.23	1.71	0.89	0.74	0.86	1.30	0.24	0.91
Spirits	0.93	1.20	3.28	1.25	0.46	1.66	1.80	2.29	1.70	1.29	1.59
Total alcohol	5.31	2.99	6.72	2.81	4.19	6.51	4.71	4.55	6.68	3.06	4.75
Conditional budget shares											
Beer	64.98	47.55	37.09	13.05	51.17	62.53	46.45	31.34	56.17	51.29	46.16
Wine	17.08	12.26	13.26	43.71	37.97	11.53	15.76	20.13	18.54	8.80	19.90
Spirits	17.94	40.19	49.65	43.24	10.87	25.95	37.79	48.52	25.29	39.91	33.93

* For Japan, 'wine' should be replaced by 'sake'.

Australia allocate about 0.9 percent of their income on spirits, Canada, France and the US about 1.2 percent, Finland 3.3 percent, Japan 0.5 percent, New Zealand, Norway and the UK about 1.7 percent, and Sweden 2.3 percent.

At the individual country level, Australians, Canadians, Japanese, New Zealanders, Norwegians, the British and the Americans allocate a larger proportion of their income on beer compared to wine and spirits while the Finnish and Swedish allocate a larger proportion of their income on spirits compared to beer and wine. The French allocate about equally between wine and spirits. The last row for 'Total alcohol' of the upper half of Table 9.3 shows that, on average, Australians allocate about 5.3 percent of their income to alcohol, Canadians 3.0 percent, Finnish 6.7 percent, French 2.8 percent, Japanese 4.2 percent, New Zealanders 6.5 percent, Norwegians 4.7 percent, Swedish 4.6 percent, British 6.7 percent and the Americans 3.1 percent. On average, in the 10 countries, consumers allocate about 2.3 percent of their income to beer, 0.9 percent to wine and 1.6 percent to spirits with a total of 4.75 percent of their income to alcohol. We shall come back to the lower half of Table 9.3 later in this section.

Figure 9.3 presents a complete time-series plot of the unconditional budget shares of beer, wine, spirits and total alcohol for each of the 10 countries. As discussed earlier, a clear picture emerges across countries that, while the wine share has been steadily increasing, beer and spirits shares have been falling throughout the time periods considered. It can also be seen that the total alcohol share has been declining during the sample periods for all countries except New Zealand. However, the plot for New Zealand should be treated with caution as the data are available only up to 1982 and recent trend could not be deduced from the data.

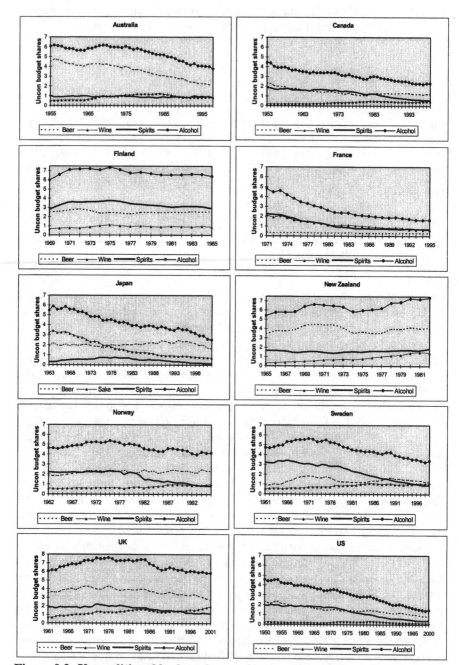

Figure 9.3 Unconditional budget shares of beer, wine, spirits and total alcohol during the sample period, 10 countries

The conditional budget shares (the proportion of total alcohol expenditure devoted to each beverage) of beer, wine and spirits are calculated as

$$w_{it}' = \frac{p_{it}q_{it}}{\sum_{i=1}^{3} p_{it}q_{it}} = \frac{w_{it}}{W_{At}}.$$

The lower half of Table 9.3 presents the conditional budget shares for beer, wine and spirits for 10 countries averaged over the respective sample periods. The last column of the table gives the mean conditional budget shares for beer, wine and spirits for each time period but averaged across countries. On average, Australians spent about 65 percent of their alcohol expenditure on beer, 17 percent on wine and the remaining 18 percent on spirits. On average, people from the ten countries allocated 46 percent of their alcohol expenditure to beer, 20 percent to wine and the remaining 34 percent to spirits. Also, consumers in all countries, except Finland, France and Sweden, allocated about half of their alcohol expenditure to beer. In general, it appears that the Australians, Canadians, Japanese, New Zealanders, British and Americans are traditional beer drinkers. It is worth noting that we have earlier observed this pattern with respect to the consumption data presented in Table 9.1 as well. In all countries except France, on average, consumers allocate somewhere in the range of 9 percent (US) to 20 percent (Sweden) of their alcohol expenditure to wine. In France, on average, consumers spend about 44 percent of their alcohol expenditure on wine and lead all the other nine nations. With regard to spirits, within alcohol, consumers in Finland, France and Sweden dominate all other countries.

Figure 9.4 graphs the complete time-series of conditional budget shares of beer, wine and spirits at the individual country level. As can be seen, in most countries, the movement of the budget share allocation to beer and spirits are in the opposite direction throughout the sample period. The allocation of budget to wine is steadily increasing over the sample period in most countries.

9.3 Divisia Moments of Alcohol in 10 Countries

We now apply conditional versions of the Divisia moments introduced in Section 7.1 to the alcohol data. That is, we summarise all the price and quantity data of the individual beverages in the form of Divisia price and quantity index, Divisia price and quantity variance and Divisia price-quantity correlations for alcohol as a whole.

The within alcohol versions of the Divisia price and quantity indices are

$$DP_{At} = \sum_{i=1}^{3} \overline{w}_{it}' Dp_{it}$$

and

$$DQ_{At} = \sum_{i=1}^{3} \overline{w}_{it}' Dq_{it},$$

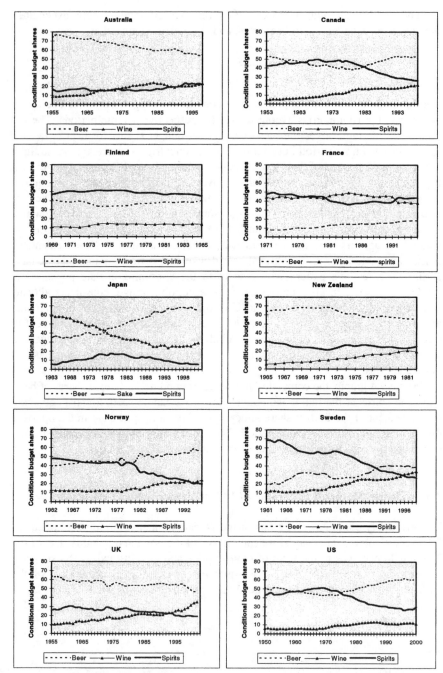

**Figure 9.4 Conditional budget shares of beer, wine and spirits during the
sample period, 10 countries**

where $\overline{w}'_{it} = \frac{1}{2}(w'_{it} + w'_{it-1})$ is the arithmetic average of the conditional budget share during periods t and t-1 with $w'_{it} = w_{it} / W_{At}$ being the conditional budget share of beverage i in period t; and Dp_{it} and Dq_{it} are the price and quantity log-changes as defined before.

To measure the variability in prices and consumption of alcohol, we use the Divisia price variance and Divisia quantity variance of alcohol defined in Section 7.1, which we reproduce here,

$$\Pi_{At} \quad = \quad \sum_{i=1}^{3} \overline{w}'_{it} [Dp_{it} - DP_{At}]^2,$$

and

$$K_{At} \quad = \quad \sum_{i=1}^{3} \overline{w}'_{it} [Dq_{it} - DQ_{At}]^2.$$

To measure the co-movement of prices and consumption of alcohol we use the Divisia price-quantity correlation coefficient, again defined in Section 7.1 and reproduced here,

$$\rho_{At} \quad = \quad \frac{\Gamma_{At}}{\sqrt{K_{At}\Pi_{At}}}, \qquad\qquad t=1, ..., T.$$

where

$$\Gamma_{gt} \quad = \quad \sum_{i=1}^{3} \overline{w}'_{it} [Dp_{it} - DP_{At}][Dq_{it} - DQ_{At}]$$

is the Divisia price-quantity covariance. Table 9.4 presents these Divisia summary measures. Columns 2-3 of the table presents the Divisia price and quantity indices, columns 4 and 5 present the corresponding Divisia price and quantity variances and the last two columns present the Divisia price-quantity covariance and correlation. As can be see from columns 2 and 3 of Table 9.4, on average across the 10 countries, the price of alcohol has increased by 2.8 to 10.4 percent per annum with a cross-country average alcohol price increase of 6 percent per annum, where the lowest price increase was in Japan (2.8 percent/annum) and the highest in New Zealand (10.4 percent/annum). Per capita alcohol consumption has increased by 0.5 to 2.7 percent per annum (except France where the per capita alcohol consumption has fallen at a rate of 0.8 percent per annum) with a cross-country average of 1 percent per annum.

As can be seen from columns 4 and 5 of Table 9.4, the consumption shows higher variation than prices. In 8 out of the 10 countries the quantity variance exceeds the price variance which is well in agreement with a number of previous studies (see Chen, 2001; Meisner, 1979; Selvanathan, 1993; Selvanathan and Selvanathan, 1994, 2003; and Theil and Suhm, 1981). The price-quantity correlation presented in column 7 of the table is negative in all countries with a cross-country average of -0.3. This reflects the tendency of the drinkers to move away from those beverages having above average price increases.

Table 9.4 Divisia Moments, 10 countries

Country	Price-index	Quantity index	Price variance	Quantity variance	Price-quantity covariance	Price-quantity correlation
(1)	(2)	(3)	(4)	(5)	(6)	(7)
1. Australia	5.83	0.53	6.12	12.72	-4.15	-0.45
2. Canada	3.90	0.89	6.81	7.32	-2.88	-0.17
3. Finland	9.78	2.69	1.89	15.39	-1.79	-0.09
4. France	4.82	-0.80	13.33	6.69	-0.97	-0.14
5. Japan	2.79	0.42	6.53	21.94	-3.32	-0.20
6. New Zealand	10.41	2.21	11.22	25.13	-6.05	-0.25
7. Norway	6.43	1.52	7.32	23.69	-2.59	-0.38
8. Sweden	6.34	0.77	7.37	19.23	-4.53	-0.30
9. UK	6.18	1.64	11.59	17.57	-8.52	-0.27
10. US	3.21	0.45	6.71	4.75	-2.10	-0.20
Mean	5.97	1.03	7.89	15.44	-3.69	-0.25

* All entries in columns 2-3 are to be divided by 100 and columns 4-6 are to be divided by 10000.

9.4 Relative Prices and Relative Consumption of Alcohol in the 10 Countries

The relative price and relative consumption of beverage i within alcohol are

$$Dp_{it}^* = Dp_{it} - DP_{At} \quad \text{and} \quad Dq_{it}^* = Dq_{it} - DQ_{At}$$

where DP_{At} and DQ_{At} are the Divisia price and volume indices, respectively, of alcohol defined in Section 9.3. Columns 2-4 and 5-7 of Table 9.5 present the mean relative growth in prices and consumption, respectively, of the three beverages for the 10 countries. As can be seen, within alcohol, in all countries (except Japan) the relative growth in price of beer is positive and that of wine is mixed while that of spirits (except in Australia and Norway) is negative. The growth in consumption of beer and spirits are mixed whereas that of wine is positive (except that in France). The relative growth in the price and consumption of sake in Japan are both negative. The above observations about the relative prices and relative consumption could be due to higher beer and spirits taxes and lower wine taxes experienced by most of these countries in the last 3 to 4 decades. The positive relative consumption growth in wine and relative negative consumption growth in spirits could be due to the shift in consumer preferences from spirits to wine due to increasing prices of spirits as well as the fact that people are moving away from high alcohol content beverages such as spirits.

The within alcohol version of equation (2.2) of Section 8.2 is

$$(Dq_{it}^c - DQ_{At}^c) = \phi^c (Dp_{it}^c - DP_{At}^c), \qquad i=1,2,3; \ t=1,\ldots,T, \qquad (4.1)$$

where we have added a country superscript to all the variables and ϕ. For a given i,

Table 9.5 Mean relative price and quantity log-changes

		Price			Quantity		
Country		Beer	Wine	Spirits	Beer	Wine	Spirits
(1)		(2)	(3)	(4)	(5)	(6)	(7)
1.	Australia	0.15	-0.23	0.03	-0.83	2.51	0.49
2.	Canada	0.69	0.45	-0.94	-0.70	2.78	-0.11
3.	Finland	0.46	0.61	-0.55	-0.74	0.96	0.37
4.	France	2.89	0.75	-1.75	0.51	-1.42	1.40
5.	Japan	-0.13	-0.08	-0.46	1.74	-1.76	0.43
6.	New Zealand	0.55	0.41	-2.08	-1.35	7.06	0.87
7.	Norway	0.38	-1.76	0.07	0.66	3.63	-2.65
8.	Sweden	0.87	-0.83	-0.03	0.93	3.57	-2.40
9.	UK	0.64	-0.25	-1.22	-1.35	2.87	0.58
10.	US	0.09	0.38	-0.19	0.18	0.90	-0.52
Mean		0.66	-0.06	-0.71	-0.10	2.11	-0.15

* For Japan, 'wine' is replaced by 'sake'. All entries are to be divided by 100.

if we regress the growth in relative consumption of i, $(Dq_{it}^c - DQ_{At}^c)$, against the growth in relative price of i, $(Dp_{it}^c - DP_{At}^c)$, for t=1,...,T, the slope of the regression line can be interpreted as ϕ^c, the income flexibility.

We plot relative consumption against relative price for each beverage in the 10 countries. Thirty such plots are presented in Figure 9.5 and estimates of the trend lines are presented in Table 9.6. As can be seen, there is a strong negative relationship between relative price and relative consumption of each beverage. The slope of the estimated trend line in all plots are negative which can be interpreted as an estimate of income flexibility. From columns 5 and 6 of Table 9.6, we can see that most of the estimates of income flexibility are estimated significantly, with an average income flexibility of –0.5, which is well in agreement with many previous econometric findings (see, for example, Chen, 2001; Selvanathan, 1993; Selvanathan and Selvanathan, 2003; Theil and Clements, 1987; and Theil and Suhm, 1981).

Under the assumption of unitary income elasticity of alcohol, the demand equation for the alcoholic beverages group given in equation (2.14) of Chapter 7 can be written as

$$[DQ_{At} - DQ_t] = \phi[DP_{At} - DP_t], \qquad t=1,...,T, \qquad (4.2)$$

where $[DQ_{At} - DQ_t]$ and $[DP_{At} - DP_t]$ are the relative consumption and relative prices of alcohol with DQ_t and DP_t being the overall Divisia quantity and price indices of all n goods. In Figure 9.6 we plot the time-series of relative consumption of alcohol against relative prices of alcohol for the 10 countries. The estimates of the trend lines from the plots are presented in Table 9.7. As can be seen, again there is a strong negative relationship between relative price and relative consumption of

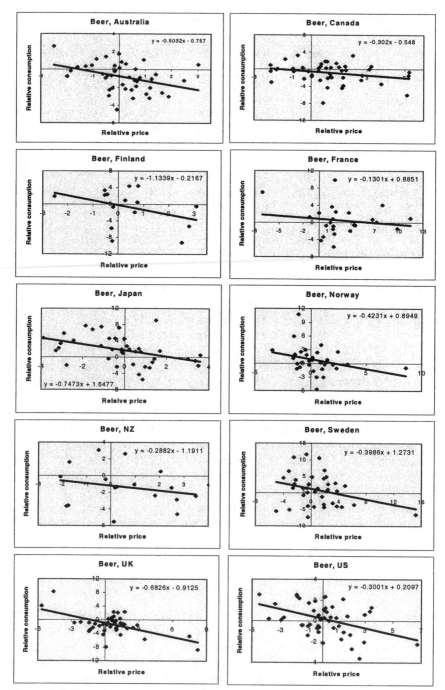

Figure 9.5 Relative consumption against relative price of beer, 10 countries

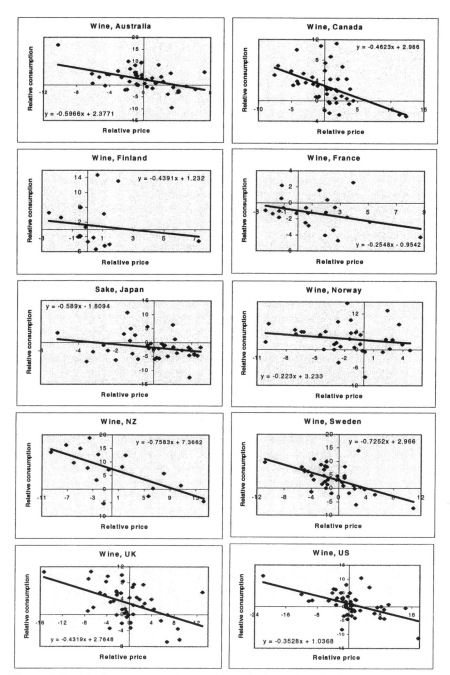

Figure 9.5 Relative consumption against relative price of wine, 10 countries (continued)

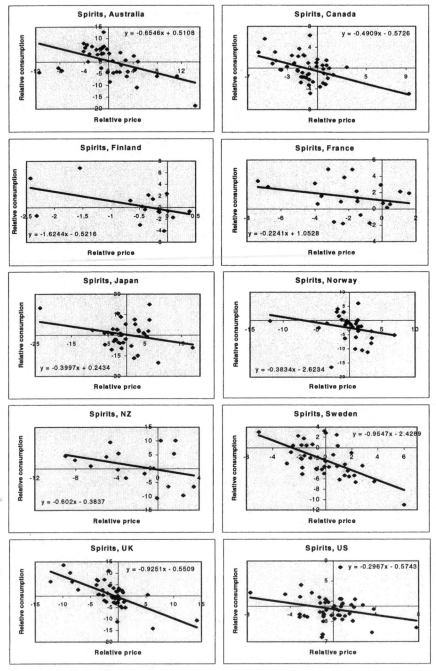

Figure 9.5   Relative consumption against relative price of spirits, 10 countries (continued)

Table 9.6 First set of estimates for income flexibility, 10 countries

Country (1)	Alcohol type (2)	Intercept term Estimate (3)	p-value (4)	Income flexibility Estimate (5)	p-value (6)
Australia	Beer	-0.757 (0.223)	0.002	-0.503 (0.199)	0.015
	Wine	2.377 (0.606)	0.000	-0.597 (0.174)	0.001
	Spirits	0.511 (0.805)	0.529	-0.655 (0.178)	0.001
Canada	Beer	-0.424 (0.338)	0.216	-0.402 (0.134)	0.004
	Wine	2.986 (0.457)	0.000	-0.462 (0.122)	0.000
	Spirits	-0.573 (0.342)	0.101	-0.491 (0.133)	0.001
Finland	Beer	-0.217 (1.110)	0.848	-1.134 (0.769)	0.162
	Wine	1.232 (1.657)	0.469	-0.439 (0.773)	0.579
	Spirits	-0.522 (0.763)	0.506	-1.624 (0.785)	0.058
France	Beer	0.885 (0.891)	0.331	-0.130 (0.188)	0.496
	Wine	-0.954 (0.430)	0.038	-0.255 (0.152)	0.109
	Spirits	1.053 (0.550)	0.070	-0.224 (0.185)	0.239
Japan	Beer	1.648 (0.509)	0.003	-0.747 (0.272)	0.009
	Sake	-1.809 (0.673)	0.011	-0.589 (0.384)	0.133
	Spirits	0.243 (1.451)	0.868	-0.400 (0.233)	0.095
Norway	Beer	0.895 (0.518)	0.095	-0.423 (0.249)	0.100
	Wine	3.233 (0.907)	0.001	-0.223 (0.221)	0.322
	Spirits	-2.623 (0.786)	0.002	-0.383 (0.261)	0.152
New Zealand	Beer	-1.191 (0.617)	0.073	-0.288 (0.339)	0.409
	Wine	7.366 (1.347)	0.000	-0.758 (0.209)	0.002
	Spirits	-0.384 (1.786)	0.833	-0.602 (0.425)	0.177
Sweden	Beer	1.273 (0.777)	0.110	-0.399 (0.216)	0.073
	Wine	2.966 (0.641)	0.000	-0.725 (0.173)	0.000
	Spirits	-2.429 (0.418)	0.000	-0.955 (0.203)	0.000
UK	Beer	-0.913 (0.350)	0.012	-0.683 (0.149)	0.000
	Wine	2.765 (0.559)	0.000	-0.432 (0.116)	0.001
	Spirits	-0.551 (0.580)	0.347	-0.925 (0.138)	0.000
US	Beer	0.210 (0.188)	0.272	-0.300 (0.095)	0.003
	Wine	1.037 (0.515)	0.050	-0.353 (0.081)	0.000
	Spirits	-0.574 (0.335)	0.093	-0.297 (0.145)	0.047
Mean				-0.547 (0.057)	

alcohol as a whole. The slope of the estimated trend line in all plots are negative which can again be interpreted as an estimate of income flexibility. From columns 4 and 5 of Table 9.7, we can see that 9 out of the 10 income flexibility estimates are estimated significantly, with an average income flexibility of –0.6, which is very close to the average of the estimates presented in Table 9.6.

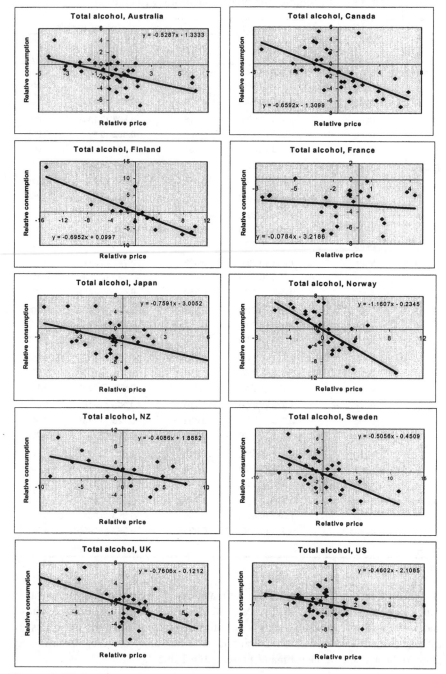

Figure 9.6 Relative consumption against relative price of alcohol, 10 countries

Table 9.7 Second set of estimates for income flexibility, 10 countries

		Intercept term		Income flexibility	
	Country	Estimate	*p*-value	Estimate	*p*-value
	(1)	(2)	(3)	(4)	(5)
1.	Australia	-1.333 (0.303)	0.000	-0.529 (0.127)	0.000
2.	Canada	-1.310 (0.433)	0.005	-0.659 (0.142)	0.000
3.	Finland	0.100 (0.702)	0.889	-0.695 (0.117)	0.000
4.	France	-3.219 (0.458)	0.000	-0.078 (0.138)	0.574
5.	Japan	-3.005 (0.714)	0.000	-0.759 (0.292)	0.016
6.	Norway	-0.234 (0.623)	0.709	-1.161 (0.213)	0.000
7.	New Zealand	1.888 (0.746)	0.023	-0.409 (0.157)	0.020
8.	Sweden	-0.451 (0.441)	0.315	-0.506 (0.123)	0.000
9.	UK	-0.121 (0.436)	0.783	-0.761 (0.155)	0.000
10.	US	-2.109 (0.420)	0.000	-0.460 (0.166)	0.009
Mean				-0.602 (0.089)	

9.5   Elasticities from Double-Log Demand Equations

In Chapter 8, we used the double-log demand equations to obtain preliminary estimates of income and price elasticities of the alcoholic beverages group as a single commodity. In this section, we use them to obtain preliminary estimates for the income and price elasticities of the individual alcoholic beverages, beer, wine and spirits. In Section 9.6, we use the differential demand systems introduced in Chapters 6 and 7 to obtain final estimates for the conditional demand elasticities and then compare the two sets of estimates.

The conditional version of the double-log demand equation (3.1) given in Section 8.3 for beverage i in finite-change form can be written as

$$Dq_{it} = \alpha_i + \eta_i\, DQ_{At} + \gamma_i\, [Dp_{it} - DP_{At}] + \varepsilon_{it}, \qquad i=1,2,3;\ t=1,\ldots,T, \qquad (5.1)$$

where $DQ_{At} = \sum_{i=1}^{3} \overline{w}_{it}' Dq_{it}$; $DP_{At} = \sum_{i=1}^{3} \overline{w}_{it}'' Dp_{it}$; α_i is an autonomous trend term; η_i is the income elasticity of beverage i; γ_i is the Slutsky own-price elasticity of beverage i; and ε_{it} is a disturbance term. It is worth noting that this double-log demand equation includes only the own-relative price of beverage i and not other prices. We estimate (5.1) by least squares (LS) for each beverage and each country separately. Table 9.8 presents the estimates for the income elasticity (η_i) and own-price elasticity (γ_i), respectively, for each beverage. The last row of the table presents the elasticities for each beverage averaged over the 10 countries. As can be seen from columns 2 to 4 of the table, all the income elasticites for beer (except that for Japan) are less than one with a cross-country average of 0.7, indicating that in all countries beer is a necessity. A majority of the wine income elasticities are larger than one with an average of 1.10 (excluding Japan), indicating that wine is a luxury in most countries. For Japan, the income elasticity for sake is less than one implying that it is a necessity. The income elasticity for spirits is greater than one in

Table 9.8 Double-log demand model estimates, 10 countries

	Country	Income elasticity			Own-price elasticitiy		
		Beer	Wine	Spirits	Beer	Wine	Spirits
	(1)	(2)	(3)	(4)	(5)	(6)	(7)
1.	Australia	0.769	1.059	1.929	-0.654	-0.612	-0.683
		(0.074)	(0.231)	(0.251)	(0.187)	(0.187)	(0.156)
2.	Canada	0.645	1.350	1.355	-0.428	-0.569	-0.486
		(0.074)	(0.124)	(0.072)	(0.109)	(0.120)	(0.107)
3.	Finland	0.424	1.630	1.245	-0.811	-0.386	-1.426
		(0.166)	(0.295)	(0.120)	(0.582)	(0.690)	(0.715)
4.	France	0.649	0.848	1.287	-0.077	-0.090	-0.145
		(0.350)	(0.235)	(0.260)	(0.161)	(0.144)	(0.160)
5.	Japan*	1.309	0.502	1.259	-0.330	-0.060	-0.445
		(0.103)	(0.116)	(0.290)	(0.284)	(0.340)	(0.239)
6.	Norway	0.400	1.379	1.635	0.092	-0.181	-0.209
		(0.106)	(0.150)	(0.112)	(0.270)	(0.206)	(0.189)
7.	New Zealand	0.818	1.150	1.533	-0.229	-0.777	-0.428
		(0.214)	(0.509)	(0.609)	(0.350)	(0.224)	(0.472)
8.	Sweden	0.814	0.399	1.150	-0.287	-0.760	-0.843
		(0.248)	(0.139)	(0.123)	(0.263)	(0.142)	(0.222)
9.	UK	0.797	0.913	1.435	-0.672	-0.408	-0.799
		(0.093)	(0.177)	(0.159)	(0.143)	(0.127)	(0.137)
10.	US	0.810	1.176	1.348	-0.287	-0.368	-0.259
		(0.070)	(0.208)	(0.124)	(0.090)	(0.084)	(0.136)
Mean		0.744	1.100	1.418	-0.368	-0.461	-0.572
		(0.080)	(0.119)	(0.073)	(0.088)	(0.080)	(0.121)

* For Japan, the 'wine' column values refer to 'sake'. The average values for wine do not include Japan.

all countries with a cross-country average of 1.42, indicating that spirits is also considered as a luxury.

The own-price elasticities presented in columns 5 to 7 of Table 9.8 are all negative as they should be. It can also be seen that they are all (except that for spirits in Finland) less than one in absolute value, indicating that demand for all three beverages, beer, wine and spirits, are price inelastic. The average own-price elasticities across countries are –0.37 for beer, -0.46 for wine and –0.57 for spirits.

9.6　Estimation and Hypothesis Testing

In this section, we present the estimation results of the differential demand model parameters and test the demand theory hypotheses, homogeneity and Slutsky symmetry, and the preference independent structure of the utility function.

The modified absolute price version of the conditional Rotterdam demand model for beverage i is given by equation (3.7) from Section 7.3, which with a constant and an error term added can be written as

$$\overline{w}'_{it}Dq_{it} = \alpha_i + \theta'_i DQ_{gt} + \sum_{j=1}^{3} \pi'_{ij}Dp_{jt} + \varepsilon_{it}, \qquad i=1,2,3;\ t=1,\ldots,T, \qquad (6.1)$$

where $\overline{w}'_{it}$ is the conditional budget share of beverage i; Dq_{it} and Dp_{it} are the quantity and price log-changes; $DQ_{gt} = \sum_{i=1}^{3} \overline{w}'_{it}Dq_{it}$ is the Divisia volume index of alcohol; α_i is a constant term; θ'_i is the conditional marginal share of beverage i and π'_{ij} is the (i,j)th modified conditional Slutsky coefficient. The parameters of equation (6.1) satisfy the adding up restrictions:

$$\sum_{i=1}^{3} \alpha_i = 0; \qquad \sum_{i=1}^{3} \theta'_i = 1; \qquad \sum_{i=1}^{3} \pi'_{ij} = 0, \qquad j=1,2,3. \qquad (6.2)$$

We specify the coefficients, α_i, θ'_i and π'_{ij} in equation (6.1) as constants. The constant terms are included in equation (6.1) to take account of autonomous trends in consumption due to variables such as advertising, demographic structure of the population, drink-driving laws, social factors etc. The zero-mean error term ε_{it} on the right-hand side of equation (6.1) is independent and multivariate normal with a constant covariance matrix. We take total alcohol consumption and prices to be predetermined and use maximum likelihood for estimation.

Now we use the tests described in Chapter 7 and applied in Chapter 8 to perform the tests of the demand theory hypotheses homogeneity and Slutsky symmetry within the alcoholic beverages group and preference independent structure among the three beverages.

Demand Homogeneity

The demand homogeneity for the three beverages, beer, wine and spirits can be written as

$$\sum_{j=1}^{3} \pi'_{ij} = 0, \qquad i=1,2,3.$$

To test homogeneity, we use the test statistic (4.1) from Section 8.4, which we reproduce here

$$\Psi_H = \frac{(\mathbf{R}\hat{\gamma})'\mathbf{S}^{-1}(\mathbf{R}\hat{\gamma})}{\mathbf{a}'(\mathbf{X}'\mathbf{X})^{-1}\mathbf{a}} \qquad (6.3)$$

For a large sample, this test statistic follows an asymptotic chi-squared distribution with n-1 degrees of freedom. We now calculate the value of the test statistic (6.3) for each country and these values are presented in column 2 of Table 9.9. The critical value of the test at the 5 percent level of significance is $\chi^2_{2,.05} = 5.99$. A comparison of data-based values in column 2 with the critical value reveals that for 8 out of the 10 countries (except for France and the US) homogeneity is acceptable.

As discussed in Section 8.4, the reason for such rejection could be due to the asymptotic nature of the test. We now perform the finite-sample test introduced by

Table 9.9 Testing homogeneity and symmetry in 10 countries

Country	Homogeneity						Symmetry		
	Asymptotic test			Exact test					
	Data-based	Critical	Conclusion	Data-based	Critical	Conclusion	Data-based	Critical	Conclusion
(1)	(2)	(3)	(4)	(5)	(6)	(7)	(8)	(9)	(10)
1 Australia	5.45	5.99	Accept	2.65	$F(2,37)=3.25$	Accept	0.24	3.84	Accept
2 Canada	4.57	5.99	Accept	2.23	$F(2,40)=3.23$	Accept	0.47	3.84	Accept
3 Finland	2.32	5.99	Accept	1.06	$F(2,10)=4.10$	Accept	0.01	3.84	Accept
4 France	12.38	5.99	Reject	5.88	$F(2,18)=6.01^*$	Accept*	2.89	3.84	Accept
5 Japan	3.64	5.99	Accept	1.77	$F(2,33)=3.28$	Accept	2.04	3.84	Accept
6 New Zealand	1.05	5.99	Accept	0.48	$F(2,11)=3.98$	Accept	4.91	6.63*	Accept*
7 Norway	0.37	5.99	Accept	0.18	$F(2,27)=3.35$	Accept	2.31	3.84	Accept
8 Sweden	0.70	5.99	Accept	0.34	$F(2,32)=3.29$	Accept	3.97	6.63*	Accept*
9 UK	1.39	5.99	Accept	0.68	$F(2,41)=3.23$	Accept	1.72	3.84	Accept
10 US	12.02	5.99	Reject	5.88	$F(2,44)=3.21$	Reject	0.99	3.84	Accept

The level of significance $\alpha = 0.05$. A * denotes critical value and conclusion at $\alpha = 0.01$.

Laitinen (1978). The test statistic (6.4), in general, follows a Hotelling's T^2 distribution which itself is distributed as a constant multiple $(n-1)(T-n-2)/(T-2n)$ of the F-distribution, $F(n-1,T-2n)$. The observed value of this F-test statistic is given in column 5 of Table 9.9 and the corresponding critical values are given in column 6. A comparison of these two columns reveals that now homogeneity is acceptable for all (except one) of the countries. Therefore, overall, we can conclude that the demand homogeneity hypothesis is generally acceptable for the 10 countries.

Slutsky Symmetry

Slutsky symmetry among the three alcoholic beverages, beer, wine and spirits, can be written as

$$\pi'_{ij} = \pi'_{ji}, \qquad\qquad i,j=1,2,3.$$

We now test symmetry using the test statistic (4.2) of Section 8.4, which we reproduce here,

$$\Psi_S = (R\hat{\gamma}^H)'\{R[S \otimes (X^{H'}X^H)^{-1}]R'\}^{-1}(R\hat{\gamma}^H), \qquad\qquad (6.4)$$

which follows a chi-squared distribution with q $(=\frac{1}{2}(n-1)(n-2)) = 1$ degree of freedom. The data-based values of (6.4) and the critical values are given in columns 8 and 9 of the table. As can be seen from the last column, the symmetry hypothesis is acceptable at the 5 percent level (except New Zealand and Sweden, for which symmetry is acceptable at the 1 percent level) for all countries.

Preference Independence

Now we test the preference independent utility structure among the three beverages, beer, wine and spirits, using data from the 10 countries. Under the preference independent utility structure, the modified price coefficients given by (3.3) of Section 7.3 can be written as

$$v'_{ij} = \eta_{AA} \theta'_i \delta_{ij}, \qquad\qquad i,j=1,2,3, \qquad\qquad (6.5)$$

where $\eta_{AA} = \phi\theta_A/\overline{W}_{At}$ is the own-price elasticity of the alcoholic beverages group defined in (8.10) of Section 6.8; ϕ is the income flexibility; θ'_i is the conditional marginal share of beverage i; and θ_A is the marginal share of the alcoholic beverages group. The group income elasticity as defined in (8.10) of Section 6.8 is $\eta_A = \theta_A/\overline{W}_{At}$. Therefore, we can write the group own-price elasticity as

$$\eta_{AA} = \phi\eta_A.$$

A point worth noting here is that, under the assumption of unitary income elasticity of alcohol (ie, $\eta_A = 1$), $\eta_{AA} = \phi$, the income flexibility.

The preference independent version of the Rotterdam model is given by equation (3.1) in Section 7.3 and equation (6.5), which we reproduce here:

$$\overline{w}'_{it} Dq_{it} = \theta'_i DQ_{At} + \eta_{AA} \theta'_i (Dp_{it} - DP'_{At}), \qquad\qquad i=1,2,3, \qquad (6.6)$$

where $DP'_{At} = \sum_{i=1}^{3}\theta'_i Dp_{it}$.

We test preference independence using a likelihood ratio test as well as Monte Carlo simulations described in Section 8.4. The data-based values of the likelihood ratio test statistic for the 10 countries are presented in column 2 of Table 9.10 and the critical chi-squared value with degrees of freedom 2 ($=\frac{1}{2}n(n-2)-1$) is given in column 3. As can be seen, preference independence is acceptable for all countries except Sweden at the 5 percent significance level. As before, the reason for such rejection for Sweden could be due the nature of the asymptotic test. We now apply the Monte Carlo simulation procedure described in Section 7.6 to test preference independence for the 10 countries in order to check the validity of the asymptotic

Table 9.10 Testing preference independence in 10 countries

	Country	Asymptotic test			Monte Carlo simulations	
		Data-based	Critical	Conclusion	Rank	Conclusion
	(1)	(2)	(3)	(4)	(5)	(6)
1	Australia	1.84	5.99	Accept	594	Accept
2	Canada	1.06	5.99	Accept	371	Accept
3	Finland	2.40	5.99	Accept	570	Accept
4	France	0.84	5.99	Accept	320	Accept
5	Japan	0.40	5.99	Accept	172	Accept
6	New Zealand	0.68	5.99	Accept	238	Accept
7	Norway	2.33	5.99	Accept	650	Accept
8	Sweden	6.19	5.99	Reject	938	Accept
9	UK	1.57	5.99	Accept	497	Accept
10	US	0.50	5.99	Accept	207	Accept

Degrees of freedom $k = \frac{1}{2}n(n-1)-1=2$. The level of significance $\alpha = 0.05$.

results in columns 2-4. The results (the rank of the data-based statistics out of 1000 simulation trials) are given in column 5 of the table. For a one-tailed test at the 5 percent level, we reject preference independence if the rank falls between 951 and 1000. As can be seen from the rank of the data-based value of the test statistic for the 10 countries, we are unable to reject a preference independent utility structure between the three beverages for all countries. Therefore, we use the model under preference independence (6.6) as our preferred demand system to derive the demand elasticities and further analysis in this chapter.

Estimation Results of the Preferred Demand System

We estimate the model under preference independence (6.6) using the ML procedure for the 10 countries and the estimation results are presented in Table 9.11. The constant terms presented in columns 2 to 4 of the table show that, in most countries, the constant term for wine is positive and for spirits is negative indicating an autonomous trend out of the latter into the former. The sign of the constant term for beer is mixed with a positive but close to zero cross-country average. For example, in Australia, the constant terms of beer and spirits are negative and that of wine is positive, indicating that there is an autonomous trend out of beer and spirits into wine.

Columns 5 to 7 of Table 9.11 present the conditional marginal share estimates. As can be seen, the conditional marginal shares are all positive and significant. For example, the estimates of the conditional marginal shares of beer, wine and spirits for Australia indicate that when consumers alcohol expenditure increases by one dollar, out of that one dollar increase, 52 cents will be spent on beer, 17 cents on wine and 32 cents on spirits. The estimates of the income flexibility (which is the same as the price elasticity of alcohol, η_{AA}, under unitary income elasticity) for the

Table 9.11 Parameter estimates under preference independence, 10 countries

Country	Intercepts			Conditional marginal shares			Income flexibility
	Beer	Wine	Spirits	Beer	Wine	Spirits	
(1)	(2)	(3)	(4)	(5)	(6)	(7)	(8)
1 Australia	-0.37 (0.13)	0.39 (0.11)	-0.01 (0.13)	0.52 (0.04)	0.17 (0.04)	0.32 (0.04)	-0.52 (0.10)
2 Canada	-0.10 (0.12)	0.28 (0.06)	-0.18 (0.13)	0.31 (0.03)	0.15 (0.02)	0.54 (0.03)	-0.47 (0.09)
3 Finland	0.36 (0.32)	-0.02 (0.20)	-0.34 (0.32)	0.16 (0.06)	0.20 (0.04)	0.63 (0.06)	-0.64 (0.43)
4 France*				0.09 (0.04)	0.39 (0.11)	0.52 (0.11)	-0.09 (0.13)
5 Japan	0.38 (0.27)	-0.39 (0.23)	0.01 (0.15)	0.65 (0.05)	0.24 (0.05)	0.11 (0.03)	-0.26 (0.19)
6 New Zealand	-0.35 (0.42)	0.74 (0.21)	-0.38 (0.47)	0.53 (0.11)	0.11 (0.06)	0.36 (0.11)	-0.44 (0.21)
7 Norway	0.72 (0.25)	0.44 (0.13)	-1.16 (0.20)	0.18 (0.05)	0.19 (0.02)	0.63 (0.04)	-0.14 (0.12)
8 Sweden	0.45 (0.23)	0.62 (0.12)	-1.07 (0.23)	0.25 (0.07)	0.09 (0.03)	0.66 (0.07)	-0.76 (0.20)
9 UK	-0.38 (0.19)	0.64 (0.13)	-0.26 (0.15)	0.49 (0.05)	0.13 (0.03)	0.38 (0.04)	-0.60 (0.10)
10 US	0.09 (0.09)	0.06 (0.05)	-0.15 (0.11)	0.41 (0.03)	0.10 (0.02)	0.50 (0.04)	-0.28 (0.06)
Mean	0.09 (0.14)	0.30 (0.12)	-0.39 (0.14)	0.36 (0.06)	0.18 (0.03)	0.47 (0.05)	-0.42 (0.07)

* No constant model for France. For Japan, the 'wine' column values refer to 'sake'. The average values for wine do not include Japan. Strictly speaking, the estimates presented in column 8 are those of the own-price elasticity of the alcoholic beverages group (η_{AA}). However, as mentioned elsewhere in the text, under unitary income elasticity of alcohol, this is the same as income flexibility.

10 countries are presented in column 8 of the table. As can be seen, all the estimates are negative as they should be with a cross-country average of -0.42. This estimated value is well in agreement with our estimates of income flexibility presented in Tables 9.6 and 9.7 as well as with previous econometric findings.

Implied Demand Elasticities

Using the parameter estimates presented in Table 9.11, we present the implied income and price elasticities (at sample means) of demand model (6.6) in Table 9.12. As can be seen, the income elasticity of beer is less than one in all countries (except Japan) indicating that beer is a necessity. In Japan, beer is a luxury. Wine is a luxury in Australia, Canada, Finland, Norway and the US and a necessity in France, New Zealand, Sweden and the UK. In Japan, sake is a necessity. Income elasticity for spirits is larger than one in all countries indicating that spirits is a luxury in all countries. The own- and cross-price elasticities are presented in columns 5-13 of the table. All the own-price elasticities (see BB, WW and SS columns of Table 9.12) are less than one in absolute value indicating that demand for all the beverages are price inelastic. The average cross-country income elasticities for beer, wine and spirits are 0.75, 0.98 and 1.39, respectively, indicating that in most countries beer is a necessity and spirits is a luxury. The average own-price elasticities across countries for beer, wine and spirits are -0.19, -0.35 and -0.31, respectively.

Table 9.12 Conditional income and price elasticities, 10 countries

	Country	Income elasticities			Own-price and cross-price elasticities								
		Beer	Wine	Spirits	BB	BW	BS	WB	WW	WS	SB	SW	SS
	(1)	(2)	(3)	(4)	(5)	(6)	(7)	(8)	(9)	(10)	(11)	(12)	(13)
1	Australia	0.79	1.00	1.80	-0.20	0.07	0.13	0.27	-0.43	0.16	0.48	0.16	-0.64
2	Canada	0.67	1.18	1.32	-0.22	0.05	0.17	0.17	-0.48	0.30	0.19	0.09	-0.29
3	Finland	0.44	1.52	1.29	-0.24	0.06	0.18	0.16	-0.78	0.62	0.14	0.17	-0.30
4	France	0.66	0.88	1.23	-0.06	0.03	0.03	0.01	-0.05	0.04	0.01	0.05	-0.06
5	Japan*	1.28	0.63	1.02	-0.12	0.08	0.04	0.11	-0.13	0.02	0.17	0.06	-0.24
6	New Zealand	0.84	0.87	1.45	-0.18	0.04	0.14	0.20	-0.34	0.14	0.34	0.07	-0.40
7	Norway	0.37	1.23	1.72	-0.04	0.01	0.03	0.03	-0.14	0.11	0.04	0.05	-0.09
8	Sweden	0.79	0.46	1.35	-0.45	0.05	0.39	0.09	-0.32	0.23	0.25	0.09	-0.35
9	UK	0.88	0.67	1.51	-0.27	0.07	0.20	0.20	-0.35	0.15	0.45	0.12	-0.56
10	US	0.80	1.06	1.24	-0.13	0.02	0.11	0.12	-0.27	0.15	0.14	0.03	-0.18
Mean		0.75	0.98	1.39	-0.19	0.04	0.14	0.14	-0.35	0.21	0.22	0.09	-0.31

* For Japan, the 'wine' column values refer to 'sake'. The average values for wine do not include Japan.

9.7 A Comparison between Previous Alcohol Studies and the Current Study

Table 9.13 presents the demand elasticity estimates of beer, wine and spirits from the current study and other (mainly system-wide) studies for a number of countries. Our study differs from these studies mainly either on the functional forms employed for estimation or on the sample periods used. As can be seen, the income and price elasticities from the current study are broadly similar to the results reported in other studies. This gives support to the reliability of the estimates and the selection of the functional form.

Table 9.13 Comparison of demand elasticities of beer, wine* and spirits from the current study with other studies, various countries

Study (1)	Period (3)	Model (4)	Restriction (5)	Income elasticities			Own-price elasticities		
				Beer (6)	Wine (7)	Spirits (8)	Beer (9)	Wine (10)	Spirits (11)
Australia									
1. Chang, Griffith and Bettington (2002)	1975-1999	AIDS		1.04	1.25	-	-0.82	-0.82	-
2. Clements and Johnson (1983)	1956-1977	Rotterdam		0.75	0.75	2.32	-0.11	-0.40	-0.53
3. Clements and E.A. Selvanathan (1987)	1956-1977	Working's		0.73	0.62	2.50	-0.12	-0.34	-0.52
4. Clements and S. Selvanathan (1991)	1955-1985	Working's	Conditional	0.73	0.61	2.51	-0.15	-0.32	-0.61
			Unconditional	0.73	0.61	2.51	-0.43	-0.37	-0.83
5. Clements, Yang and Zheng (1997)	1955-1985	Rotterdam	PI/Conditional	0.81	1.00	1.83	-0.40	-0.50	-0.91
6. Selvanathan, E A (1991)	1955-1985	Rotterdam	Conditional	0.84	0.73	1.94	-0.15	-0.60	-0.61
7. **CURRENT STUDY**	**1955-1998**	**Rotterdam**	**PI/Conditional**	**0.79**	**1.00**	**1.80**	**-0.20**	**-0.43**	**-0.64**
Canada									
8. Clements, Yang and Zheng (1997)	1955-1985	Rotterdam	PI/Conditional	0.82	1.06	1.34	-0.44	-0.57	-0.72
9. Quek (1988)	1953-1982	Rotterdam		0.77	1.12	1.20	-0.28	-0.58	-0.30
10. Selvanathan, E A (1991)	1953-1982	Rotterdam	Conditional	0.71	0.97	1.29	-0.26	-0.16	-0.01
11. **CURRENT STUDY**	**1953-1999**	**Rotterdam**	**PI/Conditional**	**0.67**	**1.18**	**1.32**	**-0.22**	**-0.48**	**-0.29**
Cyprus									
12. Andrikopoulos and Loizides (2000)	1970-1992	AIDS	Imported	1.30	0.71	1.44	-1.00	-0.56	-0.72
			Home	1.02	1.03	0.65	-0.35	-0.23	-0.17
Finland									
13. Clements, Yang and Zheng (1997)	1970-1983	Rotterdam	PI/Conditional	0.45	1.32	1.32	-0.61	-1.78	-1.78
14. Selvanathan, E A (1991)	1969-1983	Rotterdam	Conditional	0.40	1.58	1.29	-0.54	-0.86	-0.73
15. **CURRENT STUDY**	**1969-1985**	**Rotterdam**	**PI/Conditional**	**0.44**	**1.52**	**1.29**	**-0.24**	**-0.78**	**-0.30**
France									
16. **CURRENT STUDY**	**1971-1995**	**Rotterdam**	**PI/Conditional**	**0.66**	**0.88**	**1.23**	**-0.06**	**-0.05**	**-0.06**
Japan									
17. Selvanathan, E A (1991)	1964-1983	Rotterdam	Conditional	1.43	0.29	0.47	-0.25	-0.80	-0.68
18. **CURRENT STUDY**	**1955-2002**	**Rotterdam**	**PI/Conditional**	**1.28**	**0.63**	**1.02**	**-0.12**	**-0.13**	**-0.24**
New Zealand									
19. Clements, Yang and Zheng (1997)	1965-1982	Rotterdam	PI/Conditional	0.84	0.88	1.45	-0.37	-0.39	-0.64
20. Pearce (1986)	1966-1982	Rotterdam		0.85	1.14	1.31	-0.15	-0.35	-0.32
21. Selvanathan, E A (1991)	1965-1982	Rotterdam	Conditional	0.90	1.13	1.18	-0.12	-0.42	-0.52
22. **CURRENT STUDY**	**1965-1982**	**Rotterdam**	**PI/Conditional**	**0.84**	**0.87**	**1.45**	**-0.18**	**-0.34**	**-0.40**
Norway									
23. Clements, Yang and Zheng (1997)	1960-1986	Rotterdam	PI/Conditional	0.34	1.48	1.55	-0.03	-0.12	-0.12
24. Selvanathan, E A (1991)	1960-1986	Rotterdam	Conditional	0.34	1.44	1.56	-0.14	-0.07	-0.18
25. **CURRENT STUDY**	**1963-1996**	**Rotterdam**	**PI/Conditional**	**0.37**	**1.23**	**1.72**	**-0.04**	**-0.14**	**-0.09**
Sweden									
26. Clements, Yang and Zheng (1997)	1967-1984	Rotterdam	PI/Conditional	0.21	0.69	1.52	-0.30	-0.99	-2.18
27. Selvanathan, E A (1991)	1960-1986	Rotterdam	Conditional	0.22	0.48	1.52	-0.35	-0.87	-0.22
28. **CURRENT STUDY**	**1961-1999**	**Rotterdam**	**PI/Conditional**	**0.79**	**0.46**	**1.35**	**-0.45**	**-0.32**	**-0.35**

Table 9.13 continues on next page

Table 9.13 Comparison of demand elasticities of beer, wine and spirits from the current study with other studies, various countries (continued)

Study (1)	Period (3)	Model (4)	Restriction (5)	Income elasticities			Own-price elasticities		
				Beer (6)	Wine (7)	Spirits (8)	Beer (9)	Wine (10)	Spirits (11)
UK									
29. Clements and E.A Selvanathan (1987)	1955-1975	Working's		0.41	1.91	1.81	-0.19	-0.23	-0.24
30. Clements, Yang and Zheng (1997)	1955-1985	Rotterdam	PI/Conditional	0.82	1.06	1.34	-0.44	-0.57	-0.72
31. Duffy (1987)	1963-1983	Rotterdam		0.60	1.70	1.42	-0.29	-0.77	-0.51
32. Duffy (2001)	1964-1996	Rotterdam	HS/Conditional	0.77	1.34	1.25	-0.13	-0.72	-0.83
	1964-1996	AIDS	HS/Conditional	0.79	1.34	1.18	-0.12	-0.72	-0.67
	1964-1996	CBS	HS/Conditional	0.78	1.29	1.28	-0.16	-0.76	-0.82
	1964-1996	NBR	HS/Conditional	0.78	1.39	1.14	-0.10	-0.68	-0.68
33. Jones (1989)	1964-1983Q	AIDS		0.31	1.15	1.14	-0.27	-0.77	-0.95
34. McGuiness (1983)	1956-1979	Linear		0.13	1.11	1.54	-0.18	-0.38	-0.30
35. Saisu and Balasubramanyam (1997)	Long-run	ECM	Unrestricted	0.70	1.42	1.06	-0.10	-0.66	-1.16
			Hom & Sym	0.76	1.55	0.88	-0.32	-1.09	-1.28
36. Selvanathan, E A (1988)	1955-1985	Rotterdam	Conditional	0.55	1.23	1.82	-0.13	-0.37	-0.32
37. Selvanathan, E A (1989)	1955-1975	Rotterdam	Conditional	0.27	2.10	2.00	-0.25	-0.22	-0.20
38. Selvanathan, E A (1991)	1955-1985	Rotterdam	Conditional	0.52	1.31	1.83	-0.13	-0.40	-0.31
39. Selvanathan & Selvanathan (1991)	1955-1985	Rotterdam	Unconditional	0.41	1.74	2.18	-0.20	-0.49	-0.79
40. Wong (1988)	1920-1938	Rotterdam		0.94	1.62	0.94	-0.25	-0.99	-0.51
41. **CURRENT STUDY**	**1955-2002**	**Rotterdam**	**PI/Conditional**	**0.88**	**0.67**	**1.51**	**-0.27**	**-0.35**	**-0.56**
US									
42. Clements and E.A Selvanathan (1987)	1949-1982	Working's		0.75	0.46	1.34	-0.09	-0.22	-0.10
43. Nelson (1997)	1974-1990Q	Rotterdam	Conditional	0.65	0.92	1.50	-0.16	-0.52	-0.39
			Unconditional	0.14	0.20	0.31	-0.11	-0.05	-0.43
44. Nelson (1999)	1977-1994Q	Rotterdam	Conditional	0.77	1.84	1.07	-0.20	-0.69	-0.11
45. Selvanathan, E A (1991)	1949-1982	Rotterdam	Conditional	0.71	0.63	1.36	-0.11	-0.05	-0.11
46. **CURRENT STUDY**	**1950-2000**	**Rotterdam**	**PI/Conditional**	**0.80**	**1.06**	**1.24**	**-0.13**	**-0.27**	**-0.18**

* For Japan, the 'wine' column values refer to 'sake'. The average values for wine do not include Japan.

9.8 Concluding Comments

In Chapter 8, we estimated the demand for alcohol as a whole in a system-wide frame in conjunction with food, tobacco and soft drinks. In this chapter, we analysed the demand for the three beverages beer, wine and spirits within alcohol at cross-country level. We then analyse the demand for the three beverages in further detail for 10 selected countries, Australia, Canada, Finland, France, Japan, New Zealand, Norway, Sweden, UK and the US. We estimated the demand systems, tested the demand theory hypotheses and obtained implied income and price elasticities for beer, wine and spirits. The results show that:

♦ The demand hypotheses, homogeneity, symmetry and preference independence are generally acceptable.
♦ In 9 out of the 10 countries, except that in Japan, beer is considered as a necessity, in half of the countries wine is a necessity and in all countries spirits is a luxury. The cross-country average income elasticities for beer, wine and spirits are 0.75, 0.98 and 1.39, respectively.

- ♦ In all countries the demand for beer, wine and spirits are price inelastic. The cross-country average own-price elasticities for beer, wine and spirits are -0.19, -0.35 and -0.31, respectively.
- ♦ A comparison of our results with a number of previous studies revealed that the results are broadly similar, giving confidence of our analysis.

Appendix to Chapter 9

Data Source

In this appendix we present the details of the data sources for the 10 countries considered in this chapter. Per capita consumption and expenditure data were obtained by deflating the aggregate values by the respective populations. Prices are derived from dividing the expenditure by the corresponding consumption.

Australia (1955-1998)

Aggregate Consumption of beer, wine and spirits are obtained from the *Australian Bureau of Statistics* (ABS) publication, Catalogue Nos. 4306.0 and 4315.0; Population statistics are from ABS Cat. No. 3101.0; price index of beer was obtained from ABS Cat. No. 6401.0 and the price indices for wine and spirits were provided by the ABS upon written request; expenditures are obtained from ABS Cat. Nos. 5201.0, 5204.0 and 5206.0.

Canada (1953-1999)

Aggregate consumption data for the years 1963-1999 are based on volume of sales data published by *Statistics Canada* in various volumes of the *Canadian Year Book* and that for the period 1953-1962 are from the *International Survey of Alcoholic Beverage Taxation and Control Policies* (1997) published by the *Brewers Association of Canada* (which also originated from *Statistics Canada*); population and expenditure data are also from *Statistics Canada*.

Finland (1969-1985)

Aggregate consumption, expenditure and price indices are all from various issues (1978, 1979 and 1984) of the *Statistical Year Book of Finland* published by the *Central Statistical Office of Finland*. Population data are from the *International Financial Statistics* (IFS) published by the *International Monetary Fund* (1987).

France (1971-1995)

Consumption and expenditure data are from various issues of various government statistical publications of the Republic of France: *Annual Statistics of France*, Institut National De La Statistique Et Des Etudes Economiques.

Japan (1963-2002)

All per capita consumption data are from the *International Survey of Alcoholic Beverage Taxation and Control Policies* (1997) published by the *Brewers Association of Canada*. The expenditure and consumption data are used to construct the price series. These data are from the *Annual Report on the Family Income and Expenditure Survey* (various issues) published by the *Statistics Bureau, Management and Co-ordination Agency* of Japan.

New Zealand (1965-1982)

All data are from Pearce (1986). Pearce's per capita consumption data are from the *Alcohol Liquor Advisory Council* (1985) publication, which originated from the New Zealand Department of Statistics. Price data are also from the same source.

Norway (1963-1996)

Aggregate expenditures and consumption of beer, wine and spirits are from various issues of the *Statistical Year Book* of Norway published by the *Norges Offisiells Statistikk*. The population data are from the *International Financial Statistics* (IFS), various issues.

Sweden (1961-1999)

Aggregate consumption and expenditures are from various issues of *Statistical Abstract* of Sweden published by the Sveriges Officiella Statistik, Stockholm. The population data are from *International Financial Statistics* (IFS), various issues.

UK (1955-2002)

Aggregate consumption and population data are from various issues of the *Annual Abstract of Statistics* (AAOS). Aggregate expenditures are from AAOS (1973) and various issues of the *UK National Accounts: CSO Blue Book* published by the *General Statistical Services*, London.

US (1950-2000)

Data for the period 1950-1982 are from Clements and Selvanathan (1987). The aggregate consumption and expenditure data were supplied by the *Economics and Statistical Division of the Distilled Spirits Council of the US Inc.*, Washington (1984). Population data are from the US Department of Commerce publications (1982-1983). Price data for the period 1983-2000 are from various issues of the *Statistical Abstract of the United States*, US Census Bureau. Consumption data for the years 1983-2000 are from the *International Survey of Alcoholic Beverages Taxation and Control Policies* (1997) published by the *Brewers Association of Canada and WHO Statistics Alcohol Database* (2003).

Chapter 10

The Economics of Marijuana Consumption[*]

In economic terms, marijuana is an important, yet little understood and controversial commodity. In Australia for example, according to our estimates (to be discussed below), spending on marijuana in the 1990's is almost twice that on wine. But this commodity, which has been used by something like one-third of the entire adult population, generates no tax revenue. What would happen to the consumption of marijuana if it were legalised? What would happen to alcohol consumption? How much revenue could be generated if marijuana were taxed? What is the price sensitivity of consumption? At a more fundamental level, can the consumption of marijuana be analysed with the conventional utility-maximising calculus? Satisfactory answers to these and related questions are not available in the literature.

Drug taking dates back to prehistoric times and is today a major social, economic and political issue that gives rise to great controversy all over the world. Even though governments have attempted, with mixed results, to tackle consumption of illicit drugs, a substantial proportion of the population has taken drugs. The debate concerning the pros and cons of prohibition seems to be intensifying with it now being a daily issue in the media and politics in most Western countries. Advocates of prohibition argue that drugs are illegal because they are harmful to both body and mind. Brown (1995), for example, states that legalisation is not an idea whose time has come: It is nothing more than a surrender to force that would poison youths and communities. The pro-prohibition view sees the removal of criminal sanctions as only making illicit drugs more widely available and attractive, hence increasing the number of users. This increase would also lead to a larger number of addicts that could not support their drug dependency with legally-acquired income. Therefore, crime could become one way to support their habit. More users would mean more of the violence associated with the ingestion of drugs, and an increase in physical and mental illnesses associated with drug use (Inciardi and Saum, 1996).

Prohibitionists argue that marijuana is the gateway that leads to harder drugs. For example, Collins (1999) states that "Dutch supporters of their lenient soft-drug policy argue that cannabis does not inevitably thrust the heavy smoker across a threshold into hard drug use. They are right. There is no compelling physiological

[*] This guest chapter has been contributed by Professor Kenneth W. Clements and Mert Daryal.

link between cannabis smoking and heroin use, and by no means do all heavy pot smokers move on to hard drugs. But in France, for example, 80 percent of heroin addicts also are heavy consumers of marijuana and hashish. Koopman of The Hope rehab center says more than 80 percent of the heroin addicts that his institute has treated developed their habit after first becoming habitual grass smokers." DeSimone (1998) reports evidence of marijuana consumption being a gateway to cocaine. However, David Penington, former head of the Victorian Government's Drug Advisory Committee, argues that marijuana is a gateway to hard drugs for young people *because* it is illegal; in his words, "The reality is that the gateway from marijuana to other drugs is the source of the marijuana ... When marijuana is illicit, when its distribution is via an illicit trade, then the young who buy that marijuana also are offered heroin" (Penington, quoted in Malpeli and Martin, 1998).

An influential body of opinion argues that prohibition of drugs has been ineffective -- the war against drugs has been lost. Knightley (1999) states that drug-taking has now become an established practice in Western culture. It is argued that radical alternatives need to be explored such as drug policies that are consistent with a free society, that is, free will and a free market. The advocates of legalisation argue that referring to prohibited drugs as "controlled substances" is contradictory; in fact, they are now the least controlled substances in the entire economy. Governments have lost control of the distribution and manufacture of these drugs by imposing criminal penalties and pushing these activities underground. Existing drug policies benefit criminals. Law enforcement cannot eliminate the demand for illegal drugs; it only serves to raise the price of drugs, which increases traffickers' profit margins.

Freidman (1972) argues that drug taking is not a criminal matter but a medical matter, and in a free society individuals alone are responsible for their own actions as long as they do not harm others. The role of the government should be to educate people about the consequences of drug taking, not enforcing criminal restrictions. He also argues that prohibition of drugs is self-defeating and gives an example from history: Alcohol prohibition in the US in the 1920s "undermined respect for the law, corrupted the minions of the law, created a decadent moral climate -- but did not stop alcohol consumption" (Freidman, 1972, p. 104). He questions the underpinnings of current drug policies by asking, "Can any policy, however high-minded, be moral if it leads to widespread corruption, imprisons so many, has so racist effect that it destroys our inner cities, wreaks havoc on misguided and vulnerable individuals and brings death and destruction to foreign countries?" (Freidman, quoted in Knightley, 1999).

Amongst all illicit drugs, marijuana occupies a unique position (McAllister et al., 1991). It is the most popular illicit drug in Western society, probably in the world; as mentioned previously, something like one third of the adult population have used marijuana. If legalisation of drugs were to be considered, marijuana would probably be at the top of the list. A survey of public opinion on marijuana legalisation in the late 1980's indicated that less than a fifth of Australians favoured legalisation (Sullivan, 1993). However, public opinion seemed to have changed dramatically by the mid 1990's: According to the 1995 Australian National Drug Strategy Household Survey, in all states except Queensland over 40 percent of Australians aged 14 and over supported legalisation. Interestingly, the Australian Bureau of Criminal Intelligence, a Commonwealth Government agency, now advocates a softening of marijuana laws so that more police resources could be devoted to detecting offences involving hard drugs (ABCI, 1996). While marijuana is now involved in more than 80 percent of drug offences in Australia (Martin, 1998), it is mainly hard-drug users that cause violence and commit theft to support their more expensive habits. The situation in the US is not any different to that in Australia: "Last year [1998] 695,000 people were arrested in America for possessing marijuana. Perhaps ten times that number, nearly 7M, occasionally take a puff. Perhaps only jaywalkers break the law more frequently" (*The Economist*, 1999, p. 92).

In this chapter, we explore economic aspects of marijuana consumption, concentrating in particular on estimating the amount consumed, its interaction with alcohol, its price sensitivity and the likely effects of any legalisation. The structure of the chapter is as follows. Section 10.1 presents estimates of marijuana consumption and expenditure. A comparison of marijuana consumption with that of alcohol, in Section 10.2, reveals that expenditure on marijuana is almost equal to that on wine consumption *plus* spirits, or about three-quarters of beer expenditure. Sections 10.3 and 10.4 use several approaches to analyse the price sensitivity of marijuana consumption and its relationship with alcohol. The next two sections employ a specifically-conducted survey of first-year students at The University of Western Australia to estimate the effects of possible legalisation of marijuana. Concluding comments are contained in the final section.

10.1 Marijuana Consumption in Australia

In this section, we provide estimates of marijuana consumption in Australia. Our starting point is the Australian National Drug Strategy Household Surveys (NDSHS) data. These data were collected in the form of self-reported surveys completed by a random sample of the population. To maintain confidentiality, a sealed section of the questionnaire allowed respondents to indicate their usage of drugs without the interviewer being aware of their answers. The NDSHS data are given in Table 10.1 in the form of percentages of people (aged 14 years and over) who consume marijuana, as well as the frequency of consumption. The beginning and ending years in this table are determined by the availability of the NDSHS data. As can be seen, the number of people who have ever consumed increases from 28 percent in 1988 to 39 percent in 1998. But this 11 percentage-point increase is roughly offset by the growth in those who are no longer users; this category rises from 53 percent in 1988 to 68 percent in 1998. These data thus describe a pool of users of roughly the same size (relative to the population), but

Table 10.1 Marijuana consumption in Australia (Percentages of respondents)

	1988	1989	1990	1991	1992	1993	1994	1995	1996	1997	1998
Ever used marijuana	28	30	31	33	34	34	33	31	34	36	39
			Frequency of Consumption								
Daily	4	4	5	5	5	5	5	5	5	5	5
Once a week or more	11	11	11	11	10	8	9	9	9	8	8
Once a month or more	7	7	8	8	7	6	7	7	6	5	4
Every few months	11	10	9	8	7	6	6	6	6	5	5
Once or twice year	6	6	7	7	11	14	11	8	7	7	6
Less often	8	7	6	5	6	7	7	6	5	5	4
No longer a user	53	54	55	56	55	54	57	59	62	65	68
Total	100	100	100	100	100	100	100	100	100	100	100

Notes: Respondents are aged 14 and over. Source: Data for 1988, 1991, 1993, 1995 and 1998 are from National Drug Household Surveys, Canberra: Social Science Data Archives, The Australia National University. The intermediate years are estimated by linear interpolation. The data in the first row are weighted.

Table 10.2 Estimated number of marijuana users and total population
(Thousands of Australians aged 14 and over)

Frequency of consumption	1988	1989	1990	1991	1992	1993	1994	1995	1996	1997	1998
Daily	147	171	198	227	233	239	235	224	251	272	302
Once a week or more	403	435	467	499	443	383	400	403	438	437	444
Once a month or more	256	290	325	363	327	287	306	313	290	275	262
Every few months	403	396	382	363	327	287	282	269	290	291	297
Once or twice year	220	251	283	318	490	670	517	358	370	350	333
Less often	293	277	255	227	280	335	306	269	273	265	261
No longer a user	1,941	2,136	2,334	2,541	2,566	2,585	2,656	2,641	3,086	3,470	3,986
Total	3,663	3,956	4,243	4,537	4,666	4,787	4,701	4,476	4,998	5,353	5,886
Total population	13,082	13,334	13,541	13,748	13,927	14,079	14,244	14,440	14,660	14,870	15,091

Source: Population data are from ABS, *Population by Age and Sex*, Catalogue No.3201.0.

whose composition is changing with new users constantly replacing the old ones. This would seem to be consistent with elements of experimental drug taking.

Next, we use the data in Table 10.1, together with the relevant population figures, to estimate the number of users, which are given in Table 10.2. These data reveal the following: (i) The number of daily consumers has increased substantially over this period. (ii) On the other hand, the number of weekly and monthly users have grown slowly, while those using every few months have declined. (iii) The number who consume once or twice a year has increased substantially, from 220,000 to 330,000. (iv) Those who have ever used marijuana has risen from 3.7 million to 5.9 million, a 59 percent increase. However, taking out the "no longer users", the number of current users increases from 3.7-1.9 = 1.8 million to 5.9-4.0=1.9 million, which represents a more modest increase of 5 percent over the

10 years. By comparison, the overall population grew by about 15 percent over the same period.[1]

Table 10.3 presents our "guesstimates" of consumption per user, by frequency of consumption. As can be seen, we make the realistic assumption that the amount consumed by frequent and regular users is considerably more than occasional users. Table 10.4 combines the information in the previous two tables to give estimated total consumption. Our estimate of total consumption in 1998 is about 12 million ounces. The last row of the table shows that per capita (14 years and over) consumption increases from .65 ounces p.a. in 1988 to .79 ounces in 1998. In calculating expenditure, the price of marijuana is taken to be constant over time at $450 an ounce. There are several pieces of "evidence" that support this approach: (i) *The Cleeland Report* (1989) states that the street price of an ounce of marijuana was $450 in 1988. (ii) *The Illicit Drugs in Australia, Situation Report*, produced by the Australian Federal Police (1991), gives a price range of $350 to $800 for 1989 and 1990. (iii) The Australian Bureau of Criminal Intelligence provided us with unpublished data on marijuana prices for heads, hydroponic and leaves for the period 1990-1998. The weighted average of these prices falls in the range $437-$463/oz, depending on the weights.[2]

Table 10.5 gives estimated expenditure on marijuana. How do our estimates compare with those of others? The Cleeland Report (1989) estimated expenditure on marijuana to be about $1.9 billion in 1988, which is considerably less than our figure for that year of $3.8 billion. As Cleeland also use a price of $450/oz, the difference lies in the quantity consumed. Table 10.1 reveals that in 1988, 28 percent of people had used marijuana; as 53 percent are no longer users, $(1-.53) \times 28$ percent = 13 percent are currently users. By contrast, Cleeland estimate the user population to be only 6 percent, which would seem to be too low. Marks (1992) also argues that Cleeland underestimates the number of users. He takes Cleeland's assumed individual usage figures and scales them up by more realistic factors to yield estimated expenditure of $4.1 billion, which is about 1 percent of GDP in 1988. Marks' estimate is rather close to ours ($3.8 billion). Interestingly, the UN (1997) estimate that expenditure on all illicit drugs is about equal to 1.4 percent of world GDP.

Rhodes et al. (1997) estimate expenditure on marijuana in the US by taking the product of the following factors: The estimated number of users in the past month,

---

[1] This intensification of consumption is consistent with opinion polls regarding the social acceptability of marijuana. As mentioned at the start of the chapter, in the late 1980's, less than a fifth of Australians favoured legalisation (Sullivan, 1993); but by 1995 this had increased to between 40 and 50 percent, depending on the state (NDSHS, 1995, 1993).

[2] The weight given to leaves varies from 0 to .2 and the remainder is then equally split between heads and hydroponic. It should be noted that the data are in the form of price ranges and we take the mid point. Many of the price ranges are large (e.g., the upper end of the range is twice that of the lower end), reflecting the substantial uncertainty of these prices.

Table 10.3 Estimated marijuana consumption by frequency of consumption

Frequency of consumption	Weekly Grams	Monthly Grams	Annual Grams	Annual Kilos	Annual Ounces
Daily	10	43	520	.520	18.57
Once a week or more	7	30	364	.364	13.00
Once a month or more	-	4	48	.048	1.71
Every few months	-	-	3	.003	.11
Once or twice year	-	-	1	.001	.04
Less often	-	-	1	.001	.04
No longer a user	-	-	0	0	0

Note: An ounce is approximately equal to 28 grams, and a kilogram is 1000 grams or 35.7 ounces.
Source: Personal inquiries and guesstimates.

Table 10.4 Estimated marijuana consumption

Frequency of consumption	1988	1989	1990	1991	1992	1993	1994	1995	1996	1997	1998
					Thousands of ounces						
Daily	2,721	3,183	3,677	4,213	4,332	4,445	4,365	4,157	4,668	5,055	5,605
Once a week or more	5,238	5,657	6,067	6,488	5,762	4,978	5,194	5,237	5,691	5,683	5,776
Once a month or more	440	497	558	622	560	492	524	537	497	472	450
Every few months	43	42	41	39	35	31	30	29	31	31	32
Once or twice year	8	9	10	11	17	24	18	13	13	13	12
Less often	10	10	9	8	10	12	11	10	10	9	9
No longer a user	0	0	0	0	0	0	0	0	0	0	0
Total consumption	8,460	9,398	10,362	11,381	10,717	9,983	10,142	9,982	10,910	11,262	11,884
					Ounces						
Per capita consumption	.65	.70	.77	.83	.77	.71	.71	.69	.74	.76	.79

Notes: 1. Totals may not agree due to rounding. 2. Per capita consumption refers to those aged 14 years and over.

the average number of joints used, the average weight per joint and the cost per ounce. The number of users (aged 12 and over) is obtained from the US National Household Survey on Drug Abuse and the amount consumed is estimated with an ordered probit model. Using a price of $US269/oz, Rhodes et al. estimate total expenditure on marijuana to be $US7 billion in 1995. This is equivalent to $US32.5 per capita (12 years and over), or, using a long-term average exchange rate of $A1 = $US.65, $A50 per capita, much less than our estimate for Australia in 1995 of $A311 per capita. Although the US study considers past-month users only, whereas we consider past-12-months users, this should not lead to substantial differences as Table 10.5 reveals that most of marijuana expenditure is accounted for by frequent users. The difference between two estimates would seem to be due to two factors: (i) the lower relative number of users in the US (8.6 million, or 4 percent of the population 12 years and over) in comparison with that in Australia (2 million, or 14 percent of the population 14 years and over). (ii) The average

Table 10.5 Estimated expenditure on marijuana

Frequency of consumption	1988	1989	1990	1991	1992	1993	1994	1995	1996	1997	1998
					Millions of dollars						
Daily	1,225	1,432	1,655	1,896	1,950	2,000	1,964	1,871	2,100	2,275	2,522
Once a week or more	2,357	2,545	2,730	2,919	2,593	2,240	2,337	2,357	2,561	2,557	2,599
Once a month or more	198	224	251	280	252	222	236	242	224	212	202
Every few months	19	19	18	17	16	14	14	13	14	14	14
Once or twice year	4	4	5	5	8	11	8	6	6	6	5
Less often	5	4	4	4	4	5	5	4	4	4	4
No longer a user	0	0	0	0	0	0	0	0	0	0	0
Total expenditure	3,807	4,229	4,663	5,121	4,823	4,492	4,564	4,492	4,910	5,068	5,348
					Dollars						
Per capita expenditure	291	317	344	373	346	319	320	311	335	341	354

Note: Per capita expenditure refers to those aged 14 years and over.

amount of marijuana consumed in the US is estimated to be 3.1 ounces per user p.a., whereas our estimate for Australia is 5.4 ounces. A study that uses a similar approach is the Western Australian Parliament Select Committee (1997), who estimates expenditure on marijuana in Western Australia using the 1995 NDSHS. They take into account the number of users in the last year, classified by frequency of use and age, and consider three values of the average number of joints used. Using a price of $A240/oz, they estimate total expenditure to lie in the range of $A289 to $A440 million. This implies that per capita expenditure is between $A211 and $A321; our estimate of $A311 lies in the upper part of this range.[3]

10.2 Comparison With Alcohol Consumption

In this section, we present a comparison of the consumption of marijuana with that of three alcoholic beverages, beer, wine and spirits. Details of the source of the alcohol data are given in a separate Appendix, available on request.

The consumption and prices of the three alcoholic beverages and marijuana are presented in Table 10.6 and Figure 10.1 plots the consumption data. As can be seen, per capita consumption of beer decreases noticeably over this period, from more than 140 litres in 1988 to 117 in 1998. Wine consumption also decreases – by almost 1.2 litres to end up at 24.6 litres in 1998. But in contrast to beer, wine consumption increases in each of the last three years. The time path of spirits is roughly similar to that of wine – it first declines substantially, bottoms out in the early 1990s and then more than recovers to end up at 4.3 litres in 1998. Marijuana

---

[3] Both Rhodes et al. (1997) and WA Parliament Select Committee (1997) derive their estimates by considering the number of joints consumed. However, it is highly unlikely that frequent users, especially daily and more than once a week users, smoke joints. It is common knowledge amongst users that while smoking joints is enjoyable, it is not the optimal way of getting high; for example, with water pipes a better high is obtained with a smaller amount of marijuana.

Table 10.6 Quantities consumed and prices of alcohol beverages and marijuana

Year	Beer	Wine	Spirits	Marijuana
		Quantities		
1988	141.4	25.82	3.993	.6467
1989	141.6	24.32	4.048	.7049
1990	139.9	22.85	3.870	.7652
1991	134.9	23.01	3.614	.8278
1992	127.8	23.23	3.595	.7695
1993	123.8	23.14	3.982	.7090
1994	122.1	23.19	4.168	.7120
1995	120.2	22.96	4.130	.6913
1996	118.7	23.29	4.106	.7442
1997	117.6	24.18	4.158	.7575
1998	116.9	24.63	4.318	.7875
Mean	127.2	23.69	4.000	.7378
		Prices		
1988	2.819	6.190	30.578	450
1989	2.928	6.607	33.315	450
1990	3.116	6.801	36.601	450
1991	3.271	6.883	39.064	450
1992	3.361	7.056	40.532	450
1993	3.478	7.271	41.847	450
1994	3.583	7.597	43.044	450
1995	3.724	7.983	44.254	450
1996	3.891	8.306	45.687	450
1997	3.981	8.559	46.714	450
1998	4.020	8.755	47.088	450
Mean	3.470	7.455	40.793	450

Notes: 1. Quantities are per capita (14 years and over). 2. Quantities consumed of the alcoholic beverages are in terms of litres; and that of marijuana is in ounces. 3. Prices are in dollars per litre for the alcoholic beverages and per ounce for marijuana.

consumption starts off at .65 ounces in 1988, increases steadily until it reaches a peak of .83 oz in 1991, tends to decrease for the next several years and then increases again to end up at .79 oz in 1998. Retracing our steps, it can be shown that this variability in marijuana consumption is mostly due to the weekly and monthly consumers.

Table 10.7 combines the quantity and price data and presents expenditures on, and budget shares of, the four goods. The budget share is expenditure on the good in question expressed as a fraction of total expenditure on the four goods. Several interesting features emerge from this table: (i) Marijuana absorbs about 30 percent of expenditure on the four goods. (ii) Expenditure on marijuana is almost equal to

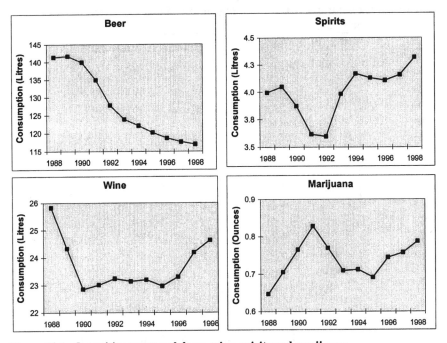

Figure 10.1 Quantities consumed, beer, wine, spirits and marijuana

that on wine *plus* spirits; and it is about three-quarters of beer expenditure. (iii) The budget share of spirits rises by almost 4 percentage points, while that of beer falls by 3+ percentage points. Table 10.8 gives the quantity and price data in terms of log-changes. The upper panel of the table shows that, on average, beer consumption decreases by 1.9 percent p.a., wine decreases by 0.5 percent, spirits increases by .8 percent and marijuana increases by 2.0 percent. The growth in consumption of both spirits and marijuana exhibit considerable volatility. For example, while spirits consumption grows at a mean rate of .8 percent p.a., in 1993 consumption of this beverage increases by more than 10 percent; and in the same year, marijuana declines by more than 8 percent, while its average growth rate is 2.0 percent.

10.3 The Price Sensitivity of Consumption, Part I: Preliminary Explorations

What is the price elasticity of demand for marijuana? By how much would usage rise if marijuana were legalised? How does its consumption interact with that of alcohol? With only ten years of data it should be acknowledged that it is not easy to answer these questions definitely. Nevertheless, it is still possible to make progress and shed some light on these important issues. In this section, we carry out a preliminary analysis of the price sensitivity of consumption; a more formal

Table 10.7 Expenditures on and budget shares of alcohol beverages and marijuana

Year	Beer	Wine	Spirits	Marijuana	Total
		Expenditures			
1988	398.41	159.84	122.10	291.02	971.37
1989	414.80	160.70	134.87	317.19	1,027.56
1990	435.91	155.39	141.67	344.36	1,077.32
1991	441.49	158.52	140.76	372.52	1,113.29
1992	429.43	163.93	145.70	346.27	1,085.32
1993	430.66	168.24	166.62	319.06	1,084.58
1994	437.49	176.17	179.40	320.42	1,113.47
1995	447.64	183.32	182.77	311.09	1,124.81
1996	461.75	193.48	187.60	334.90	1,177.74
1997	468.18	206.96	194.22	340.86	1,210.22
1998	470.11	215.61	203.31	354.37	1,243.41
Mean	439.60	176.55	163.59	332.01	1,111.74
		Budget Shares			
1988	41.01	16.46	12.57	29.96	100
1989	40.37	15.64	13.13	30.87	100
1990	40.46	14.42	13.15	31.96	100
1991	39.63	14.22	12.68	33.46	100
1992	39.57	15.10	13.42	31.90	100
1993	39.71	15.51	15.36	29.42	100
1994	39.29	15.82	16.11	28.78	100
1995	39.80	16.30	16.25	27.66	100
1996	39.21	16.43	15.93	28.44	100
1997	38.69	17.10	16.05	28.16	100
1998	37.81	17.34	16.35	28.50	100
Mean	39.59	15.85	14.64	29.92	100

Notes: 1. Expenditures are in terms of dollars per capita (14 years and over).   2. Budget shares are in percentages.

approach is used in the next section. As alcohol and marijuana share some important common characteristics, we shall analyse their consumption jointly.

As a way of summarising the data, we start with price and volume indexes of the alcoholic beverages and marijuana. Let p_{it} be the price of good i in year t and q_{it} be the corresponding quantity consumed per capita. Then, if there are n goods, $M_t = \sum_{i=1}^{n} p_{it} q_{it}$ is total expenditure and $w_{it} = p_{it} q_{it} / M_t$ is the proportion of this total devoted to good i, or the budget share of i. Let $\bar{w}_{it} = (1/2)\left(w_{it} + w_{i,t-1}\right)$ be the arithmetic average of the budget share over the years $t-1$ and t; and $Dp_{it} = \log p_{it} - \log p_{i,t-1}$ and $Dq_{it} = \log q_{it} - \log q_{i,t-1}$ be the ith price and quantity

Table 10.8 Log-changes in quantities consumed and prices of alcohol beverages and Marijuana

Year	Beer	Wine	Spirits	Marijuana
		Quantities		
1989	.21	-5.98	1.38	8.61
1990	-1.23	-6.26	-4.49	8.22
1991	-3.65	.70	-6.85	7.86
1992	-5.43	.97	-.55	-7.31
1993	-3.13	-.40	10.23	-8.18
1994	-1.42	.22	4.57	.42
1995	-1.55	-.97	-.91	-2.69
1996	-1.29	1.43	-.57	7.38
1997	-.89	3.73	1.25	1.76
1998	-.57	1.83	3.78	3.89
Mean	-1.90	-.47	.78	1.97
		Prices		
1989	3.83	6.51	8.57	0
1990	6.20	2.90	9.41	0
1991	4.86	1.19	6.51	0
1992	2.72	2.49	3.69	0
1993	3.41	3.00	3.19	0
1994	3.00	4.38	2.82	0
1995	3.85	4.95	2.77	0
1996	4.40	3.97	3.19	0
1997	2.27	3.00	2.22	0
1998	.98	2.27	.80	0
Mean	3.55	3.47	4.32	0

Note: All entries are to be divided by 100.

log-changes. The Divisia price and volume indexes are then defined as

$$DP_t = \sum_{i=1}^{n} \bar{w}_{it} Dp_{it}, \qquad DQ_t = \sum_{i=1}^{n} \bar{w}_{it} Dq_{it}. \tag{3.1}$$

The Divisia price index is a budget-share-weighted average of the n price log-changes and thus represents a centre-of-gravity measure of the prices. This index also has a statistical interpretation (Theil, 1967, p. 136): Suppose we draw prices at random such that each dollar of expenditure has an equal chance of being selected. Then, the budget share $\bar{w}_{it}$ is the probability of drawing Dp_{it} for the transition from year t-1 to t, so that the expected value of the prices is $\sum_{i=1}^{n} \bar{w}_{it} Dp_{it}$, the Divisia index. The Divisia volume index has a similar interpretation and measures the overall growth in per capita consumption.

The upper parts of columns 2 and 3 of Table 10.9 contain DP_t and DQ_t for the three alcoholic beverages plus marijuana (so that $n=4$), while the corresponding lower parts give the indexes for alcohol by itself ($n=3$). For the four goods, on average the price index rises by about 2.6 percent p.a., while the volume index falls by .1 percent p.a. The relationship between the four- and three-good indexes can be illustrated as follows. Write $\overline{W}_{At} = \sum_{i=1}^{3} \overline{w}_{it}$ for the budget share of alcohol as a whole, $DP_{At} = \sum_{i=1}^{3} \left(\overline{w}_{it} / \overline{W}_{At} \right) Dp_{it}$ for the price index of alcoholic beverages and $DP_{AM,t} = \sum_{i=1}^{4} \overline{w}_{it} Dp_{it}$ for the index of alcohol and marijuana prices. Then we have

$$DP_{AM,t} = \overline{W}_{At} DP_{At} + \left(1 - \overline{W}_{At} \right) DP_{Mt},$$

where $DP_{Mt} = Dp_{4t}$ is the change in the price of marijuana. Accordingly, the price of alcohol and marijuana as a group is simply a budget-share-weighted average of the price of alcohol and that of marijuana. As the price of marijuana is constant, $DP_{Mt} = 0$, so that the above equation becomes

$$DP_{AM,t} = \overline{W}_{At} DP_{At}.$$

From Table 10.7, the mean value of the budget share of marijuana is 30 percent, so that the alcohol share $\overline{w}_A$ is 70 percent, on average. Accordingly, the price index of alcohol and marijuana is about 70 percent of that of alcohol by itself.

The indexes defined in equation (3.1) represent weighted first-order moments of the n prices $Dp_{1t}, ..., Dp_{nt}$ and the n quantities $Dq_{1t}, ..., Dq_{nt}$. The corresponding second-order moments are the Divisia variances:

$$\Pi_t = \sum_{i=1}^{n} \overline{w}_{it} \left(Dp_{it} - DP_t \right)^2, \quad K_t = \sum_{i=1}^{n} \overline{w}_{it} \left(Dq_{it} - DQ_t \right)^2. \qquad (3.2)$$

These variances measure the dispersion across commodities of the prices and quantities. Columns 4 and 5 of Table 10.9 give (3.2) for $n = 4$ and $n = 3$. These show that usually (i) for a given year there is more dispersion in quantities than prices; and (ii) including marijuana has the effect of increasing both variances.

Finally, the Divisia price-quantity covariance is

$$\Gamma_t = \sum_{i=1}^{n} \overline{w}_{it} \left(Dp_{it} - DP_t \right) \left(Dq_{it} - DQ_t \right).$$

Given the tendency of consumers to move away from those goods whose relative prices increase, we expect Γ_t to be negative. This covariance is given in column 6

Table 10.9 Divisia moments

Year	Price index	Quantity index	Price variance	Quantity variance	Price-quantity covariance	Price-quantity correlation
	(×100)	(×100)	(×10⁴)	(×10⁴)	(×10⁴)	
(1)	(2)	(3)	(4)	(5)	(6)	(7)
		A. Alcoholic Beverages and Marijuana				
1989	3.70	1.92	8.49	24.87	-11.53	-.79
1990	4.18	.55	10.97	30.06	-13.67	-.75
1991	2.96	.33	6.39	31.57	-13.71	-.97
1992	1.92	-4.47	1.92	9.34	2.84	.67
1993	2.27	-2.34	2.30	34.02	5.60	.63
1994	2.31	.32	2.45	4.05	-.23	-.07
1995	2.77	-1.75	3.39	.64	1.30	.88
1996	2.90	1.70	3.45	13.43	-6.54	-.96
1997	1.74	.98	1.27	2.81	-.17	-.09
1998	.90	1.81	.56	4.02	-.63	-.42
Mean	2.56	-.10	4.12	15.48	-3.67	-.19
		B. Alcoholic Beverages				
1989	5.32	-1.00	3.59	7.62	-1.00	-.19
1990	6.09	-2.96	4.35	4.59	1.44	.32
1991	4.40	-3.34	3.17	5.89	-4.27	-.99
1992	2.86	-3.09	.17	8.05	.27	.23
1993	3.28	.24	.03	27.26	-.40	-.45
1994	3.26	.27	.36	5.70	-.18	-.13
1995	3.85	-1.28	.53	.09	-.01	-.06
1996	4.03	-.51	.24	1.19	-.17	-.33
1997	2.43	.67	.10	3.58	.52	.87
1998	1.25	.99	.33	3.22	.14	.14
Mean	3.68	-1.00	1.29	6.72	-.37	-.06

of Table 10.9 and, as can be seen, in 7 out of 10 cases (for $n = 4$ and 6 out of 10 cases for $n = 3$) it is negative. Column 7 gives the corresponding correlation, $\rho_t = \Gamma_t / \sqrt{\Pi_t K_t}$. When marijuana is included, the mean value of ρ is -.2; when marijuana is excluded, this mean falls to -.06, so the relationship is much weaker.

As Dp_{it} is the change in the nominal price of the ith good and DP_t is an index of the change in the prices of all goods (namely, alcoholic beverages and marijuana), $Dp_{it} - DP_t$ is interpreted as the change in the relative price of i. Similarly, as $Dq_{it} - DQ_t$ is the change in the quantity consumed of i relative to the average, this can also be termed the change in the relative quantity of i. The means (×100) of these relative price and quantity changes are:

	Quantities	Prices
Beer	-1.8	1.0
Wine	-.4	.9
Spirits	.9	1.8
Marijuana	2.1	-2.6

As in three out of the four cases the quantity change has the opposite sign to the price change, we see again that there is a tendency for consumption of those goods whose relative prices rise to grow slower than average, and vice versa.

To conclude this section, we use an alternative way of measuring the degree of interrelationship between the consumption of the four goods. Consider, for example, the consumption of beer and marijuana. Suppose that total consumption of the four goods is held constant, and that for some reason or another (such as a heat wave) beer is subject to a random shock causing its consumption to increase. If at the same time marijuana consumption falls, then, as more of one good compensates for less of the other, it would seem that both goods are capable of satisfying the same type of want of the consumer. In such a case, as these goods are competitive, it would be reasonable to describe beer and marijuana as being substitutes for one another. By a similar argument, goods whose consumption is positively correlated reinforce each other and can be described as complements.[4]

We implement the above idea by computing the correlation coefficients between the relative quantity change in good i, $Dq_{it} - DQ_t$, and that of good j, $Dq_{jt} - DQ_t$; deflating the individual quantity changes by DQ_t serves to hold constant total consumption of the group of goods. The results, presented in Table 10.10, indicate that the three alcoholic beverages are all negatively correlated

Table 10.10   Relative quantity correlation coefficients

Good	Beer	Wine	Spirits	Marijuana
Beer	1.0	.15	.61	-.70
Wine		1.0	.43	-.71
Spirits			1.0	-.90
Marijuana				1.0

with marijuana and are thus substitutes. Interestingly, for each of the beer, wine and spirits rows, the largest (in absolute value) off-diagonal correlation always involves marijuana; these correlations are beer-marijuana -.7, wine-marijuana -.7 and spirits-marijuana -.9. Accordingly, there seems to be some strength in the substitutability relationship between alcohol and marijuana. Note also that the three within-alcohol correlations are positive, indicating complementarity. While this sort

---

[4] This approach to substitutability/complementarity based on residual correlations has a long history, going back to Allen and Bowley (1935).

of behaviour cannot be ruled out, as these correlations are all lower than the others, possibly less weight should be given to this finding.

10.4 The Price Sensitivity of Consumption, Part II: A Demand System

In this section we analyse more formally the price sensitivity of consumption of marijuana, and its interrelation with alcohol, by using a system of demand equations.

The demand system we use is the Rotterdam model due to Barten (1964) and Theil (1965). We choose this model because of its straightforward nature and because it is widely used. The ith equation of this model takes the form

$$\overline{w}_{it} Dq_{it} = \theta_i \, DQ_t + \sum_{j=1}^{n} \pi_{ij} Dp_{jt} + \varepsilon_{it}, \qquad (4.1)$$

where $\theta_i = \partial(p_i q_i)/\partial M$ is the marginal share of good i; π_{ij} is the $(i, j)^{th}$ Slutsky coefficient; ε_{it} is a disturbance term; and the other notation is as before. The marginal share θ_i answers the question, When total expenditure increases by \$1, what fraction of this is spent on good i? As total expenditure is allocated to the n goods, it follows that $\sum_{i=1}^{n} \theta_i = 1$. The Slutsky coefficients deal with the substitution effects of a price change and satisfy demand homogeneity, $\sum_{j=1}^{n} \pi_{ij} = 0$ $(i=1,...,n)$, and symmetry, $\pi_{ij} = \pi_{ji}$ $(i,j =1,...,n)$. By dividing both sides of (4.1) by $\overline{w}_{it}$, it can be seen that $\theta_i / \overline{w}_{it}$ is the ith income elasticity and $\pi_{ij}/\overline{w}_{it}$ is the $(i, j)^{th}$ price elasticity. As we shall apply (4.1) for $i = 1,...,n$ to a group of goods (alcohol and marijuana), it is to be interpreted as a conditional demand system, which holds constant real total expenditure on the group. The analysis of demand within the group, independent of the consumption of other goods, is valid under the conditions of separability, whereby consumption of the group of goods forms an independent block in the consumer's utility function.[5]

To economise on the number of unknown parameters that have to be estimated, we make the simplifying assumption that tastes with respect to alcohol and marijuana can be characterised by a utility function of the preference independent form. This means that the utility function is the sum of n sub-utility functions, one for each good, $u(q_1,...,q_n) = \sum_{i=1}^{n} u_i(q_i)$. Preference independence (PI) means that the marginal utility of each good is independent of the consumption of all others. The implications of PI are that all income elasticities are positive and all pairs of goods are Slutsky substitutes. The hypothesis of PI has been recently tested with alcohol data for seven countries by Clements et al., (1997) and, using a variety of tests, they find that the hypothesis cannot be rejected.[6]

---

[5] For details, see, e.g., Clements (1987b).

[6] Earlier studies tended to reject PI (see Barten, 1977, for a survey), but it is now understood that the source of many of these rejections was the use of asymptotic tests, which were biased against the null. See S. Selvanathan (1987, 1993).

Under preference independence, the Slutsky coefficients in equation (4.1) take the form (see, e.g., Clements et al., 1995)

$$\pi_{ij} = \phi \theta_i (\delta_{ij} - \theta_j), \tag{4.2}$$

where ϕ is the own-price elasticity of demand for the group of goods as a whole; and δ_{ij} is the Kronecker delta ($\delta_{ij} = 1$ if $i = j$, 0 otherwise). Accordingly, the term involving prices in equation (4.1) becomes $\sum_{j=1}^{n} \pi_{ij} Dp_{jt} = \phi \theta_i (Dp_{it} - DP'_t)$, where $DP'_t = \sum_{i=1}^{n} \theta_i Dp_{it}$ is a marginal-share-weighted average of the prices, known as the Frisch price index. Equation (4.1) thus simplifies to

$$\overline{w}_{it} Dq_{it} = \theta_i DQ_t + \phi \theta_i (Dp_{it} - DP'_t) + \varepsilon_{it}. \tag{4.3}$$

This equation for $i=1,\ldots,n$ is the Rotterdan model under PI. The disturbances ε_{it} are assumed to have zero means and, again to economise on unknown parameters, have variances and covariances of the form

$$\text{cov}(\varepsilon_{it}, \varepsilon_{jt}) = \sigma^2 \overline{w}_i (\delta_{ij} - \overline{w}_j), \tag{4.4}$$

where σ^2 is a constant; and $\overline{w}_i$ is the sample mean of $\overline{w}_{it}$. This specification, which has been advocated by S. Selvanathan (1991) and Theil (1987), implies that (i) the variances of the disturbances increase with the corresponding budget shares (for $\overline{w}_i < .5$); and (ii) the covariances between disturbances in different equations are all negative. These are plausible implications.[7]

Before applying (4.3) to the alcohol and marijuana data, we make one further simplification. Rather than attempting to estimate the marginal shares, we shall specify their values. Recalling that the income elasticity is the ratio of the marginal share to the corresponding budget share, we can proceed by considering the values of the income elasticities and the budget shares. Columns 3-5 of Table 10.11 present some recent estimates of income elasticities for alcohol and we use them as a broad guide in Table 10.12. In column 2 of this table, beer is taken to have an income elasticity of .5 (so that it is necessity), wine 1.0 (a borderline case) and spirits 2.0 (a strong luxury); we will come back to the elasticity for marijuana. Column 3 gives the four budget shares, which approximate the sample means, while column 4 presents the implied marginal shares, computed as $\theta_i = \eta_i \times w_i$, where η_i is the income elasticity of i. As the marginal shares have a unit sum, the θ_i for marijuana can be obtained from the other three. Once we have the marginal and budget shares for marijuana, we then obtain its income elasticity of 1.2, which implies that it is a modest luxury.

---

[7] Covariance structure (4.4) corresponds to sampling from a multinomial distribution with probabilities equal to budget shares.

As the θ_i are now known, we write (4.3) as $y_{it} = \phi\, x_{it} + \varepsilon_{it}$, where $y_{it} = \overline{w}_{it}\, Dq_{it} - \theta_i\, DQ_t$ and $x_{it} = \theta_i\, (Dp_{it} - DP_t')$. Since $\sum_{i=1}^n \varepsilon_{it} = 0$, one equation is redundant and we write the above for i = 1 ,..., n - 1 as $y_t = \phi\, x_t + \varepsilon_t$, where y_t , x_t and ε_t are all vectors containing the corresponding $n-1$ elements. We estimate the one unknown parameter ϕ by generalised-least squares, i.e., by minimising the sum over t =1,...,T observations of the quadratic form $(y_t - \phi x_t)'\, \Sigma^{-1}(y_t - \phi x_t)$, where Σ is the covariance matrix defined by equation (4.4) for i, j =1,...,n -1, namely, $\sigma^2(\overline{W} - \overline{w}\,\overline{w}')$, where $\overline{W}$ = diag $[\overline{w}]$ and $\overline{w} = [\overline{w}_1,...,\overline{w}_{n-1}]'$. It can be shown (Theil, 1987, p. 126) that this amounts to minimising $\sum_{t=1}^T \sum_{i=1}^n (y_{it} - \phi x_{it})^2 / \overline{w}_i$. The alcohol and marijuana data yield the following GLS estimate of ϕ :

$$\hat{\phi} = -.429\ (.227),\tag{4.5}$$

where the standard error is given in parenthesis. This estimate of the price elasticity of demand for alcohol and marijuana as a whole is significantly different from zero. In comparison with the prior estimates of this elasticity for alcohol by itself, given in column 6 of Table 10.11, this estimate seems to be reasonable.

Table 10.11 Demand elasticities for alcohol beverages

Country	Sample Period	Income elasticities			Price elasticity of alcohol as a whole
		Beer	Wine	Spirits	
(1)	(2)	(3)	(4)	(5)	(6)
Australia	1955-85	.81	1.00	1.83	-.50
Canada	1953-82	.74	1.05	1.25	-.42
Finland	1970-83	.45	1.32	1.32	-1.35
New Zealand	1965-82	.84	.88	1.45	-.44
Norway	1960-86	.34	1.48	1.55	-.08
Sweden	1967-84	.21	.69	1.52	-1.43
United Kingdom	1955-85	.82	1.06	1.34	-.54
Mean		.60	1.07	1.47	-.68

Source: Clements et al. (1997).

We can now construct the price elasticities. To compute the Slutsky coefficients π_{ij} , we use in (4.2) the estimate of ϕ given in equation (4.5) and the values of the four marginal shares given in column 4 of Table 10.12. As the $(i, j)^{th}$ price elasticity takes the form $\pi_{ij}/\overline{w}_{it}$, we use the sample means of the budget shares given in column 3 of Table 10.12 to convert the Slutsky coefficients the elasticities and the top panel of Table 10.13 contains the results. The own-price elasticity of beer is -.2, wine -.4, spirits -.6 and marijuana -.3. Interestingly, for each alcoholic beverage, the largest cross–price elasticity is for the price of marijuana:

Table 10.12 Income elasticities, budget shares and marginal shares

Good	Income elasticity η_i	Budget share w_i	Marginal share θ_i
(1)	(2)	(3)	(4)
Beer	.5	.4	.2
Wine	1	.15	.15
Spirits	2	.15	.3
Marijuana	1.2	.3	.35
Sum		1	1

Table 10.13 Price elasticities of demand

Good	Beer	Wine	Spirits	Marijuana
(1)	(2)	(3)	(4)	(5)
		Compensated		
Beer	-.17	.03	.06	.08
Wine	.09	-.36	.13	.15
Spirits	.17	.13	-.60	.30
Marijuana	.10	.08	.15	-.33
		Uncompensated		
Beer	-.37	-.04	-.01	-.07
Wine	-.31	-.51	-.02	-.15
Spirits	-.63	-.17	-.90	-.30
Marijuana	-.38	-.10	-.03	-.69

The elasticity of beer consumption with respect to the price of marijuana is .1; wine-marijuana is .2; and spirits-marijuana is .3.   In comparison with previous studies, the values of the own-price elasticities for the three alcoholic beverages are reasonable.[8] There are only two prior comparable studies of the own-price elasticity of demand for marijuana. First, Nisbet and Vakil (1972), using US data, find it to lie in the range -.5 to -.1.5. Our estimate lies outside this range. Second, Daryal (2002) employs survey data (that we use subsequently) to estimate the elasticity to be -.4 for frequent users, -.1 for occasional users and 0 for those who are not users. Given that the bulk of marijuana is consumed by frequent users, our elasticity of -.3 is not inconsistent with Daryal's estimates.

The above price elasticities are "compensated" as they refer to the substitution effects only – real total expenditure on the four goods is held constant.

---

[8] Edwards et al. (1994) survey more than 40 studies of the demand for alcohol. Using this survey, Fogarty (2004) reports the following average price elasticities: Beer -.4, wine   -.8, and spirits -.7.

Alternatively, if we hold nominal total expenditure constant we obtain the corresponding "uncompensated" elasticities; these involve adding back the income effects of the price changes and take the form $\pi_{ij} / \overline{w}_{it} - \overline{w}_{jt} \, \eta_i$. The uncompensated elasticities, which are computed using the information contained in Table 10.12, are given in the bottom panel of Table 10.13. The own-price elasticities are now -.4, -.5, -.9 and -.7 for beer, wine, spirits and marijuana, respectively. An element-by-element comparison of the uncompensated elasticities with their compensated counterparts reveals two major differences: (i) When the income effects are included, the elasticities involving the price of beer (given in column 2) are all (algebraically) much lower; this is due to the high budget share of beer of 40 percent. (ii) The four uncompensated elasticities of spirits (given in the row for that good) are all much smaller than the compensated versions due to the high income elasticity of spirits of 2.

10.5   Legalisation of Marijuana

Suppose the consumption of marijuana were legalised. What would happen to consumption? As the elimination of criminal sanctions would have the effect of lowering the "full price" of marijuana, consumption would be expected to increase. But, on the other hand, the disappearance of the "forbidden fruit" characteristic of marijuana could tend to lower consumption. This section, which is based on Daryal (2002), explores these issues. We start with a brief review of previous research and then report the results of a specifically-conducted survey of marijuana consumption patterns of young adults.

Several studies have analysed the impact of decriminalisation in the US where marijuana consumption has been decriminalised in some states, and one study takes a similar approach for Australia.[9] Table 10.14 summarises the findings of these studies. Studies using data pertaining to the whole population (Model, 1993, Saffer and Chaloupka, 1995, 1998, Cameron and Williams, 2001) find a significant increase in marijuana consumption due to decriminalisation. By contrast, the three other studies involving youths only (Johnston et al., 1981, Theis and Register, 1993, Pacula, 1997) find that decriminalisation has no significant impact. Evidently, as the general population consume less marijuana than do the young, their consumption is more sensitive to changes in its legal status. We will return to the last column of Table 10.14 in the next section.

The data used in our analysis were collected by way of a survey in 1998 of students enrolled in the first-year unit at UWA, Macroeconomics, Money and Finance 102. Table 10.15 gives the characteristics of the students enrolled in the unit and the respondents to the survey. Table 10.16 shows that 53 percent of all

---

[9] Decriminalisation of marijuana removes criminal penalties associated with the possession of small amounts for personal use. Legalisation involves a further step whereby all sanctions are removed, so that the status of marijuana would be like that of alcohol or tobacco and perhaps have restrictions on advertising and the sale to minors.

their consumption is more sensitive to changes in its legal status. We will return to the last column of Table 10.14 in the next section.

The data used in our analysis were collected by way of a survey in 1998 of students enrolled in the first-year unit at UWA, Macroeconomics, Money and Finance 102. Table 10.15 gives the characteristics of the students enrolled in the unit and the respondents to the survey. Table 10.16 shows that 53 percent of all respondents have used marijuana, while 47 percent claimed to have never consumed it.[10] Consumption of marijuana is higher amongst males than females – 60 percent of male students have consumed it, compared to 46 percent of females. The hypothesis of independence of consumption and gender is rejected at the 5 percent significance level on basis of a chi-square test. Information on the frequency of consumption is given in the lower part of Table 10.16. Consider first the results for "all" users, given in the last column. Weekly consumption is the most popular frequency, while only a small proportion consumes marijuana daily. Interestingly, 20 percent are no longer users; these people tried it at some stage and have not used it in over a year. The most popular frequency for males is weekly (33 percent), whereas for females it is occasional (28 percent). Both daily and weekly consumption of marijuana is considerably higher among males than females; however, the hypothesis of independence of gender and the frequency of

Table 10.14 Aspects of previous studies of marijuana consumption

Author	Data	Does decriminalisation increase marijuana consumption significantly?	Relationship between alcohol and marijuana
Johnston et al. (1981)	Surveys of US high school seniors, 1975-80	No	-
DiNardo and Lemieux (1992)	Surveys of US high school seniors, 1980-89	-	Substitutes
Model (1993)	US Drug Abuse Warning Network, 1975-78	Yes[1]	Substitutes
Theis and Register (1993)	US National Longitudinal Survey of Youth, 1984-88	No	Inconclusive
Saffer and Chaloupka (1995)	US National Household Surveys on Drug Abuse, 1988-91	Yes[2]	Inconclusive
Pacula (1997)	US National Longitudinal Survey of Youth, 1984	No	Complements
Chaloupka and Laixuthai (1997)	Surveys of US high school seniors, 1982-89	-	Substitutes
Pacula (1998)	US National Longitudinal Survey of Youth, 1983-84	-	Complements
Saffer and Chaloupka (1998)	US National Household Surveys on Drug Abuse, 1988-91	Yes	Mostly complements
Cameron and Williams (2001)	Australian National Drug Strategy Household Surveys, 1988-95	Yes	Substitutes

Notes: 1. Indirect evidence from hospital emergency room data. 2. Probability of marijuana usage increases by 8 percentage points.

consumption cannot be rejected at the 5 percent significance level on the basis of a chi-square test.[11]

---

[10] William Jefferson Clinton, the former President of the US, says he has smoked marijuana, but claims "not to have inhaled." This seems sufficiently far-fetched that we did not judge it to be worthwhile to include this as a possibility in our survey.

[11] Our survey reveals that (i) more males consume marijuana than do females; and (ii) around 50 percent of all respondents are users. Bearing in mind that the mean age of our respondents is 19 years (see Table 15), these findings are consistent with results from the 1995 Australian National Drug Strategy Household Survey (NDSHS) quoted in the Penington Report (1996, p. 13). The frequency of consumption data from the two surveys for the daily and occasional users is very similar. However, the proportions that consume marijuana on a weekly or monthly basis are considerably higher in our survey; and the

Table 10.15 Characteristics of students enrolled in macroeconomics, money and finance 102 at UWA and the sample

Characteristic	Enrolled in unit	Sample
Number of students	582	327
Number of respondents	-	281
Response rate (percent)	-	86
Sex (percent)		
Male	52	48
Female	48	52
Age (years)		
Median	18	-
Mean	19	-
Origin (percent)		
Local	75	-
International	25	-

Source of the enrollment data: Unit coordinator and lecturer Paul Miller.

Table 10.16 Usage of marijuana (percentages of respondents)

	Male	Female	All
Ever used marijuana	60	46	53
	Frequency of Consumption		
Daily	9	1	6
Weekly	33	25	30
Monthly	17	25	21
Occasional	21	28	23
No longer	20	21	20
Total	100	100	100

Our survey asked, 'Suppose marijuana is legalised. Assume there is no price change. How much would your consumption of marijuana change?' Table 10.17 presents the responses, cross-classified by type of consumer and gender. All the estimated consumption changes are positive and the majority are significant at the 5 percent level. These findings do not support the "forbidden fruit" idea, whereby consumption could fall with legalisation as it may eliminate an attractive characteristic of marijuana. As indicated by the last entry in row 6, for all users,

---

proportion who are "no longer users" is much lower in our study. The reason for these differences is probably because the NDSHS covers the entire population, not only young adults, who make up our survey. These different results from the two surveys seem to say something interesting about the lifetime profile of marijuana consumption: If you are a daily or occasional user when young, then as you age and become part of the general population, you stay a daily or occasional user, at least on average. By contrast, the majority of weekly and monthly users stop using marijuana as they mature and presumably get more involved with work and family life.

marijuana consumption is estimated to increase by approximately 8 percent following legalisation. As the estimated increase in consumption of those who currently are non-users is less than 1 percent (row 7, column 4), legalisation does not draw in a substantial number of new users.[12] In general, males are relatively more responsive to legalisation than are females; the consumption of all males is estimated to increase by 6 percent, while that of all females increases by 3 percent (see row 8). Considering the differing types of consumer, daily users (row 1) have the largest response to legalisation, as expected, but this is not significant at the 5 percent level. The estimated rise for weekly, monthly and occasional users (males and females) is estimated to be 9, 8, and 7 percent, respectively, all of which are significant at the 5 percent level. None of the females who are no longer users say that their consumption will increase with legalisation, whilst for males in this category, consumption increases by 5 percent (see row 5). Going down columns 2-4, it can be seen that, in general, more frequent users are more responsive to legalisation than are less frequent users, as one would expect.

Table 10.17 **Percentage change in consumption of marijuana due to legalisation (standard errors are in parenthesis)**

Type of consumer	Males		Females		All	
(1)	(2)		(3)		(4)	
1. Daily users	21.25	(14.80)	.00	(.00)	18.89	(13.70)
2. Weekly users	8.15*	(4.07)	11.18*	(5.08)	9.32*	(3.19)
3. Monthly users	6.79*	(3.38)	9.12*	(4.07)	8.06*	(2.79)
4. Occasional users	10.88*	(4.27)	3.89*	(1.96)	7.29*	(2.35)
5. No longer a user	4.69	(4.67)	.00	(.00)	2.50	(2.48)
6. All users	9.09*	(2.28)	6.19*	(1.78)	7.79*	(1.49)
7. Non-users	.19	(.18)	.38	(.24)	.30*	(.15)
8. All types	5.55*	(1.42)	3.07*	(.86)	4.27*	(.82)

* Denotes significant at the 5 percent level.

10.6 Drinking and Legalisation

The previous section analysed the effects of legalisation on marijuana consumption. Evidence from the UWA survey indicates that there would be some increase in consumption. As we have seen that alcohol and marijuana consumption are interrelated, it is also relevant to ask, what would legalisation do to drinking? If alcohol and marijuana were substitutes, then there would likely to be a tendency for drinking to fall when marijuana usage increases as a result of legalisation; and

---

[12] This result contradicts previous findings from the US National Commission on Marijuana and Drug Abuse Surveys, conducted in 1972 and 1973. These surveys indicate that 8-12 percent of non-user youths (and 3-4 percent of non-user adults) would become users if marijuana were decriminalised (Thies and Register, 1993). It should, however, be noted that this survey refers to a period more than 25 years ago, and since then drug-taking attitudes and behaviour may have changed substantially.

conversely if alcohol and marijuana were complements. As shown by the last column of Table 10.14, prior studies of the relationship between the two types of goods are not unanimous -- four find substitutability, two/three complementarity and two are inconclusive.[13] In this section, which is based on Daryal (2002), we use additional information from the UWA survey to obtain some direct results on the effects of legalisation on drinking.

Our survey asked, "Suppose marijuana were legalised, how would your alcohol consumption change?". The responses to the question are summarised in Table 10.18. As can be seen from column 2, for each type of consumer the majority say that their alcohol consumption would not change with legalisation, which points towards the two substances being neither substitutes nor complements, but independent in consumption. Alcohol consumption of daily users is by far the most responsive, with 33 percent saying that it would increase with legalisation and 11 percent saying it would fall (see the first entries in columns 3 and 4). The responses of weekly, monthly and occasional users are all quite similar. One way of measuring the "net position" of each type of consumer is to simply subtract the "decreases" from the "increases" and column 5 contains the results. This column reveals that following legalisation, the increase in alcohol consumption outweighs the decrease in the case of the daily users by 33 - 11 = 22 percentage points, implying that alcohol and marijuana are complements for this group. For all other users, the decrease in alcohol consumption outweighs the increase, meaning that the two substances are substitutes.

Table 10.18 The effect of marijuana legalisation on alcohol consumption (percentages of respondents)

Type of consumer	None	Increase	Decrease	Increase less decrease
(1)	(2)	(3)	(4)	(5)
Daily users	56	33	11	22
Weekly users	82	4	14	-10
Monthly users	81	6	13	-7
Occasional users	77	3	20	-17
No longer a user	97	0	3	-3
All users	82	5	13	-8
Non-users	95	4	1	3
All types	87	5	8	-3

Note: For a given row, the sum of columns 2, 3 and 4 equals 100.

[13] Note that the positive compensated cross elasticities involving the price of marijuana given in the upper panel of column 5 of Table 10.13 indicate substitutability. But this is an implication of the assumption of preference independence, which was invoked to reduce the number of unknown parameters in order to make the estimation of the demand model feasible with the limited amount of data. On the other hand, the negative residual correlations for marijuana, reported in Table 10.10, indicate substitutability.

Table 10.19 gives the cross tabulations of the responses to the questions "Have you ever consumed marijuana?" and "Suppose marijuana were legalised, how would your alcohol consumption change?". We use a chi-square statistic to test the hypothesis that alcohol and marijuana consumption are independent. This yields a chi-square value of 13.51, which is significant at the 5 percent level, so we reject the hypothesis of independence. [14] Although there is a significant relationship between alcohol and marijuana consumption, this result still cannot establish whether the two substances are substitutes or complements.

Table 10.19   Change in alcohol consumption and prevalence of marijuana usage (percentages of respondents)

Have you ever consumed marijuana?	Change in alcohol consumption due to legalisation			Total
	Increase	Decrease	No change	
Yes	3	7	43	53
No	2	1	44	47
Total	5	8	87	100

10.7 Concluding Comments

This chapter has investigated economic aspects of part of the illicit drug industry, namely, the determinants of the demand for marijuana. Special attention has been devoted to the measurement of the amount of marijuana consumed, the price responsiveness of consumption, the interaction of marijuana with alcohol and the impacts of possible legalisation. In view of the large number of people who have used marijuana and the fact that, in Australia at least, expenditure on it is about twice that on wine, it is surprising that more is not known about these intriguing matters.

The main findings of the chapter are as follows:
- Per capita consumption of marijuana in Australia has increased from .65 ounces in 1988 to .79 in 1998. Expenditure of marijuana in 1998 was $5.3 billion (equivalent to about 1 percent of GDP), or $354 per capita.
- Expenditure on marijuana is almost equal to that on wine plus spirits; and it is about three-quarters of beer expenditure.

---

[14] Due to the small number of observations in some cells of Table 10.19, caution is appropriate in interpreting this result.

- The law of demand holds with respect to beer, wine, spirits and marijuana – for those goods whose prices rise faster than average, consumption grows slower than average, and vice versa.
- The own-price elasticity of demand for marijuana is about – 1/3.
- The elasticities of demand for the three alcoholic beverages with respect to the price of marijuana are: Beer-marijuana .1, wine-marijuana .2, spirits-marijuana .3.
- About 50 percent of first-year students at UWA have used marijuana, with males being heavier users than females.
- The UWA survey reveals that for all types of users, legalisation would on average cause marijuana consumption to increase by approximately 8 percent. In general, more frequent users are more responsive to legalisation than are less frequent users. Legalisation would not draw in a substantial number of new users.

Chapter 11

Alcohol Misuse and Control Policies

In Chapter 4, we presented a global picture of alcohol consumption and looked more closely at the consumption patterns of alcohol across various consumer characteristics in a selected number of countries. Following that, in Chapter 8, we analysed the demand for alcohol using a system-wide framework and data from 43 developed and developing countries. We analysed alcohol consumption in the context of the consumer utility maximizing framework and found that income and prices are two of the major economic factors that significantly influence alcohol consumption in most countries. The results also show that, in developed countries, alcohol is considered as a necessity by consumers and in developing countries it is considered a luxury. The cross-country average of income elasticities were 0.80 for developed countries and 1.13 for developing countries (see Table 8.15). The results also show that demand for alcohol is price inelastic irrespective of whether consumers are from developed or developing countries. The estimated average own-price elasticity of alcohol for developed and developing countries are very similar and are -0.57 and -0.61, respectively, with an overall cross-country average of -0.59.

In Chapter 9, we considered the consumption patterns at a more disaggregated level of individual beverages beer, wine and spirits within the alcoholic beverages group across 10 selected (developed) countries. The cross-country average estimates of income elasticities of beer, wine and spirits were 0.75, 0.95 and 1.39, indicating that within the alcoholic beverages group, beer and wine are necessities (income elasticity smaller than 1) and spirits is a luxury (income elasticity larger than 1). The cross-country averages of own-price elasticites for beer, wine and spirits were estimated as -0.19, -0.33 and -0.31, respectively, indicating that in most countries, the demand for these three beverages are price inelastic. Intuitively, these elasticity estimates mean that a 10 percent increase in the price of each beverage would lead to a 2 percent decrease in the consumption of beer, 3 percent decrease in the consumption of wine and 3 percent decrease in the consumption of spirits.

While most studies, including the present study, use time-series data there are also a number of alcohol studies available that use cross-sectional data. Like a number of cross-sectional studies, a recent US cross-sectional study by Manning (1995), based on the survey of 18,000 adults, found that higher beverage prices were significantly related to lower alcohol consumption among the overall population. However, no significant responsiveness to price was found among the heaviest drinkers, specifically on the 5 percent of the US population who are responsible for 36 percent of the US total alcohol consumption.

When people drink certain types of alcohol sensibly it is claimed that it improves a person's health and causes no harm to others in the drinking environment. But the problem starts, when people drink to become drunk. Such levels of alcohol consumption lead to several social and health problems. The cost associated with alcohol abuse and alcoholism is of continuing concern to governments, policy makers and to the society in general.

In this chapter, we consider the control policies in place in a number of countries to control excessive alcohol consumption. We consider the control policies in place in relation to sale restrictions, alcohol taxation, restrictions on alcohol consumption, drink-driving regulations, restrictions on alcohol advertising, alcohol preventative programmes and implementation of alcohol policy. As we will see below, while strict alcohol control policies are in place in most developed countries, very little or no control policies are in place in most of the developing countries. However, it should be noted that alcohol is a necessity in the developed countries and they tend to have a more serious problem of alcohol abuse compared to developing countries where alcohol is a luxury.

The countries selected in this chapter are those for which information on alcohol control policies are available. Most of the data used in this chapter are gathered from the following sources: (1) *The World Health Organisation*, WHO (2003); (2) *Brewers Association of Canada* (1997); (3) *Eurocare* (2003); and (4) various individual country reports published by the respective government bodies. Since 1997, the WHO has been engaged in constructing a global alcohol database to provide individual country information on the socio-demographic information, alcohol production/trade/industry, alcohol consumption, the prevalence of alcohol use, the health effects of alcohol use, alcohol related mortality, alcohol control measures, policies and programmes etc.

In the next section, we present some of the indicators which show the level of alcohol misuse in a selected number of countries. In the following sections we present a global picture of the various alcohol control measures such as sales restriction, drink-driving, alcohol advertising, alcohol taxes etc. In the final section we summarise the programmes in place to enhance alcohol control policies.

11.1 Alcohol Misuse Indicators

Alcohol misuse can be measured by the effect of excessive alcohol consumption on the community. There are two main indicators which are widely used to show the severity of alcohol misuse in a country, namely, deaths due to liver cirrhosis and alcohol related road accidents. In this section, wherever data are available, we analyse the plots of these two indicators over a number of years for a number of countries. First, we consider the indicators in individual countries and then we present summary tables to give a global picture.

Australia

Australians are one of the big beer drinkers in the world (see Table 4.4, Chapter 4), although the share of the beer market has fallen in recent years at the gain of wine and spirits. Almost all beer (99 percent) and wine (94 percent) consumed in Australia are locally produced and spirits are mostly (69 percent) imported. According to research published in the *Medical Journal of Australia* (*The West Australian*, 'Drinkers Ignore Safety Calls', 21/1/2002), young Australian men aged 18 to 24 were found to drink alcohol dangerously 93 percent of the time. According to another survey results reported in *The West Australian* newspaper (4/1/2002), 32 percent of women aged between 23 and 28 binge drink (binge drinking of alcohol is defined as the consumption, in a single day, of at least 8 standard units for men and at least 6 standard units for women).

Figure 11.1 shows the liver cirrhosis death rates and the rate of alcohol related road accidents per 100,000 Australian population. Death rate due to liver cirrhosis increased until the mid-1970s and is decreasing in the last 2 decades. As can be seen, the rate of alcohol related accidents have steadily declined during the sample period. These indicators show that alcohol abuse has been on the decline since 1980 in Australia.

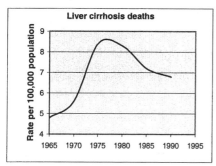
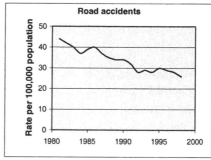

Figure 11.1 Rates of liver cirrhosis deaths and alcohol related road accidents per 100,000 population, Australia

It is also reported that alcohol consumption in excess of the national safety drinking guidelines is believed responsible for about 3300 deaths in Australia each year, costing the community A$4.5 billion. Among the 3300 deaths caused by alcohol related injuries, half of them are young people. Furthermore, Collins and Lapsley (1991) reported that the cost to the community of alcohol misuse was A$6 billion a year.

Table 11.1 presents the risk of harm in the short term of the adult population by age and gender. This data is taken from the survey results published in the 2001

The Demand for Alcohol, Tobacco and Marijuana

Table 11.1 Risk of alcohol related harm in the short term: Proportion of the population aged 14 years and over, by age and gender, Australia, 2001

Age group (1)	Abstainers (2)	Low risk (3)	Risky and high risk (4)
		Male	
14-19	27.2	30.0	42.8
20-29	8.4	27.4	64.2
30-39	9.8	39.7	50.4
40-49	11.4	50.7	37.9
50-59	12.5	59.1	28.4
60+	20.1	66.5	13.4
All ages	14.1	46.5	39.4
		Female	
14-19	25.3	28.3	46.4
20-29	11.3	32.1	56.5
30-39	16.0	47.5	36.6
40-49	16.4	55.1	28.6
50-59	21.9	62.0	16.1
60+	33.0	62.3	4.7
All ages	20.8	49.6	29.6
		All persons	
14-19	26.2	29.2	44.6
20-29	9.9	29.8	60.4
30-39	13.0	43.7	43.3
40-49	13.9	52.8	33.3
50-59	17.1	60.5	22.3
60+	27.1	64.2	8.7
All ages	17.5	48.1	34.4

Note: Abstainers are those who did not consume alcohol in the last 12 months. For males, the consumption of up to 28 standard drinks per week is considered 'Low risk', 29 to 42 per week 'Risky', and 43 or more per week 'High risk'. For females, the consumption of up to 14 standard drinks per week is considered 'Low risk', 15 to 28 per week 'Risky' and 29 or more per week 'High risk'. Source: *Statistics on Drug Use in Australia*, 2002, Table 3.4.

National Drug Strategy Household Survey (AIHW, 2002b). As can be seen, in 2001, 39 percent of male and 30 percent of female Australians consumed alcohol in a manner that put themselves at risk of alcohol related harm. For the 20-29 years age group (the high-risk group), this proportion was 64 percent for males and 57 percent for females. Among all Australians, one in three adult persons consumed alcohol in a way that put themselves at significantly increased risk of alcohol related harm in the short term.

Austria

The level of consumption of alcoholic beverages is relatively high in Austria compared to most developed countries (see Table 4.4, Chapter 4). Austria produces beer, wine and spirits. Almost all beer (97 percent), wine (93 percent) and spirits (80 percent) consumed in Austria are locally produced. Alcohol production is a government monopoly in Austria. A 1994 survey (Eurocare, 2001) of 2000 Austrians aged 16 to 99 years revealed that 28.8 percent of males and 4.3 percent of females consume on average 60 grams or more alcohol per day and 41 percent of males and 8.5 percent females consume an average of 40 grams per day. According to another 1993/94 WHO study among 15 year old boys and girls showed that 96.2 percent of boys had tried alcoholic beverages and 40.2 percent drank alcohol at least weekly. Among girls, 95 percent had tried alcohol and 25 percent drank alcohol at least weekly. According to Eurocare (2001), even though alcoholism is on the increase, the number of deaths due to alcoholism is decreasing in Austria.

Figure 11.2 plots the liver cirrhosis death rates and the rate of alcohol related road accidents per 100,000 Austrian population. As can seen the death rate due to liver cirrhosis, in Austria, has also fallen, from as high as 30 percent during the mid-70s to 20 percent in the late 1990s. The road fatality rate related to alcohol has fallen from 50 persons per 100,000 population in 1985 to 30 persons per 100,000 in 2000. These two graphs indicate a steady decline of alcohol abuse in Austria.

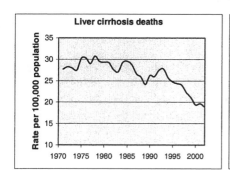
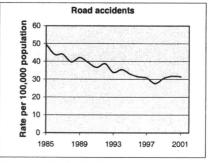

Figure 11.2   Rates of liver cirrhosis deaths and alcohol related road accidents per 100,000 population, Austria

Belgium

Belgium produces beer, wine and spirits. About 95 percent of beer consumed by the Belgians are locally produced. Imported French wine is the most popular wine in Belgium. Wine consumption in Belgium has been on the increase at the expense of beer and spirits from 1980. The overall alcohol consumption in Belgium has been declining from the early 1990s. A survey among 14 to 24 year olds in 1990 found that 19 percent never drank alcohol, 28 percent drank at least weekly, 7 percent drank 3 or more glasses per day, 36 percent had been drunk several times and 10 percent became drunk regularly.

Figure 11.3 presents the liver cirrhosis death rates and the rate of alcohol related road accidents per 100,000 Belgium population. As can be seen, the death rate due to liver cirrhosis in Belgium has fallen from about 13.5 per 100,000 in 1975 to 10.5 per 100,000 in 1990 and has increased in the last 10 years. While the alcohol related road accident rate fell during 1990-1994, it has increased since 1995. These two plots indicate that, in Belgium, alcohol abuse is on the increase in recent years.

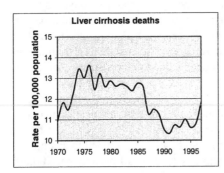 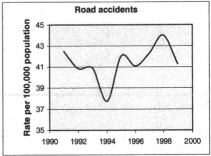

Figure 11.3   Rates of liver cirrhosis deaths and alcohol related road accidents per 100,000 population, Belgium

Canada

Canada is primarily a beer consuming country. Canada produces beer, wine and spirits. About 97 percent of beer and 50 percent of spirits consumed by the Canadians are locally produced. Most (about 75 percent) of the wine consumed in Canada is imported. Alcohol (total as well as individual beverage) consumption has been falling in the last 2 decades. According to the *1996/97 National Population Health Survey*, in Canada, 42.1 percent of drinkers reported consuming 5 or more drinks on a single occasion (6.2 percent did so on a weekly basis), 23.4 percent exceeded the low-risk guidelines of alcohol consumption and 2.5 percent reported drinking at levels associated with clinical dependence on alcohol, in the past 12 months. A study by Single et al (1996) estimates the cost associated with misuse of alcohol as approximately $7.5 billion, which is 1.1 percent of the Canadian GDP. About sixty percent of this cost is associated with loss in productivity. It is estimated that 6503 Canadians lost their lives and 80,946 were hospitalised as a result of alcohol consumption in 1995 (CCSA, 2003).

Figure 11.4 presents the liver cirrhosis death rates and the rate of alcohol related road accidents per 100,000 Canadian population. As can be seen, the rate of deaths due to liver cirrhosis peaked during the late 1970s and fell sharply during the 1980s and is stable in the last few years. The percentage of alcohol related accidents in Canada has fallen from 39 percent in 1995 to 30 percent in 2000. However, the rate of alcohol related road accidents is still high. Overall, the situation with the misuse of alcohol has been improving in Canada.

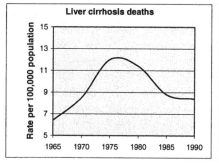 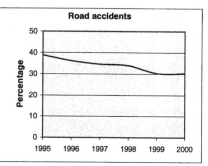

Figure 11.4   Rate of liver cirrhosis deaths and alcohol related road accidents as a percentage of total accidents, Canada

Czech Republic

The Czech Republic is one of the world's highest consumers of beer (see Table 4.4, Chapter 4). The positive trend in beer consumption is taking place at the expense of wine consumption. The Czech Republic produces beer, wine and spirits. Based on a 1995 survey among 2962 15 and 16 year olds, 54 percent reported to have drunken to intoxication in the last 12 months of the survey.

Figure 11.5 presents the liver cirrhosis death rates and the rate of alcohol related road accidents per 100,000 population in the Czech Republic. As can be seen, liver cirrhosis death rates have been fluctuating between 16 and 20 deaths per 100,000 persons over the last 30 years. The alcohol related accident rate increased initially and has slowly fallen in the last 10 years.

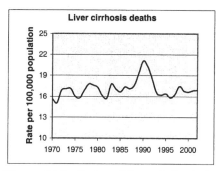 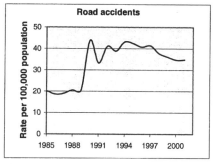

Figure 11.5   Rates of liver cirrhosis deaths and alcohol related road accidents per 100,000 population, Czech Republic

Denmark

Denmark produces beer and spirits but imports wine. Almost all beer and three fourths of spirits sold in Denmark are locally made. About 90 percent of wine sold in Denmark is imported. According to a 1995 survey among 15 and 16 years olds, 82 percent reported to have drunken alcohol to intoxication in the last 12 months. Another *1993/94 WHO Survey* conducted among 15 year olds found that boys consumed alcohol approximately twice as much as girls. The survey also found that children from high-income families are the ones who consumed alcohol the most.

Figure 11.6 presents the liver cirrhosis death rate and the rate of alcohol related road accidents per 100,000 population in Denmark. The rate of deaths due to liver cirrhosis is increasing without much improvement. On the other hand, the rate of alcohol related road accidents per 100,000 persons has fallen sharply from about 50 accidents in 1985 to 20 accidents in 2000, which is encouraging.

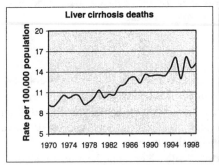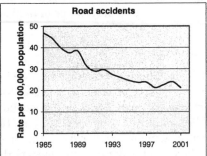

**Figure 11.6   Rates of liver cirrhosis deaths and alcohol related road accidents
per 100,000 population, Denmark**

Finland

Finland produces, exports and imports the three beverages. Almost all of beer, about 80 percent of spirits and one third of wine consumed in Finland are locally produced. Finland has been one of the countries with the most controls on alcohol consumption. In a survey among 15 to 16 year old children, 55 percent of boys and 61 percent of girls have reported to have consumed alcohol in the 30 days prior to the survey. Until the early 1960s Finnish women very seldom drank. But this changed in the 1980's where women consumed about 20 percent of all alcohol consumed in Finland. Intoxication among young women, especially in the age group 15 to 19 years, is currently very common. Women with upper-grade clerical jobs have the highest drinking frequencies and annual alcohol consumption.

Figure 11.7 depicts the liver cirrhosis death rates and the rate of alcohol related road accidents per 100,000 population in Finland. An upward trend can be seen with the rate of deaths due to liver cirrhosis which should be of concern to the government authorities. On the other hand, the rate of alcohol related road accidents have been falling from a high level of 32 accidents in 1990 but seem to have stabilized at about 20 accidents per 100,000 persons in recent years.

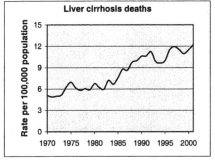 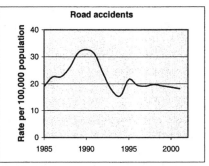

Figure 11.7   Rates of liver cirrhosis deaths and alcohol related road accidents per 100,000 population, Finland

France

France produces all three beverages. France is one of the highest wine consuming countries in the world. However, the per capita wine consumption has been halved from 125 litres in 1950 to 64 litres in 1995 and still continues to decline. About 85 percent of beer and wine consumed in France is locally produced and so is half of the spirits. A survey by WHO in 1993/94 of 15 years old boys and girls found that 38 percent of boys and 18 percent of girls drank alcohol at least once a week; 24 percent of boys and 13 percent of girls had been drunk at least twice.

Figure 11.8 shows the death rates from liver cirrhosis. As the graph shows, liver cirrhosis death rate has steadily declined from about 35 deaths per 100,000 population in 1970 to a low 14 deaths in 2000, which is very encouraging.

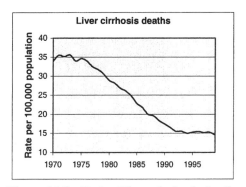

Figure 11.8   Rate of liver cirrhosis deaths per 100,000 population, France

Germany

Per capita alcohol consumption of all three beverages in Germany has increased until the 1980s and declined in the last 10 years. Germany is still one of the major beer consuming countries in the world. Almost all beer and about 70 percent of spirits consumed in Germany are locally produced. According to a survey carried out in 1995 among 18 to 59 year olds, 15.1 percent of males and 10 percent of females in West Germany and 20.5 percent of males and 11.5 percent of females in East Germany abused alcoholic beverages.

Figure 11.9 shows the liver cirrhosis death rates and the rate of alcohol related road accidents per 100,000 population in Germany. The death rate from liver cirrhosis in Germany has had a steady downward trend in the last 20 years. A similar decrease can be seen from the rate of alcohol related road accidents, falling sharply from 50 to 30 accidents per 100,000 persons in the last 10 years. Therefore, there is a lot of improvement in Germany with regard to the two alcohol abuse indicators, implying that, on the whole, alcohol misuse is on the decline in Germany.

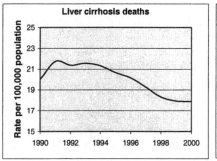 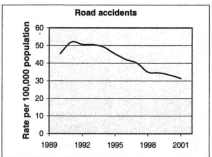

Figure 11.9   Rates of liver cirrhosis deaths and alcohol related road accidents per 100,000 population, Germany

Greece

Traditionally, Greece has been primarily a wine-drinking country. According to the results of a 1993/94 study, 83 percent of boys and 87 percent of girls had tried alcohol before they turned 15 and 8.3 percent of boys and 7.5 percent of girls drank alcohol every week.

Figure 11.10 gives the liver cirrhosis death rates and the rate of alcohol related road accidents per 100,000 population in Greece. The death rate per 100,000 persons from cirrhosis of the liver in Greece has had a steady downward trend in the last 30 years, falling sharply from 16 in 1970 to 4 in 2000. A slight decline can be seen from the rate of alcohol related road accidents, however, the rate of accidents is very high compared to any other OECD country.

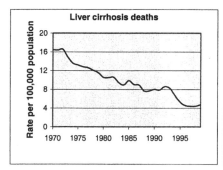 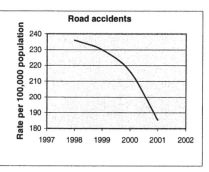

Figure 11.10 Rates of liver cirrhosis deaths and alcohol related road accidents per 100,000 population, Greece

Hungary

Hungary produces beer, wine and spirits. During the 1980s the Hungarian government introduced several measures to limit alcohol consumption in public places and alcohol availability. Since the political changes during the late 1980s, these restrictions were gradually removed. In a survey carried out in 1995 among 15 and 16 year olds, 80 percent of them reported to have drunken alcohol and 40 percent had drunken to intoxication in the last 12 months. Between 1970 and 1994 the number of alcoholic psychosis per 100,000 population had increased from 1089 to 2610.

Figure 11.11 presents time series graphs of the rate of liver cirrhosis deaths and the rate of alcohol related road accidents per 100,000 population in Hungary. The rate of liver cirrhosis deaths per 100,000 persons in Hungary has increased steadily from about 12 deaths in 1970 to 80 deaths in 1995 but has declined in the past 8 years. However, the rate is still quite high. The rate of alcohol related road accidents is fluctuating but has generally fallen in the last 10 years. The accidents per 100,000 population has decreased from 40 in 1990 to 20 in 2000.

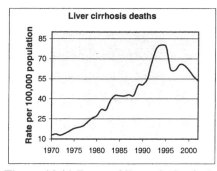 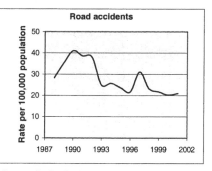

Figure 11.11 Rates of liver cirrhosis deaths and alcohol related road accidents per 100,000 population, Hungary

Ireland

Ireland is traditionally a beer consuming country. Ireland produces beer and spirits
and imports wine. There is no state monopoly but a license is required for the
production and distribution of all types of alcohol (except home-made wine and
beer). More than 90 percent of beer consumed is locally produced in Ireland. The
results from a survey among 15 to 16 year olds carried out in 1995 revealed that 86
percent had drunken alcohol and 66 percent had drunken to intoxication in the past
12 months of the survey.

Figure 11.12 presents the liver cirrhosis death rates per 100,000 Irish
population. The rate of liver cirrhosis deaths in Ireland has been stable throughout
the last three decades, fluctuating between the very low rates of 3 and 5 deaths per
100,000 persons.

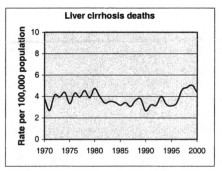

Figure 11.12 Rate of liver cirrhosis deaths per 100,000 population, Ireland

Israel

Israel produces beer, wine and spirits. The estimate of the number of alcoholics in
Israel in the year 2001 was about 2 percent of the total population. According to a
study carried out in 1998 among Jewish adolescents 12 to 18 year olds, 57 percent
reported drinking in the previous year. The same study also found that, among the
18 to 40 year old adults, about 71 percent used alcohol in the previous year.
According to a WHO 1993/94 survey, 22.8 percent of school boys and 10.4 percent
of school girls drank alcohol at least weekly.

Figure 11.13 presents the liver cirrhosis death rates and the rate of alcohol
related road accidents per 100,000 population in Israel. While the liver cirrhosis
death rate in Israel fluctuates a lot, generally, it has been on the decline. Alcohol
related road accidents declined until 1997 and steadily increased in the past 5 years,
which should be of concern to the Israel government authorities.

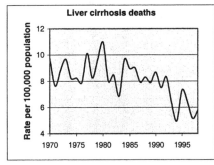
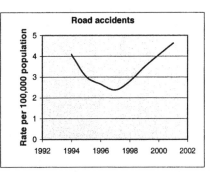

Figure 11.13 Rates of liver cirrhosis deaths and alcohol related road accidents per 100,000 population, Israel

Italy

Italy is traditionally a wine consuming country, however, per capita wine consumption has more than halved within the last two decades. While wine and spirits consumption has fallen in recent years, beer consumption has increased slightly. As a result, total per capita alcohol consumption has generally fallen in the last few years. Three fourths of the beer consumed in Italy is locally produced. A 1995 survey reported that among 15-16 year olds, 83 percent had drunken alcohol in the past 12 months and 35 percent had drunken to intoxication. In 1994, misuse of alcohol resulted in a total loss of US$7460 million in Italy. The total loss made up of primary costs in relation to treatment of alcohol dependents such as hospital care, rehabilitation, disability payment etc was US$1490 million; primary indirect costs such as lack of work following incidents or illness, loss of work through permanent invalidity, death of alcohol dependents and loss of production amounted to US$3190 million; secondary direct costs such as health treatment, destruction of properties etc amounted to US$2280 million and indirect secondary costs such as loss of production due to alcohol dependency etc amounted US$494 million.

Figure 11.14 presents the time series plots of the liver cirrhosis death rate and the rate of alcohol related road accidents per every 100,000 Italians. As can be seen, the liver cirrhosis death rate has fallen sharply from about 35 deaths in 1975 to 14 deaths in 2000 per 100,000 population, which shows a significant improvement. However, the rate of alcohol related road accidents has been increasing sharply from 1990 onwards. Even though this rate is very low compared to all other countries, the rate of increase should be a matter of concern to the Italian government authorities.

Japan

Japan is traditionally one of the highest spirits consuming countries in the world. However, over the last few years, beer and wine consumption have increased while

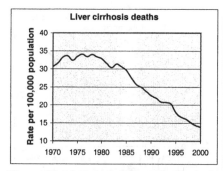
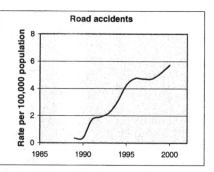

Figure 11.14 Rates of liver cirrhosis deaths and alcohol related road accidents per 100,000 population, Italy

spirits and sake consumption has fallen. Almost all beer and sake consumed in Japan are locally produced and most of the wine consumed is imported. Per capita beer consumption has increased almost five-fold in the last four decades. There is no government alcohol monopoly in Japan.

Figure 11.15 presents the liver cirrhosis death rates per 100,000 population over the period 1960-1995 and the rate of alcohol related road accidents per 100,000 population by age group in Japan. Overall, until the late 1970s, the liver cirrhosis deaths in Japan was increasing sharply but since then have stabilized or slightly decreased. However, the rate is still at a high level. Looking at the road accidents plot (Source: *Traffic Bureau of National Police Agency*, Japan), we see that the rate of accidents is high for the lower age groups (16-19 and 20-24) and the 40-49 and 50-59 age groups.

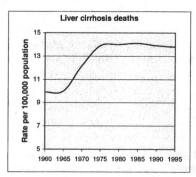
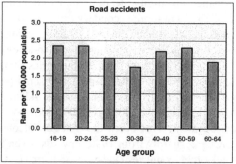

Figure 11.15 Rate of liver cirrhosis deaths and rate of alcohol related road accidents (by age group) per 100,000 population, Japan

Luxembourg

In Luxembourg, per capita consumption of wine has increased steadily (tripled in the last five decades) while that of beer has decreased. Luxembourg produces beer, wine and spirits. About 75 percent of beer and 50 percent of wine consumed in Luxembourg are locally produced and almost 95 percent of spirits is imported. A survey among adult consumers found 20 percent of people drank alcohol at least 3 to 4 days a week and among the 13 to 15 year old group, 16 percent of boys and 4 percent of girls drank alcohol weekly.

Figure 11.16 presents the liver cirrhosis death rates and the rate of alcohol related road accidents per 100,000 Dutch population. As can be seen, the liver cirrhosis death rate has declined for the last 30 years. The rate of alcohol related road accidents has mainly declined in recent years but is still quite high.

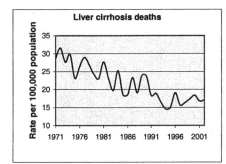 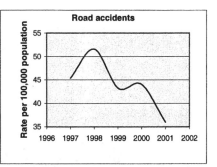

Figure 11.16 Rates of liver cirrhosis deaths and alcohol related road accidents per 100,000 population, Luxembourg

Netherlands

The Dutch consumption of beer and wine are on the increase while spirits consumption has declined from the early 1980s. About 95 percent of beer and 70 percent of spirits consumed in the Netherlands are locally produced. Most of the wine consumed is imported (which is about 80 percent). According to a 1992 survey of Dutch school children aged 10 years and over, 28 percent of the students have reported that they have consumed at least five glasses of alcohol on their last drinking occasion. In the Netherlands, drinking alcohol is banned in workplaces, transport and in parks. At least 30 percent of violent incidents with the spouse as victims took place when husband/wife was drunk at the time of the assault. In 17 percent of the families in which child abuse occurs, alcohol addiction is a contributory factor (Eurocare, 2001).

Table 11.2 presents the distribution of excessive alcohol consumption among the various age groups by gender in the Netherlands during 1997. As can be seen, 15-24, 25-34 and 35-44 age groups are the problematic age groups among both males and females. However, excessive alcohol consumption is a more serious problem among young males than young females. For example, in the 15-24 age group, the proportion of males who drink alcohol excessively is more than 8 times that of females.

Table 11.2　Proportion of excessive alcohol consumption among various age groups by gender, Netherlands, 1997

Age group	Male	Female
15-24 yrs	25	3
25-34 yrs	11	3
35-44 yrs	17	2
45-54 yrs	5	0
55-64 yrs	0	2
65+ yrs	0	1

* Excessive alcohol consumption for males means average weekly consumption of 20 or more units of alcoholic drinks plus at least on one occasion a week 10 or more units; and for females, excessive alcohol consumption means average weekly consumption of 15 or more units of alcoholic drinks plus at least at on one occasion a week 7 or more units. Source NIPO: NIPO Evaluate Campagne 'Drank maakt meer kapot dan je lief is'. Foekema 1997.

Figure 11.17 presents the liver cirrhosis death rates and the rate of alcohol related road accidents per 100,000 Dutch population. Overall, until 1983, the liver cirrhosis deaths in the Netherlands had an upward trend and since then has a downward trend. However, since 1993, the death rate is on the increase again. The number of alcohol related accidents has fallen over the years but at a very slow rate.

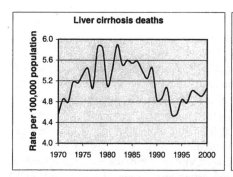 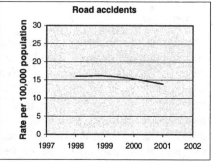

Figure 11.17 Rates of liver cirrhosis deaths and alcohol related road accidents per 100,000 population, Netherlands

New Zealand

New Zealanders most commonly consume alcohol at home but also frequently at bars, pubs, sports clubs and restaurants. Wine consumption is on the increase at the expense of beer. Beer, wine and spirits are all produced in New Zealand. About 95 percent of beer, 80 percent of wine and 65 percent of spirits consumed by New Zealanders are locally produced.

According to a 2000 nationwide survey (Habgood et al, 2001), 88 percent of male and 83 percent of female New Zealanders were drinkers in 2000. Thirty-four percent of the total volume of alcohol was consumed by women. The average annual volume consumed by women rose from 5.4 litres in 1995 to 7.3 litres by 2000. There was an increase in the percentage of males aged 16-17 years drinking more than 8 drinks from 19 percent in 1995 to 36 percent in 2000.

It is estimated that 3.4 percent of all male deaths and 1.6 percent of all female deaths in new Zealand in 1997 were related to alcohol. Alcohol related hospitalisations are estimated to cost the New Zealand government about $74 million each year (www.ndp.govt.nz/alcohol/). Easton (1997) estimated the cost associated with alcohol problems in New Zealand to be about $2.9 billion per year.

Figure 11.18 presents the liver cirrhosis death rates and the rate of alcohol related road accidents per 100,000 New Zealand population. The rate of liver cirrhosis deaths was on the increase until 1975 when it began to rapidly decrease. The death rate in recent years is approximately the same as it was before 1960. The rate of road accidents was on the increase during the 1970s and has been on the decline in the last 2 decades.

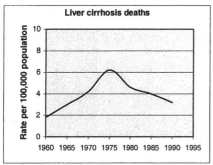
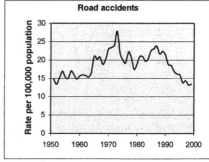

Figure 11.18 Rates of liver cirrhosis deaths and alcohol related road accidents per 100,000 population, New Zealand

Norway

Beer and wine consumption in Norway has been on the increase for the last 5 decades while spirits consumption has been falling since 1980. Almost all beer consumed by Norwegians is locally produced. About 75 percent of the spirits consumed in Norway are imported. According to a 1993 survey among 15 year old boys and girls, 80 percent of boys and 79 percent of girls have tried alcohol and 9.5 percent of boys and 6.8 percent of the girls have reported to have been drunk at least once a week.

According to police reports, 80 percent of all crimes of violence, 60 percent of all occurrences of rape, 50 percent of all sexual crimes towards children and 40 percent of all burglaries and thefts are committed while under the influence of alcohol (Source: *WHO Regional Office for Europe: Alcohol Problems, Policies and Programmes in Europe*, 1992).

Figure 11.19 presents the liver cirrhosis death rates and the rate of alcohol related road accidents per 100,000 Norwegians. The rate of liver cirrhosis deaths per 100,000 persons has been fluctuating between 3 and 8 persons over the past 30 years. The rate of alcohol related accidents is quite low in Norway and steadily falling over the last 2 decades to a low 3.4 accidents per 100,000 population in 1995.

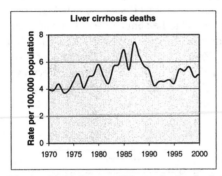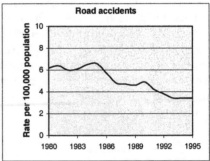

Figure 11.19 Rates of liver cirrhosis deaths and alcohol related road accidents per 100,000 population, Norway

Poland

Poland produces beer, wine and spirits. About 1 percent of the country's employment is provided by the alcohol industry. In Poland about 10.4 percent of alcohol drinkers are considered as abusers. A 1995 survey of 15-16 year olds reported that 80 percent of the respondents had drunk alcohol in the previous 12 months and 44 percent had drunk to intoxication. A 1993/94 WHO survey of 15 year old students revealed that 90 percent of boys and 87 percent of girls have tried alcohol.

Figure 11.20 presents the rate of alcohol related accidents per 100,000 population. As can be seen, the rate of alcohol related accidents fluctuates a bit but currently is on the decline.

Portugal

Beer consumption in Portugal has increased rapidly to five-fold in the last three decades while wine consumption has almost halved in the same period. Spirits consumption has stayed stable throughout. Almost all beer consumed in Portugal is locally produced. A survey conducted among 15 and 16 year olds in 1995 revealed that 74 percent had drunken alcohol and 28 percent of them had drunken to intoxication in the past 12 months.

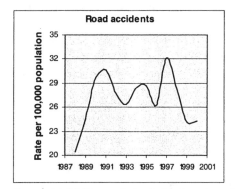

Figure 11.20 Rate of alcohol related road accidents per 100,000 population, Poland

Figure 11.21 presents the liver cirrhosis death rates and alcohol related accidents per 100,000 population in Portugal. As can be seen, the liver cirrhosis death rate has been declining steadily throughout the last three decades. The rate of road accidents related to alcohol was increasing until 1993 and has been falling since then.

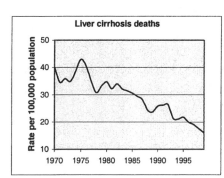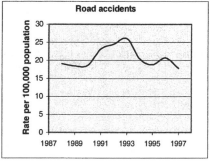

Figure 11.21 Rates of liver cirrhosis deaths and alcohol related road accidents per 100,000 population, Portugal

Spain

Until the early 1980s Spain has been largely a wine and spirits consuming country. Spanish drinkers consume mostly (about 95 percent) locally produced beer and wine and about 80 percent of locally produced spirits. That trend has changed in recent years. Currently 10 to 20 percent of beer and wine and about 50 percent of spirits consumed by the Spaniards are imported. A national survey found that in 1993, 2 percent of Spanish adults were high consumers (drinking between 415 grams and 553 grams of pure alcohol per week) and another 2 percent were classified as excessive consumers of alcoholic beverages (drinking more than 553 grams of pure alcohol per week). Another 1993/1994 *WHO Survey* found 90 percent of 15 year old boys and girls drank alcohol at least once a week and 23 percent of boys and 19 percent of girls had been drunk at least once. Drinking patterns vary in different parts of the country. Surveys found, in some parts of the country two-thirds of men and one-third of women drink alcohol daily. Another Spanish National Report, *Drug Situation 2000*, found that among the 14 to 18 age group, 24 percent get drunk at least once a month.

Figure 11.22 shows the liver cirrhosis death rates and alcohol related accidents per 100,000 population in Spain. As can be seen, the death rate due to liver cirrhosis was high in the 1970s and has been slowly falling in the last two decades. Looking at the alcohol related road accidents graph, we see that it was stable during the late 1980s but has increased slightly in recent years.

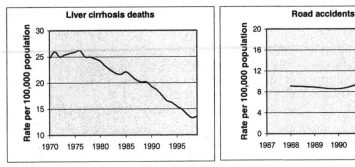

Figure 11.22 Rates of liver cirrhosis deaths and alcohol related road accidents per 100,000 population, Spain

Sweden

A positive trend in wine consumption in Sweden has continued over the last five decades while spirits consumption has declined. Beer consumption also fell during the 1980s but, in recent years, it has increased again. While more than 90 percent of beer consumed by Swedes is locally made, 75 percent of the spirits consumed by the Swedish are imported. Almost all wines consumed by the Swedish are imported. A 1993/94 survey of 15 year olds in Sweden revealed that 19 percent of boys and 11 percent of girls drank weekly and 27 percent of boys and 22 percent of girls had been drunk at least twice.

Table 11.3 presents the rate of deaths due to alcohol related illnesses per 100,000 Swedish population during 1959-1995. As can be seen, alcoholism and liver cirrhosis related deaths are the two most significant alcohol related deaths among the four types presented in the table. It can also be seen that there is a decline in the number of alcohol related deaths from the early 1980s.

The *Medical Advisory Committee, Ministry of Health and Social Welfare*, reported that alcohol is one of the major causes of production loss, illness and premature deaths. They also reported that 10 percent of the Swedish women who

Table 11.3 Rate of deaths from alcohol related illnesses (per 100,000 population), Sweden, 1959-1995

Year	Alcohol Psychosis	Alcoholism	Liver cirrhosis	Alcohol poisoning
1959	0.27	0.64	4.81	0.08
1968	0.14	1.83	7.28	1.39
1972	0.20	1.96	10.16	1.90
1977	0.10	3.08	12.39	3.88
1980	0.17	5.17	12.19	2.60
1985	0.17	5.29	7.44	2.85
1990	0.31	4.53	7.58	1.90
1992	0.27	3.47	7.29	1.63
1995	0.22	3.27	6.67	1.38

drink, drink about 50 percent of the total alcohol consumption of women. About 10 percent of men and 3 to 6 percent of Swedish women also drink heavily.

Figure 11.23 shows the number of alcohol related arrests for drunkenness and the percentage of male and female arrests. As can be seen, the total number of arrests has steadily declined over the years. The graph also shows that males are more likely to be arrested for drunkenness compared to females. Over the period, there is a slight but steady decrease in the proportion of male arrests and increase in the proportion of female arrests. However, in Sweden, drunkenness is still a more severe problem for males than females.

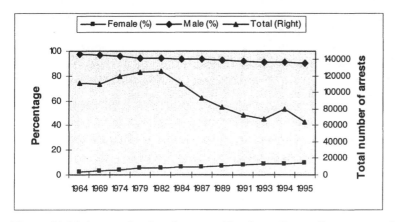

Figure 11.23 Arrests for drunkenness: Total number and percentage by gender, Sweden, 1964-1995

Figure 11.24 presents the liver cirrhosis death rates and alcohol related accidents per 100,000 population in Sweden. As can be seen, the liver cirrhosis death rate has been declining steadily from the late 1970s. The rate of road accidents related to alcohol peaked in 1989, declined since then until 1995 and has increased at a very slow rate in recent years.

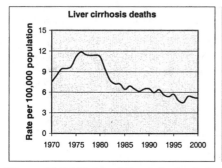 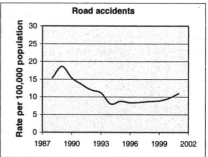

Figure 11.24 Rates of liver cirrhosis deaths and alcohol related road accidents per 100,000 population, Sweden

Switzerland

Alcohol consumption in Switzerland peaked in the mid 1970s and since then consumption of all three beverages, beer, wine and spirits has fallen. Beer, wine and spirits are locally produced in Switzerland. Eighty percent of beer, and about 40 percent of wine and spirits consumed in Switzerland are locally produced. It is also reported that the percentage of Swiss people who drink alcohol excessively is on the increase. A survey conducted among young people in 1994 showed that 60 percent of 11 and 12 year olds, and 90 percent of 15 and 16 year olds had some experience with alcohol. About 25 percent of 10 year old boys and more than 40 percent of boys in the 15-19 age group were drinking alcohol at least weekly. Five percent of boys in the 15-19 age group reported having at least one drink per day. It is estimated that, each year, about 3000 people die prematurely from alcohol related accidents and diseases in Switzerland.

Figure 11.25 presents the time series plots of the liver cirrhosis death rate and alcohol related accidents rate per 100,000 population. As can be seen, there has been a dramatic fall in the death rate over the last 30 years, which has more than halved during this period. The alcohol related accident rate is fluctuating but decreasing at a slow rate.

Ukraine

Ukraine produces beer, wine and spirits. According to a 1995 survey of 15 and 16 year olds, 79 percent reported to have drunken alcohol and 30 percent had been drunk in the past 12 months. Figure 11.26 shows the rate of alcohol-related road accidents per 100,000 persons has more than halved from 16 in 1990 to 6 in 2001.

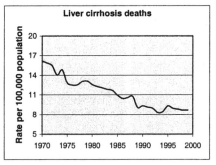 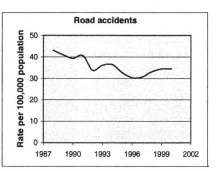

Figure 11.25 Rates of liver cirrhosis deaths and alcohol related road accidents per 100,000 population, Switzerland

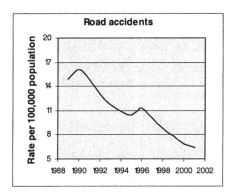

Figure 11.26 Rate of alcohol related road accidents per 100,000 population, Ukraine

UK

The UK is traditionally a beer consuming country. In the last two decades, wine consumption has increased at the expense of beer. In the last five decades, wine consumption has increased by more than 15 times. About 90 percent of beer and 70 percent of spirits consumed by the British are locally produced and about 80 to 90 percent of the wine consumed are imported. According to the UKSUAHR (2003) interim report, a report produced by the Prime Minister's Strategy Unit, almost one in three adult men and nearly one in five women now exceed the recommended guidelines of 21 and 14 units a week (21 units is equivalent to 10.5 pints of bitter, and 14 units is equivalent to 14 small glasses of wine). A current alcohol strategy is in place which has a set target of reducing the proportion of men (women) drinking more than 21 (14) standard units of alcohol per week from 28 (11) percent in 1990 to 18 (7) percent by 2005.

The report also points out that the number of women drinking above the recommended guidelines has risen by over half in the last 15 years, and that one in one hundred pregnant women drink more than 14 units of alcohol a week, although the Department of Health recommends only 1-2 units a week. British teenagers are among the heaviest teenage drinkers in Europe. According to a BBC (2/10/2003) news report, based on Department of Transport information, more people are dying in the UK in drink-drive accidents than at any time in the past decade. During 1990-1997, 4800 people died in drink-drive road accidents with injuries related to accidents involving alcohol amounting to around 135,000 over the same period.

In the UK up to 40 percent of men are binge drinkers. Heavy drinking in the UK is resulting in an increasing number of premature deaths, health problems, social disorders, and injuries. The total cost, including the costs of absenteeism, alcohol related crime, and human suffering is estimated as high as £20billion— almost three times the estimated £7billion in excise duty on alcohol that the government receives each year. Treating illnesses and injuries caused by alcohol misuse is costing the UK government up to £1.7billion per year. It is also estimated that the cost of alcohol-related crime is around £7billion. Among the people brought to hospital emergency departments, 35 percent are due to alcohol, costing the UK government more than £500million a year. The statistics also reveal that alcohol places a very significant burden on accident and emergency departments of hospitals at peak times. Among the attendees at the accident and emergency departments, 41 percent tested positive for alcohol consumption; 14 percent were intoxicated; and 43 percent were identified as problem users. In addition, up to 150,000 hospital admissions each year are related to alcohol misuse, and some 22,000 people die prematurely.

According to a survey published in 1997, four in five children in the UK started drinking alcohol at home by the age of 14 or 15. Among 14 to 15 year olds, 76 percent of boys and 79 percent of girls said they drank 'to get drunk'. Beer is the most preferred alcoholic beverage for boys and wine was the most popular among girls. It is estimated that 30 percent of the child abuse cases are related to the use of alcohol. Figure 11.27 shows the alcohol related fatal accidents, serious accidents, slight accidents and their total. As can be seen, in general, all types of accidents are on the decline, except the 'slight' accidents. This reduction in 'fatal' and 'serious' accidents and the increase in the 'slight' accidents could be due to the more advanced safety equipment (such as airbags etc) fitted in new motor vehicles in recent years which reduces the severity of the accidents, hence moving accidents which could be 'severe' to 'slight'. Overall, alcohol related accidents have decreased from 22,740 in 1988 to 16,830 in 1999.

Figure 11.28 shows the liver cirrhosis death rate as well as the alcohol related accident rate per 100,000 population in the UK. As can be seen, there is a steady upward trend in the deaths due to liver cirrhosis, which is a matter for concern. The rate of road accidents has been declining slightly but in later years, it has also increased but at a very slow rate. As can be seen, the number of alcohol related road traffic accidents per 100,000 population peaked at 25.5 in 1994 and fell to around 12 in 1998 and has increased again close to its 1993 level of 18.5 in 2001.

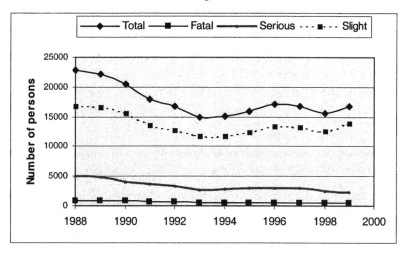

Figure 11.27 Alcohol related driving fatalities as a proportion of total fatalities (in percentages), UK, 1988-1999

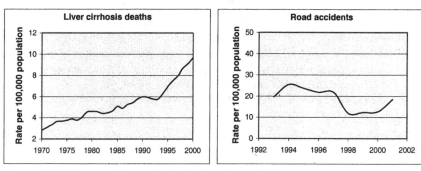

Figure 11.28 Rates of liver cirrhosis deaths and alcohol related road accidents per 100,000 population, UK

The two measures of alcohol abuse indicate that alcohol misuse is still a serious problem in the UK.

US

The US, like Australia and the UK, is a traditionally a beer consuming country. Beer consumption reached its peak in the early 1980s and has been falling since then. The same pattern can be observed for wine and spirits as well. Most of the beer (about 90 percent), wine (85 percent) and spirits (65 percent) Americans consumed are locally produced. Alcohol is considered as the number one drug problem in the US. About 43 percent of Americans are exposed to alcoholism in their families. In 1996, law enforcement agencies made about 1,467,300 arrests nationwide for driving under the influence of alcohol. Data from many sources (eg, health.yahoo.com/health/encyclopedia) indicate that about 15 percent of the population in the US are 'problem drinkers' and approximately 5 to 10 percent of male drinkers and 3 to 5 percent of female drinkers could be diagnosed as alcohol dependent (about 12.5 million people). It is estimated that 70 percent of American high school seniors have consumed alcohol within the past month despite the fact that the minimum legal age for alcohol use is between 18 to 21 years across the country. About 20 percent of the adolescents are 'problem drinkers' and 7 percent of adolescents are considered as alcoholics or dependent on alcohol. In the past, a higher percentage of men were considered to be drunkards than women but now this trend is changing.

According to the *US Federal Health Survey* (USDHHS, 1999), about 48 million Americans consume alcohol at least once in a week; and over 15 million Americans are dependent on alcohol. Sadly, 500,000 of them are between the age of 9 and 12. In 2000, almost 7 million Americans aged 12 to 20 were binge drinkers (defined as the consumption of 5 or more drinks on at least one occasion during the past month). About 7 percent of the employees in full-time jobs report heavy drinking (defined as the consumption of 5 or more drinks on at least one occasion on more than 5 days during the past month). More than 40 percent of convicted murderers being held either in jail or in a state prison reported to have used alcohol at the time of the crime (Greenfield, 1998). A study by Harwood (2000) estimated the overall economic cost of alcohol abuse was $185 billion for 1998. The major components of this estimated cost of alcohol abuse were due to lost productivity from alcohol related illness ($88 billion), premature death ($37 billion), crime ($10 billion), health care expenditure due to alcohol abuse and dependence ($26 billion).

Figure 11.29 shows the time series plots of liver cirrhosis death rate per 100,000 population and the proportion of alcohol related accidents in the US. As

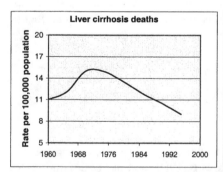
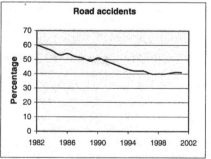

Figure 11.29 Rate of liver cirrhosis deaths per 100,000 population and alcohol related road accidents as a percentage of total accidents, US

can be seen, both the liver cirrhosis death rate and the alcohol related accidents have fallen steadily in the last 3 decades. The alcohol related road accidents as a proportion of total road accidents has dropped from 60 percent in 1982 to 40 percent in 2000. These two indicators show that there is significant improvement in alcohol misuse in the US.

11.2 Restrictions on Alcohol Sale

In this section we consider the control policies in relation to sales restrictions on alcohol. Research shows that the availability of alcohol is also one of the significant factors that determines the rate of alcohol consumption. The days of sale, hours of sale and the type of outlet, location of outlets and the type of license to sell alcohol are some of the factors used to control alcohol sales.

Australia

In Australia, unlike in some other developed countries, there are no state monopolies on the manufacturing or sale of alcoholic beverages. In each Australian state, state licensing authorities cover all aspects of licensing issues and determine the amount of licensing fee. The licensing fee differs from state to state and the average across Australia is about 11 percent of the wholesale price of alcohol. There is no license fee charged for low alcohol content alcoholic beverages (less than 3.8 percent alcohol by volume) in South Australia, New South Wales, Victoria and in the Australian capital territory.

There is no formal control imposed on the price of the alcoholic beverages in Australia. But as with any consumer good, the prices of alcoholic beverages are monitored by the *Australian Competition and Consumer Commission* (ACCC).

In terms of hours of sale, in some states 24 hour sales are permitted while in other states application can be made to obtain special permission for extended sale hours. The Federal and State Government regulations prohibit sale or serving alcohol to minors (under 18). This applies to both on-premise and retail sales. The courts are allowed to place heavy penalties on those who violate these regulations. During December 1995, a law was introduced to label the percentage alcohol content on the alcoholic beverage containers.

Austria

All alcoholic beverages are freely available at retail outlets such as supermarkets, departmental stores (from 1974) and bottle shops. To sell alcohol, the outlets need to apply for a licence from the Ministry of Finance. From 1995, there is no control on pricing, which was previously monitored by the government. There are no special restrictions on hours/days of sale and type of location of alcohol outlets. Labels with percentage of alcohol content on the containers are required by law. In eight federal states, the minimum legal age limit for drinking beer and wine in public is 16 years and in one federal state it is 15 years.

Belgium

Since 1990, stores have been required to apply for a license from local authorities in order to sell alcohol. Licensed premises must pay an annual fee, which is based on the rent paid by the establishment. Hours of sale are determined by the local authorities. Consumption of any alcoholic beverages with alcohol content over 6 percent is prohibited in workplaces. There is a minimum legal age limit of 16 years for buying alcohol which was reduced from 18 years in 1973.

Canada

The Canadian federal government works in partnership with the alcohol industry in developing guidelines on alcohol production and marketing alcohol products. In all provinces of Canada, except Alberta, government monopoly stores control the retail sales of spirits while they also sell beer and wine. Beer and wine are also being sold at producer stores. In Alberta province all beverages are being sold by licensed liquor stores. In Newfoundland and Quebec provinces grocery stores are allowed to sell beer. In Manitoba, Saskatchewan and British Columbia provinces licensed vendors are allowed to sell beer.

In Canada, hours of sale of alcoholic beverages is somewhat restricted and regulated by the liquor monopolies in each province. The hours of sale for beer are usually longer than for wine and spirits. Each Canadian province has their own legal purchase/drinking age limits. In Manitoba, Alberta and Quebec provinces the legal drinking age is 18 and in all other parts of Canada the legal drinking age limit is 19.

Czech Republic

The minimum legal age limit for buying alcohol is 18 years. There are restrictions on drinking alcohol at sports events and health premises. There are no restrictions on hours or days of sale or type of outlets. There is no requirement to print any health warnings but labels are required to state alcohol content. There is no maximum legal limit for the alcohol content of the beverages.

Denmark

There is no state monopoly but a licence is required for the production and distribution of all types of alcoholic beverages. There is also a licensing system for the sale of alcoholic beverages on-premise. However, there is no need for such license to sell beer with alcohol content less than 2.8 percent. Alcoholic beverages are commonly sold in grocery shops for off-premise consumption for which no license is required. Hours of sale for on-premise consumption are restricted to between 5am to midnight. There is no maximum legal limit for alcohol content of beverages but labels for alcohol content are required. Serving alcohol to under 18 years old is illegal. There is no age restriction on sales for off-premise consumption. Health warnings are also not required by law.

Finland

There are restrictions on hours and days of sale and on types of outlets. Sale of wine starts at 11am. Medium beer may be served from 9am. Some liquor stores are open from 10am to 6pm on Monday to Thursday, until 8pm on Fridays and until 4pm on Saturday. Some other stores are opened from 9am-8pm Monday to Friday and until 6pm on Saturdays. Labels for alcohol content are required by law and there is also a maximum legal limit of 60 percent of alcohol content in any beverage. There is a minimum legal age limit of 18 years for buying alcoholic beverages. Alcohol consumption is not allowed at the work place.

France

Restrictions on hours of sale are determined by local authorities. The maximum legal alcohol content limit is 18 percent for wine and 45 percent for spirits. By law, the labels should display alcohol content. No sale of alcohol in sports event is allowed. There are no restrictions on days of sale or on location of outlets. There is a minimum legal age limit of 16 years for buying alcohol.

Germany

To sell alcoholic beverages on-premise, a licence is required under the German law. There were no restrictions on hours or days of sale or on type or location of outlets until 1996. New legislation came into effect from late 1996 which allows the sale of alcoholic beverages between 6am to 8pm on weekdays and 6am to 4pm on Saturdays. There is no requirement for health warnings or maximum legal limit for the alcohol content of beverages but labels stating the alcohol content are required by law. There is also a differing minimum age limit for buying alcohol based on the beverage type, 16 years for beer and wine and 18 years for spirits. Sale of beer from unsupervised vending machines is also banned.

Greece

There are no restrictions on hours or days of sale of alcohol or type or location of outlets. Labels stating the alcohol content are required by law. There is also a minimum legal age limit of 18 years for buying alcohol and drinking alcohol in public places.

The maximum legal limit of alcohol content differs across the types of beverage; for beer this limit is 5 to 7 percent, for wine it is 11.5 to 12 percent and for spirits it is 40 to 42 percent.

Hungary

There is not much restriction on who, where and when alcohol can be consumed.

Ireland

There are restrictions on hours and days of sale and on type and location of outlets. Labels are not required to display health warnings or state the alcohol content. Nor is there a maximum limit on the alcohol content of beverages. The minimum legal age for buying alcohol is 18 years. There are no price controls on alcoholic beverages sold for home consumption. But there are price controls set by the Government on beer and spirits sold in public bars.

Israel

There is no state monopoly and no licence is required for production or distribution of alcohol. Health warnings are not required, but labelling of alcohol content is required by law. There is no maximum legal limit for the alcohol content of beverages. The minimum age limit for buying alcohol is 18 years.

Italy

There are no restrictions on hours or days of sale or on location of outlets but restrictions do exist on type of outlets. Sale of alcohol is not permitted to persons under 16 years old. While labels for alcohol content are required by law, there is no maximum legal limit for the alcohol content of beverages. Licences are required to serve alcohol to the public.

Japan

All types of alcoholic beverages are available from vending machines in Japan but during 5am to 11pm only. The days and hours for the retail sales of alcoholic beverages for off-premise consumption are the same for any other sale premise and on-premise are to be closed by 11pm. The minimum legal drinking age is 20 in Japan.

Luxembourg

While there are restrictions on hours of sale, there are no restrictions on days of sale or on type or location of outlets. Hours of sale are regulated by local authorities and are usually limited to between 6am and midnight. Neither health warnings nor labels for alcohol content are required by law. There is no maximum legal limit for the alcohol content of beverages. The minimum age limit for buying alcohol is 16 years.

Netherlands

There are restrictions on the open hours and days of sale by law. Shops licensed to sell food and non-alcoholic beverages are allowed to sell alcoholic beverages for off-premise consumption having content less than 15 percent of alcohol. Health warning labels are not required but labels for alcohol content are required by law.

There is no maximum legal limit for the alcohol content of beverages. The minimum legal age limit for buying beer and wine is 16 years but for spirits is 18 years.

New Zealand

Opening hours of sale for public bars are 7am to 10pm and restaurants and night-clubs could remain open until 3am. Hotels and taverns can apply for a permit to open 24 hours a day except Sundays. Wine can be sold in supermarkets from 7am till 10pm. The number of current liquor licences in New Zealand is 14,191. In December 1999, the minimum legal drinking age was reduced from 20 years to 18 years.

Norway

Norway has probably the most restrictive alcohol control policy in Europe. There are restrictions on hours and days of sale and on type and location of outlets. The Vinmonopolet shops are open from 9am-5pm on week days; half day, 9am-1pm, on Saturday and closed on Sunday. Drinking is banned in public places. Health warning labels are not required by law but labels stating the alcohol content of the beverage are required. There is a maximum legal limit of 60 percent of alcohol content in any beverage. The minimum legal age limit for buying beer or wine is 18 years and for spirits is 20 years.

Table 11.4 presents the number of licensed outlets allowed to sell alcohol in Norway. As can be seen, while there are many outlets allowed to sell medium beer, the number of outlets licensed to sell high content alcoholic beverages such as strong beer, wine and spirits are highly controlled. It can also be noted that the number of outlets hasn't increased much over the 15 years.

Table 11.4 Number of establishments licensed to sell alcohol by type of license, Norway, 1980-1996

	Medium beer	Wine	Spirits/wine/ strong beer
1980	4729	5	87
1983	4521	4	88
1985	5098	1	92
1987	5274	-	98
1990	5067	-	106
1991	5070	-	110
1992	5001	-	109
1993	4885	-	110
1994	4775	-	110
1995	4665	-	112
1996	4788	-	112

These restrictive control policies may be the reason for the low death rate due to liver cirrhosis and low rate of alcohol-related accidents in Norway (see Figure 11.19) compared to all other countries.

Poland

While labels for alcohol content are required by law, there is no maximum legal limit for the alcohol content of beverages. There is a minimum legal age limit of 18 for buying alcohol.

Portugal

There are no restrictions on hours or days of sale or on type of location of outlets. Health warnings are not required by law but labels for alcohol content are. There is a minimum legal age limit of 16 years to buy alcohol.

Spain

There is no government monopoly in Spain controlling the sale or distribution of alcohol. While there are restrictions on hours of sale, there are no restrictions on days of sale or on type or location of outlets. A license is required to produce and distribute alcohol. Cafes, restaurants and grocery stores are allowed to sell alcoholic beverages without licensing requirements. According to statistics published, Spain has more liquor outlets per capita than any other Western European country. Display of alcohol content labels on beverages are required by law but health warning labels are not. There is a minimum age limit of 16 years to purchase alcohol in most parts of the country and in some regions this limit is 18 years. Heavy fines are imposed to those who sell alcohol to minors. Vending machines selling alcohol is allowed under controlled supervision. There is also no regulation to control alcoholic beverage prices.

Sweden

The state has a monopoly on the retail sale of strong beer, wine and spirits. Strong beer may be purchased only at state monopoly stores. The state monopoly stores are opened only on Monday to Friday from 9.30am to 6pm. Sale of medium beer (2.5 to 3.5 percent alcohol content) is permitted in ordinary grocery stores. Health warning labels on alcohol containers are not required by law, but labels for alcohol content are required. There is no maximum legal limit for the alcohol content of beverages. There is also an age limit of 20 years for buying alcohol in liquor stores. There is a minimum legal age limit of 18 years for buying alcohol in restaurants and medium strength beer in grocery stores.

Switzerland

The Alcohol Board (a body of the *Financial Department of the Swiss Confederation*) regulates and controls the production, importation and sale of spirits in order to control the spirits consumption. Such controls are used as part of the management of alcohol consumption in order to promote the good health of its citizens. The cantons are mostly responsible for controlling the public sale of alcoholic beverages. There are no price control mechanisms by legislation. Beer and wine beverages can be purchased from a variety of stores between 7am and 6.30pm. Spirits sales are banned before 9am in most cantons. Labels for alcohol content are required by law, but health warning labels are not. There is a maximum legal limit of 55 percent of alcohol content for any alcoholic beverage. There is a minimum legal age limit of 16 years for buying fermented beverages and an age limit of 18 years for buying distilled beverages. But in some cantons these age limits are even lower, 14 and 16 years, respectively.

Ukraine

There are restrictions on hours of sale and location of outlets, but there are no restrictions on days of sale or on types of outlets. Warnings, such as 'Excessive alcohol use is harmful to your health' are required to be printed on alcohol containers, however, further health warning labels are not required by law. Labels informing the alcohol content of the beverage are required by the law but there is no maximum legal limit for the alcohol content of the beverages. There is also a minimum legal age limit of 21 years for buying alcohol.

UK

There is a minimum legal age limit of 18 for purchasing alcoholic beverages. However, it is possible to consume some alcoholic beverages in bars or restaurants at 16 or 17 years of age. There are restrictions on hours and days of sale and on type and location of outlets. On-licensed premises are allowed to open between 11am-11pm on weekdays; 12pm-10.30pm on Sunday and Good Friday; and Christmas day 12pm-3pm and 7pm-12.30am. Off-licensed premises are allowed to open between 8am-11pm on weekdays; 10am-10.30pm on Sundays and 8am-10.30pm on Good Friday; and 12pm-3pm and 7pm-12.30am on Christmas day. Labels stating alcohol content are required by law but health warnings are not required. There is no maximum legal limit for the alcohol content of beverages.

US

Days and hours of sale of alcohol vary from state to state in the US. The legal drinking age across the US is 21 years.

A Cross-country Comparison

Table 11.5 presents a summary of alcohol related licensing requirements for a selected number of countries in terms of import, export, production, wholesale and retail sales of the three alcoholic beverages, beer, wine and spirits. Table 11.6 presents a summary of sales restrictions such as hours of sale, days of sale, place of sale, and age limits for the purchase of alcoholic beverages at bars and bottle shops.

Table 11.5 Alcohol related licensing requirements, 45 European countries

Country	Import			Export		
	Beer	Wine	Spirits	Beer	Wine	Spirits
(1)	(2)		(3)	(4)	(5)	(6)
1. Albania	None	None	None	None	None	None
2. Armenia	Required	Required	Required	Required	Required	Required
3. Austria	None	None	None	None	None	None
4. Azerbaijan	Monopoly	Monopoly	Monopoly	Monopoly	Monopoly	Monopoly
5. Belarus	Monopoly	Monopoly	Monopoly	Monopoly	Monopoly	Monopoly
6. Belgium						
7. Bosnia	None	None	None	None	None	None
8. Bulgaria	Required	Required	Required	Required	Required	Required
9. Croatia	Required	Required	Required			
10. Czech Republic	None	None	None	None	None	None
11. Denmark	None	None	None	None	None	None
12. Estonia	Required	Required	Required	Required	Required	Required
13. Finland	None	None	None	None	None	None
14. France	Required	Required	Required	Required	Required	Required
15. Georgia	None	None	None	None	None	None
16. Germany	None	None	None	None	None	None
17. Greece						
18. Hungary	Monopoly	Monopoly	Monopoly	Monopoly	Monopoly	Monopoly
19. Iceland	Monopoly	Monopoly	Monopoly	Required		Required
20. Ireland	Required	Required	Required	Required	Required	Required
21. Israel	None	None	None	None	None	None
22. Italy	Required	Required	Required	Required	Required	Required
23. Kazakhstan	Monopoly	Monopoly	Monopoly	Monopoly	Monopoly	Monopoly
24. Kyrgyzstan	None	Monopoly	Monopoly	None	Monopoly	Monopoly
25. Latvia	None	Required	Required	None	Required	Required
26. Lithuania	Required	Required	Required	Required	Required	Required
27. Luxembourg	Required	Required	Required	Required	Required	Required
28. Malta	Required	Required	Required	Required	Required	Required
29. Netherlands	None	None	None	None	None	None
30. Norway	Required	Required	Required	Required	Required	Required
31. Poland	Required	Required	Required	Required	Required	Required
32. Portugal	Required	Required	Required	Required	Required	Required
33. Republic of Moldova	Required	Required	Required	Required	Required	Required
34. Romania	None	None	None	None	None	None
35. Russian Federation	Monopoly	Monopoly	Monopoly	Monopoly	Monopoly	Monopoly
36. Slovakia	Required	Required	Required			
37. Slovenia	None	None	None	None	None	None
38. Spain	None	None	None	None	None	None
39. Sweden	Required	Required	Required	Required	Required	Required
40. Switzerland	None	Required	None	None	None	None
41. The FYROM	Required	Required	Required	Required	Required	Required
42. Turkey						
43. Ukraine	None	Required	Required	None	Required	Required
44. UK	Required	Required	Required	None	None	None
45. Uzbekistan				Required	Required	Required

Table 11.5 continued on next page

Table 11.5 Alcohol related licensing requirements, 45 European countries (continued)

Country	Production			Wholesale			Retail		
	Beer	Wine	Spirits	Beer	Wine	Spirits	Beer	Wine	Spirits
(1)	(7)	(8)	(9)	(10)	(11)	(12)	(13)	(14)	(15)
1. Albania	Required	Required	Required	None	None	None	None	None	None
2. Armenia	Required	Required	Required	Required	Required	Required	Required	Required	Required
3. Austria	None	None	None	None	None	None	None	None	None
4. Azerbaijan	Required	Required	Monopoly	Monopoly	Monopoly	Monopoly	Required	Required	Required
5. Belarus	Required	Required	Required	Monopoly	Monopoly	Monopoly	Required	Required	Required
6. Belgium									Required
7. Bosnia	Monopoly	Monopoly	Monopoly	Required	Required	Required	Monopoly	Monopoly	Monopoly
8. Bulgaria	None	Required	Required	Required	Required	Required	Required	Required	Required
9. Croatia	Required	None	Required	Required	Required	Required	None	None	None
10. Czech Republic	None	None	None	None	None	None	None	None	None
11. Denmark	None	None	None	None	None	None	Required	Required	Required
12. Estonia	None	None	None	Required	Required	Required	None	None	None
13. Finland	Required	Required	Required	Required	Required	Required	Monopoly	Monopoly	Monopoly
14. France	Required	Required	Required	Required	Required	Required	Required	Required	Required
15. Georgia	None	None	None	None	None	None	None	None	None
16. Germany	None	None	Required	None	None	Required	None	None	None
17. Greece	Required	Required	Required				None	None	None
18. Hungary	Required	Required	Required	Monopoly	Monopoly	Monopoly	Required	Required	Required
19. Iceland	Required	None	Required	Required	Required	Required	Monopoly	Monopoly	Monopoly
20. Ireland	Required	Required	Required	Required	Required	Required	Required	Required	Required
21. Israel	Required	Required	Required	None	None	None	Required	Required	Required
22. Italy	Required	Required	Required	Required	Required	Required	Required	Required	Required
23. Kazakhstan	Required	Required	Required	Monopoly	Monopoly	Monopoly	None	None	None
24. Kyrgyzstan	None	Monopoly	Monopoly	None	Monopoly	Monopoly	None	Monopoly	Monopoly
25. Latvia	Required	Required	Required	None	Required	Required	None	Required	Required
26. Lithuania	Required	Required	Monopoly	Required	Required	Required	Required	Required	Required
27. Luxembourg	Required	Required	Monopoly	Required	Required	Required	Required	Required	Required
28. Malta	Required	Required	Required	Required	Required	Required	Required	Required	Required
29. Netherlands	None	None	None	None	None	None	None	None	Required
30. Norway	Required	Required	Required	Required	Required	Required	Required	Monopoly	Monopoly
31. Poland	Required	Required	Required	Required	Required	Required	Required	Required	Required
32. Portugal	Required	Required	Required				Required	Required	Required
33. Republic of Moldova	None	Required	Required	Required	Required	Required	None	Required	Required
34. Romania	Required	Required	None	None	None	None	Required	Required	None
35. Russian Federation	Monopoly	Monopoly	Monopoly	Monopoly	Monopoly	Monopoly	Monopoly	Monopoly	Monopoly
36. Slovakia	Required	None	Monopoly				None	None	None
37. Slovenia	None	None	None	None	None	None	None	None	None
38. Spain	Required	Required	Required	None	None	None	Required	Required	Required
39. Sweden	Required	Required	Required	Required	Required	Required	Monopoly	Monopoly	Monopoly
40. Switzerland	None	None	Required	None	None	Required	None	None	None
41. The FYROM	Monopoly	Required	Required	Required	Required	Required	Monopoly	Required	Required
42. Turkey	Monopoly	Monopoly	Monopoly				Monopoly	Monopoly	Monopoly
43. Ukraine	None	Required	Required	None	Required	Required	None	Required	Required
44. UK	None	None	None	Required	Required	Required			
45. Uzbekistan	Required	Required	Required	Required	Required	Required	Required	Required	Required

The FYROM = The former Yugoslav Republic of Macedonia; Bosnia = Bosnia and Herzegovina. Required = Licence required; Monopoly = State monopoly; None = No licence required.

Table 11.6   Alcohol sales restrictions, 44 European countries

Country	Hours of sales			Days of sale			Places of sale			Age limit for purchase in a bar			Age limit for purchase at bottle shop		
(1)	Beer (2)	Wine (3)	Spirits (4)	Beer (5)	Wine (6)	Spirits (7)	Beer (8)	Wine (9)	Spirits (10)	Beer (11)	Wine (12)	Spirits (13)	Beer (14)	Wine (15)	Spirits (16)
1. Albania	No	No	No	No	No	No	No	No	No						
2. Armenia	No	No	No	No	No	No	No	No	No						
3. Austria	No	No	No	No	No	No	No	No	No	16	16	18	16	16	18
4. Azerbaijan	No	No	No	No	No	No	Yes	Yes	Yes	18	18	18	18	18	18
5. Belarus	No	No	No	No	No	No	Yes	Yes	Yes	18	18	18	18	18	18
6. Belgium									Yes	16	16	16	16	16	18
7. Bosnia	No	No	No	No	No	No	Yes	Yes	Yes	16	16	16			
8. Bulgaria	No	No	No	No	No	No	Yes	Yes	Yes	18	18	18	18	18	18
9. Croatia	No	No	No	No	No	No	Yes	Yes	Yes	18	18	18			
10. Czech Republic	No	No	No	No	No	No	No	No	No	18	18	18	18	18	18
11. Denmark	Yes	Yes	Yes	No	No	No	No	No	No	18	18	18	15	15	15
12. Estonia	No	No	No	No	No	No	Yes	Yes	Yes	18	18	18	18	18	18
13. Finland	Yes	Yes	Yes	No	Yes	Yes	Yes	Yes	Yes	18	18	18	18	18	20
14. France	No	No	No	No	No	No	Yes	Yes	Yes	16	16	16	16	16	16
15. Georgia	No	No	No	No	No	No	No	No	No	16	16	16	16	16	16
16. Germany	No	No	No	No	No	No	No	No	No	16	16	18	16	16	18
17. Greece	No	No	No	No	No	No	No	No	No	17	17	17			
18. Hungary	No	No	No	No	No	No	Yes	Yes	Yes	18	18	18	18	18	18
19. Iceland	No	No	No	Yes	Yes	Yes	No	No	No	20	20	20	20	20	20
20. Ireland	Yes	Yes	Yes	No	No	No	Yes	Yes	Yes	18	18	18	18	18	18
21. Israel	No	No	No	No	No	No	No	No	No	18	18	18			
22. Italy	No	No	No	No	No	No	No	No	No	16	16	16	16	16	16
23. Kazakhstan	No	No	No	No	No	No	Yes	Yes	Yes	18	18	18	18	18	18
24. Kyrgyzstan	No	No	No	No	No	No	No	No	No						
25. Latvia	No	Yes	Yes	No	No	No	Yes	Yes	Yes	18	18	18	18	18	18
26. Lithuania	Yes	Yes	Yes	No	No	No	Yes	Yes	Yes	18	18	18	18	18	18
27. Luxembourg	No	No	No	No	No	No	No	No	No	16	16	16			
28. Malta	No	No	No	No	No	No	No	No	No	16	16	16			
29. Netherlands	Yes	Yes	Yes	Yes	Yes	Yes	Yes	Yes	Yes	16	16	18	16	16	18
30. Norway	Yes	Yes	Yes	Yes	Yes	Yes	Yes	Yes	Yes	18	18	20	18	18	20
31. Poland	No	No	No	No	No	No	Yes	Yes	Yes	18	18	18	18	18	18
32. Portugal	No	No	No	No	No	No	No	No	No	16	16	16	16	16	16
33. Repub of Moldova	No	No	No	No	No	No	No	Yes	Yes		18	18		18	18
34. Romania	No	No	No	No	No	No	Yes	Yes	Yes	18	18	18	18	18	18
35. Russian Federation	No	No	No	No	No	No	Yes	Yes	Yes	18	18	18	18	18	18
36. Slovakia	No	No	No	No	No	No	No	No	No	18	18	18	18	18	18
37. Slovenia	Yes	Yes	Yes	No	No	No	No	No	No	15	15	15	15	15	15
38. Spain	Yes	Yes	Yes	Yes	Yes	Yes	Yes	Yes	Yes	16	16	16	16	16	16
39. Switzerland	Yes	Yes	Yes	Yes	Yes	Yes	No	No	No	16	16	16	16	16	16
40. The FYROM	Yes	Yes	Yes	No	No	No	No	No	No	18	18	18	18	18	18
41. Turkey	No	No	No	No	No	No	Yes	Yes	Yes	18	18	18	18	18	18
42. Ukraine	No	No	No	No	No	No	Yes	Yes	Yes	18	18	18	18	18	18
43. UK	Yes	Yes	Yes	Yes	Yes	Yes	Yes	Yes	Yes	18	18	18	18	18	18
44. Uzbekistan	No	No	No	No	No	No	Yes	Yes	Yes	18	18	18	18	18	18

11.3   Advertising of Alcoholic Beverages

A number of studies have analysed the impact of advertising on alcohol sales and found that either alcohol advertising increases alcohol sales or it at least helps to reshuffle a fixed amount of total alcohol consumption among different alcoholic beverages (e.g., Duffy, 1982, 1983, 2001; McGuinness, 1980; Nelson and Moran, 1995; Selvanathan, 1989). In this aspect, alcohol advertising is considered as one of the major factors that influence alcohol sales. Promotion of alcohol products is allowed in many countries but with certain restrictions. In most countries, health warnings are not required either in the advertisement itself or on the alcohol containers.

In this section, we consider the restrictions on alcohol advertising in the print and electronic media imposed in a number of countries by governments to control alcohol sales.

Australia

Closely monitored advertising of alcoholic beverages is permitted in print and electronic media and in cinemas. On the television, alcoholic beverages advertisements are banned during Monday to Saturday between 6am and 8:30am and 4pm to 7:30pm and all day Sunday as well as Christmas day and Good Friday. Cinemas are banned to show alcohol advertisements during children's movies.

In 1991 and 1995, two government sponsored counter-advertising campaigns were launched targeting, respectively, teenagers and the 25-34 age group.

Austria

An industry based voluntary code is in place to restrict the advertising of beer and wine. Spirits advertising is banned on the TV and radio. TV advertising of beer and wine may only be shown between 6:45pm and 00.10am. No presentation of alcohol in connection with children, youth, driving and sports is allowed in advertisements for alcohol.

Belgium

There is a voluntary code restricting advertising of beer and spirits on TV, in print, on the radio and on billboards. The main restriction with this code of practice is that the advertising must not encourage excessive consumption in general and specifically must not be directed at people under the age of 21 and advertising may not show personalities popular with young people drinking or encouraging drinking.

Canada

There are certain restrictions on alcohol advertising in the Canadian media. Advertising of alcoholic beverages is controlled by the federal and provincial governments. The Canadian Radio-Television and Telecommunications Commission (CRTC) regulates the advertising of alcoholic beverages on the radio and television. Print advertising of beer and wine is permitted in almost all provinces in Canada as long as they fall under federal regulations.

Czech Republic

In the Czech Republic, a voluntary code is in place restricting advertising of alcoholic beverages.

Denmark

In Denmark, advertising of alcoholic beverages is banned on radio and TV for any beverage with alcohol content over 2.8 percent, but advertising is allowed in other media such as newspapers, billboards and cinemas by means of a voluntary code. This voluntary code stipulates things such as advertising should not be directed at minors, shall not associate alcohol consumption with improved physical performance or the driving of motor vehicles, shall not illustrate or mention success as a result of alcohol consumption, etc.

Finland

Advertising of alcoholic beverages with alcohol content less than 22 percent is allowed under restrictive rules and the advertising of beverages with over 22 percent alcohol content is banned. Any alcohol advertisement is banned if it is aimed at minors or consumption is linked to driving a vehicle.

France

There is a ban on advertising of beer, wine and spirits on TV and in cinemas and restrictions for advertising on radio, in newspapers, billboards and magazines. All advertising must include a health-related message, 'Alcohol abuse may have harmful effects on your health'. Advertising on radio is allowed at certain times of the day, usually banned between 5pm to 12 midnight. Sponsoring of sports events by alcohol producers is prohibited.

Germany

Advertising of all alcoholic beverages is allowed. The German Advertising Standards Authority controls the advertising of alcoholic beverages. Any advertisement such as encouraging the abuse of alcohol, portraying youngsters as drinking or associating athletes with drinking are not allowed. Billboard and poster advertisements are controlled by the local governments.

Israel

In Israel, there are no formal restrictions on alcohol advertising other than barring advertising that targets the youth.

Italy

Advertising of alcohol on TV is restricted in Italy.

Ireland

Advertising of alcoholic beverages is allowed in the print and broadcasting media with the exception of spirits in the broadcast media. However, advertisers must follow the alcohol and advertising industries voluntary code. It is expected that advertisements will exclude things such as targeting youths, using persons under 25 years old in the ads, sexual attraction etc.

Japan

There are no legal restrictions on alcohol advertising on TV, radio or in print media but a self-imposed alcohol industry and advertising industry voluntary code exists. The guidelines of the code include not targeting minors, not showing alcohol ads during children's TV programmes, under 20 years old may not be shown drinking alcohol etc. In the print media advertising is permitted if half the readership is under 20 years of age. On the alcohol packaging/containers warnings such as 'minors drinking is legally prohibited', 'start drinking after the age of 20', 'alcohol is for people over 20 years old' are encouraged.

Luxembourg

There are no restrictions on the advertising of alcoholic beverages but the level of alcohol content is restricted. There is voluntary agreement on alcohol advertising, the guidelines for which were established in 1992. This agreement encourages the exclusion of sports, driving, workplace and children in alcohol advertisements.

New Zealand

There are restrictions on alcohol advertising on the TV, radio and print media. Any advertisement is required to follow the Advertising Standard Authority Code and is then submitted for pre-clearance through the Liquor Pre-Vetting System. The rule under the Advertising Standard Authority Code specifies that TV advertising is not permitted between 6pm and 9pm; advertisements shall not associate liquor with vehicles, boats or hazardous activities; liquor advertisements shall not directed to minors and so on.

Netherlands

All kinds of advertising of alcoholic beverages are controlled by means of a voluntary code operated by the alcohol and advertising industries. Alcohol advertisements are prohibited during and immediately after programmes directed at youths on the radio or TV programmes or at the cinema or in print media.

Norway

All forms of advertising in the media for alcoholic beverages with alcohol content over 2.5 percent is prohibited.

Poland

In 1998, the House of Parliament voted to allow beer advertising. But the advertising of wine and spirits are banned.

Portugal

The advertising of alcohol is restricted on radio and TV and the advertising of beer and spirits is banned on billboards and cinemas. There are no restrictions on alcohol advertising in the print media. Advertising alcohol is prohibited to people younger than 18 years old.

Spain

Advertising of alcoholic beverages is allowed in Spain with some exceptions. Advertising of alcoholic beverages with over 20 percent alcohol content is prohibited by law. Advertising of all other alcoholic beverages are permitted on the radio and TV after 9.30pm. Advertising is not permitted in schools, sports centres and near health care institutions. Advertising is also not permitted in the cinemas showing films for people under 18 years old. A voluntary code governs the content of advertisements in newspapers/magazines and on billboards.

Sweden

Advertising of beer (except beers of alcohol content less than 2.5 percent), wine and spirits is banned. Other beers are allowed to be advertised in the print media under the voluntary codes agreed by the alcohol industry and the government. Advertising of alcohol is permitted in trade magazines.

Switzerland

A 1993 national referendum to continue with the ban on advertising of alcoholic beverages was defeated by 75 percent. The Swiss voted against the ban and 25 percent Swiss voters voted for keeping the ban.

Ukraine

By law, all advertising of alcoholic beverages is banned in Ukraine.

UK

Advertising of alcoholic beverages is allowed in the UK. An industry based voluntary code governs the content of advertisements of all three beverages. Advertising of alcoholic beverages are banned between 4pm and 6pm (excluding weekends and bank holidays) on TV and also before, during and after children's programmes.

US

There are no restrictions on advertising of beer, wine and spirits on the radio, TV, print media and on billboards but the alcohol and advertising industries have devised in consultation with federal and state authorities a voluntary code which has been strongly adhered to.

Summary of Advertising Restrictions

In Tables 11.7-11.9, respectively, we present the conditions under which advertising of the three beverages, beer, wine and spirits, are allowed in a number of countries. The conditions with respect to the medium of advertising such as national TVs, cable TV, satellite TV, national radio, newspapers/magazines, billboards, point of sale and cinema are given in these tables.

Table 11.7 Restrictions on beer advertising, 44 countries

Country (1)	National TV (2)	Cable TV (3)	Satellite TV (4)	National radio (5)	Newspapers/ magazines (6)	Billboards (7)	Points of sale (8)	Cinema (9)
1. Albania	NR	NR	NR	NR	NR	NR	NR	NR
2. Armenia	NR	NR	NR	NR	NR	NR	NR	NR
3. Austria	Partial	Partial	Partial	Partial	Voluntary	Voluntary	NR	
4. Azerbaijan	NR	NR	NR			NR	NR	
5. Belarus	Complete ban			Complete ban	Complete ban	Voluntary	Complete ban	Complete ban
6. Belgium	Partial	Voluntary	Voluntary	Partial	Voluntary	Voluntary	Voluntary	Voluntary
7. Bosnia	NR			NR	NR	NR	NR	NR
8. Bulgaria	NR	NR		NR	NR	NR	NR	NR
9. Croatia	NR	NR	NR	NR	NR	NR	NR	NR
10. Czech Republic	NR	NR	NR	NR	NR	NR	NR	NR
11. Denmark	NR	Partial		Complete ban	Voluntary	Voluntary	Voluntary	Voluntary
12. Estonia	Partial	NR		Partial	NR	NR	NR	
13. Finland	Partial	Partial		Partial	Partial	Partial	Partial	
14. France	Complete ban	Complete ban		Partial	Partial	NR	Partial	Complete ban
15. Georgia	NR	NR	NR	NR	NR	NR	NR	NR
16. Germany	Voluntary	Voluntary		Voluntary	Voluntary	Voluntary	Voluntary	Voluntary
17. Greece	NR	NR	NR	NR	NR	NR	NR	NR
18. Hungary	NR		NR	NR	Voluntary		Voluntary	Voluntary
19. Iceland	Complete ban	Complete ban	NR	Complete ban	Partial	Complete ban	Partial	Complete ban
20. Ireland	Voluntary	NR		Voluntary	Voluntary	Voluntary	Voluntary	Voluntary
21. Israel	Partial	Partial	Partial	NR	Partial	NR	NR	NR
22. Italy		Voluntary	Partial				NR	
23. Kazakhstan	Partial	NR		Partial	NR	NR	NR	NR
24. Kyrgyzstan	Partial	Partial	NR	Partial	Partial	Partial	Partial	NR
25. Latvia	NR	NR	NR	NR	NR	NR	NR	NR
26. Lithuania	NR	NR	NR	NR	Partial	NR	NR	
27. Luxembourg	NR	NR	NR	NR	NR	NR	NR	NR
28. Malta	Partial	Partial		Partial	NR	NR	NR	NR
29. Netherlands		Voluntary	Voluntary	Voluntary	Voluntary	Voluntary	Voluntary	Voluntary
30. Norway	Complete ban	Complete ban	NR	Complete ban	Complete ban	Complete ban	Complete ban	Complete ban
31. Poland	Partial	Partial	Partial	Partial	Partial	Complete ban	Partial	Partial
32. Portugal	Partial	Partial	NR	Partial	NR	NR	NR	NR
33. Repub of Moldova	NR	NR	NR	NR	NR	NR	NR	NR
34. Romania	NR	NR	NR	NR	NR	NR	NR	NR
35. Russian Federation	NR	NR	NR	NR	Complete ban	Partial	NR	Voluntary
36. Slovakia	NR	NR	NR	NR	NR	NR	NR	NR
37. Slovenia	Partial	NR	NR	Partial	Partial	Complete ban	NR	Partial
38. Spain	Partial	Partial		Partial	Partial		NR	Partial
39. Switzerland	Complete ban	Partial		Partial	Partial	Partial	Partial	Partial
40. The FYROM	Partial		NR	Partial	Partial	Partial	Partial	
41. Turkey	Complete ban	Complete ban		Complete ban	NR	Partial	NR	Complete ban
42. Ukraine	NR	NR	NR	NR	Partial	NR	NR	Partial
43. UK	Voluntary	Voluntary	Voluntary	Voluntary	Voluntary	Voluntary	Voluntary	
44. Uzbekistan	Partial	Voluntary	NR	Partial	Partial	Partial	Voluntary	Voluntary

Table 11.8 Restrictions on wine advertising, 44 countries

Country (1)	National TV (2)	Cable TV (3)	Satellite TV (4)	National radio (5)	Newspapers/ magazines (6)	Billboards (7)	Points of sale (8)	Cinema (9)
1. Albania	NR	NR	NR	NR	NR	NR	NR	NR
2. Armenia	NR	NR	NR	NR	NR	NR	NR	NR
3. Austria	Partial	Partial	Partial	Partial	Voluntary	Voluntary	NR	
4. Azerbaijan	Partial	Partial	Partial				NR	
5. Belarus	Complete ban			Complete ban	Complete ban	Voluntary		Complete ban
6. Belgium	Partial	Voluntary	Voluntary		Voluntary	Voluntary	Voluntary	Voluntary
7. Bosnia	NR			NR	NR	NR	Partial	NR
8. Bulgaria	NR	NR		NR	NR	NR	NR	NR
9. Croatia	Complete ban	Complete ban	Partial	Complete ban	Complete ban	Complete ban	Complete ban	Complete ban
10. Czech Republic	NR	NR	NR	NR	NR	NR	NR	NR
11. Denmark	NR	Partial		Complete ban	Voluntary	Voluntary	Voluntary	Volantary
12. Estonia	Partial	NR		Partial	NR	NR	NR	
13. Finland	Partial	Partial		Partial	Partial	Partial	Partial	
14. France	Complete ban	Complete ban		Partial	Partial	NR	Partial	Complete ban
15. Georgia	Partial	NR	NR	Partial		NR	NR	NR
16. Germany	Voluntary	Voluntary		Voluntary	Voluntary	Voluntary	Voluntary	Volantary
17. Greece	NR	NR	NR	NR	NR	NR	NR	NR
18. Hungary	Complete ban		NR	Partial	Voluntary	Voluntary		Volantary
19. Iceland	Complete ban	Complete ban	NR	Complete ban	Partial	Complete ban	Partial	Complete ban
20. Ireland	Voluntary	NR	NR	Voluntary	Voluntary	Voluntary	Voluntary	Volantary
21. Israel	Partial	Partial	Partial	NR	Partial	NR	NR	NR
22. Italy		Voluntary	Partial				NR	
23. Kazakhstan		NR			NR	NR	NR	NR
24. Kyrgyzstan	Partial	Partial	NR	Partial	Partial	Partial	Partial	NR
25. Latvia	NR	NR	NR	NR	NR	NR	NR	NR
26. Lithuania	NR	NR	NR	NR	Partial	NR	NR	
27. Luxembourg	NR	NR	NR	NR	NR	NR	NR	NR
28. Malta	Partial	Partial		Partial	NR	NR	NR	NR
29. Netherlands		Voluntary	Voluntary	Voluntary	Voluntary	Voluntary	Voluntary	Volantary
30. Norway	Complete ban	Complete ban	NR	Complete ban	Complete ban	Complete ban	Complete ban	Complete ban
31. Poland	Complete ban	Complete ban	Complete ban	Complete ban	Complete ban	Complete ban	Complete ban	Complete ban
32. Portugal	Partial	Partial	NR	Partial	NR	NR	NR	NR
33. Repub of Moldova	NR	NR	NR	NR	NR	NR	NR	NR
34. Romania	NR	NR	NR	NR	NR	NR	NR	NR
35. Russian Federation	Partial	Partial	Partial	Partial	Complete ban	Partial	NR	Volantary
36. Slovakia	Complete ban	Partial	Partial	Partial				
37. Slovenia	Partial	NR	NR	Partial	Partial	Complete ban	NR	Partial
38. Spain	Partial	Partial		Partial	Partial			Partial
39. Switzerland	Complete ban	Partial		Complete ban	Partial	Partial	Partial	Partial
40. The FYROM	Partial		NR	Partial	Partial	Partial	Partial	
41. Turkey	Complete ban	Complete ban		Complete ban	Complete ban	Complete ban	Complete ban	Complete ban
42. Ukraine	Complete ban	Complete ban	Complete ban	Complete ban	Partial	Partial	NR	Partial
43. UK	Voluntary	Voluntary	Voluntary	Voluntary	Voluntary	Voluntary	Voluntary	
44. Uzbekistan	Complete ban	Partial	NR	Complete ban	Complete ban	Partial	Partial	Partial

NR= No restrictions.

11.4   Alcohol Drinking and Driving

Most governments around the world are spending enormous resources to educate their citizens regarding the consequences of drink-driving as it is becoming a major social problem in terms of health care cost and social security issues. Table 11.10 presents the rate of alcohol related road accidents per 100,000 people in selected countries over the 1985-2001 period. As can be seen, drink-driving is still a major problem in a number of countries. In this section, we present a summary of control

Table 11.9 Restrictions on spirits advertising, 44 countries

Country (1)	National TV (2)	Cable TV (3)	Satellite TV (4)	National radio (5)	Newspapers/ magazines (6)	Billboards (7)	Points of sale (8)	Cinema (9)
1. Albania	NR	NR	NR	NR	NR	NR	NR	NR
2. Armenia	NR	NR	NR	NR	NR	NR	NR	NR
3. Austria	Complete ban	NR	NR	Complete ban	Partial	Partial	NR	
4. Azerbaijan	Partial	Partial	Partial			NR		
5. Belarus	Complete ban			Complete ban	Complete ban	Voluntary	Complete ban	Complete ban
6. Belgium	Voluntary	Voluntary	Voluntary	Voluntary	Voluntary	Voluntary	Voluntary	Voluntary
7. Bosnia	NR			NR	NR	NR	Partial	NR
8. Bulgaria	NR		NR	NR	NR	NR	NR	NR
9. Croatia	Complete ban	Complete ban	Partial	Complete ban	Complete ban	Complete ban	Complete ban	Complete ban
10. Czech Republic	NR	NR	NR	NR	NR	NR	NR	NR
11. Denmark	NR	Partial		Complete ban	Voluntary	Voluntary	Voluntary	Voluntary
12. Estonia	Partial	NR		Partial	NR	NR	NR	
13. Finland	Complete ban	Complete ban		Complete ban	Complete ban	Complete ban	Partial	Complete ban
14. France	Complete ban	Complete ban		Partial	Partial	NR	Partial	Complete ban
15. Georgia	Partial	Partial		Partial	NR	NR	NR	NR
16. Germany	Voluntary	Voluntary		Voluntary	Voluntary	Voluntary	Voluntary	Voluntary
17. Greece	NR	NR	NR	NR	NR	NR	NR	NR
18. Hungary			NR	Complete ban	Voluntary			Voluntary
19. Iceland	Complete ban	Complete ban	NR	Complete ban	Partial	Complete ban	Partial	Complete ban
20. Ireland	Voluntary	NR	NR	Voluntary	Voluntary	Voluntary	Voluntary	Voluntary
21. Israel	Partial	Partial	Partial	NR	Partial	NR	NR	NR
22. Italy	.	Voluntary	Partial				NR	
23. Kazakhstan	Partial	NR		Partial	NR	NR	NR	NR
24. Kyrgyzstan	Partial	Partial	NR	Partial	Partial	Partial	Partial	NR
25. Latvia	Complete ban	Complete ban	NR	Complete ban	NR	NR	NR	NR
26. Lithuania	Partial	Partial	Partial	Partial	Partial	Partial	NR	
27. Luxembourg	NR	NR	NR	NR	NR	NR	NR	NR
28. Malta	Partial	Partial		Partial	NR	NR	NR	NR
29. Netherlands		Voluntary	Voluntary	Voluntary	Voluntary	Voluntary	Voluntary	Voluntary
30. Norway	Complete ban	Complete ban	NR	Complete ban	Complete ban	Complete ban	Complete ban	Complete ban
31. Poland	Complete ban	Complete ban	Complete ban	Complete ban	Complete ban	Complete ban	Complete ban	Complete ban
32. Portugal	Partial	Partial	NR	Partial	NR	NR	NR	NR
33. Repub of Moldova	NR	NR	NR	NR	NR	NR	NR	NR
34. Romania	NR	NR	NR	NR	NR	NR	NR	NR
35. Russian Federation	Partial	Partial	Partial	Partial	Complete ban	Partial	NR	Partial
36. Slovakia	Complete ban	Partial	Partial	Partial				
37. Slovenia	Complete ban	NR	NR	Complete ban	Complete ban	Complete ban	Complete ban	Complete ban
38. Spain	Complete ban	Complete ban		Partial	Partial			Partial
39. Switzerland	Complete ban	Partial		Complete ban	Partial	Partial	Partial	Partial
40. The FYROM	Partial		NR	Partial	Partial	Partial	Partial	
41. Turkey	Complete ban	Complete ban		Complete ban	Complete ban	Complete ban	Complete ban	Complete ban
42. Ukraine	Complete ban	Complete ban	Complete ban	Complete ban	Partial	Partial	NR	Complete ban
43. UK	Voluntary	Voluntary	Voluntary	Voluntary	Voluntary	Voluntary	Voluntary	
44. Uzbekistan	Complete ban	Partial	Partial	Complete ban	Complete ban	Partial	Partial	Partial

NR= No restrictions.

measures such as the Random Breath Testing (RBT) introduced by governments to reduce the problems associated with drink-driving.

Australia

In 1989, the Australian Government implemented a new National Health Policy on Alcohol focusing on drink-driving and under-age drinking.

Table 11.10 Rate of alcohol related accidents per 100,000 population, 45 countries, 1985-2001

Countries	1985	1986	1987	1988	1989	1990	1991	1992	1993	1994	1995	1996	1997	1998	1999	2000	2001	Average
1. Albania	...	...	...	...	...	...	...	...	...	...	0.40	0.21	0.39	0.12	0.27	0.22	0.49	0.30
2. Andorra	...	...	...	...	...	...	...	...	...	...	123.27	43.63	104.79	27.44	22.75	16.69	...	56.43
3. Armenia	...	...	...	...	...	...	1.14	0.70	0.64	1.12	1.35	1.40	1.11	1.21	1.26	0.79	...	1.07
4. Austria	49.58	43.94	43.97	39.72	42.13	39.41	36.61	38.77	33.92	35.52	33.00	31.39	30.75	27.54	30.50	31.74	31.47	36.47
5. Azerbaijan	1.92	...	...	...	...	1.81	1.20	1.32	1.27	1.19	1.29	1.18	1.11	0.99	0.93	1.17	1.01	1.26
6. Belarus	...	...	...	...	16.77	17.36	11.01	16.70	14.79	14.46	14.24	14.55	14.28	13.82	7.48	7.37	6.82	13.05
7. Belgium	18.32	19.22	...	10.67	10.64	10.60	42.48	40.84	40.84	40.86	37.73	42.04	41.09	42.31	44.02	41.28	...	31.58
8. Bulgaria	...	...	...	...	9.93	11.28	10.16	15.67	10.78	14.64	7.35	5.40	7.12	6.42	5.98	5.78	5.42	8.92
9. Croatia	48.32	45.72	50.97	46.80	45.63	42.74	35.52	36.45	33.98	33.24	38.48	39.63	56.32	59.94	63.31	75.68	72.88	48.57
10. Czech Republic	20.23	18.59	19.04	20.63	20.39	43.77	33.24	41.07	38.82	43.18	42.40	40.75	41.40	37.71	36.12	34.71	34.79	33.34
11. Denmark	46.99	44.49	40.06	37.61	38.48	31.38	28.93	29.67	27.42	25.92	24.52	23.70	23.84	21.24	22.60	24.03	21.27	30.13
12. Estonia	23.24	...	...	...	...	32.18	35.55	23.94	30.18	42.19	43.78	30.09	35.65	38.74	31.40	32.64	38.34	33.69
13. Finland	19.01	22.51	22.63	25.80	31.38	32.61	31.00	23.90	17.65	15.49	21.59	19.49	19.13	19.75	19.24	18.76	18.16	22.24
14. Georgia	...	...	...	...	...	...	...	...	...	1.09	...	...	...	3.58	2.93	2.58	...	2.55
15. Germany	...	...	...	...	45.48	52.01	50.65	50.50	48.99	45.27	42.09	40.08	35.03	34.54	33.31	31.33	...	42.44
16. Greece	...	...	...	...	...	...	...	...	...	...	...	218.08	...	236.01	229.94	216.07	185.52	217.12
17. Hungary	31.83	28.46	...	28.33	35.21	41.04	38.64	38.04	24.92	25.76	23.60	21.64	31.07	23.17	21.73	20.19	20.99	28.41
18. Iceland	43.50	...	...	22.81	22.56	19.62	20.16	20.30	21.99	24.06	25.07	24.17	...	16.07	...	...	...	23.66
19. Israel	...	...	...	...	...	...	...	...	...	4.09	3.03	2.66	2.38	2.80	3.48	4.07	4.63	3.39
20. Italy	...	...	...	...	0.35	0.38	1.70	1.92	2.23	3.06	4.26	4.75	4.71	4.73	5.16	5.73	...	3.25
21. Kazakhstan	...	...	...	...	...	...	...	...	13.68	15.41	19.01	16.37	18.96	21.29	8.13	8.57	12.19	14.85
22. Kyrgyzstan	...	8.95	10.11	12.82	16.77	...	15.20	10.58	8.47	...	6.23	6.60	6.73	6.39	5.40	6.18	7.10	9.11
23. Latvia	...	...	...	...	...	40.22	37.95	37.18	37.88	36.34	55.33	50.87	52.78	58.92	58.69	53.60	37.92	46.47
24. Lithuania	...	...	...	...	...	27.07	31.10	21.11	23.19	20.64	19.59	23.13	28.00	32.88	31.47	31.69	29.62	26.62
25. Luxembourg	57.91	67.54	...	56.51	52.72	47.15	46.50	45.86	...	...	...	...	45.37	51.59	43.24	44.01	35.99	49.53
26. Malta	...	...	...	...	...	...	...	...	...	0.82	...	...	0.27	...	...	...	...	0.55
27. Monaco	...	...	...	...	...	...	...	...	...	...	...	...	...	53.33	...	...	...	53.33
28. Netherlands	25.61	...	...	...	...	19.16	18.27	16.17	...	...	16.48	...	...	15.99	16.10	15.25	13.91	17.44
29. Poland	24.65	21.49	...	20.48	24.55	29.72	30.67	27.65	26.32	28.38	28.66	26.28	32.15	28.33	24.11	24.24	...	26.51
30. Portugal	...	...	...	19.13	18.43	18.64	23.20	24.51	26.04	20.50	18.79	20.72	17.76	...	21.84	...	...	20.87
31. Repub of Moldova	...	...	...	...	...	...	11.01	5.77	5.84	9.73	11.38	12.25	9.75	7.21	7.84	8.04	...	8.88
32. Romania	2.51	...	...	1.71	1.70	1.66	1.83	2.31	3.28	3.61	4.03	3.88	3.52	2.13	2.57	2.42	...	2.65
33. Russian Federation	...	...	...	...	...	47.18	45.09	31.59	31.06	30.37	28.44	25.75	24.47	24.71	23.88	23.06	22.15	29.81
34. Slovakia	42.43	41.41	42.27	42.85	44.65	58.97	55.36	30.21	27.48	25.58	23.83	23.00	24.24	24.89	21.69	21.31	22.35	33.68
35. Slovenia	33.21	34.75	38.86	36.47	36.06	28.45	34.37	37.96	39.96	66.45	67.12	79.15	89.09	63.77	65.58	77.43	77.26	53.29
36. Spain	6.85	7.06	...	9.13	8.89	8.58	9.58	10.57	...	...	...	...	...	...	...	...	...	8.67
37. Sweden	12.54	14.86	...	15.36	18.65	15.36	13.58	11.97	11.14	8.01	8.76	8.34	8.47	8.72	8.88	9.60	10.98	11.58
38. Switzerland	43.80	42.53	...	43.15	40.95	39.39	40.66	33.77	36.09	36.42	32.67	30.36	30.64	33.06	34.45	34.58	...	36.83
39. Tajikistan	...	...	...	...	...	...	2.72	2.26	...	1.36	1.06	...	...	...	...	0.39	0.32	1.35
40. The FYROM*	19.60	18.77	19.85	13.50	18.24	15.53	13.63	7.58	21.16	18.91	19.63	16.19	12.47	11.61	10.06	4.98	4.08	14.46
41. Turkey	6.36	23.63	26.90	22.98	19.40	20.58	21.36	22.18	19.02	14.64	16.06	6.49	14.85	14.36	2.51	4.35	3.59	15.25
42. Turkmenistan	...	...	...	...	...	...	...	...	...	...	...	...	...	1.85	1.82	...	...	1.84
43. Ukraine	...	...	...	...	14.91	16.09	14.88	13.05	11.73	10.85	10.45	11.30	9.96	8.85	7.88	6.80	6.41	11.01
44. UK	22.43	21.49	...	...	...	...	...	...	19.69	25.51	23.69	21.82	21.83	11.97	12.27	12.66	18.45	19.26
45. Uzbekistan	...	...	...	...	...	...	...	...	...	...	2.96	3.02	2.29	2.31	2.18	...	...	2.55
46. Europe	...	...	...	...	27.93	28.25	28.61	24.85	23.23	23.10	22.42	21.69	21.79	20.69	19.69	19.37	18.84	23.11
47. EU average	31.08	30.65	...	31.55	29.33	30.75	29.33	32.07	31.74	29.67	29.08	28.51	28.98	28.57	27.47	27.28	26.68	29.55
48. Nordic average	24.11	25.30	24.12	24.29	27.46	24.31	22.41	20.01	17.39	15.02	16.60	15.63	15.59	15.12	15.43	16.00	15.75	19.68

* The former Yugoslav Republic of Macedonia. EU = European Union; Nordic = Nordic countries.

Australian Federal and State Governments have directed a lot of resources towards implementing policies that minimize the harm associated with the misuse of alcohol in the area of under age drinking, excessive drinking, drinking and driving etc and to educate the public on the misuse of alcohol. One of the areas considered as most important in terms of alcohol consumption is drinking and driving. Random Breath

Testing (RBT) is now in place in all parts of Australia. RBT was first introduced in Victoria in 1976 and was adopted nationwide in 1988. During the same period, penalties were also increased for drink driving (ie, driving under the influence of alcohol exceeding the maximum allowable limit). Across Australia there is a set Blood Alcohol Concentration (BAC) limit of 0.05g% (0.05 grams of alcohol per 100 ml of blood) blood alcohol content for general purpose drivers and a zero limit for drivers of heavy vehicles, dangerous goods, public transport, learners (L) and probationary (P) drivers. Public awareness campaigns are carried out on a regular basis mainly through the news media such as television and newspapers. Two major counter-advertising campaigns targeting youth groups, were launched in 1991 and 1995.

Austria

A Blood Alcohol Concentration (BAC) limit of 0.05g% (0.05grams of alcohol per 100ml of blood) was introduced for motor vehicle drivers in 1998. RBT was introduced in 1995.

Belgium

The BAC limit for drivers is currently 0.05g% which was reduced from 0.08g% in 1994. There is a spot fine to those who exceed the 0.05 percent limit. A 1996 study (Wydoodt et al., 1996) found that alcohol played a significant role in traffic accidents involving young people. The study also found that 48 percent of the drivers involved in weekend accidents tested positive for alcohol and the majority of them had in excess of 0.08 percent blood alcohol content. The number of alcohol-related motor vehicle traffic crashes per 100,000 population has fallen from 18.3 in 1985 to 10.9 in 1992.

Canada

Across Canada, the maximum allowable blood alcohol content level (BAC) for general purpose drivers is 0.08g%. In some provinces regulations allow an automatic 90-day suspension of driver's license for motorists who exceed the legal limit or refuse an alcohol-breath test. Among fatally injured drivers in 1996, 42 percent had some alcohol in their blood and 35 percent were over the legal limit of 0.08g% BAC.

Czech Republic

The BAC limit for motor vehicle drivers is 0.0g%.

Denmark

A BAC limit of 0.08g% for drivers was introduced in 1976. There are severe penalties for those who exceed this limit.

Finland

There is a BAC limit of 0.05g% limit for drivers. RBT is also carried out from time to time.

France

The current 0.05g% BAC limit on drivers was set in 1995; 0.03g% less than the previous restriction. RBT, introduced in 1978, is carried out infrequently. It is estimated that, in 1997, the cost of alcohol related traffic accidents were US$12.1 million.

Germany

The BAC limit is 0.05g% for drivers. RBT is carried out frequently.

Greece

The BAC limit is 0.08g% for drivers. RBT also carried out but infrequently.

Hungary

The BAC limit for drivers is 0.0g%, zero tolerance.

Ireland

The BAC limit for drivers was first introduced in 1969 with a limit of 0.125g% and then reduced to 0.10g% in 1978 and revised again in 1994 to 0.08g%. RBT is not carried out.

Israel

There is a BAC limit of 0.05g% for drivers.

Italy

The BAC limit for drivers is 0.08g%. RBT is not carried out.

Japan

The BAC limit for drivers is 0.0g%. Compared to many other countries, the penalties for drinking and driving are extreme in Japan. Temporary licence suspension, immediate imprisonment, fine and permanent loss of driver's licence are possible penalties.

Luxembourg

The BAC limit for drivers is 0.08g%.

New Zealand

The BAC limit for drivers is 0.08g%. Penalties are strictly imposed on the drivers who violate this maximum limit. RBT was replaced with Compulsory Breath Testing (CBT) in 1993. According to data released by New Zealand Transport Safety Authority (NZLTSA), the percentage of alcohol related traffic fatalities among all traffic fatalities has fallen from 43 percent in 1989 to 25 percent in 2000.

Netherlands

The BAC limit for drivers is 0.05g% and RBT is frequently carried out.

Norway

The BAC limit for drivers is 0.05g% and RBT is carried out frequently.

Poland

The BAC limit for drivers is 0.03g%. RBT is also carried out from time to time.

Portugal

BAC limit for drivers is 0.05g%.

Spain

The BAC limit varies depending on the type of vehicle used for driving. For car drivers the limit is 0.08g%; for drivers of vehicles more than 3500kg the limit is 0.05g% and 0.03g% for public service drivers and drivers of dangerous merchandise, emergency service vehicles and school bus drivers. Severe penalties are applied to those who violate these limits.

Spanish authorities estimate that 30 to 50 percent of road accidents are caused by alcohol. Based on the statistics available, it appears that the rate of road accidents involving alcohol per person is on the increase. In 1995, a number of new road safety plans were introduced to tackle the drinking-driving problems. As part of this programme the use of RBT was approved.

Sweden

The current BAC limit for drivers is 0.02g% which has been reduced from 0.05g% in 1990. These limits are quite effectively enforced in Sweden. Those who break these limits are subject to fines, licence suspension and imprisonment. Since 1977, RBT has been used effectively.

Switzerland

The BAC limit for drivers is 0.08g%. RBT is not carried out. Penalties for driving above the permitted limit vary from canton to canton.

Ukraine

The BAC limit for drivers is 0.0g%. RBT is not carried out.

UK

The BAC limit for drivers is 0.08g%. There are penalties for those found driving with alcohol above the BAC limit. RBT is not carried out in the UK.

US

According to some research studies (e.g., NHTSA, 2000), the drinking and driving problem in the US has decreased over the past decade, especially among young drivers. A 2001 survey found that 25 million (one in ten) Americans were driving under the influence of alcohol.

The BAC limit varies from state to state in the range 0.08g% to 0.10g%. Penalties also vary from state to state. For those who violate the BAC limit a penalty of between $100 to $3000 and in some cases imprisonment is imposed.

Summary of Drink-driving Restrictions

In Table 11.11 we present a summary of drink driving conditions such as maximum legal blood alcohol concentration (BAC), use of random breath testing (RBT), mandatory driver's education programme availability, disqualification of driver's licence and punishment for exceeding the BAC limits etc in a number of countries. As can be seen, in most countries, the BAC limit is 0.05 and, in some countries, the limit is 0.00. Also, in most countries, RBT is used as a tool to catch the drivers who exceed the maximum allowable blood alcohol concentration limit. Education programmes are also available in a number of countries. The period of disqualification of licence and the sentencing of persons who violate the law for alcohol related driving offences varies widely from country to country.

11.5   Taxation of Alcoholic Beverages

As discussed earlier, taxation of alcoholic beverages has a dual purpose. One purpose is to either reduce the demand for alcoholic beverages in general, or shift the demand from high alcohol content beverages to lower alcohol content beverages. The second purpose is to increase the government revenue. The tax rate, which determines the final retail price of any alcoholic beverage, varies from country to country and beverage to beverage. To give some insight into the taxation of alcoholic beverages, for each beverage, we present the total tax burden as a percentage of retail price.

The tax rates data used in this section are collected from individual country publications, BSC (1997) and Eurocare (2001).

Table 11.11 Control mechanisms and restrictions on drink-driving

Country	Maximum legal blood alcohol concentration	Use of RBT	Mandatory driver education/treatment programme for habitual offenders	License disqualification period (maximum)	Prison sentence (maximum)
(1)	(2)	(3)	(4)	(5)	(6)
1. Albania	0	Yes	No		
2. Armenia	0	Yes	No		
3. Austria	50	Yes	Yes	1 month	3 months-3 years (fatal)
4. Azerbaijan	0	Yes			
5. Belarus	50	Yes			
6. Belgium	50	Yes	Yes	8 days-5 years	15 days-3 months
7. Bosnia	50	Yes			
8. Bulgaria	50	Yes			
9. Croatia	50	Yes	Yes		
10. Czech Republic	0	Yes	No		
11. Denmark	50	Yes	No	24-30 months	-
12. Estonia	20	Yes	No		
13. Finland	50	Yes	No	3 months- 2 years	3 months
14. France	50	Yes	Yes	1 month - 1 year	2 months - 2 years
15. Georgia	30	Yes			
16. Germany	50	Yes	Yes	6 months - 5 years	5 years (fatal)
17. Greece	50	Yes		3-6 months	1-12 months
18. Hungary	0	Yes	No		
19. Iceland	50	No	No		
20. Ireland	80	No	No	1 year	6 months
21. Israel	50	No	Yes		
22. Italy	50	Yes	No	15 days - 1 year	1-6 months
23. Kazakhstan		Yes	No		
24. Kyrgyzstan	50	Yes	No		
25. Latvia	49	Yes	No		
26. Lithuania	40	Yes			
27. Luxembourg	80	Yes		3 months - 15 years	1 day - 3 years
28. Malta	80	No	No		
29. Netherlands	50	Yes	Yes	6 months - 10 years	3 months - 3 years
30. Norway	20	Yes	No		
31. Poland	20	Yes	No		
32. Portugal	50	Yes	No	15 days - 1 year	-
33. Repub of Moldova	30	Yes	No		
34. Romania	0	Yes	No		
35. Russian Federation	0	Yes	Yes		
36. Slovakia	0	Yes	No		
37. Slovenia	50	Yes	No		
38. Spain	50/30*	Yes	No	3 months - 5 years	1-6 months
39. Sweden	20	Yes		3 months - 3 years	1 month - 2 years
40. Switzerland	50	Yes	Yes		
41. The FYROM	50	Yes	No		
42. Turkey	50	Yes			
43. Ukraine	0	No	Yes		
44. UK	80	Yes	Yes	12-18 months	6 months
45. Uzbekistan	0	Yes	No		

* 50 (cars) & 30 (heavy vehicles)

Australia

In Australia, excise duties are levied on spirits and beer but not on wine. Between 1969 and 1972, a small excise duty was imposed on wine but later it was abolished on political grounds. There are many small-scale grape growers for whom the excise duty on wine posed a significant obstacle to making a living out of growing grapes for wine production. The tax structure on beer and spirits was amended in 1984/85 and again in 1988. During 1984/85, differential tax rates were introduced for ordinary low alcohol beer (between 1.15 and 3.8 percent alcohol by volume) and regular beer (over 3.8 percent alcohol by volume). This system was changed in 1988 and duty is charged on the basis of alcohol content in excess of 1.15 percent. Due to this, the beer prices fell by a significant percentage. One of the reasons for this change is to shift the beer consumers from full strength beer to low alcohol beer. According to consumption statistics, since this policy was introduced the per capita low alcohol beer consumption has doubled and it is about one fourth of the whole beer consumption. During the same period the per capita consumption of regular strength beer has fallen by about 20 percent. It can also be seen from the plot that excise duties on spirits has almost doubled in the last two decades.

The customs duties on imported beer (over 1.15 percent alcohol content) and spirits carry the same excise duties plus about a 7 percent ad valorem on beer (below 1.15 percent), wine and spirits. In addition, there is a state license tax of about 10-13 percent on regular beer, wine and spirits. Some states also charge a state licence tax on low alcohol beer, wine and spirits (4 percent in Northern Territory, 5 percent in Tasmania, 10 percent in Queensland and 7 percent in Western Australia). In 1989, the Federal government also introduced tax changes to shift consumption from the high alcohol content beverages to lower alcohol content beverages, particularly to low alcohol beers.

Figure 11.30 presents the components of tax per litre of pure alcohol in Australia and their proportions in 1997. As can be seen, tax on beer is made up of the Federal excise (45 percent), Federal sales tax (32 percent) and state license taxes (23 percent). Wine tax is made up of 61 percent Federal sales tax and the remaining 39 percent state licence taxes. With regard to spirits, Federal excise tax is 62 percent, Federal sales tax 22 percent and state licence tax 16 percent. Clearly,

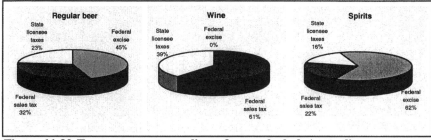

Figure 11.30 Tax components per litre of pure alcohol, Australia

Federal taxes are the most dominant tax components in the price of all three beverages. The state licensee fee is also a significant component on all three beverages.

Table 11.12 presents the tax burden on each beverage as a percentage of the retail price. As can be seen from row 1, in Australia, the tax burden is highest on the spirits (55 percent) followed by beer (43 percent) and then wine (23 percent).

Table 11.12 Total tax burden as a percentage of retail price, 22 countries

	Country (1)	Beer (2)	Wine* (3)	Spirits (4)
1.	Australia	43	23	55
2.	Austria	37	24	57
3.	Belgium	31	28	55
4.	Canada	52	44	76
5.	Denmark	41	52	76
6.	Finland	60	64	88
7.	France	24	19	53
8.	Germany	20	13	61
9.	Ireland	44	50	65
10.	Italy	31	14	40
11.	Japan	46	18	
12.	Luxembourg	17	11	54
13.	Mexico	27	28	40
14.	Netherlands	34	28	70
15.	New Zealand	36	24	64
16.	Norway	57	66	80
17.	Portugal	28	5	50
18.	Spain	20	14	55
19.	Sweden	46	66	87
20.	Switzerland	23	6	40
21.	UK	40	45	61
22.	US	19	21	45

Austria

In Austria, the latest alcohol tax law revisions were made in 1995. Beer (4 to 6 percent alcohol) is taxed at a rate of US$0.22 per litre. Table wines are taxed at US$0.12 per litre, sparkling wine is taxed at a rate of US$1.60 per litre and spirits (over 35 percent of alcohol) is taxed at a rate of US$4.90 per litre of pure alcohol.

Figure 11.31 shows the tax components in the tax of a litre of pure alcohol. In beer and table wine, the value added tax (VAT) is the dominant component and in spirits, excise tax is the major tax component. As can be seen from Table 11.12 (row 2), in Austria, the tax burden is highest on the spirits (57 percent) followed by beer (37 percent) and then wine (24 percent), which is less than half of spirits tax burden.

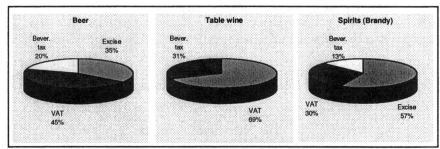

Figure 11.31 Tax components per litre of pure alcohol, Austria

Belgium

Wines with less than 8.5 percent alcohol content are not taxed in Belgium. Non-sparkling wines are taxed at a rate of US$40.10/hl and sparkling wines are taxed at a rate of US$140.40/hl. Spirits are also taxed according to the level of alcohol content. Figure 11.32 shows the tax components in the tax of a litre of pure alcohol on beer, wine and spirits. As can be seen, the value added tax (VAT) is the major component on beer and 'still' wine while excise is major component for 'sparkling' wine and spirits. As can be seen from Table 11.12 (row 3), in Belgium, the tax burden on spirits (55 percent) is the highest followed by that on beer (31 percent) and wine (28 percent - almost half of that of spirits).

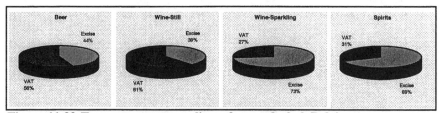

Figure 11.32 Tax components per litre of pure alcohol, Belgium

Canada

In most parts of Canada, the price of alcoholic beverages is regulated or monitored by the liquor monopolies. In 1998/99, the revenue from the control of alcoholic beverages by Canadian provincial and territorial governments increased by 4.6 percent from the previous year of $3.6 billion.

Figure 11.33 shows the components of tax on beer, wine and spirits in a litre of pure alcohol. As can be seen, the special levy component on all three beverages, beer, wine and spirits, accounts for almost half of the total tax. On a litre of pure alcohol of beer, total tax is made-up of 21 percent sales tax, 15 percent Federal tax, 18 percent GST and 46 percent special levy. As can be seen from Table 11.12 (row 4), in Canada, the total tax burden on the price of beer is 52 percent, on wine is 44 percent and spirits is 76 percent.

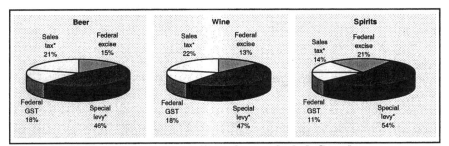

Figure 11.33 Tax components per litre of pure alcohol, Canada

Czech Republic

The tax components of the alcoholic beverages in the Czech Republic are, namely, the consumer tax and value added tax (VAT). The VAT is about 22 percent of the total tax. The consumer tax on light beer (less than 5 percent alcohol content) is at a rate of US$5.10 per 100 litres, beer (more than 5 percent alcohol content) is at a rate of US$14 per 100 litres and spirits are at a rate of US$6.30 per litre of pure alcohol.

Denmark

In Denmark, under the current tax system, there is no tax on beer with less than 2.8 percent of alcohol content. Other beers are taxed at a rate of 18 percent, table wines at a rate of 20 percent and spirits (over 35 percent proof) at a rate of 60 percent. As can be seen from Table 11.12 (row 5), the tax burden on spirits is 76 percent, wine 52 percent and beer is 41 percent.

Finland

Tax on alcoholic beverages in Finland is determined by the alcohol content of the alcoholic beverages. The tax rate for beer (4 to 6 percent alcohol) is 60 percent, table wine 56 percent and spirits 87 percent. As of 1995, restaurants and cafes have been free to set prices of alcoholic beverages after taxes.

In Finland, the two components of alcohol taxes are VAT and special taxes. Figure 11.34 shows the tax components of each beverage. As can be seen, special taxes are the main component of the total tax and VAT varies between 19 percent for fortified wine and 34 percent for beer (class 1). As can be seen from Table 11.12 (row 6), in Finland, the tax burden on all three beverages is relatively higher in Finland than in many other countries.

France

In France, beer with alcohol content not exceeding 2.8 percent alcohol by volume is taxed at a rate of US$1.04/hl and other beers with alcohol content more than 2.8 percent alcohol by volume are taxed at a rate of US$2.09/hl. Table wines are taxed

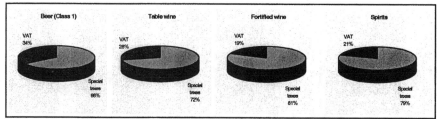

Figure 11.34 Tax components per litre of pure alcohol, Finland

at a rate of US$3.68/hl, sparkling wines are taxed at a rate of US$9.18/hl, and spirits with a pure alcohol content more than 40 percent are taxed at a rate of US$859.10/hl of pure alcohol.

As in Finland, the two tax components of alcohol tax in France are special taxes and VAT. Figure 11.35 shows the components of the taxes on beer, wine and spirits. As can be seen, the VAT is the major component in relation to beer and wine taxes and sales tax is a major component of spirits tax. As can be seen, in the price of beer, the percentage of special taxes is 29 percent; in wine it is 9 percent and in spirits it is 68 percent. The VAT component of the total tax on beer is 71 percent and for wine is 91 percent and that of spirits is 32 percent. As can be seen from Table 11.12 (row 7), in France, the total tax burden in the price of beer is 24 percent, wine is 19 percent and spirits is 53 percent. That is, the tax burden on the price of spirits is much higher than that for beer and wine.

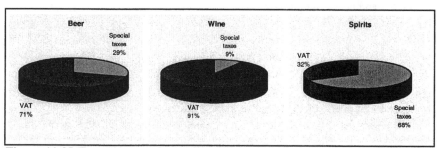

Figure 11.35 Tax components per litre of pure alcohol, France

Germany

Alcoholic beverages in Germany are taxed according to the alcohol content of the beverages. As can be seen from Table 11.12 (row 8), in Germany, except the tax on spirits (61 percent), the tax component is very low for beer (20 percent) and wine (13 percent) compared to many other developed countries.

Greece

In Greece, beer (4 to 6 percent of pure alcohol content) is taxed at a rate of 15 percent, table wines are taxed at a rate of 30 percent and spirits (over 35 percent pure alcohol) are taxed at a rate of 54 percent. In addition, a flat four percent stamp duty is also charged on each beverage.

Ireland

In Ireland, excise duty is a major source of government revenue, though in real terms it has declined somewhat since the early 1980s. The total tax revenue from alcohol in 1994 was 496 million Irish pounds (≈US$700 million). Excise tax is adjusted annually to keep par with inflation. Beer (4 to 6 percent alcohol content) is taxed at a rate of 37.9 percent per pint, table wine is taxed at a rate of 48.1 percent per bottle, spirits (over 35 percent proof) are taxed at a rate of 38.7 percent per glass, 66 percent per bottle of whisky and 65 percent per bottle of other spirits.

In Figure 11.36 we present the tax components for a litre of pure alcohol of the three beverages. As can be seen, for all three beverages, about two-thirds of the tax component is the excise and the remaining one-third is VAT. As can be seen from Table 11.12 (row 9), in Ireland, the total tax burden on the retail price of beer is 44 percent, that of wine is 50 percent and that of spirits is 65 percent.

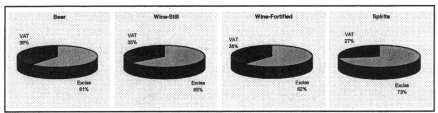

Figure 11.36 Tax components per litre of pure alcohol, Ireland

Italy

Under the Italian tax system, beer (4 to 6 percent alcohol content) is taxed at a rate of 2170 lire (about US$1.24) per 100 litres and spirits (over 35 percent proof) are taxed at a rate of 1,146,600 lire (US$653) per 100 litres. Table wine is not taxed. Figure 11.37 presents the tax components in a litre of pure alcohol for the three beverages. As can be seen, excise and VAT are about the same. For wine, as there is no excise, VAT accounts for the total tax. For spirits, about 60 percent of the tax is excise and the remaining 40 percent is VAT.

As can be seen from Table 11.12 (row 10), in Italy, the tax burden on beer is 31 percent, wine is 14 percent and spirits is 40 percent.

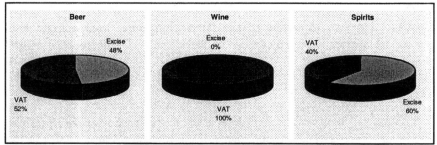

Figure 11.37 Tax components per litre of pure alcohol, Italy

Japan

In Japan, beer tax is mainly used to raise government revenue. In 1995, it is estimated that alcohol taxes contributed about 3.8 percent of the total government revenue (JNTAA, 1996).

The major components of alcohol tax in Japan are GST and special taxes. Figure 11.38 gives the components of the tax on beer, wine, sake and spirits per litre of pure alcohol. As can be seen, the special taxes component is quite large for all beverages. The GST component is a small contributor to the tax on beer (6 percent), sake (16 percent) and spirits (6 percent). As can be seen from Table 11.12 (row 11), in Japan, the total tax burden on beer is 46 percent and that on sake is only 18 percent.

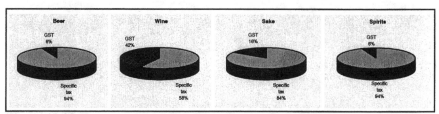

Figure 11.38 Tax components per litre of pure alcohol, Japan

Luxembourg

As in many other European countries, excise and VAT are the two major components of alcohol taxes. Figure 11.39 presents the component of taxes of beer, wine and spirits. As can be seen, excise tax on spirits (81 percent) is 3 times that of beer (24 percent). There is no excise on wine. As can be seen from Table 11.12 (row 12), in Luxembourg, the tax burden is much less for beer (17 percent) and wine (11 percent) compared to spirits (54 percent).

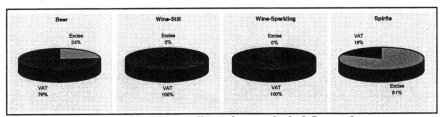

Figure 11.39 Tax components per litre of pure alcohol, Luxembourg

Mexico

In Mexico, a special tax called the Impuesto Especial Sobre Producciony Services (IEPS) is levied on all alcoholic beverages. The IEPS is applied as a percentage of the invoice price prior to dealer mark-ups. Figure 11.40 presents the percentage of the two tax components, IEPS and VAT on the total tax. As can be seen, for beer and wine the two taxes are about the same. But for spirits, IEPS component is two-thirds while the VAT component is one-third of the total tax. Table 11.12 (row 13) gives the total tax burden as a percentage of the retail price. As can be seen, the tax burden is about the same for beer and wine (about 28 percent) and for spirits it is higher (40 percent).

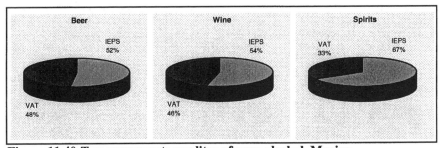

Figure 11.40 Tax components per litre of pure alcohol, Mexico

Netherlands

In the Netherlands, beer (4 to 6 percent of alcohol content) is taxed at a rate of 34 percent, table wines are taxed at 16 percent and spirits (over 35 percent proof) is taxed at 69 percent.

Figure 11.41 presents the tax components on a litre of pure alcohol. As can be seen, the excise and VAT taxes are about the same for beer and wine but is about 4:1 for spirits. Table 11.12 (row 14) shows the total tax burden as a percentage of the retail price for the three beverages in Netherlands. As can be seen, the spirits tax burden (70 percent) is more than twice that of beer (34 percent) and wine (28 percent).

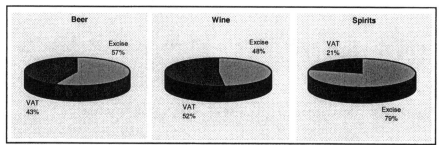

Figure 11.41 Tax components per litre of pure alcohol, Netherlands

New Zealand

Alcohol tax is a major source of revenue for the New Zealand Government. The tax rate for any beverage is based on the alcohol content. In 2002, it has collected about $500 million revenue from alcohol excise duty alone.

Figure 11.42 gives the tax components that forms the total tax of alcoholic beverages in New Zealand. As can be seen, the excise duty and GST are the two major components which determine the tax on the three alcoholic beverages. Excise duty on beer is 68 percent, wine is 53 percent and spirits is 82 percent. The corresponding GST components are 31 percent, 48 percent and 17 percent, respectively.

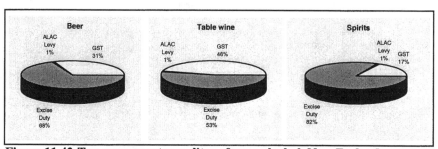

Figure 11.42 Tax components per litre of pure alcohol, New Zealand

As can be seen from Table 11.12 (row 15), the tax burden on spirits is about twice that of beer and wine. The tax burden on beer is 36 percent, wine is 24 percent and spirits is 64 percent.

Norway

In Norway, beer (4 to 6 percent alcohol content) is taxed at a rate of 61.5 percent, table wine is taxed at 65 percent and spirits (over 35 percent proof) is taxed at 90 percent. Figure 11.43 shows the tax components of alcoholic beverages. The VAT is the major component of tax on beer (80 percent) while excise tax is the major component of tax on table wine (72 percent), strong wine (85 percent) and spirits (79 percent).

As can be seen from Table 11.12 (row 16), in Norway, the tax burden on beer is 57 percent, wine is 66 percent and spirits is 80 percent.

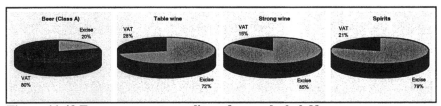

Figure 11.43 Tax components per litre of pure alcohol, Norway

Portugal

Figure 11.44 shows the tax components in a litre of pure alcohol of beer, wine and spirits. As can be seen, the special taxes and VAT are about the same for beer. For wine, there is no tax other than VAT. For spirits, the special taxes component is 71 percent while the VAT component is 29 percent. As can be seen from Table 11.12 (row 17), in Portugal, the tax burden on wine is the lowest (5 percent) and that for beer is 28 percent and for spirits is 50 percent.

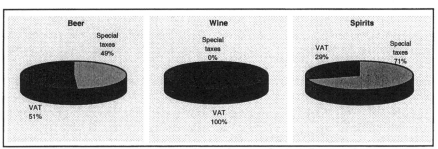

Figure 11.44 Tax components per litre of pure alcohol, Portugal

Spain

In 1994, the tax rates in Spain were 18.4 percent on beer, 13 percent on table wine and 43.4 percent on spirits. Figure 11.45 presents the tax components in a litre of pure alcohol for beer, wine and spirits. As can be seen, excise tax on beer is 30 percent, on spirits is 75 percent and there is no excise tax on wine.

As can be seen from Table 11.12 (row 18), in Spain, there is not much difference in the tax burden on the beer and wine prices but it is almost three times that of beer and wine on spirits.

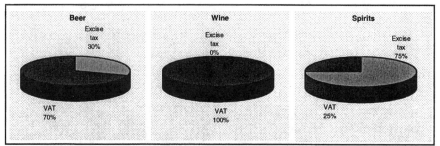

Figure 11.45 Tax components per litre of pure alcohol, Spain

Sweden

One of the most significant tools that forms part of Swedish alcohol control policy is the taxation of alcoholic beverages. The Swedish tax structure is based on the alcoholic content of beverages. Across beverages, there is a 12 percent value added tax (VAT) on all beverages with less than 3.5 percent alcohol content by volume and 25 percent VAT on all alcoholic beverages greater than 3.5 percent alcohol content by volume. The tax on a bottle of vodka is about 90 percent (including VAT) of the retail price. For moderately priced table wine, the total tax is about 60 percent. The state monopoly stores earn about 70 percent of their income from alcohol taxes. In 1994, the alcohol tax rates were: 55 percent on strong beer (alcohol content over 3.5 percent), 59 percent on table wine and 84 percent on spirits.

Figure 11.46 shows the tax components of beer, wine and spirits. In beer, 23 percent of the tax is due to VAT and the remaining 77 percent is due to excise taxes. The corresponding VAT and excise proportions for table wine are 30 percent and 70 percent, for fortified wine they are 31 percent and 69 percent, and for spirits they are 24 percent and 76 percent.

As can be seen from Table 11.12 (row 19), in Sweden, the tax burden is more than two thirds of the price of wine (66 percent) and spirits (87 percent) and is about half (46 percent) of the price of beer.

Switzerland

The tax on beer in Switzerland is fixed by the constitution at 18 percent of the price of draft lager beer. Table wines are taxed at 5 percent and different rates are applied to spirits depending on the type. While spirits production is controlled by the Federal Government, wine production is encouraged by providing subsidies and the industry is protected from imports.

Figure 11.47 presents the tax components of a litre of absolute alcohol in beer, wine and spirits. As can be seen, the excise tax on beer is about 50 percent and that on spirits is 85 percent. There is no excise tax on wine. As can be seen from Table 11.12 (row 20), in Switzerland, the tax burden on wine (only 6 percent) is very small compared to the tax burden on beer (23 percent) and spirits (40 percent).

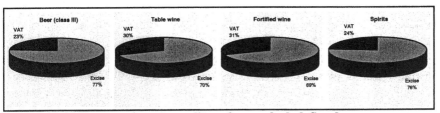

Figure 11.46 Tax components per litre of pure alcohol, Sweden

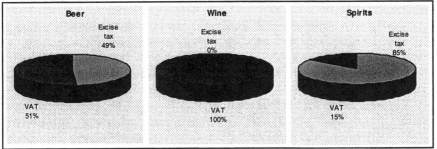

Figure 11.47 Tax components per litre of pure alcohol, Switzerland

However, compared to other countries, the tax burden on spirits is still somewhat low.

Ukraine

In Ukraine, beer (4 to 6 percent alcohol content) is taxed at a rate of 20 percent, table wines are taxed at a rate of 30 percent and spirits (over 35 percent proof) are taxed at a rate of 85 percent.

UK

In the UK, beer (4 to 6 percent alcohol) is taxed at a rate of 31 percent, table wine at 51.1 percent and spirits (over 35 percent proof) at 66.5 percent. Figure 11.48 shows the components of tax on a litre of pure alcohol for beer, wine and spirits. The two major components of alcohol taxes in the UK are VAT and excise duty. The excise duty on beer is 62 percent, table wine is 67 percent, fortified wine is 54 percent and spirits is 76 percent of the total tax. The remaining is VAT. As can be seen from Table 11.12 (row 21), in the UK, the tax burden is about 40 percent of the price of beer and wine and the tax burden for spirits is about 60 percent of its retail price.

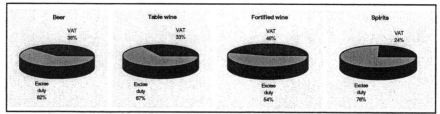

Figure 11.48 Tax components per litre of pure alcohol, UK

US

The alcohol tax system in the US is based on the alcohol content of a beverage. Below we present the tax rates on alcoholic beverages at various strength levels of pure alcohol during 1977-1990 and 1991 in Table 11.13. As can be seen, there is a sharp increase in the tax rates of regular beer and wine between the two periods 1/1/77-30/12/90 and 1/1/91 to present.

In the US, excise duty and state and local taxes are the two major components of alcohol taxes. In Figure 11.49, we show these two components. The state and local taxes form 59 percent of the beer tax, 60 percent of the wine tax and 51 percent of the spirits tax. Also, as can be seen from Table 11.12 (row 22), the tax burden on spirits (45 percent) is more than twice that on beer (19 percent) and wine (21 percent).

Table 11.13   Tax Rates, US, 1977-present

Beverage	1/1/77 - 30/12/90	1/1/91 - present
Beer		
Regular rate		
per 31 gallons barrel	$9.00	$18.00
or per 12 oz can	$0.03	$0.05
Reduced rate		
per 31 gallons barrel	$7.00	$7.00
or per 12 oz can	$0.02	$0.02
Wine		
per wine gallon		
Less than 14% alcohol	$0.17	$1.07
14% - 21% alcohol	$0.67	$1.57
21% - 24% alcohol	$2.25	$3.15
per 750 ml bottle		
Less than 14% alcohol		$0.21
14% - 21% alcohol		$0.31
21% - 24% alcohol		$0.62
Spirits		
per proof gallon	$12.50	$13.50
per 750 ml bottle	$2.14	
(at 80 percent proof)		

Source: ATF (2003)

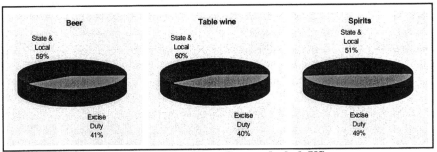

Figure 11.49 Tax components per litre of pure alcohol, US

11.6   Adults' View on Alcohol Control Policies

Table 11.14 shows the view of Australian public on various alcohol control policy options. Columns 2 and 3 of the table present the support for a number of control measures from two groups of adults, namely, abstainers or low-risk drinkers and

Table 11.14   Proportion of persons aged 14 years and over in support of introducing measures to reduce the problems associated with excessive alcohol use, by drinking status, Australia, 2001 (in percentages)

Measure (1)	Abstainers/ low-risk drinkers (2)	Risky/ high-risk drinkers (3)
1. Increasing the price of alcohol	29.1	5.7
2. Reducing the number of outlets that sell alcohol	38.3	11.8
3. Reducing trading hours for pubs and clubs	42.3	15.2
4. Raising the legal drinking age	51.5	25.1
5. Increasing the number of alcohol-free events	76.0	48.3
6. Increasing the number of alcohol-free 'dry' zones	74.5	50.1
7. Serving only low alcohol content beverages at sporting events	73.8	46.7
8. Limiting TV advertising until after 9.30pm	76.1	57.7
9. Banning alcohol sponsorship of sporting events	53.3	27.7
10. More severe penalties for drink driving	91.0	80.5
11. Stricter laws against serving drunk customers	90.2	75.6
12. Restricting late night trading of alcohol	63.3	28.9
13. Strict monitoring of late night licensed premises	80.0	60.0
14. Increasing the size of std drink labels on alcohol containers	73.4	58.2
15. Adding information on alcohol containers	77.6	59.5

Source: *AIHW* (2002b).

risky or high-risk drinkers. As can be seen, among the abstainers or low-risk drinkers, there is strong support for a number of policies such as increasing the number of alcohol-free events, increasing the number of alcohol-free 'dry' zones, serving only low alcohol content beverages at sporting events, limiting TV advertising until after 9.30pm, more severe penalties for drink driving, stricter laws against serving drunk customers, strict monitoring of late night licensed premises, increasing the size of standard drink labels on alcohol containers, adding information on alcohol containers. The risky or high-risk drinkers group strongly supported only the two policies, more severe penalties for drink driving and stricter laws against serving drunk customers. The least support, as expected, was received from the two groups for the three policies, increasing the price of alcohol, reducing the number of outlets that sell alcohol and reducing the trading hours for pubs and clubs.

11.7   Implementation of Alcohol Control Policies

In addition to the alcohol control policies considered above (through restrictions on alcohol sales, alcohol-related advertising, drink-driving and alcohol taxes), in this section, we consider other control mechanisms in place to reduce excessive alcohol consumption in individual countries.

In Table 11.15, we present the legal restrictions on alcohol consumption in public environments, such as consumption in health care buildings, educational buildings, government buildings, public transport, restaurants, parks, streets, sporting events, workplace, airports etc, in a number of countries. As can be seen, in most of the countries, there is either a voluntary or complete ban on alcohol consumption in the health care buildings, educational buildings, government buildings, public transport, sporting events and the workplace. There is not much restriction on alcohol consumption in restaurants, leisure events and domestic and international airports.

Table 11.16 presents the information on the availability of various alcohol abuse preventative programmes such as school-based alcohol education programmes, work place alcohol education programmes, drink-driving educational programmes etc available in individual countries. As can be seen, in most of the countries, there are developed or moderately developed school-based alcohol education programmes and drink-driving campaigns in place. There are not much work-based or local community based alcohol education programmes available in most countries.

We present in Table 11.17 some statistics on the implementation of alcohol control policies such as national action plan on alcohol, alcohol taxation policy, regular national survey on alcohol consumption, alcohol misuse etc. As the table shows, in a majority of the countries, there are national co-ordinating body programmes to target specific levels of alcohol consumption and carry out regular national surveys on alcohol consumption.

Table 11.15 Legal restrictions on alcohol consumption in public environments, 43 European countries

Country (1)	Health care buildings (2)	Educational buildings (3)	Government buildings (4)	Public transport (5)	Restaurants (6)	Parks and streets (7)	Sporting events (8)	Leisure events (9)	Workplace (10)	Domestic air (11)	International air (12)
1. Albania	Voluntary	Voluntary	Voluntary	Voluntary	NR	NR	NR	NR	NR	NR	NR
2. Armenia	Voluntary	Voluntary	Voluntary	NR	NR	NR	Voluntary	Voluntary	Voluntary	NR	NR
3. Austria	NR	NR	NR	NR	NR	NR	NR	NR	NR	NR	NR
4. Azerbaijan	Complete	Complete	Complete	Complete	NR	Partial	Complete	Partial	Complete	Complete	Partial
5. Belarus	Complete	Complete	Complete	Complete	NR	Partial	Complete	Partial	Complete	Complete	Voluntary
6. Belgium	Partial	Partial	Partial			Partial	Partial	Partial	Partial	Complete	Complete
7. Bosnia	Complete	Complete	Voluntary	Complete	Voluntary	NR	Partial	NR	Complete	Partial	Partial
8. Bulgaria	Complete	Complete	Partial	Complete	NR	NR	Partial	Voluntary	Partial	NR	NR
9. Croatia	Complete	Complete	Complete	Complete	Partial	Partial	Partial	Partial	Complete	Partial	NR
10. Czech Republic	Partial	Partial	Complete	Partial	NR	Complete	Partial	NR	Complete	NR	NR
11. Denmark	Voluntary	Voluntary	Voluntary	Partial	Partial	Partial	Partial	NR	Voluntary	NR	NR
12. Estonia	Complete	Complete	Partial	Complete	Complete	Complete	Partial	Partial	Partial	Partial	Partial
13. Finland	Voluntary	Voluntary	NR	Partial	Partial	Partial	Partial	Partial	Voluntary	Partial	Partial
14. France	Partial	Partial	Partial	Partial	Voluntary	NR	Partial	Voluntary	Partial	Voluntary	Voluntary
15. Georgia	Partial	Partial	Partial	Partial	NR	NR	Voluntary	Voluntary	Partial	Complete	Complete
16. Germany	Voluntary	Voluntary	Voluntary	NR	NR	NR	Voluntary	NR	Partial	NR	NR
17. Greece	NR	NR	NR	Partial		NR	Partial	NR	NR		
18. Hungary	Complete	Complete	Partial	Complete	NR	Voluntary	NR	NR	Complete		NR
19. Iceland	Voluntary	Voluntary	Voluntary	Voluntary	Voluntary	Voluntary	Voluntary	Voluntary	Voluntary	Complete	NR
20. Ireland	Voluntary	Voluntary	Voluntary	Partial	Partial	Voluntary	Partial	Partial	Complete	NR	NR
21. Israel	Partial	Complete	Partial	Voluntary	NR	NR	NR	NR	Partial	NR	NR
22. Italy	Voluntary	Voluntary	Voluntary	Voluntary	Voluntary	Voluntary	Voluntary	Voluntary	Voluntary	NR	NR
23. Kazakhstan	Voluntary	Voluntary	Voluntary	Voluntary	Partial	NR	NR	NR	Complete		
24. Kyrgyzstan	Partial	Partial	Partial	Partial	NR	Partial	Partial	NR	Complete		NR
25. Latvia	Voluntary	Voluntary	Voluntary	Voluntary	Partial	Voluntary	Voluntary	Voluntary	Complete	Partial	Partial
26. Lithuania	Complete	Complete	Complete	Complete	NR	Partial	Partial	Partial	Complete	Complete	Complete
27. Luxembourg	Voluntary	Voluntary	NR	NR	NR	NR	Voluntary	Voluntary	Voluntary		NR
28. Malta	Voluntary	Voluntary	Voluntary	Voluntary	NR	NR	NR	NR	Voluntary		NR
29. Netherlands	NR	Partial	Voluntary	NR	NR	Partial	Partial	NR	Voluntary	NR	NR
30. Norway	Partial	Partial	Partial	Partial	Partial	Partial	Partial	Partial	Partial	Partial	NR
31. Poland	Complete	Complete	Complete	Complete	NR	Complete	Complete	Voluntary	Complete	Partial	Partial
32. Portugal	Partial	Partial	Partial	NR	NR		Voluntary	NR	Partial	NR	NR
33. Repub of Moldova	Complete	Complete	Complete	Complete	NR	Partial	Partial	Partial	Complete	Partial	Partial
34. Romania		Complete	Complete	Complete	NR	Voluntary	Complete		Complete	NR	NR
35. Russian Federation	Complete	Complete	Complete	Complete	NR	Complete	Partial	Partial	Complete	Partial	NR
36. Slovakia	Complete	Complete	Complete	Complete	NR	Voluntary	Partial	Voluntary	Complete	NR	NR
37. Slovenia	Partial	Partial	Partial	Partial	Partial	NR	NR	NR	Partial	NR	NR
38. Spain	Partial	Partial	Partial	NR	NR	Partial	Complete	Partial	Partial	NR	NR
39. Sweden	Partial	NR	NR	Partial	Partial	Voluntary	Partial	Partial	Voluntary	Voluntary	NR
40. Switzerland	Partial	Partial	Partial	NR	Partial	NR	NR	NR	Partial	NR	NR
41. The FYROM	Complete	Complete	Partial	Complete	NR	Partial	Partial	Partial	Complete	Partial	Partial
42. Turkey	Complete	Complete	Complete	Complete		Voluntary	Complete	NR	Complete		
43. Ukraine	Complete	Complete	Partial	Partial	NR	Partial	Partial	Voluntary	Complete	Complete	NR
44. UK	Voluntary	Voluntary	Voluntary	Partial		Voluntary	Partial	Voluntary	Partial		
45. Uzbekistan	Complete	Complete		Complete	NR	Partial	Complete	Partial	Complete	Complete	NR

The FYROM = The former Yugoslav Republic of Macedonia; Bosnia = Bosnia and Herzegovina. Complete = Complete ban; Partial = Partial restriction; NR = No restrictions; Voluntary = Voluntary agreement with the authorities.

11.8 Concluding Comments

In this chapter, we presented detailed statistics on the level of misuse of alcohol, various alcohol control instruments such as alcohol sales restrictions, alcohol drink-driving regulations, alcohol taxes etc and various misuse preventative programmes put in place, in a number of countries. The information presented in this chapter reveals the following:

Table 11.16   Alcohol preventative programmes, 42 European countries

Country (1)	Mass media programmes (2)	School based programmes (3)	Work based programmes (4)	Local community programmes (5)	Drink driving campaigns (6)
1. Albania	Poor	Poor	DNE	DNE	Poor
2. Armenia	Poor		DNE	DNE	Poor
3. Austria	Poor	Moderate	Developed	Poor	Developed
4. Azerbaijan	Developed	Developed	Developed	DNE	
5. Belarus	Moderate	DNE	DNE	DNE	Moderate
6. Belgium	Poor	Developed	Developed	Developed	High
7. Bosnia	Moderate	Moderate	Poor	Moderate	Poor
8. Bulgaria	Poor	Moderate	Poor	Moderate	Moderate
9. Croatia	Poor	Moderate	Moderate	Poor	Developed
10. Czech Republic	DNE	Developed	Poor	Poor	Moderate
11. Denmark	High	Moderate	Developed	Moderate	Developed
12. Estonia	Moderate	Developed	DNE	Moderate	Developed
13. Finland	Developed	Moderate	Moderate	Developed	
14. France	Developed	Moderate	Poor	Poor	Developed
15. Georgia	Poor	Poor	DNE	DNE	Moderate
16. Germany	Developed	Developed	Developed	Poor	High
17. Hungary	Poor	Moderate	Poor	Developed	Poor
18. Iceland	Moderate	Developed	Moderate	Developed	Moderate
19. Ireland	Moderate	Developed	Poor	Moderate	High
20. Israel	DNE	Developed	Poor	Poor	Developed
21. Italy	Moderate	Moderate	Poor	Moderate	Developed
22. Kazakhstan	Moderate	Moderate	Poor	Poor	Developed
23. Kyrgyzstan	Poor	Poor	DNE	DNE	Poor
24. Latvia	Moderate	Developed	Developed	Moderate	Moderate
25. Lithuania	Poor	Moderate	Poor	Poor	
26. Luxembourg	Moderate	Moderate	Moderate	Poor	Developed
27. Malta	Developed	Developed	Poor	Moderate	Moderate
28. Netherlands	Developed	Developed	Moderate	DNE	Developed
29. Norway	Developed	Developed	Developed	Moderate	Developed
30. Poland	DNE	High	Moderate	High	Developed
31. Portugal	DNE	Poor	High	Poor	Developed
32. Repub of Moldova	Moderate	Poor	DNE	DNE	Moderate
33. Romania	Poor	Moderate	DNE	Poor	Poor
34. Russian Federation	Poor	Moderate	DNE	Poor	Developed
35. Slovakia	Poor	Developed	DNE	Moderate	Moderate
36. Slovenia	Moderate	Moderate	Poor	Poor	
37. Spain	Moderate	Moderate	Poor	Moderate	High
38. Sweden	Developed	Developed	Developed	High	
39. Switzerland	Developed	Developed	Moderate	Moderate	High
40. The FYROM	High	Developed	Poor	Poor	Moderate
41. Ukraine	Poor	Poor	Poor	Poor	Developed
42. Uzbekistan	Developed	Moderate	Moderate	Moderate	Developed

High - Highly developed programmes; Moderate - Moderately developed programmes; Poor - Poorly developed programmes; DNE - Does not exist.

Table 11.17 Implementation of alcohol control policies, 42 European countries

Country (1)	National action plan on alcohol (2)	National coordinating body (3)	Specific target on alcohol consumption (4)	Alcohol taxation policy aims to reduce total alcohol consumption (5)	Regular reports on consumption, harm or policies (6)	Regular national surveys on alcohol consumption (7)
1. Albania	No	Yes	Yes	Yes	No	No
2. Armenia	No	No	No	No	Yes	Yes
3. Austria	No	No	No	No	Yes	No
4. Azerbaijan	No	No			No	No
5. Belarus	No	No	Yes		No	No
6. Belgium	No	No	No	No	Yes	Yes
7. Bosnia	No	No	No		No	No
8. Bulgaria	No	Yes	Yes		No	No
9. Croatia	No	No	Yes	No	No	Yes
10. Czech Republic	No	No	Yes		Yes	Yes
11. Denmark	Yes	Yes	Yes	Yes	Yes	Yes
12. Estonia	Yes	Yes	No	No	No	Yes
13. Finland	Yes	Yes	Yes	Yes	Yes	Yes
14. France	Yes	No	Yes		Yes	Yes
15. Georgia	No	Yes	No	No	No	No
16. Germany	Yes	Yes	Yes	No	Yes	Yes
17. Hungary	Yes	Yes	Yes	No	Yes	No
18. Iceland	Yes	Yes	Yes	Yes	No	No
19. Ireland	Yes	Yes	Yes	No	No	Yes
20. Israel	Yes	Yes	Yes		No	Yes
21. Italy	Yes	Yes	Yes	No	Yes	Yes
22. Kazakhstan	No	Yes		Yes	No	Yes
23. Kyrgyzstan	No	Yes	No	No	No	No
24. Latvia	No	No	No	No	Yes	No
25. Lithuania	Yes	Yes	Yes		Yes	Yes
26. Luxembourg	No	Yes	Yes	Yes	No	No
27. Malta	No	Yes		Yes	No	Yes
28. Netherlands	Yes	Yes	No	Yes	Yes	No
29. Norway	Yes	Yes	Yes	Yes	Yes	Yes
30. Poland	Yes	Yes	Yes	Yes	Yes	Yes
31. Portugal	Yes	No	Yes	No	No	Yes
32. Repub of Moldova	No	No	No	No	No	No
33. Romania	No	No	No	No	No	No
34. Russian Federation	No	Yes	Yes		No	No
35. Slovakia	No	No	No	No	Yes	Yes
36. Slovenia	No	No	Yes		Yes	Yes
37. Spain	No	Yes	Yes		No	Yes
38. Sweden	Yes	Yes	Yes		Yes	Yes
39. Switzerland	No	Yes	Yes	No	Yes	Yes
40. The FYROM	Yes	Yes	No	No	Yes	No
41. Ukraine	No	Yes	Yes	No	No	No
42. Uzbekistan	No	No		No	No	No

1. In most countries, the statistics show that the liver cirrhosis death rate and the rate of alcohol related accidents is on the decline in the last 2 decades.

2. In many countries, restrictions on alcohol sale is used an instrument to control the supply of alcohol. Restrictions such as days of sales, hours of sale and the type of outlet/location, type of sales licence and minimum age for purchasing alcohol are mostly used to restrict alcohol sales.

3. While many governments allow alcohol advertising, a number of restrictions such as time of the day of alcohol advertisements can be shown on the electronic media, health warning labels requirements and the type of advertisements that can be telecast are in place and a strict alcohol industry code of advertising is also in place in many countries.

4. Almost all countries have put in place serious restrictions on drink-driving. Some countries has gone to the extreme level of enforcing a 0g% Blood Alcohol Concentration (BAC) limit. In many countries, Random Breath Testing (RBT) is also widely used and heavy penalties and/or imprisonment is imposed for drink-driving related offences.

5. While a majority of countries use alcohol taxes as an instrument to raise government revenue, some countries genuinely use it as an alcohol control tool. Raising taxes on alcoholic beverages obviously increases their retail prices, hence making it too expensive for middle-income and low-income groups to consume excessive alcohol. In many countries, the total tax burden as a percentage of retail price is higher for spirits (which has the highest alcohol content), followed by beer and then wine.

6. Many countries implement various alcohol misuse prevention educational programmes at schools and workplaces. A number of governments have also banned alcohol from public buildings, hospitals and sporting events. Most of the countries also attempt to implement a national action plan on alcohol and carry out regular surveys on the level of alcohol consumption among their people.

Chapter 12

Tobacco Control Policies

In Chapter 3, we presented an overview of tobacco consumption around the world. In Chapter 8, we analysed the demand for tobacco, using a system-wide framework, using data from 43 developed and developing countries. We analysed tobacco consumption in the context of consumer utility maximizing framework and found that income and prices are the two major economic factors that significantly influence tobacco consumption, in most countries. In a majority of the countries, tobacco is considered as a necessity by consumers. We also found that demand for tobacco is price inelastic. The cross-country averages of income and own-price elasticities of tobacco are 0.83 and -0.46 (see Table 8.15), respectively. These elasticity estimates mean that if income increases by 10 percent then the consumption of tobacco will increase by 8.3 percent and if the price of tobacco increases by 10 percent then tobacco consumption would fall by 4.6 percent. We also estimated the price elasticities of tobacco separately for the two groups of countries, developed and developing countries, and found that a 10 percent increase in price of tobacco would reduce the demand for tobacco by 4.2 percent in developed countries and 5.2 percent in developing countries.

While there is always a debate in the public about tolerable (moderate) level of alcohol consumption, there is a no such tolerance level acceptable to society with respect to tobacco consumption. As far as the consumption of tobacco is concerned, it is now well understood that there is no health or social benefit to smokers or to the society as a whole other than that tobacco sales generate revenue to manufacturers, governments and create employment. On the contrary, it is now scientifically proven that smoking is not only harmful to the smokers themselves but also to the people around them in the smoking environment (passive smoking). The mounting healthcare costs associated with tobacco consumption resulting from the poor health of the people of a nation is of continuing concern to governments, policy makers and to the society as a whole as the negative social impact of smoking outweighs the benefits from tobacco sales.

In this chapter, we consider the control policies implemented in a number of countries to reduce tobacco consumption. In Section 12.1, we discuss various smoking related issues which have an impact on the society as a whole. In Section 12.2, we look at the extent of prevalence of tobacco use in a number of countries. We discuss the various control measures used around the world to reduce the demand for tobacco in Section 12.3. This section also presents the control measures in relation to taxation, advertising, labelling, sales restriction etc in a number of countries. In Section 12.4, we discuss the control measures used to reduce the supply of tobacco. In the final section, we present our concluding comments.

As we will see below, while strict tobacco control policies are in place in most developed countries, very little or no control policies are in place in most of the developing countries. The data used in this chapter are gathered from *The World Health Organization* (WHO, 2003), World Bank (1999, 2001) and various individual country reports published by the respective government bodies.

12.1   Smoking Related Issues

It is now acknowledged worldwide that tobacco is toxic and contains an addictive substance (nicotine). In light of this, it is also acknowledged worldwide that the tobacco epidemic is becoming one of the biggest public health challenges faced by all countries during this century and requires a joint response from the world as a whole. In 1998, world production of cigarettes was 5.61 trillion, which is equivalent to 948 cigarettes per person or 2.6 cigarettes per day for every man, woman and child on earth (Brown, 1999). Across the world, about 1.225 billion adults (15+) smoke; 425 million from the developed countries and 800 million from the developing countries.

Table 12.1 Estimated number of smokers in the world (in millions)

Countries	Male	Female	All persons
Developed	275	150	425
Developing	700	100	800
World	975	250	1225

Source: Taylor and Bettcher (2000).

One in every three adults on earth is a regular smoker (WHO, 1999). By 2025, the number of smokers worldwide is expected to rise to more than 1.6 billion. Thirty five percent of men from the developed countries and 50 percent of the men from the developing countries smoke tobacco. About 22 percent of women from the developed countries and 9 percent of the women from the developing countries also smoke tobacco. Cigarette smoking among women is on the decline in many developing countries (for example in Australia, Canada, the UK and the US) and still on the increase in a number of developing countries in the southern, central and eastern European countries. Figure 12.1 shows the smoking trend of male and female smokers in Japan, the UK and the US. Studies also found (e.g., Jha and Chaloupka, 2000; and Gajalakshmi et al, 2004) that smoking prevalence is also related to the educational level of the people. Figure 12.2 shows the smoking

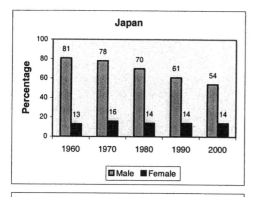

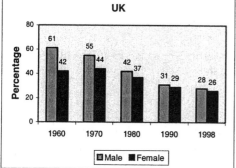

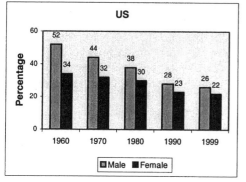

Figure 12.1 Percentage of smokers by gender, Japan, UK and US, 1960-2000

prevalence among men in Chennai, India, by education level. As can be seen, the prevalence rate decreases with the increasing level of education. The quit rates are lower in low-income countries and high in the high-income countries. For example, the smoking quit rates in China and India are in the range 5-10 percent, 15-21 percent in Hungary and Poland and 30-40 percent in the UK (Jha et al, 2002).

Smoking is a universal problem. Smoking affects people in different ways in different countries. It was earlier thought that smoking is a major problem only in the developed countries. But several research studies now show that the problem is

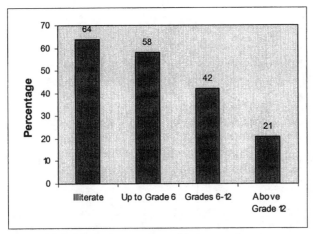

**Figure 12.2   Percentage of smoking prevalence among men by education
levels, Chennai, India, 2001**

equally serious both in the developed and developing countries. According to some
estimates (e.g. WHO, 2003; Peto et al, 2000), 4.8 million (2.4 million from
developed and 2.4 million form developing countries) peoples' death is attributable
to smoking. At the current rate of smoking, it is expected that by 2030, a total of 10
million people on earth will die from smoking, 3 million from the developed
countries and 7 million from developing countries. It is also reported that half of
these deaths will be from the middle age group (35-69 years old) population. To
highlight the seriousness of the problems associated with tobacco consumption
around the world, an anti-tobacco lobby stated that 'The death toll from tobacco is
equivalent to four fully loaded jumbo jets crashing each day, each one without any
survivors'.

While it is true that tobacco sales generate employment and tax revenue for
governments, in many countries it is also true that smokers are becoming a heavy
burden to governments as the smokers absorb larger proportions of government
revenues to look after their health problems as well as those people in their smoke
environment. In March 2002, *The Framework Convention Alliance on Tobacco
Control* (FCATC), an alliance made up of over 160 non-governmental
organisations around the world, prepared a proposal to the WHO which lead the
WHO to adopt an anti-tobacco treaty recently. The proposal demanded the UN
member countries commit to ten basic commandments such as banning all direct
and indirect advertising of tobacco products, promotion and sponsorship by
tobacco industry; stop tobacco smuggling; print explicit health warnings on tobacco
products packaging; give higher priority to human health before commercial
interests; increase tobacco taxes; remove duty free on tobacco and end all forms of
subsidy to tobacco.

While smoking is declining among males in most high income countries, cigarette consumption among males in low income and middle income countries, and amongst women worldwide has been on the increase. Many smokers in low and middle income countries are not aware of the health risks they take when they take-up smoking. Most smokers, including the ones in developed countries, start smoking during their childhood or adolescent stage when they do not understand the risks of tobacco and its addictive nature. By the time they realise the problems associated with smoking and desire to quit smoking, it may be too late to quit as they may be addicted to tobacco. For example, according to a World Bank (1999) report, 61 percent of the smokers in China surveyed thought that tobacco did little or no harm to them. Consumption of cigarettes in China has increased by 260 percent between 1970 and 1990 as US tobacco companies established their presence when China opened its doors for multinational companies. Of the 300 million current male smokers in China in the 29 years or younger age group, it is estimated that at least 100 million will die from tobacco related illness (WHO, 1999; Liu and Peto, 1998).

As the multinational cigarette manufacturing companies are finding it difficult to increase tobacco sales in the developed countries at the rate they did a few years ago, they are shifting their focus into the developing countries. A number of the British and American companies, with the help of their governments, are using their economic muscle to find new markets in Asia, Eastern Europe, Latin America and Africa. In these countries, the tobacco companies use sophisticated advertising techniques and promotional activities to increase tobacco sales. One such example is the aggressive marketing success of the multinational companies in South Korea during the 1980s. According to the WHO report (Roemer, 1993), such advertising campaigns have resulted in the smoking rate among the Korean male teenagers increasing from 18 percent to 30 percent in one year and among female teenagers the rate has increased from less than 2 percent to nearly 9 percent. Another similar example of aggressive marketing is provided by a BBC (2000) investigative team which reported that a British tobacco company was actively targeting teenagers in the African sub-continent by supplying free cigarettes in sporting events, at beaches, musical concerts and parties where many teenagers participate. Most smokers try their first cigarette when they are relatively young. In the high income countries 80 percent of them start smoking in their teens. Most starters in the low income countries take up smoking in their early twenties. Research shows that in today's environment the youths from poor families are more likely to take up smoking than the ones from the rich families. According to some published statistics (GLOBALink, 2003), it is estimated that in the high income countries as a whole about 14,000 to 15,000 young people take up smoking every day. The entries for middle- and low-income countries are in the range of 68,000 to 84,000 per day. This means that worldwide about 82,000 to 99,000 young people are taking up smoking every day.

Smokers argue that they have the right of choice to choose smoking as they have the right to choose any other consumer goods. In general by smoking what a smoker does to his/her health may be his or her business but when his/her smoking affects the non-smokers in his/her environment, it becomes other people's business as well. When people smoke, they not only impose cost on themselves but they also impose cost on non-smokers. One form of such cost is generated due to passive smoking, where the non-smokers in the environment of smokers, inhale the smoke. It is now well scientifically proven that passive smoking is a problem in society and has an impact on non-smokers. High levels of passive smoking by children can have major health effects such as brain tumours, ear infection, asthma, decreased lung function etc. It is estimated that in 1999, about 700 million children in the world, that is almost half of the children worldwide, share a home with a smoker (Bari and Yurekli, 2003). Figure 12.3 shows the percentage of children exposed to passive smoking at their homes in a number of selected countries. As can be seen, the percentage in some countries like Cuba, Argentina, Poland and Indonesia is alarming – at least two in three children are exposed to passive smoking at home.

While some smokers agree that while it is true that society has to spend extra money on their health care compared to a non-smoker, since they live for a shorter period due to smoking related health problems, their health care cost won't be much higher than a non-smoker who lives longer. However, the research based on some developed countries shows that this is not the case. Another argument put forward by the smoking lobby group is that the reduction on tobacco consumption would result in the loss of several thousand jobs. While there is some truth in this argument in the short term, it is also true that the resources saved from health care cost on smokers can be utilized to create new jobs in other areas in the long-term to counter balance the job losses in the tobacco industry.

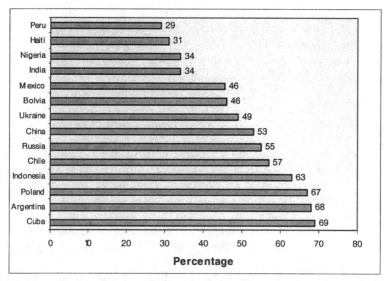

Figure 12.3   Percentage of children exposed to passive smoking at home, 14 countries, 2001

12.2   Prevalence of Tobacco Use

Table 12.2 presents the adult smoking prevalence by gender for the two sub-periods 1994-1998 and 1999-2001, for a number of European countries gathered from the WHO (2003) publications. The two sub-periods are corresponding to the second and third Tobacco Free Europe Action Plans of the WHO European Region. A comparison of the values in columns 2 and 3 reveal that the male smoking prevalence has decreased significantly (at least by 5 points) in Bulgaria, Czech Republic, Denmark, Estonia, Hungary, Iceland, Italy, Kazakhstan, Luxembourg, Norway, Romania and Slovenia and increased significantly in Albania, Georgia, Israel, Lithuania and Ukraine. In the remaining countries the change between the two periods is not that significant. A comparison of the values in columns 5 and 6 reveal that the female smoking prevalence has decreased significantly (at least by 5 points) in Croatia, Czech Republic, Denmark, Iceland, Italy, Latvia, Romania and Ukraine and increased significantly in Albania and Lithuania. In all countries, female smoking prevalence is less than 50 percent, but this is not the case with male smoking prevalence. Table 12.3 presents the smoking prevalence in young males and females for the sub-periods 1993-1996 and 1997-2001. Compared to the rate of smoking prevalence for adults, the rate for the young is somewhat lower in most countries. Surprisingly, in some countries (eg, Austria and Finland), the rate of smoking prevalence for female youth is higher than that for the male youth.

Figure 12.4 shows the smoking prevalence in a selected number of developing countries by gender (Bari and Yurekli, 2003). As can be seen, in all countries, prevalence of smoking among females is much lower than that among males. The prevalence of smoking among males is high in the Philippines (75 percent) followed by Vietnam (73 percent). The prevalence of smoking among females is high in Turkey (26 percent) followed by the Philippines (18 percent).

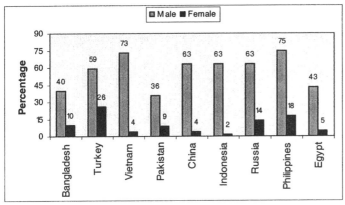

Figure 12.4 Rate of smoking prevalence in selected developing countries, 2000

Table 12.2 Prevalence of smoking among adults by gender, 1994-1998, 1999-2001, 2002

Country	Male adults prevalence			Female adults prevalence			Total adults prevalence		
(1)	1994-1998 (2)	1999-2001 (3)	2002 (4)	1994-1998 (5)	1999-2001 (6)	2002 (7)	1994-1998 (8)	1999-2001 (9)	2002 (10)
1. Albania	44	60		7	18			39	
2. Andorra	52			36					
3. Armenia	64	68			3		29		
4. Austria	30			19			24	29	
5. Azerbaijan		31			1		27		
6. Belarus	55	54	64	4	5	20	28	26	42
7. Belgium	34	36		27	26		30	31	
8. Bosnia&Herzegovina			49			30			38
9. Bulgaria	49	44		24	23		36	33	
10. Croatia	34	34		32	27		33	30	
11. Czech Republic	43	27		31	13		36	20	
12. Denmark	39	32	31	35	29	27	37	30	28
13. Estonia	52	44	45	24	20	18	36	29	29
14. Finland	29	27	27	19	20	20	24	23	23
15. France	35	33		21	21		28	27	
16. Georgia	53	60		12	15		33		
17. Germany	43	40		30	32			36	
18. Greece	46	47		28	29		37	38	
19. Hungary	44	38		27	23			31	
20. Iceland	30	25		31	23		30	24	
21. Ireland	32		28	31		26	31		27
22. Israel	32	39		25	22		28		
23. Italy	38	32		26	17		32	25	
24. Kazakhstan	60	47		7	8			24	
25. Kyrgyzstan			64			41			63
26. Latvia	53	49		18	13			29	
27. Lithuania	43	51		6	16			32	
28. Luxembourg	39	34		27	27		32	32	
29. Malta	34			15			24		
30. Netherlands	36	33		29	27		33	30	
31. Norway	36	31	30	36	32	30	36	32	30
32. Poland	44	42	40	24	23	25			32
33. Portugal	29			6			17		
34. Republic of Moldova	44	46			18				
35. Romania	62	32		25	10				
36. Russian Federation	63			10			36		
37. Serbia&Montenegro		48			34			40	
38. Slovakia	41			15			32		
39. Slovenia	35	28		23	20		29	24	
40. Spain	42	39		25	25		33	32	
41. Sweden	17	17		22	21		19	19	
42. Switzerland	39			28			33		
43. Turkey	63			24			44		
44. Ukraine	49	58		21	14			34	
45. UK	29	28		28	26		28	27	

Figure 12.5 shows the smoking prevalence by gender and regions using data from World Bank (1999). As can be seen, prevalence of smoking among males is high in the East Asia and Pacific region, and in the Eastern Europe and Central Asia region. Prevalence of smoking among females is high in the Eastern Europe and Central Asia region, and in the Latin America and Caribbean region. The overall prevalence of smoking is highest in Eastern Europe and Central Asia. It is also found that, in terms of gender, prevalence of smoking among males is higher in the low to middle income countries and prevalence of smoking among females is high in the high-income countries.

Table 12.3 Prevalence of smoking among youths by gender, 1994-1998, 1999-2001, 2002

Country	Male youths			Female youths			Total youth prevalence		
	1993-1996	1997-2001	2002	1993-1996	1997-2001	2002	1993-1996	1997-2001	2002
(1)	(2)	(3)	(4)	(5)	(6)	(7)	(8)	(9)	(10)
1. Austria	29	30	26	31	36	37	30		32
2. Bosnia&Herzegovina			11			7			
3. Bulgaria			29			26			
4. Croatia			23			25			24
5. Czech Republic		22	29		18	31			30
6. Denmark		20	17		28	21			19
7. Estonia		24	30		12	18			24
8. Finland		25	28		29	32			30
9. France	22	28	26	18	31	27	20	24	26
10. Georgia			31			6			
11. Germany		33	32		28	34			33
12. Greece		18	14		19	14			14
13. Hungary		36	28		28	29			27
14. Ireland		25	20		25	21			20
15. Israel	9	24	17	9	13	12	9		14
16. Italy			22			25			24
17. Latvia	33	38	29	14	23	21	24	30	25
18. Lithuania		24	35		10	18			27
19. Malta			17			17			17
20. Netherlands			23			24			23
21. Norway		23	20		28	27			23
22. Poland		27	26		20	17			22
23. Portugal		19	18		14	26			22
24. Russian Federation		24	27		22	19			23
25. Serbia&Montenegro			13			16			
26. Slovakia		28	31		18	28			
27. Slovenia			30			30			30
28. Spain			24			32			28
29. Sweden		18	11		24	19			15
30. Switzerland	17	25	25	18	25	24	18		25
31. Ukraine			45			23			34
32. UK			20			27			24

Figure 12.6 summarizes the prevalence of smoking in developed and developing countries (World Bank, 1999) by gender. As can be seen, the prevalence of smoking among males is high in developing countries compared to developed countries. However, the proportion of female smokers in developed countries (22 percent) is much higher than the proportion of female smokers in developing countries (9 percent). In developing countries, nearly half of the male population are smokers while only 9 percent of the female population are smokers. In developed countries, 39 percent of the male population and 22 percent of the female population are smokers. Worldwide, prevalence of smoking is 47 percent for males and 12 percent for females. Overall, for the world population, the smoking prevalence is 29 percent.

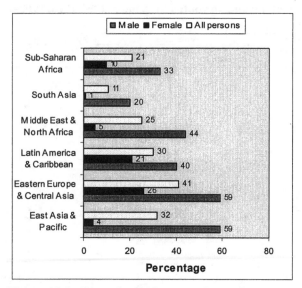

Figure 12.5 Rate of smoking prevalence (in percentages) in different regions of the world by gender and all persons, 1995

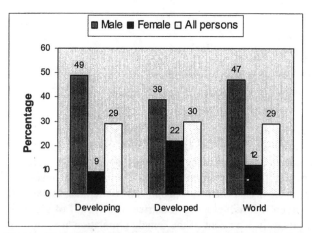

Figure 12.6 Rate of smoking prevalence (in percentages) in developed and developing countries by gender, 1997

12.3 Control Measures to Reduce Tobacco Demand

A set of effective tobacco control policies should have a combination of control measures to reduce both the demand and supply of tobacco products. In this section we discuss the measures commonly used to reduce the demand for tobacco such as tobacco tax, ban on tobacco advertising, printing warning labels on packages and providing adults with sufficient information to make an informed choice, restrictions on tobacco sales to public and restrictions on smoking in public places, increased access to nicotine replacement therapy (NRT) that would reduce the demand for tobacco products. In the next section, we look at measures to reduce tobacco supply.

Tobacco Taxes

In Chapter 8, we found that an increase in the price of tobacco, in general, would reduce tobacco consumption. Some other studies found that young and poor are the most price sensitive group in the whole population. Therefore, a price increase would reduce the tobacco consumption of regular smokers, increase the tendency for smokers to quit, prevent people from taking up smoking and reduce the chance of ex-smokers returning to smoking. Such a price increase in the tobacco products would have more impact on developing countries, as people in those countries are more sensitive to prices. According to a World Bank (1999) report, a 10 percent increase in the real price of tobacco worldwide would cause 40 million smokers alive in 1995 to quit and prevent at least 10 million tobacco related deaths.

One way of increasing the price of tobacco is by imposing a tax on tobacco products. While additional tax on tobacco would increase the price and hence reduce the demand for tobacco, in the short to medium term, it will also increase government revenue as consumers who have developed an addiction to tobacco smoking will respond relatively slowly to price increases and the government also save tax revenue from other sources as the money formerly spent on tobacco by smokers will now be spent on other consumer goods and services. The revenue from such price increase could help the governments to spend the tax revenue on several other important projects as well as to resolve problems created by smokers. The revenue generated by governments using tobacco taxes vary from country to country as the tax rates differ. The World Bank estimates that, on average, a 10 percent increase in tobacco taxes would increase tobacco tax revenue by about 7 percent. Figure 12.7 shows the cigarette tax revenue as a percentage of total government tax revenue in selected eastern European and central Asian countries (World Bank, 2001). As can be seen, there is significant difference in the percentage across countries ranging from 1 percent (Lithuania) to 11 percent (Turkey).

Figure 12.8 shows the excise (=ad valorem + specific) and total (=excise + VAT) taxes as a percentage of retail price in the year 2000, in a number of European countries, collected from World Bank (2001). As can be seen, the tax rates vary from country to country with the lowest total tax rate on tobacco in Germany (69 percent) and the highest tax rate in Denmark (82 percent).

Figure 12.9 presents the average price of a cigarette pack, average tax on a pack and tax as a percentage of price of cigarettes by country's income (Chaloupka and Nair, 2000). As can be seen, the price level and the tax levels are both high in the high income country groups. The tobacco tax as a percentage of its price is 68 percent in the high income countries, whereas it is only 40 percent in low income countries. As can be seen, there is still a lot of room available, especially in lower and lower-middle income countries, to raise cigarette taxes.

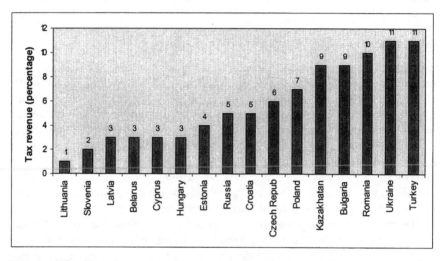

Figure 12.7   Cigarette tax revenue as a percentage of total tax revenue, European and central Asian countries, 1999

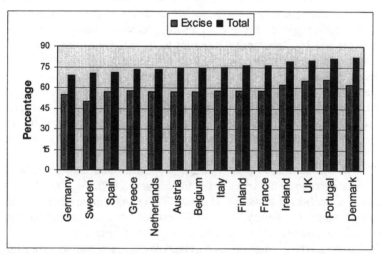

Figure 12.8   Excise and total taxes as a percentage of retail price, 14 European countries, 2000

The tobacco industry would normally argue that such an additional tax would reduce the consumption and hence reduce employment and increase tobacco smuggling. While there is some merit in their argument in the short term that reduced demand will imply reduction in production and hence less employment, it is also equally true that, in the long term, reduced consumption of tobacco will lead to less expenditure on smokers' health problems and improvement in productivity which will reduce the necessity for extra revenue by the governments.

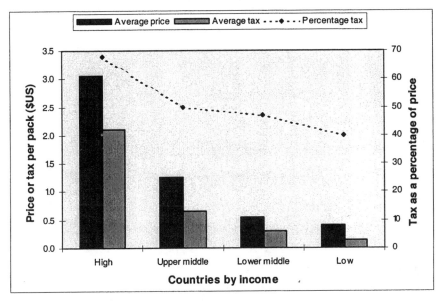

Figure 12.9   Average price of a cigarette pack, average tax per pack and tax as a percentage of price of cigarettes, country groups by income

The optimal tax rate is a complex question. Empirical evidence from the countries which adopted tax policies to control tobacco consumption and where tobacco consumption has fallen shows that the tax component of the price of a pack of cigarettes is in the range of 65-80 percent of retail price (World Bank, 1999).

Ban on Tobacco Advertising

Results from some research studies (e.g., Saffer, 2000) show that the ban on advertising has a significant effect on the demand for tobacco. Figure 12.10, reproduced from World Bank (1999), shows that there is a clear decline in the per capita cigarette consumption between 1981 and 1991 among the two groups of countries - one group had a ban on tobacco advertising and the other group did not have a ban on advertising. Due to public awareness of health problems associated with smoking, cigarette consumption fell in both groups of countries but the rate of fall is higher in the group of countries where there was a ban on advertising. Saffer (2000) estimated that a comprehensive set of tobacco advertising bans could reduce the consumption by 6.3 percent and counter-advertising messages could reduce smoking by another 2 percent.

Table 12.4 presents information on legislation on various forms of direct advertising of tobacco products in the media in a number of European countries. As can be seen, in most countries, there is a complete ban on advertising tobacco products on national TV, cable TV, national radio, national press and billboards. In a majority of countries, there is also a complete ban in the cinemas. Table 12.5 presents cross-country information on legislation on various forms of indirect advertising of tobacco products. The indirect advertising of tobacco is less restricted than direct advertising. However, in some countries, advertising tobacco products with other products on TV, sponsoring events with the name of tobacco products, direct mail giveaways and promotional discounts of tobacco products are completely banned.

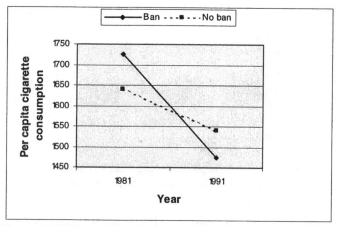

Figure 12.10 Per capita cigarette consumption with and without ban on advertising, average over 102 countries, 1981 and 1991

Nicotine Replacement Therapies

Another tool used by many countries to help smokers quit smoking is the Nicotine Replacement Therapy (NRT). Some studies (Jha and Chaloupka, 2000) found that advice by clinicians to smokers explaining the impact of smoking on their health could increase the quit rate by 2 to 3 percent in 6 months. If the clinician also discussed the use of NRT to smokers then the quit rate would increase to 6 percent and further if the clinician gave support to the quit programme

Table 12.4 Legislation on various methods of direct advertising of tobacco products, 50 European countries

Country	National TV	Cable TV	National radio	National press	International press	Billboards	Point of sale	Cinema
1. Albania	Complete ban	No restrict	Complete ban	Complete ban	No restrict	No restrict	No restrict	Voluntary
2. Andorra	No restrict	NDA	No restrict	No restrict	NDA	No restrict	No restrict	No restrict
3. Armenia	Complete ban	Complete ban	Complete ban	Partial restrict	No restrict	Partial restrict	No restrict	Partial restrict
4. Austria	Complete ban	Complete ban	Complete ban	Partial restrict	No restrict	Partial restrict	Partial restrict	Partial restrict
5. Azerbaijan	Complete ban	Complete ban	Complete ban	Complete ban	No restrict	Complete ban	Complete ban	Complete ban
6. Belarus	Partial restrict	Partial restrict	Partial restrict	Partial restrict	No restrict	Partial restrict	No restrict	Partial restrict
7. Belgium	Complete ban	Complete ban	Complete ban	Complete ban	Partial restrict	Complete ban	Partial restrict	Complete ban
8. Bosnia&Herzegovina	Partial restrict	Partial restrict	Partial restrict	Partial restrict	Partial restrict	Partial restrict	Partial restrict	Partial restrict
9. Bulgaria	Complete ban	Complete ban	Complete ban	Complete ban	No restrict	Complete ban	Partial restrict	Complete ban
10. Croatia	Complete ban	Complete ban	Complete ban	Complete ban	No restrict	Complete ban	Partial restrict	Complete ban
11. Czech Republic	Complete ban	Complete ban	Complete ban	Complete ban	Partial restrict	Complete ban	Partial restrict	Complete ban
12. Denmark	Complete ban	Complete ban	Complete ban	Complete ban	No restrict	Complete ban	Partial restrict	Complete ban
13. Estonia	Complete ban	No restrict	Complete ban	Complete ban	No restrict	Complete ban	Complete ban	Complete ban
14. Finland	Complete ban	Complete ban	Complete ban	Complete ban	No restrict	Complete ban	Complete ban	Complete ban
15. France	Complete ban	Complete ban	Complete ban	Complete ban	Complete ban	Complete ban	Partial restrict	Complete ban
16. Georgia	Complete ban	Complete ban	Complete ban	Partial restrict	No restrict	Partial restrict	Partial restrict	Partial restrict
17. Germany	Complete ban	Complete ban	Complete ban	No restrict	No restrict	Voluntary	No restrict	Partial restrict
18. Greece	Complete ban	Complete ban	Complete ban	No restrict	No restrict	No restrict	No restrict	Partial restrict
19. Hungary	Complete ban	Complete ban	Complete ban	Complete ban	No restrict	Complete ban	No restrict	Complete ban
20. Iceland	Complete ban	Complete ban	Complete ban	Complete ban	No restrict	Complete ban	Complete ban	Complete ban
21. Ireland	Complete ban	Complete ban	Complete ban	Complete ban	Partial restrict	Complete ban	Partial restrict	Complete ban
22. Israel	Complete ban	Complete ban	Complete ban	Partial restrict	No restrict	Complete ban	Partial restrict	Complete ban
23. Italy	Complete ban	Complete ban	Complete ban	Complete ban	No restrict	Complete ban	Complete ban	Complete ban
24. Kazakhstan	Complete ban	Complete ban	Complete ban	Partial restrict	No restrict	Complete ban	No restrict	Complete ban
25. Kyrgyzstan	Partial restrict	Partial restrict	Partial restrict	Partial restrict	No restrict	No restrict	No restrict	No restrict
26. Latvia	Partial restrict	Partial restrict	Partial restrict	Partial restrict	No restrict	Complete ban	No restrict	Complete ban
27. Lithuania	Complete ban	Complete ban	Complete ban	Complete ban	No restrict	Complete ban	Complete ban	Complete ban
28. Luxembourg	Complete ban	No restrict	Complete ban	Partial restrict	Partial restrict	Partial restrict	Partial restrict	Complete ban
29. Malta	Complete ban	No restrict	Complete ban	Partial restrict	No restrict	Partial restrict	Partial restrict	Complete ban
30. Monaco	NDA	NDA	NDA	NDA	NDA	NDA	NDA	NDA
31. Netherlands	Complete ban	Complete ban	Complete ban	Complete ban	No restrict	Complete ban	Partial restrict	Complete ban
32. Norway	Complete ban	Partial restrict	Complete ban	Complete ban	Partial restrict	Complete ban	Complete ban	Complete ban
33. Poland	Complete ban	Complete ban	Complete ban	Complete ban	Complete ban	Complete ban	Partial restrict	Complete ban
34. Portugal	Complete ban	Complete ban	Complete ban	Complete ban	No restrict	Complete ban	Partial restrict	Complete ban
35. Republic of Moldova	Complete ban	No restrict	Complete ban	Partial restrict	No restrict	Complete ban	No restrict	Partial restrict
36. Romania	Complete ban	No restrict	Complete ban	Partial restrict	No restrict	Partial restrict	No restrict	Partial restrict
37. Russian Federation	Complete ban	Complete ban	Partial restrict	Partial restrict	No restrict	No restrict	No restrict	Partial restrict
38. San Marino	NDA	NDA	NDA	NDA	NDA	NDA	NDA	NDA
39. Serbia&Montenegro	Complete ban	Complete ban	Complete ban	Complete ban	No restrict	Complete ban	Complete ban	Complete ban
40. Slovakia	Complete ban	Complete ban	Complete ban	Complete ban	No restrict	Complete ban	Complete ban	Complete ban
41. Slovenia	Complete ban	Complete ban	Complete ban	Complete ban	No restrict	Partial restrict	No restrict	Partial restrict
42. Spain	Complete ban	Complete ban	Complete ban	No restrict	No restrict	No restrict	No restrict	No restrict
43. Sweden	Complete ban	Complete ban	Complete ban	Complete ban	No restrict	Partial restrict	Partial restrict	Complete ban
44. Switzerland	Complete ban	Complete ban	Complete ban	Partial restrict	No restrict	Partial restrict	Partial restrict	Partial restrict
45. Tajikistan	No restrict	No restrict	No restrict	No restrict	No restrict	No restrict	No restrict	No restrict
46. The FYROM	Complete ban	Complete ban	Complete ban	Complete ban	No restrict	Complete ban	No restrict	Complete ban
47. Turkey	Complete ban	Complete ban	Complete ban	Complete ban	No restrict	Complete ban	Partial restrict	Complete ban
48. Turkmenistan	No restrict	No restrict	No restrict	No restrict	No restrict	No restrict	No restrict	No restrict
49. Ukraine	Complete ban	Complete ban	Complete ban	Partial restrict	No restrict	Partial restrict	No restrict	Partial restrict
49. UK	Complete ban	Complete ban	Complete ban	Complete ban	Partial restrict	Complete ban	Voluntary	Voluntary
50. Uzbekistan	Complete ban	No restrict	Complete ban	Partial restrict	No restrict	Complete ban	No restrict	No restrict

NDA = No data available;   No restrict = No restriction;   Voluntary = Voluntary agreement with authorities; Partial restrict = Partial restriction.

of smokers the quit rate could further increase to 8 percent. However, the price and access to NRT is a problem to most smokers. It is proposed that governments should widen access to NRT and other cessation therapies by reducing regulations and considering subsidies for low-income smokers. Table 12.6 presents the type of support available for people to quit smoking. As can be seen, in a majority of countries, some kind of support is available to those who would like to quit

Table 12.5   Legislation on various methods of indirect advertising of tobacco products, 50 countries

	Country	Product placement in TV and films	Sponsored event with tobacco brand name	Non-tobacco products with tobacco brand name	Tobacco product with non-tobacco product brand name	Direct mail giveaways	Promotional discounts
1.	Albania	No restrict	No restrict	No restrict	No restrict	No restrict	No restrict
2.	Andorra	NDA	NDA	NDA	NDA	NDA	NDA
3.	Armenia	No restrict	No restrict	No restrict	No restrict	No restrict	No restrict
4.	Austria	No restrict	Partial restrict	No restrict	No restrict	No restrict	Complete ban
5.	Azerbaijan	Complete ban	Complete ban	No restrict	No restrict	Complete ban	No restrict
6.	Belarus	No restrict	Partial restrict	No restrict	No restrict	No restrict	No restrict
7.	Belgium	Complete ban	Complete ban	Partial restrict	No restrict	Complete ban	Complete ban
8.	Bosnia&Herzegovina	Complete ban	Complete ban	No restrict	No restrict	No restrict	No restrict
9.	Bulgaria	Complete ban	Complete ban	Complete ban	Complete ban	Complete ban	Complete ban
10.	Croatia	Complete ban	Complete ban	Complete ban	Complete ban	Complete ban	Complete ban
11.	Czech Republic	No restrict	Partial restrict	Partial restrict	No restrict	Complete ban	No restrict
12.	Denmark	Partial restrict	Complete ban	Partial restrict	Partial restrict	Complete ban	Complete ban
13.	Estonia	Complete ban	Partial restrict	No restrict	Complete ban	No restrict	No restrict
14.	Finland	Complete ban	Complete ban	Partial restrict	Complete ban	Complete ban	Complete ban
15.	France	Complete ban	Complete ban	Partial restrict	Complete ban	Complete ban	Complete ban
16.	Georgia	Partial restrict	Partial restrict	Partial restrict	Partial restrict	No restrict	No restrict
17.	Germany	No restrict	No restrict	No restrict	No restrict	No restrict	No restrict
18.	Greece	Complete ban	No restrict	No restrict	No restrict	No restrict	Partial restrict
19.	Hungary	No restrict	Complete ban	Partial restrict	No restrict	Complete ban	No restrict
20.	Iceland	No restrict	Complete ban	Partial restrict	Complete ban	Complete ban	Complete ban
21.	Ireland	Voluntary	Partial restrict	No restrict	No restrict	Complete ban	Complete ban
22.	Israel	No restrict	Partial restrict	Complete ban	Complete ban	Complete ban	No restrict
23.	Italy	Complete ban	Partial restrict	Partial restrict	Partial restrict	No restrict	Complete ban
24.	Kazakhstan	Partial restrict	Partial restrict	Partial restrict	No restrict	Complete ban	No restrict
25.	Kyrgyzstan	No restrict	No restrict	No restrict	No restrict	No restrict	No restrict
26.	Latvia	Partial restrict	No restrict	No restrict	No restrict	No restrict	No restrict
27.	Lithuania	Complete ban	Partial restrict	No restrict	No restrict	Complete ban	Complete ban
28.	Luxembourg	No restrict	Partial restrict	Complete ban	No restrict	No restrict	No restrict
29.	Malta	Complete ban	No restrict	No restrict	No restrict	Complete ban	Complete ban
30.	Monaco	NDA	NDA	NDA	NDA	NDA	NDA
31.	Netherlands	No restrict	Complete ban	Partial restrict	Partial restrict	Complete ban	Complete ban
32.	Norway	Complete ban	Complete ban	Complete ban	Complete ban	Complete ban	Complete ban
33.	Poland	Complete ban	Complete ban	Complete ban	Complete ban	No restrict	No restrict
34.	Portugal	Complete ban	Complete ban	Partial restrict	No restrict	No restrict	Complete ban
35.	Republic of Moldova	No restrict	No restrict	No restrict	No restrict	No restrict	No restrict
36.	Romania	Complete ban	Partial restrict	Partial restrict	No restrict	No restrict	No restrict
37.	Russian Federation	Partial restrict	No restrict	No restrict	No restrict	No restrict	No restrict
38.	San Marino	NDA	NDA	NDA	NDA	NDA	NDA
39.	Serbia&Montenegro	Complete ban	No restrict	No restrict	No restrict	No restrict	No restrict
40.	Slovakia	No restrict	No restrict	No restrict	No restrict	No restrict	No restrict
41.	Slovenia	Complete ban	Partial restrict	Partial restrict	Complete ban	No restrict	No restrict
42.	Spain	Complete ban	No restrict	No restrict	No restrict	No restrict	No restrict
43.	Sweden	Partial restrict	Partial restrict	Partial restrict	Partial restrict	Complete ban	Partial restrict
44.	Switzerland	No restrict	Partial restrict	No restrict	No restrict	Partial restrict	No restrict
45.	Tajikistan	No restrict	No restrict	No restrict	No restrict	No restrict	No restrict
46.	The FYROM	Complete ban	Partial restrict	Partial restrict	No restrict	Complete ban	Complete ban
47.	Turkey	Voluntary	Partial restrict	Partial restrict	Voluntary	No restrict	No restrict
48.	Turkmenistan	No restrict	Voluntary	No restrict	No restrict	No restrict	No restrict
49.	Ukraine	No restrict	Complete ban	Partial restrict	No restrict	No restrict	No restrict
49.	UK	Complete ban	Complete ban	No restrict	No restrict	Complete ban	Voluntary
50.	Uzbekistan	No restrict	Partial restrict	Partial restrict	No restrict	No restrict	No restrict

NDA = No data available; No restrict = No restriction; Voluntary = Voluntary agreement with authorities; Partial restrict = Partial restriction.

Table 12.6 Type of support available for people to quit smoking

Country	Training of health professionals and medical students?	Cessation clinics?	Help lines?	Price incentive or reduced cost for treatment?	Pharmacotherapies available for cessation?	Pharmacotherapies available through prescription only?	Pharmacotherapies available without prescription?
1. Albania	No	No	No	No	No	No	No
2. Andorra	NDA	Yes	NDA	NDA	Yes	NDA	NDA
3. Armenia	Yes	No	No	No	Yes	NDA	Yes
4. Austria	Yes	Yes	Yes	No	Yes	Prescription	Yes
5. Azerbaijan	No	No	No	No	No	No	No
6. Belarus	Yes	Yes	Yes	No	Yes	No	Yes
7. Belgium	NDA	NDA	NDA	NDA	Yes	Prescription	No
8. Bosnia&Herzegovina	Yes	Yes	Yes	NDA	Yes	Yes	Yes
9. Bulgaria	Yes	Yes	No	No	Yes	Prescription	Yes
10. Croatia	Yes	Yes	Yes	No	Yes	NDA	Yes
11. Czech Republic	Yes	Yes	Yes	No	Yes	Prescription	Yes
12. Denmark	Yes	Yes	Yes	Yes	Yes	Prescription	Yes
13. Estonia	Yes	Yes	Yes	No	Yes	Prescription	Yes
14. Finland	Yes	Yes	Yes	No	Yes	Prescription	Yes
15. France	Yes	Yes	Yes	Yes	Yes	No	Yes
16. Georgia	NDA	Yes	Yes	NDA	Yes	No	Yes
17. Germany	Yes	NDA	Yes	NDA	Yes	Prescription	Yes
18. Greece	Yes	Yes	No	No	Yes	Yes	Yes
19. Hungary	Yes	Yes	Yes	Yes	Yes	Yes	Yes
20. Iceland	Yes	Yes	Yes	Yes	Yes	No	Yes
21. Ireland	Yes	Yes	Yes	Yes	Yes	Prescription	Yes
22. Israel	NDA	NDA	NDA	NDA	NDA	NDA	NDA
23. Italy	Yes	NDA	Yes	NDA	Yes	Prescription	Yes
24. Kazakhstan	Yes	Yes	No	No	Yes	No	Yes
25. Kyrgyzstan	Yes	Yes	No	No	No	No	No
26. Latvia	Yes	No	NDA	No	Yes	Prescription	Yes
27. Lithuania	Yes	Yes	NDA	No	Yes	Prescription	Yes
28. Luxembourg	NDA	NDA	NDA	NDA	NDA	NDA	NDA
29. Malta	Yes	Yes	Yes	No	Yes	Prescription	Yes
30. Monaco	NDA	NDA	NDA	NDA	NDA	NDA	NDA
31. Netherlands	Yes	No	Yes	Yes	Yes	Prescription	Yes
32. Norway	No	No	Yes	No	Yes	Prescription	Yes
33. Poland	Yes	Yes	Yes	Yes	Yes	Prescription	Yes
34. Portugal	Yes	Yes	Yes	No	Yes	Prescription	Yes
35. Republic of Moldova	No	No	No	No	Yes	NDA	Yes
36. Romania	No	No	No	No	Yes	NDA	Yes
37. Russian Federation	Yes	Yes	No	No	Yes	Yes	Yes
38. San Marino	NDA	NDA	NDA	NDA	NDA	NDA	NDA
39. Serbia&Montenegro	Yes	Yes	No	No	Yes	No	Yes
40. Slovakia	Yes	Yes	No	No	Yes	Prescription	Yes
41. Slovenia	Yes	Yes	No	No	Yes	Yes	Yes
42. Spain	Yes	Yes	NDA	NDA	Yes	Prescription	Yes
43. Sweden	Yes	Yes	Yes	No	Yes	Prescription	Yes
44. Switzerland	Yes	Yes	Yes	No	Yes	Prescription	Yes
45. Tajikistan	No	No	No	No	No	No	No
46. The FYROM	NDA	No	NDA	No	Yes	No	Yes
47. Turkey	Yes	Yes	No	No	Yes	NDA	Yes
48. Turkmenistan	NDA	No	No	No	Yes	No	Yes
49. Ukraine	Yes	Yes	No	No	Yes	No	Yes
49. UK	Yes	Yes	Yes	Yes	Yes	Prescription	Yes
50. Uzbekistan	NDA	NDA	NDA	NDA	Yes	No	Yes

NDA = No data available; Prescription = Bupropion and nasal spray are only available on prescription.

smoking. These supports include, training the health profession, cessation clinics and pharmacotherapies without prescription.

Educational Programmes, Warning Labels and Restriction on Smoking Locations

Research shows that various types of educational programmes at schools and to the public would also help reduce the level of people taking up smoking and increase the rate of cessation. 'Information shocks' such as the publication of research studies to show the severe health problems associated with smoking to counter the tobacco advertising can also have a positive impact on reducing the tobacco consumption. Researchers also found that printing consumer information through large clear warning labels on the cigarette boxes will also have significant impact on reducing tobacco consumption. Evidence from Australia, Canada and Poland (World Bank, 1999) suggests that such labels are effective, provided that they are large, prominent, and contain hard-hitting and specific factual information. In Poland, warning labels that occupy 30 percent of each of the two largest sides on the cigarette pack were introduced in the late 1990s have been found to be strongly linked with smokers' decision to quit or cut down their smoking. In Australia and Canada, smokers reported that they were motivated to quit or cut back their consumption after reading the warning labels on the cigarette packs. Table 12.7 presents the requirements of printing health-warning labels on tobacco products. As can be seen, in many countries, tobacco companies are required by law to print health warning labels on all tobacco products, print contents of the cigarette on all cigarette packets etc.

Another tool used by governments to reduce the level of smoking and passive smoking is to impose restrictions on smoking locations (e.g. bans on smoking in workplaces, hospitals, cinemas, restaurants, public transport and other public places).

Tables 12.8 and 12.9 present various restrictions on smoking in public places and public transport, respectively. As can be seen, in most countries, a complete smoking ban is imposed in places such as health care facilities, educational institutions, government buildings, workplace/offices, theatres and cinemas, buses, taxis, trains, trams and domestic and international airports. However, in most countries, a complete ban is not imposed in restaurants, pubs and bars.

Another form of controlling tobacco availability is to impose a legal age limit for buying cigarettes. The research shows that a majority of smokers initiate smoking before age 25, often in childhood or adolescence. For example, in China between 1984 and 1996, there was a significant increase in the number of young men who took up smoking. Table 12.10 presents data on various forms of bans and restrictions on tobacco sale. As can be seen, in most countries, there are no restrictions on selling tobacco products at self-serve shops, mail order or internet sales and the sale of duty-free tobacco products. However, in most countries, there is a complete ban on selling single or unpacked products and giveaway free samples.

12.4   Control Measures to Reduce Tobacco Supply

A number of governments have introduced control measures to reduce the demand for tobacco as well as to reduce the supply of tobacco. Empirical evidence from a number of studies shows that control measures used to reduce the demand for tobacco are more effective than the measures used to control the supply of tobacco. In this section we look at control measures associated with tobacco supply.

Table 12.7 Health warning labels on tobacco products, 51 countries

	Country	Health warnings on tobacco products?	Specification of message placement?	Specification of colour, contrast and font?	Specification of the area to cover?	Specification of the warning size?	Specification of the content?	Specification of the number of messages?	Specification of the language?	Health warnings in tobacco advertising?
1.	Albania	No	No	No	No	No	No	No	No	Yes
2.	Andorra	Yes	Yes	NDA	No	No	Yes	No	NDA	NDA
3.	Armenia	Yes	Yes	Yes	Yes	Yes	Yes	No	Yes	Yes
4.	Austria	Yes	Yes	Yes	Yes	Yes	Yes	Yes	Yes	Yes
5.	Azerbaijan	Yes	No	Yes	No	No	No	No	Yes	NDA
6.	Belarus	Yes	No	No	No	No	Yes	No	Yes	Yes
7.	Belgium	Yes	Yes	Yes	Yes	Yes	Yes	Yes	Yes	NA
8.	Bosnia&Herzegovina	Yes	Yes	Yes	No	No	Yes	Yes	Yes	No
9.	Bulgaria	Yes	Yes	Yes	Yes	Yes	Yes	Yes	Yes	NA
10.	Croatia	Yes	Yes	Yes	No	No	Yes	Yes	Yes	NA
11.	Czech Republic	Yes	Yes	Yes	Yes	Yes	Yes	Yes	Yes	Yes
12.	Denmark	Yes	Yes	Yes	Yes	Yes	Yes	Yes	Yes	NA
13.	Estonia	Yes	Yes	Yes	Yes	Yes	Yes	No	Yes	NA
14.	Finland	Yes	Yes	Yes	Yes	Yes	Yes	Yes	Yes	NA
15.	France	Yes	Yes	Yes	Yes	Yes	Yes	Yes	Yes	NA
16.	Georgia	Yes	Yes	Yes	Yes	Yes	No	No	Yes	Yes
17.	Germany	Yes	Yes	Yes	Yes	Yes	Yes	Yes	Yes	Yes
18.	Greece	Yes	Yes	Yes	Yes	Yes	Yes	Yes	Yes	Yes
19.	Hungary	Yes	Yes	Yes	Yes	Yes	Yes	Yes	Yes	NA
20.	Iceland	Yes	Yes	Yes	Yes	No	Yes	Yes	Yes	NA
21.	Ireland	Yes	Yes	Yes	Yes	Yes	Yes	Yes	Yes	Yes
22.	Israel	Yes	Yes	Yes	No	No	Yes	Yes	Yes	Yes
23.	Italy	Yes	Yes	Yes	Yes	Yes	Yes	Yes	Yes	NA
24.	Kazakhstan	Yes	Yes	No	Yes	Yes	No	No	Yes	No
25.	Kyrgyzstan	No	No	No	No	No	No	No	No	Yes
26.	Latvia	Yes	Yes	No	Yes	Yes	Yes	Yes	Yes	Yes
27.	Lithuania	Yes	Yes	Yes	Yes	Yes	Yes	Yes	Yes	NA
28.	Luxembourg	Yes	Yes	Yes	Yes	Yes	Yes	Yes	Yes	Yes
29.	Malta	Yes	Yes	Yes	Yes	Yes	Yes	Yes	Yes	Yes
30.	Monaco	NDA	NDA	NDA	NDA	No	NDA	NDA	NDA	NDA
31.	Netherlands	Yes	Yes	Yes	Yes	Yes	Yes	Yes	Yes	Yes
32.	Norway	Yes	Yes	Yes	Yes	Yes	Yes	Yes	Yes	NA
33.	Poland	Yes	Yes	Yes	Yes	Yes	Yes	Yes	Yes	NA
34.	Portugal	Yes	Yes	Yes	Yes	Yes	Yes	Yes	Yes	NA
35.	Republic of Moldova	Yes	No	Yes	No	No	Yes	No	Yes	Yes
36.	Romania	Yes	Yes	Yes	Yes	Yes	Yes	Yes	Yes	Yes
37.	Russian Federation	Yes	Yes	Yes	Yes	Yes	Yes	Yes	Yes	Yes
38.	San Marino	NDA	NDA	NDA	NDA	NDA	NDA	NDA	NDA	NDA
39.	Serbia&Montenegro	Yes	Yes	No	No	No	Yes	Yes	No	NA
40.	Slovakia	Yes	Yes	Yes	Yes	Yes	Yes	Yes	Yes	NDA
41.	Slovenia	Yes	Yes	Yes	Yes	Yes	Yes	Yes	Yes	Yes
42.	Spain	Yes	Yes	Yes	Yes	Yes	Yes	Yes	Yes	No
43.	Sweden	Yes	Yes	Yes	Yes	Yes	Yes	Yes	Yes	NA
44.	Switzerland	Yes	Yes	Yes	Yes	Yes	Yes	Yes	Yes	No
45.	Tajikistan	No	No	No	No	No	No	No	No	No
46.	The FYROM	Yes	No	No	No	No	Yes	No	No	No
47.	Turkey	Yes	No	No	No	No	Yes	No	No	NA
48.	Turkmenistan	No	No	No	No	No	No	No	No	No
49.	Ukraine	Yes	Yes	No	Yes	Yes	Yes	Yes	No	Yes
50.	UK	Yes	Yes	Yes	Yes	Yes	Yes	Yes	Yes	Yes
51.	Uzbekistan	No	No	No	No	No	No	No	No	Yes

NDA = No data available; NA = Not applicable.

Table 12.8　Restrictions on smoking in public places, 49 countries

	Country	Health care facilities	Education facilities	Government facilities	Restaurants	Pubs and bars	Workplaces and offices	Theatres and cinemas
1.	Albania	Voluntary agree	Voluntary agree	Voluntary agree	NR	NR	Voluntary agree	Voluntary agree
2.	Andorra	NDA	Complete ban	Complete ban	NR	NR	NR	NDA
3.	Armenia	NR	NR	NR	NR	NR	NR	NR
4.	Austria	Partial restrict	Partial restrict	Partial restrict	NR	NR	Partial restrict	Complete ban
5.	Azerbaijan	Complete ban	Complete ban	Complete ban	Partial restrict	NR	Complete ban	Complete ban
6.	Belarus	Complete ban	Complete ban	Complete ban	Partial restrict	Partial restrict	Partial restrict	Partial restrict
7.	Belgium	Complete ban	Complete ban	Partial restrict	Partial restrict	Partial restrict	Partial restrict	Complete ban
8.	Bosnia&Herzegovina	Complete ban	Complete ban	Partial restrict	Partial restrict	Partial restrict	Partial restrict	Complete ban
9.	Bulgaria	Complete ban	Complete ban	Complete ban	Partial restrict	Partial restrict	Complete ban	Complete ban
10.	Croatia	Complete ban	Complete ban	Complete ban	Partial restrict	Partial restrict	Complete ban	Complete ban
11.	Czech Repub	Complete ban	Complete ban	Partial restrict	Partial restrict	Partial restrict	Partial restrict	Complete ban
12.	Denmark	Partial restrict	Partial restrict	Partial restrict	NR	NR	Partial restrict	Partial restrict
13.	Estonia	Complete ban	Complete ban	Complete ban	Partial restrict	Partial restrict	Complete ban	Complete ban
14.	Finland	Complete ban	Complete ban	Complete ban	Partial restrict	Partial restrict	Complete ban	Complete ban
15.	France	Partial restrict	Partial restrict	Partial restrict	Partial restrict	Partial restrict	Partial restrict	Partial restrict
16.	Georgia	Partial restrict	Partial restrict	Partial restrict	Partial restrict	Partial restrict	Partial restrict	Partial restrict
17.	Germany	NR	Partial restrict	Partial restrict	NR	NR	Partial restrict	Partial restrict
18.	Greece	Complete ban	Complete ban	Complete ban	Partial restrict	Partial restrict	Complete ban	Complete ban
19.	Hungary	Complete ban	Complete ban	Complete ban	Partial restrict	Partial restrict	Complete ban	Partial restrict
20.	Iceland	Complete ban	Complete ban	Complete ban	Partial restrict	Partial restrict	Complete ban	Complete ban
21.	Ireland	Partial restrict	Partial restrict	Partial restrict	Partial restrict	NR	Partial restrict	Partial restrict
22.	Israel	Complete ban	Complete ban	Complete ban	Partial restrict	Partial restrict	Complete ban	Partial restrict
23.	Italy	Complete ban	Complete ban	Complete ban	Partial restrict	NR	Complete ban	Complete ban
24.	Kazakhstan	Complete ban	Complete ban	Complete ban	Partial restrict	Partial restrict	Partial restrict	Complete ban
25.	Kyrgyzstan	NR	NR	NR	NR	NR	NR	NR
26.	Latvia	Complete ban	Complete ban	Partial restrict	Partial restrict	Partial restrict	Partial restrict	Partial restrict
27.	Lithuania	Complete ban	Complete ban	Complete ban	Partial restrict	NR	Complete ban	Complete ban
28.	Luxembourg	Complete ban	Complete ban	NR	NR	NR	NR	Complete ban
29.	Malta	Complete ban	Complete ban	NR	NR	NR	NR	Complete ban
30.	Netherlands	Complete ban	Complete ban	Complete ban	NR	NR	Complete ban	Partial restrict
31.	Norway	Complete ban	Complete ban	Complete ban	Complete ban	Complete ban	Complete ban	Complete ban
32.	Poland	Complete ban	Complete ban	Complete ban	Partial restrict	Partial restrict	Complete ban	Complete ban
33.	Portugal	Partial restrict	Partial restrict	Partial restrict	Voluntary agree	Voluntary agree	Partial restrict	Complete ban
34.	Repub of Moldova	Complete ban	Complete ban	Partial restrict	NR	NR	Partial restrict	Partial restrict
35.	Romania	Complete ban	Complete ban	Complete ban	Partial restrict	Partial restrict	Complete ban	Complete ban
36.	Russian Federation	Complete ban	Complete ban	Complete ban	NR	NR	Complete ban	Complete ban
37.	Serbia&Montenegro	Complete ban	Complete ban	Partial restrict	Partial restrict	NR	Partial restrict	Complete ban
38.	Slovakia	Partial restrict	Complete ban	Complete ban	Partial restrict	Partial restrict	Complete ban	Complete ban
39.	Slovenia	Complete ban	Complete ban	Partial restrict	Partial restrict	NR	Partial restrict	Complete ban
40.	Spain	Complete ban	Complete ban	Partial restrict	NR	NR	Partial restrict	Complete ban
41.	Sweden	Complete ban	Complete ban	Complete ban	Partial restrict	Partial restrict	Complete ban	Complete ban
42.	Switzerland	Voluntary agree	Voluntary agree	Partial restrict	NR	NR	Partial restrict	Voluntary agree
43.	Tajikistan	NR	NR	NR	NR	NR	NR	NR
44.	The FYROM	Complete ban	Complete ban	Complete ban	Partial restrict	Partial restrict	Complete ban	Complete ban
45.	Turkey	Complete ban	Complete ban	NR	NR	NR	Partial restrict	Complete ban
46.	Turkmenistan	Complete ban	Complete ban	Complete ban	NR	NR	Complete ban	Complete ban
47.	Ukraine	Complete ban	Complete ban	Complete ban	NR	NR	Partial restrict	Complete ban
48.	UK	NR	NR	NR	Voluntary agree	Voluntary agree	NR	NR
49.	Uzbekistan	NR	NR	NR	NR	NR	NR	NR

NDA = No data available; NR = No restriction.

The Global Tobacco Industry

While several countries in the world grow tobacco, it is estimated that about 25 countries produce more than 90 percent of the world's tobacco production (WHO, 1997). Table 12.11 provides the top ten tobacco producing countries in the world. As can be seen, China is by far the largest producer of tobacco products producing 36 percent of the world's tobacco followed by the US (11.2 percent) and India (8.3 percent).

Table 12.9 Smoking restrictions on public transport, 51 countries

	Country	Buses	Taxis	Trains	Domestic air transport	International air transport	Domestic water transport	International water transport
1.	Albania	Voluntary agree	Voluntary agree	No restrict	No restrict	Partial restrict	No restrict	Partial restrict
2.	Andorra	Complete ban	NDA	NDA	NDA	NDA	NDA	NDA
3.	Armenia	No restrict	No restrict	No restrict	Not applicable	No restrict	Not applicable	Not applicable
4.	Austria	Complete ban	Voluntary agree	Complete ban	Complete ban	Complete ban	No restrict	No restrict
5.	Azerbaijan	Complete ban	Complete ban	Complete ban	Complete ban	Complete ban	Complete ban	Complete ban
6.	Belarus	Complete ban	Complete ban	Complete ban	Complete ban	Complete ban	Complete ban	Complete ban
7.	Belgium	Complete ban	Complete ban	Partial restrict	Complete ban	No restrict	No restrict	No restrict
8.	Bosnia&Herzegovina	Complete ban	Complete ban	Complete ban	Complete ban	Complete ban	Complete ban	Complete ban
9.	Bulgaria	Complete ban	Complete ban	Partial restrict	Complete ban	Complete ban	No restrict	No restrict
10.	Croatia	Complete ban	Complete ban	Partial restrict	Complete ban	Complete ban	Partial restrict	Partial restrict
11.	Czech Republic	Complete ban	Complete ban	Partial restrict	Complete ban	Complete ban	Complete ban	Not applicable
12.	Denmark	Partial restrict	No restrict	Partial restrict	Voluntary agree	Voluntary agree	Voluntary agree	No restrict
13.	Estonia	Complete ban	Complete ban	Complete ban	Complete ban	Complete ban	Partial restrict	Partial restrict
14.	Finland	Complete ban	Complete ban	Complete ban	Complete ban	Complete ban	Complete ban	Complete ban
15.	France	Complete ban	Complete ban	Partial restrict	Complete ban	Voluntary agree	Partial restrict	Partial restrict
16.	Georgia	Partial restrict	No restrict	Partial restrict	Partial restrict	Partial restrict	Voluntary agree	Voluntary agree
17.	Germany	Complete ban	Partial restrict	Partial restrict	Partial restrict	Partial restrict	No restrict	No restrict
18.	Greece	Complete ban	Complete ban	Partial restrict	Complete ban	Complete ban	Partial restrict	Partial restrict
19.	Hungary	Complete ban	Voluntary agree	Partial restrict	Not applicable	Complete ban	Partial restrict	Partial restrict
20.	Iceland	Complete ban	Complete ban		Complete ban	Complete ban	Partial restrict	Partial restrict
21.	Ireland	Voluntary agree	Complete ban	Partial restrict	Partial restrict	Partial restrict	Partial restrict	Partial restrict
22.	Israel	Partial restrict	Partial restrict	Partial restrict	Complete ban	Complete ban	No restrict	No restrict
23.	Italy	Complete ban	Voluntary agree	Complete ban	Complete ban	Voluntary agree	Complete ban	Voluntary agree
24.	Kazakhstan	Partial restrict	No restrict	Partial restrict	Partial restrict	Partial restrict	Partial restrict	Partial restrict
25.	Kyrgyzstan	No restrict	No restrict	No restrict	No restrict	No restrict	No restrict	No restrict
26.	Latvia	Complete ban	Complete ban	Partial restrict	Complete ban	Partial restrict	Complete ban	Partial restrict
27.	Lithuania	Complete ban	Complete ban	Partial restrict	Complete ban	Complete ban	Complete ban	Complete ban
28.	Luxembourg	Complete ban	No restrict	Partial restrict	Partial restrict	Partial restrict	No restrict	No restrict
29.	Malta	Complete ban	Complete ban	Not applicable	Not applicable	Complete ban	Complete ban	Complete ban
30.	Monaco	NDA	NDA	NDA	NDA	NDA	NDA	NDA
31.	Netherlands	Complete ban	Partial restrict	Complete ban	Complete ban	Complete ban	Complete ban	Complete ban
32.	Norway	Complete ban	Complete ban	Partial restrict	Complete ban	Voluntary agree	Partial restrict	No restrict
33.	Poland	Complete ban	Complete ban	Partial restrict	Complete ban	Complete ban	Partial restrict	Partial restrict
34.	Portugal	Complete ban	Complete ban	Partial restrict	Partial restrict	Voluntary agree	Partial restrict	Partial restrict
35.	Republic of Moldova	Complete ban	Complete ban	Partial restrict	Complete ban	Complete ban	Partial restrict	Not applicable
36.	Romania	Complete ban	No restrict	Complete ban	Complete ban	Voluntary agree	Complete ban	No restrict
37.	Russian Federation	Complete ban	No restrict	Partial restrict	Complete ban	Partial restrict	Complete ban	Partial restrict
38.	San Marino	NDA	NDA	NDA	NDA	NDA	NDA	NDA
39.	Montenegro	Complete ban	No restrict	Partial restrict	Partial restrict	Partial restrict	Partial restrict	Partial restrict
40.	Slovakia	Complete ban	Complete ban	Partial restrict	Complete ban	Partial restrict	Partial restrict	No restrict
41.	Slovenia	Complete ban	Partial restrict	Partial restrict	Partial restrict	Partial restrict	Partial restrict	Partial restrict
42.	Spain	Complete ban	Partial restrict	Partial restrict	Complete ban	Partial restrict	Partial restrict	Partial restrict
43.	Sweden	Complete ban	Complete ban	Complete ban	Complete ban	Complete ban	Complete ban	Partial restrict
44.	Switzerland	Voluntary agree	No restrict	Voluntary agree	Voluntary agree	Voluntary agree	Voluntary agree	Voluntary agree
45.	Tajikistan	No restrict	No restrict	No restrict	No restrict	No restrict	No restrict	No restrict
46.	Republic of Macedonia	Complete ban	Complete ban	Complete ban	Complete ban	Complete ban	Not applicable	Not applicable
47.	Turkey	Complete ban	Voluntary agree	Complete ban	Complete ban	Complete ban	No restrict	No restrict
48.	Turkmenistan	Complete ban	Complete ban	Complete ban	Complete ban	Complete ban	Complete ban	Complete ban
49.	Ukraine	Complete ban	Complete ban	Complete ban	Complete ban	Complete ban	Complete ban	Complete ban
50.	UK	Partial restrict	No restrict	Partial restrict	Partial restrict	Partial restrict	Partial restrict	Partial restrict
51.	Uzbekistan	Partial restrict	No restrict	Partial restrict	No restrict	No restrict	Not applicable	Not applicable

NDA = No data available.

Most of the world tobacco manufacturing industry is controlled by a small number of state monopolies and multinational corporations of which the largest state monopoly is China which produced 1.7 trillion cigarettes in 1997 (about one third of the world production (WHO, 1999). Figure 12.11 shows the top five cigarette producers and their share in total production.

Table 12.10 Various types of bans and restrictions on the sale of tobacco products, 50 countries

	Country	Vending machines	Self-service displays	Mail order or electronic sales	Single or unpacked cigarettes	Sale of duty free tobacco products	Free samples of cigarettes
1.	Albania	No restrict	No restrict	No restrict	No restrict	No restrict	No restrict
2.	Andorra	No restrict	No restrict	No restrict	No restrict	No restrict	No restrict
3.	Armenia	No restrict	No restrict	No restrict	No restrict	No restrict	No restrict
4.	Austria	No restrict	No restrict	No restrict	Partial restrict	Partial restrict	Partial restrict
5.	Azerbaijan	Complete ban	No restrict	No restrict	Complete ban	No restrict	Complete ban
6.	Belarus	Complete ban	Partial restrict	No restrict	No restrict	Partial restrict	Partial restrict
7.	Belgium	Partial restrict	No restrict	No restrict	Complete ban	Partial restrict	Complete ban
8.	Bosnia&Herzegovina	Complete ban	No restrict	No restrict	Complete ban	No restrict	No restrict
9.	Bulgaria	No restrict	No restrict	No restrict	No restrict	No restrict	No restrict
10.	Croatia	Complete ban	Partial restrict	Partial restrict	Complete ban	Partial restrict	Complete ban
11.	Czech Republic	Partial restrict	No restrict	No restrict	Complete ban	No restrict	Complete ban
12.	Denmark	No restrict	No restrict	No restrict	Complete ban	Partial restrict	Complete ban
13.	Estonia	Complete ban	No restrict	No restrict	Complete ban	No restrict	No restrict
14.	Finland	Partial restrict	Partial restrict	No restrict	Complete ban	Partial restrict	Complete ban
15.	France	Complete ban	Complete ban	Complete ban	Complete ban	Partial restrict	Complete ban
16.	Georgia	No restrict	No restrict	No restrict	Complete ban	No restrict	No restrict
17.	Germany	Partial restrict	No restrict	No restrict	Partial restrict	Partial restrict	Partial restrict
18.	Greece	No restrict	No restrict	No restrict	Complete ban	Partial restrict	Partial restrict
19.	Hungary	Partial restrict	No restrict	No restrict	Complete ban	No restrict	Complete ban
20.	Iceland	Complete ban	Complete ban	No restrict	Complete ban	No restrict	Complete ban
21.	Ireland	No restrict	No restrict	No restrict	Complete ban	Partial restrict	Complete ban
22.	Israel	Partial restrict	No restrict	No restrict	No restrict	No restrict	Complete ban
23.	Italy	Partial restrict	Complete ban	Partial restrict	Complete ban	Partial restrict	Complete ban
24.	Kazakhstan	Complete ban	Complete ban	Complete ban	Complete ban	No restrict	Partial restrict
25.	Kyrgyzstan	No restrict	No restrict	No restrict	No restrict	No restrict	No restrict
26.	Latvia	Complete ban	No restrict	No restrict	Complete ban	No restrict	Complete ban
27.	Lithuania	Complete ban	No restrict	No restrict	Complete ban	No restrict	Complete ban
28.	Luxembourg	No restrict	No restrict	No restrict	No restrict	Partial restrict	Complete ban
29.	Malta	Partial restrict	No restrict	No restrict	Complete ban	No restrict	Complete ban
30.	Monaco	NDA	NDA	NDA	NDA	NDA	No restrict
31.	Netherlands	Partial restrict	No restrict	No restrict	Complete ban	Partial restrict	Complete ban
32.	Norway	Complete ban	No restrict	Complete ban	Complete ban	No restrict	Complete ban
33.	Poland	Complete ban	No restrict	No restrict	Complete ban	No restrict	Complete ban
34.	Portugal	Partial restrict	No restrict	No restrict	Complete ban	Partial restrict	Partial restrict
35.	Republic of Moldova	No restrict	No restrict	No restrict	Complete ban	No restrict	No restrict
36.	Romania	Partial restrict	No restrict	No restrict	Complete ban	No restrict	No restrict
37.	Russian Federation	Complete ban	No restrict	No restrict	Complete ban	No restrict	No restrict
38.	San Marino	NDA	NDA	NDA	NDA	NDA	No restrict
39.	Montenegro	No restrict	No restrict	No restrict	No restrict	No restrict	No restrict
40.	Slovakia	Complete ban	Complete ban	Complete ban	Complete ban	Complete ban	Complete ban
41.	Slovenia	Complete ban	No restrict	No restrict	Complete ban	No restrict	Complete ban
42.	Spain	Partial restrict	No restrict	No restrict	No restrict	Partial restrict	No restrict
43.	Sweden	Partial restrict	Partial restrict	Partial restrict	Complete ban	Partial restrict	Partial restrict
44.	Switzerland	No restrict	Voluntary	Voluntary	No restrict	No restrict	Partial restrict
45.	Tajikistan	No restrict	No restrict	No restrict	No restrict	No restrict	No restrict
46.	The FYROM	No restrict	No restrict	No restrict	No restrict	No restrict	Complete ban
47.	Turkey	No restrict	No restrict	No restrict	Complete ban	No restrict	Complete ban
48.	Turkmenistan	No restrict	No restrict	No restrict	No restrict	No restrict	No restrict
49.	Ukraine	Complete ban	Partial restrict	No restrict	Complete ban	No restrict	Complete ban
49.	UK	Partial restrict	Voluntary	Partial restrict	Complete ban	Partial restrict	Complete ban
50.	Uzbekistan	No restrict	No restrict	No restrict	No restrict	No restrict	Partial restrict

Table 12.11   World's 10 leading producers of un-manufactured tobacco, 1994

Rank	Country	Production (000' tonnes)	Percentage of world total
1	China	2,088	36.3
2	US	641	11.2
3	India	475	8.3
4	Brazil	365	6.4
5	Turkey	176	3.1
6	Zimbabwe	153	2.7
7	Indonesia	137	2.4
8	Greece	125	2.2
9	Italy	114	2.0
10	Pakistan	96	1.7

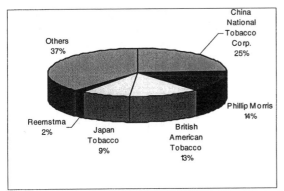

Figure 12.11   Top five cigarette producers and their percentage share in the total world production, 1997

While empirical evidence from a number of countries shows that the demand based tobacco control policies used to reduce the demand for tobacco are having a positive impact, the tobacco supply control measures are not as effective as expected. The supply control measures considered by various governments include control of tobacco cultivation, import bans and trade restrictions. To control tobacco cultivation, some governments encouraged farmers, especially in the developing countries, to undertake a crop substitution. However, as tobacco is considered to be a cash crop by many farmers, especially in the developing countries, crop substitution is not considered as an attractive option to many farmers unless they were given a lot of incentive to change crop. So far there is no research evidence available to show that crop substitution has reduced the tobacco consumption.

Smuggling

The trade and import restrictions of tobacco led to tobacco smuggling in a number of countries. Figure 12.12 shows the smuggled cigarettes from the US/UK as a percentage of consumption in a selected number of countries in 1999 (Joy de Beyer, 2002). As can be seen, in some countries like Israel, the percentage is as high as 44 percent. Tobacco smuggling has now become an important component of the tobacco control policy equation. Some research shows that it has now become essential to put in place control measures to reduce the supply of smuggled tobacco into the market in order to have an effective tobacco control policy.

Smuggling of tobacco is a major problem to a number of governments for several reasons. The higher taxes and price differentials between countries encourage smugglers to smuggle tobacco to make quick profits. When a government uses tax on tobacco as a tobacco control policy tool to reduce the demand for tobacco, the tobacco made available through smuggling in the black market defeats the effort by making cheaper tobacco available to smokers. In addition, tobacco smuggling effectively reduces government revenue through lost taxes and hence public health care facilities. Some tobacco companies encourage tobacco smuggling as it lowers the price of tobacco which will in turn simulate the

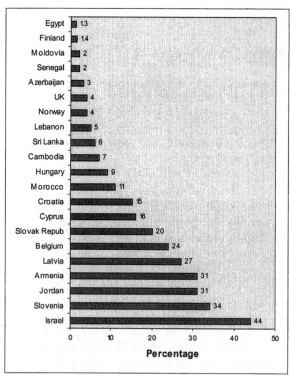

Figure 12.12 Smuggled cigarettes as a proportion of consumption, 1999

demand for tobacco products. As evidence to this fact, a number of senior tobacco company executives have been convicted by courts for being actively involved in tobacco smuggling in a number of countries.

Like any other smuggling, tobacco smuggling could also increase the level of crime and corruption in the society, adding another problem for governments. Evidence (e.g., see Joy de Beyer, 2002) shows that in countries where more than 10 percent of tobacco supply comes from smuggling (for example in Spain, Italy, Pakistan, Nigeria, Yugoslavia, Ukraine, Moldova, Colombia, Iran, Austria, Cambodia), the price of tobacco is low and on the other hand in countries where smuggling tobacco forms less than 5 percent of total tobacco supply (for example in Sweden, Denmark, Norway, France, Finland and Ireland) the price of tobacco is higher. Research also shows that, in a number of countries, effective control measures have been placed on tobacco smuggling. This, together with the imposition of higher tobacco taxes, has resulted in increases in government revenue, whilst, at the same time, reducing the consumption of tobacco.

In order to reduce the level of smuggling, governments put in place a number of measures such as high penalties for smuggling, printing special markings on cigarette packets to confirm that taxes have been paid, banning unlicensed tobacco manufacturers, importers/exporters, sellers and distributors and asking them to keep records of all their activities, having links with all customs departments around the world to capture tobacco smugglers.

12.5 Concluding Comments

In this chapter we looked at both demand and supply tobacco control measures used to reduce tobacco consumption. One of the important demand side control tools is additional taxes on tobacco products. While it is universally accepted that a price increase through additional tax on tobacco products would decrease consumption of tobacco, some argue that it may also significantly reduce the government tax revenue and employment. A number of studies showed that in the short to medium term while tobacco tax reduces consumption it will also increase government revenue (for example, a 10 percent tax would increase the revenue by 7 percent). It is also found that in the medium to long-term, the revenue saved in health costs would increase resources that could be deployed to find new employment for tobacco industry workers who may loose their jobs. The non-price control measures such as bans on tobacco advertising, printing bigger warning labels on packages and providing adults the needed information to make an informed choice, restrictions on tobacco sales to the public and smoking in public places, increased access to nicotine replacement therapy (NRT) would also help to reduce the demand for tobacco products.

On the supply side tobacco control measures such as the crop substitution and controlling the smuggling of tobacco are widely discussed. While crop substitution is a possibility, it does not appear to be working effectively. However, it has been found that measures to control smuggling of tobacco could help reduce tobacco consumption and have been successfully implemented.

Table 12.12 presents the information on national action plans and co-ordinating bodies available across countries. As can be seen, in most countries, some kind of national tobacco action plan, government policies specifically targeting tobacco consumption, national co-ordinating body for tobacco control and intervention to prevent initiation of tobacco and to protect non-smokers exists.

Table 12.12 National action plans and co-ordinating bodies, 50 countries

	Country	National tobacco action plan exists?	Specific targets on tobacco in government policy?	National coordinating body for tobacco control?	Interventions to prevent initiation of tobacco use?	Interventions to protect non-smokers?
1.	Albania	No	No	No	Yes	Yes
2.	Andorra	No	NDA	No	Yes	No
3.	Armenia	Yes	Yes	Yes	Yes	No
4.	Austria	No	No	No	Yes	Yes
5.	Azerbaijan	Yes	Yes	Yes	Yes	No
6.	Belarus	No	No	Yes	Yes	Yes
7.	Belgium	No	No	No	Yes	Yes
8.	Bosnia&Herzegovina	Yes	Yes	Yes	Yes	Yes
9.	Bulgaria	Yes	Yes	Yes	Yes	Yes
10.	Croatia	No	Yes	Yes	Yes	Yes
11.	Czech Republic	No	Yes	No	Yes	Yes
12.	Denmark	Yes	Yes	Yes	Yes	Yes
13.	Estonia	Yes	Yes	Yes	Yes	Yes
14.	Finland	Yes	Yes	No	Yes	Yes
15.	France	Yes	Yes	Yes	Yes	Yes
16.	Georgia	Yes	Yes	Yes	Yes	Yes
17.	Germany	No	Yes	No	Yes	Yes
18.	Greece	No	No	Yes	Yes	Yes
19.	Hungary	Yes	Yes	No	Yes	Yes
20.	Iceland	Yes	Yes	Yes	Yes	Yes
21.	Ireland	Yes	Yes	Yes	Yes	Yes
22.	Israel	NDA	NDA	NDA	NDA	NDA
23.	Italy	Yes	Yes	No	Yes	Yes
24.	Kazakhstan	No	No	Yes	Yes	Yes
25.	Kyrgyzstan	No	Yes	No	Yes	Yes
26.	Latvia	No	No	Yes	Yes	Yes
27.	Lithuania	Yes	Yes	No	Yes	Yes
28.	Luxembourg	NDA	NDA	NDA	NDA	NDA
29.	Malta	No	No	Yes	Yes	Yes
30.	Monaco	NDA	NDA	NDA	NDA	NDA
31.	Netherlands	Yes	Yes	Yes	Yes	Yes
32.	Norway	Yes	Yes	Yes	Yes	Yes
33.	Poland	Yes	Yes	Yes	Yes	Yes
34.	Portugal	Yes	Yes	Yes	Yes	Yes
35.	Republic of Moldova	No	Yes	Yes	No	Yes
36.	Romania	No	No	NDA	Yes	No
37.	Russian Federation	Yes	Yes	Yes	Yes	No
38.	San Marino	NDA	NDA	NDA	NDA	NDA
39.	Serbia&Montenegro	Yes	Yes	Yes	Yes	Yes
40.	Slovakia	Yes	Yes	Yes	Yes	Yes
41.	Slovenia	Yes	Yes	Yes	Yes	Yes
42.	Spain	Yes	Yes	Yes	Yes	Yes
43.	Sweden	Yes	Yes	Yes	Yes	Yes
44.	Switzerland	Yes	No	Yes	Yes	Yes
45.	Tajikistan	No	No	NDA	No	No
46.	The FYROM	Yes	Yes	Yes	Yes	Yes
47.	Turkey	No	No	Yes	Yes	Yes
48.	Turkmenistan	No	No	No	Yes	Yes
49.	Ukraine	No	NDA	Yes	Yes	Yes
50.	UK	Yes	Yes	Yes	Yes	No
51.	Uzbekistan	No	No	No	Yes	No

NDA - No data available.

Chapter 13

Consumption Patterns of
Five Consumer Goods: A Summary

Many of the issues related to the consumption of food, soft drinks, tobacco, alcohol and marijuana are common to most countries. The cross-country analysis presented in this book involved a number of countries with similar lifestyles and provides convincing evidence regarding the consumption of these commodities. We have presented an extensive three-dimensional analysis on the consumption patterns of five consumer goods across countries and over time. The consumer goods considered in this book are both important and controversial. The commodities included in the analysis are (1) food, one of the basic necessity for all consumers; (2) soft drinks, a necessity for some consumers and a luxury for others; (3) alcohol and tobacco, two of the most commonly used licit drugs; and (4) marijuana, the most commonly used illicit drug. The countries considered in the study are a number of developed as well as developing countries. The time period considered are the most recent wherever possible. This chapter presents an overall summary of the conclusions about the consumption patterns of the five consumer goods presented in Chapters 1 to 12.

13.1   Food Consumption

An overview of the basic data for food shows that, at sample means, while consumers in the developing countries allocate about one-third of their income on food (ranging from 15 percent for Singapore to 53 percent for the Philippines), consumers from developed countries (OECD) allocate less than one fifth of their income on food (ranging from 12 percent for the US to 32 percent for Greece). For the world as a whole, on average, consumers allocate about one fourth of their income on food. Aggregate food prices, on average, increased in the developing countries at about double the rate of increase in the developed countries (about 6 percent). However, the consumption of food increased, on average, at about the same rate in both groups of countries (about 0.8 percent per annum).

A plot of the food budget share versus the income for a number of countries identifies an approximate inverse linear relationship between the two variables, supporting the well-known *Engel's law*, which states that the budget share for food falls with increasing income. A plot of the relative consumption of food against the relative price of food for a number of countries shows an approximate negative linear relationship supporting the basic law in economics, the *law of demand*. The slope of this plot is -0.4, which can be interpreted as an estimate of the consumption parameter, the income flexibility (which is considered as an international constant and equal to a value between -0.4 and -0.7). The average estimated marginal share of food for a world consumer is 0.144 indicating that when income increases by one dollar, 14.4 cents of that increase will be allocated to food. The estimated average income elasticity across countries for food is 0.6 (less than one) implying that food is a necessity for consumers in any country. When the countries are grouped into developed and developing countries, the average food income elasticity is 0.5 (for developed countries) and 0.7 (for developing countries). The estimated average own price elasticity across countries for food is -0.3 and indicates that internationally the demand for food is price inelastic.

13.2   Soft Drinks Consumption

In developing countries, the proportion of income allocated to expenditure on soft drinks by consumers is almost as twice as that of consumers in developed countries. On average, world consumers allocate about one percent of their income on soft drinks. The prices of soft drinks increased at a faster rate in the developing countries (at a rate of about 12 percent per annum) than in the developed countries (at a rate of about 7 percent per annum). However, the consumption of soft drinks grew at a rate of 3-4 percent in both group countries. A plot of the soft drinks budget share versus the income identifies an approximate inverse linear relationship between these two variables (as in the case of food), supporting the well-known *Engel's law*. A plot of relative consumption of soft drinks against relative price of soft drinks shows an approximate negative linear relationship supporting the basic economic law, the *law of demand*. The slope of this plot is -0.9, which can be interpreted as an estimate of the consumption parameter, the income flexibility. The average estimated marginal share of soft drink for a world consumer is 0.097 which indicates that when income increases by one dollar, 9.7 cents of that increase will be allocated to soft drinks. The estimated average income elasticity across countries for soft drinks is 1.1 (greater than one) which indicates that it is internationally a luxury. When the countries are grouped into developed and developing countries, the average income elasticity for soft drink is 0.97 (for developed countries) and 1.34 (for developing countries) indicating that soft drink is a necessity in developed countries and a luxury in the developing countries. The estimated average own price elasticity across countries for soft drink is -0.6 which indicates that internationally the demand for soft drinks is price inelastic.

13.3   Tobacco Consumption

On average, world consumers allocate about 3 percent of their income on tobacco consumption. Even though tobacco is well-known for its harmful health effects, consumer allocation on tobacco expenditure is still 3 times the allocation on soft drinks. Across the world, on average, tobacco consumption has fallen at a rate of 0.6 percent per annum and tobacco prices have increased at a rate of 10.5 percent per annum. A plot of the tobacco budget share versus the income identifies an approximate inverse linear relationship between these two variables, supporting the well-known *Engel's law*. A plot of relative consumption of tobacco against relative price of food shows an approximate negative linear relationship supporting the basic economic law, the *law of demand*. The slope of this plot is -0.7, which can be interpreted as an estimate of the consumption parameter, the income flexibility. The average estimated marginal share of tobacco for a world consumer is 0.023 which indicates that when income increases by one dollar, 2.3 cents of that increase will be allocated to tobacco. The estimated average income elasticity across countries for tobacco is 0.8 (less than one) indicates that it is internationally a necessity (while in a number of individual countries it is considered a luxury). When the countries are grouped into developed and developing countries, the average income elasticity for tobacco is 0.7 (for developed countries) and 0.97 (for developing countries). The estimated average own-price elasticity across countries for tobacco is -0.5, which indicates that internationally the demand for tobacco is price inelastic.

One of the important surveys on students' daily smoking among the 10th grade students (ESPAD, 2000) reveal that among the European countries the highest rate of smoking among the school students has been reported in the UK (20 percent) followed by Ireland (18 percent) and Moscow (16 percent). The least students smoking has been reported in Greece, Former Yogoslav Republic of Macedonia and Romania (all 4 percent). Recent data on annual per capita cigarette consumption reveals that all around the world the per capita cigarette consumption has fallen from 1980, except the South East Asian countries. The recent mean per capita cigarette consumption in the regions Africa, America, East Mediterranean, Europe, South East Asia and Western Pacific are 553, 1023, 1120, 2132, 640 and 1621, respectively. It also appears in all these regions, the average price of a packet of foreign brand cigarettes is higher than the domestic brand cigarettes.

In terms of 1996 per adult consumption of number of cigarettes among the population aged 15 and over, the top 6 countries are Greece (3474 cigarettes), Japan (3193 cigarettes), Poland (3180 cigarettes), South Korea (2993 cigarettes), Switzerland (2658) and Hungary (2645 cigarettes).   The number of cigarettes consumed per person has declined in a number of countries over the last two decades. On a scale where 1 indicates country with the highest consumption, the most significant improvements between 1986 and 1996 have been observed in Australia (rank improved from 9th to 17th), Canada (8th to 16th) and the US (6th to 14th). On the other hand, a decline in performance have been observed in China (35th to 20th), Germany (27th to 15th), Netherlands (38th to 30th), Portugal (32nd to

18th) and Turkey (24th to 9th). A cross-country comparison of prevalence of daily smoking of the adult population in a number of OECD countries reveals that the prevalence has declined in the last three decades. This prevalence is about one in three of the adult population in Japan, Korea, Luxembourg, Netherlands and Norway and less than one in five in Australia, Canada, Sweden and the US. Data from a number of countries also shows that there is not much significance in the difference of male and female smoking. However, socioeconomic characteristics such as level of education, labour force status, income status, ethnic background and marital status have some influence on the level of smoking.

13.4   Alcohol Consumption

On average, world consumers allocate about 3 percent of their income on alcohol consumption. Across the world, on average, alcohol consumption has increased at a rate 0.8 percent per annum and alcohol prices have increased at a rate of 9.6 percent per annum. A plot of the alcohol budget share versus the income identifies an approximate inverse linear relationship between these two variables, supporting the well-known *Engel's law*. A plot of relative consumption of alcohol against relative price of alcohol shows an approximate negative linear relationship, supporting the basic economic law, the *law of demand*. The slope of this plot is -0.3, which can be interpreted as an estimate of the consumption parameter, the income flexibility. The average estimated marginal share of alcohol for a world consumer is 0.03 which indicates that when income increases by one dollar, 3 cents of that increase will be allocated to alcohol. The estimated average income elasticity across countries for alcohol is 0.96 (less than one) which indicates that it is internationally a necessity or near luxury (in a number of individual countries it is considered a luxury).   When the countries are grouped into developed and developing countries, the average income elasticity for alcohol is 0.8 (for developed countries) and 1.1 (for developing countries) indicating that alcohol is a necessity in most developed countries and a luxury in developing countries. The estimated average own price elasticity across countries for alcohol is -0.5 which indicates that internationally the demand for alcohol is price inelastic.

The ESPAD (2000) also reveals that the proportion of 10th grade students who have reported that they have consumed any alcohol in the past 30 days was 40 percent for the US and 61 percent for the European countries. Proportion of these students who have reported that they have used alcohol at least 10 times during the last 30 days of the survey is the highest in Malta (20 percent) followed by Denmark (18 percent) and the UK and Ireland (16 percent). The lowest percentage has been reported in Finland and Iceland (both 1 percent). Recent per capita pure alcohol consumption data of the world shows that Ireland is ranked as number 1 (12.3 litres of pure alcohol per capita), Luxembourg as number 2 (12.1 litres of pure alcohol per capita) and Romania as number 3 (11.7 litres of pure alcohol per capita).

Among the ranks, the first 18 countries are from Europe, followed by Australia (7.8 litres of pure alcohol per capita).

The 1996 per adult international consumption figures from 147 countries reveal that Czech Republic (9.83 litres), Ireland (9.32 litres) and Germany (8.01 litres) lead the world in beer consumption and France (8.91 litres), Portugal (8.81 litres) and Slovenia (8.50 litres) leads the world in wine consumption and Guyana (13.05 litres), South Korea (11.97 litres) and Bahamas (9.82 litres) leads the world in spirits consumption. Results from a number of surveys reveal that alcohol is mostly consumed at home, friends' home, private parties and in licensed premises. The results also reveal that a significant section of youngsters (about 10 percent) consume alcohol in cars, which is a matter for concern for the road traffic authorities. Data from a number of countries also shows that there is a significant difference in the amount of drinking between the male and female populations. Also socioeconomic characteristics such as level of education, labour force status, income status, ethnic background and marital status have some influence on the level of drinking. The risk of harm in the long term due to alcohol consumption appears to be high among the 20-29 year age group.

The cross-country disaggregated analysis of alcohol into beer, wine and spirits for the ten OECD countries (Australia, Canada, Finland, France, Japan, New Zealand, Norway, Sweden, UK and US) reveal that in most countries there is a shift in consumption into wine at the expense of beer and spirits. The prices of beer, wine and spirits have increased in all ten countries. On average, consumers allocate 2.3 percent of their income on beer, 0.9 percent of their income on wine and 1.6 percent of their income on spirits with a total of 4.8 percent of their income on alcohol as a whole. Within alcohol, the alcohol expenditure is divided as 46 percent on beer, 20 percent on wine and the remaining 34 percent on spirits. A plot of relative consumption of each beverage against its relative price shows an approximate negative linear relationship, again supporting the basic economic law, the *law of demand*. The estimated average income elasticity across the ten countries for beer, wine and spirits are, 0.75, 0.98 and 1.39, respectively indicating that beer is a necessity, wine a near luxury and spirits is a luxury. The estimated average own-price elasticity for beer, wine and spirits are -0.2, -0.4 and -0.3, indicating that the demand for all three beverages is price inelastic. These elasticity estimates are reasonably well in agreement with the results reported in previous studies.

13.5   Marijuana Consumption

The ESPAD survey also reveals that the proportion of students who have used marijuana during the last 30 days among the European countries and the US is the highest in France (22 percent) followed by US (19 percent) and the UK (16 percent). The least percentage has been reported in Cyprus, Faroe Island and Romania (all 1 percent). This survey also reveals that the proportion of boys and girls who have used marijuana during the last 30 days of the survey is higher for boys than girls in all European countries with highest incidence being in France (25 percent for boys and 19 percent for girls). Another survey that compares the once a week marijuana use among 14-25 years from CDHFS (1997) reveals that the proportion of males consuming marijuana are almost twice that of females. The proportion of males in the UK and Australia is about 37 percent. A comparison of the illicit drug use in the past month among the over 15 year old population in 2000/01 among Australia, Canada, New Zealand, UK and the US reveals that the proportion of New Zealanders consuming marijuana (20 percent) is more than two times that of all other countries, except Australia (15 percent). The other popular illicit drugs in these countries are amphetamines, ecstasy and opiates in that order. Survey data from a number of countries also reveals that the main route of access to marijuana is through friends/relatives and there is significance difference in the amount of consumption of marijuana between male and female. Also socioeconomic characteristics such as level education, labour force status, income status, ethnic background and marital status have some influence in the level of marijuana consumption.

Based on Australian data we estimated the income elasticity of marijuana as 1.2 (grater than one) indicating that it is a luxury. The own-price elasticity of marijuana is -0.3, indicating the demand for marijuana is price inelastic. All the cross-price elasticities between marijuana and the other three beverages are positive indicating that marijuana, beer, wine and spirits are pairwise substitutes.

13.6   Overall Drug Usage

In general, it appears that among the three drugs alcohol, tobacco and marijuana, alcohol is the most consumed (every 4 in 5 adults) followed by tobacco (every 1 in 4 adults) and marijuana (every one in 10). Based on the analysis, it also appears that tobacco and alcohol are not considered as associated with a 'drug problem' by most consumers while a significant proportion believe that marijuana is. Many consumers also believe that the consumption of alcohol and tobacco either directly or indirectly cause death but not marijuana. While every one in three persons gave personal approval for the regular use of tobacco and every two in three persons gave personal approval for the regular use of alcohol, only every one in five persons gave personal approval for the regular use of marijuana. This indicates that there is a greater concern in society about the use of marijuana compared to the use of tobacco and alcohol.

13.7   Empirical Regularities in Consumption Patterns

The book also identified a number of empirical regularities in the consumption patterns of food, soft drinks, alcohol (beer, wine and spirits), tobacco and marijuana. These empirical regularities include,

- The *Engel's Law* (an inverse relationship between budget share and income)
- The Law of Demand (all other things being equal, an increase in the relative price of a commodity causes its consumption to fall)
- Demand homogeneity (demand functions are homogeneous of degree zero or an equiproportionate change in income and prices results in unchanged consumption of each good or, in other words, the consumer does not suffer from money illusion)
- Substitution effects are symmetrical (when real income is held constant, the effect of an increase in the price of commodity j on the demand for i is equal to the effect of a price increase of commodity i on the demand for j also known as Slutsky symmetry)
- Consumers' tastes are preference independent (marginal utility of good i is independent of the consumption of j or consumers' taste can be described by means of a utility function which is the sum of *n*-sub utility functions, one for each good).

13.8   Alcohol and Tobacco Control Policies

In this book, we also presented detailed statistics on the level of misuse of alcohol and the various alcohol control instruments and preventative programmes put in place by governments in a number of countries. In summary, the statistics show that, in most countries, liver cirrhosis death rate and the rate of alcohol related accidents has declined in the last 2 decades. In many countries, restrictions on alcohol sale are used as an instrument to control the supply of alcohol. While many governments allow alcohol advertising, a number of restrictions such as time of the day that alcohol advertisements can be shown on electronic media, health warning label requirements and the type of advertisements that can be telecast are in place and a strict alcohol industry code of advertising is also in place in many countries. Almost all countries have put in place serious restrictions such as lowering the allowable Blood Alcohol Concentration (BAC) limit using Random Breath Testing (RBT) and heavy penalties and/or imprisonment for drink-driving related offences. While a majority of countries use alcohol taxes as an instrument to raise government revenue, some countries genuinely use it as an alcohol control tool. Raising taxes on alcoholic beverages obviously increases their retail prices, hence making it too expensive for middle-income and low-income groups to consume excessive alcohol. In many countries, the total tax burden as a percentage of retail price is higher for spirits (which has the highest alcohol content), followed by beer and then wine. A number of governments have also banned the consumption and sale of alcohol from public buildings, hospitals and sporting events. Most of the countries also attempt to implement a national action plan on alcohol and carry out regular surveys on the level of alcohol consumption among their population.

The analysis in the book also revealed that a number of demand and supply control measures are put in place by many governments to reduce the consumption of tobacco. One of the important demand control tools is additional taxes on tobacco products. While it is universally accepted that a price increase through additional tax on tobacco products would decrease consumption of tobacco, some argue that it may also significantly reduce the government tax revenue and employment. A number of studies also showed that in the short to medium term while tobacco tax reduces consumption it will also increase government revenue (for example, a 10 percent tax would increase the revenue by 7 percent). It is also found that in the medium to long-term, the revenue saved in health costs would increase resources that could be deployed to find new employment for tobacco industry workers who may lose their jobs. The non-price control measures such as bans on tobacco advertising, printing bigger warning labels on packages and providing adults the needed information to make an informed choice, restrictions on tobacco sales to the public and smoking in public places, increased access to nicotine replacement therapy (NRT) would also help to reduce the demand for tobacco products.

On the supply side tobacco control measures such as the crop substitution and controlling the smuggling of tobacco are widely discussed. While crop substitution is a possibility, it does not appear to be working effectively. However, it has been found that measures to control smuggling of tobacco could help reduce tobacco consumption and have been successfully implemented.

In most countries, some kind of national tobacco action plan exist and many include, government policies specifically targeting tobacco consumption, a national co-ordinating body for tobacco control and intervention to prevent initiation of tobacco use and to protect non-smokers.

Bibliography

AIHW (2000a). '1998 National Drug Strategy Household Survey – Detailed Findings,' *Drug Statistics Series*, No.6, AIHW Cat. No. PHE-27, Australian Institute of Health and Welfare, Canberra.

AIHW (2000b). 'Statistics on Drug Use in Australia 1998,' *Drug Statistics Series*, No.7, Australian Institute of Health and Welfare, Canberra.

AIHW (2001). 'Statistics on Drug Use in Australia 2000,' *Drug statistics series*, No.8, Australian Institute of Health and Welfare, Canberra.

AIHW (2002a). '2001 National Drug Strategy Household Survey – First Results,' *Drug Statistics Series*, No.9, Australian Institute of Health and Welfare, Canberra.

AIHW (2002b). '2001 National Drug Strategy Household Survey – Detailed Findings,' *Drug Statistics Series*, No.11, Australian Institute of Health and Welfare, Canberra.

AIHW (2003). 'Statistics on Drug Use in Australia 2002,' *Drug statistics series*, No.12, Australian Institute of Health and Welfare, Canberra.

Allen, R.G.D. and A.L. Bowley (1935). *Family Expenditure*. London: P.S. King and Son.

Andrikopoulos, A.A and J. Loizides (2000). 'The Demand for Home-Produced and Imported Alcoholic Beverages in Cyprus: The AIDS Approach,' *Applied Economics* 32: 1111-1119.

ATF (2003). Bureau of Alcohol, Tobacco, Firearms and Explosives, US Department of Justice. http://www.atf.treas.gov/alcohol/stats/.

Australian Bureau of Criminal Intelligence (1996). *Australian Illicit Drug Report*. Canberra: ABCI.

Australian Federal Police (1991). *Illicit Drugs in Australia, Situation Report*. Canberra: AFP.

Bari, E. and A.A.Yurekli (2003). *Children's Exposure to Environmental Smoke*. World Bank, Washington DC, USA.

Barnard, G.A. (1963). 'In discussion,' *Journal of the Royal Statistical Society*, Series B, 25: 294.

Barnett, W.A. (1979). 'Theoretical Foundations for the Rotterdam Model,' *Review of Economic Studies* 46: 109-130.

Barnett, W.A. (1981). *Consumer Demand and Labour Supply: Goods, Monetary Assets and Time*. Amsterdam: North-Holland Publishing Company.

Barten, A.P. (1964). 'Consumer Demand Functions Under Conditions of Almost Additive Preferences,' *Econometrica* 32: 1-38.

Barten, A.P. (1969). 'Maximum Likelihood Estimation of a Complete System of Demand Equations,' *European Economic Review* 1: 7-73.

Barten, A.P. (1977). 'The Systems of Consumer Demand Functions Approach: A Review,' *Econometrica* 45: 23-51.

Barten, A.P., L. Bettendorf, E. Meyermans and P. Zonderman (1989). *Users' Guide to DEMMOD-3*. Kathlieke Universiteit Leuven, Belgium.

BBC (2000). *BBC News: 20 September 2000*, British Broadcasting Corporation; http://news.bbc.co.uk/l/hi/health/933430.stm.

Bera, A.K., R.P. Byron and C.M. Jarque (1981). 'Further Evidence on Asymptotic Tests for Homogeneity and Symmetry in Large Demand Systems,' *Economics Letters* 8: 101-105.

Besag, J., and P.J. Diggle (1977). 'Simple Monte Carlo Tests for Spatial Patterns,' *Applied Statistics* 26: 327-333.

BBC News (2000). 'Huge Rise in Alcohol Related Deaths,' BBC World Service, 10 May 2000. http://news.bbc.co.uk/1/hi/health/.

Bewley, R.A. (1983). 'Tests of Restrictions in Large Demand Systems,' *European Economic Review* 20: 257-269.

Bewley, R.A. (1986). *Allocation Models: Specification, Estimation and Applications.* Cambridge, Mass.: Ballinger Publishing Company.

Blundell, R. (1988). 'Consumer Behaviour: Theory and Empirical Evidence - A Survey,' *Economic Journal* 98: 16-65.

Brewers Association of Canada (1997). *Alcoholic Beverage Taxation and Control Policies: International Survey,* Ninth Edition, Ottawa, Ontario, Canada.

Brown, A. and A. Deaton (1972). 'Surveys in Applied Economics: Models of Consumer Behaviour,' *Economic Journal* 82: 1145-1236.

Brown, L.P. (1995). 'Why the United States Will Never Legalise Drugs,' *Vital Speeches of the Day* 61: 628-9.

Brown, L.R (1999). *Vital Signs.* Worldwatch Institute, Washington DC, USA.

Cameron, L. and J. Williams (2001). 'Cannabis, alcohol and cigarettes: substitutes or complements?' *Economic Record* 77(236): 19-34.

CASH (2002). Media Release, Cancer Council of Australia, Canberra, Australia, January 8, 2002.

Cassel, G. (1932). *The Theory of Social Economy.* Edition translated from the Fifth German Edition by S.L. Barrow. New York: Harcourt, Brace.

CCSA (2003). Canadian Center on Substance Abuse, Canada. www.ccsa.ca/profile/.

CDHFS (1997). *Marijuana in Australia: Patterns and Attitudes, National Drug Strategy.* Monograph Series 31, Commonwealth Department of Health and Family Services for the National Drug Strategy, Canberra.

Chaloupka, F. and A. Laixuthai (1997). 'Do Youths Substitute Alcohol and Marijuana? Some Econometric Evidence,' *Eastern Economic Journal* 23: 253-76.

Chaloupka, F.J. and R. Nair (2000). 'International Issues in the Supply of Tobacco,' *Recent Changes and Implications for Alcohol Addiction* 95 (Supplement 4): 477-489.

Chang, H., G. Griffith and N. Bettington (2002). 'The Demand for Wine in Australia Using a Systems Approach: Industry Implications,' Paper 9, *Agribusiness Review* 10: 1-12.

Chen, D.L. (2001). *World Consumption Economics.* New Jersey, London, Singapore: World Scientific.

Cleeland Report (1989). Parliamentary Joint Committee on the National Crime Authority. Drugs, Crime and Society. Canberra: Australian Government Publishing Service.

Clements, K. W. (1987a). 'Alternative Approaches to Consumption Theory,' Chapter 1 in H. Theil and K. W. Clements (eds.), *Applied Demand Analysis: Results from System-Wide Approaches.* Cambridge, MA: Ballinger Publishing Company.

Clements, K.W. (1987b). 'The Demand for Groups of Goods and Conditional Demand,' Chapter 4 in H. Theil and K. W. Clements (eds), *Applied Demand Analysis: Results from System-Wide Approaches.* Cambridge, MA: Ballinger Publishing Company.

Clements, K.W. and M. Daryal (1999). 'The Economics of Marijuana Consumption,' Paper presented at the 28th Conference of Economists, Economic Society of Australia, La Trobe University, September.

Clements, K.W., P.S. Goldshmidt and H. Theil (1985). 'A Conditional Version of Working's Model,' *Economics Letters* 18: 97-99.

Clements, K.W. and L.W. Johnson (1983). 'The Demand for Beer, Wine and Spirits: A System-wide Approach,' *Journal of Business* 56: 273-304.

Clements, K.W. and E.A. Selvanathan (1987). 'Alcohol Consumption,' in *Applied Demand Analysis: Results from System-Wide Approaches*, Theil, H. and Clements, K.W. (eds), Ballinger, Cambridge, MA. pp. 185-264.

Clements, K.W., E.A. Selvanathan and S. Selvanathan (1996). 'Applied Demand Analysis: A Survey,' *Economic Record* 72: 63-81.

Clements, K.W. and S. Selvanathan (1991). The Economic Determinants of Alcohol Consumption.' *Australian Journal of Agricultural Economics* 35(1991): 209-231.

Clements, K.W. and S. Selvanathan (1994). 'Understanding Consumption Patterns,' *Empirical Economics* 19: 69-110.

Clements, K.W., S. Selvanathan and E.A. Selvanathan (1995). 'The Economic Theory of the Consumer,' Chapter 1 in E.A. Selvanathan and K.W. Clements (eds), *Recent Developments in Applied Demand Analysis: Alcohol, Advertising and Global Consumption.* Berlin: Springer Verlag. Pp. 1-72.

Clements, K.W., W. Yang and S.W. Zheng (1997). 'Is Utility Additive? The Case of Alcohol,' *Applied Economics* 29: 1163-1167.

Collins, D.J. and H.M. Lapsly (2002). *Counting the Cost: Estimates of the Social Costs of Drug Abuse in Australia in 1998-99.* National Drug Strategy Monograph Number 49, Department of Health, Canberra.

Collins, L. (1999). 'Holland's Half-Backed Drug Experiment,' *Foreign Affairs* 78: 82-98.

Cournot, A. (1838). *Recherches Sur Les Principes Mathematiques de La Theorie Des Richesses.* Paris: L. Hachette.

Daryal, M. (2002). 'Price, Legalisation and Marijuana Consumption,' *University Avenue Undergraduate Journal of Economics 2002.* (available at www.econ.ilstu.edu/uauja).

Deaton, A.S. (1974). 'The Analysis of Consumer Demand in the United Kingdom, 1900-1970,' *Econometrica* 42: 341-367.

Deaton, A.S. (1975). *Models and Projections of Demand in Post-War Britain.* London: Chapman and Hall.

Deaton, A.S. (1986). 'Demand Analysis,' in Z. Griliches and M.D. Intriligator (eds), *Handbook of Econometrics.* Volume III, Amsterdam: North-Holland Publishing Company, 1768-1839.

Deaton, A.S. and J. Muellbauer. (1980a). *Economics and Consumer Behaviour.* Cambridge: Cambridge University Press.

Deaton, A.S. and J. Muellbauer. (1980b). 'An Almost Ideal Demand System,' *American Economic Review* 70: 312-326.

DeSimone, J. (1998). 'Is Marijuana a Gateway Drug?' *Eastern Economic Journal* 24: 149-64.

DiNardo, J. and T. Lemieux (1992). 'Alcohol, Marijuana and American Youth: The Unintended Effects of Government Regulation,' Working Paper No. 4212, National Bureau of Economic Research.

Divisia, F. (1925). 'L'Indice Monetaire et la Theorie de la Monnaie,' *Revue d'Economie Politique* 39: 980-1008.

Drug Situation 2000, *Spanish National Report to the European Monitoring Centre for Drugs and Drug Addiction (EMCDDA)*, Spanish Focal Point, Reitox Ref/2000, Madrid, November 2000.

Duffy, M.H. (1982). 'The Effects of Advertising on the Total Consumption of Alcoholic Drinks in the UK: Some Econometric Estimates,' *Journal of Advertising* 1: 105-107.

Duffy, M.H. (1983). 'The Demand for Alcoholic Drinks in the UK: 1963-1978,' *Applied Economics* 15: 125-140.

Duffy, M.H. (1987). 'Advertising and the Inter-Product Distribution of Demand: A Rotterdam Model Approach,' *European Economic Review* 31: 1051-1070.

Duffy, M.H. (2001). 'Advertising in Consumer Allocation Models: Choice of Functional Forms,' *Applied Economics* 33: 437-456.

Duffy, M.H. (2003). 'On the Estimation of an Advertising Augmented, Cointegrating Demand System,' *Economic Modelling* 20(1): 181-206.

Dupuit, J. (1934). *De L'utilite et De Sa Mesure*. Turin: LaRiforma Sociale (Reprint).

Easton, B. (1997). *The Social Cost of Tobacco Use and Alcohol Misuse*. Report prepared for ALAC, Health Research Council and Public Health Commission, Wellington, New Zealand.

Easton, B. (2002). *Taxing Harm: Modernising Alcohol Excise Duties*. Report commissioned by the Alcohol Advisory Council of New Zealand, Wellington, New Zealand.

Edgeworth, F.Y. (1881). *Mathematical Psychics*. London: C. Kegan Paul.

Edwards, G., et al. (1994). *Alcohol Policy and the Public Good*. Oxford: Oxford University Press.

Engel, E. (1857). *Die Productions- und Consumtionsverhaltnisse des Konichreichs Sachsen. Zeitschrift des Statistischen Bureaus des Koniglich Sachsischen Ministeriums des Innern*, 8-9: 1-54. Reprinted in the *Bulletin de l'Institut International de Statistique*, 9 (1895).

ESPAD (2000). *1999 ESPAD Report: Alcohol and other Drug use Among Students in 30 European Countries*, The European Schools Survey Project on Alcohol and Drugs, Swedish Council for Information on Alcohol and other Drugs, Sweden; and the State University of New York.

Eurocare (2001). *Overview of National Alcohol Policies in the 15 Countries of the European Union*. Institute of Alcohol Studies (A member of Eurocare), Cambridgeshire, United Kingdom. http://www.eurocare.org/profiles/.

Fisher, I. (1892). 'Mathematical Investigations in the Theory of Value and Prices,' *Transactions of the Connecticut Academy* 9: 1-124.

Fogarty, J. (2004). 'The Own-Price Elasticity of Alcohol: A Meta Analysis,' *Economics Program Discussion Paper No. 04.01*, The University of Western Australia.

Frisch, R. (1932). *New Methods of Measuring Marginal Utility*. Tiibingen: J.C.B. Mohr.

Freidman, M. (1972). 'Prohibition and Drugs,' *Newsweek*. May, p. 104.

Gajalakshmi, V., S. Asma, C.W. Warren (2004). 'Tobacco Survey Among Youth in South India,' *Asian Pacific Journal of Cancer Prevention* 5: 273-278.

GLOBALink (2003). www.globalink.org/tobacco/wb/wb01.shtml.

Goldberger, A.S. (1987). *Functional Form and Utility: A Review of Consumer Demand Theory*. Boulder and London: Westview Press.

Gossen, H.H. (1927). *Entwicklung der Gesetze des Menschlichen Verkehrs und der Daraus Fliessenden Regeln Fiir Menschliches Bandeln*. 3d Edition. (1st Edition, 1854). Berlin: R.L. Prager.

Greenfield, L.A. (1998). *Alcohol and Crime: An Analysis of National Data on the Prevalence of Alcohol Involvement in Crime*. US Department of Justice, Bureau of Justice Statistics, Washington, DC.

Habgood, R., S. Casswell, M. Pledger and K. Bhatta (2001). *Drinking in New Zealand: National Survey Comparison 1995 and 2000*. Alcohol and Public Health Research Unit, University of Auckland, Auckland, New Zealand.

Harwood, H. (2000). *Updating Estimates of the Economic Costs of Alcohol Abuse in the United States: Estimates, Update Methods and Data.* Report prepared by the Lewin Group for the National Institute on Alcohol Abuse and Alcoholism, United States.

Hicks, J.R., and R.G.D. Allen (1934). 'A Reconsideration of the Theory of Value,' *Economica,* n.s., 1: 52-76, 196-219.

Houthakker, H. S. (1952). 'The Econometrics of Family Budgets,' *Journal of the Royal Statistical Society, Series A,* 115: 1-21.

Houthakker, H.S. (1960). 'Additive Preferences,' *Econometrica* 28: 244-257.

ILO (1998). *Fighting Drug and Alcohol Abuse in the Workplace.* International Labour Office Report, http://www.ilo.org/public/english/bureau/inf/pr/1998/3.htm, International Labour Office, Geneva, Switzerland.

Inciardi, J. A. and C. A. Saum (1996). 'Legalisation Madness,' *Public Interest* 123: 72-82.

Jevons, W. S. (1931). *The Theory of Political Economy.* 4ᵗʰ Edition. (1st Edition, 1871). London: Macmillan and Co.

Jha, P., and F.J. Chaloupka (2000). *Tobacco Control in Developing Countries.* New York: Oxford University Press for The World Bank and WHO.

Jha, P., M.K. Ranson, S.N. Nguyen and D. Yach (2002). Estimates of Global and Regional Smoking Prevalence in 1995, by Age and Sex,' *American Journal of Public Health* 92: 1002-1006.

JNTAA (1996). *A Guide to Japanese Beverages.* Japan National Tax Administration Agency, Japan.

Johnson, L.W. (1985). 'Alternative Econometric Estimates of the Effect of Advertising on the Demand for Alcoholic Beverages in the United Kingdom,' *International Journal of Advertising* 4: 19-25.

Johnston, L., P. O'Malley and J. Bachman (1981). *Marijuana Decriminalisation: The Impact on Youth, 1975-1980.* Ann Arbor, Michigan: Institute for Social Research.

Jones, A. M. (1989) 'A Systems Approach to the Demand for Alcohol and Tobacco,' *Bulletin of Economic Research* 41, 86-101.

Joosens, L., and M. Raw (1998). 'Cigarette Smuggling in Europe: Who Really Benefits?' *Tobacco Control* 7: 66-71.

Joy de Beyer, (2002). 'Tobacco Smuggling: Issues and Evidence,' *International Conference on Illicit Trade,* New York.

Keller, W.J., and J. van Driel (1985). 'Differential Consumer Demand Systems,' *European Economic Review* 27: 375-390.

Knightley, P. (1999). 'War on Drugs Lost to Market Forces,' *The Australian,* March 6, pp. 6-7.

Laitinen, K. (1978). 'Why is Demand Homogeneity So Often Rejected?' *Economics Letters* 1: 187-191.

Liu B. and R. Peto (1998). 'Emerging Tobacco Hazards in China. Retrospective Proportional Mortality Study of One Million Deaths,' *British Medical Journal* 317: 1411-22.

Lluch, C., A.A. Powell and R.A. Williams (1977). *Patterns in Household Demand and Saving.* Oxford: Oxford University Press.

Malpeli, G. and B. Martin (1998). 'Law Pushes Young onto Heroin: Expert,' *The West Australian,* November 2, p. 11.

Manning, W., L. Blumberg and L.H. Moulton (1995). 'The Demand for Alcohol: The Differential Response to Price,' *Journal of Health Economics* 14(2): 123-148.

Marks, R.E. (1992). 'The Costs of Australian Drug Policy,' *The Journal of Drug Issues* 22: 535-547.

Marshall, A. (1898). *Principles of Economics.* 4th Edition (lst Edition, 1890). London: Macmillan and Co., 1898.

Martin, R. (1998). 'Majority Back Drug Reform,' *The West Australian,* February 2, p. 9.

McAllister, I., R. Moore and T. Makkai (1991). *Drugs in Australian Society: Patterns, Attitudes and Policies.* Longman: Melbourne, Australia.

McGuinness, T. (1980). 'An Econometric Analysis of Total Demand for Alcoholic Beverages in the U.K., 1956-75,' *Journal of Industrial Economics* 29: 85-109.

McGuiness, T. (1983). 'The Demand for Beer, Wine and Spirits in the UK, 1956-1979,' in *Economics and Alcohol,* Grant, M., Plant, M. and Williams, A. (eds), Croom Helm, London.

Meisner, J.F. (1979). 'The Sad Fate of the Asymptotic Slutsky Symmetry Test for Large Systems,' *Economics Letters* 2: 231-233.

Menger, C. (1871). *Grundsatze der Volkswirthschaftslehre.* Vienna: Wilhelm Braumulller.

Model, K. (1993). 'The Effect of Marijuana Decriminalisation on Hospital Emergency Drug Episodes: 1975-1980,' *Journal of the American Statistical Association* 88: 737-747.

MTF (2002). *2002 Monitoring the Future Study,* Survey Research Center, Institute for Social Research, University of Michigan, USA.

Natcen (2003). *Smoking, Drinking and Drug Use among Young People in England in 2002: Provisional Results,* National Centre for Social Research and Department of Health, United Kingdom.

National Drug Strategy Household Survey (computer file, various issues). Canberra: Social Data Archives, The Australian National University.

Nelson, J.P. (1997). 'Economic and Demographic Factors in U.S. Alcohol Demand: A Growth-Accounting Analysis,' *Empirical Economics* 22: 83-102.

Nelson, J.P. (1999). 'Broadcast Advertising and U.S. Demand for Alcoholic Beverages,' *Southern Economic Journal* 65: 774-990.

Nelson, J.P. and J.R. Moran (1995). 'Advertising and US Alcoholic Beverages Demand: A System-wide Estimation,' *Applied Economics* 27: 1225-1236.

NHSDA (2003a). 'Alcohol and Tobacco Use Tables,' The NHSDA Report, *2001 National Household Survey on Drug Abuse,* Office of Applied Statistics, US Department of Health and Human Services, www.samhsa.gov/oas/NHSDA/, SAMHSA, Michigan, USA.

NHSDA (2003b). 'Marijuana Use and Drug Dependence,' The NHSDA Report, *2001 National Household Survey on Drug Abuse,* Office of Applied Statistics, US Department of Health and Human Services, www.samhsa.gov/oas/NHSDA/, SAMHSA, USA.

NHTSA (2000). *Traffic Safety Facts 1999.* Alcohol. National Centre for Statistics and Analysis, Washington DC.

Nisbet, C.T. and Vakil, F. (1972). 'Some Estimates of Price and Expenditure Elasticities of Demand for Marijuana Among UCLA Students,' *Review of Economics and Statistics* 54: 473-475.

NS (2002). *Smoking Related Behaviour and Attitudes,* United Kingdom National Statistics, Office for National Statistics, London.

NS (2003). *National Statistics,* Data Results for Alcohol Misuse, United Kingdom National Statistics Online, http://www.statistics.gov.uk/CCI/.

NZHIS (2001). *New Zealand Drug Statistics.* New Zealand Health Information Service, Wellington, New Zealand.

ONDCP (2003). Drug Policy Information Clearing House, Fact Sheet, Office of National Drug and Control Policy, Executive Office of the President, http://www.whitehousedrugpolicy.gov.

Pacula, R.L. (1997). 'Does Increasing the Beer Tax Reduce Marijuana Consumption?' *Journal of Health Economics* 17: 577-585.

Pacula, R.L. (1998). 'Adolescent Alcohol and Marijuana Consumption: Is There Really a Gateway Effect?' Working Paper No. 6348, National Bureau of Economic Research.

Pareto, V. (1909). *Manuel d'Economie Politique*. Paris: V. Giard et E. Briere.

Pearce, D. (1986) The demand for alcohol in New Zealand, Discussion Paper no. 86.02, Department of Economics, The University of Western Australia.

Penington Report (1996). *Drugs and Our Community: Report of the Premier's Advisory Council*. Melbourne: Victorian Government.

Peto, R., A.D. Lopez and J Boreham (2000). *Mortality from Smoking in Developing Countries 1950-2000*. Indirect Estimates from National Vital Statistics, New York, Oxford University Press.

Phlips, L. (1974). *Applied Consumption Analysis*. Amsterdam: North-Holland Publishing Company. Second edition 1983.

Pollak, R.A and T.J. Wales (1987). 'Pooling International Consumption Data,' *Review of Economics and Statistics* 69: 90-99.

Pollak, A.A. and T.J. Wales (1992). *Demand System Specification and Estimation*. New York and Oxford: Oxford University Press.

Powell, A.A. (1974). *Empirical Analytics of Demand Systems*. Lexington, Mass.: D.C. Heath and Company.

Quek, K.E. (1988). 'The Demand for Alcohol in Canada: An Econometric Study,' Discussion Paper No. 88.08, Department of Economics, The University of Western Australia.

Rhodes, W., S. Langenbahn, R. Kling and P. Scheiman (1997). *What America's Users Spend on Illegal Drugs, 1988-1995*. Washington: The Office of National Drug Policies. Web site address: http://www.whitehousedrugpolicy.gov/drugfact/retail/contents.html.

Ridolfo, B. and C. Stevenson (2001). 'The Quantification of Drug-Caused Mortality and Morbidity in Australia, 1998,' AIHW Cat. No. PHE 29, Drug Statistics Series No. 7, AIHW, Canberra.

Roemer, R. (1993). *Legislative Action to Compact the World Tobacco Epidemic*, World Health Organisation.

Saffer, H. (2000). *The Control of Tobacco Advertising and Promotion*. Background Paper, World Bank, Washington DC, USA.

Saffer, H. and F. Chaloupka (1995). 'The Demand for Illicit Drugs,' Working Paper No. 5238, National Bureau of Economic Research.

Saffer, H. and F. Chaloupka (1998). 'Demographic Differentials in the Demand for Alcohol and Illicit Drugs,' Working Paper No. 6432, National Bureau of Economic Research.

Saisu, M.A. and V.N. Balasubramanyam (1997). 'Income and Price Elasticities of Demand for Alcoholic Drinks,' *Applied Economics Letters* 4: 247-251.

SAMHSA (2001). *National Household Survey on Drug Abuse*, 2000 and 2001, Office of Applied Statistics, US Department of Health and Human Services, http://www.samhsa.gov.

SAMHSA (2003). 'Marijuana Incidence and Initiation: Trends, Patterns and Implication,' Office of Applied Statistics, US Department of Health and Human Services, http://www.samhsa.gov.

Samuelson, P.A. (1965). 'Using Full Duality to Show that Simultaneously Additive Direct and Indirect Utilities Implies Unitary Price Elasticity of Demand,' *Econometrica* 33: 781-96.

Sandwijk, J.P., P.D.A. Cohen, S. Musterd and M.P.S. Langemeijer (1995). *Licit and Illicit Drug Use in Amsterdam II*. Amsterdam: University of Amsterdam.

Scales, B., B. Croser and J. Freebain (1995). *Winegrape and Wine Industry in Australia*. AGPS, Canberra.

Selvanathan, E.A. (1987). *Explorations in Consumer Demand*, PhD Thesis, Murdoch University, Western Australia.

Selvanathan, E.A. (1988). 'Alcohol Consumption in the UK, 1955-85: A System-wide Approach,' *Applied Economics* 20, 1071-1086.

Selvanathan, E.A. (1989). 'Advertising and Alcohol Demand in the UK: Further Results.' *International Journal of Advertising* 8: 181-188.

Selvanathan, E.A. (1991). 'Cross-Country Alcohol Consumption Comparisons: An Application of the Rotterdam Demand System,' *Applied Economics* 23: 1613-1622.

Selvanathan, E.A. and K.W. Clements (1995). *Recent Developments in Applied Demand Analysis: Alcohol, Advertising and Global Consumption*. Berlin: Springer Verlag.

Selvanathan, E.A., and S. Selvanathan (2003). *International Consumption Comparisons: OECD vs LDC*. New Jersey, London, Singapore: World Scientific.

Selvanathan, S. (1987). 'A Monte Carlo Test of Preference Independence,' *Economics Letters* 25: 259-261.

Selvanathan, S. (1991). 'The Reliability of ML Estimators of Systems of Demand Equations: Evidence from 18 Countries,' *Review of Economics and Statistics* 73: 338-346.

Selvanathan, S. (1993). *A System-Wide Analysis of International Consumption Patterns*. Advanced Studies in Theoretical and Applied Econometrics, Boston: Kluwer Academic Publishers.

Selvanathan, S. and E.A. Selvanathan (1994). *Regional Consumption Patterns: A System-Wide Approach*. London: Avebury Publishers.

Single, E., L. Robson, X. Xie and J. Rehu (1996). *The Cost of Substance Abuse*. Canadian Centre on Substance Abuse, Ottawa.

Slutsky, E. (1915). 'Sulla Teoria del Bilancio del Consumator,' *Giornale degli Economisti* 51: 1-26; Translation, 'On the Theory of the Budget of the Consumer,' in G.J. Stigler and K.E. Boulding (eds), *Readings in Price Theory*. Chicago: Richard D. Irwin, 1952.

Stone, R. (1954). 'Linear Expenditure Systems and Demand Analysis: An Application to the Pattern of British Demand,' *Economic Journal* 64: 511-527.

Sullivan, L. (1993). 'Who Says Banning Marijuana Doesn't Work?' *News Weekly*, November 20, pp. 12-13.

Taylor, A.L. and D.W. Bettcher (2000). 'WHO Framework Convention on Tobacco Control,' *Bulletin of the World Health Organisation*.

The Economist (1999). 'Mary Jane Rathbun,' April 24, p. 92.

Theil, H. (1965). 'The Information Approach to Demand Analysis,' *Econometrica* 33: 67-87.

Theil, H. (1967). *Economics and Information Theory*. Amsterdam and Chicago: North-Holland and Rand McNally.

Theil, H. (1971). *Principles of Econometrics*. New York: John Wiley and Sons.

Theil, H. (1975/76). *Theory and Measurement of Consumer Demand*. Two volumes. Amsterdam: North-Holland Publishing Company.

Theil, H. (1980). The System-Wide Approach to Microeconomics. Chicago: The University of Chicago Press.

Theil, H. (1987). 'The Econometrics of Demand Systems,' Chapter 3 in H. Theil and K.W. Clements (eds), *Applied Demand Analysis: Results from System-wide Approaches*. Cambridge, MA: Ballinger Publishing Company. pp. 101-162.

Theil, H., C-F. Chung and J.L. Seale, Jr. (1989). *International Evidence on Consumption Patterns*. Greenwich, Connecticut: JAI Press, Inc.

Theil, H. and K.W. Clements (1987). *Applied Demand Analysis: Results from System-Wide Approaches*. Cambridge, MA: Ballinger Publishing Company.

Theil, H. and F.E. Suhm (1981). *International Consumption Comparisons: A System- Wide Approach*. Amsterdam: North-Holland Publishing Company.

Thies, C. and F. Register (1993). 'Decriminalisation of Marijuana and the Demand for Alcohol, Marijuana and Cocaine,' *The Social Science Journal* 30: 385-399.

Thomas, R.L. (1987). *Applied Demand Analysis*. London: Longman Group.

Tu, Y. and Q. Ye (1999). 'The Economic Laws of Alcohol Consumption,' Unpublished paper, The University of Western Australia, forthcoming.

UKSUAHR (2003). *Interim Analytical Report*. The Strategy Unit Alcohol Harm and Reduction Project. The Prime Minister's Office, United Kingdom. www.number10.gov.uk/.

United Nations (1997). *United Nations International Drug Control Programme: World Drug Report*. Oxford: Oxford University Press.

UNODCCP (1999). *Global Illicit Drug Trends 1999*, UN Office for Drug Control and Crime Prevention, New York: UNODCCP.

UNODCCP (2002). *National Drug Strategy Household Survey 2001*, Alcohol and Public Health Research Unit, Substance Abuse and Mental Health Services Administration, United Nations Office for Drug Control and Crime Prevention, New York, UN.

USDHHS (1999). *National Household Survey on Drug Abuse: Population Estimates 1998*. Substance Abuse and Mental Health Services Administration, US Department of Health and Human Services, Washington DC.

Walras, L. (1896). *Elements d'Economie Politique Pure*. 3rd Edition. Lausanne: F. Rouge.

WDT (1997). *World Drink Trends 1997*, Productschap voor Gedistilleerde Dranken Commodity Board for the Distilled Spirits Industry, World Advertising Research Center Ltd.

WDT (2001). *World Drink Trends 20021*, Productschap voor Gedistilleerde Dranken Commodity Board for the Distilled Spirits Industry, World Advertising Research Center Ltd.

WDT (2003). *World Drink Trends 2003*, Productschap voor Gedistilleerde Dranken Commodity Board for the Distilled Spirits Industry, World Advertising Research Center Ltd.

Western Australian Parliament Select Committee (1997). *Taking the Profit Out of Drug Trafficking. An Agenda for Legal and Administrative Reforms in Western Australia to Protect the Community from Illicit Drugs*. Interim Report. Perth: Legislative Assembly.

WHO (1997). *Tobacco or Health*, A Global Status Report: World Health Organisation.

WHO (1999). *Tobacco - Health Facts*. Fact sheet 221, World Health Organisation. April 1999.

WHO (2003a). World Health Organisation Regional Office for Europe. http://data.euro.who.int/.

WHO (2003b). *Adult Per Capita Alcohol Consumption*, World Health Organisation Statistics Alcohol database. http://www3.who.int/whosis/alcohol.

Wold, R., in association with L. Jureen (1953). *Demand Analysis*. New York: John Wiley and Sons, 1953.

Wong, A.Y-T. (1988). 'The Demand for Alcohol in the UK 1920-1938: An Econometric Study,' Discussion Paper No. 88.13, Department of Economics, The University of Western Australia.

Working, H. (1943). 'Statistical Laws of Family Expenditure,' *Journal of the American Statistical Association* 38: 43-56.

World Bank (1999). *Curbing the Epidemic: Government and the Economics of Tobacco Control*. World Bank, Washington DC, USA.

World Bank (2001). *Tobacco Control in Bulgaria*. A presentation prepared for Dr Dominic Haazen, World Bank Bulgaria Health Task Team, World Bank, Washington DC, USA.

Wydoodt, J. and B. Noels (1996). *Alcohol, Illegal Drugs en Medicatie - Recent Otnwikkelingen in Vlannderen*. VAD, Brussels.

Yang, W., K.W. Clements and D. Chen (2003). 'The Demand Analysis Package 2000,' Appendix in E.A. Selvanathan and S. Selvanathan, *International Consumption Comparisons: OECD versus LDC*, World Scientific, pp. 295-320.

Subject Index

Author Index